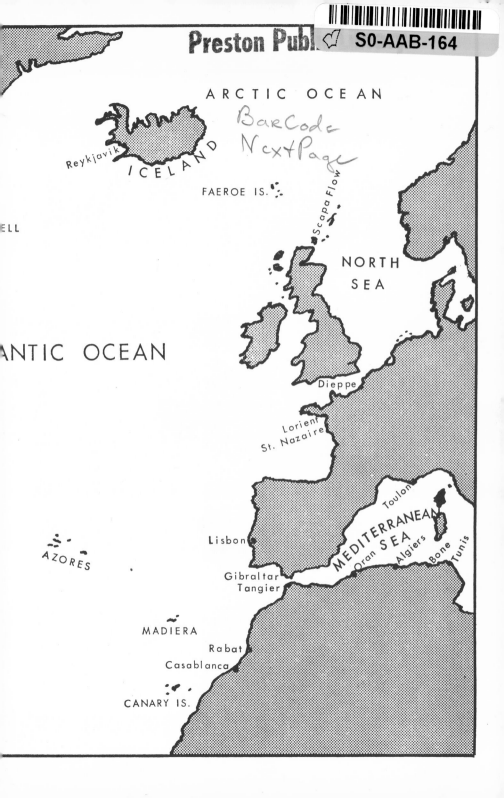

Preston Publ░ S0-AAB-164

ARCTIC OCEAN

BarCode
NextPage

Reykjavik ICELAND

FAEROE IS.

Scapa Flow

NORTH SEA

ELL

ANTIC OCEAN

AZORES

Lisbon

Dieppe

Lorient
St. Nazaire

Toulon

MEDITERRANEAN SEA

Oran Algiers Bone Tunis

Gibraltar
Tangier

MADIERA

Rabat
Casablanca

CANARY IS.

946.54
Ada

Years of Deadly Peril

Preston Public Library
389 Route 2
Preston, CT 06365

ALSO BY THE AUTHOR:

1942: The Year That Doomed the Axis

940.53
Ada
Y2

Years of Deadly Peril

by

HENRY H. ADAMS

DAVID McKAY COMPANY, INC.
New York

Preston Public Library
389 Route 2
Preston, CT   06365

YEARS OF DEADLY PERIL

COPYRIGHT © 1969 BY HENRY H. ADAMS

All rights reserved, including the right to reproduce
this book, or parts thereof, in any form, except for
the inclusion of brief quotations in a review.

Library of Congress Catalog Card Number: 73–87777

MANUFACTURED IN THE UNITED STATES OF AMERICA

VAN REES PRESS   •   NEW YORK

Preface

THIS book is the story of two years of folly and heroism. Historians have shown us how the unsettled issues of the First World War inevitably led to the Second. Here I have tried to reconstruct the story of how the citizens of the Western world paid in blood and treasure for the incredible blindness of their leaders in the Twenties and Thirties.

In every land the people suffered and died while the black stain of Nazism flooded across Europe. Yet while they lived, they worked and played, read books, went to the movies, listened to the radio, went to ball games, played golf, tennis, cricket, or what have you, while their call to the colors or their turn to die came inexorably closer.

This book is not military history as such, although military operations are inevitably involved. It is the story of the people, great and small, who fought in the battles and endured the blows of war. The life at home, as it was affected by the war, is as important as the battles, for what the people were at home, how they lived, how they thought, affected the outcome of battles perhaps even more than the strategy and tactics of the generals and the admirals, the diplomacy and politics of the statesmen.

The story of the total experience of World War II is the theme of this book and the others in the series. This volume deals with the politics, the strategy, the tactics, the people, the trivia of the dark years from the beginning of the war in September, 1939, up to the Japanese attack on Pearl Harbor on December 7, 1941. The second book in the series (already published), *1942: The Year That Doomed the Axis,* carries the story through the Casablanca Conference in January,

1943. Succeeding books will complete the story of the war. The scale is panoramic, not specialized; the focus is on people, not events.

Friends at home and abroad have contributed more than they realized to this book. I should especially like to thank Commander Rolf Sheen of the Norwegian Navy, Vice Admiral Friedrich Ruge of the Federal German Navy, Dr. Harve Cras (Jacques Mordal), head of the Section Historique du Ministère de la Marine, Lieutenant Commander David W. Waters, RNR, FRHS, the late Commander F. Barley, RN, Captain T. Armour, RN, Commander G. Titterton, RN, Lieutenant Commander Peter Kemp, RN, Captain S. W. Roskill, RN, Admiral Romeo Bernotti, Rear Admiral G. Fioravanzo, and Commander C. Levi of the Italian Navy, and countless officers of the U.S. Navy, Marine Corps, and Army who have patiently endured questions.

To my former colleagues at the U.S. Naval Academy, Professors E. B. Potter and W. W. Jeffries, I wish to give special thanks for encouragement and advice.

Most of all I owe thanks to my wife Catherine for her loyal support throughout the writing and revisions. In a very real sense, this book is hers as much as mine.

HENRY H. ADAMS

Illinois State University
July, 1969

Table of Contents

Years of Deadly Peril

CHAPTER ONE

The Never Never Land

There is nothing in this world constant,
but inconstancy.
Swift, "A Critical Essay upon
the Faculties of the Mind"

IT WAS a strange time. It was a time of war when few were fighting.
It was a time of peace that brought no assurance.

It was the time of "The Phony War," "The Sitzkrieg," "The Great
Bore War." In America, life went on as though nothing had happened. Men went off to their offices and factory jobs, their trucks and
taxicabs, their stores and sales counters as usual. Europe could mind
its own business—it was no concern of Americans.

In London, as day followed uneventful day, people set the example
for the rest of the country. They relaxed tensions built up through
the fall and the long, cold winter. Gas masks, which had been issued
to all the previous autumn, were often gathering dust at home. It
was "a bit windy" to carry them, no matter what the regulations said.
A.R.P.* wardens made nuisances of themselves over the lighting
regulations. In a few parks and village squares, small groups of dedicated men practiced drilling just in case—but they were more likely
to be figures of fun than of admiration.

But the British could not relax completely. Nor could the French.
They were at war, and throughout both countries, homes had vacant
beds, empty chairs at the dinner table, for armies and navies had
mobilized. In the elaborate underground fortifications of the Maginot
Line, the homesick soldiers of the French Army looked to their comfort and well-being between the times they mounted guard and stared

* Air Raid Precautions.

1

across at the barrier of strongpoints called the Siegfried Line. Along the Belgian border, from the thickets of the Ardennes Forest to the sea, the French defenses were lighter. Would it not have been unfriendly to erect massive fortifications on the border of an ally?

When Hitler had begun the war on September 1, 1939, without bothering to declare it, his troops had crushed the Polish armies in less than four weeks. The Polish Government—what was left of it— had set up a Government in Exile in London. Britain and France had dutifully declared war on Germany on September 3. At 11:15 that morning, an ashen-faced Prime Minister arose to speak in the House of Commons. The man with the umbrella, the appeaser of Munich, the man whose actions had stood for peace at any price, now prepared to lead his nation to war.

> This is a sad day for all of us [said Mr. Chamberlain, and his words went by radio to the homes of Britain], and to none is it sadder than to me. Everything that I have worked for, everything that I have hoped for, everything that I have believed in during my public life, has crashed into ruins.

His poignant words attracted little sympathy for his personal tragedy, and the nation doggedly began to take up the burden of arms.

Scarcely had Neville Chamberlain finished speaking when the air-raid sirens began to keen. In the crisp, cool September morning, the skies seemed clear enough, but the shaken, bewildered people of London sought cover. Barrage balloons stood as mute sentinels against the oncoming raiders. But they never came that day. Ten minutes later the All Clear sounded.

That seemed to be the pattern of events for Britain and France during the fall and winter of the war's first year. Once hapless Poland had been eliminated, with Russia claiming her price of half the country in payment for her non-aggression pact with Germany, a lull settled over the battlefields. A few men died in light patrolling actions, and only their families remember them. At sea the war was real. A few hours after Chamberlain's speech, the liner *Athenia* was some 200 miles west of the Hebrides. On board were 1400 passengers fleeing the coming storm in Europe. It was 9 o'clock that night; the passengers had been warned and carried life jackets. The ship was darkened and heading toward the setting sun and the safety of the New World.

Suddenly there was a crash, an explosion. The ship shuddered. Not far away Leutnant Fritz-Julius Lemp was peering through the periscope of the *U-30,* noting with satisfaction that his torpedo spread had struck fair. He soon decided that no further torpedoes would be needed and turned his U-boat away to continue his patrol.

The ship's officers and crew worked efficiently, and there was no panic. Soon the lifeboats were in the water, and in a few hours rescue vessels took over a thousand survivors aboard. But 112 persons lost their lives, 28 of them Americans.

Germany promptly proclaimed that no U-boat had done the deed. Goebbels rushed proclamations of innocence so swiftly that the denial reached some people before news of the sinking. It might have been better if he had waited, for when *U-30* returned to port, a grim-faced Lemp confessed to Commodore * Dönitz, commander of Germany's U-boat arm, that he believed he had sunk the *Athenia* under the impression that she was an auxiliary cruiser.† Dönitz told him to keep quiet about the whole affair and reported the facts to his superior, Grand Admiral Erich Raeder. The offending page was removed from the log of the U-boat, and the crew was placed under an oath of secrecy.

Did the discovery of the real facts embarrass Goebbels? Not at all. He blandly announced that the *Athenia* had been sunk on the personal orders of Winston Churchill in order to bring America into the war.

Mr. Churchill had more than the *Athenia* to worry about. On September 3 he had entered the somewhat gloomy building that stands by the Horse Guards Parade at the head of the Mall leading down to Buckingham Palace. Walking along the familiar corridors of the Admiralty building, Churchill must have cast his mind back to the First World War when he had had to resign his post as First Lord of the Admiralty ‡ as a result of the Gallipoli failure. Now he was back, and his cries of disaster had all been justified. The Navy was his again, to do with as he would.

One of the first things the new First Lord did was to send a message to that Navy he loved so well—"Winston is back." Then he took off his coat and went to work.

---

* Dönitz was promoted to Rear Admiral on October 1, 1939, and to Admiral shortly thereafter.

† That is, a merchant ship fitted with guns and commissioned in the Navy. She could be employed in convoy escort and on patrol.

‡ The First Lord of the Admiralty is a civilian Cabinet post, somewhat corresponding to the American Secretary of the Navy in World War II. The highest naval command is First Sea Lord, which corresponds to the American Chief of Naval Operations.

There was much work to be done, both on land and on the sea. Especially at sea, for it would be there and there alone that Britain would fight for the first months of the war.

But, first, what could be done to help Poland? It was far away, and the Baltic was closed to the British fleet. Mines, submarines, and aircraft all barred the way. There was no place Britain could hurl an army against Germany, and she had no army to hurl—only a handful of men that she could soon form into four divisions to put in France.

France, according to treaty, was supposed to attack Germany's rear when she moved against Poland. But the French stood idly by. French plans, said Commander in Chief Maurice Gustave Gamelin, were based on action in 1941 or 1942.

But Poland needed the help in 1939.

A handful of men in Polish uniforms moved toward the radio station near Gleiwitz, a German town close to the Polish border. A few shots were fired, and the men seized the station, leaving one or two dead outside. An officer spoke a few words in the Polish language into the microphone, and then the men disappeared.

A few other incidents of the same type took place all along the border that separates Poland from Germany. It was the evening of August 31, 1939.

The next morning, at 0445, German troops crossed the Polish border, and World War II had begun. Proclaimed the Führer in a broadcast:

> The Polish state has refused the peaceful settlement of relations which I desired, and has appealed to arms. . . . A series of violations of the frontier, intolerable to a great power, prove that Poland is no longer willing to respect the frontier of the Reich.
>
> In order to put an end to this lunacy, I have no other choice than to meet force with force from now on.

He met force with force, but the original force had been provided by Germany, not Poland. The frontier violations had occurred, but the men in Polish uniforms were Germans, a special group of S.S. men who were to give Germany a pretext. The corpses were those of concentration camp inmates, already condemned to death. They had been given lethal injections, and the bullet holes were added by the S.S. men to give a touch of realism to the whole affair.

It was, perhaps, inconsiderate of the Poles not to have provided the pretext themselves, but no matter. Hitler had been able to arrange it all, for he was determined to extend Germany's *Lebensraum* to the east. Ever since he had come to power in 1933, the existence of the Polish Corridor to the Baltic and the presence of the Free City of Danzig, all taken from German territory, had rankled in Hitler's soul. It was not to be borne that the Polish nation had any right to exist. Hitler would take what he wanted, and Russia could have the rest.

That Russia had to be placated, Hitler knew full well. Had he not made a deal, no Russian leader could have endured the fact of German troops advancing east across Poland. Who could know where or when they would stop? But, if Russia shared the spoils—

On August 23, 1939, Nazi Foreign Minister Ribbentrop for Germany and Molotov for Russia signed a non-aggression pact, which kept Hitler from the worry of Russian intervention on the Polish side. A secret "Additional Protocol" provided that Russia would get eastern Poland. Everything was most satisfactory. Germany had a free hand in western Europe. Russia had purchased time, for it would be a year and a half before Hitler tossed the non-aggression pact out the window and turned on his former partner.

Meanwhile, there was the little task of finishing off Poland.

Two German Army Groups, totaling 1,400,000 men, made the attack on Poland, while only some 800,000 Poles were available to defend their country. The tiny Polish Air Force was destroyed in a matter of hours, and the defenders were overwhelmed by the Germans on the ground. In truth, the Germans and Poles were fighting different wars. Polish tactics and strategy seemed to go back, not to World War I, but to the Crimean War, while the Germans gave the world an opening performance of the Blitzkrieg. Poland could not stop it, nor could France eight months later.

The Blitzkrieg can best be described as an expanding penetration. Spearheaded by armor, it drives fast and hard, exploiting weak points. Behind come motorized infantry, and then regular infantry. Air power disrupts enemy countermoves, so that confusion soon is the order of the day in the enemy ranks. Positions intended to hold up advances for days at a time are bypassed or quickly overrun by the combination of tanks, bombing, and mechanized artillery. The classic static defense offers little in the way of a barrier to the Blitzkrieg, and the Polish commanders were not capable of anything else.

The German plan for the conquest of Poland was a double envelopment. In the north, General Fedor von Bock's Army Group North,

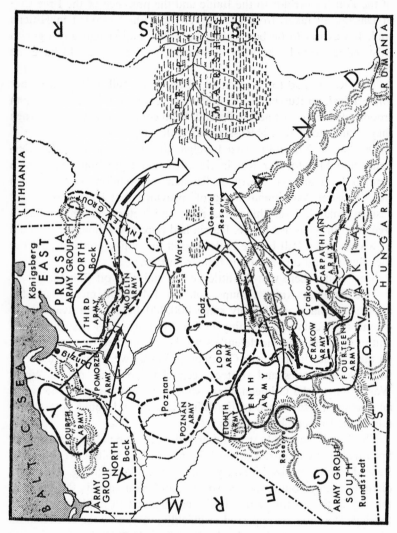

German invasion of Poland.

consisting of two armies, would cross the Polish Corridor and head south toward Warsaw and Kutno. The three armies of General Gerd von Rundstedt's Army Group South would head east toward Lodz, northeast toward Warsaw, and east to Cracow.

The speed of the German advance gave the Poles no time to reorganize their defenses, and one after another their armies were cut off and annihilated.

On September 3, General Heinz Guderian, commanding the Nineteenth Panzer Corps, could hardly believe his eyes. A cavalry brigade was charging his tanks!

The Pomorska Cavalry Brigade was a splendid sight. The colorful uniforms were bright, the horses were well groomed, and the leather gleamed. Officers drew their sabers and signaled the charge. The troopers dropped their lances into position and followed nobly. Horses' hooves thundered, and the dust and dirt flew up behind them. The charge had all the splendor and élan of one in a spectacular movie.

But it was not a movie, and the time was not 1854, and the opponents were not hapless infantrymen.

Horses against tanks! Lances and sabers against cannon and rifles!

Let those who will dwell on the slaughter that followed. Those men had nothing but their courage and their lives to offer.

Unfortunately, they were not enough.

And it was as true for the whole Polish nation as it was for the Pomorska Brigade. The Germans rushed on, giving no chance at all to the hapless Poles. Warsaw capitulated on September 27, alone and unaided, beset by two enemies. For on September 17, the Russians had poured in from the east. It was only a case of mopping up and dividing the spoils.

A few patriots escaped and made their way to London to set up a Government in Exile. There would be more such governments later, too many more.

Poland was left to become nothing. It was to disappear.

> We have no intention of rebuilding Poland [wrote General Franz Halder, Army Chief of Staff, in his diary]. Not to be a model state by German standards. Polish intelligentsia must be prevented from establishing itself as a governing class. Low standard of living must be conserved. Cheap slaves . . .
>
> Total disorganization must be created! The Reich will give the Governor General the means to carry out this devilish plan.

The Reich kept this promise.

Jews were rounded up and put in the cities, where they would be easy to find and deal with later. Firing squads kept busy. Resettlements were often carried out in blizzards, so that thousands froze or died of exposure. This loss was all gain from the German point of view.

On February 21, 1940, S.S. Oberführer Richard Gluecks informed the notorious Heinrich Himmler that he had found a suitable spot for a new "quarantine camp." Its name—Auschwitz.

*   *   *

"I have no war aims against Britain and France," declared Hitler at the Guild Hall in Danzig on September 19. "My sympathies are with the French *poilu.*"

Somehow, the people of Britain and France didn't believe him. The war went on.

To live, Britain must import food and materials. All these must come by sea, and it was at the ships of Britain that Germany launched her most telling offensive, by means of the deadly U-boats.

Because of Hitler's shortsightedness in all things maritime, Germany was ill-equipped to pursue submarine warfare in the fall of 1939. In contrast to the huge numbers which were to prowl the seas a few years later, Germany had only 56 operational U-boats when the war began. Of these only 26 were ocean-going types. Seventeen of these were on station when the war began, but Dönitz could not hope to maintain such a large number in the future.*

The sinking of the *Athenia* had more importance than might have been supposed, for it convinced the Admiralty that Germany was at once adopting unrestricted submarine warfare, and the order went out to begin ocean convoys. Originally the idea had been to wait and see, to let ships continue to sail independently according to peacetime methods, believing them to be more efficient.

Such methods are more efficient if the ships survive. But evidence from both World Wars proves conclusively that independently sailed ships in time of war tend to get sunk at a much greater rate than those in convoy. So, grumbling and only half-convinced, the Admiralty instituted the convoy system.

It is perhaps charitable to call it a system at this early date, for

* A good rule of thumb for submarine employment is that one-third can be on station at any one time. Another third will be in transit and the rest in for refit and training.

preparations for convoy had been neglected during the years of peace. Few escorts were available, and many of them were not capable of dealing with the U-boat on the surface, having less speed and smaller guns. Still, they went to sea and they did their part. An escort type that soon came into service was the "Flower-class" corvette. These were only 900 tons, about 200 feet in length, and fitted with obsolete asdic.* They were said to roll in a heavy dew, and their motions in the stormy winter North Atlantic are best imagined, not felt. Their designer had placed the mast directly in front of the bridge, so that the conning officer was unable to take a center-line bearing on a target. The crews who manned them so faithfully often in a Dantesque mood suggested that the appropriate punishment for the designer would be to send him to sea in one of his creations.

Many of the escorts were manned by enthusiastic amateurs, reservists called up, rather short on experience, but willing to "have a go" at almost anything. There was just enough leavening of experienced officers and men to make the whole thing work—just. And it was upon these enthusiastic amateurs that Britain's lifeline depended.

A typical convoy of the early days consisted of some 30 to 35 merchant ships, escorted by a venerable "V and W-class" destroyer of World War I vintage, a minesweeper, and a couple of drifters or trawlers fitted with depth-charge racks. Experience was short on the merchant ships as well, for the watch-keeping officers were accustomed to being out alone, not cramped in a close convoy with other ships only a few hundred yards away. There was temptation to strike out on one's own, to get away from the stifling, confining convoy and the acrimonious signals of the harried escort commander. But gradually the merchant skippers learned better. They discovered the little tricks of keeping station, and they began to develop some degree of faith in the protectors. The convoy system was there to stay throughout the war.

At first the convoys were patchy and limited in coverage. Shortage of escorts meant that convoys dispersed at 15° West longitude if they were going across the Atlantic or 47° North latitude if they were bound for Gibraltar or Africa. It was all that could be done.

In spite of the small number of U-boats at sea, the inexperienced escorts could not prevent losses. By the end of the year, 114 ships

* Asdic is the British equivalent of the American sonar, an ultrasonic device that gives an indication of the range and bearing of an underwater object. It takes considerable training to enable an operator to distinguish a submarine from a reef, a school of fish, a whale, or even a thermal layer in the water.

had been lost to U-boats, for a total of 421,156 tons.* Unfortunately, the figures would get worse in the months and years to come.

The U-boats had other successes, too. In the Western Approaches area, *U-39* narrowly missed the carrier *Ark Royal* with a spread of torpedoes and was promptly sunk for her pains. But on September 17, at about 2000, *U-29* let off torpedoes at the carrier *Courageous*. Two of them hit and she went down in fifteen minutes, taking 519 of her officers and men with her.

It was Friday, the thirteenth of October. H.M.S. *Royal Oak* swung peacefully at her anchorage in Scapa Flow. This was to be the main anchorage for the British Home Fleet. Located north of Scotland in the Orkney Islands, it offered little in the way of creature comforts for the men whose ships were based there. Bleak rocks jutted up out the roaring, pounding Atlantic, and screaming sea birds battled for bits of garbage and small fish. The Romans called these islands *Ultima Thule*—the end of the world. The Vikings found them to their taste, but not so the men of the Home Fleet. The men of the *Royal Oak* were content to stay aboard their ship where they were warm and dry and safe.

In these bleak waters the German High Seas Fleet had immolated itself following World War I, and for the German Navy, the words Scapa Flow carried a connotation of disaster and defeat. Its men hoped to avenge that defeat someday.

As the drab Friday faded into darkness, men of the *Royal Oak* thankfully settled down to their rest after a busy day of taking on provisions and stores. At 2230 the ship's entertainment system played the last record for the night, "Goodnight, My Love." All was peaceful.

While the men of the *Royal Oak* were still at work, some of them joking about Friday the thirteenth, the 500-ton *U-47* under command of Leutnant Günther Prien was moving toward the entrance to Scapa Flow. In the First World War, two U-boats had attempted to attack the fleet at Scapa, and neither had ever come back. Now Prien was going to give it another try.

* Sinkings of merchant ships by U-boats in 1939.

Month	Number of Ships	Tons
September	41	153,879
October	27	134,807
November	21	51,589
December	25	80,881

Only twelve of these ships were sunk in convoy. All the rest were independents or stragglers from convoys.

Sunken blockships guarded the entrance to Scapa, but Prien chose his time well, at high tide. Also, there was a gap in the blockship line. The hulk intended to fill it had been sunk on the way north, and another had not yet been sent. Navigating carefully, Prien got through. There had been a nasty moment when she fouled a blockship's anchor cable with her stem, but no damage was done. Without further incident, *U-47* entered the Scapa Flow anchorage. The time was just after midnight.

On the *Royal Oak* one of the men thought he heard something. A messmate reassured him: "Don't worry—it's Saturday the fourteenth."

The jar and the slight sound the man had heard was from Prien's first torpedo attack. The torpedo apparently hit way forward or possibly the anchor cable. It made little impression on the ship, and the captain and crew believed that if it was an explosion, it was internal.

Prien swung away to reload, and at 0116, he fired three more torpedoes. From the moment of the order, *"Torpedo los!"* Prien and his crew scarcely dared breathe. This was the last chance. There were no more torpedoes. If these missed, the daring penetration would have been in vain.

Never fear. Two of the torpedoes hit fair and square. Thirteen minutes later the battleship rolled over and sank, taking with her 833 officers and men.

Prien made his way out the way he came, and the passage out was the most difficult and dangerous part of his exploit, for the falling tide caused a race in the passage he had to use. The U-boat almost swung out of control at one point, but Prien managed to get her back on course. By 0215 he was clear and took his departure for Wilhelmshaven, which he reached on October 17. Met by Dönitz, Prien was flown to Berlin for personal congratulations by the Führer, who presented him with the Knight's Cross of the Iron Cross. Prien went on to become one of Germany's U-boat aces. He and his U-boat were lost on March 8, 1941, while attacking a convoy.*

On the last day of November, the Russians mounted an attack on Finland. But the scrappy Finns put up such a battle, aided by the winter, that the Russian-Finnish War became a joke and the Red

* Alexander McKee in his book *Black Saturday: The Death of the* Royal Oak (New York: Holt, Rinehart and Winston, Inc., 1960), argues that Prien never penetrated Scapa Flow and that the *Royal Oak* was sunk by internal explosions. He points out many discrepancies, but his case is not convincing.

Army a laughing stock. Of course, the situation was hopeless, and the Finns had eventually to give up in March. Hitler looked on smugly and decided that the Russians were hopelessly incompetent in the business of war. They could be polished off without much trouble when the time came.

* * *

The American Hog Islander, S.S. *City of Flint,* was steaming peacefully from New York to the United Kingdom, carrying general cargo. It was a routine voyage, perhaps seeming a little dull to the crew, for on the previous voyage, the *City of Flint* had rescued 236 survivors from the *Athenia.* Improvising dormitory space, feeding arrangements, and care for the sick, Captain Joseph A. Gainard had brought his passengers safely to Halifax and New York. That had been the voyage of excitement.

They had had their excitement. This voyage would be routine.

It was the afternoon of October 9, 1939. Cadet Officer Manuel Codoner, who was on the bridge, pointed to something on the horizon. "Isn't that cloud moving fast, compared with the others?"

Captain Gainard looked and wondered if it was indeed a cloud. In a few minutes he knew the answer. It was a ship, and it was moving toward them. Worse, it was a large warship.

Codoner spoke again. "I think she's German."

"What would a German ship be doing way out here, only three days off the Grand Banks?" someone wanted to know.

"I wouldn't know," replied the cadet, "but she looks like the *Deutschland.* I've been aboard the *Deutschland* in Germany when I visited there."

Codoner was right. It was the *Deutschland.* One of Germany's three pocket battleships, she displaced well over her official 10,000 tons, carried six 11-inch guns in two turrets, and could make some 28 knots on her diesel engines.* She was a formidable foe and could be expected to dispose of any cruiser that dared to meet her. Certainly an unarmed merchant ship was helpless in her presence.

The 11-inch guns were pointed at the *City of Flint,* and as Captain Gainard brought his vessel to a stop, two flag-hoist signals appeared: "You must not use your radio" and "I am going to send you a boat."

---

* The other two were the *Admiral Graf Spee* and the *Admiral Scheer.* When she returned to Germany, the *Deutschland* had her name changed to *Lützow.*

Three German officers boarded the *City of Flint* and came up to the bridge. "Captain, I am sorry," said one of them, "to cause you inconvenience, but this is war. I must ask to see your papers."

The Germans studied the manifests. The cargo consisted of apples, asphalt, machinery, wax, lumber, tractors, canned goods, cereals, tobacco, lard, flour, grease, and general cargo.

The senior German officer, Leutnant Hans Puschbach, looked grim. "This is bad," he said. "You have 20,000 drums of oil on board. What kind of oil is it?"

"Lubricating oil."

"That is bad. And this flour; what is it?"

"White-bread flour."

"Under the laws of my country," said the German, "you are guilty of carrying contraband to the enemy. I must signal back to the ship."

"This is a United States ship," retorted Captain Gainard. "And this cargo is not contraband under the laws of the United States."

His words were of no effect. Soon came the order from the *Deutschland.* "We are sending a prize crew. The ship will go to Germany. We are also sending thirty-eight English prisoners who have given their parole."

And so, under a prize crew, the American *City of Flint* began a new journey. Under command of her own captain, whose every move was directed by Leutnant Puschbach, she set out far to the north to avoid British patrols. Puschbach was polite, but he was firm. "You are now bound for Germany," he told the crew. "My sailors will be a military guard and you will get all your orders from your captain. You must obey these. If there is any interference or refusal, I will kill you. I have sufficient means here to sink the ship. If there is any interference in any way, I must act with war measures. My country is at war, and whether we like it or not, we must do certain things we would not do ordinarily."

As the ship plowed her way northeast, the crew started several plots to recapture their ship, but they were always discovered.

When the ship reached the far north, it made an emergency call at Tromsø, Norway, for water, and then Puschbach decided to go on to Murmansk. Captain Gainard hoped the Russians would release the vessel according to international law, and at first, it seemed he would get his wish.

Russian boarding officials were suspicious, but after examining the papers of the *City of Flint,* they took off the German prize crew and stated that the ship was free to leave. Free, that is, as soon as "your papers are returned by the customs men." But it was always tomorrow that the papers would be returned.

Gainard attempted to send a message to American Ambassador Laurence Steinhardt, but somehow the message never got through. One "tomorrow" followed another, and still the ship was held in Murmansk.

Four days passed with no change in the situation. On the fifth the German prize crew returned, and the Russians announced the ship was free to sail—for Germany.

Down the long Norwegian coast went the *City of Flint,* keeping in territorial waters. Then Leutnant Puschbach decided to take the ship into Haugesund to get medical treatment for a man who had an injured leg. Under international law, such an emergency would permit the Germans to keep custody of the vessel, if the emergency was bona fide. But the Norwegians decided the injury was too slight. The *City of Flint* had entered illegally. A Norwegian military guard escorted the German prize crew off the ship, and the captain of the minelayer *Olaf Tryggvason* sent for Captain Gainard.

"Captain," he said with a broad grin, "I congratulate you, I am glad you are free. I am glad that we were a part of this successful operation; so are your minister and my admiral. Incidentally, your minister and my admiral want me to inform you that the *Olaf Tryggvason* sails for Bergen in an hour, and Bergen is a delightful place to spend a weekend."

Captain Gainard and his crew did find Bergen a delightful place to spend the weekend. The American minister, Mrs. J. Borden Harriman, handled most of the technicalities, and the men of the *City of Flint* enjoyed themselves. They had a dinner given by the American Club of Bergen, and afterwards, everyone joined in Norwegian folk dances.

The vessel stayed in Bergen until after Thanksgiving while the State Department sent protesting notes to both Russia and Germany. Toward the end of November, she sailed for home. Her troubles were over, for the time being, at any rate.*

The incident of the *City of Flint* was Germany's first challenge to America. Neither side was willing to make an issue of the matter, and it was soon forgotten. But there would be other incidents, other irritations, some far more serious.

The *Deutschland* was not the only German pocket battleship at

* She was sunk on January 27, 1943, while carrying supplies to the American forces in North Africa.

14

sea. Her sister, *Admiral Graf Spee,* had sailed from Germany before the war broke out and skulked in the South Atlantic, out of sight of ships, waiting, waiting for permission to begin her activities against British shipping. The hunter was ready, but Hitler decided that the hunting season had not yet begun.

The British steamer *Clement,* 5050 tons, was rolling gently in the brisk easterly breeze. It was just after 1115, and Third Officer H. J. Gill stared intently out over the port bow. Then he returned to the speaking tube and called down to Captain F. C. P. Harris, who was in his cabin just below the bridge. "There is a man-o'war about four points on the port bow, coming in fast."

Captain Harris was not worried. "I expect that is the *Ajax,*" he replied, "or a Brazilian cruiser."

He was wrong on both counts. It was no cruiser, and it was neither British nor Brazilian. It was the *Graf Spee.* Hitler had opened the hunting season.

The pocket battleship approached end on, and Captain Harris could see no flag. A seaplane circled the *Clement,* spraying machine-gun bullets toward the bridge. Harris ordered the vessel stopped and the boats lowered. A distress message went out by radio, and the confidential books went overboard. All hands took to the lifeboats.

A boarding officer in one of the *Graf Spee*'s boats came up and took Captain Harris and Chief Engineer W. Bryant with him. They were not mistreated, for they had had the good fortune to be captured by a gentleman.

Captain Hans Langsdorff had been an officer in the Imperial German Navy. Although he belonged to the Nazi Party, he was naive on political matters, and had been genuinely shocked when Hitler led his beloved Germany into the alliance with Russia. The Navy was his life, and his entire career had pointed to the command he now held. He did not like the role he had to play, that of the wolf attacking the helpless sheep. He had his orders, however, and he intended to do his duty, but as humanely as possible.

He turned to greet the two British officers as they were led to the bridge of his ship. Saluting Harris, he said, "I am sorry, Captain, I will have to sink your ship. It is war. I believe you have destroyed your confidential papers?"

"Yes," replied Harris.

"I expected it. That it the usual thing."

It was a source of considerable embarrassment to Captain Langs-

15

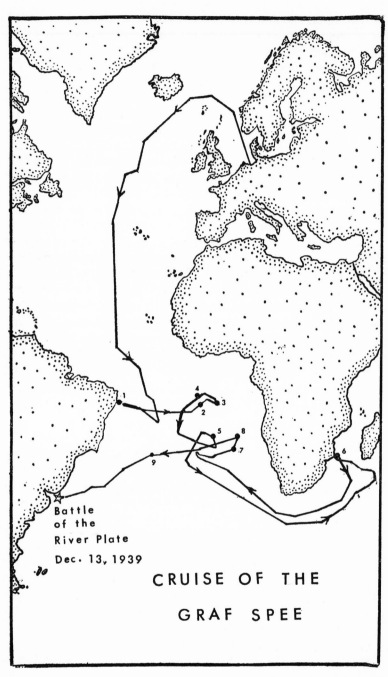

Battle
of the
River Plate

Dec. 13, 1939

CRUISE OF THE

GRAF SPEE

see caption on opposite page

dorff that it took so long to sink the *Clement*. Two torpedoes missed, and it took the main battery guns to finish the helpless merchantman off. Then the *Graf Spee* turned away, displaying the name board with *Admiral Scheer* on it to the crew of the *Clement*, left behind in their boats.*

Langsdorff was not callously leaving the men to their deaths. The sea was moderate, and it was less than 200 miles to the South American coast. The men were in no grave danger. But Langsdorff took considerable risk to see to it that they were saved. Using the call sign of the *Admiral Scheer*, he called up the radio station at Pernambuco: PLEASE SAVE THE LIFEBOATS OF THE CLEMENT X ZERO NINE FOUR FIVE SOUTH THREE FOUR ZERO FOUR WEST.

Back came the answer: THANKS X OKAY X HASTA LUEGO.

Harris and Bryant were transferred to a neutral ship and reached the Cape Verde Islands ten days later.

The *Graf Spee* sped eastward to pass between St. Helena and Ascension Island, in order to move as far from the scene as possible. She knew her presence had been revealed by radio and by the neutral. It was time to hunt elsewhere, for the British would soon be after her.

The next day a message clattered out of the message tube at the Admiralty.

BRITISH SHIP MBBL [*Clement*] SUNK BY SURFACE RAIDER SEVEN FIVE MILES SOUTHEAST OF PERNAMBUCO FOURTEEN HUNDRED LOCAL TIME YESTERDAY

This was the confirmation of suspicions the Admiralty had long held, that at least one German raider was at sea, and very possibly it might be a pocket battleship. This presented them with a nasty problem, for she could outrun any battleship the Allies possessed at that

---

* Langsdorff had decided to disguise his ship as the *Admiral Scheer*, one of her two sisters, in order to confuse the British. False name plates were prepared, and the crew had the *Scheer*'s name on their cap bands.

Victims of the *Graf Spee*

1. S.S. *Clement*, Sept. 30, 1939	6. S.S. *Africa Shell*, Nov. 15, 1939
2. S.S. *Newton Beach*, Oct. 5, 1939	7. S.S. *Doric Star*, Dec. 2, 1939
3. S.S. *Ashlea*, Oct. 7, 1939	8. S.S. *Tairoa*, Dec. 3, 1939
4. S.S. *Huntsman*, Oct. 10, 1939	9. S.S. *Streonshalh*, Dec. 7, 1939
5. M.V. *Trevanion*, Oct. 22, 1939	

time, and she could blow any cruiser out of the water with her 11-inch guns. In fact, there were only five ships in the British and French navies capable of both catching her and sinking her: H.M.S. *Hood,* H.M.S. *Repulse,* H.M.S. *Renown,* and the French battle cruisers *Strasbourg* and *Dunkerque.* And these five ships could not be everywhere.

To cover as much as possible of the area the pocket battleship might infest, with the cooperation of the French, the Admiralty established a number of "killer groups," based on the West Indies, the east coast of South America, Cape Town, Ceylon, Brest, Dakar, and a roving group to patrol between Pernambuco and Freetown. Most of these groups consisted of two heavy cruisers, and their composition changed from time to time as the days and weeks went on without success. The *Graf Spee* was proving hard to find.

Her real value to Germany was not in the number of ships she sank. Many U-boats were to do better on a single patrol. The *Graf Spee* sank 9 ships for a total of 50,088 tons.* But she caused nearly three times that number of warships to be drawn from other duties in an effort to track her down. This is the real measure of her effectiveness.

On December 7, 1939, the *Graf Spee* parted from her supply ship *Altmark* for the last time. To the tender mercies of Captain Heinrich Dau, Langsdorff had left 299 British seamen from his victims. The *Graf Spee* would make one more foray before heading for home. This time she would strike at the busy approaches to the River Plate on which lie the cities of Buenos Aires in Argentina and Montevideo in Uruguay. In that area Langsdorff had two rendezvous. The first would cost the British the steamer *Streonshalh.* The second would cost Germany the *Graf Spee* and Langsdorff and 37 of his men their lives. The trap was about to close around him.

Commodore Henry Harwood, RN, was working with his staff in the chartroom of H.M.S. *Ajax.* Using all the information he could gather, he boldly predicted that the German raider would arrive off the River Plate on December 13. And he would be there to meet her.

His little squadron might—just might—be able to grapple with the

* These were *Clement* (5050 tons), September 30; *Newton Beach* (4651 tons), October 4; *Ashlea* (4222 tons), October 7; *Huntsman* (8196 tons), October 10; *Trevanion* (5299 tons), October 22; *Africa Shell* (706 tons), November 15; *Doric Star* (10,086 tons), December 1; *Tairoa* (7983 tons), December 2; *Streonshalh* (3895 tons), December 7.

Graf Spee. His most powerful ship, H.M.S. *Exeter,* was ten years old, and, unlike all other British heavy cruisers, mounted six instead of eight 8-inch guns. She had an antiaircraft battery of eight 4-inch guns, which would be useless in a surface action. Her skipper, Captain F. S. Bell, had confidence in his ship and would give a good account of himself.

Harwood's other two ships were sisters, light cruisers with eight 6-inch guns, and eight 21-inch torpedo tubes. They were fast and maneuverable, but thin-skinned. Eleven-inch armor-piercing shells from the *Graf Spee* would go through their 4-inch side armor with ease. His flagship, *Ajax,* carried four more antiaircraft guns than her sister and also two scouting aircraft. The third ship, *Achilles,* was on loan to the Royal New Zealand Navy, and had only recently made the long voyage across the Pacific and around through the Strait of Magellan to join the Commodore.

It was a chancy thing to send this little force against the powerful German raider, for her six 11-inch guns hurled projectiles two and a half times as heavy as those of the 8-inch *Exeter.** Her secondary battery of 5.9-inch guns was nearly the equivalent of the main batteries of the two light cruisers. Here was Harwood's only gunnery advantage; he had sixteen 6-inch guns in his two light cruisers, while Langsdorff had only eight. Harwood also had a 3- to 4-knot speed advantage. It was scarcely a comfortable situation.

It was 0450 on the morning of December 13. The darkness of the night changed moment by moment into the gray light of dawn. All three British ships were at Dawn Action Stations, as they were every morning. On the bridge of the *Ajax,* Commodore Harwood exchanged an occasional word with Captain Charles H. L. Woodhouse, commanding the flagship. But mostly he looked out at the sea, seeking something he could not find. This was the moment of the decision. If Harwood had judged right, the *Graf Spee* would soon be putting in an appearance. If he was wrong, then it would be his fault, and any further victims of the raider would lie on his conscience.

It grew light and soon the horizon was clearly visible. Around the entire circle of sea at whose center he kept watch, there was nothing. Only the other ships of his squadron marred the perfect symmetry.

Grievously disappointed, Commodore Harwood exercised his ships in the maneuvers he intended to use if he caught up with the German.

At 0540, the ships resumed normal cruising stations and Commo-

---

* The weight of metal of *Exeter*'s broadside was 1536 pounds, that of the *Graf Spee* 4020 pounds. These figures are for main batteries only.

19

dore Harwood and Captain Woodhouse retired to their sea cabins. So did Captain Bell in the *Exeter*.

Aboard the *Achilles,* Captain W. E. Parry lingered on his bridge to talk to Lieutenant Richard Washbourn about the gunnery exercises scheduled for later in the day. He finished the discussion and was turning to go below for a shave and bath when a lookout reported a sighting.

"Smoke bearing Red one double oh, Sir." *

The time was 0611, and, though they did not yet know it, the British had found the *Graf Spee*.

At first Harwood believed the smoke came from a merchant ship. Certainly a well-run warship had no business making that volume of smoke. He ordered the *Exeter* to investigate.

At 0616 Bell signaled, "I think it is a pocket battleship." A moment later came the signal, "Enemy in sight, bearing 322." †

The battle was about to begin. And 37 men of the *Graf Spee,* 5 officers and 48 men of the *Exeter,* 7 men of the *Ajax,* and 4 men of the *Achilles* had less than two hours to live.

Commodore Harwood's only chance was to force the enemy to divide her fire. This had been his plan all along. As the ships went to action stations, the two light cruisers continued to the northeast as a unit, while the *Exeter* sheered off to the southwest. They would engage the *Graf Spee* from either bow.

The British ships ran up battle ensigns, four each, in case one was shot away. The White Ensign of the Royal Navy is an inspiring looking flag, and as these huge ensigns flapped and fluttered in the breeze, they displayed perhaps the only remnant of pageantry permitted in modern war.

The *Graf Spee* had spotted the British force some minutes earlier. Her higher fighting top gave her lookouts a greater range of visibility. The first report was of a single ship, but even as the pocket battleship went to action stations, the correction came: three ships.

If they were merchantmen, this would be the richest haul yet. Langsdorff permitted his hopes to rise. Then a lookout identified the largest ship as the *Exeter*. An officer hurriedly thumbed through a copy of *Jane's Fighting Ships*. There was no doubt about it. It was the *Exeter,* all right. Then the two ships with her must be destroyers. And

* The British report relative bearings by color corresponding to the running lights, red for port and green for starboard. Thus the *Graf Spee* was spotted slightly abaft the port beam.
† This is a true bearing, roughly northwest.

20

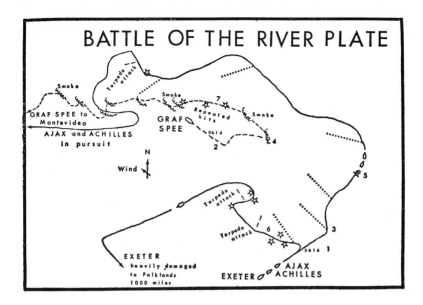

BATTLE OF THE RIVER PLATE

Smoke

Torpedo attack

GRAF SPEE to Montevideo

AJAX and ACHILLES in pursuit

Smoke

7

Repeated hits

Smoke

GRAF SPEE

0614

2

4

N

Wind

0
0
5

Torpedo attack

Torpedo attack

1
6
3

0614

EXETER
heavily damaged
to Falklands
1000 miles

EXETER

AJAX
ACHILLES

just beyond, out of sight, Langsdorff believed, lay a convoy. It was an opportunity too good to be missed. He would close, polish off the *Exeter* and the destroyers. Then the convoy would be helpless. It would be a wonderful climax to his cruise.

He ordered full speed and closed the distance.* Already his 11-inch guns were training on the *Exeter*. In a few short moments, he would be in range.

Five minutes later an officer reported that the two smaller ships were not destroyers, but cruisers of the *Ajax* class. In an instant, Langsdorff knew he had made a mistake. He could not afford to engage three cruisers, for a lucky hit by any of them might incapacitate him. A raider has no friends, and any damage he sustained could be repaired only in Germany. He could not afford *any* damage.

But it was too late. All three cruisers were faster than the *Graf Spee,* and the two sides were closing at a combined speed of 50 knots or more. There was no avoiding battle.

At 0617 the *Graf Spee* opened fire on the *Exeter* at a range of 21,000 yards. Three minutes later, the *Exeter*'s guns roared defiance, then those of *Achilles* and *Ajax*.

On board the *Graf Spee*, Langsdorff properly regarded the *Exeter*

* The speed increase undoubtedly caused the smoke that betrayed the *Graf Spee* to the British.

as the major threat and trained his main battery to starboard to engage her. Division I, the two light cruisers, he would hold at bay with his secondary batteries.

The *Exeter*'s third salvo straddled * the *Graf Spee,* and almost at the same instant an 11-inch shell from the raider landed alongside the *Exeter.* The explosion sent a shower of splinters on the ship, killing most of the crew in the starboard torpedo mount, cutting electrical leads, and starting a small fire. Then came the first direct hit, which went completely through the deck and out the ship's side without exploding. Things were getting too hot.

A moment later the *Exeter* was nearly knocked out of action. Captain Bell reported: "After the eighth salvo B turret received a direct hit from an 11-inch shell and was put out of action. The splinters also killed or wounded all the bridge personnel with the exception of the Captain, Torpedo Control, and Firing Officers, and wrecked the wheelhouse communications."

In that instant the *Exeter* was changed from a splendid fighting ship to a weaving, erratic wreck. Captain Bell was wounded in the face; the men who had been standing on either side of him were dead. A and Y turrets were still firing as Bell hastened aft to the secondary control station, and through the thunder of the guns, he shouted to bring his vessel back on course. Arriving there, he found all communications and control equipment shot away there as well, and had to establish a human chain to relay his commands to the after steering position deep down in the ship, where sweating men strained their hearts out to move the heavy rudder by hand.

Still Captain Bell and the *Exeter* would not quit. They continued to fire, and had the satisfaction of seeing a shell hit near the funnel of the German raider. It was shortly after this that the *Graf Spee* began to make a smoke screen and turned away.

Meanwhile Division I, *Ajax* and *Achilles,* was peppering the *Graf Spee* with 6-inch guns. Many of the shells hit, doing superficial damage, for they could not penetrate the armor of the German. Annoyed, Langsdorff turned his big guns on the light cruisers, giving *Exeter* a much-needed respite. The *Ajax* and *Achilles,* while maintaining rough formation, were weaving independently, dodging shells as best they could. *Achilles* used the trick of steering toward the last shell splashes, so that the corrections applied by the *Graf Spee*'s

---

* A straddle is the term applied when some shells of a salvo fall short and others pass over the target. The range is then established. It is only a matter of time and luck until the shells begin hitting.

gunnery officer would always be in the wrong direction. But neither ship escaped damage. Captain Parry of *Achilles* was wounded in both legs, and a shell hit on the *Ajax* destroyed the cabins of Captain Woodhouse, the Executive Officer, and Commodore Harwood.

The battle went on. More hits reduced the *Exeter* to a near-wreck; only one gun was still firing, and her speed was reduced to 18 knots. Desperately, Bell got off his three starboard torpedoes, and then ordered his ship swung to starboard to unmask his port tubes. Cursing, straining men got the rudder over, and eleven minutes later three more torpedoes entered the water and streaked toward the raider.

The *Exeter* had shot her bolt. She could no longer keep up with the battle. As long as she was able, she continued to fire her one remaining gun. At one point, Bell considered trying to ram; it would finish the *Exeter,* but it would finish the *Graf Spee,* too. But there was no chance. The battle passed on.

Now Langsdorff was able to concentrate on the two light cruisers, and the game looked hopeless for Harwood. His 6-inch shells seemed unable to do any serious damage, and at about 0740 he received a report that *Ajax* had only a fifth of her ammunition remaining and that only three guns were able to fire.

> *Graf Spee*'s shooting was still very accurate and she did not appear to have suffered much damage.
> I therefore decided to break off the day action and try to close in again after dark. Accordingly at 0740 *Ajax* and *Achilles* turned away to the east under cover of smoke.

So wrote Commodore Harwood in his report of the battle. *Exeter*'s torpedoes had missed, and so had four fired earlier from *Ajax*. His own force was near to being knocked out, and the *Graf Spee* seemed immune to damage. He could only shadow and hope.

But the *Graf Spee* was in far worse shape than Commodore Harwood imagined.

Strangely enough, it was not the 8-inch shells of the *Exeter* that had done the most damage. Only two of those had hit. One of them hit the armor belt and started only small leaks. The other passed through the director tower and the admiral's bridge without exploding. But a large number of 6-inch hits were in vital places. One opened a hole in the bow. Another destroyed the galley; another disrupted damage control communications. Captain Langsdorff was wounded by the thirteenth hit, being knocked off his feet and rendered unconscious for a few minutes. It is just possible that this misfortune affected his judgment in the crucial hours and days ahead.

As the two light cruisers swung away under smoke screens, Captain Langsdorff, too, had had enough for the moment. When he came to, he continued the fight while he must. Then, after inspecting the ship, he said to his navigator, Lieutenant Commander Wattenberg: "We must run into port; the ship is not now seaworthy for the North Atlantic."

So began the day-long run toward the River Plate and the death trap of Montevideo. Neither Captain Langsdorff nor the *Graf Spee* would ever come out again.

Commodore Harwood, who had won but still did not know it, tagged along in the *Ajax, Achilles* playing "Follow Father" in her wake. They kept a respectful distance, but Commodore Harwood was determined not to lose touch. The *Graf Spee* might double back and turn on him.

First things first, however. Harwood had to determine the condition of his force. He had lost sight of the *Exeter* and did not even know if she was still afloat. Unable to raise her by radio, he sent his search plane to look. Half an hour later, the plane returned and signaled: *"Exeter* severely damaged and joining you as best she can." It was noon before the Commodore received word from her directly in reply to a signal asking what speed she could make. EIGHTEEN KNOTS X ONE GUN IN Y TURRET AVAILABLE IN LOCAL CONTROL X ALL OTHER MAIN ARMAMENT PERMANENTLY OUT OF ACTION X ONE FOUR INCH GUN AVAILABLE NO AIR IN SHIP.

It took little reflection for the Commodore to realize that the *Exeter* could be of no further service. He ordered the gallant ship to make for the nearest British base, Port Stanley in the Falkland Islands, 1200 miles away.*

Now the Commodore had, as he put it, "only one and a half cruisers" to handle the *Graf Spee* if she turned back on them, but the German ship showed no such intention. Once or twice she fired when the British ships edged too close, but that was all. On ran the three ships toward Montevideo, all day and far into the night. On the

* The *Exeter* reached the Falklands safely and made temporary repairs. On her return to England in February, Captain Bell and his crew were feted, and Mr. Churchill visited the ship to speak to all hands. She had a distinguished war career until she was sunk by the Japanese on March 1, 1942, in Sunda Strait. See the author's *1942: The Year That Doomed the Axis* (New York: David McKay Company, Inc., 1967), pp. 84–88.

way in, the *Graf Spee* encountered the British merchant ship *Shakespeare*, put a shot across her bow, but did not sink her when the *Shakespeare* refused to obey the signal. At 2350 the *Graf Spee* entered Montevideo harbor and dropped her anchor.* Her raiding career was over.

The *Ajax* and *Achilles* took station outside the three-mile limit and waited. It was all the Commodore could do. The next moves were up to the Admiralty and to the diplomats.

Commodore Harwood's first thought was the necessity of keeping the *Graf Spee* in port long enough for reinforcements to reach him. And no reinforcements were close at hand. The nearest was the heavy cruiser *Cumberland,* already pounding north from the Falklands, bringing her eight 8-inch guns to join the fray. She arrived off the Plate on the evening of December 14. There would be no further reinforcements until December 19, when the carrier *Ark Royal,* the battle cruiser *Renown,* and the cruiser *Neptune* would be on hand.

Captain Langsdorff's first thought was to make his ship seaworthy once again. Much of the work could be accomplished by his own ship's company with the materials they carried on board. But some was beyond his capacity; he needed a shipyard. To assist him, he had the services of the German ambassador to Uruguay, Dr. Otto Langmann, who seemed to be more interested in blaming Captain Langsdorff than in aiding him.

Almost his first words to Langsdorff were to castigate him for entering Montevideo at all. He should, said the ambassador, have gone on to Buenos Aires. There the strong German colony would see to it that he had more assistance than was likely from the "politically weak" Uruguay. Langsdorff had not taken his ship the additional distance up the River Plate because the channel is shallow. He felt he could not risk grounding or fouling his cooling intakes, which, on the *Graf Spee,* were in the bottom of the ship. He was not particularly interested in politics and did not know that Uruguay was much more closely tied with Britain and France than was Argentina.

Meanwhile, he had other things to worry about. There were the prisoners from the sunken ships to set free. There were the dead to bury. And, above all, he had his ship to get ready for sea once more.

He demanded fifteen days to repair the damage. The British Minister, Mr. Eugen Millington-Drake, and the French Minister, M. Gentil, demanded that the *Graf Spee* go back to sea in twenty-four

---

* This was 0050, December 14, according to the time kept aboard both the British and the German ships.

hours or be interned. It was not until he received an urgent signal from Commodore Harwood, imploring him to delay the sailing of the German raider, that Mr. Millington-Drake realized that he had put his wrong foot forward. He began to maneuver to delay the ship without seeming to.

As Mr. Millington-Drake left Dr. Guani, the Uruguayan Foreign Minister, by one door, Dr. Langmann, looking sulky, and Captain Langsdorff came in by another. It began to seem as though Dr. Guani needed traffic signals, for, of course, the British and French could not meet the Germans, either officially or unofficially.* Before he gave the Germans the decision of the Uruguayan commission that had examined the damage to the *Graf Spee,* Dr. Guani could not resist the temptation to heckle the Germans. When Dr. Langmann opened by saying, "Your Excellency is well aware of the facts," Dr. Guani said quickly:

> "Let me see if I have got them right." He picked up a paper and read from it. " 'Early yesterday morning off Punta del Este, a naval battle took place. The German pocket battleship, *Admiral Graf Spee,* was engaged by three British cruisers, the *Exeter,* the *Ajax,* and the *Achilles.* In the course of this engagement, the German battleship gained a victory. The British cruiser *Exeter* was seen to be shot to pieces and the other British cruisers fled. The *Graf Spee* herself received a few minor hits—' "
>
> Langsdorff interrupted. "That is not correct."
>
> "No?" inquired Guani politely.
>
> "No. The *Graf Spee* has suffered serious damage. She is not seaworthy."
>
> "But," protested Guani, "I am quoting the official communiqué of your own Government, quoted by your own official agency, the *Deutsches Nachrichtenbureau,* issued today at 1315 Greenwich Mean Time." †

Then followed the decision. The *Graf Spee* could have seventy-two hours in port, beginning from the time the investigating commission had left the ship. That meant that the ship would have to leave the harbor at 2000 on Sunday, December 17. If she did not, she would be interned.

The Uruguayan Government had satisfied neither party in this

* Sir Eugen Millington-Drake has told the author that he did not, in fact, meet Captain Langsdorff, even off the record. He would have liked to, for he has a high regard for him.

† From an account given the author by Sir Eugen Millington-Drake.

decision. It had not given the British time to gather additional forces, nor had it given the Germans time to complete the repairs Langsdorff desired to make. But Uruguay had been strictly correct according to international law.* Langsdorff would have to sail by the time appointed. He could, of course, sail earlier, if he desired. Uruguay would put no barriers in his way. She would be only too happy to be rid of her unwelcome visitor.

The British, meanwhile, embarked on a great program of deception to convince the Germans that heavy naval forces were just over the horizon. Stories were leaked in bars, in taverns, and over the insecure telephone lines that the *Renown* and *Ark Royal* were waiting, accompanied by several cruisers and destroyers. Langsdorff's gunnery officer believed that he had spotted both the *Renown* and *Ark Royal* on the horizon. What he saw can never be known—fishing vessels, clouds, coastal steamers? Imagination is a wonderful thing, and we all have a tendency to see what we expect to see. For the vessels he believed he saw were over 2000 miles away.

Langsdorff could have discounted stories from the shore, but the report of one of his own officers weighed heavily with him. He realized his trap. He needed instructions, and he needed them from Berlin, not from the testy, disapproving Langmann. He sent off a message.

(1) *Renown* and *Ark Royal* as well as cruisers and destroyers off Montevideo. Close blockade at night. No prospect of breaking out to the open sea and getting through to Germany.

(2) Intend to proceed to the limit of neutral waters. If I can fight my way through to Buenos Aires with ammunition still remaining I shall endeavor to do so.

(3) As a breakthrough might result in the destruction of *Spee* without possibility of causing damage to the enemy, request instructions whether to scuttle the ship (in spite of the inadequate depth of water in the Plate estuary) or to submit to internment.

Admiral Raeder took the message to Hitler, and the Führer himself made the decision, which was duly sent back to Langsdorff:

(1) Attempt by all means to extend the time in neutral waters in order to guarantee freedom of action as long as possible.

* Under international law a warship of a belligerent nation must leave a neutral port within twenty-four hours or be interned. However, if she is damaged, she is permitted to remain long enough to make the repairs required to render her seaworthy, but she may not add in any manner whatever to her fighting force. The local authorities of the neutral power are the sole judges of what repairs are necessary.

(2) With reference to No. 2. Approved.

(3) With reference to No. 3. No internment in Uruguay. Attempt effective destruction if ship is scuttled.

Raeder

On the evening of December 16, Langsdorff had been considering the possibility of a breakthrough. His best chance was to sail that night, hoping to escape the British ships, and make his way to Buenos Aires. Then he was informed that a British merchant ship had sailed at 1815 that day and that he would not be allowed to depart until 1815, December 17.* Since he *had* to leave by 2000 that date, it left him only an hour and three-quarters to make his move. All chance of surprise was lost.

He decided he would scuttle his ship.

He felt he could not fight his way out. The *Graf Spee* would be trapped in the narrow channel, unable to maneuver to avoid gunfire or torpedoes. If she sank in the Plate estuary, he would be unable to destroy secret equipment which could be captured by divers. Even if he took the ship to sea, he could not feed his crew, in the unlikely event they made it to the open Atlantic. His galleys were knocked out, and he could not get them repaired in time. But mostly, he did not want to sacrifice his men in a futile battle. If there had been the possibility of inflicting further damage to the enemy, he would have gone out.

Sunday, December 17, was a busy day. The British were readying themselves for new battle, the Germans for scuttling. The British were now led by a Rear Admiral, for the day before, Harwood had received a signal informing him of his promotion and of his elevation to Knight Commander of the Bath, while the captains of the *Exeter, Ajax,* and *Achilles* were made Companions of the Bath. A sailor on the *Ajax* pointed out wryly that though his admiral and his captain were both members of the Order of the Bath, they did not have a bathroom between them, since their quarters had been destroyed by a shell from the *Graf Spee*.

Harwood reported his intentions to the Admiralty. They began, "My object destruction."

"Whose?" quipped one of his officers.

Langsdorff spent most of the day transferring his crew to the

---

* This is in accordance with Article 16 of the Hague Convention of 1907, which reads, in part: "A belligerent warship may not leave a neutral port or roadstead less than twenty-four hours after the departure of a marine ship flying the flag of its adversary."

chartered German steamer *Tacoma,* which would take them to Buenos Aires. Only 43 men would take the *Graf Spee* on her last, brief voyage.

At 1815, December 17, as thousands watched from the waterfront of Montevideo, the *Graf Spee* got under way, her colors flying.* She was followed by the *Tacoma.* She did not go far before she turned westward, as if toward Buenos Aires. Instead she put her nose on a mudbank. The *Tacoma* waited some 3000 yards away. Langsdorff stood quietly on the bridge while his men set the fuses on the scuttling charges. He was a lonely figure, a man who had been defeated, a man who was scuttling his ship. He was a man who had lost everything—reputation, ship, command.

But not self-respect, not honor. These, he knew, he had kept. And he would prove it a little later.

With Germanic love for the dramatic, the charges were set to go off just at sunset, at 2054. Langsdorff and his scuttling party watched from a launch, while the rest of his men observed from the *Tacoma.* Promptly, as the sun dipped below the horizon, the explosions began. Wreckage leaped up as one shattering roar followed another. The ship lurched, shuddered, and began to crumple. She heeled part way over and sank, most of her top hamper remaining above the water.

The fires continued for a long time. It was a Wagnerian scene, which delighted the heart of Goebbels, who made the most of it for propaganda effect.

The next day in Buenos Aires, Langsdorff, cheerful and confident, saw to the comfort and well-being of his crew. Contrary to his hopes, the Argentinian Government decided they should be interned. He made a last address to the crew and then retired to his hotel room.

There he wrote three letters. The first was to his wife, the second to his parents, and the third to Baron von Thermann, German ambassador to Argentina. It concluded:

> It was clear to me that the decision [to scuttle the ship] might be consciously or unwittingly misconstrued by persons ignorant of my motives as being attributable partly or entirely to personal considerations. Therefore I decided from the beginning to bear the consequences involved in this decision.
>
> For a captain with a sense of honor, it goes without saying that his personal fate cannot be separated from that of his ship. . . .
>
> I alone bear the responsibility for scuttling the pocket battleship

* Observers placed the crowd at nearly three-quarters of a million people. Broadcasters carried the story to the world as the events took place.

29

Admiral Graf Spee. I am happy to pay with my life for any possible reflection on the honor of the flag. I shall face my fate with firm faith in the cause and the future of the nation and of my Führer.

I am writing this letter to Your Excellency in the quiet of the evening, after calm deliberation, in order that you may be able to inform my superior officers, and to counter public rumors if this should become necessary.

> Langsdorff,
> Captain,
> Commanding Officer of the
> sunk pocket battleship
> *Admiral Graf Spee.*

The next morning Langsdorff was found dead by his own hand. His body lay on the ensign of the Imperial German Navy. He was buried with full military honors, and one of the captains he had captured, Captain H. C. Pottinger of the *Ashlea,* attended the funeral to represent the officers and men who had been prisoners in the pocket battleship.

So ended possibly the last sea battle that was marked by chivalry on both sides. Neither gave quarter and neither asked it, but each respected the other. After the war was over, survivors met on occasion and joined in ranks of mutual respect and friendship. The Battle of the River Plate seems an episode taken out of the context of the brutality of modern war. It was isolated, and there was time to stop and consider each move, each motive of the enemy.

Soon there would be no time. Soon there would be only agony and bloodshed, devastation and ruin. There would be no time for the brotherhood of arms, for the respect great warriors have for each other.

Such attitudes from another age could not long survive the utter ruthlessness with which Hitler waged war and the utter ruthlessness with which the Allies learned to respond.

* * *

The Battle of the River Plate took place far from Britain, far from Europe. It seemed remote, good for a two or three days' story in the paper, then to be buried in history. For the "Phony War" was still on. Many people in London and Paris believed that Hitler was bluffing, that he would let things drift for a while and then call it all off. So why carry your gas mask? In the music halls of London a hit song was sung, "We're Going to Hang Out Our Washing on the Siegfried Line." But they didn't really think they would have to.

Occasional alerts disturbed the routine of life as usual. But for the most part, Londoners went about their business, enjoyed "a cuppa" at work, went to their pubs, to the pictures and the theater. Their surroundings had changed somewhat, for no bright lights turned Piccadilly Circus into a wonderland of adventure and make-believe. There were signs indicating "A.R.P. Shelter for 200 Persons," or "First Aid Station for Slightly Wounded Persons," or "Your King and Country Need YOU." Windows had strips of gummed paper running across them to reduce the danger from shattered glass in the event of bomb blasts. Everywhere there were uniforms; everywhere there were bustling crowds, pushing through the darkness to the cheer of brilliant lights inside the theaters themselves.

The London theater season had been dull. Except for a few serious plays, such as Elmer Rice's *Judgment Day,* a *Julius Caesar* in modern dress at the Embassy, and a new translation of Machiavelli's cynical sex comedy *Mandragola,* the West End theaters featured thrillers, farces, bedroom comedies, and revues. Even the revues, usually so sparkling with witty satire on government politics, limped with only routine bawdiness to attract their audiences. The best was probably *Black Velvet* at the Hippodrome, a little freer and more imaginative in its innuendos than the rest. The Windmill Theater, one of London's institutions, maintained its formula of striptease, satire, dancing, vaudeville, and nudes, throughout the afternoon and evenings. It never closed during the entire war, the only theater in London that could make that claim. Many famous British comedians got their start on its stage.

The story in Paris was similar. A few old classics held the stage at the Comédie Française and elsewhere. Farces and melodramas drew the dreary audiences in hope of some entertainment. The Folies Bergère and Casino de Paris sadly missed the tourists as they carried on with their displays of splendid scenery, beautiful nudes, and artistic pageantry.

But the theater, the cinema, the entertainments were not London and Paris of that winter. The little men and women went about their business, making believe that there was no war, trying to make believe that their only problems were those of daily life, that nothing could happen to them.

But there was a real difference between London and Paris, between England and France. It did not seem to cross the mind of the

31

average Britisher that they might be beaten. There might be unpleasant days ahead. There might be days of strain and sorrow, of disaster and death, but the life of Britain would go on. The little man would still enjoy his pub and his tea, his daily flutter on the races, his holidays at Brighton. He might have to wait, but in the end, he would enjoy all these again.

Did the Frenchman dream of his café, of his *pain et vin ordinaire?* Perhaps. But he was tired, suffering from a nationwide tiredness that the twenty-one years of the Long Armistice had not been able to give surcease to. A million and a half Frenchmen had died on the battlefields of the First World War, and France had profited little from this outpouring of blood. The disillusionment of Versailles gave way to the cynicism of the Lost Generation and to the despair of the Great Depression. French moves to block a resurgent Germany received no support from her recent allies. Britain and the United States refused to back the French when Hitler reoccupied the Rhineland in violation of the Versailles Treaty. Now, when Hitler smashed into Poland, the French had no desire to die for Danzig and Warsaw. They felt the British had dragged them into the war. And they were tired.

The French Army was the finest in the world. Everyone—except Hitler and a few of his officers—agreed with this estimate. Was not every able-bodied Frenchman trained to arms through universal conscription? Had not all the French high commanders sat at the feet of Papa Joffre and Père Foch? Was not the supreme military genius Gamelin in overall supreme control?

But this army, so imposing in parades and reviews, when crack units paraded, showing off the latest in modern weapons, was mostly show. The glittering weapons were barely enough for the parades, totally lacking in numbers for war. The crack divisions were few; for the most part, the French Army was made up of reserves—tired men, hating the war, suspicious of foreigners, ill-disciplined, demoralized. Wrote British General Alan Brooke after reviewing part of the French Ninth Army that fall: "Seldom have I seen anything more slovenly and badly turned out. Men unshaven, horses ungroomed, clothes and saddlery that did not fit, vehicles dirty, and complete lack of pride in themselves or their units. What shook me most, however, was the look in the men's faces, disgruntled and insubordinate looks . . ."

Such was the weapon the military genius Gamelin was preparing to use. He and his government were in perfect agreement. This was to be a war without casualties! The Germans could hurl themselves on the Maginot Line, which was impregnable.

But suppose they outflanked it?

An attack through the Low Countries was the most likely German move, but Gamelin and Premier Daladier relegated countering it to a secondary part of their plans. To do otherwise would violate the cardinal rule of the defensive. Lest the Germans be prodded into action, French and British forces were forbidden to use artillery or to drop bombs on German territory. For the first six months of the war, only propaganda leaflets were dropped from British bombers over German soil.

Thus, grumbling French troops manned their positions throughout that winter, and the civilians at home grumbled with them. They damned the British for having got them into the war and for failing to support it. Only 4 British divisions were in France, with 6 more to come that spring, while the French had mobilized nearly 90. One Frenchman in eight was in uniform, and only one Britisher in forty-eight.

German propaganda skillfully played on French suspicions of the British. Britain, said the voice of Goebbels, was willing to fight to the last Frenchman. *"Toujours les poitrines française!"*

But still, as time went on, nothing happened. It was so quiet, as one English wit put it, "you could hear a Ribbentrop."

Across 3000 miles of ocean, few Americans even sensed the malaise of Europe. Commentators like Edward R. Murrow and William Shirer reported the facts, but the people of the United States preferred not to hear. In the United States, it was a time to work and play as usual, to let Europe work out its own mess. Had we not been called "Uncle Shylock" in demanding payment of war debts? Had we not once saved Europe? And now look at it! This time we'll stay out! We'll tend to our own business and The American Way of Life.

In work and play, the American people steadfastly ignored the war. There was little to read about it in any case, so you could turn your attention to other things.

The New York theatrical season was booming, with such attractions playing as Gertrude Lawrence in *Skylark,* Monty Woolley in *The Man Who Came to Dinner,* Eddie Dowling in Saroyan's *The Time of Your Life,* Howard Lindsay in *Life With Father,* Elliott Nugent in Thurber's *The Male Animal.* One of the biggest smashes was *DuBarry Was a Lady,* starring Ethel Merman and Bert Lahr, with music by Cole Porter. Perhaps the burlesque show touches would not have been to the taste of the court of Louis XV, but they exactly suited those of American theatergoers.

Across the country, people went about their daily activities, untouched by the war. The only ones seriously disturbed were those who planned yearly trips to Europe, for the season in Paris and London. But all was not lost. They still could travel to the Mediterranean on the United States Line's ships *Manhattan* and *Washington,* or to the Caribbean, South America, or the Pacific. Pan Am, with its Boeing Clippers, would fly you to these places, four days to Rio de Janeiro or five to Buenos Aires. If you wanted a leisurely sea voyage, the American President Lines advertised round trips to Japan for $630, or a complete round-the-world voyage westbound via Japan, China, the Philippines, Singapore, Ceylon, India, Egypt, Italy, and home for $1143, first class.

The fledgling airlines were making a plea for holiday business, as well. Miami-bound New Yorkers could get away from the snows and winds for only $71.75 one way via American Airlines and be enjoying Florida weather only eight hours and twenty minutes later. It cost $149.95 to cross the continent and took sixteen hours.

If you preferred to drive a new car to see the country, you could get a new Chevrolet for $659, F.O.B. Detroit, a Packard for $867, a Buick for $845, and the top-of-the-line Cadillac "Seventy-Two" for $2670.

For those who weren't going anywhere, the local theater, the radio, and the public library offered entertainment. The movies were featuring such shows as *Pinocchio,* with Walt Disney's endearing Jiminy Cricket, *The Grapes of Wrath, The Primrose Path, My Son! My Son!, Strange Cargo,* and other less notable fare. One of the most important books published that spring was William Faulkner's *The Hamlet,* which seems to have confused reviewers and readers alike. The radio carried on with the unending feud between Jack Benny and Fred Allen. Puppet Charlie McCarthy quipped and leered to the straight man of his creator, Edgar Bergen. The most popular daytime show was "Fibber McGee and Mollie"—" 'Tain't funny, McGee!" Thousands listened for their telephones to ring during the hour on Tuesday night when "Pot o' Gold" was on the air, refusing to go out, for their house might be the fabulous end of the rainbow. Major Bowes's "Amateur Hour" on Sunday nights started many a professional career in show business. Newscasts tended to be highly personalized, from the acidulous Fulton Lewis, Jr., to the frenetic Walter Winchell, to the overemotional Gabriel Heatter—"Ah, there is sad news tonight!"

There was the clipped, careful voice of H. V. Kaltenborn, the rushed, crisis-laden words of Raymond Gram Swing, the calm tones of Elmer Davis and Edward R. Murrow. It wasn't always an act. Mr. Heatter read his commercials for Kreml Hair Tonic with the same drama-filled intensity that he reported a world disaster.

On the whole, life was rather good that winter. No one, except the Poles and Finns, Germans and Russians, was seriously incommoded by the war. Of course, some unfortunates shivered on the outposts or died in torpedoed ships, but that was their hard luck. In Paris and London, it was a nuisance to have to stumble around in the dark of the blackouts, but there was nothing to worry about—nothing to worry about.

German Major Helmut Reinberger sat back as comfortably as he could in the passenger seat of the small "Taifun" plane that was carrying him from Muenster to Cologne. At the controls was his friend Major Erich Hoenmann, a reserve aviator and commanding officer of an airfield at Loddenheide. Reinberger had to get to Cologne, and he was grateful to his friend for giving him a ride.

For several weeks, Reinberger had been attached to the staff of Luftwaffe Major General Kurt Student, working on plans for the invasion of the Low Countries and France. The attack was scheduled to begin in just a week.

Gazing out at the clouds that filled the January sky, Major Reinberger felt a bit uneasy. He had been urgently summoned to a conference at Cologne to iron out final details. He had taken the train as far as Muenster, but then the tangle of traffic in the Ruhr made it impossible for him to get any farther. He had sought inspiration in a few drinks at the local officers' club, and there he ran into his friend Hoenmann. Reinberger poured out his troubles, and Hoenmann was delighted to assist. "I'll fly you there, myself, tomorrow," he offered. After all, he needed flight time, and it would give him a chance to see his wife in Cologne.

Reinberger accepted, but he knew he shouldn't. It was strictly forbidden to fly carrying secret papers. And Reinberger had papers so secret that they would reveal the entire German campaign plan to any Allied intelligence officer.

But it would be a black mark on his record if Reinberger missed the meeting at Cologne, so he climbed into the plane the next morning and off they went. If his superiors found out what he had done, he would be in trouble.

35

He was already in trouble, although he did not know it yet. Unable to see the ground well, Hoenmann was steering too far to the west. He was unfamiliar with the plane, having flown it only once before, and he accidentally cut off the gasoline supply to the engine. He fought to restart it, but it would not respond. Down, down they went, inside Germany, they hoped. At last they broke through the clouds and beheld a river below. "The Rhine!" exclaimed Hoenmann. Reinberger nodded.

Hoenmann brought the plane down to a crash landing near the river and the men breathed more easily. Neither was injured, but since they were not sure just where they were, Reinberger decided to destroy his papers.

He had just begun when soldiers appeared. To the horror of the German officers, the soldiers wore Belgian uniforms. The river they had seen from the air had not been the Rhine; it had been the Meuse, and they were about a mile or so from the Belgian town of Mechelen-sur-Meuse.

Some of the soldiers seized the two German officers while others snatched the scorched papers from the fire. Later at police headquarters, Reinberger made a desperate effort to complete the destruction of the documents but failed. He and his companion were interned and the documents were turned over to the British and French.

After they had analyzed these papers, Allied military and political leaders refused to believe them!

All the circumstances suggested a plant, for the security violations on the part of Major Reinberger had been so gross that French, British, and Belgian officials considered that not even the stupidest officer could have been guilty of them. And they realized from interrogations that Major Reinberger was not a stupid officer. So nothing was done to prepare to meet the Germans when they would come. Major Reinberger's blunder proved to be no gain to the Allies.

But it was a major loss for the Germans. The "Phony War" existed only on the surface. Hidden from the public, officers at all levels of the German High Command worked on plans for the future. The "Phony War" was going to become very real—and soon.

After he had crushed Poland, Hitler made peace overtures to Britain and France during the month of October, and when these were turned down, he was surprised and hurt. Although he had little use for the French, Hitler admired the British and included them in his "Aryan" peoples. But if they were to be so stupid as to fight a profitless war to the finish against the Reich, then, so be it. They would be crushed.

Alas, regardless of their doom,
The little victims play!
No sense have they of ills to come,
Nor care beyond today.

And so the inexorable calendar crept round to April. Easter, with its message of hope, came and went. But the hope was spiritual, for the true, awful folly of real war was about to come.

CHAPTER TWO

Onslaught in the North

People don't do such things.
Ibsen, Hedda Gabler

F FOR Freddie" and "K for King," two Hudson patrol bombers of
Coastal Command, droned out over the North Sea. Pilot Officer
C. W. McNeill, a Canadian, puzzled over his orders as he peered
through the windshield of "K for King." "The ship must on no
account be attacked. She is carrying hundreds of British prisoners.
Note her exact position and report—in code, of course. Her name is
Altmark."

The Nazi supply ship *Altmark* had been milch cow for the ill-fated
Graf Spee before her demise in the harbor of Montevideo in December, 1939. In the course of her cruising, the *Graf Spee* had sunk
9 British ships. Before sending them to the bottom, Captain Hans
Langsdorff, commanding officer of the pocket battleship, had removed
all the crews safely. He soon showed himself to be a gentleman and
sympathetic captor in dealing with his prisoners. But not so with Captain Heinrich Dau, commanding the *Altmark,* when Langsdorff felt
forced to transfer 299 of his prisoners to the supply ship. "These men
are our enemies, who are out to annihilate us. They may not like
being our prisoners, but we cannot help that. That's no reason why
we should sympathize with them. War knows no pity!" The prisoners
were kept in the forward hold, with only primitive sanitary facilities.
Limited periods were allowed on deck for exercise and fresh air, and
officers were segregated from the crews. Ventilation was poor, and
lighting was worse. But worst of all was the utter boredom. Once the
prisoners had made their spaces habitable—barely—there was nothing to do.

The *Altmark* skulked in the South Atlantic for over a month after the death of the *Graf Spee*. Then, with crew and prisoners alike demoralized from idleness, she set out on the long, risky voyage home to Hamburg.

The British knew she was bound to come sometime, and they knew that there were prisoners aboard. It became a point of honor to free them.

Aboard the *Altmark,* southern summer changed to northern winter as the ship crossed the Equator and headed up toward Iceland and the British blockading forces. The days turned cold and gray and the nights colder and black. Lookouts peered constantly into the rain and mist, and the watch officers were ready to alter course at once if anything should be seen. But luck was with the Germans, and the *Altmark* evaded the British blockade and reached Norwegian territorial waters near Trondheim. Captain Dau drew a long breath of relief. He had succeeded. The voyage was as good as over.

To the east of the *Altmark* lay some of the most gorgeous scenery in the world. The mountainous coast, slashed by fjords of incredible grandeur, provide an experience no one can ever forget.

But Dau had no eyes for the beauty before him. His satisfaction came from quite another kind of geography.

Along the coast of Norway, a thousand miles and more from North Cape to Ryvingen on the southern tip, lie thousands of islands, forming a passage known through the ages as the Leads. Its waters have known the keels of Viking raider ships, fishing boats, peaceful traders of the Hanseatic League, warships of all nations of the older world. In times of war to which Norway is not a part, ships in them are protected by Norwegian neutrality and under international law may laugh at would-be pursuers, however great their strength. Even warships enjoy this protection, as long as they are on what is known as "innocent passage." Although Dau was carrying prisoners of war, his passage was still innocent from a legal point of view. He looked forward to an easy trip to the Kattegat; from there he would have only a 200-mile dash to reach Danish waters, which would protect him all the way to Germany. He planned to make the dash at night, free from British detection.

Dau's plans were vain, for there was no hope of escaping British detection. Less than twenty-four hours after the *Altmark* had entered Norwegian waters the British knew about it, tipped off by Norwegian friends. The First Lord of the Admiralty, Winston Churchill, was determined to intercept her and release the prisoners at all costs. That

39

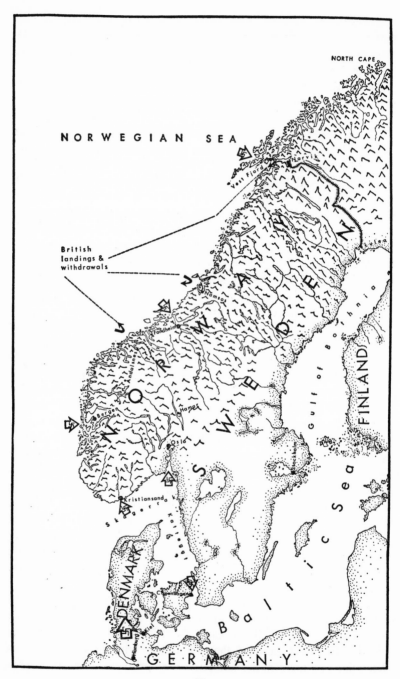

NORTH CAPE

NORWEGIAN SEA

British
landings &
withdrawals

Vest Fjord

Narvik

Luleå

Namsos

Trondheim

Åndalsnes

S W E D E N

N O R W A Y

Gulf of Bothnia

FINLAND

Bergen

Hamer

Oslo

Stockholm

Kristiansand

Skagerrak

Kattegat

Baltic Sea

DENMARK

Copenhagen

G E R M A N Y

was why "F for Freddie" and "K for King" were out searching; that was why Captain Philip Vian was leading a flotilla of destroyers and a cruiser toward Norway.

Three times the Norwegians stopped the *Altmark* and examined her, while the prisoners, battened down in their hold, screamed and shouted to attract attention of the boarding officers, but each time Dau ordered deck winches and other noisy machinery set in operation to drown their shouts. Three times he lied to the examining officers, stoutly proclaiming he had no prisoners on board. Three times he protested the examination, maintaining his vessel was a state ship and immune from search.* The Norwegians respected his lies and his claims of immunity and did not search the vessel. Dau drew a long breath of relief each time and continued his voyage.

Shortly after noon on February 16, 1940, the *Altmark* was approaching Egersund and Jøssing Fjord. The worst was over.

Then Dau saw two aircraft approaching his ship. They bore British markings. "Criminals!" sputtered Dau angrily. "They are violating Norwegian neutrality!" He cast a baleful glance at his wake where a Norwegian gunboat plodded after him.

Pilot Officer McNeill in "K for King" spotted a large tanker. "Could be," he called to his crew. "Let's have a look." He headed for the deck and roared toward the ship. Skimming along the wave tops, "K for King" passed under the bows. There was the name: ALTMARK.

Reaching for altitude, McNeill thought rapidly. He had been instructed to report the sighting in code, but he knew it might take hours for the process of encoding, transmission, reception, decoding, and forwarding to proper authority. And there weren't many hours of daylight left. If the British failed to capture the *Altmark* that afternoon or evening, she would be safe. So he took a chance. He transmitted in plain language.†

Aboard H.M.S. *Cossack,* flagship of the Fourth Destroyer Flotilla, Captain Vian intercepted the message from "K for King" and headed for the prison ship. At 1445 Dau angrily turned away from sweeping

---

* Under international law a state-owned vessel such as a warship is in effect a floating piece of the territory of the country to which she belongs. On board all the laws and authority of the parent country apply even when the vessel is in a foreign port. She is immune to search or to seizure of personnel aboard. A merchant ship, on the other hand, comes under the laws of the country she is visiting.

† McNeill received the expected "rocket" from his commander when he returned to base, but history has shown his judgment to be correct.

the western horizon with his binoculars. *"Englische Kriegschiffe!"* he muttered.

The *Altmark* turned toward Jøssing Fjord to avoid the British warships, which were closing rapidly. The destroyer *Intrepid* fired a shot across her bows, but a Norwegian patrol boat intervened, and the *Altmark* made it into the fjord. Another patrol boat appeared, and the two Norwegian craft took up stations near the German. Baffled, Commander R. C. Gordon withdrew the *Intrepid* to await the arrival of further orders.

A little later, Vian arrived in the *Cossack*. He consulted the senior Norwegian officer, who told him he had orders to oppose the British with force if they moved on the *Altmark*. Vian informed him that he would withdraw from Norwegian waters to request instructions.

When Churchill received Vian's message, he consulted with the Foreign Secretary, Lord Halifax. They agreed that the prisoners must be freed, even if it meant violating Norway's neutrality.

> Unless [wirelessed Churchill] Norwegian torpedo-boat undertakes to convoy *Altmark* to Bergen with a joint Anglo-Norwegian guard on board and a joint escort, you should board *Altmark*, liberate the prisoners and take possession of ship pending further instructions. If Norwegian torpedo-boat interferes, you should warn her to stand off. If she fires upon you, you should not reply unless attack is serious, in which case you should defend yourself using no more force than is necessary and cease fire when she desists. Suggest to Norwegian destroyer that honour is served by submitting to superior force.

Once more back at the scene, Vian gave the Norwegian commander the gist of this message and invited him to board the *Altmark* with him and escort her to Bergen. The Norwegian refused.

Vian's reply was characteristic of the man. "Half ahead both," he ordered. "We're boarding."

The Norwegian officer decided to submit to superior force. He moved his little ship out of the way.

Confidently, Vian conned the *Cossack* into the fjord and headed for the German prison ship. But Dau had one last play to make in the game. He came astern at full power in an attempt to ram and drive the *Cossack* onto the side of the fjord. Between the *Altmark*'s 20,000 tons and the sheer rock of the fjord, the *Cossack* would have been crushed like a tin can when someone steps on it.

Nimbly maneuvering his ship, Vian evaded the ponderous *Altmark* and brought his port bow to her so that the German vessel lay between the *Cossack* and the shore. With a rush the boarding party was away, swarming over the decks of the prison ship.

The fight that followed was sharp and vicious. Six Germans were killed and one Englishman was wounded. Six Germans suffered wounds. A member of the boarding party made his way to the holds. Yelling down Number 1, he called, "Any British down there?"

The bewildered men, prisoners for so long, had no idea of what was going on. They had heard the scuffles and shots, but what they portended, they had no way of knowing. But they knew a countryman's voice.

"Yes!" A tremendous yell. "We're all British!"

"Come on up. The Navy's here!"

Laughing, shouting, weeping with joy, the men came out of their prison, clambered across to the *Cossack*. One man spotted Dau. "Lend us your revolver," he pleaded to a British officer. "I want to shoot this bloody captain. He's a bastard and a Nazi."

The man was hustled aboard the *Cossack,* disappointed at not being able to carry out his intention. The *Cossack* left the scene, Dau raging futilely at the departing British destroyer. The liberated men landed safely in England, where the press and public made much of them. After a few weeks ashore, most of them returned to the sea, undaunted by their experiences.

This little episode, scarcely a footnote in the history of the Second World War, bears an importance far beyond what might be expected, for it was the last straw as far as Hitler was concerned. Because of it he decided to invade Norway.

It was no new idea to Hitler or to the German High Command. The importance of Norway to Germany's prosecution of the war can hardly be overstated. Not only did the Leads afford a safe passageway for German shipping and U-boats around the British blockade. Not only was Norway a window to the north. It was through Norway that Germany got most of her high-grade iron ore.

Far to the north in Sweden is the Galiväre iron range, which provided Germany with some 70 percent of her iron ore. A single railroad led from these mines to the Swedish town of Lulea on the Gulf of Bothnia, where German ships could readily pick up the rich cargo and take it to the Fatherland without fear of British opposition, except, possibly, an occasional British submarine.

From December to April each year Lulea is icebound, and all shipping ceases. In 1902, rather than be deprived of four to five months of production, the Swedes had pushed a railway to the northwest, through almost impossible country, involving, at one part, a descent of 1700 feet in 23 miles, through nineteen tunnels, to reach the small fishing village of Narvik on the end of Vest Fjord, nearly 150 miles north of the Arctic Circle. Thanks to the Gulf Stream, Narvik is open to shipping all year, and the town grew to be a major source of Swedish ore for the rest of the world.

As early as October 10, 1939, Grand Admiral Erich Raeder, Commander in Chief of the German Navy, had brought the Norwegian problem to Hitler's attention. As long as Norway was neutral, he argued, it was all to Germany's advantage. But if Britain were to violate Norwegian neutrality, then Germany must be prepared to act, ruthlessly, and without delay. This was the first step leading to a campaign that would bring death or misery to thousands of Norwegians, death in battle to Britishers and Germans, would bring Raeder to trial for his life at the Nuremberg Tribunal, and would give the world a new synonym for traitor.

Raeder first met Vidkun Quisling in December in Berlin. The little Norwegian traitor had been dismissed from his former post of minister of defense, and had formed a political party of his own, the National Union Party. Although it never had very many members, it attracted extremists, for it was modeled on the Nazi Party of Germany. In spite of his sound and fury, Quisling was not even able to win a seat in the Storting, the Norwegian parliament. In despair, he turned to the Nazis for help.

His plea could not have come at a better time. The German leaders were becoming conscious of their vulnerability on the northern front. Thus Quisling received a reception all out of proportion to his real worth. Circumstances also played into his hands in his choice of contact, for it was to Alfred Rosenberg, the self-styled philosopher of the Nazi Party, that he addressed himself. This conceited man delighted in his title of chief of the party's Office of Foreign Affairs, and he dreamed of forming a northern "Aryan" empire, embracing northern Europe and Scandinavia under the German Reich. This empire would ruthlessly exclude Jews, Slavs, and other "impure" races and rule for the greater glory of Germany. Let the rest of the world take heed. Nothing will block the inevitable destiny of Greater Germany! *Heil Hitler!*

Rosenberg had met Quisling as early as 1933, but it was not until this meeting that anything fruitful developed. This time, Quisling had a plan. It was to be the Anschluss of Austria all over again. "Experienced and die-hard National Socialists who are practiced in such operations" would seize key points with the assistance of contingents of the German Army and Navy. Impressed, Rosenberg took Quisling along to see Raeder. In spite of himself, Raeder, as he later testified at Nuremberg, thought the little Norwegian traitor made sense. As he recorded in the archives, "Quisling stated . . . a British landing is planned in the vicinity of Stavanger, and Christiansand is proposed as a possible British base. The present Norwegian government as well as the Parliament and the whole foreign policy are controlled by the well-known Jew, Hambro [Carl Hambro, at the time president of the Storting], a great friend of Hore-Belisha [also a Jew, at that time British Secretary of State for War]. The dangers to Germany arising from a British occupation were depicted in great detail."

Raeder took Quisling along to see Hitler, who listened to the arguments and ordered his staff to set to work with Quisling on a draft plan for occupation of Norway, with Denmark thrown in for good measure.

Yet Hitler was cautious. Although he sent a special agent to Norway to work with Quisling on plans, he kept emphasizing to his officers that the Norwegian study *was* a study, not an operation order. He and Raeder agreed that for the time being, at least, "the most favorable solution is definitely the maintenance of the status quo." Planning continued, but it was desultory, for the entire proposal was very much on the back burner.

So matters continued until February 17, when Hitler learned of the impudent action of Captain Vian in daring to remove the British prisoners from the *Altmark*. He was outraged. At the very least, the crew of the *Altmark* should have acquitted themselves like men and Germans. "No resistance! No British losses!" stormed Hitler.* Two days later he ordered General Alfred Jodl, head of the Operations Section of the OKW,† to get moving. "Equip ships. Put units in readiness." To command Operation *Weserübung,* as it was now called, he appointed General Nikolaus von Falkenhorst, a career soldier in his middle fifties.

Hitler didn't give Falkenhorst much time. After seeing him on

---

* Hitler's fury at the lack of resistance on the *Altmark* ended Dau's career. When the ship finally got back to Germany, he was relieved of command and was never heard from again.

† OKW: *Oberkommando der Wehrmacht,* the High Command organization of all the German armed forces. The head was Hitler himself and the Chief of Staff was Colonel General, later Field Marshal, Wilhelm Keitel. The word *Wehrmacht* refers to all the armed forces, not merely to the army.

the morning of February 21, Hitler told him that he would be given 5 divisions for the job and ordered him to return with an outline plan that afternoon. He failed to tell him that the plans had been under study for over two months.

Falkenhorst went out and bought a copy of that bible of travelers, a Baedeker on Norway. When he returned that afternoon, he submitted a plan to land one division each at Narvik, Trondheim, Bergen, Stavanger, and Oslo. "There wasn't much else you could do," he remarked later, "because they were the large harbors."

Falkenhorst was given a small staff and set to work on his plans. He was given access to the studies already underway for the aggression to the north, but no troops. There comes a point when actual units must be assigned to plans, and that point soon came. Accordingly, on February 26, Falkenhorst paid a call on General Halder, Chief of the General Staff under OKH,* and requested that a number of crack mountain troops be assigned to *Weserübung*. Halder was stiffly indignant. No one had told him or his superior, Colonel General Walter von Brauchitsch, head of the Army, anything about forthcoming Scandinavian operations! "Not a single word on this matter has been exchanged between the Führer and Brauchitsch," Halder testily noted in his diary. "That must be recorded for the history of the war!"

Falkenhorst got his troops. There was nothing Brauchitsch could do about it. The Führer had spoken. To make matters worse, when Hitler issued the formal order for the operation on March 1, Falkenhorst was placed directly under his command, independent of OKH altogether. The directive for *Weserübung* is remarkable for its cynical self-justification.

> The development of the situation in Scandinavia requires the making of all preparations for the occupation of Denmark and Norway by a part of the German Armed Forces (*Fall Weserübung*). This operation should prevent British encroachment on Scandinavia and the Baltic; further, it should guarantee our ore base in Sweden and give our Navy and Air Force a wider starting line against Britain. The part which the Navy and the Air Force will have to play, within the limits of their capabilities, is to protect the operation against the interference of British naval and air striking forces.
>
> In view of our military and political power in comparison with that of the Scandinavian states, the force to be employed in the *Fall Weserübung* will be kept as small as possible. The numerical weakness

* OKH: *Oberkommando des Heeres*—Army High Command.

46

will be balanced by daring actions and surprise execution. On principle, we will do our utmost to make the operation appear as a *peaceful* occupation, the object of which is the military protection of the neutrality of the Scandinavian states. Corresponding demands will be transmitted to their governments at the beginning of the occupation. If necessary, demonstrations by the Navy and Air Force will provide the necessary emphasis. If in spite of this resistance should be met with, all military means will be used to crush it.

If Brauchitsch and Halder had their noses out of joint at being left out of the proceedings and at Falkenhorst's independent command, Field Marshal Hermann Goering, head of the Luftwaffe, was outraged, for Falkenhorst would have operational command of all Luftwaffe units in Scandinavia. It was not to be borne. "The Fat One" claimed jurisdiction of everything in the air. If flights of angels flew over Germany, Goering would have claimed them as subject to his orders.

Goering stormed off to see Hitler. "The Luftwaffe is mine!" he fumed. "The stupid army officers cannot be expected to employ it properly!" Hitler yielded the point. Falkenhorst would have to request air support as needed from Luftwaffe headquarters. To appease his sybaritic friend, Hitler sacrificed unity of command, a grave military mistake. As it turned out, however, it hardly mattered, for the British and French so botched their response to the German invasion of Norway that the Germans could have gotten away with almost any military folly.

Swelling with pride in his victory over Falkenhorst, Goering swaggered into a meeting with Hitler on March 5. This was a general conference on *Weserübung,* attended by all high military commanders. As the only *Generalfeldmarschall* on active duty, Goering outranked everyone in the room except Hitler, and he was prepared to throw his weight about. "Field Marshal [Goering] vents his spleen," recorded Jodl in his diary, "because he was not consulted beforehand. He dominates the discussion and tries to prove that all previous preparations are good for nothing."

Goering was successful in this conference as he had been with the Führer. Heavier tasks were laid on the Army and Navy to spare his precious Luftwaffe, particularly in view of the important role it was to play a month later in the campaign in the west. With these revised plans, the operation began to move. D-day was to be April 9, 1940.

It was not only in Germany that eyes were being turned on Scandinavia. As early as September, 1939, Winston Churchill proposed to the War Cabinet that the Norwegian Leads be mined, as had been done in World War I. Met by Chamberlain's desire to avoid upsetting the apple cart, the proposal got nowhere, although Churchill continued to press it. Then, with the outbreak of the Russo-Finnish War on November 30, 1939, ideas began to be tossed about for methods of aiding Finland.

In spite of the Non-Aggression Pact signed between Germany and Russia in August, 1939, Joseph Stalin trusted Hitler as he would adders fanged. His principal reason for claiming half of Poland had been to form a defensive barrier against possible German attack from the west. He then turned his eyes upon the north.

A provision of the Non-Aggression Pact assigned the Baltic to Russia as a sphere of influence. Stalin lost little time in taking advantage of it. On September 29 he forced little Estonia to grant Russia rights to establish and garrison military, naval, and air bases. A week later it was the turn of Latvia, and then in another five days, Lithuania.

But Finland was the main stumbling block. Stalin and his military chiefs regarded the Karelian Isthmus as a dagger pointed at Leningrad. This isthmus is a narrow neck of land joining Finland to Russia and lies between the Gulf of Finland and Lake Ladoga. From Finnish territory, long-range artillery could shell Leningrad. So, a series of stern demands went from the Kremlin to Helsinki. Cede part of the Karelian Isthmus and much other territory along the Russo-Finnish border. Let Russia build a naval base at Hangö near the entrance to the Gulf of Finland. In return, we will give you 2000 square miles of useless snow-covered lands in the north.

The beleaguered Finnish Government agreed to the territorial deal, but refused the naval base. This, they declared, would be a violation of national sovereignty. The Russian press responded. "Finns Plot Aggression Against USSR." "The Soviet Union Will Reply to Finnish Threat."

On November 30, without a declaration of war, the Red Air Force bombed Helsinki. At the same time, the Red Army attacked the Mannerheim Line across the Karelian Isthmus and several places along Finland's eastern border.

In America and in the rest of the free world, the plight of the Finns attracted great sympathy. Although most Americans could not have told you where Finland was exactly, they all knew that she had been the only one to pay the war debts growing out of the First World War. Naturally, everyone expected that she would be crushed

48

in a few days, as Poland had been. Observers watched with bewilderment, then amazement, and then with glee as the mighty Russian war machine ground to a halt, repelled by tiny Finland. Shades of David and Goliath!

Alas for the myth. Goliath won in the end. At first, David had many advantages. The territory of Finland has been said to consist "almost entirely of natural obstacles to military operations." Only a fraction of Russia's military power was directed against Finland, for the Reds were not interested in obliterating Finland as a country or in destroying the military installations they might want to use themselves later. Still, it was a dramatic story as the world saw it: three and a half million Finns opposed and held off a hundred and eighty million Russians.

The Red Air Force hit Helsinki repeatedly in terror attacks, with the aim of breaking the spirit of the Finns, for had not the air strategist Douhet stated that after a few attacks the civilians, "driven by the instinct of self-preservation, . . . would rise up and end the war"? Hitler and Goering might have learned a lesson had they been willing to learn. The ruthless bombing increased the Finnish will to resist.

The Russians had no better luck in the land attacks. On the eastern border of Finland, Soviet heavy equipment, tanks and large guns, bogged in snowdrifts. The railways and primitive roads of northern Russia could not supply the stranded Russian forces. Finnish ski troops, white-clad for camouflage, sped around the ponderous Soviet formations, cutting them off, striking down stragglers, blowing up vehicles, causing terror and demoralization wherever they went. Even the much-vaunted attack on the Mannerheim Line failed. The Russians simply did not have the strength to penetrate it.

While the Western world hooted in derision, Russian military men temporarily called off the attacks. The emphasis is on *temporarily*. They had not given up. They set to work with great thoroughness to discover the causes of their failures. In February they came back. This time they had the proper equipment and the number of men that would be needed. Troop-carrying sledges gave them flexible mobility. Supplies had been stockpiled. They were ready.

On February 1 the drive opened, a massive frontal assault on the Mannerheim Line. Twenty-seven Soviet divisions—almost equal in number to the entire population of Finland—began a slow, grinding drive. Men fell in tens, in hundreds, in thousands, but the drive never slackened. Artillery support was massive. Experts in the West

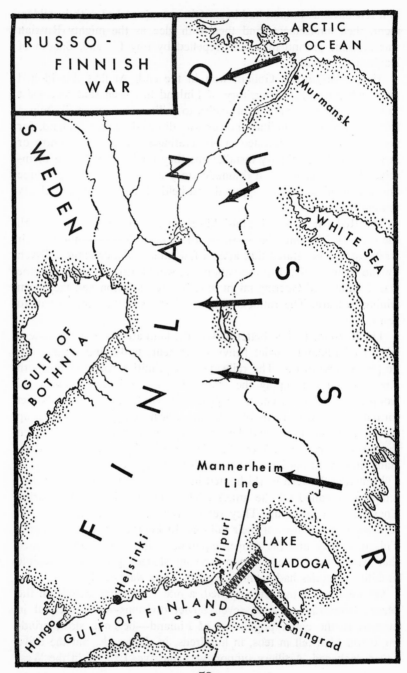

RUSSO-
FINNISH
WAR

ARCTIC OCEAN

Murmansk

SWEDEN

FINLAND

U S S R

WHITE SEA

GULF OF BOTHNIA

Mannerheim Line

LAKE LADOGA

Helsinki

Viipuri

Hango

GULF OF FINLAND

Leningrad

snickered over the poor aim of the Russian guns. What they did not know was that the Russians had constructed duplicates of the Finnish fortifications and had tested them to learn the best methods of destruction. They had learned that hits near the foundations would gradually weaken the entire structure or tilt them out of line so that their guns were disoriented.

On February 1 the attack began, and minute by minute, hour by hour, day by day, the guns roared out, and the Red Air Force struck from the skies. As many as 3000 shells a day were hurled against the Mannerheim Line and the gallant defenders manning their posts. There could be but one end. On February 13, the Mannerheim Line was breached at Summa, near the western end. The Finns fell back, mounting desperate rearguard actions to the outskirts of Viipuri. Ice on the Gulf of Finland gave the Russians the opportunity to outflank the exhausted Finns.

There was no hope of help from overseas. Nearly 12,000 volunteers—mostly from Norway, Sweden, and Denmark, and even a few Americans—had joined the fighting; Britain and France were in the process of preparing an expeditionary force of some hundred thousand men to send to the aid of Finland, but it came to naught when Norway and Sweden refused to allow this force to cross their territories.

The inevitable end came on March 12. The Finns yielded to the Russian demands, and the free world sorrowed. A few weeks later, at the Alvin Theater in New York, Robert E. Sherwood's play, *There Shall Be No Night,* paid tribute to Finnish courage. To Mr. Sherwood, the hopeless resistance of the Finns was a step to "help speed the day when man becomes genuinely human, instead of the synthetic creature—part bogus angel, part actual brute—that he has imagined himself in the dark past."

To Mr. Churchill's adroit mind, the proposal to send an expeditionary force to the aid of Finland seemed a perfect opportunity to do something about the German iron ore traffic in the Leads. In the strange miasma of the Twilight War, however, the Chamberlain government could not bring itself to stir up trouble, so the weeks passed by and nothing was done. Then it was too late. The Russians had won, and there was no excuse for sending troops to Scandinavia.

Now that it was too late, both the French and British Governments woke up to the opportunities and dangers in the northern countries. Premier Édouard Daladier, who had rashly promised 50,000 troops to Finland without being able to make good his word, was forced to resign, and he was replaced as Premier by Paul Reynaud on March 21. A week later the Supreme War Council—the highest officials of the French and British Governments—met in London. Out of their deliberations came two decisions: that neither country would negotiate or conclude an armistice or treaty of peace except by mutual agreement, and that the British would lay mines in the Norwegian Leads.

This was a bold decision, a clear violation of Norwegian neutrality. Therefore, the British decided, they would first put the mines in place and then inform the Norwegian Government. In the First World War such mining had been done, but with the acquiescence of the Norwegians. This time there was no possibility they would agree. Hitler's saber rattled too loudly in the south.

The British realized that Hitler might react strongly to the threat to the iron ore traffic, so they prepared a force to seize Narvik, Trondheim, Bergen, and Stavanger, to deny them to the Germans.

We have heard those names before. Except for Oslo, they were the identical targets in Norway told off for capture by General Falkenhorst's troops.

The British intended to land their units only if the Germans reacted to the mining of the Leads. They had no intention of occupying Norway. Their men would come as allies to assist in defense of Norwegian soil. It was well to be forehanded and have units ready.

The date selected for the mining operation was April 8, 1940.

The date selected for the German invasion of Norway was April 9, 1940.

The British would be comfortably ahead of the German invasion forces. Confidence was high. A complacent Prime Minister Chamberlain addressed a labor union meeting on April 4. It was strange, he said, that Hitler had not acted when the Germans were so ready and the British were not. "One thing is certain," concluded Mr. Chamberlain; "he missed the bus."

Unknown to Chamberlain, the German bus was in motion, and the British one was about to suffer a breakdown.

The first part of the British operations went off as scheduled. In the early morning hours of April 8, four British destroyers laid mines in the approaches to Narvik. As expected, the Norwegians protested. And the German invasion forces drew nearer.

And where were the British troops which had so forehandedly been prepared in the case of German reaction?

At the moment, they were disembarking from the ships which were to take them to Norway.

The German moves toward Norway did not escape all notice. Reports came in of ship movements. A source in Copenhagen reported that a German division embarked in 10 ships was scheduled to land in Narvik in a few days. The RAF on a leaflet bombing raid over Hamburg noted unusual activity. All of these reports were accepted in London with steadfast incredulity. It couldn't be happening. In passing them on to Commander in Chief Home Fleet, the Admiralty added a soothing note: "All these reports are of doubtful value and may well be only a further move in the war of nerves."

Admiral Sir Charles Forbes in his flagship *Rodney* pondered over these reports, and on receipt of a scouting report from aircraft, at 1727 on April 7 gave orders for the fleet to raise steam. Soldiers embarked for Norway were landed from the units based at Rosyth in the Firth of Forth, while Sir Charles prepared to take his main units out of Scapa Flow in the Orkney Islands. By 2015 that day the ships were under way.

But the Germans were ahead of them.

Five German units were moving toward Norway by sea. Two other groups moved toward Denmark, while German army units were poised on the Danish border.

At 0500, April 9, 1940, Dr. Curt Bräuer, German minister to Norway, roused Foreign Minister Dr. Halvdan Koht from his bed in his home in Oslo. At the same moment Cecil von Renthe-Fink, German minister to Denmark, was spoiling the slumbers of Foreign Minister Edvard Munch. Twenty minutes later the no-longer-sleepy foreign ministers in Oslo and Copenhagen were reading nearly identical notes:

... The German troops ... do not set foot on Norwegian [Danish] soil as enemies. The German High Command does not intend to make use of the points occupied by German troops as bases for operations against England as long as it is not forced to.... On the contrary, German military operations aim exclusively at protecting the north against the proposed occupation of Norwegian [Danish] bases by Anglo-French forces....

In the spirit of the good relations between Germany and Norway [Denmark] which have existed hitherto, the Reich Government declares to the Royal Norwegian [Danish] Government that Germany has no intention of infringing by her measures the territorial integrity and political independence of the Kingdom of Norway [Denmark] now or in the future....

Any resistance would have to be, and would be, broken by all possible means... and would therefore lead only to absolutely useless bloodshed.

The Danes yielded quickly even as German troops poured across the border on the mainland and other troops landed from their transports on the Langelinie Pier in Copenhagen, near where the beloved Little Mermaid broods over the harbor. A battalion quickly moved on and seized the Amalienborg Palace where King Christian X lived. Unwilling to allow his subjects' blood to be spilled in a hopeless resistance, the King gave in.

The response of the Norwegian Government was quite different. Dr. Bräuer telegraphed it to Berlin. "We will not submit voluntarily: the struggle is already under way."

While the *Völkischer Beobachter* carried the headline, GERMANY SAVES SCANDINAVIA!, frustrated Foreign Minister Ribbentrop urgently telegraphed Bräuer, "You will once more impress on the Government there that Norwegian resistance is completely useless."

Resistance was useless. It accomplished nothing. It only inspired free men to courage in the face of tyranny, torture, and death rather than submit to barbarian strength masquerading as a civilized nation.

A series of warnings of invasion had reached the Norwegian Government by April 8. In Oslo, as in London, disbelief was the order of the day. On that very afternoon the Free Polish submarine *Orzel* had sunk a German ship off Lillesand, near the southern tip of Norway. The ship turned out to be the transport *Rio de Janeiro,* and Norwegian rescuers learned from survivors that they were a part of a German military force going to "protect" Bergen. That evening the Norwegian Storting met, as did the Cabinet. They ordered limited defense preparations but denied permission for local commanders to mine the fjords or for airfields to alert their garrisons to the possibility of paratroop attacks. Even the next morning, after the shocked Foreign Minister Koht had received the German note, orders to call up reserves for the Army were sent out by ordinary mail!

At sea, the British had already encountered the Germans. H.M.S. *Glowworm* pitched and rolled along through the dark night in a rising westerly gale which had reached full strength by the time the sun cast a grudging light over the gray, storm-tossed sea. The previous day she had been a part of a destroyer and minelayer force headed for Vest Fjord. Riding along in solid dignity, protecting them and

54

protected by them, was the venerable battle cruiser *Renown,* her six 15-inch guns at the moment mute symbols of British superiority at sea.

But somebody fell overboard while this little force under Vice Admiral W. J. Whitworth headed toward Narvik. There was little chance to save him as the seas rose and darkness fell. But they tried. *Glowworm* was sent off on the task. She did not find the man, but she found something bigger. Much bigger.

As that gray dawn broke on the morning of April 8, Lieutenant Commander G. B. Roope peered over the spin-drift sea, looking for the consorts he had been seeking all night. There was nothing but the sea and the clouds and the wind. The normal routine of life went on. Dawn action stations were followed by breakfast, men joking and grousing over their mugs of tea.

Suddenly a lookout called out. To starboard a shape loomed up through the gray. It was a destroyer plunging wildly in the heavy seas. The *Glowworm's* four 4.7-inch guns trained on her when she was recognized as German. Two salvos roared out before the German disappeared in the mist.

Scarcely had she gone before a second German destroyer, the *Bernd von Arnim,* hove into view. Immediately the two little ships were in a desperate dogfight, difficult as it was in the spray and heavy seas. Although the *Arnim* was larger and more heavily armed than her opponent, she was less stable, and this made matters more even. She called for help, and help was near at hand.

Running down upon the hapless little British destroyer was the heavy cruiser *Hipper,* a bone in her teeth and her eight 8-inch guns ready. She carried more firepower in her secondary battery than the *Glowworm* had in all. Roope struggled with the hopeless fight, trying to maneuver to escape as hit after devastating hit smashed into his ship. His most important task was to get news of this encounter to his superiors. One can imagine him saying to his signals officer, "Make to *Renown,* repeated Admiralty . . ." The message sent and acknowledged, his whole duty was done. What else could he do?

Escape was impossible. Clinging to the wreckage of his battered bridge, Roope maneuvered his ship close to the German cruiser and launched torpedoes. It was a forlorn hope. The *Hipper* combed the torpedo tracks.

Black smoke was now pouring from the stacks of the destroyer, and it gave her momentary respite from the *Hipper's* shells. The German, coming on doggedly to finish off the little gadfly, plunged into the cloud of smoke after her. As she came out the other side, her commanding officer, Captain Hellmuth Heye, stared in amazement and admiration. The *Glowworm* had turned to face her foe and was coming in to ram. Collision was inevitable. Men on both ships braced themselves to meet the shock. British sailors knew that the time it would take to cover the few yards of water separating the two ships represented the last seconds of life for some of them.

Then it came. With a shriek of tortured metal, the two ships smashed together. The twisted wreck of the *Glowworm* fell away, revealing a scar where the armor plate had been ripped for 130 feet from the *Hipper*'s starboard side. Wallowing, burning, asking for no mercy, the *Glowworm* lay in the trough of the sea, waiting for the coup de grâce. It never came. Captain Heye was too chivalrous to torment her further. About 9 o'clock it was all over. The *Glowworm* blew up and sank. Only a few survivors swam feebly about in the churning waters. Captain Heye ordered his ship stopped and rescue work begun. A few men were saved, but not Lieutenant Commander Roope. He had lived through the ramming; he had even survived the explosion of his own ship, but when he took the line thrown him from the *Hipper,* he was done. Just as he had nearly reached the deck of the cruiser, his nerveless fingers lost their grip. With a gentle splash his body hit the water as life departed from him.

After the war, when the details of the *Glowworm*'s gallant fight were learned, Lieutenant Commander Roope was posthumously awarded the Victoria Cross, Britain's highest decoration.

"Resistance is to be broken ruthlessly!" This was the command to the five German invasion groups headed for Norway, that small country whose only offense was geographic. Relentlessly the German groups swept on across waters supposedly controlled by the most powerful navy in the world. British naval units scoured all likely regions, but they were too late, misdirected, unlucky. Only the *Glowworm,* to her cost, and the *Renown* found anything before the jaws of the trap closed on Norway.

Far to the north, about 50 miles from the entrance to Vest Fjord, the midwatch was drawing to a close on the *Renown*. At 0337 on April 9, two ships loomed out of the mist to eastward. They were the two German battle cruisers *Scharnhorst* and *Gneisenau*. While the *Renown* maneuvered to close the range, her crew went to action stations. The Germans did not sight her at first, and when the *Gneisenau* in the lead spotted her, she held fire, not knowing whether the ship was friend or foe.

56

The men of the *Scharnhorst* remained in ignorance of the Britisher's presence for a time. The flagship *Gneisenau* had not bothered to warn her consort. On the *Scharnhorst*'s bridge, her navigator was preparing to take advantage of a brief clearing of the western sky to take a star shot. It would be the strangest one of his life, for his sextant revealed on the horizon not the tiny image of the star but the flash of guns.

The brief battle was inconclusive. Although the German ships were superior in strength to the single British vessel, it was the *Renown* that scored the first hit. Admiral Günther Lütjens decided to break off the action and disappeared into a rain squall. For two hours the three ships pounded northwest at high speed, but the *Renown* dropped slowly behind. At 0615 the German ships disappeared, having inflicted two hits on the *Renown,* but they did little damage. At 0800 *Renown* broke off the chase. The two German ships, each with a turret out of action, made a wide sweep around and returned to Germany, arriving three days later.

Meanwhile the German occupation of Norway was proceeding with all the ruthlessness the orders had demanded. At Stavanger, at Bergen, and at Trondheim, the Germans, using deception, force, and surprise, were able to get control of their targets quickly, even though the cruiser *Königsberg* was damaged by three shell hits as she entered Bergen harbor.

It was at the two extreme ends of the attack, at Narvik and at Oslo, that the Germans ran into trouble.

In the Norwegian capital, the German diplomatic officials were having a merry time on the night of April 8/9. Led by the naval attaché, Captain Richard Schreiber, the party moved down to the waterfront and waited. Occasionally Dr. Bräuer joined them as they looked to the south down the long Oslofjord. As the hour of five approached, expectations grew. At any moment they would see the shapes of big German naval ships coming into view. They slapped themselves to keep warm, and they waited.

They waited in vain.

Oslofjord is a beautiful passage, almost eighty miles long, running north from the Kattegat to Oslo. The sides of the fjord are by no means as spectacular as those farther north, but they afford opportunities for defense, as the Germans learned to their cost.

It was about 2300 on April 8 that the German naval group for Oslo entered the fjord. In the van was the proud heavy cruiser *Blücher*. She was a spanking new ship, having entered service only the previous September. Her eight 8-inch guns were trained in, for no trouble was expected by either of the flag officers on board. On her flag bridge Rear Admiral Oskar Kummetz turned to his passenger-guest, Major General Erwin Engelbrecht, commander of the 163rd Infantry Division, who was to take charge in Norway until General Falkenhorst could arrive. Kummetz pointed astern at the other ships of the group following along behind. Next astern of the flagship was the pocket battleship *Lützow,* over 10,000 tons of sleek fury, mounting six 11-inch guns.* Next came the cruiser *Emden,* with eight 5.9-inch guns. After her were three smaller ships, jammed with troops for the occupation.

In their path lay the tiny Norwegian patrol vessel, *Pol III.* Her captain, Lieutenant Commander Welding Olsen, looked out calmly to see his death coming toward him. But he gave no thought to that. He flashed a challenge to the Germans, and receiving no reply, sounded the alarm by radio to the naval authorities, and hurled his 216-ton craft against the three German heavy ships and their charges, his 76-mm. popgun firing the first Norwegian shots of the war.

There could be but one end to such a match. Ablaze from stem to stern, her skipper mortally wounded, *Pol III* went down quickly, but not before she had rammed and seriously damaged the German torpedo-boat *Albatross.* The Germans pressed on.

Near the island defenses of Rauoy and Bolaerne came the next opposition. It amounted to nothing. The defenders there had received no orders from Oslo and hesitated to act on their own responsibility. They illuminated the German ships with searchlights and put a few warning shots across their bows, which the Germans ignored. Soon they had disappeared into a mist.

Once past these defenses, the Germans stopped to offload troops to take Rauoy and Bolaerne from the rear. Other detachments were sent to take the unprotected naval base of Horton on the west side of the fjord. Its only defense was the minelayer *Olaf Tryggvason,* and her skipper, Commander T. Briseid, ordered her into action. She sank the minesweeper *R-17* and drove off the torpedo-boat *Albatross,* which was having a bad day.

Pressing on at 12 knots, the Germans approached the crucial Drøbak Narrows. At this point, the fjord narrows to less than 600

---

* *Lützow* had originally been named *Deutschland,* but Hitler was superstitious about the possibility of losing a ship by that name, so she was re-christened in late 1939. She was a sister ship of the *Graf Spee.* The third ship of that class was the *Admiral Scheer.*

yards, and just beyond, where it widens again, the venerable fortress of Oscarsborg stands on an island in the middle of the fjord. Although the fort itself dates from Crimean War times, the 8-inch guns it mounted were comparatively modern Krupp reliables. And the commander of the fortress had no doubt where his duty lay. Shells tore into the *Blücher,* starting fires in her aircraft hangar, which spread to the army trucks and ammunition stowed on the main deck. The ship lurched to starboard and changed course to the east a few degrees to draw away from the punishing fire.

This move brought her close to another fort at Kaholm on the eastern shore of Oslofjord. Here were not only 11-inch guns but torpedo tubes. The guns promptly joined in with those of Oscarsborg, raining more death upon the stricken ship.

Over the years the torpedo tubes at Kaholm had been tenderly cared for by a group of elderly reservists. The compartment which contained the weapons gleamed with typical Scandinavian sparkle. The paintwork was spotless, and the brightwork glistened. The torpedoes in the tubes had been checked and rechecked, but no one believed they would ever be used. The care lavished on them was the dedication of the hobbyist. Perhaps the men hated to send the torpedoes on their deadly work. But send them they did. As the German cruiser pulled into their sights, the men stood to their stations. A jerk on the firing lever, then another, and another. The torpedoes were running.

Two of them smashed into the starboard side of the *Blücher,* exploding in the engine rooms. Men died by the score, seared in an instant by the fires or boiled alive by the steam. The little way the ship still had on carried her past the arc of fire of the guns, and she came to anchor. For nearly three hours her crew fought the fires and tried to repair the engines. They seemed to be having some success, but one fire reached a magazine and the ship blew up. Although hundreds reached shore safely, including Admiral Kummetz and General Engelbrecht, it was a long swim in the icy waters, and over 1000 men lost their lives.*

The command of the invasion group passed temporarily to Captain August Thiele of the *Lützow,* who very sensibly withdrew when the *Blücher* was hit. His own ship did not get away unscathed, for three 11-inch shells put her foremost turret out of action. Thiele went back

* The wreck of the *Blücher* still lies at the bottom of Oslofjord. It was pointed out to the author by Captain Ivar Grønbukt, master of the Norwegian-America Line ship *Sagafjord.*

down the fjord a few miles, landed troops, and waited for them to capture the shore defenses. It was not until the following day that the ships were able to proceed to Oslo.

Meanwhile, the Luftwaffe had saved the day for the Germans at Oslo. By nine in the morning, planes were over the city, while others dropped paratroops. Transport planes landed at Fornebu Airport, and by nine-thirty, the Germans held the field. They had lost a few planes to antiaircraft fire, but the Norwegians were too surprised to organize effective resistance. With 6 companies of infantry, Oberstleutnant Pohlman marched on the city, a military band playing the "Horst Wessel Lied" and other martial marching airs. The stunned citizens of Oslo looked on in grim silence.

The futile resistance at Drøbak and at Fornebu had cost Norwegian lives, but it was important. It gained time for the center of Norwegian resistance to escape.

At seven-thirty that morning of April 9, a special train pulled out of the station at Oslo, heading north. Among the passengers aboard were King Haakon VII, the royal family, Dr. Halvdan Koht, Foreign Minister, Colonel Otto Ruge, who would become Commander in Chief of the Norwegian Army, and most of the members of the Storting. It was a dispirited group that got off the train at Hamar, 100 airline miles north of Oslo, but their courage had not faltered. The Storting convened and authorized Dr. Koht to enter into peace negotiations with the German minister, Dr. Bräuer.

Meanwhile the Germans had acted with typical psychological obtuseness. They proclaimed that the traitor Quisling was the head of the new Norwegian Government, but the presence of the legitimate Government at Hamar robbed Quisling of even the appearance of legality.

Colonel Ruge wisely insisted that the road to Oslo be watched. Some of the members of the Storting, holding vestiges of faith in the honor of war, refused to believe that the Germans might try to capture the king. But Colonel Ruge had his way. The Government moved another 25 miles, this time to the east, to the town of Elverum, near the Swedish border, and two infantry battalions set up barricades between there and Hamar.

It was just in time. The German air attaché in Norway, Captain Spiller, piled two companies of paratroops into buses and set out on just such a raid to capture the king. It was something of a lark. There had been no serious resistance on land near Oslo, and there was no reason to suspect there would be any at Hamar or Elverum. The

German soldiers were like tourists, enjoying the scenery and snapping pictures of one another and of the sights with cameras they had concealed during their jumps.

As their buses left Hamar for Elverum, they ran into a barricade, and a withering rifle fire pinned them down. Captain Spiller was mortally wounded, and the force raced back to Oslo.

This little example of German treachery during negotiations made Dr. Bräuer's task no easier. Meeting with King Haakon at Elverum, he flatly demanded that the monarch recognize Quisling as head of the Government and that all resistance cease forthwith.

King Haakon, the only monarch in this century who held his throne as a result of a popular vote, explained that such a decision was not his to make. Political decisions rested with the Cabinet and with the Storting. He agreed to consult with them and inform Dr. Bräuer by telephone of their decision.

Bräuer left and the Norwegian Government prudently withdrew to the nearby village of Nybergsund—just in case the Germans had other tricks up their sleeves—and there the king assembled members of the Government as a formal Council of State. In grave tones he addressed them.

> For my part, I cannot accept the German demands. It would conflict with all that I have considered my duty as King of Norway since I came to this country nearly thirty-five years ago. . . . I do not want the decision of the Government to be influenced by or be based upon this statement. . . . I cannot appoint Quisling Prime Minister, a man in whom I know neither our people . . . nor its representatives in the Storting have any confidence at all.
>
> If, therefore, the Government should decide to accept the German demands—and I fully understand the reasons in favor of it, considering the impending danger of war in which so many young Norwegians will have to give their lives—if so, abdication will be the only course open to me.

These words rallied the waverers, and Dr. Koht telephoned Dr. Bräuer, who had reached Eidsvoll, halfway back to Oslo. It was a stunned German minister who telegraphed Berlin:

> The king will name no government headed by Quisling, and this decision was made upon the unanimous advice of the Government. To my specific question, Foreign Minister Koht replied: "Resistance will continue as long as possible."

Ribbentrop and Hitler were furious. Dr. Bräuer was recalled and disappeared into the obscurity of an army uniform and was soon employed on the western front.

Since they could not persuade the King of Norway, the Germans decided to kill him. On April 11, the Luftwaffe sent planes over Nybergsund. High explosive and incendiary bombs dropped on the hapless village. Men, women, and children trying to escape the fires were mercilessly machine-gunned.

"Resistance is to be broken ruthlessly!"

The sorrowing king stood knee-deep in snow in the woods, watching the benefits Nazism was bringing his people. When the attack was over, the grimly resolute members of the Government set out to make their way through the rugged Gudbrandsal which led northwest through Lillehammer, Dombas, and on to Åndalsnes, whence they might reach British protection and could rally their countrymen to resist.

CHAPTER THREE

Norway Lost

And thus the native hue of resolution
Is sicklied o'er with the pale cast of thought,
And enterprises of great pith and moment
With this regard their currents turn awry,
And lose the name of action.
Shakespeare, Hamlet

TEN German destroyers made their way up Vest Fjord, picking their way along through the darkness and snow flurries. Leading the way was the *Wilhelm Heidkamp*, flying the broad pennant of Commodore Friedrich Bonte. These were the ships bound for Narvik, the key objective of the whole Norwegian operation, and they represented exactly half of Germany's available destroyers.

Not one of them would ever see home port again.

At 0300, April 9, Bonte's ships passed the pilot station at Trangøy and about an hour later entered Ofotfjord, an extension of Vest Fjord, which leads to Narvik. Men stood tensely to their guns as they entered, for Quisling had informed the Germans that the mouth of Ofotfjord was heavily fortified. The fortifications existed only in the imagination of the traitor, even though the British shared the illusion of their existence. Only two small patrol vessels barred the way, and they made no attempt to stop the German flotilla. Indulging in a little psychological warfare, they informed the commodore that eight warships were in Narvik. This was a fourfold exaggeration, if, indeed, the two ships actually there could be classed as warships in comparison with the sleek destroyers headed their way. The little patrol vessels then sounded the alarm on their radios.

Commodore Bonte detached three of his destroyers to land troops to deal with the imaginary fortifications at Ramnes and sent others

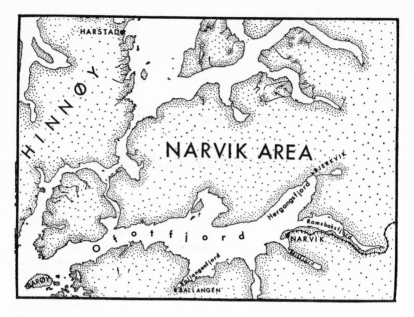

into the side fjords to capture small villages where military stores were located. With the *Arnim* and *Thiele* he pushed on to Narvik.

At the very time he was supposed to reach his goal, the snow-storm lifted as if on cue, and the port of Narvik lay open before him. The ancient coastal defense ship *Eidsvold* lay in his path. Even though she was old, the *Eidsvold* presented a threat. She was armed with two 8.2-inch guns and six 5.9-inch guns. They were pointed at the Germans, and they were much bigger than the 5-inch guns of the destroyers. A warning shot splashed in front of the *Heidkamp*. Commodore Bonte ordered his ships to stop.

Unwilling to expose his ships to danger, Commodore Bonte decided to resort to treachery. Calling an officer to him, he instructed him to take a boat and board the *Eidsvold* to demand free passage. He told the officer that the negotiations would fail. Therefore, as soon as his boat was safely out of the line of fire on the trip back, he was to fire a red Very light.

While he waited for the officer to complete his fruitless mission, Commodore Bonte maneuvered his engines at slow speeds to keep his torpedo tubes lined up on the Norwegian ship. The officer climbed up a ladder to the *Eidsvold,* held a brief conference, and departed. The boat hastily moved out of the way, and the Very light signal soared up into the sky. Immediately two torpedoes leaped out of the

Heidkamp's tubes. Both of them hit the *Eidsvold*. She broke in two and sank immediately, carrying all but eight of her crew to their deaths.

The German ships moved toward the piers. The *Arnim* had just reached there when the sister ship of the *Eidsvold* appeared through the merchant ships anchored in the crowded harbor. This ship, the *Norge,* managed to get off a few rounds before she was blown out of the water by German shells and torpedoes.

"Resistance is to be broken ruthlessly."

On board the German destroyers were two battalions of German troops led by Major General Eduard Dietl. Since only three of the ten destroyers had yet arrived at Narvik, it was only a small force that General Dietl could assemble to march on the town. The local garrison had about 450 men and could have put up some resistance, but its local commander, Colonel Sundlo, was the only highly placed Norwegian officer who was an adherent of Quisling. He surrendered without firing a shot. Two companies of his men fled over the border into Sweden, and General Dietl was in firm command of the town. It was all over by 0800 that morning.

Commodore Bonte now faced a major problem. By his orders, he was to get his flotilla back to Germany as soon as possible. But all his ships were low on fuel and could not make the long passage until they had filled up. Two tankers were supposed to have been waiting in Narvik, but only one, the *Jan Willem,* had arrived, having come down from Murmansk, where the Russians had kindly allowed her to load oil. The other tanker had been sunk on the way to Narvik.

The Commodore was not particularly worried. He knew that the *Jan Willem* could not supply enough oil for all his destroyers to fill up completely, but he felt they could take on enough to get out and rendezvous with a tanker at sea or perhaps reach Trondheim or Bergen. The real danger lay in delay, for the *Jan Willem* could service only two destroyers at a time, and it took several hours for each pair.

Still, he could be long gone before the British could possibly reach him so far north. He planned to sail his destroyers on the evening of the next day, April 10. Satisfied with his plans, he stationed two of his destroyers in Hergangsfjord to the northeast of Narvik and three others in Ballangenfjord, ten miles to the west.

At 2022 a report reached him that five British destroyers were in Vest Fjord. This was a surprise, but not alarming, since they were steering southwest toward the open sea.

The commodore turned in for a good night's sleep.

It was to be his last in this life.

The British destroyers which had caused Commodore Bonte such little concern were under command of Captain B. A. W. Warburton-Lee. During the course of April 9, as the story of the German invasion of Norway began to be pieced together in London, all sorts of information and misinformation had poured in to the Admiralty and War Office. Originally a part of the escort for the *Repulse,* Warburton-Lee's ships had been detached with instructions to "send some destroyers up to Narvik to make certain that no enemy troops land." This message came in several hours after Narvik was in German hands.

Then, about noon, the Admiralty took a hand and sent a message to Warburton-Lee directly: "Press reports state one German ship has arrived Narvik and landed a small force. Proceed Narvik and sink or capture enemy ship. It is at your discretion to land forces if you think you can recapture Narvik from number of enemy present."

Such intervention, over the head of the Commander in Chief, was one of Mr. Churchill's most unfortunate habits. It raised doubts in Captain Warburton-Lee's mind on whether he was still under the Home Fleet or was a special detached unit. It raised similar doubts in Admiral Forbes's mind, and also in the mind of Admiral Whitworth, to whom Warburton-Lee's force had originally been assigned. If the information and orders had been passed to either of those commanders, the attack on Narvik might have been beefed up with happier results for the British. Indeed, Admiral Whitworth considered sending support to the prospective attack on Narvik, but doubt over the question of command relationship held his hand. With four ships, Captain Warburton-Lee sped on up Vest Fjord to attack the German ten.

The more he thought about the situation, the less he liked it. A press report seemed an unreliable source on which to base military action. And the idea that the Germans had sent only one ship to take such an important objective was scarcely to be believed.

He decided to stop at the pilot station at Tranøy to see what the Norwegians could tell him. The pilots had quite a bit of news for him, but it was not all accurate. They told him that six destroyers, each larger than any of the British ones, had gone to Narvik, that there was a U-boat in the fjord, and that the entrance had been mined. The Norwegians predicted with some gloom that Captain Warbuton-Lee would need twice as many ships as he had with him.

Captain Warburton-Lee had no way of getting twice as many ships, but he did find one more, the *Hostile* of his own flotilla, which had been on detached service. This ship, with the *Hardy, Hunter, Hotspur,*

66

and *Havock,* formed a kind of "Five-H Club," and the flotilla commander felt he could mount some sort of attack with them. He decided to go in at dawn, when a fortunate high tide would carry his ships over moored mines if they existed. He signaled the Admiralty: INTEND ATTACKING AT DAWN, HIGH WATER. He turned away down the fjord to kill a few hours before he began his run in. It was while he was on this course that he was reported to Commodore Bonte. But the German commodore seems to have given no consideration to the possibility that the British might come back.

The Admiralty approved Captain Warburton-Lee's proposal, but about midnight, they began to have second thoughts. NORWEGIAN COAST DEFENCE SHIPS EIDSVOLD AND NORGE MAY BE IN GERMAN HANDS [they signaled]. YOU ALONE CAN JUDGE WHETHER IN THESE CIRCUMSTANCES ATTACK SHOULD BE MADE. WE SHALL SUPPORT WHATEVER DECISION YOU TAKE.

Having set his course, Captain Warburton-Lee was not one to turn aside. His reply: GOING INTO ACTION.

Going up the long fjord in darkness with snow falling almost constantly was no business for the faint-hearted or the unskilled mariner. In Norwegian fjords deep water goes right up to the towering cliffs, so a ship does not run aground. It will simply collide with the cliff with all the effect of a car hitting a stone wall. Soundings give no warning of danger. The fjords twist and turn, and even with the best charts, you must be *very* sure of your position.

Captain Warburton-Lee could not be sure of the position of his flagship, the *Hardy,* as he led the flotilla in. There was nothing to be done about it. He went on.

A lookout cried a warning. A snowy cliff dead ahead. The *Hardy* heeled far over as she scrambled clear. The water boiled in froth as reversed screws on other ships avoided collisions. A few miles farther on, they had to maneuver wildly again to avoid a passenger steamer coming down the fjord.

About 0430 the five British ships reached their goal. Narvik lay just ahead, and through the light of dawn five German destroyers could be seen. Wasting no time, Captain Warburton-Lee ordered a torpedo and gunfire attack.

The bewildered Germans had no inkling of danger. As shells began to drop among them, they first thought they were under air attack. Then the torpedoes began to hit. The first ship to go was the flagship *Heidkamp.* A torpedo struck her after magazine, and the explosion tore the ship apart. Most of her crew died in that awful second, including Commodore Bonte. Then the *Schmidt* rose partly out of the water as two torpedoes hit her at the same instant. She broke in half and both parts sank in a matter of moments. Three other ships, the *Lüdemann,* the *Künne,* and the *Roeder* were all heavily damaged.

Well pleased with the results of the attack, Warburton-Lee withdrew a little way to take stock. Finding all his ships in good shape, he decided to strike once more. This attempt was not as successful, since a mist was settling over the harbor and only occasionally could a target be seen. It was time to retire.

As he turned away, he was startled to see three German destroyers coming down from Hergangsfjord. Something was clearly wrong. There had been only six German ships in the area, according to the Norwegian pilots, and he had accounted for five of them. So much for Norwegian information.

He ordered his ships to engage the newcomers, called for 30 knots, reported the contacts to his superiors, and led the way down the fjord. A running fight developed, but the Germans were so low on oil that they soon had to give up the chase. It looked as though the British flotilla had got away with it.

It was not to be. The last two German destroyers, the *Thiele* and *Von Arnim,* which had been in Ballangenfjord, had received the alarm and set out to avenge their comrades. Because Warburton-Lee thought the two ships might be reinforcements coming to his support, he challenged by signal light before opening fire. It was a bad mistake. The challenge was answered by highly accurate 5-inch gunfire. A shell smashed the *Hardy*'s bridge, mortally wounding Captain Warburton-Lee, and killing or wounding everyone else there.

The only officer on the bridge to escape serious injury was Paymaster-Lieutenant G. H. Stanning. Although his left foot was dragging uselessly, he made his painful way from the bridge to the wheelhouse, pushed aside the dead coxswain, and steered the ship until a seaman relieved him. Whereupon Stanning painfully crawled up the ladder to the bridge again to resume control.

Since the ship had been hit in the engine room and was losing all power, Stanning turned to port to beach her before she sank. She made it, even though she was on fire and settling lower in the water at every second. The survivors escaped into the care of sympathetic Norwegians until they were rescued a few days later.

The *Hunter,* next in line, had been badly hit and swerved across the bow of the *Hotspur.* As Commander H. F. N. Layman gave the orders that would swing the *Hotspur* clear, a shell burst below the bridge, knocking out both his steering and his engine-order telegraph. Helpless to steer or stop his ship, Layman watched with horrified eyes as his bow drove like a knife into the *Hunter*. *Hotspur*'s engines kept the two ships locked together, and they spun slowly in a circle.

Commander Layman raced aft to the secondary control station, and he had no sooner left the bridge than it took a direct hit, killing everyone who remained there. Layman pulled his ship clear and made a wavering passage down the fjord, covered by a smoke screen and shellfire from the other two British ships.

By this time the *Hunter* had sunk, and the three surviving British destroyers made good their escape down the fjord. The Germans let them go. Once again the reason was fuel shortage. On the way out, the British came upon a merchant ship standing in. It turned out to be the German supply ship *Rauenfels*. The crew abandoned ship, and the *Havock* fired two shells into her. It was an imprudent thing to do, for the *Rauenfels* had been loaded with ammunition, and the explosion sent a tower of flame and smoke 3000 feet into the air. Debris rained on the *Havock,* but fortunately there were no casualties.

So ended the first Battle of Narvik. There would be more.

For his attack, Captain Warburton-Lee was awarded the first Victoria Cross to be given in World War II.*

When the story of the attack was released to the press and radio, it helped to inspire the Norwegians to resist with all their power the despoilers of their homeland. It so demoralized the Germans at Narvik that they hesitated before extricating their ships. When they next tried, it was too late.

A few days later, on April 13, the battleship *Warspite,* supported by nine destroyers and by aircraft from the carrier *Furious,* entered the fjord to finish off the work so ably begun by Captain Warburton-Lee. It was the first time so large a ship had gone into action in such restricted waters. She was in danger from mines and submarines, but she made it safely. A plane from the *Furious* sank a U-boat at the entrance to Ofotfjord, and then the fury was upon the Germans. All five of the remaining German destroyers were sunk or beached.

Admiral Whitworth, aboard the *Warspite,* was tempted to try to retake the town. But he had no troops, and he felt that the small force which could be spared from his ships could be easy prey to the

* Warburton-Lee's Victoria Cross was the first to be *awarded.* Lieutenant Commander Roope of the *Glowworm* had been the first to *earn* his, but it was not awarded until after the war when the story became known.

Germans in the area. Regretfully he withdrew but sent a message to his superiors: MY IMPRESSION IS THAT ENEMY FORCES IN NARVIK WERE THOROUGHLY FRIGHTENED AS RESULT OF TODAY'S ACTION AND THAT PRESENCE OF WARSPITE WAS THE CHIEF CAUSE OF THIS. I RECOMMEND THAT TOWN BE OCCUPIED WITHOUT DELAY BY MAIN LANDING FORCE.

The next morning he jogged his superiors again. INFORMATION FROM NORWEGIAN SOURCES ESTIMATES 1500 TO 2000 TROOPS. I AM CONVINCED NARVIK CAN BE TAKEN BY DIRECT ASSAULT WITHOUT FEAR OF MEETING SERIOUS OPPOSITION ON LANDING.

These two attacks on Narvik were very nearly the only things that went right in the entire British response to the Norwegian invasion. Only once more would they know success in this campaign. Once more the scene would be Narvik, but it would be too late.

The Supreme War Council met in emergency session in London on the afternoon of April 9, Premier Reynaud and a group of French leaders flying over for the purpose. What could be done about Norway without weakening too much the Allied positions facing the Germans on the French border? The French agreed to supply a detachment of Chasseurs Alpins, specially trained mountain troops. The rest would be British. Operations would be under British command—if they could only figure out what to do.

It quickly became clear that the British could not do anything at all in southern Norway. The Luftwaffe had moved efficiently from the first, and soon German fighters and dive bombers were operating out of many airfields in the area between Bergen and Oslo. Soon they would extend their operations farther north.

Since there was no possible way of establishing a Royal Air Force base in Norway, and since Norway was far beyond the range of fighters based on the British Isles, whatever air opposition the British could throw at the Luftwaffe would have to come from the Navy. From their air base in the Orkney Islands, Skua dive bombers could just reach the Norwegian coast at Bergen. Fifteen of them took off in the early morning hours of April 10 and set out on the 275-mile journey to the second city of Norway, their pilots nursing their throttles to conserve fuel. Guiding the flight was Lieutenant Commander Hale, who had been over Bergen the day before in a Coastal Command Blenheim bomber. He knew exactly where the German ships were berthed. The timing had to be exact, for if the planes had to waste any time searching, their crews would have to swim the last few miles home.

As the 15 Skuas roared into the fjord, Hale looked anxiously for the place where he had seen ships the previous day. Nothing. He did not know it, but the cruiser *Köln* had sailed for home the previous night. But the *Königsberg* was still there; she had shifted berth and was tied up alongside a pier.

The raid was a complete surprise to the German defenders. As the Skuas screamed down in the attack, led by Captain R. T. Partridge, Royal Marines, the German gunners could be seen running to their stations. One by one the planes reached the pull-out point, dropped their bombs, and dashed on their way home. It was not until the eighth or ninth plane was releasing its bomb load that the German guns snarled their angry defiance. But it was too late. Not a single British plane was shot down, and before the last one was out of sight, the *Königsberg* was rolling on her side. In a few minutes she was gone, the first major warship ever to be sunk by air attack alone.

The triumph of the Skuas against the *Königsberg* was very nearly the only success that Britain had in the air during the Norwegian campaign. Only one aircraft carrier was available to the Home Fleet at that time, the *Furious*. She had sailed so hastily that she had no fighters on board, and the Swordfish torpedo planes had no success whatever in a raid on Trondheim and little at Narvik. It was not until the *Ark Royal* and *Glorious* put in an appearance on April 24 that the British had any further luck in the air.

Meanwhile the Luftwaffe reigned supreme where it would, operating from an increasing number of airfields in Norway. British ships were almost impotent to protect themselves from the shrieking Stukas. Although cruisers and larger ships had an adequate, or reasonably adequate, number of high-angle antiaircraft guns, the destroyers and smaller vessels—those which would bear the brunt of the attacks— were not so fortunate. Most had only .50-caliber machine guns and the unreliable 2-pound pom-pom. On most British destroyers in the Norwegian operations, the main battery guns, usually 4.7-inchers, could not be elevated above 40 degrees. As the Stukas attacked at an 80-degree dive angle, the destroyers could do little to defend themselves. The destroyer *Gurkha* was the first to suffer. Caught alone, some miles from the British main body on the afternoon of April 9, she was dive-bombed, hit, hit again and again, until she was a burning wreck. Most of her crew were picked up, but the lesson was clear.

The attack on the *Gurkha* was only a part of the operations of the Luftwaffe that afternoon. For over six hours they attacked a force of 4 cruisers and 6 destroyers, damaging 2 cruisers. By the time darkness had fallen and the German planes had roared away, the British discovered that they had expended over 40 percent of their antiaircraft ammunition without shooting down a single plane. There was only one thing to do: move the fleet units out of range of German air. For the time being, the British ships would be able to operate in the Trondheim area and north. But how long would it last?

The Supreme War Council had approved striking back at the Germans in Norway with a view to liberating the land and restoring the king. The French gladly left the strategic direction of operations in British hands, and the British had to make up their minds what they were going to do. The two obvious places to attack were Trondheim and Narvik. But which? Or both?

Since troops were already selected for operations against Norway and were ready, the British War Cabinet decided they should be employed to free Narvik as quickly as possible. After considerable debate, the Cabinet decided to try to take Trondheim, as well, so preparations were set in motion. Thus began what Churchill called "this ramshackle campaign."

For Narvik, the War Office selected Major General P. J. Mackesy as troop commander, while the Admiralty picked Admiral of the Fleet Lord Cork and Orrery as naval commander. Although a five-star admiral is vastly senior to a two-star general, Lord Cork was not given supreme command of the operation. Instead, the two commanders were vaguely told to "cooperate." And they sailed with vastly different instructions.

From the War Office, General Mackesy brought away an attitude of caution. He must not allow himself to be rushed into anything. Take it slow and easy, and all will yet be well.

The object of the force will be to eject the Germans from the Narvik area and establish control of Narvik itself . . . Your initial task will be to establish your force at Harstad, ensure the cooperation of Norwegian forces that may be there, and obtain the information necessary to enable you to plan your further operations. It is not intended that you should land in the face of opposition. You may, however, be faced with opposition owing to mistaken identity; you will, therefore, take such steps as are suitable to establish the nationality of your force before abandoning the attempt. The decision whether to land or not will be taken by the senior naval officer in consultation with you. If landing is impossible at Harstad, some other suitable locality should be tried. A landing must be carried out when you have sufficient troops.

Seldom have a set of orders been more irrelevant to the situation. All of the warnings, all of the admonitions, read as though it would be the *Norwegians* that would oppose the British and later French troops. From Harstad on the island of Hinnøy to the northwest of Narvik, Mackesy would have no means of reaching Narvik without another naval lift. The only way to reach that key city before the middle of May was by water. If Mackesy intended to approach the city by land, he would have to cross a narrow fjord and march around. But that would have to wait. There was too much snow on the ground.

The Chief of the Imperial General Staff, General Edmund Ironside, gave Mackesy a letter which had a slightly different tone to it. "You may have a chance of taking advantage of naval action and should do so if you can. Boldness is required."

General Mackesy pocketed the letter; it seems to have made little impression on him, and he went ahead with his preparations with a calm confidence in settling in for an indefinite stay at Harstad.

The naval commander, Lord Cork and Orrery, was personally briefed by Churchill and by Sir Dudley Pound, the First Sea Lord. Here there was no cautious admonition on how to handle possible suspicious Norwegians. The objective was to strike and strike hard at Narvik. "My impression on leaving London [wrote Lork Cork] was quite clear that it was desired by His Majesty's Government to turn the enemy out of Narvik at the earliest possible moment, and that I was to act with all promptitude in order to attain this result."

Lord Cork embarked in the cruiser *Aurora* on April 12 at Rosyth with the firm intention of "turning the enemy out." About the same time, General Mackesy sailed in the cruiser *Southampton* from Scapa Flow with the firm intention of establishing a base at Harstad, where he could sit down and draw up a plan. So the two commanders headed on their way, their minds made up in advance and their ideas poles apart.

On receipt of the encouraging message from Admiral Whitworth,* Lord Cork decided the moment was right and radioed the *Southampton* to rendezvous with the *Aurora* in Skjelfjord in the Lofoten Islands, near the entrance to Vest Fjord. By some quirk of atmospherics, the *Southampton* failed to receive the message, which was picked up clearly in London. By the time the relay through the Admiralty had

---

* See above, p. 70.

73

been received on board, the *Southampton* had reached Harstad, and General Mackesy was busily unloading his troops. Thither charged the *Aurora,* Lord Cork impatiently urging speed so as not to throw away the opportunity that offered.

He was toying with the idea of having a try at Narvik all by himself, using sailors and Marines to form landing parties if he could not get the general to agree to his plans. He had to abandon this notion on receipt of a wireless from the Admiralty: WE THINK IT IMPERATIVE THAT YOU AND THE GENERAL SHOULD BE TOGETHER AND ACT TOGETHER AND NO ATTEMPT AT LANDING SHOULD BE MADE EXCEPT IN CONCERT.

In the forenoon of April 15, the *Aurora* reached Harstad, followed by transports bringing the rest of Mackesy's troops. The general boarded Lord Cork's flagship, and the admiral was flabbergasted. He had spent most of the passage from Rosyth devising alternate plans for a quick decision at Narvik, and the realization that General Mackesy was only now gathering information preparatory to devising a plan came as a great shock to him. Mackesy had, he reported, come into the town, made contact with the Norwegian officials, and determined that no Germans were present. He thereupon had begun unloading. He could not do otherwise, he argued. His ships were not combat loaded. Men were separated from their equipment, and even the Scots Guards, who were accustomed to snow and rugged terrain, found movement almost impossible. He calmly proposed to continue his unloading and wait for the snow to melt. Then he would take the road to Narvik.

There were no snows on the road to Narvik, retorted the Admiral, if that road was the water one his ships could traverse up Ofotfjord. Troops could land and take the town at once.

The General refused to be swayed, and Lord Cork reported the impasse to London. Back flashed a wireless message composed by Mr. Churchill himself. Although it was addressed to both commanders, the real target was General Mackesy.

YOUR PROPOSALS INVOLVE DAMAGING DEADLOCK AT NARVIK AND THE NEUTRALISATION OF ONE OF OUR BEST BRIGADES. WE CANNOT SEND YOU THE CHASSEURS ALPINS. THE WARSPITE WILL BE NEEDED ELSEWHERE IN TWO OR THREE DAYS. FULL CONSIDERATION SHOULD, THEREFORE, BE GIVEN BY YOU TO AN ASSAULT UPON NARVIK COVERED BY THE WARSPITE AND THE DESTROYERS, WHICH MIGHT ALSO OPERATE AT ROMBAKSFJORD.

THE CAPTURE OF THE PORT AND TOWN WOULD BE AN IMPORTANT SUCCESS. WE SHOULD LIKE TO RECEIVE FROM YOU THE REASONS WHY THIS IS NOT POSSIBLE, AND YOUR ESTIMATE OF THE DEGREE OF RESISTANCE TO BE EXPECTED ON THE WATERFRONT. MATTER MOST URGENT.

Lord Cork summoned the general again the next day to discuss action in view of the message from London. The general again refused, pointing to categorical prohibitions against heavy bombardment in his orders from the War Office. "Bombardment must be carried out in such a way that there is a reasonable expectation that damage will be confined to the objective and that civilian populations in the neighbourhood are not bombarded through negligence.

"Thus it is clearly illegal to bombard a populated area in the hope of hitting a legitimate target which is known to be in the area, but which cannot be precisely located and identified . . .

"Thus an anti-aircraft or coast defence gun situated in the centre of a populous area could not be bombarded with reasonable expectation that damage would be confined to it."

The pleasantly humane views in these instructions were not long for this world. A few weeks would see their end, not out of choice, but out of "military necessity." War, never humane at best, would become a little more inhuman.

General Mackesy agreed to a personal reconnaissance in the *Aurora* to see for himself whether bombardment would enable him to land troops as desired and still not endanger any civilians. Perhaps he was looking for evidence to support the position he had been defending so vehemently. Perhaps he was right. "I am convinced that a naval bombardment cannot be militarily effective, and that a landing from open boats in the above conditions must be ruled out absolutely. Any attempt of the sort would involve not the neutralisation but the destruction of the 24th [Guards] Brigade." Such a landing would, he told Lord Cork, result in the "snow of Narvik being turned into another version of the mud of Passchendaele."

There was nothing to be done. Lord Cork tried a bombardment on his own, hoping the Germans might surrender. But he had little faith in it. The weather was against him; snows were falling, reducing visibility and obscuring targets. For three hours the 15-inch guns of the battleship *Warspite,* the 8-inch guns of the *Effingham,* and the 6-inch guns of the *Enterprise* * and *Aurora* shattered the calm of

* Not to be confused with the American carrier of the same name.

75

Ofotfjord, the echoes reverberating through the mountains and combining with blast and concussion to shake the houses and break windows in Narvik. Little damage was done, and there were no signs that anyone was ready to surrender. Considering the visibility, it seems unlikely that the British could have seen a surrender signal in any case. But General Dietl's troops were safely hidden away in the hills east of Narvik and were not affected by the bombardment at all.

There was nothing for it. Lord Cork signaled the recall, and the force retired to Harstad. General Mackesy continued to unload his troops and began to prepare a plan. They would wait for the snow to melt.

In retrospect it seems clear that, with the Germans demoralized from the sinking of their 10 destroyers and the attack on April 13 by the *Warspite,* an attack delivered on April 15 or 16, as Lord Cork wished, might have succeeded. But every hour of delay increased the strength of the defenders. The destroyer crews were integrated into the German army defenses; positions were strengthened; machine guns and light artillery were sited. The surprise and psychological impact the British might have exploited were frittered away.

* * *

Trondheim, Norway's ancient capital, lies some 400 airline miles south of Narvik. Founded in 997 by Norway's first Christian king, Olaf Tryggvason, it is now the third largest city in Norway. In its 12th-century cathedral the kings are still crowned, and there they are buried.

From the first, both the Germans and the British realized the importance of Trondheim. All roads leading north pass through the city, and the magnificent harbor in Trondheimsfjord afforded ample space for ships to supply troops ashore. If Britain could retake the city and hold it, then the Germans to the north could only surrender to the British or flee across the border to interment in neutral Sweden. It was a tempting, dazzling prospect. "I threw myself with increasing confidence into this daring venture [wrote Churchill], and was willing that the Fleet should risk the weak batteries at the entrance to the fjord, the possible minefields, and, most serious, the air."

Briefly, the British planned a triple thrust at Trondheim. Some 90 miles north of Trondheim, at the head of Namsenfjord, is the little lumber-shipping town of Namsos. A small force would be landed here to fight its way down to invest Trondheim from the north. A hundred miles south of the city, on Romsdalsfjord, is the timber port of Åndalsnes at one end of the long road leading through the magnificent Gudbrandsdal Valley to Dombas, Lillehamar, and Oslo. Here another force would land, proceed down the valley to Dombas, and then turn northwest to fall upon Trondheim from the southeast. Hopefully, they would be joined by loyal Norwegian troops retiring up the Gudbrandsdal falling back before the German advance.

The major blow at Trondheim would come from the sea. Up to 50,000 men would eventually hold the city and establish a barrier to all German advance further north.

Such was the plan. Such was the dream. But it was to prove only a dream.

Troops went into Namsos and Åndlasnes, but they didn't stay long. The main drive against Trondheim never came off.

Mauriceforce, the code name for the Namsos group, landed on April 14, when spirits were running high in Britain and France as a result of the victory of the *Warspite* at Narvik. Under command of the much-decorated Major General Sir Adrian Carton de Wiart, the expedition got off to a good beginning. On the first day only a few men were landed, but not their commander, who was still in England being briefed by the War Office. A highly colorful character, Carton de Wiart wore a black eye-patch; his left sleeve was empty, but his mind was not. When his telephone shrilled during the night hours, he quickly guessed that his assignment would be Norway. It was fitting, since that was one of the few parts of the world where he had not left some part of himself.

With a sardonic view of the War Office's grasp of reality, Carton de Wiart embarked with a single staff officer in a seaplane, which duly landed him at Namsos. His welcome set the tone for the few days that Mauriceforce remained there. As his plane skimmed down on the waters of Namsenfjord it was followed by others—Germans. Some dropped bombs on the town, but one energetically turned its attention to the British commander's aircraft. It was quickly riddled, the staff officer wounded, and the General was pinned down in the sinking plane until the German attacker ran out of ammunition. Unruffled, Carton de Wiart stepped ashore, rounded up two officers he found, detailed them to his staff, and set to work to get the rest of Mauriceforce ashore.

For the next few days they came in, always in driblets, and always under air attack, if they tried it by day. So they turned to night operations, when the Luftwaffe pilots turned in for a few hours of rest. They managed to get a brigade of British troops ashore, followed on April 19 by 3 battalions of French Chasseurs Alpins. Carton de Wiart especially welcomed these well-trained troops, who had wide experience in fighting in mountainous terrain and in snow. Unfortunately, some vital part of their ski harness had been left behind, and nothing could be improvised. "They would have been invaluable to us [recorded the General later] if only I could have used them."

Meanwhile, overhead the Luftwaffe was unchallenged. Ships, with their hopelessly inadequate antiaircraft weapons, merely attracted bombs that might have fallen on the troops and on the town. As it was, the Germans methodically and efficiently obliterated the village of Namsos, while the infuriated Norwegians and their allies looked on impotently.

It was quickly clear to Carton de Wiart that he had been given a hopeless task. When he was informed that he was to be an acting lieutenant general, he did not bother to put on the insignia of his new rank, for he knew the operation would be coming to an end. Evacuation would be necessary, and no one was likely to promote the leader of an expedition that ended in failure. The fact that the shortcomings of the War Office and of the years of peace doomed Mauriceforce would make no difference. The commander was responsible.

I SEE LITTLE CHANCE OF CARRYING OUT DECISIVE OR, INDEED, ANY OPERATIONS UNLESS ENEMY AIR ACTIVITY IS CONSIDERABLY REDUCED.

This message from Namsos was not well received by the War Office. Something might turn up. Åndalsnes might be different.

Åndalsnes was different. It had a rail line from which the troops could move into the interior and join forces with General Ruge's Norwegians coming up the Gudbrandsdal. So, under the command of Brigadier H. de R. Morgan, Sickleforce men were sent down the road to Dombas to meet the Norwegians.

Otherwise Åndalsnes was the same. German aircraft ruled the skies; ships were bombed and strafed. Åndalsnes and the nearby towns of Ålesund and Molde were blasted into rubble. Other planes strafed the troops making their way down the narrow road leading to Dombas. What it was like can be learned from Brigadier Dudley Clarke.

> The German pilots flew now just as they liked, up and down that one narrow road along which everything had to move. In relays of two and three they would come out to bomb the bridges and the

cross-roads and then, with the bombs spent, they would drop down on their remaining petrol for the sport of shooting up anything left in sight. The hum of engines soon became so regular that there was no more chance to stop the car and streak for shelter before each made his initial run in.

That first attack either got you or it missed you; and only then, after it was over, would there follow the exhausting process of tumbling out and ploughing through snow to the nearest tree or wall, or even the roadside drain, in the few minutes that were left before the next one . . .

Looking back upon it I believe the "Evil Eye" feeling was the worst part, the sensation of being watched at every turn by birds of prey who could swoop with deadly suddenness whenever they chose the moment. It was largely that which drove us to the flimsy cover of trees and sheds, and it was that which reduced "Sickleforce" to something near complete immobility during each eighteen hours of daylight.

If anything was to be done in Norway, the British would have to have air power. The carriers *Ark Royal* and *Glorious* had joined the *Furious* in Norwegian waters, but they were primarily needed to give protection to the fleet, and their aircraft were of too low performance to do anything effective against the German Stukas and Messerschmitts.

In a desperate measure, a squadron of 18 Gladiators was ordered to use an improvised airfield on the frozen Lake Lesjaskog near the road between Åndalsnes and Dombas. The Gladiator was scarcely a plane to pit against the Luftwaffe's Messerschmitt 109. The British plane was a biplane, with a top speed of 253 miles per hour; the trim ME-109 could practically fly rings around it. Even if a Gladiator could catch the German fighter, its four .303 Browning machine guns had little chance against the two machine guns and two 20-mm. cannons mounted in the wings of the German plane.

It made little difference, for the Gladiator squadron never really had a chance. Its members flew their obsolescent aircraft off from the flight deck of the *Glorious* on the afternoon of April 24, and they all landed safely on the impromptu airfield in a blinding snowstorm. Overhead Luftwaffe pilots watched the proceedings. They may have smiled indulgently. They didn't even bother to attack. There would be time enough the next day when the British pilots had learned some of the facts of life of operating aircraft in the arctic conditions Norway was providing so amply.

As if the weather was not bad enough, the chaos born of improvisation and carelessness plagued the Gladiator pilots. During the bitterly cold night, the planes froze up solid, so that the engines would not

79

turn over and the controls could not be moved. A starter truck was pushed up to a plane. Its ample batteries would turn the engine over. A press of a switch. Nothing. Someone had forgotten to send acid for the batteries. There were no reserve stocks of lubricating oil for the engines.

After two hours of frantic scrambling, involving jumper cables, calls for oil to be sent in, shoveling the makeshift runway, the exhausted ground crews and pilots managed to get two Gladiators into the air, just as the Luftwaffe sent its bombers over. A couple of more Gladiators managed to get off the ground—God knows how—and they bravely took off after the bombers. Most of the rest of the Gladiators were destroyed where they stood.

The remaining handful, the bomb attack ended, made off in support of their troops and tangled with the Stukas which made life a snowy hell for the weary soldiers. The Stuka, a dive bomber, had nearly the speed and fighting capacity of the Gladiators, but the British planes did good work, shooting down several Germans and bringing solace to the hearts of the men on the ground. At last, at last they had some air cover.

Then, in the early afternoon, the Gladiators ran out of ammunition.

The gallant pilots kept flying their missions, bluffing the Stukas, but it could not last. By evening, when they flew to an alternate airfield, only 5 of the 18 remained. By the end of the next day, there was but one.

By this time it made little difference. The campaign for central Norway was at an end.

The British had linked up with the retreating Norwegians, and fighting gallantly in the snow, they were all retiring on Åndalsnes for evacuation.

What of Trondheim? What of the main thrust, for which the Namsos and Åndalsnes expeditions were supposed to be the supporting operations? When was it going to take place?

The answer was, never.

While the hapless Namsos and Åndalsnes operations floundered in the snow, preparations for Operation Hammer, the main stroke against Trondheim, were going forward in spite of Admiral Forbes's on-the-scene forebodings. "I do not consider operation feasible unless you are prepared to face very heavy losses in troops and transports." Churchill, in particular, pushed for action. "We still think," he signaled Admiral Forbes, "that the operation described should be further studied. . . . Danger from air would not be appreciably less wherever these large troopships are brought into the danger zone. . . . The aerodrome at Trondheim, which is close to the harbour, could be dealt with by Fleet Air Arm bombers and subsequently by bombardment. . . . Pray, therefore, consider this important project further."

Admiral Forbes replied discouragingly. "I do not anticipate any great difficulty from the naval side, except that I cannot provide air defence for transports whilst approaching and carrying out an opposed landing—the chief air menace being JU-88's from Germany. And I know, from personal experience, what an opposed landing is like, even without air opposition."

Even in the face of this, Mr. Churchill was not disposed to be discouraged. At his elbow, urging, urging, urging, was the highly respected Admiral of the Fleet Sir Roger Keyes, Member of Parliament, and hero of the daring raid on Zeebrugge in 1918. Keyes's career had been marked by boldness. He had never been one to hold back when cooler and wiser heads urged caution. As chief of staff to the commanding admiral at the ill-fated Dardanelles operation of 1915, he had urged yet one more attempt at passing the Narrows. His chief overruled this advice, but throughout his long career, Keyes passionately believed that Constantinople could have been taken if he had had his way.

Now Keyes saw his chance for vindication. He, in person, would lead the ships of the Home Fleet against the forts and planes defending Trondheim. He, in person, would retrieve the disasters of Norway.

His counsel fell on willing ears, for Mr. Churchill, as in 1940, had been First Lord of the Admiralty in 1915. He had believed then that only overcaution had prevented success, that with more determination, the way to Constantinople could have been opened, and all the might-have-beens would have followed inevitably. The Western Front might have been broken; the Russian collapse and Revolution might never have taken place; the Central Powers might have been crushed before their economic collapse, so there would have been no fertile grounds for the rise of Hitler. All this Mr. Churchill perceived, and in Norway a chance beckoned once again. The opportunities could not be as great as those he saw before him in 1915, but great they were nonetheless.

But they were not to be. To appoint Admiral of the Fleet Sir Roger Keyes over the head of the Commander in Chief, Admiral Forbes, in face of Forbes's opposition, would probably have induced his resignation. The political consequences would be insupportable.

On April 18, the Chiefs of Staff presented a paper to the Prime Minister. They had changed their minds. The risks at Trondheim were too great, and they were now unanimously opposed to the direct assault. Let the Trondheim operation go and those at Namsos and Åndalsnes be beefed up. Surely they would accomplish the purpose at far less risk and cost.

But events moved faster than plans. As has been told, both attempts failed. There was nothing for it but evacuation, and so it came about.

The decision to withdraw from central Norway had reached the commanders concerned by the morning of April 28. It was bitter news to the Norwegian Commander in Chief, General Ruge, who had protected the king so well at Elverum and had led the long, fearful retreat up through the snows and ice of the Gudbrandsdal. "So, Norway must go the way of Czechoslovakia and Poland," he said. "But why? Why withdraw when your troops are still unbeaten? . . . But these things are not for us to decide, General. We are soldiers and we have to obey. Let us return to our plans. Please tell me what help I can give you to carry out your orders."

Major General B. C. T. Paget, who had taken over command in the Åndalsnes area, sympathized with Ruge, but there was nothing to be done about it. He agreed with the decision to evacuate, and the task was to get as many men out safely as possible.

The first concern was for the safety of the Norwegian king and his family, as well as the members of the Norwegian Government. Under the protection of Ruge's troops, they had reached Molde, not a great distance from Åndalsnes. On the night of April 29/30, the cruiser *Glasgow* with an escort of two destroyers was sent to Molde to take the royal party off to safety. Although the British urged that the Norwegians seek safety in Britain, they respected the king's desire to remain on Norwegian soil as long as there was any hope of resistance. Accordingly, King Haakon and his followers were landed on May 1 at Tromsø, a hundred miles north of Narvik.

During the night hours of the last day of April and the first two of May, 4400 men were evacuated from Åndalsnes and about 5500 from Namsos. Not a ship was lost, nor a man.

But wars are not won by evacuations. There was still fighting to do, and the time was approaching when they would do it, in larger measure than they dreamed at that moment.

On May 10, Germany unleashed her long-awaited offensive in the west.

Norway had become a sideshow.

But the story of Norway was not over. There was still the opportunity at Narvik.

In the Narvik area by this time, the snows were beginning to melt. More troops had arrived, including 3 battalions of Chasseurs Alpins and 2 battalions of the famed French Foreign Legion. In command of this French detachment was a man whom Lord Cork found in accord with his own ideas. General Béthouart proposed immediate action, but General Mackesy still held back. On May 7, however, he gave reluctant approval for preliminary steps to be undertaken during the night of May 11/12. It was his last order, for a new army Commander in Chief had arrived on the scene. His name is one to be remembered, for he will be heard from again in another year and another clime. He is the man who later was to save the British position in North Africa. His name? Lieutenant General Claude Auchinleck.*

On the night of May 12/13, twenty-four hours behind schedule, in the broad daylight of the midnight sun, the big guns of the battleship *Resolution* and the cruisers *Aurora* and *Effingham* roared out in Hergangsfjord. At the head of this fjord was the target area, the village of Bjerkvik. The echoes resounded and crashed from one rock wall to the other, while the shells smashed to a rubble the houses and sheds in which the German troops had taken cover. General Béthouart calmly took his troops ashore at Bjerkvik and at Øyjord, a few miles away. By morning, the operation had succeeded, at a cost of only 36 casualties.

But then came further delays. The abandonment of the British position in central Norway had freed the Germans to drive farther north. A column of land forces was drawing inexorably closer, from Trondheim to Grong, from Grong to Mosjøen, from Mosjøen to Mo, from Mo to Bodø. Soon the German forces would press on Narvik from the south. If Narvik was to be taken at all, it would have to be soon.

Meanwhile, the Luftwaffe had moved even more rapidly than the infantry. Newly established airfields in the north of Norway made it impossible for operations against Narvik to proceed until the Allies could establish some air power in the area.

Not until May 20 could airfields be prepared in the region to receive British aircraft, and on the next day a squadron of Gladiators and a squadron of Hurricanes landed on an improvised strip at Bardu-

* See the author's *1942: The Year That Doomed the Axis* (New York: David McKay Company, Inc., 1967).

foss, 50 miles north of Narvik. They were able to keep the Luftwaffe in check, and plans went on apace for the final seizure of Narvik.

Before they could be implemented, however, the grim news from France forced a reappraisal. The 24,500 Allied troops in the area could be better used on the main front. They would have to be evacuated. But first, they would seize the ore city, destroy its facilities, and pull out. Norway would be left to her fate. There was no other way.

On May 27 the British, the French, and a Polish brigade mounted the final assault. By afternoon the next day, Narvik had fallen, and only the grim work of destruction lay ahead. When it was over, more than 20 wrecked ships littered the harbor; the wharves and storage facilities were demolished. It was over nine months before the city and harbor were of any use except for fishing activities.

As soon as the city had fallen, preparations for evacuation began. Large liners picked their way through the fjords and embarked troops which sailed for home, covered by such naval forces as could be spared. By the end of the first week in June, the operation was in full swing. King Haakon and his party, bowing to the inevitable, left Tromsø in the cruiser *Devonshire* and crossed to Britain to establish a Government in Exile. No word of recrimination ever passed the lips of Norway's beloved king. Throughout the war he remained a staunch symbol of resistance, an inspiration to his countrymen and to free men everywhere.

The Norwegian venture seemed to be ending in a whimper. But fate intervened once more to take a hand, and there is one more deed of high valor to be told.

For weeks, Grand Admiral Erich Raeder had contemplated with disfavor the reports of British ships sailing with impunity the waters between Britain and Norway, bringing men and supplies to Harstad for operations against Narvik. On May 21, Hitler approved his proposal to send the *Scharnhorst, Gneisenau, Hipper,* and 4 destroyers to attack these ships and stir up what trouble they could in the northern waters. Operation Juno, as this venture was called, began when the 7 ships sailed from Kiel on the morning of June 4.

Strangely enough, the Germans had no inkling that the Allies were evacuating Narvik, and when the German ships reached their hunting grounds, Admiral Wilhelm Marschall made a serious blunder. A scouting plane spotted 6 large passenger liners to the southeast, heading south, away from the German force. Admiral Marschall considered that they were empty transports, not worth his bother. He would look for a more rewarding prize.

But he who seeks to grasp too much may end by holding nothing. These liners were the *Monarch of Bermuda, Batory, Franconia, Lancastria, Sobieski,* and *Georgic,* and they bore in their holds and cabins and public rooms 15,000 men. The ships continued their voyage peacefully, and the men they carried lived to fight other battles in other lands.

No prizes appeared before the eyes of Admiral Marschall's lookouts. The German force put in at Trondheim briefly for fuel and information and then resumed the hunt. Another large troop convoy sailed from Harstad for Britain, but of this Admiral Marschall knew nothing. He sailed to the northwest, largely on hunch.

No one knew it, but his course was taking him directly toward the second convoy. The scene was being set for tragedy on a grand scale for the 7 transports had 10,000 troops on board.

By this time, the British had wind of the presence of the German force in the area, but the only surface ships that might have been able to cope with the *Scharnhorst*'s and *Gneisenau*'s 11-inch guns were far out of position, having gone off on a wild-goose chase as a result of a faulty sighting report. Only a few cruisers and the two aircraft carriers *Ark Royal* and *Glorious* were available.

But the *Glorious* could be of little use. The overworked Gladiator and Hurricane pilots, who from their improvised airfield at Bardufoss had met the challenge of the Luftwaffe, could not bring themselves to obey orders and destroy their planes. They begged to be allowed to fly them off to a carrier.

Such a request appeals to the imagination, and there was little hesitation in permitting the pilots to try it. None of them had ever landed on a carrier deck before, but that did not stop them. With a Swordfish from the carrier *Glorious* leading the way, the 10 surviving Gladiators and 8 Hurricanes flew out over the sea, entered the landing pattern, and skillfully brought their planes safely to a stop on the treacherous, tiny deck. It was incredible, for none of the aircraft had arrester hooks in the tails, but not a plane or pilot was lost.

Because she was low on fuel, and because the presence of the Gladiators and Hurricanes made flight operations nearly impossible, the *Glorious* was sent off to make the passage to Britain on her own, shepherded by the destroyers *Ardent* and *Acasta.*

This was the group that the German force found. This was the sacrifice. The gallantry of the pilots in bringing their aircraft aboard the *Glorious* was to be wasted.

But, while the Germans were destroying this little group, the transports with their 10,000 passengers got clean away.

At 1545 on June 8, a German lookout spotted a masthead to the eastward, and the battle cruisers turned toward it. In a few minutes the target was discerned as an aircraft carrier, and Admiral Marschall had a few anxious moments, expecting a swarm of planes around his head at any time. On closer examination, he could see no signs of flight operations, so he pressed on, opening fire at a range of 28,000 yards with his 11-inch guns. The best the British could do was to flee, for their 4.7-inchers could not reach so far, nor could they do any real damage if they did hit.

Helpless to get her planes in the air, the *Glorious* sped on. But the Germans were faster, and the range inexorably closed. The *Ardent* and *Acasta* took station astern and covered the retreat with a smoke screen, but still the German shells began to hit. The *Ardent* turned back through the smoke screen and delivered a torpedo attack, but the Germans dodged and promptly blew the British destroyer out of the water.

By 1700 the *Glorious* was in a sinking condition, uncontrollable fires raging in her hangar deck. There was nothing to be done.

It was time for Commander C. E. Glasfurd, commanding the *Acasta,* to take his ship out of there. He looked around his bridge calmly and then gave his order. But it was not to escape. They would attack.

"You may think we are running away from the enemy," he told his crew. "We are not. Our chummy ship has sunk, the *Glorious* is sinking, the least we can do is make a show. Good luck to you all."

Back they turned through the smoke screen. Her bows creamed the water as she rushed in, her guns blazing, her White Ensign fluttering defiance. Closer and closer they bore in on the surprised enemy. At point-blank range, the *Acasta* sheered to starboard and torpedoes leaped over the port side. One slammed into the *Scharnhorst,* putting her out of action for a year.

But now the *Acasta* had to pay the price. There was no escape. Shells began hitting and, in the words of her sole survivor, one "seemed to lift the ship out of the water." The captain ordered "Abandon ship," and the crew went over the side. Leading Seaman C. Carter continues the story. "Before I jumped over the side I saw Surgeon Lieutenant H. J. Stammer, RNVR, still attending to the

86

wounded, a hopeless task, and when I was in the water I saw the captain, leaning over the bridge, take a cigarette from a case and light it. We shouted to him to come on our raft. He waved 'Goodbye and good luck'—the end of a gallant man."

So ended the Norwegian campaign—a story of frustration and failure, of heroism and horror, of caution and conservatism, of bewilderment and betrayal.

The Norwegian campaign gave the name of Quisling to the world, but the world would better remember the names of the men whose courage and devotion to duty made their mark, names such as King Haakon, General Ruge, Lieutenant Commander Roope of the *Glowworm*, Captain Warburton-Lee of the *Hardy*, Lord Cork and General Béthouart at Narvik, and Commander C. E. Glasfurd of the *Acasta*.

CHAPTER FOUR

The Occasion and the Man

*You have sat too long here for any good
you have been doing.
Depart, I say—let us have done with you.
In the name of God, go!*
Cromwell to the Long Parliament

ILLUSIONS shattered, hopes dashed, assurances unrealized, Parliament on May 7 turned to rend the Prime Minister and his Government. The fair words were all untrue. "Today," Sir Samuel Hoare, Secretary of State for Air, had proclaimed to the nation when Norway was invaded, "our wings are spread over the Arctic. They are sheathed in ice. Tomorrow the sun of victory will touch them with its golden light."

The disastrous fiasco in Norway was not only a rude awakening; it was a revelation of how deep the slumber had been. Although Prime Minister Chamberlain's leadership of the war had been less than inspired, it could hardly have been otherwise. He was a man wholly dedicated to peace, and his role, just as with his predecessors in his high office, had been that demanded by the people. Had not the war to end wars been fought? Was not the world secure before the guns of the Royal Navy? Was Britain not mistress of the seas? Had not mankind learned from the incredible folly of Verdun and Passchendaele, of the Marne and Château Thierry?

No Prime Minister during the years between the wars and no government, whether Conservative, Liberal, or Labour, could have survived in office had it proposed more than a minimal sum of money to be spent on Britain's national defenses. It was a time of disillusion with war, and the voice of the turtle was heard in the land.

In 1919, the Great War safely won, the Navy and the Army were informed by the Prime Minister to prepare their annual budget estimates on the assumption that there would be no war for ten years. At the time, it was a reasonable assumption, and the monies saved by cutbacks of the services could be well used to help the nation regain its economic stability. But, and it was a big but, the ten-year rule was unending, for it was automatically extended, year by year, even day by day, as time went on. It hampered all planning and served to deny requests for necessary replacements. It was a curious argument, which went something like this: It takes four years to build a battleship. But there will be no war for ten years. Therefore, the battleship will be six years old when war breaks out, and hence obsolete. Accordingly, there is no point in building a new battleship. That knocks £7,000,000 from the estimates. What else can we cut?

In 1933, Hitler came to power in Germany and soon began to rattle the saber. And what was the British reaction? It was to elect a Labour Government under Ramsay MacDonald on the slogan, "A Vote for the Tories Is a Vote for War." Instead, rely on the League of Nations and on the Brotherhood of Man. While Germany was busily rearming, Britain proposed the "MacDonald Plan," calling upon Britain and France to cut their armies and limit the size of guns to 105 millimeters. Although the MacDonald Plan had little actual effect, it was symptomatic of an attitude. Spoke Mr. Clement Attlee to an approving House of Commons: "The Labour Party will oppose increase of armaments on the plea of either national defence or parity."

It need scarcely be added that the ten-year rule remained in effect.

By the following year, with Hitler growing more bellicose daily, responsible ministers agreed that something would have to be done about Britain's defenses. Yet when the Army reported that it would require £50,000,000 to modernize its existing facilities, the Government promptly denounced the sum as fantastic and cut it in half. By the time of Munich, the Army had only 50 field guns, only 375 tanks, 300 of them obsolete. They depended on the Vickers machine gun, designed in the 1880s, and on the Lewis, first produced in 1912. As for the Royal Air Force, its newest fighter, the Gauntlet, had a speed of 230 miles an hour, while its bombers, the Hind and the Hendon, were sadly deficient in bomb load and range. The Hind could carry a 500-pound bomb—*one* 500-pound bomb—for a range of 430 miles, and the Hendon a single 1500-pound bomb 920 miles.

In view of the extreme myopia displayed by national governments toward national defense, it was only the vision and dedication of private citizens that saved Britain in the forthcoming Battle of Britain.

Nearly every one of the fighters that faced the Luftwaffe over England was conceived, designed, and built by a private person. After the Blenheim fighter had been built by the Bristol Aeroplane Company on the order and plans of Lord Rothermere, it was tested and flown widely around the country. Lord Rothermere then presented the aircraft to the nation, and from his prototype the RAF set the specifications for the production models. A similar story can be told for the Gloucester Gladiator, and the Hawker Hurricane. Only the fabled Spitfire came about as a result of Air Force designs, and it was built first as a racing plane, not as a fighter.

The very year that dedicated citizens were building and flying the first prototypes of these planes, the Government tentatively asked for a modest increase in appropriations for the Royal Air Force in view of the rapid increase in the German aircraft building program.

In response to this diffident request, the Labour Party moved a vote of censure.

The motion was defeated, but it was a clear warning. The House of Commons was in no mood for an arms program. Germany kept on building aircraft.

The Royal Navy, perhaps, fared best in peacetime of any of the services, as far as appropriations were concerned, but it, too, had been dangerously weakened. In 1918, the Royal Air Force had replaced the Royal Flying Corps, and responding to the plausible argument that the RAF should be responsible for all military aircraft, the Government had decreed that the Navy should transfer its 2500 planes and 55,000 flying personnel to the RAF. The RAF would fly the naval missions and furnish the planes. Although, in theory, the Navy was to specify the types and number of aircraft it needed, in practice, the Navy got what was left over. Its carrier aircraft were usually adaptations of land fighters. The result of such modifications was to slow the plane down, reduce its rate of climb and service ceiling, and make it clumsy in the air. This would have been bad enough, but it seemed that the naval aircraft were always one model behind those provided for the RAF.

In 1937, the Fleet Air Arm was restored to the Navy, but the transfer only accentuated an even greater problem. A whole generation of airmen had grown up knowing little about naval operations and caring little, for it was on their performance as RAF officers that their advancement had depended. Equally serious, a whole generation of senior naval officers had come to positions of command knowing little about the use of air power in connection with the fleet. Such separation of training and ways of thought could not augur well for the battles to come.

In 1935 the Government made another decision, questionable at the time, and folly in its outcome. The Anglo-German Naval Treaty, signed that year, permitted Germany to build its surface navy up to 35 percent of that of Britain's, its submarine arm to 45 percent, unless "a situation arose which in their [Germany's] opinion made it necessary" to exceed this limitation. In that case, they could build all they wanted.

The British interpreted this treaty as putting a limitation on German naval building and therefore justifying a limit on their own. What they did not know was that the 35 percent allowed Germany just matched the maximum building capacity of German shipyards. In other words, Germany was given a green light for all the naval ships she could turn out. When the terms of the treaty became bothersome to Hitler in the spring of 1939 he blandly abrogated it. It had served its purpose. It had lulled the British into a lesser building program for the Navy than they would otherwise have undertaken. They would pay and pay again for heeding the voice of economy, for, when the hour of battle arrived, they would have to face the new ships of their enemy with the old ones that they possessed.

So then stood Britain's defenses in the face of a resurgent, aggressive Reich. Wishful thinking, ignorance, and a refusal to see the threat brought Britain to the verge of annihilation. It was by the courage, the sacrifice, the unprotected bodies of her young men that Britain would survive the follies of her older and wiser heads.

On May 7 a harassed Prime Minister entered the House of Commons. He looked, as one member put it, like a toothbrush in a stiff collar. The Opposition had demanded a debate on the war in Norway, and this was to be their day.

It was their day indeed. Mr. Chamberlain started the proceedings with a defense of his leadership in the war, a defense of the Conservative Party. As he spoke, he could sense the temper of the House. It was not favorable. As he had come in, he had been greeted by cries of "Here's the man who missed the bus!" "Missed the bus!"

His speech was lackluster. He began with a solemn tribute to Britain's soldiers, sailors, and airmen, but his critics were not to be placated by sentimentality. He was buying sympathy with the blood of Britain's men. It would not do. He outlined military operations in progress, constantly being interrupted and heckled by the Labour members. This was not so surprising. Much more significant was the attitude of his own party. Backbenchers sat stolidly, most determined to support their leaders, but not a few were leaving the fold.

Chamberlain announced that Mr. Churchill was acting in a new position, "giving guidance and direction to the Chiefs of Staff Committee on behalf of the Military Co-Ordination Committee." Most members sensed this was a sorry compromise, as, indeed, it was. As Churchill put it, "I was thus to have immense responsibilities, without effective power in my own hands to discharge them."

When Mr. Chamberlain had stood up to make his presentation, he had been greeted with applause and cheers lasting thirteen seconds. When he sat down after his speech, a polite ripple of applause, mostly from loyal Conservatives, lasted no more than two seconds as a reporter for the *Daily Express* timed it.

Clement Attlee opened the debate for the Opposition, but his speech failed to provide much light. Then occurred the first of several dramatic moments of that day in the House of Commons.

In strode Admiral of the Fleet Sir Roger Keyes, a Member of Parliament and a member of Chamberlain's own Conservative Party. He was in full uniform, six rows of combat ribbons gleaming on his breast.

Although Keyes was usually a terrible speaker, he had special incentive on this occasion. He was a bitterly disappointed man, for he had seen himself reliving the glory of his days at the Dardanelles and at Zeebrugge in World War I. Ceaselessly he had urged that he be permitted to take the heavy surface ships into Trondheimfjord. One man, he thought, had stood in his way, his lifelong friend, Winston Churchill. Now he turned to attack, not his friend, but the Government he held responsible for muddle and timidity in the Norwegian campaign. He laid the blame squarely in Chamberlain's lap, for, he felt, the vacillations of the Conservative Government hamstrung those like Churchill who urged more vigorous persecution of the war. Since Churchill had held the responsibility for naval matters in connection with Norway and a technical responsibility as a member of the War Council, it was inevitable that any attack upon Chamberlain must be upon Churchill, as well. This fact Keyes ignored. He slashed into Chamberlain to the cheers of even the rank and file of the Prime Minister's own party.

"Immediately the campaign opened," said Keyes, "I went to the Admiralty to attempt to suggest action based upon my considerable experience in amphibious warfare in the Dardanelles and on the Belgian coast in the last war. I was foolish enough to think my suggestions might be welcome, but I was told that it was astonishing to think these had not been examined by people who knew the resources available and what the danger would be. . . .

"It [the Norwegian campaign] is a shocking story of ineptitude. The Gallipoli tragedy has been followed step by step."

When Keyes sat down, the Chamberlain Government was doomed, although no one quite realized it at that moment. Keyes's peroration, a glowing tribute to Churchill—the man, according to the admiral, that the whole country looked to to help win the war—gave impetus to what followed.

Leo Amery, another of the rebellious Conservatives, delivered the next attack, a pitiless, scathing dissection of Chamberlain's direction of the war. "The Prime Minister," he said scornfully, "gave us a reasoned, argumentative case for our failure. It is always possible to do that after every failure. Making a case and winning a war are not the same thing. Wars are won, not by explanations after the event, but by foresight, by clear decision and by swift action. I confess that I did not feel there was one sentence in the Prime Minister's speech this afternoon which suggested that the Government either foresaw what Germany meant to do, or came to a clear decision when it knew what Germany had done."

Reviewing the conduct of the war to date, he charged that plans had always been "based on the feeblest common denominator."

Then he delivered the most crushing blow. Looking straight at the occupants of the leaders' bench, he spoke terrible words intended for the ears of his lifelong friend, Prime Minister Chamberlain: "I do [this] with great reluctance, because I am speaking of those who are old friends and associates of mine, but they are words which, I think, are applicable to the present situation. This is what Cromwell said to the Long Parliament when he thought it was no longer fit to conduct the affairs of the nation: 'You have sat too long here for any good you have been doing. Depart I say, and let us have done with you. In the name of God, go!' "

Although the Prime Minister was not present to hear those words, they were carried to him, and some observers have dated Mr. Chamberlain's decision to resign from that moment.

Loyal Conservative members took the floor in an attempt to save the day, but the damage had been done. One by one, members left the floor to dine, to talk, to plan. What could be done? Most were agreed that the Government as presently constituted was doomed. Whether Mr. Chamberlain could reorganize it and continue as Prime

Minister was a leading question. But vastly more important in the minds of many was whether Winston Churchill could be saved from the wreck.

Churchill was obviously the one man whose energy and imagination could reverse the complacent drift. But he was tainted by his reputation for impulsive action. The fiasco of the Dardanelles-Gallipoli campaign, so forcefully brought to mind by Keyes that very afternoon, had cost Churchill his post of First Lord of the Admiralty in 1915. Throughout the peacetime years, Churchill, as an outspoken Member of Parliament, had been a voice crying in the wilderness, pleading for the arms Britain would need in the event war came upon her. He was mocked and ridiculed. It was to be peace in our time!

Now he had been proven tragically right. But it was no help to his position in the minds of many. In the minds of some people there is nothing more unforgivable than a man proved right by events. The most vindictive are those who have been proved wrong. Somehow they must make the prophet of doom responsible for that doom.

A whispering campaign against Churchill intensified. He was too impulsive, too volatile, too emotional, too determined to poke a finger into everyone else's pie. Lord Halifax, who admired him, summed him up as "a child's emotion and a man's reason."

Responsible parliamentary leaders by now were convinced, if the Prime Minister was not, that the Government would have to be reorganized. No longer could the Conservatives keep the helm. It would have to be a coalition government, and Labour, up to this point, had steadfastly refused to serve under Mr. Chamberlain. Because of his party loyalty and his personal loyalty to his leader, Churchill stood in grave danger of being destroyed by the attacks on the Prime Minister. At no point would he be in graver peril than when he would rise on the last day of debate to give the Government's reply to its critics.

Before that moment should come, Chamberlain had more hard knocks to take in the House. Labour member Herbert Morrison opened the proceedings the next day with a brutal speech, attacking Chamberlain and others in his administration. He conspicuously omitted Churchill from the list of those assailed. He concluded by calling for a division of the house, that is, a vote of censure against the Government.* Morrison's manner was that of a schoolmaster before a particularly stupid class and it irritated Chamberlain intensely.

* Technically the vote was on a motion of adjournment, but it was in fact a vote of censure on the Chamberlain Government's conduct of the war.

94

The Prime Minister had not planned to speak at that moment, but in the face of the call for a division, he changed his mind. His gaunt frame rose from its seat. "It may well be," he simpered, "that it is a duty to criticise the Government. I do not seek to evade criticism, but I say this to my friends in the House—and I have friends in the House. No Government can prosecute a war efficiently unless it has public and parliamentary support. I accept this challenge, I welcome it indeed. At least I shall see who is with us and who is against us, and I call on my friends to support us in the Lobby tonight."

Some men are gifted with the ability to turn phrases which will ring down through time. Such a man, who in a few hours would become Britain's Prime Minister, was Winston Churchill. Chamberlain, unhappily, was not one of these. He is remembered not only as the man with the umbrella but more as the man with the foot in his mouth. "It is peace in our time," he had said after Munich. "Hitler has missed the bus," he jibed just before the invasion of Norway. Now he had done it again. He had called upon his "friends" to support him. To an American, these words might seem harmless enough, but to a Briton, it was a call for party support. But the moment was beyond party, as the members seemed to sense.

Lloyd George made the most of Chamberlain's ill-judged remarks when he rose to speak. "It is not a question of who are the Prime Minister's friends," he said, his voice scornful. He and Chamberlain cordially disliked each other, a dislike dating back to the First World War when Lloyd George had been Prime Minister. "It is a far bigger issue. The Prime Minister must remember he has met this formidable foe of ours in peace and in war, and he has always been worsted. He is not in a position to appeal on the ground of friendship. He has appealed for sacrifice. The nation is prepared for every sacrifice, so long as it has leadership. . . . I say solemnly, that the Prime Minister should give an example of sacrifice, because there is nothing which can contribute more to victory in this war than that he should sacrifice the Seals of Office."

Lloyd George then turned to trying to separate Churchill from his responsibility in the Norwegian affair. "I do not think that the First Lord [of the Admiralty, Churchill] was entirely responsible for what happened there [in Norway]."

Churchill, however, would have none of it. In a flash he was on his feet, saying, "I take complete responsibility for everything that

95

has been done by the Admiralty, and I take my full share of the burden."

But Lloyd George was too experienced a parliamentarian to allow himself to be diverted or thwarted. "The Right Honourable Gentleman," he retorted, "must not allow himself to be converted into an air-raid shelter to keep the splinters from hitting his colleagues."

When Churchill rose to speak and close the debate, he faced an impossible task. His loyalty to his party and his loyalty to his leader demanded that he defend the conduct of the war. Yet it was indefensible, and he knew it. He began on a quiet note, frankly owning responsibility when it was his, but by his very defense showing where the Government had failed. He was beset with hecklers, one in particular who was hidden under the steps, resorting to nose-blowing, honking, and generally making an ass of himself. Churchill stood it as long as he could, and then turned on his adversary accusing him of making noises indistinguishable from brays while skulking out of sight.

"On a point of order," shouted a Labour member, "is 'skulk' a parliamentary word?"

The Speaker, too, had had enough. "It depends whether it applies accurately or not," he replied scornfully.

As Churchill continued to talk, reports began to circulate in the lobbies on the floor that the expected German attack on the Low Countries would begin within forty-eight hours. It has been suggested that the Conservatives planted this rumor in an attempt to save the Government. If so, they reckoned better than they knew, for it would be little more than thirty-six hours before the Nazis crossed the Belgian and Dutch borders. But, even more decisive at the moment, the rumor, if the Government spokesmen did start it, recoiled upon their heads, for not a few members, both Labour and Conservative, were thinking upon the botched Norwegian campaign and were appalled to think of the same Government dealing with this new and vastly greater threat.

When Churchill concluded, the House began its division. A large number of Conservatives abstained, and 44 voted against the Government. When the results were announced, the vote for the Government was 281, against 200. The Chamberlain Government had won, but its majority was down to 81 from its usual 200. Mr. Chamberlain's friends had become fewer.

Amid cries of "Resign!", "Missed the bus!", and "In the name of God, go!", Mr. Chamberlain rose, smiled a frosty smile, and left the

House through the door behind the Speaker's chair. He knew as he left that never again would he enter the House as Prime Minister in fact. He might hold the shadow of that office for a day or two until his successor was appointed, but it would be only the shadow. He had failed. He had not been able to keep the peace, and he had not been able to lead in war. Many friends and not a few enemies looked on his departure with pity, but scarce a one could have cried "Well done!"

The next day, Chamberlain made a few half-hearted efforts to save his Government, but he seems to have known in advance that they would be futile, for he had told his close friends on the night before that he intended to resign. The only question remaining was, therefore, who would succeed him.

Looking back from the perspective of nearly three decades, one wonders how the question even arose. History has recorded that Churchill was the man of the hour, the man whose leadership would take Britain through the dark weeks and months and years ahead up to the eve of victory.

But the choice was by no means so clear then. Churchill's own reputation was in his way, and he had been tarred with some of the stigma of Chamberlain's policies. It was far from certain that Churchill would be Britain's next Prime Minister.

Chamberlain's formal attempts to form a coalition government foundered on the refusal of Labour leaders to serve under him. Failing in these efforts, he sought to hand the reins over to Lord Halifax, his closest friend and colleague, then serving as Foreign Secretary. Halifax was a man respected by all, a deeply religious man who often went down on his knees to ask for help through the many crises he faced in his lifetime. He never sought high office, but it continually sought him, and he discharged his duties conscientiously and well. But his very aristocratic virtues would have stood in his way at that hour, for he was not a man to rally the people, to lead them through sacrifice and blood.

On the morning of May 10 the long-expected German blow fell on the west. The German armies smashed through the frontiers of both Belgium and Holland. German aircraft roared ahead of the troops, their bombs and bullets raining death, destruction, and confusion.

Against this somber news, three men gathered in a room at Number Ten Downing Street, the residence of the Prime Minister. They were Churchill, Chamberlain, and Halifax. Chamberlain opened the proceedings by summarizing the political position as he saw it. He said he was satisfied that he could no longer serve as Prime Minister and that he was not prepared to state whether Halifax or Churchill should be his successor. As he spoke, he looked pointedly at Halifax, making his own preference perfectly clear.

A silence followed, which Churchill described as seeming longer than the two minutes of silence at Armistice Day. Halifax noted in his diary that the moment gave him a bad stomachache. Then he spoke, emphasizing Churchill's greater fitness to lead at such a moment. Then he pointed out the real barrier. As a peer of the realm, and unable to sit in the House of Commons, he would have to work through a kind of Deputy Prime Minister in the Commons. "The inevitable result would be," he noted in his diary, "that outside both these points of vital contact, I should speedily become a more or less honorary P.M., living in a kind of twilight just outside the things that really mattered."

Chamberlain reluctantly agreed with Halifax's arguments, and so it was that the mantle fell on the stocky shoulders of the man who would bear it for five years.

That night at 6 o'clock, Winston Churchill was ushered into the presence of the king at Buckingham Palace.

"I suppose you don't know why I have sent for you?" inquired His Majesty.

Playing the traditional game, Churchill replied, "Sir, I simply couldn't imagine why."

"I want to ask you to form a Government."

It was a Government truly national in scope that Winston Churchill organized. Including Labour and Liberal leaders as well as members of his own Conservative Party, Churchill's organization was soundly conceived and changed little throughout the war. Chamberlain became Lord President of the Council. Clement Attlee was a member and so was Anthony Eden. It would be pointless to give a full list here. The important thing is that they worked together and better than they had ever done before, for the time had arrived when they must place country before party, and they all knew it.

That night, as their brutal assault on the Low Countries drove on, the German people heard a broadcast from Berlin. "Mr. Chamberlain has resigned and is followed by Winston Churchill.

"Thus the post of the man who walked with prayerbook in hand is taken over by Churchill, most brutal representative of the policy of force—the man whose program is to dismember Germany—this man whose hateful face is well known to all Germans."

It did not take the Germans long to recognize their most fearsome enemy.

Could there have been the voice of fear in that broadcast?

On May 13 the new Prime Minister entered the House of Commons to make his first speech in office. The scene has been superbly described by Major General Sir Edward Spears, at that time a Member of Parliament.

He [Churchill] was quite calm; in the queer light of the House, which so often seems to trail a veil of last winter's fog across the beams of its ceiling, he seemed rather white, but his jaw was set.

His first sentences were simple, matter-of-fact, strongly worded; they were an explanation of the reasons which had led him to recall the House.* Then suddenly he was transformed into an inspired leader, the High Priest of a great religion dedicating a nation to measureless sacrifice. The ancient table was the altar before which he spoke; looking up and above the crowded benches at the high, narrow, cathedral-like windows which let in broad slits of light, he said slowly: "I have nothing to offer but blood, toil, tears and sweat."

The House had been silent and attentive; a great hush now came over it as when the roar of London is stilled for two minutes on Armistice Day.

Then followed deep murmured approval as if the House was saying Amen.

But something had happened. Each man had taken Churchill to himself as his leader, adopted his doctrine, silently taken his vow just as, moved by the same spirit, great crowds had taken the Cross as they listened to St. Bernard preaching the Crusade 800 years ago.

The Commons, whose very essence consists in its division, had undergone a strange transformation. Just as a mob of recruits, uncertain and desperate, can become an embryo army when the men have taken the oath in the presence of a leader who has impressed his personality on them, so the House, awed and hushed just now, was transformed into a vociferously confident assembly. It was one entity as with deep-throated cheers it now punctuated every new sentence Churchill uttered. Ten minutes earlier it had been a strong-willed, earnest, worried assembly, well disposed, but still smarting from many deep slashes; now it was a cohesive force whose heart throbbed in unison with that of its leader. They cheered his words almost before he had uttered them, so well did they know he would voice their thoughts as they would have wished to have expressed them. "You ask, what is our policy?" the great voice was saying. And, as if he were baring the heart of the nation before Heaven, he went on: "It

* The House had been in recess for the long Whitsun weekend.

99

is to wage war, by sea, land and air, with all our might and with all the strength that God can give us; to wage war against a monstrous tyranny, never surpassed in the dark, lamentable catalogue of human crime, that is our policy."

The House, moved to an ever higher level of emotion, roared its approval.

"You ask, what is our aim? I can answer in one word: it is victory, victory at all costs, victory in spite of terror, victory, however long and hard the road may be...."

There can have been no more solemn dedication in the history of the world. He pledged himself, the Commons and the people, to follow the path from which there was no turning. Wherever he led, all would follow, however hard the road; and the Commons, truly voicing the very mind of the people, pledged its troth to him for better or for worse until victory was achieved.

But splendid words alone were not enough. Hitler's war machine smashed on as *poilu* and Tommy advanced to meet it. Their confidence was high, those unconsidered men of both nations. There was no way for them to know that their equipment was obsolete, that their leaders would be outguessed at every turn by the enemy.

And so they marched, those men who would pay in blood for two decades of folly, two decades of living in a dream world.

That dream was about to turn into dreadful nightmare.

CHAPTER FIVE

Onslaught in the West

Seest thou a man wise in his own conceit?
There is more hope of a fool than of him.
Proverbs

MARCHING as to war, the British troops advanced smoothly into Belgium. Happily they left behind them the irksome toil of preparation of defenses along the border where no Maginot Line existed. Thankfully they put behind them inspections, drills, formations, and marched on through the glorious spring day of that fateful May 10. Only a few bombers were overhead. More in evidence were the birds, whose happy singing showed no concern for the awful folly of the men below them. Their songs were echoed by the troops as their voices bellowed out "There'll Always Be an England," "Roll Out the Barrel," or the unprintable versions of "Even 'Itler 'ad a Mother."

Neither the airborne nor the foot-borne singers had any idea of what lay ahead.

Those were the last moments of the Age of Innocence. The troops manning the lines in France had not learned the hard lessons of Norway. They had no experience of the kind of war the Germans had perfected in Spain and in Poland.

Confidently the French and British people put their trust in the soldiers at the front and in the military genius of the French generals. It was a misplaced trust.

From the point where the Maginot Line ended south of the Ardennes Forest, the line to the sea was held by the French First Army Group, of which the British Expeditionary Force was a part. Here only light fortifications existed, for the French did not expect to use them for defense. Instead, this massive group would wheel, advancing past Brussels to the River Dyle, and there lock the Germans in the decisive battle. The French Commander in Chief, General Maurice Gamelin, believed this move would be the perfect counter to the 1940 version of the classic Schlieffen Plan which had so nearly worked in 1914.

And now the German attack had come as foreseen. In the early morning hours, the German tanks and troops poured across the borders of Holland and Belgium. It was all as it should be. While the German waves broke against the strength of the prepared defenses in the Low Countries, the Grebbe-Peel Line, and the Albert Canal Line, General P. Bilotte's First Army Group would have time to reach its positions. The German drive would be stalled. It was a perfect countermove—for 1914.

But in 1940, there were two fatal weaknesses in the plan so lovingly drawn up by Gamelin and his staff. The tank and the dive bomber proved the British and French tactical conceptions as obsolete as those of Caesar. And their strategy was based on their assumption that the Germans would again use the Schlieffen Plan.

But the Germans were not using the Schlieffen Plan.

Originally they had proposed to do so. But the weather and the unfortunate plane ride of Major Reinberger * gave time for reconsideration. Gradually a whole new concept emerged.

As late as February, Army Group B under General Fedor von Bock was to make the main drive through Holland and Belgium. It comprised 3 armies and 43 divisions, well over half a million men. On its left, General Gerd von Rundstedt's Army Group A, with 2 armies and 22 divisions, had the role of protecting Bock's flank from Allied counterattack. This was a relatively passive role, little to Rundstedt's liking.

Opposite the Maginot Line was drawn up General Wilhelm Ritter von Leeb's Army Group C, with only 19 divisions. It had the most inactive role of all, merely creating enough disturbance to pin down the French troops in his area when they might be needed elsewhere as reinforcements.

Rundstedt's brilliant Chief of Staff, Major General Fritz Erich von Lewinski, *gennant* von Manstein, is generally credited with the stroke of genius that transformed the campaign in the west. We see him brooding over the plan put forward by OKH,† his aquiline nose seem-

---

* See above, p. 35.

† *Oberkommando des Heeres,* the Army High Command.

ing a pointer to the piercing eyes that probed, darting everywhere, taking in everything. We see him smite the map with his gloved hand and hear him exclaim, "There! There is the point!" His hand sweeps magnificently over the map. "There is the key blow!"

The real story is less simple and less dramatic. Manstein was surely no admirer of the OKH plan. But it would be more than the truth to say that the whole conception came to him as a result of a single *coup d'oeil,* all at once, and in its magnificent and deadly simplicity. He makes no such claim in his memoirs. But together he and Rundstedt worked out a new scheme, only to have it ridiculed by both General von Brauchitsch, Commander in Chief of the Army, and by his industrious Chief of Staff, General Franz Halder. "The plan lacks positive aspects," noted Halder crushingly.

Apparently, by coincidence, Hitler himself had been thinking along the line of the Manstein-Rundstedt proposal, but his ideas had not been taken very seriously by the Army.

Either Halder or Brauchitsch or both decided it would be as well to free the relatively straightforward Rundstedt from the insidious arguments of Manstein. Accordingly Manstein was given command of the newly-created XXXVIII Corps and committed to the general reserve. This actually was a promotion for Manstein, but in view of the timing, it is impossible to escape the conviction that the new assignment was suspiciously opportune for Brauchitsch and Halder. It was all very neat.

The neat little scheme backfired. On the evening of February 17, Hitler held a reception for the newly created corps commanders. Manstein was present and soon caught the Führer's ear. A long private conversation ensued, and from that moment the OKH plan was doomed.

By this time, almost in spite of themselves, Halder and Brauchitsch, who were by no means unintelligent men, had begun to feel the force of Rundstedt's repeated memoranda. They took another look at their own plan, and the more they looked, the less they liked it. They began to wonder if there was not something in the Rundstedt-Manstein proposals after all.

Once they had reached this frame of mind, the plan quickly took form.

The main point of attack was shifted from Bock's Army Group B opposite Holland and Belgium to Rundstedt's Army Group A. Bock, however, would advance first, across the border into the Low Countries to pull the French and British armies into Belgium. Then Rundstedt, with most of Germany's Panzer divisions, would penetrate the Ardennes Forest and sweep west behind the Allied main forces and cut them off in Belgium. Isolated from reinforcement and supplies, they must inevitably surrender.

The French General Staff had foreseen the possibility that Germany might attack through the Ardennes and Sedan, but they had dismissed it. Everyone knew that the thick Ardennes Forest, with its jumble of rivers, was impassable to organized military forces.

The French reputation for omniscience in all things military had led the British to agree to French command of the land war in France. Nine of the 10 divisions in the B.E.F. then in France were in the line, with headquarters at Arras, forming a single army in the First Army Group. General Lord Gort commanded this force as it set bravely off for the Dyle Line. On its left was the French Seventh Army under General Henri Giraud, which was supposed to speed on to the relief of stricken Holland. To the right of the B.E.F. was the French First Army under General Blanchard, then came General André-Georges Corap's inexperienced Ninth Army, and last, with its right flank on the Maginot Line and its left joining Corap's Ninth at Sedan, was General Charles Huntziger's Second Army. With an infallible instinct for blunder, the French High Command had placed the boundary —always the weakest point—between the Second and Ninth Armies at the precise point where the main German blow would fall.

As the roar and crash of battle opened, the two sides were not unevenly matched in manpower and in tanks. The Germans had 136 divisions committed to the western offensive in three army groups. The combined French, British, Belgian, and Dutch forces amounted to 135 divisions. But the Germans were organized, the Allies were not. The Germans had a sound plan, the Allies had not. Germany had 2,439 tanks, and they were concentrated where they would be needed. The Allies had 2,689, scattered at random all along the front. In the air, Germany had a marked superiority, with some 3,700 aircraft, nearly all modern, while the Allies had about 2,000 combat planes, nearly all obsolete.

In Holland the war lasted only five days. Since the Dutch placed heavy reliance on their canals and on flooding the lowlands, the Germans simply went over those obstacles. General Kurt Student's Seventh Airborne Division, reinforced with two regiments from the Twenty-Second Infantry Division, landed in gliders near Rotterdam, Dorndrecht, Moerdijk, and Maastricht. They were supported by 4000

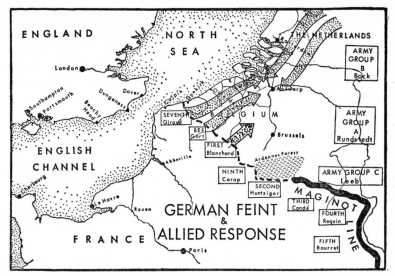

The map shows:

ENGLAND
London

NORTH SEA

THE NETHERLANDS

ARMY GROUP B Bock

ARMY GROUP A Rundstedt

ARMY GROUP C Leeb

Southampton
Portsmouth
Dungeness
Dover
Beachy Head
Calais
Dunkirk

ENGLISH CHANNEL
Cherbourg
Le Havre
Rouen

Antwerp
BELGIUM
Brussels

SEVENTH Giraud
BEF Gort
FIRST Blanchard
NINTH Corap
SECOND Huntziger
THIRD Condé
FOURTH Requin
FIFTH Bourret

Ardennes Forest
Abbeville
MAGINOT LINE

GERMAN FEINT
&
ALLIED RESPONSE
FRANCE
Paris

paratroops. Quickly these men seized control of key bridges and canal locks, all at a cost of 180 killed.

Many myths have risen over these paratroopers. They were supposed to have landed in Dutch uniforms, women's clothes, even in the habits of nuns, machine guns concealed under the robes. There is a modicum of truth in these stories, but they grew with the telling out of all proportion to the truth. A British paper published a cartoon of a cigar-smoking German soldier dressed in a nun's garb, his wounded arm supporting a machine gun, reporting to his officer, "Herr Leutnant, I have definite proof that the inhuman Dutch are firing upon women."

In the land war, the Eighteenth Army of General Georg von Kuechler drove rapidly into Holland. The first real barrier was the Maas River. In some places the Dutch had blown the bridges, but not everywhere.

About four that morning, three men in Dutch uniforms approached the east end of the bridge at Gennep. The sleepy guards waved them on. Suddenly the three men whirled and seized the weapons of the surprised bridge custodians. One of the men was a German in a Dutch uniform; the other two were Dutch traitors. The three formed an advance guard of a force known as "Trojan Horse," especially trained to seize the Maas' bridges. A few minutes later Leutnant Wilhelm Walther appeared with seven more men. This tiny group held the bridge until the German army appeared a few hours later.

It was not always so easy, but by noon the Germans had established several strong points on the far side of the Maas and were beginning to roll.

The Dutch were never able to form an organized line of resistance, for a few traitors in the rear, paratroops, and airborne troops had all combined to spread confusion. In addition many of the roads were clogged with pitiful refugees, setting out, they knew not where, their few loved belongings on their backs or in pushcarts, wagons, wheelbarrows. And over it all the planes of the Luftwaffe reigned supreme. The scream of the Stuka as it swooped down brought terror even before its bombs or bullets hit. The Stuka pilots displayed a grim impartiality, strafing and bombing troops and refugees alike.

On May 14, a regiment captured Doorn, the place of exile of the former Kaiser. The commander, Colonel Fritz Neidholdt, recognized the old man, saluted smartly, and posted a guard of honor.

Wilhelm II's renewed glory did not last long. When Hitler learned of the matter, he would have nothing to do with such royalist activities. The guard of honor was withdrawn, and the city of Doorn was declared out of bounds for all German personnel.*

Rotterdam, the principal port city of Holland, was approaching desperate straits. The bridges which had been blown over the Oude Maas and Nieuwe Maas meant that there was no hope for assistance from the advancing French Seventh Army, even if it had been able to get there. On May 13, Lieutenant Colonel Dietrich von Choltitz, commanding the battalion holding the only unblown bridges in Rotterdam, sent a Dutch merchant and a Dutch priest into Rotterdam to urge the commander, Colonel Scharoo, to surrender the city. The Colonel sent back a stiff reply that civilians had no business meddling with military affairs.

A day later a demand came from corps headquarters, and Choltitz sent the officer in under a white flag. While a Dutch messenger, Captain Bakker, was running back and forth, bearing the terms for surrender, the Luftwaffe roared over. The agreed capitulation signal, a series of red rockets, shot up into the air, but the Luftwaffe came on. Either the smoke over the city hid the rockets from the pilots, or they were under orders to ignore them. Goering may well have wanted to finish off the defenders in a hurry, or, more likely, wanted to prove

---

* The former Kaiser continued to live at Doorn Castle, ignored by the Germans all around him. He had not long to endure his insulting isolation, for he died a little over a year later, on June 4, 1941. Then, danger of a restored monarchy safely past, Hitler gave him a lavish state funeral.

to his Führer that his Luftwaffe could destroy a large, modern city. And destroy it they did. The heart of the city was leveled to the ground, and 78,000 persons were made homeless. The only bright spot—if it can be called that—was that so few were killed, only about 800. It is a measure of the brutality of the German attack that one can refer to the deaths of 800 persons in terms of "only."

When the bombers left, Rotterdam citizens fought the fires, tended the wounded, picked up their dead, and offered no resistance to anything. The formal capitulation of the city followed that evening, and the Dutch soldiers made their painful way back to their barracks or command posts, averting their eyes as they passed the horrors they had been unable to prevent. They still carried their weapons, for they had been instructed to proceed to their home posts to turn them in. They were dumb with shock, but at least there was no more shooting.

Then there was a roar and rumble of tanks and trucks. Around the corner came the advance elements of Obergruppenführer Sepp Dietrich's Leibstandarte Adolf Hitler SS Regiment.* Seeing the Dutch soldiers, the trigger-happy SS men opened up with machine guns. A scene of wild shooting took place, although the Dutch do not seem to have fired back.

Out rushed General Student, the senior officer on the scene, only to fall unconscious from a stray bullet in the head. Choltitz, who was with him, kept his nerve and ordered the Dutch into a church. Gradually the firing died away.

With the bombing of Rotterdam, Dutch resistance soon ceased. The Germans had hoped to capture Queen Wilhelmina, but she was taken off from the Hook of Holland at noon on May 13 by the British destroyer *Hereward*. That evening H.M.S. *Windsor* rescued most of the officials of the Government and Allied legation staffs.

Although the soil of her country was occupied, the Dutch queen established a Government in Exile in London. Like Norway, the Netherlands never surrendered as a country. Her troops made capitulations in the field. But the Netherlands remained at war with Germany from across the sea while her people suffered the agonies of five years of merciless occupation.

---

* The SS [Schutzstaffeln] was Hitler's personal army under Heinrich Himmler. It was an élite force, looking down on the regular army. For military operations units of division size called "Waffen-SS" were formed and were subject to the strategic and tactical command of the Army, but all matters of discipline, training, promotion, and the like remained with Himmler and his staff. The rank Obergruppenführer corresponds to Lieutenant General.

In Belgium, hopes of resistance to the Germans rested on the forts guarding Liége. In World War I, Liége had held the German advance for eleven days, and it would hold again, but once the Germans had captured the protective forts, they could flow past the old city.

Strongest of all the forts was the massive Fort Eben Emael. Regarded by Allies and Germans alike as the most impregnable fortress in Europe, it was stronger than any point in the Maginot Line. Below ground a series of steel and reinforced-concrete galleries provided for the needs of its 1200-man garrison. It had two 120-mm. (4.7-inch) guns, twenty-eight 60- and 75-mm. guns, twenty-five double and twelve light machine guns, a half-dozen antiaircraft guns, and many automatic rifles. Its field of fire was unrestricted, so that it was death for anyone to approach.

An hour before the first Germans crossed the Belgian border on the morning of May 10, Oberleutnant Rudolf Witzig and 80 men of his special detachment were sitting in gliders at an airfield near Cologne. The time was 0430. One by one Junkers 52s towed the gliders down the runway and up into the air. They crossed the peaceful land below, a few lights visible in the early morning darkness. Witzig's glider and another parted their towlines. The others went on until they were over Aachen, some 20 miles from Fort Eben Emael.

At 0525, five minutes before the official time of the invasion of Belgium, 9 gliders landed on the roof of the fort. In the absence of his leader, Sergeant Wenzel took charge. They dropped hollow-charge explosives on the turrets. The force of the explosions drove down through the turrets and gun bores, filling the interior of the fort with fire and fumes. Other gunports they took care of with flame-throwers. In a matter of minutes the fort was out of action, blind and helpless. It did not fall until the next day, but it mattered not at all. It had ceased to be a barrier to the German troops.

By the evening of May 11, General Walter von Reichenau's Sixth Army had driven the Belgians back from the Albert Canal to the Dyle Line, where the vanguard of the French and British were even then arriving. Amid a certain amount of confusion—the result of lack of planning before hostilities broke out—the Allied troops dug in and gave a good account of themselves for the next five days. But by that time, their positions had become untenable, not because of Reichenau's army in front of them, but because of General Ewald von Kleist's Panzer Army at their backs.

On the evening of May 9, Major General Erwin Rommel, later to win fame in North Africa, wrote his wife: "We're packing at last.

Let's hope not in vain. You'll get all the news for the next few days from the papers. Don't worry yourself. Everything will go all right."

Everything did go all right. Rommel's Seventh Panzer Division was one of seven poised along the Belgian border south of Aachen, poised to deliver the main blow. In the north, Hoth's Fifteenth Panzer Corps had the Fifth and Seventh Panzer Divisions, under command of Kluge's Fourth Army. Kleist's Panzer Army had two corps, the Forty-First under General Georg-Hans Reinhardt, and the Nineteenth under General Heinz Guderian.

> At our first clash with French mechanized forces [wrote Rommel], prompt opening fire on our part led to a hasty French retreat. I have found again and again that in encounter actions, the day goes to the side that is the first to plaster its opponent with fire. The man who lies low and awaits developments usually comes off second best.

The advance into Belgium went off with scarcely a hitch as far as the Meuse River, the most difficult natural obstacle for the German armor. Kleist's Order of the Day on the eve of the attack spelled out its importance.

> This side of the Meuse River there can be no rest or halt for a man of this column. The organization must advance day and night without stopping, without looking right or left, and without yielding for a moment its calm control. The only way for us to carry out our orders is to take full advantage of the enemy's surprise and the disorder of his positions for the purpose of putting some of our detachments across the Meuse quickly. Our losses will be smaller if we do not allow the enemy time to get his bearings and make plans for the defense.

On the afternoon of May 12, the Panzer divisions had reached the Meuse. They had taken some pounding from French aircraft and long-range artillery, but casualties had been less than expected. But they had outrun their own heavy artillery, and would have to force the Meuse with their own efforts, supported by the Luftwaffe, if they were not to lose the momentum required for the German success. The French, however shaken by the onslaught, had not failed to destroy the bridges spanning the Meuse.

The key crossings of the Meuse were those by Rommel at Dinant and by Guderian at Sedan and Bazeilles. Guderian himself went across in the first assault boat, with extremely heavy air support pinning the French defenders down. By the end of the day at least substantial parts of all three of Guderian's divisions were across the river and were ready to drive on.

In the north, Rommel's Seventh Panzer Division was the first to cross the river. Under heavy fire from the defenders on the opposite bank, Rommel reorganized the attack, crossing himself in a rubber boat, to take care of arrangements on the far side. He had far less air support than Guderian, but in the course of a few hours, his division was well established on the other side and his engineers were constructing pontoon bridges for the crossing of the tanks. The French and British airmen tried hard to destroy the pontoons, but were decidedly ineffective. Despite their lack of success, the pilots deserve all honor, pressing on and on, despite fearful losses. That day, attempting to stop the crossings at any cost, the French and British pilots saw 150 of their planes knocked out of the air by German fighters and flak.

As night fell on May 13, all 7 Panzer Divisions were across the river, in part at least. It was not until May 15 that Reinhardt was able to build his bridges and get his tanks moving again.

But the rest did not wait. On they rushed, Guderian toward the fatal hinge between Huntziger's French Second Army and Corap's Ninth. Rommel, meanwhile, headed for Corap's right flank and center, supported by Walsporn's Fifth Panzer Division.

That night, General Corap made a disastrous decision to abandon the Meuse Line and withdrew to the west. But the advancing Germans allowed no time for organized retreat. The withdrawal turned into a rout, and a hole 60 miles wide opened between Huntziger's smashed left wing and Corap's routed right wing.

The way to the Channel lay open.

On the morning of May 15, at (for him) the unheard-of hour of 7:30, Mr. Churchill was aroused from his slumbers by a nervous aide, who reported that French Prime Minister Paul Reynaud was on the telephone.

"We have been defeated," said Reynaud in English.

Churchill made no immediate reply, so Reynaud repeated.

"We are beaten. We have lost the battle."

"Surely it can't have happened so soon," replied Churchill.

"The front is broken near Sedan. They are pouring through in great numbers with tanks and armored cars."

Churchill hoped the German drive would soon run out of steam, but it did not. With the main French and British forces in Belgium, facing Bock's Army Group B, and the rest futilely waiting in the

Maginot Line for an attack that never came, there was nothing to halt the German advance to the sea.

And what of the French Commander in Chief, General Gamelin, whose strategy had dissolved before his eyes?

He viewed the situation with calm.

His calm was not completely reassuring to Churchill, who decided the next day to go and see for himself. With only General Sir John Dill, Vice Chief of the Imperial General Staff, and Sir Hastings Ismay, his own representative to the Chiefs of Staff, Churchill embarked in a Flamingo, a passenger plane outfitted in considerable luxury for the Prime Minister's use. An escort of fighters went along, but it was not needed, as most of the flight was through cloud.

Arriving safely at Le Bourget Field, the spot where, thirteen years earlier, Lindbergh had been greeted by wildly enthusiastic crowds as he brought the *Spirit of St. Louis* triumphantly to a stop after the first non-stop New York to Paris crossing, Churchill and his party found only gloom. A British liaison officer, Colonel H. Redman, met the plane and informed Churchill that things were even worse than he imagined. There was nothing between the Germans and Paris. Already, bearded ministers and junior clerks, gray, bespectacled gentlemen and young would-be diplomats were busily feeding bonfires with the archives of the Third Republic. Panic had gripped the Quai d'Orsay. As they drove through the streets toward Paris, passing Clichy, the Gare St. Lazare, the Madeleine, and turned right from the Rue Royale onto the Rue du Faubourg Saint-Honoré where the British Embassy is located, they saw only apathy, resignation, listlessness. Even the sight of the police escort and the handsome limousine brought no stirring of interest.

After a brief stop at the Embassy, Churchill and his party went on to the Quai d'Orsay, where Premier Paul Reynaud was waiting with Édouard Daladier, former Premier and then Minister of Defense, and the Commander in Chief, General Gamelin. All were utterly dejected, and the normally courteous French were so far lost that they forgot to offer seats to their visitors.

Churchill refused to be downcast. He strode into the room as if it were his own office, saying in his execrable and inimitable French, "Things seem pretty bad, but this is not the first time we have been in a mess together. We will get out of it all right. Now, what is the situation?"

Gamelin took up a pointer and displayed the situation on a map. The whole front between the Second and Ninth Armies had broken

111

wide open; German tanks were driving through at impossible speed, followed by masses of infantry. Over all the Luftwaffe reigned supreme.

The Germans might head for the Channel at Abbeville or they might turn on Paris. There was nothing to stop them.

Gazing at the ominous bulge sketched on the map between Montmédy and Namur, Churchill slapped the diminutive Gamelin on the back. Gamelin winced. "Evidently," exclaimed Churchill, "this will be known as the Battle of the Bulge!" His French failed him on the last word, which he rendered as *"le Boolge."* "Now, my General, when and where are you going to counterattack—from the north or the south?"

The General replied briefly that he had nothing—no troops to order into a counterattack. He shrugged his shoulders. Ismay noted that he seemed beaten already.

"But," said Churchill, thoughtlessly reverting to English. "Where is the strategic reserve?" He checked himself and tried again in French. *"Où est la masse de manoeuvre?"*

Another shrug. *"Aucune,"* responded the General briefly.

That a captain commanding a company should not keep a reserve is incredible. That a Commander in Chief should commit his forces with no reserve is as impossible of belief as that an airplane should be built with no wings. Churchill was stunned. "Why," he wrote, "had the British Government, and the War Office above all, not known more about it? It was no excuse that the French High Command would not impart their dispositions to us or to Lord Gort except in vague outline. We had a right to know. We ought to have insisted. Both armies were fighting in the line together. I went back again to the window and the curling wreaths of smoke from the bonfires of the state documents of the French Republic."

There was nothing to be gained from recriminations. The hard-pressed Gamelin sulkily agreed to pull several divisions from the Maginot Line to try to cut into the bulge from the south, or at least to defend Paris. He seemed unclear which he would do.

Most of all, the French demanded more fighter squadrons from Britain. At that moment German aircraft were making organized movement difficult in areas well removed from the breakout and impossible near the bulge.

There had never been enough Allied aircraft from the beginning. The French had about 450 and the British 400 in France. These

850, less than a quarter of the number the Germans were employing in the west, were being systematically shot out of the sky.

As if mere lack of numbers was not enough of a handicap, the French Air Force was a mockery of a modern war-ready organization. Its leaders were ultraconservatives, who had devoted their peace-time activities to seeing that young men with courage and initiative were not promoted. Typical of this breed was the French Air Commander in Chief, General Vuillemin, whose creaky organization had collapsed in two days. Since the French Air Force was helpless, let Britain send more.

Churchill had come to France with the permission of the Cabinet to send four more fighter squadrons to French bases, but when he learned the full gravity of the situation, he wired London for Cabinet concurrence in sending an additional six, for a total of ten. "I again emphasise the mortal gravity of the hour," he cabled, "and express my opinion as above. Kindly inform me what you will do. Dill agrees. I must have answer by midnight in order to encourage the French. Telephone to Ismay at Embassy in Hindustani."

From his long experience in India, General Ismay spoke fluent Hindustani, and he had a staff officer in London equally proficient in the language. In case the telephone lines were tapped, it would do the average German little good to hear the unintelligible sounds of the East.

Half an hour before the deadline, the telephone rang in the Embassy. It was Captain A. T. Cornwall-Jones, who spoke the single word *"Han"* [Hindustani for Yes].

Churchill rushed to Reynaud's apartment and told him the good news and then insisted that Daladier be sent for so he could be told. Churchill's attitude seems to have been that of a man giving valuable presents. He liked to see the expressions of pleasure on their faces.

Although Reynaud and Daladier were not on speaking terms with each other socially, they had to work together in their official capacities. Grumbling, Reynaud sent for Daladier, and grumbling, Daladier came. Wrote Churchill, "Daladier never spoke a word. He rose slowly from his chair and wrung my hand."

Churchill spent the night at the Embassy, flying back to London the next morning to report on his doings in Paris. He had made clear to the French that unless they pulled themselves together for a supreme effort, the ten squadrons could not be sent, for there was no point in throwing them away on a lost cause. They would be needed for the defense of Britain.

As a matter of fact, they were not sent, at least not all of them. Air Chief Marshal Sir Hugh C. T. Dowding, Commander in Chief, Fighter Command, on the day Churchill was talking in Paris had written a lengthy letter, protesting the wastage of planes.

> I must therefore request [he concluded] that as a matter of paramount urgency the Air Ministry will consider and decide what level of strength is to be left to the Fighter Command for the defences of this country, and will assure me that when this level has been reached, not one fighter will be sent across the Channel however urgent and insistent the appeals for help may be.
>
> I believe that if an adequate fighter force is kept in this country, if the Fleet remains in being, and if Home Forces are suitably organized to resist invasion, we should be able to carry on the war single-handed for some time, if not indefinitely. But, if the Home Defence Force is drained away in desperate attempts to remedy the situation in France, defeat in France will involve the final, complete and irremediable defeat of this country.

Air Marshal Sir Arthur Barratt, Commanding British Air Forces in France, informed the Air Ministry that only three squadrons could be accommodated in the available airfields. Such petty details seem never to have occurred to Reynaud, Daladier, and Gamelin, in their demands for more and more aircraft. Churchill, with his tremendous grasp of detail, should have thought of them, but he was too emotionally caught up in his anxiety for France to pose such a simple question.

For the next few days, three fighter squadrons flew to France from Britain each morning, operated until the afternoon against the Luftwaffe, and then—fewer in numbers—flew back to their home fields. Each afternoon three more squadrons flew over to relieve their comrades who had fought that morning. Each evening the survivors flew back to Britain.

Meanwhile Guderian's, Reinhardt's, and Hoth's three Panzer Corps swept on, followed by motorized troops and by infantry. On May 19, Rommel reached Cambrai, and Guderian had gone all the way to Péronne. Two days later, Guderian reached Abbeville and the sea. The French Seventh Army had escaped the trap, running back south to reinforce the shattered Ninth. But the rest, the Belgian Army, the French First Army, and the B.E.F., were cut off in Belgium. They would have to fight their way back to France, through the German penetration, or they would have to fall back on the sea.

Pressed by Bock's Army Group B coming through northern

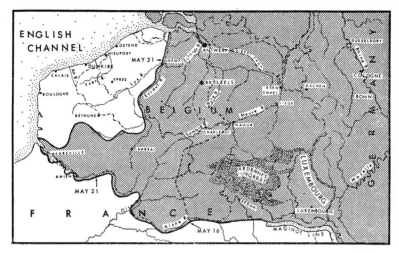

German advances, May 16–21.

Belgium, the Allies had to abandon the Dyle Line and fall back on the Escaut (Scheldt) River. But the French First Army was in a salient near Douai, and Hoth's Panzer Corps threatened to bypass it and fall upon the B.E.F. from the rear. On May 19, Gort extended his flank all the way to Arras, behind Blanchard's First Army, but if the German advance continued to the sea, his position would be untenable.

On the morning of May 19, General Gamelin had stirred himself and come up with his master plan to redeem the battle. It was a masterpiece of the obvious. The encircled French First Army and the B.E.F. would attack southward from Arras, while the French reconstituted Seventh Army and the Sixth would make an effort at Cambrai. Gamelin would cut the Germans in two.

That evening Gamelin was relieved as Commander in Chief by General Maxime Weygand.

Nor was this the only change made by Reynaud. He reshuffled his cabinet, taking over himself the post of Minister of Defense from Daladier. Also, he brought in one of the great names from the past, Marshal Henri Philippe Pétain, hero of Verdun in the First World War. Pétain became Vice President of the Council. He "will remain at my side until victory is won," declared Reynaud in a broadcast announcing the changes.

In her most desperate hour, France turned to her old men. These were the survivors of a glory that had never existed, survivors of a

115

myth, survivors of a dream. Pétain and Weygand were both tired men, tired of the day-to-day problems, set in their ways, closer to the past than to the present. Pétain was 84 and Weygand 73. While the pessimistic Pétain looked every year of his age, Weygand was youthful-appearing, his step springy, his bearing exuding confidence. But it was all show. A doctor observed of him that he presented one of the rare cases where the body remained young while the mind aged with the passing of the years.

These, then, were the men brought in at the fifty-ninth minute to be the saviors of France. They will play their appointed roles in the days ahead.

Within moments of taking over command, Weygand made his first and perhaps decisive mistake. He canceled Gamelin's last order for a simultaneous drive north and south near Arras to try to cut off the German penetration. He had decided that he would see for himself.

If there was ever a time that Gamelin's plan might have worked, it was when it was ordered. Any delay would be fatal, for each hour the German breach widened. More troops poured in. It was like a giant wedge. With the passing of time, the wedge went deeper and the part that would have to be cut became wider.

For twenty-four hours after assuming command, Weygand did nothing except cancel Gamelin's offensive. He did arrange, however, to be flown the next day to a conference with General Bilotte, King Leopold, and Lord Gort, so that he could discuss forthcoming operations with them.

Nearer the fighting than Weygand in his Paris headquarters was Lord Gort north of Arras. His evaluation of the situation was considerably more realistic. Watching Hoth's Panzer divisions pushing westward, he saw there was nothing to stop them. At any hour they might fall upon his unprotected back, for the only troops to hold the entire position from the mouth of the Somme to Ostend were the nine divisions of the B.E.F. The French First Army and the Belgian Army had already been outflanked on the south and were fighting desperately to hold off the Sixth and Eighteenth German Armies from the east.

Worse still, the B.E.F. was split, for the three divisions of Sir Alan Brooke's Second Corps were plugging the gap between the Belgians and the French in the vicinity of Lille. As early as May 19, Gort had informed London that the situation was far more serious than anyone on that side of the Channel seemed to realize. He said there were only three things that might be done. First, maintain the present defense of the Escaut Line. This required a successful drive to cut the German corridor separating them from France. Second, retire to the line of the Somme which "would obviously be unwelcome to the Belgians who would be faced with the alternatives of withdrawing with us and abandoning Belgian soil, fighting on a perimeter of their own, or seeking an armistice." The third possibility was to retire on the Channel ports of Calais, Gravelines, Dunkirk, Nieuport, and Ostend. "I realized that this course was in theory a last alternative," wrote Gort later. "It involved the virtual certainty that even if the excellent port facilities at Dunkirk continued to be available, it would be necessary to abandon all the heavier guns and much of the vehicles and equipment. Nevertheless, I felt that in the circumstances there might be no other course open to me. It was therefore only prudent to consider what the adoption of such a plan might entail."

May 19 being a Sunday, both Churchill and Chamberlain were in the country when Gort's report came in, and it was not possible to hold a meeting of the War Cabinet until that afternoon. The news was by no means to Churchill's liking. In spite of the things he had seen and heard on his visit to Paris three days earlier, he still had a lingering faith in the French generals and the armies they commanded. At all costs, he declared, Gort must fight his way south to France. There must be no thought of evacuation. However, the canny Prime Minister ordered that "as a precautionary measure the Admiralty should assemble a large number of small vessels in readiness to proceed to ports and inlets on the French coast."

To reinforce their instructions, the War Cabinet sent General Sir Edmund Ironside, Chief of the Imperial General Staff, to Gort's headquarters, just in case.

At this moment we see the typical Churchill. Undaunted by the gravity of the news, he knew there must be a way out, and he further knew that he was the man to find it. In issuing the order for Gort to drive toward Amiens, he was not only taking over the role of British Commander in Chief, he was usurping the functions of both General Gamelin and of General Georges, who commanded the Northwest Region, and of General Bilotte, commanding the Army Group to which the B.E.F. was assigned. "Was the War Cabinet in London," wondered Air Commodore J. S. Slessor, who was to accompany Ironside, "in a position to direct operations of the B.E.F. from London, not really knowing the latest situation?"

Slessor and Ironside set off from Charing Cross Station in a special

117

train to Dover, where they took passage in H.M. destroyer *Keith*. Arriving at Boulogne, they found a heavy bombing raid in progress and had to wait several hours to disembark. Once the raid lifted, the two men went ashore, seated themselves in Gort's official Rolls-Royce, under the watchful eye of aide de camp Captain J. Crawshay. Across relatively clear roads they traveled to Gort's headquarters at Wahignies, near Carvin. It was still early. The breakfast table had not been laid, and only one man was up and stirring—Lord Gort himself.

It quickly became obvious to Ironside that the orders he carried were impossible, already outdated by the pressure of events. Even as they talked, word came in that Panzer forces were already close to Arras, and unless they could be stopped, the entire position of the B.E.F. would be turned. Gort ordered two divisions, the Fifth and the Fiftieth, under command of Major General H. E. Franklyn, to attack toward Arras. He would carry out this attack if he could get some support from the French. In fact, he would carry it out in any case, but to have any chance of success, it would require strong, decisive action by the French on his left. But the French seemed to be doing nothing.

Ironside charged off to General Bilotte's headquarters at Bethune, 18 miles away. Arriving at the girls' school pressed into military service, the Britisher found both Bilotte and Blanchard in the depression that stultifies thought. No action seems possible, for the consequences will not bear thought.

"Tiny" Ironside, a huge man of six feet four inches, built like a bear, lost his temper. Seizing Bilotte by the jacket, he looked as though he would shake some life into the French commander. "You must make a plan!" shouted Ironside. "Attack at once to the south with all your forces on Amiens!"

No amount of jacket-seizing could put fire in General Bilotte. Although he promised that he would mount a two-division attack toward Cambrai in support of Franklyn's drive toward Arras on May 21, he did very little. As Franklyn poised himself, word came that the two French divisions could not arrive before May 22, unless it was May 23.

Franklyn's attack of two divisions, known as Frankforce, stepped off bravely, but it had not advanced far before it ran head on into Rommel's Seventh Panzer Division. Although the British had only 74 tanks, they brought consternation to the Germans, not only those in Rommel's division, but as far up as Hitler's headquarters. Wrote Rundstedt, Commander of Army Group A: "A critical moment in the drive came just as my forces reached the Channel. It was caused by a British counterstroke southward from Arras on May 21. For a short time it was feared that our armored divisions would be cut off before the infantry divisions could come up to support them. None of the French counterattacks carried any serious threat as this one did."

Alas for the British, the counterstroke had been too weak. Because the attack had to be mounted in a tearing hurry, it was not a two-division assault; it was merely a matter of two tank battalions and two infantry battalions. Such a small force came so close. What could a larger one have done?

Ironside sped back to London, while the new Commander in Chief, General Weygand, flew to Belgium and drove to Ypres for a meeting with Bilotte, Gort, and Leopold, King of the Belgians. No one thought to inform Lord Gort of the time and place of the meeting, so he waited at his headquarters, hearing the details of the failure of Frankforce, and waiting for the summons that never came. Such was the state of disorganization that the message notifying him of the time and place of the meeting had gone astray. The telephone call had to go through London, and no one thought of sending a messenger. In fact, it would have been difficult to do so, for no one at First Army Headquarters had any idea where Gort's command center was located. Gort had duly notified the French, but the coding officer had considered the information so secret, he had locked it away in the security files before showing it to anyone!

Weygand waited for a time and then left, breathing fire at what he considered a deliberate snub by Gort. He was convinced that Gort had avoided the meeting as a sign that he would not accept Weygand's orders.

Gort eventually made his way to Ypres, word finally having reached him, but in the absence of Weygand, he had to deal with Bilotte, of whose professional capacities he had the gravest misgivings. Bilotte explained the plan for the concerted north and south drives, the same as set forth by Gamelin some days earlier. But now, it was called "the Weygand Plan." And, by now, it was too late.

While returning from the Ypres meeting, General Bilotte was fatally injured in an automobile crash. Command of the combined French, British, and Belgian force fell upon General Blanchard of the French First Army. Of the three army commanders in the beleaguered region, he was the only one who knew nothing of "the Weygand Plan." To make matters worse, he was not confirmed in command for several days. In such circumstances, he felt he had no authority to issue orders to Gort or to Leopold. In his state of mind, he probably felt relieved.

He should have done something. Each hour the peril grew greater; each hour reduced the options available to any commander in his position. With two army groups pressing from the east and from the south, only desperate, decisive actions could prevent utter, final, ruin.

To try to stir something up, Churchill flew back to Paris the next day, May 22. He met with Reynaud and Weygand in the headquarters of the French Supreme Commander at the Château de Vincennes, guarded by Spahis with white cloaks and long curved swords, symbols, perhaps, of the state of France's military position.

Weygand appeared cheerful and confident, but he had little to offer other than "the Weygand Plan." He demanded increased numbers of British aircraft, and he had a few nasty remarks to make about Lord Gort for missing the scheduled meeting at Ypres. Both Churchill and Ismay were encouraged, and the meeting ended on a note of restrained optimism.

When the official text of "the Weygand Plan" reached General Ironside and Lord Gort, it seemed to them to have been drafted on preconceptions rather than facts. It was vague, a dream rather than a plan. It assumed too much, and always on the most favorable side. The French First Army was rested and well equipped. False. The B.E.F. casualties had been light. False. There was no real threat from Bock's Army Group B on the east. False. Time was on the side of the Allies. False. There was unified command under Blanchard. False, because Blanchard was not commanding.

On May 23, Gort evacuated the Arras position. It could not be held in the face of German strength. In fact, General Franklyn was lucky to get his troops out through a gap five miles wide between the closing jaws of a pincer movement by the Germans.

Weygand was furious. Gort's withdrawal had ruined all his schemes. "The Weygand Plan" lay in ruins. Nonetheless, both Paris and London continued to push it upon Blanchard, Leopold, and Gort.

Gort, his lines shortened by his retreat from Arras, informed Blanchard that he would not be ready for a major drive south in accordance with the Weygand Plan before May 26. The effort at Arras had cost him most of his vehicles, and his new supply arrangements through Dunkirk were not yet working efficiently. The B.E.F. went on half-rations, even though some commanders showed a remarkable gift of improvisation. Major General Bernard L. Montgomery, later

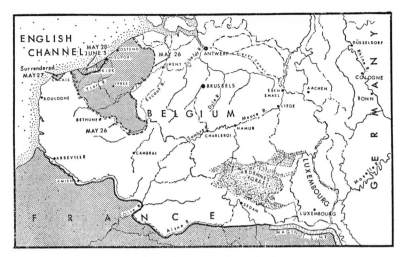

German advances, May 26–June 5.

to become famous at El Alamein, rounded up a herd of cattle and drove the animals with his Third Division, as a kind of food train on the hoof.

Unexpectedly the situation eased. It was no doing of the French High Command nor yet of the British. Fearful of the wear and tear on his tanks and armored vehicles, mindful of the bold and telling attack of Frankforce near Arras, and rather appalled at the very success his troops had won, Rundstedt halted his tanks. The order was given on May 24, and Hitler, motivated by perhaps the same reasons, confirmed it.

Already Guderian's and Reinhardt's Panzers were turning toward Calais and Dunkirk. If they reached either, there would be no possible chance of either keeping the forces in the pocket supplied or evacuating them. Forty-six Allied divisions would be rounded up en masse. It seems clear that General Franklyn's attack at Arras played a major role in the salvation of over 300,000 men from the Dunkirk beachhead.

The stop order lasted until May 26, but the time the Allies had gained was enough—just.

The French First Army, meanwhile, had pulled itself together and made a two-division thrust toward Cambrai, but when it was heavily attacked by dive bombers, the force retired to its starting position.

There was no sign of any supporting movement from the south. Instead of the eight divisions that Weygand had ordered to attack from the north and an unspecified number to coordinate from the south, this was the sum and substance of the drive. Weygand, however, reported that the French Seventh Army driving up from the south had captured Péronne, Albert, and Amiens.

"It later transpired," wrote Gort bitingly, "that this information was incorrect." No advance of any consequence had been made. But Gort's withdrawal from Arras could be blamed for everything.

In this vacuum of leadership, for no orders had reached either Blanchard or Gort for three days, something had to be done, and Lord Gort did it. On the evening of May 25, he was sitting in his room in his headquarters. His maps were spread out in front of him, and he gazed at them silently for a long time. Then, about 6 P.M., he got up and walked into the room where his Chief of Staff, Lieutenant General Sir H. R. Pownall, was working.

"Henry," he said, "I've got a hunch. We've got to call off the Fifth and Fiftieth Divisions from the attack to the south and send them over to Brookie * on the left."

"Well, you do realize, sir," replied Pownall, "that that's against all the orders that we've had and that if we take those two divisions away, the French First Army is very unlikely to attack without British support?"

Gort thought a moment and then spoke quietly. "Yes, I know that quite well. All the same, it's got to be done." Under pressure from Bock's Army Group B, a gap had opened between Brooke's left flank and the right of the Belgian troops. Unless it was plugged, the B.E.F. would find enemy troops on three sides of them. It would not be long before the Germans would be behind them as well, and then it would be one long good night for the British troops in Flanders.

The decision Gort had made was a most difficult one, for it effectively removed the B.E.F. from the strategic command of the French. Under agreement between the two governments, the French had complete direction of the land war on the Western Front. Even the King of the Belgians had placed himself and his army under that command. Now, on his own responsibility, consulting no one, asking none to share the blame, Lord Gort had taken the first move toward saving his army to fight again. In time to come, the British would call his move the salvation of the Army. The French called it betrayal.

Lord Gort's decision was the only one he could have made under the circumstances. With the failure of the attack on Arras on May 21,

* Lieutenant General Sir Alan Brooke, commanding the British Second Corps. His left flank rested on the Belgian right.

all chance of linking up the northern and southern segments of the Allied armies went glimmering. On May 25 or 26 the only hope that existed was in the minds of those too uninformed or too stupid to know otherwise. All that was left was to make for the sea.

In thinking of a retreat to Dunkirk, Lord Gort was acting in the reflexive action of a general whose country was a sea power. It was automatic for a British general whose position was threatened to retire to the coast, where the Navy would take him off. It had happened time and time again in British history, and it would happen again. In 1781 Cornwallis had fallen back on Yorktown before the troops of Mad Anthony Wayne, Lafayette, and Steuben. This time the Navy failed, for the French under Admiral le Comte de Grasse had defeated the British Admiral Sir Thomas Graves in the Battle of the Virginia Capes. Cornwallis had to surrender to Washington. In January, 1809, the Navy had rescued over 20,000 men of Sir John Moore's army in Spain after a masterful retreat which captured the imagination of the public and had brought Moore the title of "England's greatest soldier."

To the British generals, the sea was a highway, easily traveled, capable of bearing troops, guns, and supplies to any point in the world, putting them ashore, and taking them off as necessary. To a sea-faring nation such a concept comes naturally. In Lord Gort's mind, Dunkirk was a door to freedom and opportunity.

Except for a small part of their people, the French do not follow the sea. Their Channel and Biscay fishermen yield to no one in seamanship, and the French Navy has fought many gallant fights, but it has never had the tradition of victory earned by the Royal Navy. Driven from the seas during the Napoleonic Wars, it had come back to become a first-rate navy, but its men and officers lacked the hard experience that was a natural part of the tradition of the British. It never exerted the weight in strategic planning that its British counterpart did. France is basically a land power, and its High Command was land-minded. To Weygand, to Blanchard, to the *poilu* in the ranks, the idea of falling back on Dunkirk was drawing into a bastion at best or a trap at worst. Behind them would be the impenetrable sea. It might as well be boiling hot, for all the good it would do them.

The day following Gort's decision, Churchill ordered the Admiralty to begin the evacuation of the troops that had managed to reach Dunkirk. Also he gave one of the hardest orders of his life.

The only obstacle to the German advance on Dunkirk from the southwest was the port of Calais. If it fell, there was nothing to stop the Panzers from smashing the evacuation beaches. Some six battalions of French and British defended Calais under command of Brigadier Cameron G. G. Nicholson. He and his men must fight it out to the end.

> EVERY HOUR YOU CONTINUE TO EXIST [telegraphed Churchill] IS OF THE GREATEST HELP TO THE B.E.F. GOVERNMENT HAS THEREFORE DECIDED YOU MUST CONTINUE TO FIGHT. HAVE GREATEST POSSIBLE ADMIRATION FOR YOUR SPLENDID STAND. EVACUATION WILL NOT (REPEAT NOT) TAKE PLACE, AND CRAFT REQUIRED FOR ABOVE PURPOSE ARE TO RETURN TO DOVER.

After dispatching this telegram, Churchill was unnaturally silent. When dinner came, he ate little and drank even less. As he rose from the table, he remarked to Ismay, "I feel physically sick."

To a French Government, badly shaken by the utter failure of its High Command, its strategy, and its leadership, it was convenient to have in Lord Gort a whipping-boy, a scapegoat. On him could be laid the blame for all the deficiencies of two decades. No one could trust the British, they said. Look at Poland. Look at Norway. They didn't fight, or if they did, they ran away. A German propaganda leaflet fed these feelings with the message, "In the autumn the leaves fall. So fall the *poilus* fighting for the English."

Soon the French had another scapegoat. The day Gort began his retreat toward Dunkirk, on May 26, Leopold informed his allies that the Belgian armies would soon collapse. On May 27, he asked for terms, and the next day he surrendered unconditionally.

"There never has been such a betrayal in history!" cried Reynaud on hearing the news. "To think that this is the man to whose succor we flew is unbelievable. It is monstrous, absolutely monstrous."

But Weygand would not leave it at that. He felt he had to implicate the British, as well. "If only Gort had counterattacked with more vigor," he wailed, "the Belgians, feeling themselves better supported, might have resisted longer."

Commented General Spears, Churchill's representative to Premier Reynaud, summing up his impressions of an evening of recriminations: "In the last war, when things were going wrong and I, a solitary liaison officer with the French, had felt, as I often did, lonely, hurt and angry, I always knew these were passing difficulties I must surmount, for the essential unity of Britain and France remained, since they were at one in their will to fight. Now, for the first time, I sensed a break in the relationship between the two nations, no more perceptible than a crack in crystal, but going right through, irreparably. We were no longer one."

It was at this time that the wisdom of Gort's move in sending the Fifth and Fiftieth Divisions to Brooke on the left flank became painfully apparent. With the collapse of the Belgian Army, the road to Dunkirk lay open to the German Eighteenth Army. With these two divisions at his disposal, Brooke was able to plug the gap—barely. Now all that remained was to get the B.E.F. and the French First Army to the beaches for evacuation.

It was a long, weary retreat, beset at every hour by dangers from the skies and on the ground. Ever hampering the orderly retreat of the soldiers were the mobs of refugees, pitiful bits of humanity, cast out of their homes by the merciless tides of war. In every sort of conveyance they came, bound they knew not where. There were two main currents of these refugees, one moving northeast to get away from the Panzer armies to the south. This current inevitably collided with the second one moving west, fleeing Bock's Eighteenth and Sixth Armies. Where the two streams met, at nearly every crossroad, were scenes of unbelievable confusion. Terrified people tried to push through each other, overturning pushcarts and baby carriages loaded with household goods, and scattering family treasures to be trampled underfoot by uncaring strangers.

Most of the refugees were the very old and the very young, women, and men too crippled to be on duty with the armies. Children clutched their toys, their dolls, their blankets, while the carts and wheelbarrows were loaded with mattresses, pots and pans, bottles of wine, heirloom clocks, *prie-dieux,* crucifixes, rakes, hoes, apparently anything the heart-broken people could lay their hands on when they left their homes, perhaps forever.

Every so often, apparently for sport, a German Stuka or Heinkel or ME-109 would slide down out of the sky, its machine guns blazing. With shrieks of terror, the old and the young, the hale and the infirm, all dived for cover until the merciless aircraft had passed. Then the survivors would climb to their feet to mourn their dead and to plod on.

Even where there was no fighting, the Luftwaffe was occasionally hitting at civilians. Near the village of Trois Maisons in Alsace, about 20 boys were playing football when they were suddenly strafed by a captured French Curtis biplane, still bearing French colors. Spurts of dust rose from their football field as the boys threw themselves on their faces. When the triumphant plane had passed, two of the boys did not rise. One moaned, and the other lay still. Five bullets had pierced his back as he lay quivering on his face.

There was a ruthless military advantage in these terror attacks, for they spread panic, and the crowds of refugees, panic-stricken and unreasoning, interfered with troop movements. It was grim, it was horrible. But it was war as the Germans waged it in 1940.

As nearly half a million men began to retire on Dunkirk like lemmings marching on the sea, they had to be kept from becoming an unruly mob. An organized retreat in the face of vastly superior forces is the most difficult of military operations. Most men have no goal but personal safety, and for many it simply seems safer to quit, surrender, lay down the burden, or simply flee, forgetting friends. There were units which looked for the nearest Germans so they could be done with the fighting and spend the war in the safety of a prison camp. There were a few cases of *sauve qui peut,* as weaker men cast down their rifles and fled. Few of them made it, for if they were not cut down by the Germans, their own officers or non-commissioned officers finished them off to keep panic from spreading.

It was not the first time in history that the discipline and devotion to duty of British and French non-coms had kept their units from disintegration. With an encouraging slap on the seat of the trousers, a rough word of praise or admonishment, a refusal to be stampeded, these men, some of them recently barrow-pushers or tradesmen, kept their units together so that their officers could organize the defenses and the retreat on which all their lives depended.

The Royal Air Force and some French aircraft did their best to assist. As the perimeter around Dunkirk shrank, the available airfields became fewer. Although many French pilots fought gallantly and many met their deaths supporting the troops in the retreat, others were infected by the general rot of despair. At one French airfield, where three British pilots were awaiting a pickup by one of their own planes, the French pilots were eating their lunch. A German flight of aircraft came over and dropped bombs. A few people were killed, including some children. Not a single French fighter went up to meet the Germans, and not a French pilot left his lunch. The three Britishers were so furious that they volunteered to take the French planes up to fight the Germans. With lackluster eyes the French commander refused their request.

General Weygand shared the attitude of most Frenchmen that to retreat to the sea was to retire into a redoubt that must be held. He saw no opportunity in the use of the sea as a highway, and issued stern orders to General Blanchard about forming a defensive perimeter around Dunkirk, based on the Yser and Aa Rivers. For this reason, and for the reason that Blanchard felt that if his men embarked in ships, they would be abandoning France, the French retirement on Dunkirk was tardy. Let this be remembered when the French complain of the comparatively low number of Frenchmen evacuated from Dunkirk beaches.

If any troops at all were to be evacuated from the Dunkirk area, it would require a superhuman effort on the part of both the Navy and the Royal Air Force. Thanks to Churchill's precautionary instructions to the Admiralty on May 19, there had been a full week to get ready before the first of the soldiers were to be taken off. Upon the capable shoulders of Vice Admiral Sir Bertram H. Ramsay fell the naval arrangements.

On May 26, the British War Cabinet gave Lord Gort permission to withdraw on Dunkirk and that evening gave orders for Operation Dynamo, the Dunkirk evacuation, to commence. At that time, the more optimistic hoped that Ramsay's forces would be able to take off 45,000 men in the next two days. The rest would inevitably be lost.

Captain W. G. Tennant went across to Dunkirk as Senior Naval Officer, Dunkirk, to organize the evacuation, where he would meet conditions of incredible difficulty. On the way across in the destroyer *Wolfhound* he experienced dive-bombing attacks every half-hour. On arrival, he found the town blazing, most of the facilities in ruins, and reports of disaster everywhere.

PLEASE SEND EVERY AVAILABLE CRAFT TO BEACHES EAST OF DUNKIRK IMMEDIATELY [he signaled]. EVACUATION TOMORROW NIGHT IS PROBLEMATICAL.

From such an unlikely beginning the Miracle of Dunkirk ensued. It is a tale of heroism and devotion, of cowardice and ineptitude, of extemporization and success. But, above all, it is a tale of courage.

In response to Tennant's request, Admiral Ramsay dispatched everything he could find to the beaches east of Dunkirk. The motley armada included destroyers, Channel ferries, sloops, patrol vessels, gunboats, corvettes, trawlers, drifters, schuyts, yachts, tugs—even hospital ships. If a vessel had a bottom, engines, and was over 30 feet in length, it went.

It would be impossible to tell completely the story of the Dunkirk evacuation, for 858 * vessels of all types were involved, and some made as many as ten round trips. Each trip was an adventure filled with desperate danger. We can only follow the broad outline and fill in a few details. They are merely typical of thousands of similar equally stirring tales.

The first day, May 26, was a day of fumbling and improvisation. The ships ran the normal channel from Dover to Dunkirk, and this brought them under the guns of Calais, which had fallen to the Germans that very day. This route, however, was by far the shortest one to use, being only 29 miles long.† It soon had to be abandoned, however, and two others of 55 and 87 miles had to be employed.

Contrary to popular belief, it was not the spontaneous effort of amateur yachtsmen that brought off the soldiers. Channel steamers and destroyers brought off over half the total number. It is not surprising that this should be so. The Channel steamers were designed for carrying passengers, and they could carry a lot of them. The destroyers decidedly were not designed for passengers, but they took them, anyway, and they were fast. On several occasions these destroyers, small by American standards, carried over a thousand men on a trip. How they packed them in must remain a mystery, not only to landsmen, but also to any seaman who has ever served in "the small boys," as the Navy calls them.

The private yachts simply did not have the carrying capacity that was needed. Yet they did their best, and that they succeeded in taking off over 5000 men in the days of the evacuation makes them and their owners and their crews worthy of every praise. Picture a 38-foot cabin cruiser, if you will. It may be yours, or you may have been a guest on board. Now imagine 30 or 40 filthy, dog-tired men, some of them wounded perhaps, climbing aboard. At any moment you may be machine-gunned from the air, or a bomb or shell may drop nearby. You move out, the boat lower in the water than you have ever known it. Ahead lies some 50 to 90 miles of sea. The weather, fortunately, remains good, but there is a swell. Will your boat take it? No wonder you breathe a sigh of relief when your boat passes the Dover breakwater. You unload, have a bite to eat, refuel.

Then you go back.

Retired Reserve Commander Charles H. Lightoller had had a long

---

* There were probably many more small craft never reported to the Admiralty.

† Because of the many shoals in the southern part of the North Sea, it was imperative to stick to well-marked channels.

career at sea in the merchant navy. As a young second officer he had sailed in the *Titanic* on her only voyage and had been the senior surviving officer of that tragedy. Now "on the beach," he kept in touch with the sea by piloting his 60-foot cruiser *Sundowner*. With his son, a Sea Scout, and three others, he set out from Southend for Dunkirk by the prescribed route. On the way across, he rescued the crew of another vessel which had broken down. Then, proceeding to Dunkirk, he laid his vessel alongside a destroyer moored to the mole. But let Commander Lightoller tell his own story.

My son, as previously arranged, was to pack the men in and use every available inch of space—which I'll say he carried out to some purpose. On deck I detailed a naval rating to tally the troops aboard. At fifty I called below, "How are you getting on?" getting the cheery reply, "Oh, plenty of room yet." At seventy-five my son admitted they were getting pretty tight—all equipment and arms being left on deck.

I now started to pack them on deck, having passed word below for every man to lie down and keep down; the same applied on deck. By the time we had fifty on deck, I could feel her getting distinctly tender, so took no more. Actually we had exactly 130 on board, including crew.

During the whole embarkation we had quite a lot of attention from enemy planes, but derived an amazing degree of comfort from the fact that the *Worcester*'s A.A. guns kept up an everlasting bark overhead. . . .

Arriving off the harbour I was at first told to "lie off." But when I informed them that I had 130 on board, permission was at once given to come in (I don't think the authorities believed for a minute that I had 130), and I put her alongside a trawler lying at the quay. Whilst entering, the men started to get to their feet and she promptly went over to a terrific angle. I got them down again in time and told those below to remain below and lying down till I gave the word. The impression ashore was that the fifty-odd lying on deck plus the mass of equipment was my full load.

After I had got rid of those on deck I gave the order "Come up from below," and the look on the official face was amusing to behold as troops vomited up through the forward companionway, the after companionway, and the doors either side of the wheelhouse. As a stoker P.O., helping them over the bulwarks, said, "God's truth, mate! Where did you put them?" He might well ask.

Most of the men who were saved during the evacuation were taken from the port of Dunkirk itself, for loading from the moles was far faster than taking the men off the beaches. As the days went on, it became possible to move a ship into position, march the men on in a very short space of time, get the ship away, turn her around, and head off for Dover, all incredibly fast.

But over it all was the constant threat of air attack. The RAF did its best, but they flew their planes from bases in Kent, and time over the loading area was limited. German bases were closer, and their planes were better—except, that here, for the first time, the British unveiled the famous Spitfire.

To the men struggling to embark, to the men on the ships picking their way through the wrecks that strewed the harbor, to the men fighting to hold off the German troops and maintain the precarious perimeter, it seemed there were never enough British planes. What the soldiers could not see, could not know, were the many battles that took place in the air, well away from the beaches. To this day, many veterans of Dunkirk are convinced that the RAF let them down. Yet, during the evacuation, Fighter Command aircraft flew an average of 482 hours a day and lost 106 of their number. It was not a maximum effort, but Air Marshal Dowding was thinking about the forthcoming Battle of Britain.

The Luftwaffe was making a maximum effort, for Hermann Goering had persuaded Hitler to call off the ground troops closing in on the perimeter, bragging that the Luftwaffe could stop the Allied soldiers completely. The skies were filled with all sorts of German aircraft, mercilessly bombing and strafing. Yet on the shore they did strangely little harm. The city of Dunkirk was already in ruins, and a few more bombs merely stirred the rubble. Their bombs never did demolish the vital moles, and those that fell on the beaches did little damage, for the soft sand damped the explosions.

They were the most danger to the ships, and it was here that they did their gravest damage. Six British and 3 French destroyers were lost in this manner, and 19 others damaged. Nine of the big passenger steamers were lost, most of them from bombing. Not even the hospital ships were spared, although they adhered strictly to the Geneva Convention, displaying large red crosses and operating lighted at night.

On June 1, losses to aircraft became so great that Admiral Ramsay ordered that henceforth all embarkations would take place during the hours of darkness.

One of the reasons for Ramsay's decision may have been the story of the Channel passenger steamer *Prague*. Arriving at Dunkirk in the middle of the morning at the height of an air attack, she, nevertheless, made her way alongside and loaded about 3000 French troops on board. On the way back, she was shelled off Gravelines and dive-bombed as well. Both attacks missed, but the shock of the explosions caused severe damage.

Although he drove at his best speed on one engine, her master, Captain Baxter, could feel the ship gradually sinking under him. And there was still a long way to go. He moved the men forward to try to get the damaged stern further out of the water. But still the ship continued to settle.

Baxter spotted the destroyer H.M.S. *Shikari* and signaled to her. She came alongside as the *Prague* continued on her way—no mean feat of seamanship. The *Shikari* took 500 men from the sinking ship and then called up the steamer *Queen of Thanet,* which took off 2000 more. The corvette *Shearwater* and a sloop took off the rest.

In peacetime such a story, a sinking ship, transfers at sea between vessels that did not stop, the water gaining inside the *Prague* and threatening outside, all these would have made world headlines. During the Dunkirk evacuation, it was merely routine.

The French Navy also played an important part in the Dunkirk operations, although they got off to a late start as a result of the inefficiencies of the French High Command. In proportion to the number of ships they had at Dunkirk, they did their share. But they could have brought in more ships if Reynaud and Weygand had been able to face the idea of evacuation earlier and had ordered Admiral Darlan to get things moving.

On May 31, Churchill was once again in Paris to attend a meeting of the Supreme War Council. Weygand and Reynaud complained that at that time only 15,000 Frenchmen had been taken off as opposed to 165,000 British troops. Was Britain leaving its allies to die while her men ran away?

Churchill ingenuously pointed out that the city of Dunkirk had been manned largely by British forces, and that naturally these had been taken off first to leave room for the fighting men as they came in. But this was begging the truth. Perhaps Churchill at that time did not know, perhaps he could not bring himself to tell the French leaders, that it was Blanchard's dilatoriness that kept the French troops so far away. While the British had fallen back in good order, the French had temporized. As a result, eight divisions had been cut off around Lille, and only the equivalent of three or four could be expected at the beachhead. And they would be late.

It has pleased some French writers commenting on these operations to call this move a gallant rearguard action which saved the British.

At the meeting, Churchill issued the order that British and French troops would go aboard the ships *bras dessus, bras dessous*—that is, arm in arm.

It was an order impossible to enforce, for by the time it reached Dunkirk there were few British troops left and the French ones were just coming in large numbers. And it has been a favorite charge of the French against the British ever since that they took care of their own men first.

The French troops that did arrive after they had been cut off from the rest of their forces tended to be often undisciplined. Many examples of indiscipline and panic had appeared among the British troops, but in the main the sense of discipline and fair play prevailed. On the beaches, for example, men stood in lines in the water, out through the shallows and up to their shoulders, waiting for small boats to come by and take them out to the waiting ships. When a boat had taken off a dozen or so, the others would move up. It was as though they were standing in line waiting for a bus. On a mole in Dunkirk a sergeant had his men drawn up in ranks, six across the front. The master of a ship announced he had room for 60 more. "Sixty, you say, sir? Right, sir." Turning to his charges, he barked, "First ten ranks, quick march, forward—march!"

Not so well led, and more ignorant of the sea, the French soldiers sometimes got out of hand. They would rush the boats, swamping them. They could not seem to get the idea that a boat sitting on the bottom because of the weight of men aboard was not going to go anywhere. It never seems to have occurred to them for some to get out, pull the boat out into deep water, and then climb back aboard.

Part of the trouble with getting the French on board was the language barrier. Unable to understand, the French soldier often took matters into his own hands. The British sailor, on the other hand, failing to grasp that the French could not understand plain English, especially when it was shouted at them, simply lost patience. It is more amazing that there were so few incidents than that there were so many.

Yet, on the last day, one fact threatens to blot the memory of all the triumph of Dunkirk. On the night of June 3, Admiral Ramsay called upon his depleted force to make one more effort. The exhausted men—some of them had slept only four hours in the last week—set forth again. The French commander had reported that there were approximately 30,000 men still to be picked up.

This was the last chance. The Germans were within three miles of Dunkirk. This would be it.

As the ships reached Dunkirk, the waterfront was swarming. But it was not swarming with those they had come to rescue. Those troops were still falling back. But from the basements, from the shell holes, from the sewers, emerged 40,000 demoralized French soldiers, deserters in the retreat. They had lain hidden all during the evacuation, and now they sensed it was the last moment. They swarmed aboard the ships, which were soon filled to capacity and set off, their skippers not knowing the truth. At 0340, H.M.S. *Shikari* cast off from the mole with 383 French troops aboard.

The Dunkirk evacuation was over. On the beach, the brave men who had held off two army groups watched the ships sail away and leave them, bearing in the places they should have had the rag-tag and bob-tail, the stragglers and deserters, as well as some brave men who managed somehow to get aboard.

Yet this sorry ending cannot detract from the magnificent accomplishment. At the beginning, the hope was to get 45,000 men off in two days. The operations extended nine days, and 338,226 men were landed in Britain, plus an unknown number in French ports.* The price was grim: over 100 aircraft and 235 ships and boats were lost.

Yet the evacuation at Dunkirk was more than the gallantry that made it possible. The 300,000 trained troops that came back from Dunkirk had lost their equipment, but they had not lost their self-respect or their courage. From them would come the cadre to train the British soldiers who would fight in Africa, in Greece, in Crete, and again in France. From them would come the dependable non-commissioned officers and the junior and middle grade officers, without whom no military organization can function. This was the real victory of Dunkirk.

But, as Churchill put it in his report to the House of Commons

---

* This table gives the number of men safely delivered to England each day.

May 26	26,746	May 31	68,014
May 27	7,669	June 1	64,429
May 28	17,804	June 2	26,256
May 29	47,310	June 3	26,175
May 30	53,823	TOTAL	338,226

on June 4, "Wars are not won by evacuations." The triumph of Dunkirk obscured in the minds of many the deadly peril that lay ahead.

But that peril was clear enough to Churchill, and to Reynaud, and to Roosevelt.

CHAPTER SIX

Giddy Minds and Foreign Quarrels

> *We that have free souls, it touches us not:*
> *let the galled jade wince,*
> *our withers are unwrung.*
>
> *Shakespeare*, Hamlet

As Spring picked her cautious way across the face of the United States, nothing could have been of less interest to the ordinary American than the war in Europe. He was little incommoded by the "Sitzkrieg," for he saw no reality in the fighting in Europe, what there was of it. When the gallant Finnish resistance collapsed, and little Finland—"the only country that paid its war debts"—knuckled under, there was nothing to worry about. Hadn't America bailed the Old World out once before? And what were our thanks? To be called Uncle Shylock. To be called Babbitts, uncultured and uncouth. We were insensitive money-grubbers.

Now that Europe had committed the supreme idiocy of going to war once more—not that the people showed much in the way of fight —the only thing to do was to let Europe stew in its own juice. Don't expect America to come to the rescue again. Once was enough!

The voice of Isolation was dominant in the United States that spring, and it lacked nothing for spokesmen. And it was not the lunatic fringe alone that denounced Europe and its quarrels. Respected Senators and Representatives, Republicans and Democrats alike, spoke out against Europe and against even the most uncertain, toddling, steps toward preparation of the nation's defenses. Wrote Representative John G. Alexander, a Minnesota Republican, in a letter to President Roosevelt:

> Why take our youth from their homes and out of the wholesome environment in which most of them are living, and transplant them

into the lonely, inhospitable and disturbing and discouraging arena of a training camp? Their mental, moral and physical well-being is too important to be disregarded in that way. . . . Mr. President, we want no foreign wars, we want none of our American boys to fight in foreign lands or seas, we want only to prepare to protect and defend our own shores and border.

Perhaps it really seemed preferable to Mr. Alexander to fight on our own soil, with few, ill-trained mercenaries, and suffer the destruction of American cities. He does not seem to have realized the implications of his proposals, if they can be dignified by such a name.

Even the most prominent candidate for President in the Republican Party, Senator Robert A. Taft, shared Mr. Alexander's logic.

I do not know what the Germans may do, and no one knows what they may do until they are freed from the present war and have an opportunity to show. When they do, we can adopt the same methods. We can take the same steps that may be necessary to meet the particular kind of German "blitzkrieg," if there is such a blitzkrieg, at the time we find out what it is.

Did Mr. Taft really mean that the time to begin the manufacture of arms was after the Germans had already invaded the United States?

Even John Nance Garner, Vice President of the United States, was not exempt. Shortly before the war broke out in Europe, Mr. Roosevelt called a meeting of Congressional leaders, in an attempt to get them to repeal the Neutrality Act, which forbade sale of munitions to any belligerent. Such repeal, argued Roosevelt, strongly backed up by Secretary of State Cordell Hull, might well make Germany think twice, for she would be in no position to take advantage of American arms, while France and Britain would have ready access. Not so, retorted Senator William E. Borah of Idaho. He had private sources of information which he considered superior to those of the State Department. There would be no war, he stated; "Germany isn't ready for it." The Vice President listened and then said happily to Roosevelt, "Well, Captain, we may as well face the facts. You haven't got the votes, and that's all there is to it."

This meeting was a revelation to Roosevelt, and he was thereafter very careful in his dealings with the Congress to make sure he had the votes. If he didn't, he worked through executive decree or he waited. He knew that time, unhappily, would prove him right.

If such were the voices of respected leaders, what of the irresponsible, the bigots, the rabble-rousers? The coming of war brought them out from under every rock. The Russo-German Non-Aggression Pact of August, 1939, produced a strange alliance between the Communist Party of the United States and the German-American Bund, led by prime hater Fritz Kuhn. In their desire to aid Germany in every way, both found themselves supporting the isolationists. This alliance was ruptured on the morning of June 22, 1941, when Hitler attacked Russia. Then Germany became, *and always had been,* proclaimed *The Daily Worker,* the power of evil that must be defeated at all costs. But up until that moment, the Communists, under the leadership of Earl Browder, did their best to impede not only aid to Britain and France, but the rearmament program of the United States.

One of the most vicious, because seemingly respectable, isolation voices was that of Father Charles E. Coughlin, a Catholic priest of Royal Oak, Michigan. As early as 1930, Father Coughlin had begun his weekly Sunday afternoon broadcasts over station WJR in Detroit. Gifted with a rich speaking voice, with just a touch of Irish brogue, Father Coughlin wheedled his way into the hearts of many of the so-called little men, the jobless, the despairing. In the midst of the Depression, he gave them, not a program, but someone, something to blame. He railed at the bankers, the "money-changers," the elements of "subversive Socialism." Soon dollar bills were raining in on his Shrine of the Little Flower. They came from everyone who felt himself aggrieved—from Catholics, Protestants, and Jews, from Southern Baptists and Northern Presbyterians, from clerks in San Francisco, from stevedores in New York, from sweatshop workers in Brooklyn, from cab drivers in Chicago. All those caught up in the Depression heard their resentment voiced by Father Coughlin. His main targets were the bankers and the Communists. By some miracle that defies logic, he made them one and the same enemy. His listeners, estimated at 30 to 45 million, loved it.

He supported Roosevelt for election in 1932, and his slogan, "Roosevelt or Ruin," brought him to the favorable attention of party bigwigs. He was courted and feted. It was wonderful. He founded a weekly newspaper, *Social Justice,* and its pages were filled with equal parts of denunciation of "the money interests" and gratuitous, half-baked economic and political advice.

Gradually he drifted away from the New Deal, and ugly tones began to creep into his broadcasts and into the pages of *Social Justice.* His heroes now were Huey Long, Gene Talmadge, Adolf Hitler, and Benito Mussolini. Praising William Randolph Hearst, he began to

137

sound more and more isolationist, and now his worst vituperation was reserved for Franklin D. Roosevelt, "the betrayer of the people." Posing as a strong union supporter, Father Coughlin printed *Social Justice* in a non-union printing shop.

In 1936, he formed the "Union Party," with "Liberty Bill" Lemke of North Dakota as its candidate for President. The platform of the Union Party was based on a mixture of the pension plan of Dr. Francis Townsend and the "Share the Wealth" scheme of Huey Long, with a touch of Fascist methods of discipline for the people.

The Union Party was a flop, and for the time being, Father Coughlin was under a cloud, but he came back, this time on a deliberate policy of anti-Semitism. "The international Jewish bankers" had brought on World War I, the Russian Revolution, and the Great Depression. One article in *Social Justice* proved to have been taken, almost word for word, from a speech by Nazi Propaganda Minister Joseph Goebbels. The name of Roosevelt was frequently misprinted as "Rosenfeld" in *Social Justice*.

By 1940, his platform for action had solidified around such propositions as these: A Jewish-British-Roosevelt conspiracy had started the war. Germany and Italy were only defending themselves against Jewish-Wall Street economic plots. Great Britain was going Communist. Britain would presently make a deal to save the Empire and leave the United States to pick up the pieces. Increased taxes would not go into defense but into increased bureaucracy. Roosevelt, if not a Jew himself, was run by the Jews, who were the ones profiting from the war.

Heil, if not Hitler, then Coughlin!

Between the extremes of the responsible isolationists—Taft, Senator Vandenberg of Michigan, Borah—and the conscienceless demagogues of the Father Coughlin ilk, there were all ranges of isolationist opinion. Many businessmen, General Robert E. Wood of Sears, Roebuck & Co., Jay Hormel, James D. Mooney, believed that Hitler and Nazism were the wave of the future and that American businessmen had better learn to do business with them.

Colonel Charles A. Lindbergh was one of the most respected spokesmen for isolation. For many people he had never lost the luster of "Lindy, the Lone Eagle"; and, while the personal tragedy of his kidnapped and murdered son led him into seclusion, the image remained. The sensational press had made a recluse of him, and he had lived abroad a great deal. In England he had seen the enervation of national will under the flaccid governments of Stanley Baldwin and

Neville Chamberlain. He had seen France's disunity bordering on chaos. In contrast he had seen the efficiency, ruthless organization, and national sense of purpose of resurgent Germany under Hitler and the Nazi Party, and he had been impressed. Goering recognized in him a powerful voice which might be directed toward German aims, in all innocence on Lindbergh's part. Goering saw to it that he visited aircraft factories, showing him the latest model planes. He had seen industry humming with war production. Although Lindbergh dutifully reported what he had learned to the United States Government, he was convinced in his own mind that France and Britain were done for, that Germany held the future of Europe in her hand, and that if the United States was not to share the fate of the decadent Western democracies, she should mind her own business and let the inevitable German victory take place.

> We are in danger of war today [he proclaimed], not because Europeans attempted to interfere in our internal affairs, but because Americans attempted to interfere in the internal affairs of Europe.
> Our dangers are internal. We need not fear invasion unless Americans bring it through their own quarreling and meddling with affairs abroad. If we desire peace, we need only stop asking for war. Nobody wishes to attack us, and nobody is in a position to do so.

Such men as these formed the America First Committee, a strong lobby bent on keeping America out of war. They proposed to do this by any means, even if it meant crippling the defenses of the United States.

Although spokesmen for isolation flooded the air and swamped the newspapers with speeches and press releases, there is no doubt that in May, 1940, they spoke for a large segment of the American public. In a Roper poll, nearly 76 percent voted for answers of one form of isolationism or another. Thirty percent picked "Have nothing to do with any warring country—don't even trade with them on a cash and carry basis."

William Allen White, the respected editor of the *Emporia Gazette,* was appalled at the counsels of retreat and run voiced by the America First Committee and others of the sort. He formed the Committee to Defend America by Aiding the Allies from among his newspaper friends and other prominent citizens. "Our idea," he wrote, "is to fill the radio and the newspapers and the Congressional mail with the voice of prominent citizens urging America to become the nonbelligerent ally of France and England. I am afraid it is too late. . . ."

The response to the appeals of the CDAAA was overwhelming. Letters poured in on the Congress, for it seemed there was a substantial minority that saw the war as a struggle against tyranny. While few wished to enter the war, millions saw that the more America tried to stay out, the more certain it was that war would come to her. Or, if it did not, the country would not be the America they knew and loved.

The success of White's committee can perhaps be measured by the virulence of the attacks upon it.

Like thieves who operate under the cover of night [wrote Father Coughlin in *Social Justice*], there are in our midst those who operate beneath the cloak of protected auspices to steal our liberty, our peace and our autonomy.... "The Committee to Defend America by Aiding the Allies" is a high-sounding name composed of high-handed gentlemen who are leaving no stone unturned to throw everything precious to an American to the dogs of war.... Sneakingly, subversively and un-Americanly hiding behind a sanctimonious stuffed shirt named William Allen White, these men form the most dangerous fifth column that ever set foot upon neutral soil. They are the Quislings of America. They are the Judas Iscariots within the apostolic college of our nation.

They are the gold-protected, Government-protected, foreign-protected snakes in the grass who dare not stand upright and speak like men face to face.

And who were these men and women afraid to "stand upright and speak like men face to face"? They were such men as Robert E. Sherwood, dramatist, James B. Conant, president of Harvard University, Henry R. Luce, publisher of *Time* and *Life*, J. Roscoe Drummond, writer, and even Mrs. Dwight W. Morrow, the mother-in-law of the isolationist Colonel Lindbergh. None of them has ever been accused of "un-Americanly hiding."

When, in September, 1939, President Roosevelt proclaimed a state of Limited National Emergency, the cry of the isolationist began to rise, and it reached a real crescendo during those tragic months of April, May, and June, 1940. But the isolationists were making so much noise that perhaps they did not realize there had been by then large defections in their ranks. As the Nazi juggernaut rolled on, the overwhelming response of the American people was not fear, but resolution. Let us look to our defenses. Let us be ready.

During the fall of 1939, the repeal of the Neutrality Act to permit "cash-and-carry" of war goods satisfied no one. To those in favor of aid to Britain and France it was not enough. To the isolationists, it was a step toward war, since it was obviously unneutral. British and French ships could use the Atlantic, for the U-boat peril was not yet great, but Germany could not get her ships through the British blockade. Yet, at that time, it was all that could be done. For once, the isolationists did not have the votes. Neither did those who prayed for an Allied victory.

As spring came on, after six months of inactivity in the war, Americans were pursuing their cautious, customary affairs. War might erupt in blazing vigor in Europe with the good campaigning weather, but it all seemed so far away. The baseball teams went to their training camps, played the Grapefruit League games, and began the regular season. Everyone looked for Joe McCarthy's New York Yankees to sweep the American League pennant as they had done for the last four years. Cincinnati was favored to repeat in the National League. In the opening game of the season, Cleveland pitcher Bob Feller had a no-hit game against the Chicago White Sox, the Indians winning 1–0.

Broadway was ending a rather poor season. One of the outstanding plays was *Ladies in Retirement* by Edward Percy and Reginald Denham. *There Shall Be No Night* was still *a succès d'estime,* probably more from sympathy for the Finns than for intrinsic artistic merit. Gladys George starred in *Lady in Waiting,* a rather slight farce which depended for its success largely on Miss George's talents. *The Man Who Came to Dinner,* a take-off on Alexander Woollcott, was still going strong, as was *Life With Father.* Maurice Evans played both *Hamlet* and *Richard II,* but otherwise Shakespeare was not doing very well that season. The Lunts' *Taming of the Shrew* and the highly publicized *Romeo and Juliet,* starring Laurence Olivier and Vivien Leigh, both closed after short runs. Probably the most overrated play of the season was William Saroyan's *The Time of Your Life,* which ran for 185 performances at the Booth Theatre. It is a weird story of a night in a San Francisco waterfront dive. The principal characters, a prostitute who "used to be in burlesque," and a drifter who likes to observe life, are spokesmen for the author's theme, that even in ugliness there is beauty, even in vice there is goodness.

Among the popular songs, some of them holdovers from previous years, were "Lazy River," "Too Marvelous for Words," "Green Eyes" as arranged by Jimmy Dorsey, and "Beat Me, Daddy, Eight to the Bar."

At the end of April the results of the annual radio popularity poll were announced. The winners:

Star of Stars—Nelson Eddy
Best Comedian—Jack Benny, replacing Edgard Bergen and
                    Charlie McCarthy
Best Actor—Don Ameche
Best Actress—Barbara Luddy
Singers of Popular Songs—Bing Crosby and Kate Smith
News Commentators—Lowell Thomas and Dorothy Thompson
Best Variety Program—Breakfast Club
Best Children's Program—*The Lone Ranger*
Best Dramatic Serial—*One Man's Family*
Best Sports Commentator—Bill Stern
Best Educational Program—*Information, Please*
Best Dance Orchestra—Wayne King

The movies were staging a strong comeback from the Depression doldrums. Double features were still common, and a few theaters still featured "bank nights" and free china, but the Gallup Poll stated that 54,000,000 Americans went to the movies each week. Of the hundreds of films made, some have memories for today. The biggest splash was made by *Gone With the Wind,* a 4-hour supercolossal, starring Clark Gable and Vivien Leigh. Few films had received such advance publicity, beginning with a nationwide search for a Scarlett O'Hara. In the end it was a British actress who won the coveted role. Bette Davis and Charles Boyer starred in *All This and Heaven Too,* a tear-jerker of murder, suicide, and scandal. The Andy Hardy films kept going with Mickey Rooney in *Andy Hardy's Private Secretary.* A well-known Western-type actor, Ronald Reagan, appeared in *An Angel From Texas.* W. C. Fields made another of his magnificent one-man shows, *The Bank Dick.* It was one-man only in the sense that the audience never looked at anyone else. A long movie tradition began that year with the release of *The Road to Singapore,* starring Bob Hope and Bing Crosby. They had many roads to follow in the coming years, when they were later joined by Dorothy Lamour.

All in all, Americans were more concerned with life as usual, business as usual, than they were with the war in Europe. Even the attack on Norway scarcely disturbed the normal way of life. There were new headlines, new unpronounceable names, and then a growing feeling of bewilderment as the famed British Navy was not able to throw the invaders out. But still, it all seemed so far away.

Sumner Welles, who had been sent by President Roosevelt to try to keep the war from exploding further in Europe, returned at the end of March, having visited the kings of Great Britain and Italy, Hitler, Mussolini, Chamberlain, Daladier, Reynaud, and Pope Pius XII. "I wish to state categorically," he said on his return, "that I have not received any peace plan or proposals . . . that I have not conveyed any such proposals . . . nor am I bringing back to the President any such proposals." In other words, Hitler and Mussolini had no intention of being stopped, even by the U.S. Under Secretary of State.

His boss, Cordell Hull, was even then being heckled in the Congress over reciprocal trade agreements. At stake was an agreement with Argentina, for the cackling Senators, happy to have a chance to get their digs into the white-haired Tennessean, Secretary of State Hull, argued that four and a half million dollars worth of imported canned meats was a threat to the billion-dollar canned meat industry of the United States. Eventually, as everyone expected, the Senators tired of the game, and Mr. Hull was allowed to go back to his office to keep an eye on the war in Europe.

This being an election year, Congress was having a wonderful time with the usual pork-barrel bills. Appropriations for farmers went up to a billion dollars, and the popular Civilian Conservation Corps got $280 million for the coming year, $50 million more than it had asked, and in spite of a legal ruling that the extra money could not be spent. It made no difference. The lawmakers had the bit between their teeth.

Election year or no, the National Labor Relations Board was a favorite whipping boy, and Congress gave vent to its displeasure by cutting the NLRB budget some 11 percent.

The war seemed far away, both to Congress and to the people. There was plenty to do at home. In addition to the usual recreations, many families had plans for travel this summer, for both World's Fairs would be open again. The New York World's Fair reopened in May and the San Francisco Fair at Treasure Island the following month. There were the usual exhibits of science and industry. Both fairs were making every effort to recoup the financial losses of the previous year by emphasizing the folksy touch. "Elmer," a small-town hick, became the symbol of the New York Fair, and posters of him were everywhere. The midways were rejuvenated, and new shows were added. Scattered throughout the New York Fair were thousands of signs: "HELLO FOLKS!" Among the shows were *The Streets of Paris,* where Gypsy Rose Lee performed an absent-minded strip tease, *Twenty Thousand Legs Under the Sea,* retitled from the previous year's *Dream of Venus,* designed by Salvador Dali. There was a show entitled *Battle of Emotions* where male subjects were attached to lie detectors and their emotional response to dancing girls measured in wiggly lines. In *Dancing Campus,* couples could dance to name bands for a quarter apiece.

Food and lodging were reasonable. Many hotel rooms were available at prices between $1.50 and $5.00. At one restaurant in the fair, lunch was available for 75 cents, and it was served on a tablecloth. At the "5 and 10 Cent Restaurant" no item cost more than a dime, for which you could get pork chops, beef stew, meat loaf, or spaghetti. Hamburgers were also a dime.

In San Francisco, the Golden Gate International Exposition opened two weeks later, with some of the best shows held over from the previous years. There was the *Aquacade,* which also had a version in New York. The San Francisco version starred Esther Williams. Sally Rand's *Nude Ranch* was back, as was Clifford Fischer's production of *Les Folies Bergère.* New was a pretentious pageant, *America! Cavalcade of a Nation.* There were the usual quotas of scientific and industrial exhibits, and prices compared favorably with those in New York.

As Sally Rand's fan dance had been the best-remembered feature of the Chicago Fair of 1933 and 1934, so her *Nude Ranch* seemed to capture the imagination of Americans in 1939 and 1940. On the radio Edgar Bergen's puppet Charlie McCarthy would chuckle lasciviously and was always packing his bags for a trip to Treasure Island. "I'm one of her fans," he would snigger.

Transportation to the two fairs received a big boost from the Association of American Railroads and the Pullman Company. For $90 in day coaches or $135 plus $34.50 for minimum Pullman accommodations (upper berth), you could travel from your home town to both coasts and back home again. These Grand Circle tours were extremely popular and induced many Americans to leave their home regions for the first time to see the world. Many of the travelers little realized that in two or three years they would be seeing a great deal more of the world, and not in such comfort as they enjoyed that summer. And there would be no Sally Rand as a feature of the journey.

Those who stayed at home tended to mind their own business, to work the farms, turn out the tools, machines, toys, furniture, automobiles, tires, and all the other things man needs or thinks he needs. There were those with time on their hands to be their brothers' keepers. With the announcement of German paratroopers and spies in Holland and of Quislings in Norway, the FBI began to receive reports of suspicious behavior on the part of German-Americans, Italian-Americans, French-Americans, Spanish-Americans, Afro-Americans, Norwegian-Americans, Danish-Americans, Chinese-Americans, Japanese-Americans, and even American-Americans. Not only might these men and women be spying, but they might be corrupting the morals and minds of the innocent youth of defenseless America.

A Brooklyn housewife brought suit in a New York court to upset the appointment of Lord Bertrand Russell (who was still in a comparatively rational state) to teach mathematics and logic at the College of the City of New York. His outspoken theories on matters of sex brought him under the lady's ire. His writings were, her attorney charged, "lecherous, salacious, libidinous, lustful, venerous, erotomaniac, aphrodisiac, atheistic, irreverent, narrow-minded, untruthful and bereft of moral fiber." Judge John E. McGeehan agreed with the charges and revoked the appointment.

The time of the singing of birds was come, and the voice of the candidate was heard in the land. Once each four years in the United States, men from the east and the west, the north and the south look in the mirror and see visions. Each one, in his own mind, is standing on the steps of the Capitol, his right hand upraised, repeating the oath of office after the Chief Justice of the United States. It is a long road from the dream to the fulfillment, and many call themselves, but only one is chosen.

In the early spring, it seemed anyone's race. The incumbent, Franklin Delano Roosevelt, was completing his eighth year at 1600 Pennsylvania Avenue. Although there was no constitutional prohibition on a third term, tradition harking back to Washington and Jefferson was against it. When queried on his intentions, Mr. Roosevelt brushed the questions aside in an airy manner that gave no hint whatsoever of his real plans. Probably at that early date he had no idea himself. His careful, noncommittal answers could be read as anyone liked, and the hopefuls were careful to read them as *they* liked.

True to form, the Socialist Party nominated veteran Norman Thomas, while the Communist Party in a rally at Madison Square Garden in New York nominated Earl Browder for President and James William Ford, a Negro, for Vice President. Their platform: oppose all war loans and credit to warring imperialist powers. Stop the sale and shipment of munitions and armaments to belligerents. Resist the militaristic and armaments programs of the Administration and the Congress. Since this program was announced after France

145

was clearly beaten and Germany, it seemed, had no need for munitions, the partiality of this platform is not difficult to discern.

Roosevelt's silence caused some confusion in the Democratic Party. Both James A. Farley, Roosevelt's campaign manager in former years and his Postmaster General, and Cordell Hull, Secretary of State, believed they had the blessing of the Old Man in their bids for the Presidency. Old Cactus Jack, John Nance Garner, Roosevelt's ornery Vice President, made a try in the Illinois primary, and his *lèse majesté* may have cost him a place on the ticket in July. John L. Lewis made a few gestures in the direction of the nomination, largely on a program of hate everyone else. Paul V. McNutt of Indiana was observed to have a hopeful glint in his eye. An opponent referred to him as "merely a Garner in a high hat."

On the Republican side, the field was wider, for no one was held back to see if Mr. Roosevelt would announce his intentions. Cheered by a Gallup Poll in May that gave the Republicans their best chance since 1928, candidates on every side could be seen, hands outstretched, smiles dazzling the eye of the beholder. The leading contender was Thomas E. Dewey of New York. As district attorney of New York City, he had attracted wide fame in his racket-busting endeavors. His tiny mustache provided much fun to his detractors, who promptly hung on him the sobriquet of "Buster" Dewey.

His principal rival for the nomination was Robert Alphonso Taft, "Mr. Republican" from Ohio. Taft was one of those extremely intelligent, hard-working Senators who form the backbone of the Government. Yet he never had the magic quality of capturing the public's affection. A dedicated isolationist, Mr. Taft that spring was comfortably ahead in pledged delegates to the Republican convention, and the political pundits were confidently asserting that he was the one to watch.

Another isolationist candidate, Senator Arthur Vandenberg of Michigan, was counted pretty well out of it as a result of a poor primary showing. He would go to the convention with a few delegates as Michigan's "favorite son" candidate. But—you never could tell. . . .

Other hopefuls, with little chance of success but who might be able to deliver delegates to the highest bidder, were Senator Burton K. Wheeler, Representative Joseph Martin, Charles L. McNary, Arthur H. James, Governor of Pennsylvania, Bruce Barton, Justice Owen J. Roberts, John Bricker of Ohio, and publisher Frank Gannett of Rochester, New York.

Working in the wings, his amateurish campaign giving considerable merriment to the professionals of both parties, was a bumbling political innocent from Indiana. His irresponsible interventionism made him an anathema to most of his party leaders. He was a dangerous man, this Wendell Willkie, who, on May 8, had told the National Institute of Social Sciences meeting in New York that he opposed Hitler and all his works.

I hope that, within the limits of international law and with due regard to keeping ourselves out of the war, America hands a brass knuckle to the democracies so that they can take another sock at the dictatorships.

To me it makes an enormous difference who wins the war. First of all it makes a spiritual difference, but more than that, if England, France, Norway, and other democratic nations pass out, we Americans will meet with the triumphant and truculent dictatorships in another field of battle some day.

The man was a positive menace! A warmonger! And worse, his words were being reported in the foreign press. It might give those Britishers, those Frenchies, a lot of queer ideas!

The fall of Norway Americans contemplated without much emotion. It was an unfamiliar land, and Germany did not seem very menacing from the Land of the Midnight Sun. But, when the Nazis began to roll into the Low Countries, when the old names, half forgotten, half venerated, of World War I began to appear in the headlines, the public began to take notice. Such names as Sedan, Namur, and Liége brought back bitter memories. Pictures of refugees, of dive bombers, of trainloads of soldiers, of the wounded and the dead began to appear in *Life* and in *Look,* in *Time* and in *Newsweek,* in the newsreels and in the pages of *The New York Times, The Philadelphia Inquirer, The Washington Post, The Los Angeles Herald-Examiner, The San Francisco Chronicle, The Bangor Daily News, The Fargo Forum, The Council Bluffs Nonpareil,* in newspapers great and small, from one end of the country to the other. Suddenly the war seemed closer, more dangerous. The ruthless efficiency of the German war machine could be ignored when it was directed against Poland or Denmark or Norway. But now it seemed closer to home. Could it happen here?

There was no rush, no demand that America hasten to declare war. Far from it. People watched the headlines and gazed at the spreading stain of Nazi advances as depicted in newspaper maps, and they were fascinated and they were fearful. But they were a little suspicious, too, suspicious of Britain and France, and suspicious of "That Man in the White House," who seemed more sympathetic than he had any business being of the plight of Holland and Belgium, of France and Britain.

British propaganda of the First World War, which had told of raped nuns, of little children with their hands cut off by ruthless Germans, of old men and women used as targets for bayonet practice, had roused America in 1914, 1915, 1916, and 1917. But later revelation that many of the accounts had been exaggerated had left a bitter taste, and 1940's real atrocities were often taken with a knowing smile and a shake of the head.

Yet the overwhelming majority of the American people sympathized with the Allied cause. The wreck of one more or less democratic state after another shocked and horrified them, yet they seemed afraid that their sentiments might lead them into rash action. And in Mr. Roosevelt, the ordinary citizen recognized his own feelings dangerously amplified. Carried away by his love of Britain and France and their cultures, the President might be impelled to do something rash. All at costs he must be protected from himself, for only in this way could Mr. and Mrs. John Q. Familyman be protected from themselves. A rabid isolationist like John T. Flynn might write, "If anything was needed to demonstrate the utter absurdity of all the dishonest gab in Washington about a foreign invasion, this Norwegian adventure supplies it." But Mr. and Mrs. Familyman did not really believe it. They tended to agree with Wendell Willkie; it made a tremendous difference to them who would win the war. But they didn't know what they could do about it.

One thing they knew must be done, and this was look to the state of America's arms. And any view of the defense establishment of the United States in the summer of 1940 was bound to be gloomy. In 1920 the Congress had established the peacetime Regular Army with a ceiling of 280,000 men. But during depression years, Congress had never appropriated enough money to support even this modest establishment. Career officers had to be dedicated men, for promotions were slow. It was not uncommon for a West Point graduate to find himself only a captain after twenty years of service. Even the most gifted had a troublesome time of it. General George C. Marshall, who was appointed Chief of Staff of the Army on September 1, 1939, found the road rocky. A full colonel on Pershing's staff in World War I, he reverted to captain (although for only one day) in 1920. As a major he put in three years and then had ten years as lieutenant

148

colonel. In 1936 he was promoted to brigadier general, which he remained until his appointment as Chief of Staff. That job automatically carried the rank of full general.

He had little to command when he took over. While Germany was riding roughshod over the armies of Poland, the American Army and Army Air Corps stood at 227,000 men. As Germany drove into Norway, into Holland, into Belgium, the figure had climbed somewhat, and on July 1, 1940, after France had surrendered, it had reached the grand total of 257,730 officers and men. Thus, ten months after the war had broken out in Europe, the Army of the United States was 22,270 men short of its authorized *peacetime* strength.

National Guard units were supposed to beef up the Army in case of war, but most of these were far from ready. Some were completely inefficient, politics-ridden, and more interested in a good time for the boys than in realistic training.

The Navy was in slightly better shape than the Army, for President Roosevelt, as a former Under Secretary of the Navy, had always had a keen interest in that service. The bombing of the *Panay* by the Japanese in 1937 had given excuse for a naval construction program of some proportions, and in January, 1940, Congress authorized a further 11 percent increase, even though Admiral Harold R. Stark, Chief of Naval Operations, had requested 25 percent.

With so few shots in America's locker, it was time to do something about it. Although there remained a certain resistance in Congress to increased expenditures for arms, a poll in *The New York Times* revealed that 83 percent of those questioned desired an increase for the Navy, 90 percent for more air strength for both Army and Navy, and 88 percent desired a larger Army. And the voters were fully aware that such expenditures would mean increased taxes.

Roosevelt needed no urging, no persuasion. Better than anyone he knew that unforeseen demands might be made on America's armed services at any time. Although public attention was fixed on Europe, Mr. Roosevelt remembered Asia and the festering war between Japan and China.

On May 16 he went before Congress to ask for additional appropriations. In characteristic fashion, he neglected to discuss what he was going to say with either Secretary Hull or with Chief of Staff Marshall, so both were listening with some apprehension as he spoke.

The theme of the address was in the sentence, "The American people must recast their thinking about national production." While trying to say that the money spent during his Administration for armaments was wisely spent, he rather spoiled his point by indicating huge deficiencies in military equipment. Using the most optimistic figures he dared on the speed of modern aircraft, he showed how near the United States was to Europe and Africa in terms of flying time. Suddenly the Atlantic Ocean did not seem so wide.

Secretary of War Harry Woodring and General Marshall were shocked out of their wits by Roosevelt's next item. He demanded that the country produce 50,000 aircraft a year. The War Department had been thinking in terms of perhaps 19,000. "My God!" said Marshall. "We don't know whether it will be ten thousand, fifty thousand, or one hundred thousand."

Roosevelt demanded that $1,182,000,000 be added to the appropriations of $1,748,796,578 already in the budget for the Army and Navy. He wanted a special fund of some $200 million to be spent at his discretion on plane production and "to provide for emergencies affecting the national security and defense. . . . Our defenses must be invulnerable, our security absolute. But our defense as it was yesterday, or even as it is today, does not provide security against potential developments and dangers of the future."

Ten days later, the President took his message to the people in a Fireside Chat. He gave a lengthy justification of the Administration's actions in providing additional beef for America's armed forces. Then warming to his subject, he castigated the isolationists and all special interest groups.

"There are some among us who were persuaded by minority groups that we could maintain our physical safety by retiring within our continental boundaries. . . . Obviously a defense policy based on that is merely to invite future attack.

"And, finally, there are a few among us who have deliberately and consciously closed their eyes because they were determined to be opposed to their Government, its foreign policy and every other policy, to be partisan, and to believe that anything that the Government did was wholly wrong. . . .

"The Trojan Horse. The Fifth Column that betrays a nation unprepared for treachery. . . .

"The method is simple. It is, first, a dissemination of discord. A group—not too large—a group that may be sectional or racial or political—is encouraged to exploit its prejudices through false slogans and emotional appeals. The aim of those who deliberately egg on these groups is to create a confusion of counsel, public indecision, political paralysis and, eventually, a state of panic. . . .

"As a result of these new techniques, . . . the unity of the State can be so sapped that its strength is destroyed. . . .

"These dividing forces are undiluted poison."

With nominating conventions only weeks away, it would be strange if the President's remarks were not interpreted politically and equally strange if he did not have some political implications in them. "Damned warmonger!" snapped the Republicans. "Damned fools!" retorted the Democrats. And the President said nothing. He had had his say—for the moment.

Shortly after his Fireside Chat, Mr. Roosevelt took the first tentative step toward organizing the nation for possible war. As well as anyone, he realized that a nation could not run a war industry and a war economy on principles of *laissez faire*. Someone had to give direction, and, preferably, it should be some agency outside the normal channels of Government. First he appointed the Office for Emergency Management, which was supposed to coordinate Government agencies and offices and to give guidance in emergencies. Then, to replace the functions of the moribund National Defense Council, which consisted of six Cabinet officers, he created the National Defense Advisory Commission, responsible for the coordination of America's productive resources. The members were William S. Knudsen, for Industrial Production; Sidney Hillman, for Labor; Edward R. Stettinius, Industrial Materials; Leon Henderson, Price Stabilization; Ralph Budd, Transportation; Chester C. Davis, Farm Products; and Dr. Harriet Elliott, Consumer Interests. The secretary was William H. McReynolds. Later Donald M. Nelson was added as Coordinator of National Defense Purchases.

No one was appointed chairman. Such a procedure should be no surprise to anyone. Mr. Roosevelt simply had all the members report directly to him. It took more time, but it left no doubt about who was boss.

The NDAC began to function quickly, and, like Abraham, it soon became the father of, if not many nations, then agencies, commissions, committees, boards, groups, and administrations. From it are descended all the wartime organizations of vivid memory, such as OPM, OPA, WPB, and the like.

Such an organization was needed, for the regular departments of the Government simply were not geared to work with the speed and imagination the desperate hours required. There is a kind of bureaucrat, well known to all who have to do with him, who protects his career by avoiding decision. It is so much easier to say no. Then his neck is never on the chopping block. Let someone else take the risk. His pension is only a few years off.

Of course, each of the new agencies would inevitably develop its own bureaucrats, but it would be time enough to deal with that problem when it arose. In the meantime, Mr. Roosevelt proposed to give the NDAC its head, let it use people who had no stake in the Government and who were simply motivated by a desire to get the job done so that they could "get the hell out of Government service and have done with Government ways forever!"

That such an organization was needed can be seen from the experience of Robert Stevens, a textile manufacturer, who was nosing around the War and Navy Departments in response to Donald Nelson's instructions to "find out what their requirements are in textiles and figure out a way to meet them."

Stevens investigated the obvious—blankets, uniforms, tarpaulins—and then thought of parachutes. How many parachutes would be needed for the new, vastly increased military air program? With some difficulty, for the information was labeled as "restricted," he discovered that four parachutes per airplane was the average, allowing for reserves. Some bombers carried as many as eleven men, but fighters and pursuit planes had only one man. So four made a reasonable average.

Procurement officers in the Army informed him that they thought they would need perhaps 6,500 parachutes for the year beginning July 1, 1940. The Navy was more modest, asking only for 2,500. Stevens mildly replied that he thought they would need 200,000. The procurement officers shook with laughter and asked how he arrived at such a fantastic number.

"The President," he replied, "has asked for 50,000 warplanes. I just multiplied that by four."

It was difficult for both the Army and the Navy to realize that the lid was coming off. All the training of officers during the peacetime years had taught caution in dealing with budgetary matters. A would-be spendthrift officer soon found himself exiled and saw more realistically minded officers promoted over him. The habit of caution still prevailed.

There was still another complication. Even though money was becoming available, there was little to spend it on, for Amercian industry simply was not turning out enough in the way of war materials, and most of what they were turning out was on contract to

Britain and France. While typewriters and desks, cooking equipment and garbage cans, might be taken from the civilian market, guns, planes, tanks, warships, and radars could not. It would not be long before Marshall, tirelessly building the Army, would ask not to have men sent until their equipment was ready for them.

The wheels began to turn, but infinitely slowly at first. It would have been even slower had it not been for French and British war orders, for the process of tooling up had begun. It would be a long, long time before those responsible for production could be comfortable, and it was not until 1943 that American production really caught up. Even then there were shortages.

On June 10, Mussolini declared war on an already defeated France in order to share the spoils at the victors' banquet. That day the President was scheduled to deliver the graduation address at the University of Virginia in Charlottesville. Mr. Roosevelt was outraged, for he had gone so far as to risk his personal dignity, and more important, the dignity of the United States, in appeals to Mussolini to refrain from the step he had just taken. He used the term "stab in the back," and had it included in the speech he had prepared for the graduation.

Sumner Welles, Under Secretary of State, persuaded him to take it out on the grounds that it would needlessly endanger Italian-American relations.

Riding in the car to Charlottesville, Mr. Roosevelt felt his indignation boiling up all over again. "I was so hot I was grumbling about it," he confessed later. He was still seething as he gripped the lectern.

The speech began mildly enough, generalities about America and America's young men. Then followed a brief summary of American efforts to keep Italy out of the war.

Then he took a deep breath. It was not until December 8, 1941, in his "Day of Infamy" speech, that such scorn was heard again in the voice of Franklin Delano Roosevelt.

On this tenth day of June, 1940, the hand that held the dagger has struck it into the back of its neighbor.

In our American unity, we will pursue two obvious and simultaneous courses: we will extend to the opponents of force the material resources of this nation, and at the same time we will harness and speed up the use of those resources in order that we ourselves in the Americas may have equipment and training equal to the task of any emergency and every defense.

All roads leading to the accomplishment of these objectives must be kept clear of obstructions. We will not slow down or detour. Signs and signals call for speed—full speed ahead.

Here, then, was the program. It was not war. It was not peace. It was distinctly not neutral. It would cause shrieks of anguish from the isolationists, and it would raise false hopes in some of the leaders of nations struggling for their lives. Would it be enough?

It was all the United States had to offer.

CHAPTER SEVEN

The Fall of France

> *He which hath no stomach to this fight,*
> *Let him depart; his passport shall be made,*
> *And crowns for convoy put into his purse:*
> *We would not die in that man's company*
> *That fears his fellowship to die with us.*
>
> Shakespeare, King Henry V

THE fires of Dunkirk's rubble were not yet out when the fatal thrust was driven at the heart of France. Every Frenchman, no matter how far from the scene of the fighting, shivered, his flesh crawling, as in expectation of the lash.

On June 5, 1940, Bock's Army Group B began a drive across the Somme aimed at Rouen, Château Thierry, and Paris. He had about 50 divisions. Three days later, Rundstedt's Army Group A, of 45 divisions, attacked to Bock's east. He would move toward Dijon and Lyons and south. Part would swing against the rear of the Maginot Line. Army Group C, with only 24 divisions, was to cooperate with Rundstedt by attacks on the Maginot Line near Saarbrücken, not so much to take the positions as to keep Weygand from using those troops to reinforce the west.

Against this total of 119 German divisions (plus 23 in strategic reserve) Weygand could dispose only 65 French divisions and one British. Many of these were tied down in the Maginot Line or were facing the Italian border, in expectation that "the jackal would join the feast," as Churchill put it. Weygand tried to form a defense in depth behind the Somme and Aisne Rivers, but there was too little time, too little material, too few men. He had no hope. His men were beaten in mind, body, and spirit.

Every road between Paris and the front held tragedy. The mind rejects as mere useless repetition descriptions of refugees aimlessly moving, ever moving, men and women, young and old, without goal, without hope. Yet, it must be told again, this sorry tale, for it is a part of the story of France, a part of the story of war, more revealing than precise accounts of high strategy, brilliant tactics, dazzling bravery. These are the ones who asked only to be let alone, who have no comprehension of what is happening to them. Their wanderings began long before our time, and they will go on as long as man's folly brings war upon this world.

On the day before the new German drive into France opened, Churchill had addressed Parliament, reporting on the deliverance of Dunkirk. His conclusion, one of his greatest statements, should be recorded here, in spite of its familiarity, because the story cannot be told without it. Also it played its part in the decisions of President Roosevelt and Premier Reynaud.

> Even though large tracts of Europe and many old and famous states have fallen or may fall into the grip of the Gestapo and all the odious apparatus of Nazi rule, we shall not flag or fail. We shall go on to the end, we shall fight in France, we shall fight in the seas and oceans, we shall fight with growing confidence and growing strength in the air, we shall defend our island, whatever the cost may be, we shall fight on the beaches, we shall fight on the landing-grounds, we shall fight in the fields, and in the streets, we shall fight in the hills; we shall never surrender, and even if, which I do not for a moment believe, this island or a large part of it were subjugated and starving, then our Empire beyond the seas, armed and guarded by the British Fleet, would carry on the struggle, until, in God's good time, the New World, with all its power and might, steps forth to the rescue and the liberation of the Old.

When General Spears, still acting as Churchill's liaison officer to Reynaud, read this passage to the French Premier the next day, he saw Reynaud was visibly moved, even though the full flavor was lost by extempore translation into French.

"Your Prime Minister was speaking for France as well as for England," replied Reynaud.

Such unity of purpose was becoming unhappily rare in Paris. The effect of Churchill's words was but fleeting in the room where Spears rendered them. Two other men were present, Weygand and Pétain, and they were voices of despair, although they preferred to call it "realism."

Weygand demanded that the British troops evacuated at Dunkirk be returned to France immediately and thrown into the battle along the Somme. It made no difference that they were exhausted; so were the French. It made no difference that they had lost their heavy weapons in the retreat. Rifles and pistols could be used. He handed Spears a note: "The Commander in Chief is compelled to observe that the appeals to the British Government have been without avail. The German attack against us is being launched without our having received any further help from the British; neither fighters nor fresh divisions."

Despite Weygand's recriminations, Churchill's patience never broke. He was determined to do all he could to save France. But not if it meant losing Britain in the process.

When the French demanded that *all* British aircraft be thrown into the battle at this point, half of them to be based in France, Churchill balked. The RAF would do what it could, but on its own terms. Unity of command was possible for bomber forces, declared the Air Ministry, but under a British officer. It was not practicable to impose unified command on the fighter forces.

If the British seem intransigent in their demands on control of their own aircraft, it resulted from a deep suspicion that the French were not using their own efficiently, that it was easier to blame the British. After the war, the Riom Trials revealed that large numbers of French fighters were available in the central areas of France, that they were never committed to the battle, and were later taken by truck to Unoccupied France.

Churchill was getting fed up with the continual cries for help from France, especially demands such as those of General Vuillemin, French Air Commander in Chief, who demanded much, delivered little from his own air forces, and was ever ready to minimize the British participation. Particularly irritating were such statements as this commenting on British support in the air during the first phase of the battle: "Such reinforcements, although produced tardily and in insufficient numbers at the time of the battle which started on May 10th, proved however to be of value."

What were the facts? The French had about 450 aircraft in the battle zone, the British 400. Most of the French aircraft were lost, including a substantial number assigned to other parts of France. Since the French had a total of 1450 aircraft of all types and some survived until after the armistice, it is reasonable to assume a maximum loss of 1200 French aircraft to all causes. The French records are silent on this point, perhaps because of the confusion of shifting bases and capitals so many times.

During the period from May 10 to June 20, the RAF lost 944 aircraft and 915 men. This then was what Vuillemin referred to as the force "produced tardily and in insufficient numbers."

On the French side, it must be noted that French leaders sincerely believed that if France was lost, all was lost. It was wrong for Britain to withhold *anything*.

Churchill, however, as early as the Dunkirk evacuation, had made up his mind that France might be knocked out of the war and Britain would have to fight alone. Nothing, not even his emotional ties to France, his very real love and admiration of the French people, would allow him to strip Britain of all her defenses.

Given these attitudes on both sides, it was inevitable that Britain and France would be drawing apart day by day. Quarrels, misunderstandings, recriminations were inevitable.

On the evening of June 5, Reynaud reshuffled his cabinet, with the principal aim of excluding Daladier. Paul Baudouin replaced him as Foreign Minister. Newly appointed as Under Secretary for War was General Charles de Gaulle.

On the morning of June 6, Weygand, at a meeting of the War Council, turned on General Spears with all the venom he could muster, and his supply was not inconsiderable. It started with a demand for an explanation of the movements of the British 51st Division, which, Weygand claimed, had fallen back without orders. How could he, Weygand, conduct operations with such as these mingled with his own reliable and disciplined forces? What did General Spears have to say about it? The division's commanding general, Victor Fortune, should be renamed Misfortune!

Naturally Spears had nothing to say, having no connection with operations. He said he would find out.* To soothe matters, Reynaud suggested they would do better to discuss the future than the past. What of air operations?

The still fuming Weygand now exploded. According to Spears, he was literally yelling, in a high-pitched, broken voice. "What is happening in the air now is but a repetition of what happened in the north when the British refused to attack on Arras. I support and

* What Spears found out was that the British 51st Division had fallen back, but so had the French 31st Division on its right. Since they were attacked by three German divisions, the retreat is not surprising. Both Frenchmen and Britons fought well and gallantly.

endorse every word that General Vuillemin has written. Mr. Churchill may think General Vuillemin's demands unreasonable. Perhaps if he saw the condition of our Army he would think we were unreasonable to go on fighting.

"I will not accept," he went on in a scream, "that La Royale Air Force should send out reconnaissances of its own and bomb objectives of its own choosing. I, the Commander in Chief, I alone am the person to select targets!"

Spears broke in. *"Mon général,* we have not got pet objectives of our own, we are trying to strike where it hurts most. Again this is not my business, but have you indicated to Air Marshal Barratt * the targets you have in mind, or the reconnaissances you require?"

Weygand looked blank.

"When did you see the Air Marshal last?" asked Spears. As there was no answer, he demanded incredulously. "Do you mean to say that you have not seen him at all, have never seen him?"

Weygand sheepishly admitted he had never seen Barratt.

Spears offered to arrange a meeting as soon as possible. Weygand was somewhat chastened, but his vituperation went on.

For the first time in the discussions, the possibility of a retreat to French North Africa came up. It was a relatively casual mention, largely in connection with safe training of recruits. But the idea would grow in importance.

The same day Churchill informed Reynaud that a British division was even then preparing to embark for France, and should be there by June 13, that it would be followed by three others, and by a corps commander, General Brooke. Reynaud was delighted. *"Ce brave Churchill! Vraiment c'est un brave type!"* he kept murmuring.

Unfortunately, when the British got there, it would be too late for four divisions—or forty—to reverse the course of the battle.

By the next morning, the Weygand Line from the River Oise to the sea had been breached and the French were falling back. They were retreating in good order, but retreating they were. Two days later, some of the western German elements had reached the Seine.

Then, to the east, the second blow fell, as Rundstedt's Army Group A began its smashing drive, thrusting past Rheims and Verdun. In the lead were Guderian's Panzers, headed for the Swiss border.

That same day, June 9, General de Gaulle arrived in London on an official visit to plead for more British air support in France.

* Air Chief Marshal Sir Arthur S. Barratt, commanding all British air forces in France.

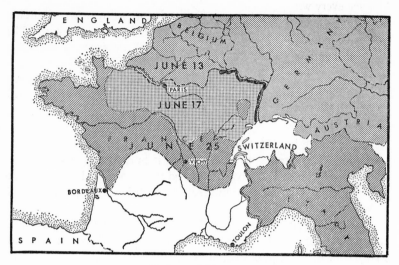

Defeat of France.

Although Churchill does not record this meeting in his memoirs, it made an impression on de Gaulle, as it was the first time the two men had met. "The impression that he made on me," wrote de Gaulle, "strengthened my conviction that under such a fighter Great Britain would certainly not falter. Mr. Churchill struck me as being up to the toughest task, so long as it was a grand one. . . . The very humor with which he flavored his words and gestures and the way in which he used charm at one moment and anger at another made one aware of the degree to which he was master of the terrible game in which he was engaged."

De Gaulle made his official request that British aircraft be assigned to French fields south of the Loire. Mr. Churchill categorically refused, and de Gaulle did not press the point. In that moment it became clear that Mr. Churchill had little or no hope of reversing the tide of battle in Europe. He was already thinking ahead to the next phase of the war. Then Britain would be the target of the blows now falling on France.

On June 10, Weygand formally notified Reynaud that "the events of the past two days of battle make it my duty to warn the Premier that the final breaking of our lines of defense may occur at any moment."

Utterly worn out, his troops were fighting doggedly, without fear or hope. There were no reserves to throw into the fray. They could only fall back, fall back, trading time for distance, until something happened to bring the horror to an end.

Since the military position was obviously hopeless, there remained only bitter alternatives. One was to try to establish a redoubt in Brittany. This course would abandon all the rest of France to the Germans. In any case, Weygand considered it harebrained from a military point of view. The other choice was yet more bitter: to abandon all of France to the occupying Nazis and fight on from North Africa and the colonies beyond the seas.

Paul Baudouin, the new Foreign Minister, spoke the word hidden in the back of everyone's mind—surrender. "The situation is deteriorating day by day," he added.

"If the situation is deteriorating, it is because we are allowing it to deteriorate," declared de Gaulle.

Reynaud refused to think of an armistice or surrender. Either alternative was better. In Brittany they could be reinforced by the troops Britain was even now sending.

Little time remained for consideration. Onrushing events gave no opportunity for committee meetings, calm deliberation, parliamentary procedures. As the rumble of tanks and the roar of guns grew closer, Reynaud and his officials had to make a heartbreaking decision. They must leave Paris, abandon the capital to the invaders. Soon the swastika would fly from the Eiffel Tower. Soon the Champs Elysées would ring to the hobnailed boots of goose-stepping Nazis.

Or would Paris be destroyed? Would the heritage of centuries be lost forever?

In face of danger from the north, there was little time to heed a new threat from the south. At this juncture, Italy's declaration of war was but one more irritation. It was like a mosquito bite on the leg while your arms were being slowly mangled.

Before the Government left Paris for Tours, Reynaud directed a desperate appeal to President Roosevelt.

We shall fight in front of Paris; we shall fight behind Paris; * we shall ensconce ourselves in one of our provinces and, if we are driven out of it, we shall go to North Africa and, if need be, to our American possessions . . . I beseech you to declare publicly that the United States

* Reynaud's words sound like a paraphrase of Churchill's "We shall fight on the beaches" speech. Actually, the allusion is to a statement of Clemenceau in World War I, "Fight outside Paris, inside Paris, behind Paris." The words "inside Paris" were carefully omitted this time.

will give the Allies aid and material support by all means short of an expeditionary force. . . .

Before midnight the limousines of the ministers of state were on their way. Leaving Paris through the Porte de Châtillon, overtaking and passing cars of Parisians who had started earlier, they went on through Orléans to Tours, which they reached the following morning. However, Weygand set up his headquarters in Briare, southeast of Orléans, and it was there that circumstances summoned the French Premier.

Determined to stiffen French resistance, Churchill invited himself to a meeting of the War Council at Briare, arriving at the airport late that afternoon. He was met by a French colonel who, as Spears put it, "might have been welcoming poor relations at a funeral reception." Other members of Churchill's party bundled in other cars and set off for Le Château de Muguet and a council of despair which would lead to no meeting of minds. General Weygand was in his normal form, but perhaps even more vituperative than usual of Britain and all her works. So often had he sounded this theme that perhaps Churchill took too little heed of his solid truths on the military situation. If, argued Churchill, France could stabilize a front and hold out till the spring of 1941, then Britain would have 20 to 25 divisions to throw into the fray. By that time, the United States might be ready to take an active part. Warming to his subject, the Prime Minister urged resolution, courage, fortitude. The whole problem was to hold out until the vast potential strength of the Allies could be gathered and hurled at Germany.

"I cannot guarantee that our troops will hold out for another hour," replied Weygand coldly. "If the last line of defense is broken, I cannot see how a coordinated defense on French territory will be possible."

It was clear that Weygand had nothing left. No reserves, no suggestions, no ideas. He was a defeated man. Churchill suddenly recognized this fact and ignored the French Commander in Chief for the rest of the conference.

But Weygand was not to be ignored. He returned to his theme. He demanded that the Government seek an armistice. Furiously Reynaud reminded him that the question of an armistice was the responsibility of the Government and of the Government alone. Unabashed, Weygand went on. Britain had not borne her share. She must throw in the entire RAF. They must send more troops, more supplies, more machines, more everything.

"Here," he shouted, "is the decisive point! Now is the decisive moment! It is therefore wrong to keep *any* squadrons back in England."

"This is not the decisive point," replied Churchill calmly, "and this is not the decisive moment. That moment will come when Hitler hurls his Luftwaffe against Great Britain. If we can keep command of the air, and if we can keep the seas open, as we shall certainly keep them open, we will win it all back for you."

"If France is lost," Weygand retorted, "then all is lost. What," he continued, "would Britain do if France surrendered, releasing a hundred German divisions to use against Britain?"

Broadly speaking, replied Churchill, he proposed to drown as many as possible on the way across the Channel and to knock the others on the head as they crawled ashore.

Weygand shrugged impatiently. From that day on, he never ceased in his efforts to force the Government into an armistice. Still he kept on demanding more and more from Britain. Was he determined to drag Britain down in the ruins of France? Could he not bear the thought that another might succeed where he had failed?

The conference adjourned for the night, Churchill occupying quarters in the château. The next morning, as the French officers were enjoying their *café au lait* and their *croissants* in the dining room, an apparition, looking, as they said, like an angry Japanese genie, appeared in a long, voluminous, red silk kimono, over flowing white pajamas, white disheveled hair crowning an angry face. *"Uh ay ma bain?"* demanded the apparition furiously. Even in disaster Mr. Churchill demanded his morning bath. *Fiat lavatium, ruat coelum!*

After he had bathed, the Prime Minister learned from Air Marshal Barratt an ugly story. So fearful were the French of reprisals from Italy that General Vuillemin had prevented British bombers flown to the south of France the night before from taking off for an attack on Genoa and the industrial centers of northern Italy. Vuillemin had caused trucks, wagons, and cars to be driven out onto the runways to keep the planes from taking off. Churchill was outraged, but he decided to say nothing about it to Reynaud and Weygand. It was too late, and recriminations would not help. The bombers returned to England.

The discussion that morning added little, for it seemed all had been said. Again the French demanded aircraft, and again Churchill refused to denude the defenses of the British Isles.

Reynaud summed up the French position. Unless a miracle happened, France was lost. There was still the Brittany redoubt. There were still the colonies, and France might continue to fight from overseas. "Our only hope," he concluded, "is in the industrial resources of the United States."

"We are in the closest touch with the United States," replied Churchill, "and will continue to impress on their Government the gravity of the situation and the urgency of our needs, but there is a matter the importance of which overshadows all others, and which I must put to you. Should there be a fundamental change in the situation, I must request you, before coming to a final decision which may govern French action in the second phase of the war, to let the British Government know at once. They will come over immediately to meet the French Government at any convenient place which you choose to indicate to discuss the new circumstances with you."

Stripped of its politeness, this statement was a fair warning, a reminder that the French Government had entered into a solemn agreement that neither Britain nor France would conclude an armistice or peace without the consent of the other. Churchill's statement was a formal request from one government to another. And it foreshadowed the ominous rift between the two nations that lay ahead.

As the conference concluded, Churchill drew the French naval Commander in Chief aside. "Darlan," he said, "you must never let them get the French fleet."

"Never," promised Darlan.

On the other side of the Atlantic, President Roosevelt felt the bitter hopelessness of France. There was so little he could do. The Neutrality Laws severely limited the contributions that America could make to the Allies, and the constantly increasing demands of America's defense buildup made it even more difficult to consider diverting materials from America's own needs on the unlikely chance that they could stem the tide in Europe.

There was grave danger, Mr. Roosevelt knew, that if he sent arms and munitions abroad, he might inadvertently be betraying his own country. Many of his advisers assured him that Britain and France would soon be beaten, and any arms sent over would merely fall into the hands of the Germans and might well be used against the United States. As clearly as anyone, the President realized that the French could not hold out in France, but he did hope he could sustain Premier Reynaud in his determination to fight on from North Africa. One of the ways in which France could still make a vital contribution to the war was with her navy. Let the ships flying the *tricouleur* join those flying the White Ensign.

It was a bitter moment for Mr. Roosevelt. He could offer only words. Reynaud and France needed so much more.

Your message of June 10th [cabled Mr. Roosevelt] has moved me very deeply. As I have already stated to you and to Mr. Churchill, this Government is doing everything in its power to make available to the Allied Governments the material they so urgently require, and our efforts to do still more are being redoubled. This is so because of our faith in and our support of the ideals for which the Allies are fighting.

The magnificent resistance of the French and British Armies has profoundly impressed the American people.

I am, personally, particularly impressed by your declaration that France will continue to fight on behalf of Democracy, even if it means slow withdrawal, even to North Africa and the Atlantic and other oceans; also to remember that vital materials from the outside world are necessary to maintain all armies.

I am also greatly heartened by what Prime Minister Churchill said a few days ago about the continued resistance of the British Empire, and that determination would seem to apply equally to the great French Empire all over the world. Naval power in world affairs still carries the lessons of history, as Admiral Darlan well knows.

When Roosevelt's message arrived in France, it merely confirmed the armistice party in their views. Weygand now had a powerful ally. The old Marshal, the "Hero of Verdun," the venerable Pétain, had prepared a paper on the necessity of surrender, but he had not yet presented it to Reynaud. According to the French Premier, he was still ashamed to hand it to him. No man was held in such awe by the French people as Pétain, but the people did not realize that only the shell remained. According to Georges Mandel, Minister of the Interior, Pétain had given up. He lived in the past, a walking monument. He believed that only soldiers could be relied on in the final moments. He preferred to trust the "honor of soldiers," even German ones, to the politicians of France or Great Britain.

In a conversation with Spears, Mandel said, *"C'est un Conquistador,"* of Pétain. But he punned it into, *"C'est un comte qui s'adore."*

As the British leaders left for London, Premier Reynaud was left behind to face a fight for his political survival. Realizing that Reynaud was unyielding in his determination to oppose the Germans to the last, the defeatists knew there could be no armistice as long as he was Premier. He must go.

Moves were already underway to sap his authority. Cliques and cabals spread. In corners and in rooms not being used for anything else, men gathered and talked and schemed and plotted. The gravest affront to Reynaud's authority was the decision made by Weygand on June 11 to declare Paris an open city. He did not bother to mention this fact during the meeting of the War Council.

Scarcely had the wheels of Churchill's Flamingo touched down at the airport in London than the pressures began to rise for him to return to France, for one last appeal. He put in an evening at Whitehall and Downing Street, and then the next morning, June 13, was off again for Tours.

This time when the British leaders arrived, the situation was so confused that no one was on hand to meet their plane. Churchill commandeered a car, and the party drove toward Tours looking for the French leader. Finally, overcome by the pangs of hunger, they found a shuttered café and persuaded the proprietor to open it for them. The grumbling innkeeper provided cold chicken, bread, cheese, and Vouvray wine. It was better than nothing.

While they were eating, the British found their meal spoiled by the arrival of Foreign Minister Baudouin, whose soft, silky hopelessness grated on Churchill's nerves. Churchill was furious because he had learned from Spears that Baudouin was spreading the lie that Churchill had agreed to France seeking an armistice if the United States did not enter the war.

It was in no pleasant mood that Churchill and his party accompanied Baudouin to the Préfecture in Tours. He shrugged it off, however, when Reynaud entered the room, and there, for the last time, Mr. Churchill and M. Reynaud met face to face. This time Churchill was full of sympathy for France in her plight. To the defeatism around him, even that in the voice and words of the French Premier, Churchill had but one answer. England would fight on. When Reynaud hinted at a possible release from the pledge of no single surrender of March 28, Churchill replied firmly. "Under no circumstances will Great Britain waste time in reproaches and recriminations. But that is a very different matter from becoming a consenting party to a peace made in contravention of the agreement so recently concluded."

Reynaud believed that he might be able to persuade his ministers to fight on from overseas if need be, if he could make President Roosevelt's telegram public, so a request went off to Washington for permission.

Churchill took up his theme again. England would never surrender.

Her major weapon at this time was her navy and the blockade it imposed on Germany. If France were occupied by the Germans, she would be blockaded, too, in spite of all the suffering that measure would bring to France. He paused to let that idea sink in. It should have had more effect than it did on his listeners, but they were landsmen and knew little of the importance of sea trade in the life of France, nor could they envision what blockade would mean. France cannot feed herself, and they would have to rely on their conquerors for the necessities of life. Or they would sink to a starvation level of subsistence.

But Baudouin, Weygand, Pétain, and the rest were uncomprehending. In any case, if France fell, what chance was left for England? The blockade would be over long before France would feel its effects.

"We shall listen to no peace proposals emanating from Hitler," declared Churchill; "to do so would merely be to court another Munich followed by another occupation of Prague.

"The war will continue, and it can but end in our destruction or our victory."

Before the conference adjourned, Churchill requested that Reynaud deliver to the British some 400 captured German Luftwaffe pilots, so that if France surrendered, these particular pilots would be unable to join in the battle against Britain. Reynaud readily agreed. Yet in the confusion of the next few days, his orders were either forgotten or ignored.

"We had to shoot them down a second time in the Battle of Britain," reported Churchill wryly.

The British leaders thereupon left the France they were not to see again for four long years of war. After speeding their guests on their way, the French Council of Ministers met in the late afternoon. Scarcely had the call to order taken place than Weygand seized the floor. In the most insulting manner he shouted that the ministers would be mad to consider carrying on the war in Brittany, or in North Africa, or anywhere else. It would be desertion, he said, for the ministers to go to North Africa. Let them emulate the Roman Senate, which continued its deliberations as the barbarians entered Rome. How would the ordinary Frenchman accept the sacrifices, suffering, privations demanded of him, when he saw his ministers flee to the sanctuary of North Africa? Let no one suggest that it was yet a greater sacrifice for the ministers to leave the soil of the Motherland. No one would believe it, not for a moment. The ordinary Frenchman would feel that his ministers were merely perpetuating the slaughter, the bombing, the burning, and the suffering of the people, while they themselves had taken good care to seek sanctuary in North Africa or elsewhere.

And suppose that they could find it in their consciences to leave the Motherland in her hour of trial. What welcome would they receive in the colonies? People prefer to receive victors, not the vanquished. Yet even suppose they did receive a warm welcome. What authority could they exercise in the Motherland? How long would they be abroad? How long would it take America to build the planes and the tanks to reconquer France? How would this be done? Shall we bomb our own towns? Our fellow countrymen? It is an absurd and hateful program. Your Commander in Chief will not follow it. He will not leave the soil of France even if he is put in irons.

Then, losing all control, Weygand stormed out of the room shouting, "They sit with their backsides in their armchairs, and they don't give a damn that the French Army is in the process of being massacred!"

Here was the outright challenge. Here was direct insubordination and insolence. Weygand was not a minister of state. He was Commander in Chief of the Army. The issue was clear: were the armed forces the masters or the servants of the state? There could be but one answer. If Reynaud was to retain his position as head of Government, he must deal drastically with this insubordination. The only thing that he could do would be to relieve Weygand of his command.

Instead, Reynaud temporized. He hesitated to take so drastic a step. Weygand had held his post only a little over three weeks. He had been called upon as a savior, when all seemed lost, to redeem the Battle of France. To remove him now might destroy any remaining confidence the French had in their military and political leaders.

Instead of relieving Weygand, Reynaud refused to permit him to attend any further meetings of the Council of Ministers. This was merely a half-measure, and did nothing to strengthen Reynaud's position or to weaken that of the opposition.

After Weygand's departure, Marshal Pétain took the floor and repeated the arguments of the Commander in Chief. He, Pétain, would under no circumstances leave France for North Africa. Let there be an armistice, he demanded, in spite of the agreement of March 28 with Britain; it was not the British whose citizens were dying by the thousands under the German guns.

"No," declared Reynaud. "This is contrary to the honor of France!"

Following the close of their deliberations, Reynaud took his case to the people of France. Yet the people of France could only look to their leaders. Their leaders were divided; those who counseled resolution had little power; those who counseled surrender gained power day by day.

Meanwhile the French Government had had to move once again: this time to Bordeaux, where they arrived on the evening of June 14th. In these new surroundings, the advocates of surrender, headed by Pétain, Weygand, and the anglophobic, German-sympathizing Pierre Laval, were able to perfect their arrangements. Their advance guard took care of arranging office space and communications. Under their influence, the bewildered French civil servants followed their orders. The result was, Reynaud declares in his memoirs, that his enemies managed to place a tap on his private telephone line, so that all of his communications, political discussions, instructions to his supporters, and even his conversations with London, were overheard by his opponents.

By this time the military situation had deteriorated to such an extent that any hope of establishing a redoubt in Brittany was gone. The British forces already there, commanded by General Sir Alan Brooke, found their position untenable, and Brooke recommended to Churchill immediate evacuation. Churchill agreed, and Brooke formally notified his French superiors that he was removing his troops without delay. To Churchill this seemed a vitally necessary act to preserve those men to fight again another day. To Pétain, Weygand, and their supporters, it was another betrayal by Perfidious Albion.

Barred from the deliberations of the Council of Ministers, Weygand sought an interview with the Premier. He again demanded an armistice. Reynaud recognized by this time that nothing further could be done in France. Any further resistance must come from North Africa. He therefore ordered Weygand to arrange a surrender in the field.

This would be a far different situation than an armistice sought by the French Government. Surrender in the field means only that the armed forces under a particular commander will lay down their arms. It is not binding upon a government. The Government could continue the fight from its colonies overseas, could raise another army, could do all in its power to continue resistance. This was the course which the Norwegians, the Poles, and the Dutch had employed, while their Governments in Exile waited in London, doing what they could to speed the day of victory.

Weygand angrily and vehemently refused to obey this order. He would not, he said, assume such a responsibility. Reynaud offered to give him a written order directing surrender in the field. Again Weygand refused.

"The honor of the Army," he declared, "is at stake!"

"What," retorted Reynaud, "of the honor of France?"

Once again Reynaud should have relieved Weygand. Once again he hesitated. Instead, he attempted to persuade the General through an intermediary to accept the idea of surrender in the field. He could have chosen no worse intermediary, for he selected Marshal Pétain. In view of Pétain's statements during the last few days, it seems incomprehensible that Reynaud should have chosen him. Yet Pétain was the only man whose judgment on such a matter Weygand would have accepted; perhaps Reynaud had no other choice.

At any rate, Pétain agreed to undertake the assignment. Fifteen minutes later he returned to Reynaud. Pétain had not convinced the Commander in Chief; the Commander in Chief had convinced him.

From that moment Reynaud's position grew weaker hour by hour.

In a meeting of the Council of Ministers, Camille Chautemps, Vice President of the Council, proposed that the ministers inquire what terms the Germans would demand for an armistice. He did not, he said, believe that these terms would prove to be acceptable. At the same time he felt that the ministers ought to ask the Germans what their demands would be. If they should prove impossible, the French ministers could then continue the war from Algeria or French Morocco with clear consciences.

This deceptively reasonable proposal won immediate support from most of the ministers, but not from Reynaud and his few stalwarts. Reynaud was not deceived for an instant. When the troops in the field learn that their government is asking for armistice terms, the will to fight quickly goes out of them. No soldier is anxious to be killed at any time; he regards it the height of stupidity to risk his life when the next few days will probably see a cease-fire. Chautemps's proposal, then, was nothing more than a parliamentary maneuver to weaken Reynaud's position. Reynaud's opposition was in vain; the Council of Ministers voted overwhelmingly in favor of Chautemps's proposal.

Before the French could in conscience approach the Germans concerning such an armistice, they were honor bound to seek British agreement and release from their obligations under the agreement of March 28th. Accordingly they sent a message to London outlining the proposition.

Not awaiting a British answer, meanwhile, the defeatist party was engaged in lively backstage maneuvering to unseat Premier Reynaud, in their eyes the chief stumbling block to an armistice and its "peace with honor." Having already won to their camp the valuable Weygand, their next obvious target was Admiral Jean Xavier François Darlan, the head of the French Navy, and the most powerful officer the Navy had seen for generations.

Darlan had been a highly energetic leader, whose balanced tours of sea and shore duty had won for him a thorough knowledge of his profession and of the political world. From 1925 until the outbreak of war, Darlan had been instrumental in building the Navy into a modern, well-balanced, and well-equipped force, manned by tough, well-trained fighting men. Yet Darlan's greatest success was his greatest weakness, for his actions indicate that Darlan thought that *he* was the Navy. "I command . . . I order . . . I promise . . ."—these phrases leap from his dispatches to the fleet, his communications with the Cabinet ministers. He was highly intelligent, highly devoted to the Navy and to France, highly ambitious, highly conceited, and highly dangerous.

From the beginning of the catastrophe, Darlan had been an advocate of resistance, and he had promised that the French fleet would fight to the end. On June 3rd he had said, "If one day they ask for an armistice, I shall finish my career with a splendid act of disobedience and leave with the fleet." Ten days later in a secret note to the Council of Ministers, Darlan wrote: "If we are driven into a corner over an armistice, I wish to be informed ahead of time, so that I may give orders to the fleet, which ought not to be included in an armistice and which, in any case, I refuse to surrender." As late as the morning of June 15th, Darlan had drawn Édouard Herriot aside and inquired, "Is it true that those b——'s Pétain and Weygand want to ask for an armistice? If that is so, I tell you that I am going to get the hell out with the fleet!" *

But Darlan's position was not as adamant as it seemed. Every man has his price, they say, and the defeatist party found Darlan's. These men were determined to overturn Reynaud's ministry and to replace it with one under Pétain. Obviously, before they could strike, they needed to have a tentative government organized ahead of time that could immediately pick up the reins of office. That very afternoon, Pétain sought out Darlan and offered him the post of Minister of

* "Est-il vrai que ces . . . de Pétain et Weygand veulent demander l'armistice? S'il en est ainsi, je vous previens que je f . . . le camp avec la flotte." Albert Kammerer, *La Passion de la Flotte Français* (Paris, 1951), p. 67.

171

Marine (roughly equivalent to the American Secretary of the Navy or the British First Lord of the Admiralty).

From that moment Darlan changed. No longer did he talk of sending the fleet to Britain or to the West Indies. No longer did he talk of getting the hell out with the fleet. Except for the new battleship *Richelieu,* which was moved to Dakar, and the unfinished battleship *Jean Bart,* which sailed to Casablanca, the French fleet remained where it was.

The next day, Sunday, June 16, events moved rapidly toward a climax. During the morning, Premier Reynaud busied himself with preparations for the move to North Africa. Breaking off only to attend the meeting of the Council of Ministers, Reynaud encountered his most serious parliamentary challenge to date. Pétain tendered his resignation. He demanded an immediate armistice. "The daily deliberations of the Government," he wrote in his letter of resignation, "seem to me to be purely delaying maneuvers bordering on the final abdication of French sovereignty." To this beaten man it seemed that French sovereignty could better be preserved by surrendering to Germany, rather than by fighting on with the British.

Pétain was shamed out of his maneuver by being reminded that the French had already set the machinery in motion for seeking an armistice by their request for a release from Great Britain. In all decency, they must allow the British time to answer.

Reynaud had pinned his hopes upon American aid. It is possible that even in his wildest dreams he had permitted himself to believe, as he had certainly prayed, that America would intervene militarily in the struggle against the German tyranny. That afternoon a message from President Roosevelt shattered these hopes.

The President, after expressing admiration for the resplendent courage with which the French armies were resisting the invaders on French soil, noted that American efforts to provide aircraft, artillery, and munitions of all kinds were being redoubled. "I believe," he wrote, "it is possible to say that every week that goes by will see additional material on its way to the Allied nations." The President went on to say that the United States Government would not recognize any attempts on the part of the Germans to infringe upon the independence and territorial sovereignty of France.

At the end of the cable came the crushing blow for Reynaud. "I know that you will understand," cabled Roosevelt, "that these statements carry with them no implication of military commitments. Only Congress can make such commitments."

If Mr. Roosevelt's cable brought small comfort to Premier Reynaud, it greatly strengthened the hands of his enemies, slamming the door as it did on any possibility of active American intervention. The hope of both Reynaud and Churchill had been that the disastrous events in the Low Countries and in France would swing American public opinion toward intervention, so that Congress must perforce declare war.

Now this hope was gone.

The second important message Reynaud received that day came from London. It outlined the conditions under which Britain would agree to release France from her promise not to seek a separate peace. British Ambassador Sir Ronald Campbell presented him with the following note:

Foreign Office to Sir R. Campbell:
Please give M. Reynaud the following message, which has been approved by the Cabinet:
Mr. Churchill to M. Reynaud. 16 June 1940, 12:35 P.M. Our agreement forbidding separate negotiations, whether for armistice or peace, was made with the French Republic, and not with any particular French administration or statesman. It therefore involves the honour of France. Nevertheless, *provided, but only provided, that the French Fleet is sailed forthwith for British harbours pending negotiations,* His Majesty's Government give their full consent to an inquiry by the French Government to ascertain the terms of an armistice for France. His Majesty's Government, being resolved to continue the war, wholly exclude themselves from all part in the above-mentioned inquiry concerning an armistice.

This note was followed by a second, equally direct, equally uncompromising:

Foreign Office to Sir. R. Campbell:
You should inform M. Reynaud as follows:
We expect to be consulted as soon as any armistice terms are received. This is necessary not merely in virtue of the treaty forbidding separate peace or armistice, but also in view of vital consequences of any armistice to ourselves, having regard especially to the fact that British troops are fighting with French Army. You should impress on French Government that in stipulating for removal of French Fleet to British ports we have in mind French interests as well as our own, and are convinced that it will strengthen the hands of the French Government in any armistice discussions if they can show that the French Navy is out of reach of the German forces. As regards the French

Air Force, we assume that every effort will be made to fly it to North Africa, unless indeed the French Government would prefer to send it to this country. We count on the French Government doing all they can both before and during any armistice discussions to extricate the Polish, Belgian, and Czech troops at present in France, and to send them to North Africa. Arrangements are being made to receive Polish and Belgian Governments in this country.

Reynaud would not agree to sending the French fleet to Britain. Since he had no intention of seeking an armistice, he intended to send it to North Africa, where it could continue the fight against the Germans and the Italians. The point soon became academic, however, because within the hour Sir Ronald requested the return of the two telegrams. The British were withdrawing the permission they had given.

The British turnabout was not a case of vacillation; rather it resulted from one last attempt to save the situation with a dramatically imaginative proposal—union between the Republic of France and the United Kingdom.

The idea had been born in London where several Frenchmen and Britons had conceived the plan as the most impressive statement possible of the solidarity of the Allies. After initial reluctance, Churchill accepted the proposal and made it his own. The energetic young General Charles de Gaulle telephoned Reynaud the outline of the proposal.

The Premier seized upon the idea wholeheartedly, for it offered the last chance of keeping France in the war. He told de Gaulle that he must have the text of the proposal before the meeting of the Council of Ministers that afternoon. Otherwise he feared the Council would take some drastic action and so make any consideration of the union impossible.

At 4 o'clock de Gaulle called back. Without a dissenting voice the British War Cabinet had approved the union. All afternoon men had worked on the language of the proposal, Churchill adding his inimitable spirit and style to the draft. At last all was ready, and de Gaulle's voice spanned the miles to Bordeaux, where Reynaud scribbled the words as fast as he could with the stub of a pencil.

DECLARATION OF UNION

At this most fateful moment in the history of the modern world, the Governments of the United Kingdom and the French Republic make this declaration of indissoluble union and unyielding resolution in their common defence of justice and freedom against subjection to a system which reduces mankind to a life of robots and slaves.

The two Governments declare that France and Great Britain shall no longer be two nations, but one Franco-British Union.

The constitution of the Union will provide for joint organs of defence, financial, and economic policies.

Every citizen of France will enjoy immediately citizenship of Great Britain; every British subject will become a citizen of France.

Both countries will share responsibility for the repair of the devastation of war, wherever it occurs in their territories, and the resources of both shall be equally, and as one, applied to that purpose.

During the war there shall be a single War Cabinet, and all the forces of Britain and France, whether on land, sea, or in the air, will be placed under its direction. It will govern from wherever it best can. The two Parliaments will be formally associated. The Nations of the British Empire are already forming new armies. France will keep her available forces in the field, on sea, and in the air. The Union appeals to the United States to fortify the economic resources of the Allies, and to bring her powerful material aid to the common cause.

The Union will concentrate its whole energy against the power of the enemy, no matter where the battle may be.

And thus we shall conquer.

De Gaulle concluded by saying that Reynaud would probably be chosen to preside over the War Cabinet of the Union.

Greatly moved by the proposition, and pinning all his hopes on its capturing the imagination of the French ministers, as it had those of the British, Reynaud prepared to preside at the vital meeting of the Council. After the preliminaries were out of the way, Reynaud read the text of the Declaration of Union and stated that he proposed to meet with Churchill the following day to work out details. Then he waited expectantly for an answer.

There was none.

The Pétainists, thanks to their tap on the Premier's telephone, knew as much about the British offer as Reynaud did himself. Since they had first heard of the idea in de Gaulle's earlier telephone call, they had set about to discredit it. Their labors had borne such fruit that even Reynaud's supporters sat mute during the session.

Not so the Pétainists.

It would reduce France to the status of a Dominion, shouted one. It was a mere scheme to seize the French colonies. Since Britain herself would soon be defeated, said Pétain, it would be "fusion with a corpse." "Better be a Nazi province," blustered another; "at least we know what that means."

"I prefer," retorted Reynaud, "to collaborate with my allies rather than with my enemies!"

The proposal was dead. There was no point in further discussion. Chautemps returned to the armistice proposal. Reynaud reminded him stiffly that the British had withdrawn their agreement. The debate turned into a quarrel. The Premier adjourned the session abruptly to prevent an open rupture.

Reynaud then made his supreme gamble. He immediately sought out President Lebrun and tendered his resignation. He hoped he would be told to form a new government which he could staff with men of stout heart, men who favored carrying on the struggle to the end. But the Pétainists had thought of that maneuver. They threatened Lebrun with disaster, chaos, and civil war unless France capitulated.

Lebrun told Reynaud that France would seek an armistice.

"If you want such a policy carried out," responded Reynaud stoutly, "go and ask Marshal Pétain."

Both Presidents of the Chambers supported Reynaud's position, but Lebrun had made up his mind. He sent for Marshal Pétain.

The old Marshal was ready for the summons. He had his officials all selected. Conspicuously absent from his list were the names of Paul Reynaud and any of the ministers who had supported him. Chautemps, the author of the armistice proposals, was again Vice President of the Council; Weygand, Minister of National Defense; and Darlan, Minister of Marine.

At 11 o'clock the same night, the reconstituted Council of Ministers voted to ask for an armistice. No one mentioned the agreement with Britain. No one mentioned the fleet.

Just after midnight, a note of inquiry addressed to the Germans was handed to the Spanish ambassador for forwarding to Berlin. The next morning a similar note was given to the Papal Nuncio to be delivered to Rome.*

The French fleet was still in France. Since it was obvious to Churchill that France was going to sue for an armistice, he ordered Sir Ronald Campbell to redeliver the British note of acquiescence which contained the British demand for the French fleet. The French paid no attention. The note had been canceled, they argued. Therefore the provisions concerning the fleet did not arise. They conven-

---

* Hitler refused the Pope as intermediary between France and Italy, so the French request to Rome also had to go through Spain.

iently disregarded the fact that its cancellation also canceled British acquiescence to France's seeking an armistice at all!

The choice of the word "canceled" was an unfortunate one, for it led to a dubious situation when the note was reinstated. "Suspended" might have been a happier choice of word from the British point of view. Since the note agreeing to a French armistice had been officially received only after the request had in fact been made, the French could consider themselves under no obligation to accede to any conditions the British imposed, granting of course that they had not kept the terms of the agreement of March 28.

That morning, June 17, Churchill sent a message to Pétain, Lebrun, Weygand, and Darlan.

> I wish to repeat to you my profound conviction that the illustrious Marshal Pétain and the famous General Weygand, our comrades in two great wars against the Germans, will not injure their ally by delivering over to the enemy the fine French Fleet. Such an act would scarify their names for a thousand years of history. Yet this result may easily come by frittering away the few precious hours when the Fleet can be sailed to safety in British or American ports, carrying with it the hope of the future and the honour of France.

To reinforce this message, Churchill sent Sir Dudley Pound, the First Sea Lord, Mr. A. V. Alexander, First Lord of the Admiralty, and Lord Lloyd, Secretary of State for the Colonies, to Bordeaux to confer with Admiral Darlan and other French leaders. Darlan received them on the afternoon of June 18. Clearly and forcibly the British party explained the mortal peril in which Britain would be placed if the Germans gained control of the French ships. Darlan repeated his previous promise that under no circumstances would the fleet be delivered to the Germans. He would take all possible precautions to keep the Germans from seizing it by force. He promised that the ships would be gathered and demobilized in ports not occupied by the Germans, and that if they were threatened by the Germans or Italians, they would be scuttled. All this Darlan pledged on his word of honor.

The British still believed that the French fleet should be sailed to British waters, but it was probably already too late for such an action. Since the French had already requested armistice terms, the Germans would have interpreted the move as evidence of bad faith. Darlan knew this full well, for he said as much in a letter to Churchill written only a few weeks before his death at the hand of an assassin in December, 1942. "If I did not consent to have the French ships sailed to British ports, it was because I knew that that decision would have been followed by the occupation of all of Metropolitan France and that of North Africa." This statement is to some extent hindsight, for Darlan did not know the German armistice terms at the time of his conversation with the British leaders.

It would be a mistake to assume that the new Pétain government was anxious to ally itself with Germany. Probably Laval was the only important French politician who actively sought full partnership. Chautemps sincerely believed that it would do no harm to ask for terms, and he and many others felt that the terms would be so harsh that no man of honor could accept them. Thus it would, as Reynaud admitted to the American Ambassador, A. J. Drexel Biddle, free the hands of the French. "Only by such a move," said Reynaud, "could he show the French people, who have been kept in utter ignorance of the real gravity of the military situation, the severity of the German terms, and justify a flight of the Government to Africa or to England."

The French were understandably concerned over how their overtures to the Germans would be interpreted on the other side of the Atlantic. Baudouin, the Minister of Foreign Affairs, sent Roosevelt a telegram explaining their position.

> The French Government is resolved not to yield to any condition contrary to national honor, dignity, or independence. If, in reply to the overtures made to Germany, unacceptable demands should be returned, it is with fierce resolution that the whole country, preferring to suffer what it could not accept, would continue the struggle on bases in the French Empire until the day when the common effort of all free peoples would lead to its liberation.

Most Frenchmen sincerely believed that having defeated France, Germany had won the war. It was merely a case of accommodating one's self to live in the world that Germany had created by the force of arms. While the British might protest their determination to continue the fight, the French, while wishing them well, could not bring themselves to believe that Britain could hold out where they had failed. Had not the great Weygand said, "Within three weeks, Britain will have her neck wrung like a chicken"?

While the French were willing within reason to accommodate themselves to Britain's desires, it was not reasonable to abandon Metropolitan France to the invader. It was not reasonable to turn their fleet over to Britain so the British could use it as a pawn in their own peace negotiations, which could obviously not be long delayed. The French were willing to let Britain have the things which could no longer benefit France. Thus Weygand ordered that French contracts for aircraft being built in the United States should be transferred to the British. The planes later did prove of great use to the RAF.

The question of the French fleet caused deep concern both to President Roosevelt and to the American Navy Department. The Office of Naval Intelligence estimated that the combined naval forces of Germany, Italy, and France would be a third stronger than the Royal Navy and far stronger than the U.S. Navy, most of which was, in any case, stationed in the Pacific. In view of these dangers, Roosevelt urged upon the Congress a huge building program for a two-ocean navy. At the same time, he ordered the funds of the French Government frozen, and he directed a stiff warning to the French Government, to be delivered in person by Ambassador Biddle.

The President desires that you obtain immediately an interview with Admiral Darlan and subsequently, if possible, with the Minister for Foreign Affairs, and state that the views of this Government with regard to the disposition of the French Fleet have been made very clear to the French Government on previous occasions. The President desires you to say that in the opinion of this Government, should the French Government, before concluding any armistice with the Germans, fail to see that Fleet is kept out of the hands of her opponents, the French Government will be pursuing a policy that will fatally impair the preservation of the French Empire and the eventual restoration of French independence and autonomy. Furthermore, should the French Government fail to take these steps and permit the French Fleet to be surrendered to Germany, the French Government will permanently lose the friendship and good will of the Government of the United States.

This message, intemperate in diplomatic usage, had only the effect of getting a repetition from Darlan of his previous promise not to surrender the fleet. *"La question ne se pose pas,"* he declared. But the French fleet remained where it was.

What measures was Darlan taking to ensure that the fleet would not fall into German or Italian hands? He ordered French merchant vessels in British convoys to leave the convoys and head for French ports. "You are not to enter British ports," he radioed to them on June 18. The following day he telegraphed to Admiral Oden'hal,

179

Chief of the French Naval Mission in London, "Do not (repeat not) obey the English. Obey the English only after confirmation."

On June 20, Darlan sent an important message to the fleet:

N° 5057–5059 13h.30, 20 June 1940

1. The Admiral of the Fleet believes it possible to continue in command of the maritime forces and hereby takes the necessary steps to enable him to do so.
2. In case the Admiral of the Fleet should be prevented from exercising his command freely, the maritime forces will be placed under the orders of Admiral Laborde, then those of Admiral Estéva, then those of Admiral Abrial, followed by those of Admiral Gensoul.
3. All flag officers, or those who may be called upon to succeed them, are required to conform to the general orders given below:
   a. Fight fiercely to the end so long as a regularly constituted French Government which is independent of the enemy has not given orders to the contrary.
   b. Refuse to obey any other government.
   c. No matter what orders may be received, I shall never abandon an intact warship into the hands of the enemy.

Admiral of the Fleet

Darlan's position was clear. He was not going to let the fleet get away from *him,* whether into German, Italian, or British hands. It was *his* fleet, and he had given *his* word that the enemy should not have it. Unfortunately, the British felt that more than Darlan's word was needed for their security.

The French request for an armistice caught Hitler somewhat unprepared. He expected the French to capitulate, but he did not expect it quite so soon. Since his aim was to destroy the French armies, he deliberately stalled to give his troops time to finish the job. To coordinate his terms with those of Mussolini, he summoned the Italian dictator to a meeting at Munich on June 18.

Hitler had decided to be reasonable. His curious admiration for the British and for the British Empire led him to seek an understanding with them by almost any means. Surely, he argued, the British, having seen their last ally on the Continent defeated and their own army pushed into the sea, would accept the inevitable and recognize that Europe belonged to Germany. If the British would but return the German colonies wrested from the Fatherland in the Versailles Treaty and accept Germany's role in Europe, there was no reason for the war to continue.

On these assumptions, Hitler reasoned that if he made outrageous demands on France, it might drive her to desperation, send the French Government scurrying to North Africa and the French fleet to join the British. In that case, he knew, stubborn pride would cause the British to fight to the end. On the other hand, he argued, when they saw how reasonable he was with France, they would think twice, throw out the pig-headed Churchill, and make peace.

As for the French fleet, "the best thing we can hope for," Hitler said, "is that the French will sink it. The worst is that the fleet should go over to the British."

Mussolini's son-in-law, Count Galeazzo Ciano, a perceptive observer of the conference and Foreign Minister of Italy, noted in his diary, "The *Duce* is an extremist. He would like to go so far as the total occupation of French territory and demands the surrender of the French fleet.

"Hitler," he continued, "is now the gambler who has made a big scoop and would like to get up from the table risking nothing more."

Hitler's policy at this meeting with Mussolini was to see that the junior partner did not upset the apple cart with outrageous demands.

As he feared, Mussolini's grandiose ideas of his due for his week in the war threatened Hitler's strategy. The *Duce* wanted Germany and Italy jointly to occupy all of France; for himself, he wanted all French colonies in North Africa and a substantial portion of the French fleet. The discussion lasted three days, but Hitler had his way. Big Brother had spoken. Mussolini's miserable performance in the war to date had won him no more consideration.

CHAPTER EIGHT

Not Since Waterloo

*It is upon the navy under the Providence
of God that the safety, honour, and
welfare of this realm do chiefly attend.*

Charles II, Articles of War

H. M.S. *Hood* steamed through the blue waters of the Mediterranean. On her flag bridge, a tall, spare, white-clad figure stood looking out over the North African coast to starboard. He could see the white-stuccoed native houses and the collection of European-style buildings which made up the city of Oran. A little to the west lay the French naval base at Mers el Kebir. A long jetty projected from the shore toward the open sea, and on the far side of the jetty, moored with their sterns toward him, the white-clad figure could make out the shapes of four of the most important ships in the French Navy. The figure in white was Vice Admiral Sir James Somerville, Royal Navy, and he was anxiously but determinedly waiting for the French to reply to a communication he had sent them. He dreaded their answer, for he thought he knew what it would be. If he was right, he would have to take action, and he would remember it with dismay for the rest of his life. It was an action which could please no one but Hitler and Mussolini.

Britain's Army had tried and failed. Until it could be rebuilt, re-equipped, and retrained, it could do nothing toward winning the war. It could man the beaches and fields in case of invasion, but it could not be used elsewhere for some time to come. Only the small force in Egypt, mostly Dominion troops, might consider offensive action in the weeks and months ahead.

The Royal Air Force had spent its blood and its aircraft lavishly during the Dunkirk evacuation and the Battle of France. It was licking its wounds, but it was ready to fight if it had to. Its time would come in August. At the moment it was time to rebuild, to get ready for the fray.

It was on the Navy, once France had fallen, that the chief burden fell. The Royal Navy was the largest in the world, and it was the best trained. But it was stretched thin. Demands for convoy, for patrol, for guarding the German fleet had kept it busy enough during the fall, winter, and spring. The French Navy had had the principal responsibility for the Mediterranean, and the Italian Navy had been idle, snug in its country's neutrality.

Now all that had changed. Italy had joined the war, and her fine, fast ships had already been in action against the British. And what of the French Navy?

Hark back to the days before the French laid down their arms. The scene is Rethondes in the forest of Compiègne. A railway carriage, which had been the private car of Marshal Foch, has been dragged to the very spot where it stood on November 11, 1918. At that time, in that carriage, Foch had dictated terms of armistice to a defeated Germany. Now, on June 21, 1940, Hitler, an unknown corporal in 1918, occupies Marshal Foch's seat. The Germans this time are there as the victors, the French as the vanquished. With Hitler are his High Command officers, Goering, strutting in his light-blue Luftwaffe uniform, Raeder, in the darker blue of the Navy, Keitel of the Army and Brauchitsch in field gray. Foreign Minister Ribbentrop in the lighter uniform affected by the Foreign Office, and Rudolf Hess, Deputy Chancellor and Hitler's heir apparent, in a gray Nazi Party uniform. All are spotless, stiffly correct.

The French arrive, rumpled from their journey to this spot, their uniforms no match for the splendor of the triumphant Germans. Salutes are exchanged, the French officers take their seats, and Keitel begins to read on a nod from Hitler.

He has read only a few lines, when Hitler rises, salutes again, and strides from the car, accompanied by everyone but General Keitel. They pass the guard of honor, and the band blares out "Deutschland über Alles" and the "Horst Wessel Lied."

France was to be divided. Germany would occupy three-fifths of the country, including all the Channel and Atlantic coasts, and, ignominy in the minds of all Frenchmen, Paris would lie in the occupied zone. Only the southeast section of the country would be free of the Nazi boot and the twisted cross of the swastika.*

Harsh as the armistice conditions were to France, the British and American Governments had one major concern—the French fleet. Would Germany or Italy demand it? Added to the fleets of Italy and Germany, it could make Britain inferior at sea. Without use of the sea, Britain could not survive. The naval clauses were a matter of life and death to Britain.

When, at length, a copy of the armistice conditions reached London, the War Cabinet turned its most searching scrutiny on Articles VIII and IX, which read: †

Article VIII. The French war fleet, with the exception of that part which is left to the disposition of the French Government for the safeguarding of French colonial interests, will be assembled in ports to be determined and will be demobilized and disarmed under the control of Germany or of Italy.

The determination of these ports will be made according to the home ports of the vessels in time of peace. The German Government solemnly declares that it has no intention during the present war of utilizing for its own purposes the French warships stationed in ports under German control except for those units necessary for coastal surveillance and for minesweeping.

It further solemnly and formally declares that it has no intention of formulating demands with regard to the French war fleet after the conclusion of peace. Except for that part of the French fleet to be determined as necessary for the safeguarding of the French colonial interests, all warships outside of French territorial waters shall be recalled to France.

Article IX. The French High Command shall furnish to the German High Command precise indications of all mines laid by France, both the mine barrages in the ports and along the coast as well as the military installations for defense and protection.

Minesweeping shall be carried out by French forces to the extent that the German High Command shall direct.

Not only the British, but even the French, were highly dissatisfied with these clauses. To require that the ships be demobilized in their

* The German armistice would not become effective until the one with Italy had been accepted. The French feared that Mussolini would demand all that Hitler had not—that is, the occupation of the rest of France. When Italy's proposals were received, they were modest, demanding only a narrow strip of land on the Riviera.

† The conditions imposed in the Italian armistice were nearly identical as far as the French fleet was concerned.

home ports would mean that a substantial portion of the French Navy would be situated in German-controlled and occupied ports at Brest and Lorient on the Atlantic coast and in Cherbourg on the Channel. Not only would the French have no power over these vessels; if officers of the French Navy wished to inspect them, they would have to cross Occupied France to do it. Would the Germans permit such inspections?

On the orders of Admiral Darlan, General Huntzinger suggested the following:

> The French fleet ... after having been demobilized and having offloaded its munitions under the control of Germany or Italy respectively, shall be based in French ports in North Africa.

He told the Germans that if the French ships were based on Atlantic or Channel ports, the British would surely seek to destroy them by air raid or by sabotage landing parties. General Keitel haughtily refused to consider the suggested modification. The French, he went on, stubbornly showed a complete lack of appreciation of the liberal terms of Article VIII. He claimed that in the phrases "will be assembled" and "will be made according to the home ports in time of peace," the German text employed the word *soll,* which merely states that something will be done in the future; they might have used the word *muss,* which would state that something had to be done. In the French text both words were translated by the same word, *doit.*

"The German text has authority, and my word is good," pontificated Keitel. "It is up to you to straighten out the translation."

Later, at meetings with the Armistice Commission at Wiesbaden, the French were to find that the most rigid interpretations of the armistice provisions were the invariable practice.

In Britain the reaction to Articles VIII and IX was unanimously unfavorable. The French, being perfectly sure that Britain would soon be overcome by Germany and would be seeking her own armistice, were in reality making only a *pro forma* objection to the naval clauses. But no member of the British War Cabinet was for a moment entertaining the idea of surrender, and the British were most keenly concerned over maintaining their tenuous superiority at sea. The addition of the Italian fleet to that of Germany had already posed a grave problem. If the fine French ships should actually be used against her, Britain might find her naval requirements impossible of fulfillment. Even though the Royal Navy might have near equality in mere numbers of ships to the combined German, Italian, and French fleets, its worldwide commitments meant that this seeming equality was actually inferiority in practice. The German, Italian, and French ships could come out when and if they chose. The British had to be ready at all times and in widely scattered areas of the world. With her warships engaged in protecting trade, Britain simply did not have enough ships to meet the combination which could be arrayed against her.

Determined to continue the war, the British accepted ruthlessness as a necessity in salvaging what they could from the wreckage. Churchill made it clear that Britain would fight on, regardless of others, regardless of cost, and regardless of consequences.

> However matters may go in France or with the French Government or other French Governments, we in this island and in the British Empire will never lose our sense of comradeship with the French people. . . . If final victory rewards our toils they shall share the gains —aye, and freedom shall be restored to all. . . .
>
> What General Weygand called the Battle of France is over. I expect that the Battle of Britain is about to begin. Upon this battle depends the survival of Christian civilization. Upon it depends our own British life, and the long continuity of our institutions and our Empire. The whole fury and might of the enemy must very soon be turned on us. Hitler knows that he will have to break us in this island or lose the war. If we can stand up to him, all Europe may be free and the life of the world may move forward into broad, sunlit uplands. But if we fail, then the whole world, including the United States, including all that we have known and cared for, will sink into the abyss of a new Dark Age, made more sinister, and perhaps more protracted, by the lights of perverted science. Let us therefore brace ourselves to our duties, and so bear ourselves that, if the British Empire last for a thousand years, men will say, "This was their finest hour."

The more the War Cabinet examined Article VIII, the less they liked it. First the terms specified that the ships were to be demobilized in ports under German or Italian control. The term "demobilized" might mean the ships would actually be placed out of commission, with major machinery disabled. Or it might merely mean that they would have their fuel offloaded, a situation which could be remedied in a few hours of pumping. In the same way, the term "disarmed" might mean as little as having the ammunition placed ashore. Then, too, the phrase "under German or Italian control" suggested to the British that German or Italian officers would be issuing all orders to French ships, wherever they might be situated.

Again confusion occasioned by translation may have entered into the picture. In English the word "control" is far stronger than the corresponding French word *contrôle,* which implies administrative rather than operational authority.

Also the provision that the Germans might employ certain units necessary for "coastal surveillance and for minesweeping" the British interpreted to mean that the Germans might find all ships of the French Navy useful for this purpose. Since the Germans and Italians were to be the sole judges of what units were necessary to effect these functions, it seemed not unlikely to the British that the Germans might well decide that they needed the entire French battle fleet to conduct coastal surveillance. This surveillance might easily extend to the British coast as well.

Although the armistice terms provided that neither Germany nor Italy would make use of the French fleet during the current war, the British War Cabinet felt that they could not permit the survival of Britain to rest on the promises of Hitler and Mussolini. Hitler had scarcely been a man of his word with respect to international agreements. If they needed any reminders of this fact, the members of the War Cabinet could have received them from the throngs of Czech, Austrian, Danish, Norwegian, Polish, Belgian, and Dutch refugees then in London, victims of their Governments' faith in Hitler's pledged word. Why would he keep his word to France if at any time it was to his purpose to violate it?

The final consideration was that the armistice could be voided at any time by the Germans upon any pretext whatever—or none at all. In that case, even Hitler's paper promises would vanish.

Hitler did keep his promises up until the time of the Allied landings in North Africa in 1942; then he denounced the armistice, occupied all of France, and strove to seize the French ships at Toulon. But the real reason for his softness regarding the French fleet was that he totally failed to appreciate the strategic importance of the Mediterranean. Hitler was land-minded, and his strategic vision was continental. The Mediterranean he regarded as a sideshow; he did not commit any forces there until the spring of 1941, and then it was largely for the purpose of coming to the rescue of his junior partner, Mussolini, who was in grave trouble in Albania, Greece, and Libya.

In his lack of appreciation of the Mediterranean, Hitler was gravely shortsighted. The British position in Egypt was the one bastion outside the United Kingdom where the British could gather for a future offensive. It was the one place where Britain could oppose the Axis on the ground. In the Mediterranean rested Britain's hopes for the future, for a return to the Continent, and for eventual victory. If Britain were to have oil for her Navy, gasoline for the Royal Air Force, and oil for her industry, she must keep the Middle East accessible, for the transatlantic convoys could not bring enough from America to supply her needs. Hitler should have had his eyes on this oil as well, for the shortage of fuel by 1943 was seriously handicapping the Navy, the Army, and the Luftwaffe.

Although Britain could no longer use the Mediterranean for transport, she had to prevent its becoming an Axis lake. The War Cabinet believed Britain could manage to hold the essential positions in the Mediterranean if she had only the Italian fleet and the Italian Air Force to face. At the western end of the Mediterranean, Britain had her traditional stronghold of Gibraltar, impregnable from sea, but dangerously exposed to capture from the land side, should Spain join the Axis powers. In the Rock itself existed strong fortifications, stores of provisions, naval supplies, quarters for the garrison, and the naval dockyard.

Midway along the length of the Mediterranean, southeast of Sicily, Britain held the fortress of Malta, its Grand Harbour at Valetta offering an additional, but perilously exposed, base for naval operations. Malta lay under the threat of naval and air attack from Italy and might well prove untenable. No one could then foresee the heroism and endurance the Malta garrison and the Maltese people would show in the coming years. They were to endure attacks which made the tiny island the most heavily bombed place in the history of the world. As the British saw it in mid-June, 1940, Malta was fit only for air operations against Italian shipping to Libya and as a naval base for submarines and small vessels.

At the eastern end of the Mediterranean, the British maintained the Mediterranean Fleet at Alexandria, supported by a well-equipped base. The Eighth Army bore the responsibility of defending Egypt and the Suez Canal. It was on this army that any hope of early offensive action rested. Both army and navy were entirely dependent on overseas supplies. But ships bringing them could no longer use the direct Mediterranean route; they had to come the long way around the Cape of Good Hope, through the Indian Ocean, the Red Sea to Suez. Then the supplies went overland to the "Desert Rats."

Recognizing Germany as the principal adversary, Britain could not afford to send the major strength of the Royal Navy into the Mediterranean to seek a decisive engagement with the Italian fleet. The first charge on the Royal Navy was to protect trade; second, and of almost equal importance, was to blockade, to keep German warships penned up and to keep supplies of all kinds from reaching the Axis powers.

It was on economic blockade that the Chiefs of Staff pinned their principal hopes for defeating Germany. Every ship which had to be withdrawn from the Home Fleet would have the effect of reducing the pressure on Germany.

United States officials shared these apprehensions with the British. President Roosevelt foresaw also that the addition of the French fleet to those of the Axis might well unsettle South American nations. The principal danger lay in Argentina, with her many German nationals and citizens of German descent. The need of keeping a substantial part of the U.S. Navy in the Pacific as a make-weight against Japan meant accepting grave risks in the Atlantic. The Americans thus reacted much as the British had to the armistice terms. The armistice, Under Secretary of State Summer Welles said to the French ambassador, "apparently threw the entire fleet directly into German hands."

In London, matters were moving to a head. The Chiefs of Staff made the difficult decision to strengthen the naval forces in the Mediterranean. Meanwhile they were concerting plans for action should the worst occur.

When the French Government agreed to Germany's terms of surrender, Foreign Minister Paul Baudouin recognized that the French must inform the British Ambassador, Sir Ronald Campbell, without delay. Unwilling, however, to face Sir Ronald himself, he delegated the task to François Charles-Roux, the Permanent Secretary of the Foreign Office. Charles-Roux was instructed to put the best face on the matter and impress upon the British ambassador the French efforts to modify the naval terms and German intransigence in refusing to alter them in any particular.

At 7 P.M., June 21, Sir Ronald Campbell appeared while Charles-Roux was talking to André François-Poncet, formerly French ambassador to Italy. M. François-Poncet remained through the interview at the request of Charles-Roux and furnishes valuable testimony of the progress of the meeting. He remained standing near a window.

On reading the naval terms, Sir Ronald lost his composure. He stammered and stumbled, forgetting in his agitation how to express himself in French, which he normally spoke fluently. France had agreed "to hand over the fleet in spite of her promises," he charged. Solemnly and composedly Charles-Roux stated that he was mistaken, that the fleet would never be handed over, and that it would be disarmed in French ports.

"But a disarmed ship, with only an anchor watch, in an occupied port, would be at the mercy of a sudden seizure by the occupying force," objected Sir Ronald.

"No," replied Charles-Roux, "because Admiral Darlan has already taken the necessary measures so that no ship can fall into the hands of the enemy."

"But the execution of those measures prescribed by Admiral Darlan can be prevented by a sudden attack by a German detachment."

Charles-Roux bade Sir Ronald put his trust in Darlan. This remark revealed the crux of the disagreement between the British and the French. The French view was that Admiral Darlan had repeatedly given his word, and that should end the matter. Sir Ronald and his Government were not content to put their trust in any one man— not when the security of Britain depended upon it. The two men had reached an impasse. Charles-Roux declared that they had no choice. "The knife is at our throats," he stated dramatically.

Sir Ronald left the room. François-Poncet declared mournfully to his colleague, "He will never forgive us for this!"

Sir Ronald next had a talk with Weygand. The general declared that the documents had been signed and there was nothing more to be said. The British ambassador replied that there was nothing left for him to do in France and that he would return to London for discussions. He tried to make courtesy calls on President Lebrun and on Marshal Pétain. Both refused to receive him, their attendants blandly asserting that they had retired. He was received by Baudouin in a brief, formal, and proper interview; then he took passage for home in a British warship.

Thus, during the critical days following the French armistice, no British representative above the rank of a junior minister was available to make Britain's views heard by the French Government.

In spite of all that had happened, the British still clung to hope that the French might fight on in North Africa. In the colonies, and thus removed from the passions and terrors current in Metropolitan France, men of stout heart might declare themselves not bound by the armistice. They might flock to the banner of General Charles de Gaulle, who was organizing a group of patriots in London. They called themselves the Free French. On June 20, just before the armistice was signed, some twenty-five French leaders, including Georges Mandel, César Campinchi, and Édouard Daladier, left Bordeaux about the steamer *Massalia,* bound for Casablanca. They were confident they could rally the Resident General, Auguste Paul Noguès, to the cause. Noguès, Mandel believed, would break with Bordeaux and become the focus of resistance.

On June 19, de Gaulle had telegraphed Noguès, offering to place himself under his orders, and on June 24 he telegraphed him again, and also the commanding generals in Syria and in Indochina, calling on them to defy the German conditions. From Indochina and Syria came prompt messages to Noguès urging him to adopt de Gaulle's plan for organized colonial resistance.

Noguès apparently wavered for a time; but when an officer from Weygand arrived, Noguès sided with Pétain. Thus when the *Massalia,* bearing the French resistance leaders, reached Casablanca on June 24, Noguès was ready for them. Daladier, as a former Premier of France, sent ashore a proclamation of the formation of a resistance government. Instead of broadcasting the proclamation, Noguès sent it to Pétain.

The British hurriedly dispatched Lord Gort and Mr. Alfred Duff Cooper, British Minister of Information, to Rabat to confer with Daladier and Mandel. But Noguès prevented the meeting. He placed the French resistance leaders under arrest aboard the *Massalia,* and detained the vessel in the harbor for several weeks. Thus Daladier and his associates could neither send nor receive communications and were effectively rendered useless for the resistance movement. It bcame perfectly clear to Churchill that there was no possibility of organized French resistance from North Africa. The Vichy Government was in control, and relations between Britain and France approached the nadir.

Accordingly the British abruptly ceased attempts to do business with the government of Pétain. They backed General Charles de Gaulle, who promptly issued a proclamation calling on Frenchmen everywhere to rally to the Cross of Lorraine. "Our fleet, our aircraft, our vehicles . . ." he declared, "have been delivered intact to the enemy for use against our own allies."

The last hope of French cooperation was gone. Britain prepared to take stronger measures. If the French would not take the steps necessary to prevent their fleet from menacing Britain, then Britain would have to remove the menace.

The British had already taken action to strengthen their naval forces in the Mediterranean. There was not much to worry about at the eastern end, where Admiral Cunningham had a reasonable force.

He could, however, do with a few more heavy ships, and they would be sent in good time.

At the other end of the Mediterranean there was a real weakness. Only a handful of destroyers and other small ships were available, and they were busy with escort duty, contraband control, and general patrolling. And it was in this end of the Mediterranean that most of the French warships were located, at Toulon, Algiers, and Mers el Kebir.

The few ships Britain had at Gibraltar were under command of Admiral Sir Dudley North, Flag Officer Commanding North Atlantic (F.O.C.N.A.). North had no responsibilities inside the Mediterranean, so something had to be done.

Even before the French armistice, the ships which were to take over primary responsibility for the western Mediterranean were being selected and told to get moving. Since Force H, as it was designated, would operate both in the Mediterranean and in the Atlantic, the Admiralty retained operational control, ordering its commander to cooperate with Admirals North and Cunningham as necessary.

The ships began to arrive at Gibraltar on June 23. There were the carrier *Ark Royal,* the battleship *Valiant,* which had fought at Jutland, the slightly younger battleship *Resolution,* the battle cruiser *Hood,* considered by many to be the most powerful ship in the world, the light cruisers *Arethusa* and *Enterprise,* and 4 destroyers. A week later, on June 30, 1940, Vice Admiral Sir James Somerville hoisted his flag in the *Hood.* Now the British had available at Gibraltar a powerful force, weaker, to be sure, than either the Italian or French forces in the Mediterranean, but one that would be able to give a good account of itself in an emergency.

As Force H was assembling, the British War Cabinet had reached a painful decision: to force the French Navy to continue the war on Britain's side or to neutralize it. If neither of these goals could be attained, then the French fleet must be destroyed. Churchill called it a "hateful decision, the most unnatural and painful in which I have ever been concerned." Yet the British believed that their lives depended upon it. On June 28 they grimly began planning Operation Catapult, action against the navy of France. They did not even inform General de Gaulle of their intentions. They have since said it was to prevent any word leaking back to France. Perhaps they simply could not bring themselves to tell him.

At this time the French fleet was somewhat widely scattered. In British ports were 2 old battleships, 2 super-destroyers, 8 destroyers, and 6 submarines, as well as some 200 small minesweeping and coastal craft. The British felt they could deal with them readily. In the West Indies were an aircraft carrier and 2 light cruisers. A substantial number of ships was at Toulon, France's chief naval base in the Mediterranean, and out of reach of any British action. At Alexandria, where they could be watched by Admiral Cunningham, were a battleship, 4 cruisers, and several smaller vessels. At Algiers there were 7 cruisers, and at Mers el Kebir there were 2 modern battle cruisers, 2 battleships, and several light cruisers, as well as a substantial number of destroyers, submarines, and smaller vessels. A few vessels were scattered about smaller ports of the Inland Sea from North Africa to Syria. Meanwhile, the unfinished battleship *Jean Bart* had just arrived in Casablanca, and her sister ship *Richelieu* had reached Dakar. These sisters the British regarded with particular suspicion, since they were of the latest design and were superior in armament to Britain's newest *King George V*-class battleships.

No French vessel of any significant size remained in port in German-occupied France.

Admiral Darlan was punctilious in keeping his word about the French fleet, as he interpreted his word. He sent a special series of messages to his principal commanders ordering resistance to *any* efforts directed against their ships. Since many previous messages had instructed these same commanders to resist the Germans and Italians, the new messages were clear instructions to oppose the British.

Admiral Darlan knew his commanders. He would not have to spell it out for them. Britain was the only nation with both the desire and the capability of taking any action against the French naval forces.

Darlan's first message was sent on June 24.

24 June 1940, 12h.45.
To Admirals West, South, Africa, Antilles, French Forces in the Far East, Third Squadron, Force X, Naval Division in the Levant. Maritime Prefects, Third and Fourth Maritime Regions.

The clauses of the armistice are being sent you in clear by other means. I am profiting by the last communications which I can send in code to make known my views on the subject. These orders remain in effect, whatever orders to the contrary you may receive in the future, even if they are signed by me.

First—The demobilized warships are to stay French, under French flag, with reduced French crews, remaining in French metropolitan or colonial ports.

Second—Secret precautions for sabotage are to be made in order that

193

any enemy or *ex-ally* seizing a vessel by force may not be able to make use of it.

Third—Should the Armistice Commission charged with interpreting the text come to a decision different from that in paragraph one, warships are, without further orders, to be dispatched to the United States or, alternatively, scuttled, provided that no other action is possible to preserve them from the enemy. Under no circumstances are they to fall intact into enemy hands.

Fourth—Ships that seek refuge abroad are not to be used in operations against Germany or Italy without prior orders from the Commander in Chief.

Fifth—In no case obey the orders of a foreign admiralty.

The following day, Admiral Odend'hal delivered a copy of this message to the British Admiralty. However, the text which he gave them omitted the word "ex-ally" from paragraph two, and omitted paragraph five altogether.* Since this message obviously had an effect in shaping the instructions the Admiralty was to send out, the importance of these omissions cannot be overstated.

Two days later, Darlan sent another message to the same commanders. In it he wrote as a father to his children, calling upon their personal loyalty as he told them the unpleasant facts of life. In fact he misstated the case, claiming that the armistice negotiators had obtained relaxations of the naval terms; as he wrote, there was no chance of obtaining any until the Armistice Commission met some time later.

Order of June 26, 1940, 8h.54.

I have the terms of the two armistices in my hand: neither one is dishonorable. Our navy and our air force can be seen by their exceptional treatment to be paid homage for their conduct and recognition for their valor. You will receive from me the complete texts and *the verbal processes of discussion which have eased the rigor of certain points*. We keep all our ships and all our aircraft of naval aviation; our effective seamen on active service are not limited, and our adversaries have undertaken a solemn engagement not to touch our navy in the peace treaty. What more could we hope, being defeated? It now remains to accept the signed conventions with dignity. To do otherwise would bring about the definitive ruin of our country, gravely wounded by defeat. To respond to outside interests would lead our territory into becoming a German province. *Our former allies are not to be listened to:* let us think French, let us act French. The uneasiness

---

* Paragraph five has not previously appeared in any English account of actions at this time.

of the navy has come about from insufficient information as to what has been done and what decisions taken. I appeal to the spirit of discipline which has upheld our service during the hostilities. I cannot believe that those who have faithfully obeyed me when I have demanded their lives for the country will not have the moral courage to obey me with assurance of support, however hard that may be in actuality.*

There can be no doubt that Admiral Darlan was sincere in his belief that the French ships should remain French and that they were to be relied upon to scuttle themselves rather than submit to any enemy. Also he was perfectly certain in his own mind that if the French fleet made any move to join the British, the Germans would forthwith denounce the armistice and occupy all of France. Once having laid down her arms, France was helpless to oppose any German military pressure.

Darlan, in common with Pétain and Weygand, sincerely believed that Britain would soon be defeated. Then the French fleet would survive, and it would be the only undefeated military force of all those which had opposed the Axis. Even supposing Britain should survive the attack about to be hurled against her, it would still be useless for France to continue the fight from North Africa, these men believed; in that case Spain would enter the war on the Axis side.

As the Axis documents have become available since the war, it is clear that this apprehension was fully justified. As a result of the Civil War, Spain was too weakened to embark upon a lengthy campaign, but General Franco was tempted, as Mussolini had been, at the prospect of gaining a seat at the victors' table. He was eager to gain territory in North Africa at the expense of the French, and he desired above all to win Gibraltar back for Spain. On June 14, troops from Spanish Morocco had seized the international city of Tangier across the Strait from Gibraltar. On June 19 he went a step further, writing to Hitler that he was prepared to enter the war on the Axis side in return for Gibraltar and for several large pieces of French territory in North Africa, including French Morocco and the Oran Province of Algeria.

Hitler was less than delighted by the receipt of Franco's letter. He had no desire to win huge victories by the force of German arms, only to have others cluster around to share the feast. He had one uninvited guest already in Mussolini. Accordingly he returned a chillingly noncommittal letter to Franco. Later, in October, 1940,

* Italics supplied.

when Hitler was anxious for Spain to enter the war, Franco had raised his price.

In June, 1940, however, no one could foresee that Spain would not become a belligerent. And if France had continued to resist from North Africa, there can be little doubt that Hitler would have acceded to Franco's terms, especially if Spanish troops could have been used against the French in North Africa, leaving him free to devote his attention to knocking out Britain.

As the dark month of June, 1940, drew to a close, Britain's fortunes had never seemed lower. In a lightning campaign, Germany had knocked Holland, Belgium, and France out of the war. German bombers stood poised, ready to drop their deadly loads on British cities. German U-boats were moving into western French ports, making them greater threats than ever to the merchant ships carrying to Britain the goods on which her very life depended. In French observation posts, German officers looked across the Channel at the cliffs of Dover, planning how they might cross. German Army, Navy, and Luftwaffe High Commands studied the possibilities of an invasion of Britain.

Amidst these dangers from the enemy, the British felt that they had been betrayed by an ally. Not only had France guaranteed not to seek a separate peace, but she had violated the condition on which the British had agreed to her approaching Hitler for an armistice. The French had not first removed their fleet to a place of safety or to ports whence it might continue the war. The ships could well be seized by the Germans and thus used against them; against this, the British had only the word of Admiral Darlan and other French leaders. Any promise was too slender a reed where the survival of Britain was concerned.

The French, too, felt aggrieved. British contributions to the land campaigns had been pitifully small. The British had refused to stake their last hopes on the Battle of France and had withheld a reserve of aircraft which might have stopped the Nazi Panzers. They had demanded sacrifice after sacrifice from the French, withholding their own final efforts from the struggle. Then, when France had given her all, Britain demanded more, that she expose all of the soil of France to the occupation of the Hun in order to maintain a futile struggle a few days longer. Let's face it, argued the men of Bordeaux; Germany has won the war, and it is no kindness either to France or to Britain to refuse to admit the fact. We must prepare ourselves to live in the world Germany has made.

The French position was the more logical of the two, but there is that in the soul of the Anglo-Saxon that defies logic. It is to be found in the old ballad:

> I'll lay me doun and bleed awhile,
> Then rise and fight again!

* * *

Two men sat talking in the admiral's cabin. One, wearing the summer white uniform of a captain in the Royal Navy, spoke earnestly, desperately. The other, wearing a vice admiral's uniform of the French Navy, listened carefully to the fluent French of his visitor. Both men's expressions were grim, for their conversation did not deal with a subject they liked. It was not the way two old friends should meet after several years.

Outside the portholes of the ship could be seen the naval anchorage of Mers el Kebir, and a few miles to the east the city of Oran, second largest in Algeria. Birthplace of the Nobel Prize-winning novelist Albert Camus, Oran is a city of mixed French and Arab population. Although much of the city is modern, large sections of the native quarter date far back into the past. Settled by the Arabs in the 10th century, it has known Spanish, Arab, and French possession. As an important center of trade, it has rail lines running east along the coast connecting it with Algiers and toward the south through Sidi bel Abbes. It is also an important port, 195 nautical miles from Gibraltar, 120 miles from Cartagena, and 305 miles from Marseilles.

About four miles to the west of Oran Harbor is situated the naval base of Mers el Kebir, once a lair of pirates, but since the early 19th century used by the French as a naval base. Here in June, 1940, lay the principal strength of the French Mediterranean Fleet. At this time there was a long wharf extending from the tip of a small peninsula in a southeasterly direction for approximately 1000 yards. Tied up stern first to this wharf in what is known as a "Mediterranean moor" were the battle cruiser *Dunkerque,* the battleship *Provence,* the battle cruiser *Strasbourg,* the battleship *Bretagne,* and the seaplane tender *Commandant Teste.* Anchored forward of these ships were 6 super-destroyers, the *Volta, Mogador, Tigre, Lynx, Kersaint,* and *Terrible.* The squadron was under the command of Vice Admiral Marcel Gensoul. Gensoul was nearly sixty years of age at the time. Most of his adult life had been spent at sea, for he had joined the navy as a young man. Patriotic beyond all calls of personal considerations, he was completely and unreservedly devoted to Admiral Darlan, whom he knew as a personal friend as well as his military superior. He could be counted upon to give unswerving obedience to any commands from Darlan, whatever the cost might be to him personally. He was well known to many officers in the Royal Navy, where his courteous bearing and professional abilities had gained him many friends. One of them, Captain C. S. Holland, was fated to be the unwilling bearer of a British ultimatum to him.

The ships under Gensoul's command comprised some of the finest in the active French fleet. Although the battleships were old, both dating from the First World War, the battle cruisers *Strasbourg* and *Dunkerque* were brand-new ships, expressly designed to be superior to the German battle cruisers *Scharnhorst* and *Gneisenau*. They were 702 feet in length, with 101¾-foot beam, drawing 28 feet. Each had a standard displacement of 26,500 tons. They mounted eight 13-inch guns in two quadruple forward turrets. In addition they carried sixteen 5.1-inch dual-purpose guns, as well as 44 smaller antiaircraft machine guns. In their sea trials, the ships had logged 31.5 knots, two knots better than their designed speed. Admiral Gensoul flew his flag in the *Dunkerque*.

The 6 super-destroyers were, for the most part, new ships, and of a type not used in other navies at the time. Displacing from 500 to 1000 tons more than the standard British or American destroyers, these ships were also more heavily armed and faster.

As events in France were moving toward their conclusion, the British had already begun efforts to persuade Gensoul to preserve his ships for the Allied cause. Admiral Sir Dudley North visited him on June 24. After a lengthy conference, the best Sir Dudley could obtain was the bleak promise that Gensoul would obey the orders of Marshal Pétain and those of Admiral Darlan. As it happened, the next day the Admiralty asked North whether there was any chance that the French ships at Oran and Mers el Kebir would submit to *force majeure* if a strong detachment of British ships appeared off the port. North was forced to reply that he saw no possibility whatever that Admiral Gensoul would yield. Thus, from the beginning, the Admiralty knew as a near certainty that any attempts to subvert or to seize the French ships would be met with force.

On July 1, Admiral Somerville, commanding Force H, received orders to be prepared to carry out his share of Operation Catapult. He was to take action against the French ships at Mers el Kebir on

July 3. Somerville was greatly disturbed. He believed that the Admiralty and the War Cabinet had a totally false view of French attitudes in North Africa. In particular Captain Holland, the commanding officer of the *Ark Royal,* warned against presenting Gensoul with any kind of ultimatum. Captain Holland had recently been naval attaché in Paris. As a personal friend of Admiral Gensoul he was better able than any other British officers to predict Gensoul's reactions.

In view of what he had learned, Somerville sent the following message to the Admiralty.

From F.O. (H) to Admiralty 1220/I

I have had further opportunity to discuss situation with Holland, Spearman, and Davis and am impressed by their view that use of force should be avoided at all costs.

They consider now that armistice terms are known, there is distinct possibility of French accepting first alternative. To achieve this end and, in accordance with their experience of French, they propose— Holland arrives 0800 and signals in P/L [plain language] addressed to Gensoul: "The British Admiralty have sent Captain Holland to confer with you. The British Navy hopes that their proposal will enable you and your glorious French Navy to range yourself side by side with them. In these circumstances your ships would remain yours and no one need have anxiety for them. A British fleet is at sea off Oran waiting to welcome you." One hour after Holland enters harbour, Force H off Oran repeats same message addressed to French Admiral, using signal projectors turned on as many ships as possible. This is to ensure purport of message received by officers and men other than French Admiral.

If French refuse first alternative then the second alternative must be worded as follows: "proceed to sea with a minimum steaming speed," demilitarized and allowing themselves to be captured by Force H. Strictly assuring ships be returned to France on completion of hostilities. French may say they acted under force and that they were unable to oppose British action.

Third and fourth alternatives to be in form of invitation to French.

They hold strongly that offensive action or threat would immediately alienate Frenchmen wherever they are and transfer a defeated ally into an active enemy. They believe our prestige would be enhanced if we withdrew from Oran without taking offensive action.

These views based on very recent contact with French naval authorities. Unless their Lordships send more definite and contrary information, I consider these proposals merit very careful consideration. Very early reply requested as possible acceptance first or second alternative depends on immediate action.

The Admiralty replied the next day with a terse rejection of the estimate of the men on the spot.

It is the firm intention of HMG * that if the French will not accept any of the alternatives which have been sent you, their ships must be destroyed. The proposals in your 1220/I are not therefore acceptable.

With a heavy heart, Admiral Somerville took Force H to sea on the afternoon of July 2, bound for Oran. By early morning Force H was off the harbor, and at 6:30 A.M., Captain Holland in H.M. destroyer *Foxhound* appeared off the entrance of the harbor and requested permission to enter. He then made the following signal which had been approved by the Admiralty:

The British Admiralty has sent Captain Holland to confer with you. The British Navy hopes their proposal will enable you and your glorious French Navy to range yourself side by side with them. In these circumstances your ships would remain yours and no one need have any anxiety for the future. A British fleet is at sea off Oran waiting to welcome you.

On receipt of this signal, Admiral Gensoul sent his barge to the *Foxhound* with his Flag Lieutenant, Lieutenant Dufay, to present his compliments. When Captain Holland requested permission to see Admiral Gensoul in person, Dufay returned to the *Dunkerque* for instructions. By this time lookouts had sighted Force H off the coast, and Admiral Gensoul sensed that he was being presented with an ultimatum. Stiffly he refused point-blank to meet Captain Holland or to associate in any way with those who would threaten him. At 8:47 A.M. he demanded that the *Foxhound* leave the harbor.

Captain Holland ordered the destroyer to comply and set out by ship's boat for the *Dunkerque*. Arriving on board, he was disappointed that he could not discuss the terms personally with the admiral. He gave the note to Lieutenant Dufay and returned to the boat to wait.

In the Flag Quarters of the *Dunkerque,* Gensoul, his Gallic pride already offended, sat down in no conciliatory frame of mind to read over the British communication.

To Monsieur l'Amiral Gensoul from Admiral Somerville.

His Majesty's Government have commanded me to inform you as follows:

They agreed on the French Government approaching the German Government only on condition that, if an armistice was concluded,

* His Majesty's Government.

the French Fleet should be sent to British ports. The Council of Ministers declared on 18th June that, before capitulating on land, the French Fleet would join up with the British or sink itself.

Whilst the present French Government may consider the terms of the Armistice with Germany and Italy are reconcilable with these undertakings, H.M. Government find it impossible from their previous experience to believe that Germany and Italy will not at any moment which suits them seize French warships and use them against Britain and Allies. Italian Armistice prescribes that French ships should return to metropolitan ports, and under armistice France is required to yield up units for coast defence and minesweeping.

It is impossible for us, your comrades up to now, to allow your fine ships to fall into the power of the German or Italian enemy. We are determined to fight on until the end and, if we win, as we think we shall, we shall never forget that France was our Ally, that our interests are the same as hers, and that our common enemy is Germany. Should we conquer, we solemnly declare we shall restore the greatness and territory of France. For this purpose we must be sure that the best ships of the French Navy will not be used against us by the common foe.

In these circumstances, H.M. Government have instructed me to demand that the French Fleet now at Mers-el-Kebir and Oran shall act in accordance with one of the following alternatives:

A. Sail with us and continue to fight for victory against the Germans and Italians.

B. Sail with reduced crews under our control to a British port. The reduced crews will be repatriated at the earliest possible moment. If either of these courses is adopted by you, we will restore your ships to France at the conclusion of the war, or pay full compensation if they are damaged meanwhile.

C. Alternatively, if you feel bound to stipulate that your ships should not be used against Germans or Italians, since this would break the Armistice, then sail them with us with reduced crews to some French port in the West Indies—Martinique, for instance—where they can be demilitarized to our satisfaction, or perhaps be entrusted to the United States of America, and remain safely until the end of the war, the crews being repatriated.

If you refuse these fair offers, I must with profound regret require you to sink your ships within six hours. Finally, failing the above, I have the orders of His Majesty's Government to use whatever force may be necessary to prevent your ships from falling into German or Italian hands.

The last paragraph of the message was clearly an ultimatum. Whether Gensoul would have responded more favorably had the message omitted the last paragraph will never be known. Those who knew the admiral believed he would.

When he read the actual message, he saw only the ultimatum. He ordered his ships cleared for action. At 10 A.M. he sent Dufay to Holland with the message:

> The assurances given to Admiral Sir Dudley North remain unchanged. In no case, anytime, anywhere, any way, and without further orders from the French Admiralty, will the French ships fall intact into the hands of the Germans or the Italians.
>
> Given the form and substance of the veritable ultimatum which has been sent to Admiral Gensoul, the French ships will defend themselves with force.

Thus with British *gaucherie* and Gallic pride the lines were drawn. The tragedy had to be played to its inevitable conclusion.

Before he sent his message to Captain Holland, Admiral Gensoul ordered his ships to raise steam and to clear for action. Through their glasses, British observers could see the awnings over quarterdecks being unrigged, the canvas covers being removed from the guns, and tompions being taken from the muzzles of the main batteries.

Fifteen minutes earlier, Admiral Gensoul had dispatched a highly misleading message to the French Admiralty.

> An English force composed of three battleships, an aircraft carrier, cruisers and destroyers before Oran has sent me an ultimatum: "Sink your ships; six-hour time limit, or we will constrain you to do so by force." My reply was: "French ships will answer force with force."

Admiral Gensoul bears a heavy responsibility before history for this telegram. While the British message to him had been an ultimatum, it had not been in the nature of a simple challenge: sink your ships or we will do it for you. The British had presented three options to these drastic measures; join them, turn their ships over to the British after sailing them to a British port, or accept demobilization in the West Indies or in the United States. Gensoul did not even give the French Government an opportunity to consider these propositions. Yet all three of the positive proposals involved political considerations far beyond his responsibilities as Commander in Chief of the Atlantic Raiding Force. The proposals had been drafted by the British War Cabinet, but Gensoul took it upon himself to see that the French Government had no opportunity to consider them.

Gensoul believed he was following Darlan's orders, as contained in his message of June 24, especially the crucial fifth paragraph which had not been communicated to the British: "In no case obey the orders of a foreign admiralty."

Gensoul's action reveals an essential weakness of the French military system. The loyalty of officers tends to be too much to the man, too much to the great leader rather than to the office the leader represents. Many French officers throughout history have shown that they look upon the Government as something transient, while their own leaders represent permanence and continuity. Often in French history the armed forces have not been the servants of the Government, arms by which the Government may implement its policy. They become the masters, and their decisions and their judgments commit the country to actions which the Government must accept. Admiral Gensoul in his reaction to the British ultimatum was conducting himself as he believed Darlan would desire. He ignored his responsibility of putting the political alternatives before those men whose duty it was to make political decisions.

Long afterwards, Admiral Gensoul admitted that he had acted under the press of emotions rather than reason. He testified before the High Commission investigating the acts of the Vichy Government:

How shall I explain the fact that in my telegram I did not reproduce the terms of the ultimatum as I did later in my report? I believe it was a consequence of an obsession which haunted me at that moment, which, to my mind left me but one alternative: to sink my ships or to see them sunk by the English. My sole thought was that it was absolutely impossible to obey and to submit to an ultimatum under the menace of English guns. I did not consider for a single moment the possibility of accepting the offer of sailing my fleet to the Antilles or the United States under the escort and menace of English ships. I perhaps could have accepted sailing freely for the United States, but not with English guns trained upon my ships. I did not at that moment recall Paragraph 3 of the telegram of the Admiralty of June 24 [which spoke of sending the ships to the United States]. Perhaps I should have thought of it, just as I should have sent the Admiralty a more complete extract of the English ultimatum. I can no longer explain why I did not do that nor why my staff officers (Admiral Danbé, Captain Clatin, now deceased, and Lieutenant Dufay) did not call my attention to this omission. The telegrams were prepared very hastily and this must be attributed to the circumstances of the moment.

At that crucial moment, the French Admiralty was in the process of moving from Bordeaux to Vichy, with an intermediate stop at Nerac, Admiral Darlan's family home, well to the south in Gascony.

The temporary establishment at Nerac was in the process of closing down. Darlan himself had left; with him he had taken a third of his staff. Half the remainder had departed a few hours later, leaving only a skeleton crew under Rear Admiral Le Luc. Le Luc was the one who received Gensoul's telegram and who had to take action upon it, since Darlan was completely out of reach.

Given Gensoul's distorted report of the British ultimatum, there could be but one reply any naval officer could have given: to resist force with force. Le Luc therefore quite properly ordered the admirals commanding the 4 heavy cruisers and 3 divisions of destroyers at Toulon and the 6 cruisers at Algiers: "Prepare for combat and rally to Oran under the orders of the admiral in the *Dunkerque*."

Only after issuing these orders did he succeed in reaching Darlan by telephone.

Darlan was, of course, outraged. He tried to open direct communication with Gensoul but could not get through. All his orders to Mers el Kebir had to go by telephone to Nerac, thence by telephone to Marseilles, and finally by cable to Oran. The French did not dare to use radio communications, for the British would be sure to intercept and read them. The French had been forbidden by the terms of the Armistice to employ codes and ciphers for military purposes. Also, if they used the radio with their messages uncoded, the Germans might intercept them and issue orders themselves which would be calculated to work to German and not necessarily to French interests.

Meanwhile, Lieutenant Dufay was conferring with Captain Holland aboard the *Foxhound*. Holland, keenly aware that Gensoul might be blind to everything but the threat contained in the last paragraph, urged Dufay to impress upon the admiral the several honorable alternatives to the disaster of Frenchmen fighting Englishmen. Such a tragedy could be of benefit only to the Germans and Italians. Holland stressed the point that the British in no way questioned Darlan's good faith in the promises he had made for the French fleet. What they did fear was that Darlan might not be able to carry out his promises. Implicit in this statement, although a point Holland did not put in words, was the British feeling that Pétain's Government could not be relied upon to permit Darlan to keep his word.

Dufay emphasized that Darlan had already given the necessary orders and that all preparations had been made to prevent the French ships from falling into enemy hands. No further orders from Darlan were necessary should the Germans or Italians attempt to seize control of the French ships. Dufay then made the tentative suggestion that the French ships might be disarmed at Mers el Kebir, since it was within easy reach of Gibraltar. From there the British could keep an eye on the fleet, where it would be far removed from Metropolitan France and from any threat of a German or Italian seizure by a *coup de main*. Holland returned a cautious answer, but suggested that some such arrangement might be possible.

At 10 A.M. Gensoul sent his Chief of Staff, Captain Danbé, with a curt written statement which seemed to bar the door to any further negotiations.

> Admiral Gensoul can only confirm what has already been communicated by Lieutenant Dufay.
>
> Admiral Gensoul is determined to defend himself by every means at his command.
>
> The first cannon shot against us will have the practical result of setting the entire French Fleet against Great Britain, a result which would be diametrically the opposite of that sought by the British Government.

Upon receiving this communication, Captain Holland saw his visitors to their boat. He then directed the commanding officer of the *Foxhound* to leave the harbor and set a course for the *Hood*. There seemed to be no hope left.

Then the Admiralty—and Mr. Churchill—increased the pressure on Admiral Somerville. In spite of French efforts at security, the British had intercepted Admiral Le Luc's message directing the French ships at Toulon and Algiers to rally to Mers el Kebir. The Admiralty passed this information on to Somerville with the advice: "Settle matters quickly or you will have reinforcements to deal with." In view of this development, Somerville signaled Gensoul, even as the *Foxhound* was making her way out of the harbor: "I regret that I shall be forced to open fire if you get under way without accepting one of my proposals."

Meanwhile, Admiral Gensoul, unable to believe that the British were deadly serious, had canceled his orders for the ships to prepare for action. He was not so sanguine, however, as to cancel the order for them to prepare to get under way. Perhaps the sight of their funnel smoke combined with the prospect of French reinforcements prompted Somerville to send his warning.

Somerville alternately displayed the velvet glove and the iron hand. An early message, "We hope that the propositions will be acceptable to you and that we will find you at our side," was followed later in the morning by a stern warning: "I regret to inform you that in conformity to my instructions I cannot permit you to leave the harbour until the terms of His Majesty's Government have been accepted."

At 12:30, a British plane made what the French have since charged was the first belligerent move. It dropped several mines in the main ship channel of Mers el Kebir.

Just a few minutes before the mines were placed, Admiral Gensoul sent a fuller but no less inaccurate report of the situation to the French Admiralty.

> Initial English ultimatum was: either to rally to the English Fleet or to destroy the ships within five hours to prevent their falling into German or Italian hands. Have replied: 1. The latter eventuality is not to be envisaged. 2. Shall defend myself by force at the first cannon shot, which will have a result diametrically opposed to that desired by the British Government.
>
> English reply: If you sail without accepting the British propositions which are reasonable and honourable, I shall open fire with regret. Captain Holland, who has served as intermediary, has indicated that disarmament at Mers el Kebir would appear to give a basis for arrangements, the latter under all severe reservations.

Gensoul's tentative reference to the possibility of local disarmament was undoubtedly a feeler, a request for the French Admiralty either to approve his inflexible stand or to issue him instructions for a local solution to the problem.

In the light of the signals between Gensoul and the French Admiralty the words, "which are reasonable and honourable," are puzzling. It would seem that Gensoul must have remembered the phrase from Lieutenant Dufay's report of the conversation with Captain Holland. The words appear nowhere in the messages sent by Admiral Somerville. They ought to have suggested to the French naval authorities in Nerac and Vichy that there were intermediate British proposals and not merely the extremes Gensoul had presented. But the French Admiralty, merely a distant spectator of the events, was in no mood to seek nuances. They had sent aid; now events must run their course.

As the deadline approached, Admiral Gensoul resumed his preparations to fight. He alerted the air forces and the coastal batteries. To the ships: turn over your main engines and prepare for action.

Only fifteen minutes of grace remained, when at 1:15 P.M. three messages were transmitted simultaneously. Admiral Somerville warned: "If you accept our propositions hoist a square white flag at the mainmast. If not, I will open fire." At the same time the radio room on the *Dunkerque* picked up a message from the French Admiralty ordering Gensoul to stop any demobilization of his force. A French reprisal was to be undertaken against Gibraltar. It is not clear whether Gensoul had seen this message before he sent his next one to Admiral Somerville. Most probably he had not, for Gensoul, as a man of honor, could not have said he was awaiting a reply from his Government if he had already received it. He must have replied to Somerville before he read the message from Vichy. He signaled:

I have no intention of getting under way. I have telegraphed to my Government from whom I am awaiting a reply. Do not create the irreparable.

On the receipt of this message, Admiral Somerville extended his deadline for two hours, until 3:30 P.M. Then Gensoul signaled that he was ready to receive Captain Holland personally for honorable discussions. When he reached the *Dunkerque* at 3:15 P.M., Captain Holland was conducted immediately to Admiral Gensoul's quarters. The meeting between these old friends was tense, for both men realized that unless they could find some way out of their horrible dilemma, tragedy would come. Admiral Somerville once again extended his deadline for another two hours, and the two men plunged into desperate negotiations, each vainly trying to find a formula consistent with his orders and acceptable to the other side.

Captain Holland opened the proceedings by assuring Admiral Gensoul that the British did not intend to confront him with an ultimatum. No one doubted Admiral Darlan's word, not for a movement. But the British Government believed the admiral would not be allowed to keep his promises. The Germans would in some way manage to seize the French ships by surprise. Admiral Darlan would be placed in such a position that he could not issue the orders necessary to stop it.

Admiral Gensoul showed Captain Holland Darlan's message of June 24. He emphasized Paragraph 3, which directed that if the armistice clauses were not respected by the Germans, the ships would, without further orders, be sailed to the United States or be scuttled. This paragraph went a long way toward allaying British fears. Gensoul added his personal word of honor that he would demobilize his ships. He also promised that he would reply by force to any German moves against his vessels. If the Germans threatened him, he would sail to Martinique or to the United States. But he would not do it under the compulsion of British guns.

Captain Holland argued that he could prevent disaster. He had only to do at the moment what he promised he would if the Germans threatened him. No, said the admiral. Not under British pressure. Holland gave up. He could do no more. He sent word:

> Admiral Gensoul says crews being reduced and if threatened by enemy would go to Martinique or U.S.A. but this is not quite our proposition. Can get no nearer.

This message reached Admiral Somerville at 5 P.M. Thirty minutes remained. In his flag quarters in the *Hood,* with the ship cleared for action, Somerville was making his painful decision. He knew that he could not accept the conditions Gensoul had set. German troops might infiltrate French North Africa and suddenly seize the ships. Even if they did not, the French ships in North Africa would be totally dependent on the Germans for fuel. If the Germans knew their business, and they did, they would not permit the French to have enough fuel to cross the Atlantic.

Meanwhile, French reinforcements were speeding toward Oran. Shortly he might have to face both surface and submarine attack. In addition to possible French attack, the Italians might well be on him. By this time the whole world knew of his presence. He had been in one place for twelve hours, and each passing moment cut into his margin of safety.

He simply could not afford to risk longer delay. Accordingly he sent a final message to Admiral Gensoul:

> If none of the British proposals are acceptable by 17:30 BST,* I repeat 17:30 BST, it will be necessary to sink your ships.

When Admiral Gensoul receive this message, he silently read it and handed it to Captain Holland without a word. There was nothing more to be said. The admiral rose, nodded briefly to Captain Holland, and left the room. French officers conducted him to the ship's side. They rendered him departing honors as he left the ship.

As he departed, Holland could see the crews of the French ships running to their battle stations.

On the flag bridge of the *Dunkerque,* Gensoul said sorrowfully to an aide: "I have done everything to gain time. Now it is finished!"

The ghosts of Napoleon and Wellington, of Nelson and Villeneuve, might have looked on grimly at the events of the next hour. Admiral

---

* 17:30 BST—5:30 P.M. British Summer Time, one hour ahead of Greenwich time.

Gensoul, on the flag bridge of the *Dunkerque,* faced the consequences to which national pride and a stubborn, literal obedience to orders had driven him. At any moment British salvos might come hurtling down on him and on this fleet which he had commanded so proudly.

He had done his full duty. He had resisted all pressure, he had obeyed the orders of his admiral, François Darlan, to the letter. The fact that he was responsible for those orders because he had sent Darlan incomplete and misleading information did not seem to enter his mind.

Whatever happened now, he had fulfilled his role. It only remained to accept the inevitable consequences.

Whatever happened, he must let history justify him by accepting the first blow. He made no move to train his guns or to get his ships under way. The British must be the ones to end the cease-fire which had endured for a century and a quarter.

Aboard the *Hood,* Admiral Somerville unflinchingly contemplated the task before him. The Prime Minister had sent a message which goes far to describe his feelings. "You are charged," wrote Churchill, "with one of the most disagreeable and difficult tasks that a British Admiral has ever been faced with, but we have complete confidence in you and rely on you to carry it out relentlessly."

His horror at his task in no way weakened Somerville's determination. In his desperate efforts to avert tragedy he had violated his instructions from the Admiralty by twice extending the deadline. Now he could wait no longer. Even at this last moment he held off, hoping against hope that something might yet save the situation at the last moment.

The deadline of 5:30 P.M. came and went. The *Foxhound,* bearing Captain Holland, cleared the harbor and set course for Force H.

He looked in vain for any signal from her. Turning his long glass on the *Dunkerque,* he saw only French battle colors—no sign of the square white flag which would have meant French submission. The moments passed. Nearly half an hour went by. Finally, at 5:55 P.M., his face set in grim determination, Somerville quietly gave his order.

"Open fire!"

The *Hood's* eight 15-inch guns crashed out their first salvo. Seconds later the shells struck the wharf astern of the French capital ships. Immediately Admiral Gensoul ordered the fire returned. At 6 P.M. he telegraphed to Vichy: "In action against the British Force."

A hundred and twenty-five years of peace and friendship between Britain and France had come to an end. Not since the Battle of

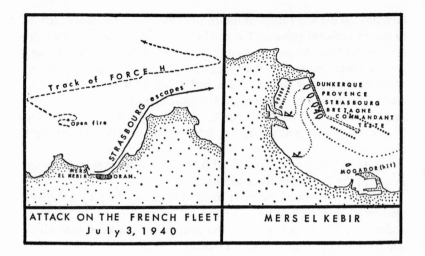

ATTACK ON THE FRENCH FLEET July 3, 1940	MERS EL KEBIR

Waterloo in 1815 had French and British forces exchanged fire in anger.

Meanwhile, aircraft from the *Ark Royal* were pressing in on Mers el Kebir to drop mines and to spot the fall of shot for the *Hood, Resolution, Valiant, Arethusa,* and *Enterprise.* Civilians and sailors on the dock waved gaily to the pilots. No one had told them of the danger. Many of the wavers suddenly became grisly fragments of shredded flesh. For this horrible, needless slaughter, Admiral Gensoul must bear a large share of responsibility. Knowing that shells might fall at any second, he had done nothing to clear the pier of civilians or needless personnel. It was incomprehensible negligence.

As the first shells burst, Gensoul ordered all ships to make a dash for the open sea. All crews worked feverishly to cast off moorings, raise anchors, and maneuver their ships out of their cramped berths. Now the consequences of their positions became dreadfully apparent. The two battle cruisers, *Dunkerque* and *Strasbourg,* had been designed with all their main-battery guns forward and could not reply to British fire unless they could turn. Only the four after guns of the battleships *Bretagne* and *Provence* could bear. Only the *Dunkerque* had a clear angle of fire, but her guns could not bear at the moment. While she was slipping her anchor chain and casting off the final hawser which bound her to the dock, she received a 15-inch hit, followed quickly by three others. Her electrical system went out. Her guns were useless for the moment, for her turrets could not train. She moved well up into the bay and anchored. On the way, she managed to get off four

210

salvos at the *Hood,* fired under local control, the turrets painfully trained by sweating men.

The *Bretagne* took a hit in her after magazine at 5:58 while her crew struggled to free her from her moorings. A massive column of flame shot up from her stern. The fires spread rapidly, and by 6:07 she was ablaze from the bridge aft. Two minutes later, she sank, taking 977 men to their deaths.

The *Provence* slipped her lines and then swung wide to give the *Dunkerque* room to get out. As she pulled clear, a 15-inch shell slammed into her stern. Another, barely missing, raised a huge column of water which helped to smother the flames. The water turned to steam as she burned even more fiercely. In grave danger of sinking and blocking the channel, her captain beached her in 5 fathoms of water. There she remained, out of the fight.

Another 15-inch shell blew the stern off the destroyer *Mogador.* Thanks to excellent damage control, she did not sink and was able to anchor in shallow water, absolutely helpless to move with no rudder and screws. Miraculously the *Commandant Teste* remained untouched during the battle.

More fortunate than her consorts, the *Strasbourg,* unable to weigh her anchors in time, let the chains run out through the hawse holes and, casting off her stern lines, got under way. Captain Collinet rang for full speed. A 15-inch salvo fell in the berth the ship had just vacated. Twisting and turning through the crowded and narrow harbor, he made a dash for the entrance. By 6:10 she had reached the mouth of the harbor and was making 15 knots. Escaping the British mines by some miracle, she set out for Toulon, her speed increasing all the time. She drove off an inquisitive British destroyer with her 13-inch guns. The destroyer promptly took refuge behind a smoke screen. Accompanied by 5 French destroyers from Oran, the *Strasbourg* succeeded in making good her escape.

The initial phase of the action lasted but seventeen minutes. At 6:10 P.M., Admiral Gensoul signaled to Admiral Somerville, "All my ships are out of action. I request that you cease fire."

"Hoist the designated signal," Somerville replied.

A brief search on the *Dunkerque* for a square white flag ended when someone brought out a light tan blanket with pale blue stripes. Admiral Gensoul ordered this hoisted to the mainmast. It had the desired effect.

At 6:12, Force H ceased fire.

Gensoul was not accurate when he stated that all his ships were out of action, for the *Strasbourg* was well on her way. Perhaps, literally speaking, she was no longer a part of Gensoul's command. At any rate, her captain did not allow his admiral's capitulation to change his actions.

As the *Strasbourg* made her dash from the harbor, Force H was well to the westward to avoid the shore batteries east of Oran. Thus Somerville's ships were in poor position to intercept the French battle cruiser and her guardian destroyers speeding northeastward. Because of the haze and gunsmoke, Somerville could not see their movements. When an aircraft from the *Ark Royal* reported them ten minutes later, Somerville at first discredited the report. Gensoul had said that all his ships were out of action. In another ten minutes, the sighting confirmed, Somerville gave chase with Force H. He recalled a flight of 6 Swordfish torpedo bombers from the harbor and sent them after the fleeing *Strasbourg*. All torpedoes missed. Nor was a later strike, launched about 8:20 P.M., any more successful.

By this time the French ships were some 25 miles ahead of Force H, and Somerville gave up the pursuit.

Taking advantage of the distraction of the *Strasbourg*'s dash, the destroyers *Poursuivante* and *Bordelaise* and the auxiliary *Rigault de Genouilly* broke from Oran. The two destroyers got through to Toulon successfully, but the *Rigault de Genouilly* fell victim to the British submarine *Pandora,* which had lain off Oran with her sister *Proteus.* The *Strasbourg* and her consorts reached Toulon safely on the evening of July 4. The *Commandant Teste* followed the next day.

Meanwhile Somerville, sick at heart, recalled all forces and shaped his course for Gibraltar.

At Mers el Kebir Admiral Gensoul sadly regarded the ruins of his fleet. Not only the wreckage of the Atlantic Raiding Force lay in the waters of Mers el Kebir. With those ships lay the wreckage of Anglo-French friendship.

CHAPTER NINE

The Gentlemen's Agreement

He that is slow to anger is better than
the mighty; and he that ruleth his
spirit than he that taketh a city.
Proverbs

Two admirals at Alexandria flew their flags proudly from their respective flagships. Each had the highest regard for the other's professional ability. They were close friends. They had sailed together against the Italians, and they had talked together, dined and wined together.

The fact that one was British and one was French had hardly seemed to matter.

When the British resumed responsibility for the eastern Mediterranean in late May, 1940, Admiral Sir Andrew Browne Cunningham shifted his flag from Malta to Alexandria. By early June he had assembled under his command a force of 4 battleships, a small aircraft carrier, 5 cruisers, 2 antiaircraft cruisers, and a number of smaller vessels, including destroyers, minesweepers, and auxiliaries. To this fleet the French had added a detachment known as Force X, consisting of the battleship *Lorraine,* the heavy cruiser *Duquesne,* flying the flag of Vice Admiral René Godfroy, 2 other heavy cruisers, a light cruiser, 3 destroyers, and 6 submarines. Force X had originally had 3 battleships, but 2 of them had been shifted to the west during the Battle of France. They had been at Mers el Kebir.

As soon as Italy entered the war, Admiral Cunningham had taken his fleet to sea on a sweep against Italian shipping in the eastern Mediterranean. The French cruisers had taken part in this operation. The sweep was worse than unsuccessful, for they found no Italian units, but lost the cruiser *Calypso* to an Italian submarine. But the operation was symbolic of the brotherhood in arms shared by the two fleets at that stage of the war.

The French collapse caused a particularly serious embarrassment at Alexandria, because the British could not leave port. Instead of being free to seek the enemy, they had to remain in the harbor to keep watch over a friend.

It was an intolerable situation.

Cunningham knew Godfroy as a man of honor who would never attempt to hinder the British from carrying out their missions. On the other hand, no one could doubt that he would obey orders if Darlan directed him to take his ships to some port under French control. As long as the French ships were seaworthy and battleworthy, Cunningham had to keep his ships swinging idly around their anchors. And his ships were vitally needed at sea.

In the last days of France's belligerency Admiral Cunningham received instructions from the First Sea Lord, Sir Dudley Pound, to urge Godfroy and Force X to fight on, regardless of the actions of the French Government. Failing that, he must gain control of the French ships before the surrender, or if this proved impossible, have them sunk. This British pressure arose from War Cabinet fears that they might have to evacuate the eastern Mediterranean. If such a move had to be made, the British would have to deal with Force X first.

Admiral Cunningham vigorously opposed the withdrawal of his command from Alexandria. He radioed that he considered the position in the eastern Mediterranean vital in spite of the paramount importance of the Atlantic. Withdrawal of the fleet would mean the collapse of General Wavell's command in Egypt, followed by the inevitable loss of Egypt, Palestine, Cyprus, and Malta. In addition, Britain would forfeit the respect of the whole Moslem world and lose the benefit of Turkey's benevolent neutrality. He felt that if the Mediterranean Fleet remained, it could stand off the Italian Navy and avert disaster in the Middle East.

But before the Mediterranean Fleet could accomplish this task, it must throw off the shackles of the now useless and potentially dangerous French squadron at Alexandria.

The French and British units were anchored together in Alexandria Harbor. The crews enjoyed all the friendship and camaraderie suitable for brothers in arms. British officers enjoyed the French cooking aboard the ships of Force X, while French officers talked shop over pink gins with their opposite numbers in British wardrooms. Nothing

214

was further from the minds of these comrades of the sea than the thought that events might put them in deadly hate of one against the other.

On June 24 Admiral Godfroy received a message from Bordeaux ordering him to take his fleet to join a small French detachment at Beirut in Syria. Admiral Cunningham, too, had received orders, and in a courteously worded memorandum the same day requested Godfroy to immobilize his ships. The French admiral was, naturally, helpless to comply with the directive from France. It was out of the question for Godfroy to fight his way out of the harbor; he was badly out-gunned, and his ships were so intermixed with those of the British that any display of force would inevitably result in a confused melee in which no one could fire on a foe without endangering a friend. When Darlan learned of Godfroy's helpless position, it did nothing to mollify his attitude toward the British.

In common with other Frenchmen of the time, Admiral Godfroy spiritedly supported the war until his Government surrendered and most of his native land was occupied. Then the fight seemed to drain out of him; his thoughts reverted more and more to returning his ships to France and his men to their homes.

The situation remained at an impasse for several days. Then, on June 29, the Admiralty sent Admiral Cunningham the plans for Operation Catapult, the moves to be taken against the French ships at Mers el Kebir, Alexandria, and elsewhere. Cunningham detested the instructions sent him, feeling that they were dishonorable. He had been told to seize the French ships by a *coup de main*. The ties of friendship between him and Godfroy, the ties of brotherhood between the crews, and the ties of amity between the two nations would all be severed by such an act of treachery. In his view, no such violent measures were necessary; the helplessness of the French ships, the desire of their men to return to France, the lack of pay and provisions would, in time, solve the problem without either bloodshed or dishonor. In some heat he dispatched a strongly worded message to London the following day.

I cannot see what benefit is to be derived from forcible seizure of ships in Alexandria, and am most strongly opposed to the proposal. Request urgent consideration of the following points.
1. Apparently situation at Alexandria is quite different from that elsewhere in Mediterranean. . . .
2. If ships are to be seized, what is the object? If it is to prevent ships falling into enemy hands, that has already been achieved.

3. I am convinced that the French would resist most strongly, so that if it is desired to obtain ships for our own use it is unlikely to be achieved by forcible seizure. Such action would be more likely to result in ships being scuttled at their moorings, a harbour filled with wrecks and unnecessary British and French casualties.

4. Moreover, the effect is likely to be disastrous in the Middle East, particularly in the Suez Canal and at Djibuti, where French co-operation is vitally important, and in Syria, whose friendly attitude is very necessary.

5. On the other hand, it is quite likely that if things are allowed to go on as they are, the ships may drop into our hands under pressure of lack of pay and food. . . .

6. However, this appreciation makes no allowance for the repercussions which would follow the use of force at Oran. I am strongly opposed to such action there if it can possibly be avoided. I am not in full possession of the facts, but may remark that the whole of the friendly French element may be alienated, and in particular I would mention the effect in North Africa where friendly attitude may greatly affect naval operations later on. . . .

In reply he received a much more moderate set of instructions. There was to be no violence. Those Frenchmen who chose to serve on board their ships would be paid by the British Government. Then followed two choices to be given the French: one to immobilize their ships in Alexandria, and the second to scuttle them at sea. Admiral Cunningham was to present Admiral Godfroy with these alternatives at promptly 7 A.M. on July 3 so that it would be simultaneous with the actions to be taken against the French fleet elsewhere. Cunningham was strictly charged to complete the affair by dark the same day.

It should detract in no way from the triumph of Admiral Cunningham's diplomacy to note that he had a much easier situation to face than the one at Mers el Kebir. At Alexandria the French had no freedom of action with their ships penned up in a harbor controlled by the British. The personal friendship between the two commanders made it possible for them to negotiate face to face. Also Admiral Cunningham was considerably senior to Admiral Somerville and could afford to take more liberties with Admiralty instructions.

Yet all of these advantages could have been nullified had not both Admiral Cunningham and Admiral Godfroy displayed tact, good judgment, and independence of decision. Both ignored instructions from their respective admiralties. Both showed common sense when they received stupid instructions.

Punctually at 7 A.M. on July 3, Admiral Godfroy presented himself on board H.M.S. *Warspite,* flagship of the British Mediterranean Fleet. Nearby, apparently calm, but ready for any eventuality, the other British ships rode at their anchors. In addition to the *Warspite,* 3 other battleships, *Ramillies, Malaya,* and *Royal Sovereign,* lent imposing weight to the scene. Not far off swung the small aircraft carrier *Eagle,* accompanied by the cruisers *Orion, Neptune, Sydney, Gloucester,* and *Liverpool.* Admiral Godfroy was well aware that something important was in the wind because of the unusual hour of the meeting. He could scarcely have been unimpressed by the powerful force lying so peacefully in the blue waters of the harbor.

In Admiral Cunningham's after cabin the two commanders sat down to a formal discussion, speaking English except when there was a possibility of misapprehension on Godfroy's part, at which time Commander R. M. Dick of Cunningham's staff would interpret.

Admiral Cunningham then gave him a message from the British Government. It expressed the hope that he would agree to have his ships continue in the war against the common enemy. As this message was only a vague generalization designed to set the tone of the meeting, the two admirals then got down to specifics. Instead of presenting all the proposals at once as Somerville and Holland had been forced to do at Mers el Kebir, Admiral Cunningham presented his one by one, allowing for discussion of each. At the outset, he told his guest that his instructions required him to reach agreement before nightfall. He then read the first proposal.

The British Government asks you to put at their disposition the Naval units under your command so that they can continue to struggle against the enemy side by side with the British Navy.

For those who wish to join us the conditions of service and pay will be the same as that of officers, petty officers and men of corresponding rank in the British Navy. Those who do not wish to continue the fight are entirely free to return to France and arrangements will be made as soon as practicable for them to do so.

You are asked to announce these proposals in such a way that they are known to all officers and ships' companies and to make it clear that they are free to make their choice without any constraint.

The British Government guarantees to return to France at the end of the war all ships which have thus taken part with us in the struggle against the enemy.

Admiral Godfroy had several objections. He had no authority to hand his ships over to a foreign government; if he did, he and his men would be deserters. Also, such a move would be a clear viola-

217

tion of the armistice and would expose France to severe retaliation on the part of her conquerors.

Admiral Cunningham rejoined that he could bypass Godfroy and make the offer directly to the French officers and enlisted men with, perhaps, a fair chance of success. He was, he hastened to add, reluctant to appeal to subordinates over their commander's head and would do it only if there seemed no other way.

With no agreement in sight on the first proposition, the two admirals passed on to a consideration of the second:

> If you remain convinced that it is not possible to allow your forces to help the British Navy, the British Government asks you to put your ships in a condition in which they cannot go to sea, and leave on board only skeleton crews sufficient to keep the ships in good order.
>
> In this case the British Government guarantees the pay and supplies for the officers and men thus left on board, and that the ships will only be used if the enemy breaks the terms of the armistice between France, Germany, and Italy.

This proposal seemed to make an immediate appeal to Godfroy. He asked for a little time to think it over, and agreed to give his answer by 11:30 A.M.

To make the record complete, Admiral Cunningham then presented the third proposal.

> If these proposals are neither of them acceptable, the British Government asks you as a third alternative to order your forces in Alexandria to sea in order to sink them outside the port in deep waters.

In his memoirs, Admiral Cunningham noted that the second proposal would be most suitable. It would permit Godfroy to preserve his ships so that they could be used again if Italy or Germany should break the armistice, as he fully expected they would. Admiral Cunningham then argued that Godfroy would not be violating the armistice or his honor by accepting any of the British proposals since he was confronted with overwhelming force. *Force majeure* would prevent any blame from falling on him or on France by his acceptance of the British terms.

As Admiral Godfroy rose to take his departure, Admiral Cunningham assured him that he hoped his decision would be to accept the first proposition so that they could continue as comrades in arms.

Jubilant at Godfroy's reasonable behavior, Admiral Cunningham sent a dispatch to the Admiralty stating his belief that Godfroy would accept the proposal to immobilize his ships.

At noon Godfroy sent a disappointing answer to Cunningham. He proposed to accept the third proposal; he would sink his own ships. If he had been able to communicate with France,* he went on to say, he would have recommended the second proposition. But on his own responsibility, his sense of duty would not allow him to disarm his ships in a foreign port under the constraint of a foreign navy.

In using this argument, Godfroy does not appear to have been thinking very clearly. It was precisely the fact that he was under the constraint of a foreign navy that would have given legal weight to a decision to immobilize the ships. He could do this on his own responsibility under threat of *force majeure*. The French Government could not have ordered him to accept this proposition without violating the armistice. The government could disavow Godfroy's actions; they could not disavow their own.

Since he could not initiate radio communications with his Government, Admiral Godfroy's letter went on to say, he had no choice but to accept the third proposal and sink his ships, as the only way open to him as a French naval officer and a man of honor.

He asked to be given forty-eight hours to make his preparations. To this distressing letter Admiral Cunningham replied:

> My instructions leave me with no alternative but to accept your choice to take your ships to sea and to sink them in open waters.
>
> I am prepared to accept the delay of forty-eight hours during which you are making arrangements for the safety and transport of your ships' companies and will gladly facilitate any action you wish taken in this respect.
>
> I am therefore under the painful necessity of asking you to proceed to sea to carry out your purpose at 1200 on Friday, 5th July.

This official letter was quickly followed by a personal one in which Cunningham proposed some suggestions for relieving the unhappy situation. Since Godfroy felt that he could not set his crews ashore in a foreign port, Cunningham suggested that he might be willing to remove his fuel and to take the warheads off his torpedoes. Under these conditions, his ships would not be able to proceed to sea, and thus the Mediterranean Fleet would be released from its onerous and undesired surveillance of the French ships. It would then be free to go about its business of carrying on the war.

* This was because of the move of the French Admiralty as noted in the previous chapter. Later in the day, communications were restored.

Godfroy quickly agreed to this proposal, and by late afternoon the French ships had begun pumping fuel into fuel barges.

After he had reported to London his satisfaction at the way events were going, Cunningham was outraged to receive the following from the Admiralty:

> Admiralty note that oil fuel is being discharged by French ships. Reduction of crews, especially by ratings, should begin at once by landing or transfer to merchant ships, before dark tonight. Do not, repeat NOT, fail.

This, Admiral Cunningham wrote, is "a perfect example of the type of signal which should never be made." It was clearly calculated to undermine the confidence of the man on the spot who knew the situation far more clearly than anyone could at Whitehall, some 3000 miles distant from the scene. Throughout the war the Admiralty displayed a lamentable desire to get its finger in the pie and interfere in the operational decisions of the man on the scene. In particular, Winston Churchill, both as First Lord of the Admiralty and as Prime Minister, permitted his impatience to lead him to actions and orders which disturbed or frustrated the local commander. So long as the commander is conforming to the intent of the High Command, he should be left alone. If one has to tell the local commander how to do his job, it is time to get a new commander.

The final idiocy of the message was that when it was sent, it was already dark in Alexandria. It could not be obeyed. Therefore Admiral Cunningham simply ignored it.

Admiral Godfroy, too, had received a message from his superiors: "Get under way, by force if necessary."

He made the obviously truthful reply. "The conditions of the anchorage do not permit us to leave port, even by fighting our way out. We will defend ourselves where we are if we are attacked, remaining ready, if necessary, to scuttle ourselves."

By this time, Godfroy had received news of Somerville's ultimatum at Mers el Kebir. Shaken as he was, he penned a moderate letter in his own hand to Admiral Cunningham.

Admiral,

I have just learned that an ultimatum has been addressed to our Atlantic Fleet by the British Admiralty.

On the other hand my Admiralty has ordered me to sail, though I have asked to be assured that the order is authentic.

I have replied that sailing is impossible, but that the situation is definitely changing.

So that I may not incur reproach for having discharged oil-fuel after receiving an order to sail, I have stopped the discharge of oil-fuel pending events.

But that changes nothing. I give my word as to my intentions, which remain unchanged from those which I expressed to you in writing this morning.

This note meant that Cunningham's personal appeal had failed. The intentions expressed in writing had been to sink his ships. The compromise to offload fuel oil had been oral. Cunningham sent his Chief of Staff, Rear Admiral Sir Algernon U. Willis, to the *Duquesne* to try to bring Admiral Godfroy around once more. If anything, Willis found the situation worse than suggested by Godfroy's letter, for the French admiral now refused to take his ships to sea to sink them peacefully.

"If I am permitted to leave harbor," he said, "I will make a dash for freedom!"

"But, sir—" objected Admiral Willis.

"I know, sir. It will mean a running battle with you. I cannot help that, I have my duty. And if you threaten me in port, I will scuttle my ships where they lie anchored."

The two men talked on, but they could make no headway.

As Sir Algernon rose to take his leave, Admiral Godfroy drew him aside for a moment, an expression of grim humor on his face.

"If I am forced to scuttle my ships, *mon Amiral,*" he confided, "I shall take care to do it where the hulks will inconvenience you as little as possible."

Admiral Cunningham realized that the situation could not be allowed to remain as it was. In a midnight conference, he and his staff considered three possibilities. First, they could attempt to board and capture the French ships at their anchorages. They rejected that idea, since it would be almost impossible, now that the French had been alerted. The second option was to sink them by gunfire and torpedoes where they were. This action could only cause useless bloodshed and would expose the British ships to damage so they could not pursue the war against Italy. And like the first possibility, it would be dishonorable. The only other possibility they saw was to demand that Admiral Godfroy intern or surrender his ships. They knew what his answer would be; he would forthwith sink them. In spite of the obvious disadvantages of this plan, the other two had even more, so Admiral Cunningham radioed to the Admiralty that he intended to implement it on Friday morning, July 5.

Admiral Cunningham then retired for the night. Early the next morning he was awakened by the arrival of another letter from Admiral Godfroy. The Frenchman had learned of the attack on the French ships at Mers el Kebir. Curtly he informed Admiral Cunningham that he was repudiating any and all agreements he had made the day before and was reserving to himself complete freedom of action. That meant he might try to fight his way out of the harbor at any moment.

Cunningham prepared for action. It would be a stupid battle. Hitler and Mussolini would be overjoyed. No one else would.

While the French ships raised steam, a process which would take several hours, Cunningham ordered his ships to be kedged around so that their broadsides or torpedoes could bear on the French. Meanwhile, he and Commander Dick had their heads together to draft another appeal to the French commander. What else could they do? They would have to be quick before the French ships were ready to get under way.

They decided that the best thing would be to try to win over the French officers and men. Commander Dick composed suitable messages in French. Signalmen busily clacked the shutters of their signal lights. *Matelots* and French officers read the appeals, letter by letter. Other officers copied these messages on large blackboards. Boat crews passed close to the French ships, holding the boards up so the *matelots* could read them.

The French, meanwhile, ostentatiously refrained from any move which could be interpreted as a menace or threat. With British guns trained on French ships, the French guns remained steadfastly amidships. The destroyer *Duguay Trouin* rigged a scaffold, and soon a working party was on it, touching up the paintwork. The *Lorraine* sounded swimming call; in a few moments many of her crew could be seen splashing in the waters alongside.

The commanding officers of the British ships paid visits to their opposite French numbers. These visits quickly revealed that there was no hostility in the minds of the French.

"When I saw the tompions being removed from your guns, I immediately ordered the tompions to be placed in mine," remarked one French captain to his guest.

In the midst of this scene of high comedy which might have turned to stark tragedy at any moment, an Italian airplane flew over the harbor. British antiaircraft guns opened up on the intruder; the French merrily joined in, perhaps savoring a welcome relief from tension.

The situation was approaching the ridiculous. Admiral Godfroy, while attempting to adhere to the stiff, unyielding instructions he was receiving from France, had but to look about him to see spontaneous signs of friendship and affection on all sides. It seemed that the British appeals were having their effect, and Godfroy knew that he might be unable to count on obedience on the part of his crews if he forced matters to a show-down. About noon, Godfroy ordered all his captains to meet aboard the *Duquesne*. This conference, which lasted about an hour, might be termed a "council of peace," rather than a council of war, for it led to a way out.

Shortly after lunch, Admiral Godfroy repaired on board the *Warspite* and told Admiral Cunningham that he yielded to overwhelming force. This declaration protected France from retaliation by Germany or Italy, since the French Government had not authorized his actions.

It also meant that he would face court-martial should he return to France.

The two admirals quickly agreed upon the conditions.

(a) All oil fuel to be discharged from the French ships forthwith.
(b) Ships to be placed immediately in a condition in which they cannot fight.
(c) Discharge of ships' companies to be a matter for further discussion; but it was agreed that they should be reduced.

"The Gentlemen's Agreement" was reached in the early afternoon of July 4, and a more formal undertaking was signed on July 7. By this time the French crews had been reduced by some 70 percent, while those who remained on board were being paid and fed by the British Government.

The "Gentlemen's Agreement" was never violated on either side. Godfroy never missed an opportunity to express sympathy or congratulations to Admiral Cunningham as the occasion warranted. Once he wrote:

> Since we cannot fire our guns during these bombing attacks, we are reduced to watch. It is a pity we can do nothing, because our excellent stereoscopic range-finders would be very valuable at night when hostile aircraft are unlighted by searchlights. But we shall use our small guns and machine-guns against dive-bombers if they seem to fly against us. My thoughts were with you during all these last days we have

passed. . . . In spite of the fact that many things are turning more difficult for us here, I try to remain patient in that long ordeal. The idea of your understanding so well our situation helps me.

Almost as soon as the Gentlemen's Agreement had been signed, Admiral Cunningham took the Mediterranean Fleet to sea, confident in Admiral Godfroy's honor, that he could do so in safety. Out of the harbor steamed the *Warspite, Malaya, Royal Sovereign, Eagle, Orion, Neptune, Sydney, Gloucester,* and *Liverpool.* Two days later they were in action in the first major fleet engagement of the war. In this action, the British gained the moral edge over the Italians, who became increasingly circumspect in sending their convoys to Libya. The result was that Marshal Graziani, drawn up with his army near the Egyptian border, was continually on short rations. Thus the Italians were in a poor position to attack General Wavell's position in the Eastern Desert. Perhaps it is not too much to say that the Gentlemen's Agreement reached at Alexandria not only prevented another catastrophe like the one at Mers el Kebir, but indirectly preserved the whole British position in the Middle East.

There was still more to Operation Catapult. Several other groups of French warships had to be dealt with.

At Portsmouth Navy Yard Nelson's flagship *Victory,* permanently enshrined in drydock, flies the flag of the Flag Officer Commanding Portsmouth. On the early morning of June 3, nearby the *Victory* lay the old French battleship *Courbet,* the super-destroyer *Leopard,* 5 destroyers, 2 submarines, and several auxiliaries. The watch had been relieved, and the men of the duty section settled down to the routine, waiting for the sun to rise.

Farther west at Plymouth was another small group of French ships, the venerable battleship *Paris,* the super-destroyer *Triomphant,* 3 destroyers, the gigantic submarine *Surcouf,* 2 smaller submarines, and a few lesser warships and auxiliaries. At several other ports, Falmouth, Swansea, and Dundee, were other units bringing the grand total to 50 French ships.

On news of the French surrender, the British War Cabinet issued an order forbidding these ships to sail. The French reacted strongly to this order through their Chief of Naval Mission in London, Admiral Oden'hal, who wrote the First Sea Lord, Admiral of the Fleet, Sir Dudley Pound:

I just receive [sic] a message from Admiral Darlan stating that the dispositions of the Armistice have been accepted by the French on the only condition that the French Fleet must definitely remain French under the French Flag with a French reduced complement and is to remain French finally.

Admiral Darlan considers that these dispositions have nothing contrary to the British interests.

But he has been sadly impressed in learning that the British Admiralty opposed the departure of the French warships now in the United Kingdom ports; such a position, if maintained, could only be considered as unfriendly by the French Government. Therefore, Admiral Darlan requests me to ask you most pressingly to alter your decision at an early date.

In normal times, these ships, immobilized in British ports, could be no conceivable menace to Britain. But the times were not normal. Under pressure of events, the Cabinet decided that these ships must be seized at the same time that moves were made against the French units elsewhere. Seizure would give de Gaulle a naval force. Then, too, the French sailors would be unable to do anything when they learned what had happened to their brothers at Mers el Kebir. There would be no bloody battles in Portsmouth and Plymouth.

Churchill had early fixed upon General Charles de Gaulle as the one man likely to inspire French resistance. But Frenchmen seemed in no hurry to rally to the Cross of Lorraine. If de Gaulle had a naval and military force, things might get better. Loyal Frenchmen would, Churchill thought, rush to de Gaulle if only he had something to fight with. The 50 French ships in British ports would serve as a naval nucleus. At the very least, many of these ships could be immediately useful as convoy escorts in the Atlantic.

As the morning watch * on the French ships was passing, stealthy, silent groups of British bluejackets moved into position. At 4:30 A.M. a British officer presented himself at the quarterdeck of each French ship and announced that he desired to see the commanding officer. At the same time, the British sailors disarmed the French sentries and quickly penetrated the berthing spaces. They turned the indignant French sailors out and sent them ashore still dressed in sleeping garments. Later, the Frenchmen were allowed to return to their vessels in small groups to dress and gather their personal belongings.

* The morning watch runs from 4 A.M. to 8 A.M. The watch from 8 A.M. to 12 noon is known as the forenoon watch.

225

On nearly all the French ships the coup worked smoothly. Aboard the submarine *Mistral* at Plymouth, alert officers were able to open scuttles, and the submarine began to settle at her moorings. The British boarding officer calmly stood by and made it clear that if the submarine sank, her crew would go down with her. No one would be allowed ashore as long as she continued to sink. Rather than commit suicide, the French stopped the flooding. On the giant submarine *Surcouf*, also at Portsmouth, a hand-to-hand fight broke out. Before British reinforcements could get the upper hand, one Frenchman and one British seaman were killed and two Britons wounded.

So far everything had gone smoothly for the British. All ships had been seized with no damage and at the cost of only four casualties. But then the stupidity of officialdom took over. The dispossessed French sailors were treated as prisoners of war and loaded at bayonet point into railroad carriages. They heard the doors slam and the locks turn. The trains moved off. No one told the French where they were going. No one gave them any food or water. They had had no breakfast. Hours later they arrived at a prison camp near Liverpool. The camp, hurriedly thrown together, lacked even primitive facilities.

Psychological warfare began at once. Join General de Gaulle! Rally to the Cross of Lorraine! The men had no officers to guide them. Their leaders were in custody on the Isle of Man. To join the Free French meant immediate release from the prison camp. To refuse to join meant an indeterminate stay under appalling conditions.

A few days later Churchill announced in the Commons that some 800 or 900 had joined de Gaulle. The number sounds impressive until we recall that nearly 10,000 French sailors had been removed from the 50 ships.

Those who would not join the Free French movement were eventually repatriated to France.

The British seizure of the French ships demonstrated how easy it would have been for the Germans or Italians to do the same thing in ports under their control. The French have since asserted that the scuttling of the French fleet in Toulon in November, 1942, proved that they could and would keep their word and therefore that the whole of Operation Catapult was unnecessary. However, Toulon was in unoccupied France, and the French had several days to get ready to destroy their fleet while the Germans took over southern France. Had the French fleet been at Brest or Lorient, ports under German control, the story might have been closer to what it was in

Britain. There was no warning given, and 48 of the 50 ships involved offered no resistance.

Another group of French ships lay at Martinique in the West Indies: the aircraft carrier *Béarn*, the cruiser *Émile Bertin*, the auxiliary cruisers *Percy*, *Esterel*, and *Barfleur*, the school ship *Jeanne d'Arc*, and 10 patrol vessels. These ships were under the command of Admiral Georges Robert, who was also High Commissioner for the Antilles and Guiana. Aboard the *Béarn* were 106 American-built aircraft, while the other ships had on board large quantities of gold bullion sent from France before the armistice. The British made several overtures to Admiral Robert to induce him to join the Free French cause. Robert refused, so they sent the West Indian squadron to blockade the island.

The spectacle of two European nations playing power politics in the Western Hemisphere was distasteful to Washington and other American capitals. Such action was a clear violation of the Monroe Doctrine. If unchallenged, it might lead to a German take-over of French colonies in the New World.

Hull issued a stern warning: "In accordance with its traditional policy relating to the Western Hemisphere, the United States would not recognize any transfer and would not acquiesce in any attempt to transfer, any geographic region of the Western Hemisphere from one non-American Power to another non-American Power."

Foreign Minister Ribbentrop replied on July 1 that Germany would respect the Monroe Doctrine only so long as the United States did not interfere in European affairs. This statement was no assurance at all, since the United States was already giving considerable aid to Britain. At any moment Germany chose, she might accuse the United States of interfering in European affairs. In a public statement, Secretary Hull tried to make the American position quite clear. Hitler's "new order," which Ribbentrop had likened to a European Monroe Doctrine, had no bearing or parallel. The Monroe Doctrine "never has resembled," wrote Hull, "and it does not today resemble, policies which appear to be arising in other geographical areas of the world, which are alleged to be similar to the Monroe Doctrine, but which, instead of resting on the sole policies of self-defense and of respect for existing sovereignties, as does the Monroe Doctrine, would in reality seem to be only the pretext for carrying out of conquest by the sword, of military occupation, and of complete economic and

227

political domination by certain powers of other free and independent peoples."

The real fear in both Washington and London was that France might cede Martinique to Germany, or at the least grant her rights to establish a U-boat base at Fort de France, Martinique's principal harbor. The problem, therefore, was considerably larger than merely a few ships.

These fears were strengthened by the attitude of Admiral Robert. He supported the Vichy Government wholeheartedly. No one in either London or Washington trusted the men who now led France.

A British naval blockade of Martinique could not be tolerated by the United States. Having invoked the Monroe Doctrine, Secretary Hull found himself in the position of having to apply it to friend as well as foe. "My Government is concerned," Hull told Ambassador Lord Lothian, "over possible developments of an undesirable nature at Martinique. Our Navy thinks that the British may seize the French vessels and also occupy Martinique with military forces. If this is done, it will involve real trouble between your Government and mine."

Lord Lothian disclaimed any such British intention and agreed to cooperate with the United States in every way. But still President Roosevelt and Secretary Hull agreed that it would be just as well if an American naval force kept a wary eye on Martinique. A heavy cruiser and 6 destroyers were sent on this duty. Thus emerged the ludicrous spectacle of an American force keeping tabs on a British force which was blockading a possession of a former ally, all at a time when both navies had many other important things to do.

British and American diplomats now worked together to try to find some way out of the mess. It had to be acceptable to the British, to Vichy France, and to the United States, all without violating the Monroe Doctrine. It was going to be a neat trick.

The joint Anglo-American diplomats appealed to France to permit the ships in Martinique to go to ports in the United States for internment. They suggested that the new planes aboard the *Béarn* be transferred to the British or be repurchased by the American manufacturers, who would sell them to the British. The French ambassador to Washington, M. le Comte de Saint-Quentin, was agreeable, but his Government turned thumbs down. Although the negotiators at the time did not know it, the German Armistice Commission refused to allow the Vichy Government to transfer ships or planes to any other nation. Thus 106 aircraft which might have been used in the

Battle of Britain deteriorated and became useless aboard the idle *Béarn*.

The United States sent Rear Admiral John W. Greenslade to Fort de France to try his hand with Admiral Robert. Admiral Greenslade found Robert uncooperative. He shared the Vichy view that once France had fallen, it was all over. The West would have to learn to live with Germany, the new master of Europe. As the summer wore on, however, and Britain showed no sign of yielding, British defiance and British resistance impressed Admiral Robert. He finally agreed to demobilize the French warships at Martinique. He also let the United States station a naval observer at Fort de France. In return, the United States agreed to keep the island supplied with food and other necessities. By the end of August, 1940, the problem of Martinique was settled. Vichy did not like it, but there was nothing they could do about it.

* * *

Unquestionably the most powerful vessels in the French Navy were the two unfinished battleships, *Jean Bart* and *Richelieu*. When Germany smashed into France they were still in the yards where they had been built, the *Jean Bart* at St. Nazaire and the *Richelieu* at Brest. Each had been designed with a 35,000-ton standard displacement, was to have eight 15-inch guns, and would be capable of over 30 knots. Although not so rugged as the German battleships *Bismarck* and *Tirpitz,* they were roughly equivalent to these two vessels and therefore superior to Britain's new *King George V*-class battleships with their 14-inch batteries. When France was collapsing, Admiral Darlan decided to remove both the battleships beyond the reach of the Nazis.

Although the *Jean Bart* had only one of her two turrets installed, she could be made ready to steam. Her commanding officer, Captain Pierre J. Ronarc'h, was determined to save her at all costs. The ship had been long a-building, and even when war broke out, the French had seen no reason to authorize overtime or night shifts to speed her construction. At the German breakthrough in May, Captain Ronarc'h became alarmed for the safety of his ship. He bent his efforts to the twin problems of getting her sufficiently completed to take to sea and the task of getting her out of her building dock to open water.

The task of preparing the ship to face the Atlantic was at length overcome by cajolery, bullying, desk-pounding, and back-slapping. Pieces of machinery were installed bit by bit, and joint by joint, essential connections were made so the boilers could furnish steam to the turbines and the turbines furnish power to the shafts. Realizing that his ship could not be completed, Captain Ronarc'h concentrated on making sure that what was installed was placed so that it could do its job most efficiently. Only one fireroom with its three boilers was made ready; only two of the four propeller shafts were equipped with screws, but at length all was ready for departure. It was just in time, for the tide conditions were right almost the very moment that the ship was ready to steam, and the Germans were only 40 miles away in Nantes.

Getting the huge ship safely to sea presented innumerable difficulties. She had been built in drydock, and the channel to the drydock was several feet too shallow to accommodate the 30-foot draft of the *Jean Bart*. A program of extensive dredging had been planned, but it had lagged when one of the dredges sank in the winter of 1940. Captain Ronarc'h pleaded with the authorities to set all available dredges to work deepening the channel. He met typical bureaucratic obstruction. With no one willing to accept the responsibility and issue the necessary orders, Captain Ronarc'h had to undertake a personal trip to Paris to gain the approval of Admiral Michelier, Chief of Staff to the French Admiralty, before the dredges could begin the vital work. When it was completed, there was a pie-shaped area 885 feet long into which Captain Ronarc'h had to insert the *Jean Bart*'s 812-foot length and then swing her 35 degrees to line her up with the channel. The channel itself had been deepened to a depth of twenty-eight feet, one foot, nine inches greater than the planned draft of the *Jean Bart,* which had been especially lightened for the passage. She had on board only enough fuel to reach open water; she would have to refuel at sea, with all the risks that were entailed in stopping in possible submarine operating areas.* As a final hazard, the channel had been made only some 148 feet wide, while the *Jean Bart* had a beam of 108 feet, 7 inches. When we remember that the sortie was to be made at night, in a ship whose handling characteristics were unknown, we can begin to appreciate the problem which lay before Captain Ronarc'h.

Shortly after midnight on June 19, the *Jean Bart* completed her preparations for sea. The drydock in which she had been built was flooded; her boilers were lighted off and her turbines warmed up. She was ready to move, if all went well. It remained only to wait for

* The French had not yet developed the techniques of underway fueling which enabled ships later in the war to minimize the risks of fueling at sea.

230

the flood tide. She could not go out before 3:11 A.M. nor after 4:57 A.M.

The moment of 3:11 came and went. The tugs were late. At last they appeared, puffing up importantly, and secured their hawsers. At 3:20 the *Jean Bart* started out of the dock. A few moments later she was hard aground. The tugs churned the water to muddy foam, and their efforts combined with the rising tide to set her free. A second time she went aground and remained fast until 4:25. Fifteen minutes later, German planes roared in, dropping bombs all around her. One hit, but there was little damage and there were no casualties. As she worked her way toward the open sea, still under tow of the tugs, her engineers worked feverishly to get power on the main engines. At last at 4:50 A.M. came the welcome word that the engines were ready to steam. The towlines were cast off, and the *Jean Bart* proudly set out to sea.

A welcoming committee of French and British destroyers and smaller ships formed up to give her escort. The British were confident that she would proceed to a British port where she could finish her fitting out. However, it was not to be. Admiral de Laborde, riding the destroyer *Hardi,* informed the British commander that the *Jean Bart* was bound for Casablanca. Thereupon, the British ships discreetly withdrew.

After tense hours spent in fueling, the great battleship set out for Casablanca. Time after time during the next few days, she wallowed to a stop as untested machinery broke down. Perseverance and courage at length paid off. Under the watchful care of 3 French destroyers, she reached Casablanca on the afternoon of June 22, 1940. Captain Ronarc'h expected to refuel there and then cross the Atlantic to the United States, where the ship could be completed. The Franco-German armistice put an end to this plan, and at Casablanca she remained. She lay idle until her guns went into action against the United States battleship *Massachusetts* on November 8, 1942.

The *Richelieu,* sister ship of the *Jean Bart,* had no such dramatic voyage. Completed some time earlier, she had finished her trials. As the Germans were closing in on Brest, her commanding officer, Captain Marzin, took her to sea hurriedly on June 18 and shaped his course for Dakar, arriving on June 23.

In surveying the results of Operation Catapult, the British had small cause for satisfaction. Only at Alexandria had the goal been accomplished completely. French crews in England for the most part remained aloof from the Free French cause. The *Strasbourg* and several destroyers had made good their escape from Mers el Kebir to reach Toulon, where the Germans could get their hands on them more easily than if the vessels had remained in North Africa. The fate of the ships at Martinique was still unsettled. For these dubious gains the British had alienated the French Government, the French people, and many neutrals.

Since the French had not immediately declared war after the attack at Mers el Kebir, the British decided that they might as well finish the job. There remained untouched outside of metropolitan France the *Jean Bart* at Casablanca and the *Richelieu* at Dakar. The former they believed they could safely ignore in view of her unfinished state. The *Richelieu,* on the other hand, represented a strong potential menace. Aerial reconnaissance over Oran and Mers el Kebir confirmed intercepted French radio traffic that the *Dunkerque* was not as heavily damaged as first reports had indicated. To finish off what had been begun, the Cabinet ordered a second attack to be made at Mers el Kebir and one on the *Richelieu* at Dakar.

Three waves of torpedo planes from the *Ark Royal* roared in over the harbor of Mers el Kebir at dawn on July 6. The French, caught completely by surprise, hurriedly sounded Action Stations. While men ran to their guns, the planes launched their torpedoes. One hit the tug *Esterel,* moored alongside the *Dunkerque.* Unhappily, the tug had on board some 50 depth charges. When the tug went down, the depth charges did not explode. A second torpedo rushed over where she had been and smashed into the *Dunkerque.* The force of the explosion set off the depth charges. A gigantic column of water, debris, and bits of human flesh shot 300 feet into the air; fragments of metal and scraps of wood fell over the deck of the *Dunkerque* and the dock, mowing down sailors and civilians. The battle cruiser, with a huge hole torn in her side, settled to the mud of the harbor bottom as 25,000 tons of water poured in. The British goal was accomplished; she would be out of action for at least a year.*

* * *

The former French city of Dakar in Senegal is the westernmost port on the continent of Africa. An easy port of call for ships plying between South America or South Africa and Europe, the port in 1939 ranked as the third most important in the French Empire, only Le Havre and Marseilles exceeding it in annual tonnage. Situated just a

---

* She never saw action again. In February, 1942, she was moved to Toulon, where she was scrapped.

thousand miles north of the Equator, Dakar, with its delightful climate and economic advantages, had, by the outbreak of war, attracted some 15,000 Europeans to make their homes there, where they constituted 15 percent of the population of the city. Possessing a fine, improved harbor, and a naval base with repair yards and a small drydock, Dakar had proved to be a useful stopping point for convoys running between South Africa and British or French ports.

In Dakar, local commanders and the European population as a whole favored continuing on the side of the Allies even though France was collapsing. The governor, M. Cayla, and the military commander, Rear Admiral Plançon, refusing to credit the signing of the armistice, planned to pursue the war with all their resources. The arrival of the *Richelieu,* however, soon undermined their determination, for her commanding officer, Captain Marzin, felt that he was bound by the orders of Darlan and secondarily by those of Admiral de Laborde at Casablanca, not those of Admiral Plançon. Meanwhile, the sailors of the *Richelieu* who had witnessed the horrors of the German advance into France began to spread the tale of German invincibility. Gradually the attitude of the city began to solidify against fighting on.

Since he saw little chance of winning the allegiance of Captain Marzin in defiance of Vichy, Plançon felt that it would be a good idea for the *Richelieu* to go to Casablanca. This scheme accorded well with the feelings of Captain Marzin, who was not happy with the situation at Dakar. At 1:30 P.M. on June 25, he took his ship out of the harbor and shaped a course for Casablanca.

Patrolling off the port of Dakar was the British aircraft carrier *Hermes,* under the command of Captain R. F. J. Onslow. The British had followed the French battleship, just to keep an eye on her. They felt it would be useful to know where all the French ships were going and what they were doing.

As the *Richelieu* emerged from the harbor, the *Hermes* signaled, inquiring her intentions. Captain Marzin replied briefly that he was shifting anchorages. He neglected to state that his new anchorage was nearly 1350 miles away! Setting a course north, he set out for Casablanca at 20 knots. Having no orders to intercept, the *Hermes* let her proceed on her way.

At Casablanca, Admiral Ollive, the sole superior in West Africa to both Admiral de Laborde and Admiral Plançon, unaware of the situation at Dakar, and noting that the harbor at Casablanca was crowded, radioed Captain Marzin to take the *Richelieu* back to

Dakar. Captain Marzin received this message on the morning of June 26 and turned around to head back. At 7:30 A.M. the same day, the British cruiser *Dorsetshire* made contact with the *Richelieu* and took station on her, sending frequent invitations for the *Richelieu* to join the British naval forces. In order to gain time for the invitation to filter through to the crew, the *Dorsetshire*'s captain invited the *Richelieu* to help search for a lost aircraft. Captain Marzin blandly replied that he had seen no lost aircraft but would alert the search facilities at Dakar. The two ships kept company during the night, and the next morning, June 27, the *Richelieu* reentered the harbor of Dakar. There she found the newly arrived First Auxiliary Cruiser Division, consisting of the armed former merchant ships *El Djezïr, El Mansour, El Kantara,* and the *Ville d'Oran,* laden with 2000 tons of gold belonging to the Bank of France.

Soon after the *Richelieu* reached port, Rear Admiral Cadart, the division commander, and Captain Marzin won Admiral Plançon over to the necessity of remaining loyal to Darlan's orders. Once Plançon had agreed, the troop commander, General Barrau, quickly fell into line, and the military commanders now presented a united front to Governor Cayla.

Too late to preserve the colony from the men of Bordeaux, the British Commander in Chief, South Atlantic, Vice Admiral G. H. d'Oyly Lyon, appeared at Dakar for a "courtesy call." Finding the city firmly in the Vichy orbit, d'Olyly Lyon dropped the pretense. "I request," he stated, "that you will obtain from the Admiral commanding in chief the French naval forces the assurance that the enemies of the British Empire will not have the right to use the port of Dakar."

Admiral d'Oyly Lyon received a rather unsatisfactory reply. On direct orders of the French Admiralty, he was informed that British merchant ships would be interned if they entered Dakar harbor and that British warships would be forbidden all communication with the shore. There was nothing for the British commander to do but withdraw and await further orders.

In the several undisturbed days which followed, French military forces firmly established control of the city. When the news of Mers el Kebir arrived, all commanders began preparations to fight the British, if necessary. Darlan sent a petulant command to attack British ships on sight. But cooler heads prevailed at Vichy, and Darlan modified his instructions. Only if the British came within 20 miles of the coast were they to be attacked. The few British merchant ships unlucky enough to be in Dakar were seized by way of reprisal.

The British considered intolerable the presence at Dakar of the powerful *Richelieu* in view of the threat she presented to trade convoys bound for the South Atlantic. These convoys represented the only means of supplying General Wavell's army in Egypt. They passed close to Dakar, often stopping or changing escorts at Freetown in Sierra Leone, some 400 miles farther south.

If France should declare war, the presence of the *Richelieu* at Dakar would threaten the existence of these convoys. One ship could conceivably cause the surrender of General Wavell and the Eighth Army.

Another cause for concern, and one shared by the United States, was that Germany might take over Dakar as a surface or submarine base. Accordingly, although an operation against Dakar was not part of the original Catapult plan, the British belatedly added it.

At 2 P.M. on July 7, the British auxiliary *Milford* appeared off the port and hoisted a flag of parley. "I urgently request," her blinkers flashed, "permission to enter harbor for the purpose of transmitting a vitally important message to the Admiral commanding the naval forces in French West Africa."

"Withdraw or I will open fire," replied the Harbor Control Post coldly.

The *Milford* did not withdraw immediately, but stopped some two miles from the harbor entrance and began lowering a boat.

"It is useless to put a boat in the water," warned the Control Post. "If you do not withdraw immediately, I will open fire on you."

The *Milford* yielded. "I am retiring to inform my admiral," she signaled, "since you will not reconsider your decision. The message with which I am charged comes from His Majesty's Government."

In about three hours the *Milford* returned, this time escorted by the cruisers *Dorsetshire* and *Australia,* while, some 30 miles out, the carrier *Hermes* kept watch. Under these circumstances, the Control Post condescended to accept the message of the British Government.

This message presented the French with virtually the same terms that had been offered at Mers el Kebir. After the Control Post acknowledged receipt of the message, a grim silence followed. Dakar went about its daily business, ignoring the presence of the British ships. Captain Richard F. J. Onslow, the man on whose shoulders the responsibility lay, waited impatiently.

About 10 P.M. he warned the French that time was running out.

The French made no reply.

The placid scene ashore which was proving so irritating to Captain Onslow masked a state of near chaos in the harbor. Something approaching mutiny had broken out on some of the ships as the crews learned of the British proposals. News of the ruthless attack at Mers el Kebir had been broadcast throughout the French Navy as propaganda of the perfidy of a former ally. Now the scheme backfired.

To a man, they all wanted to avoid the fate of the crews at Mers el Kebir. Reservists organized meetings on some ships. The war was over, they declared. Let the navy send them home. Their brothers in the army had already been demobilized. Groups of men walked off their ships, intending to disappear in the byways of the city.

Unfortunately for them, most of these latter-day Jacobins had no more imagination than to head for the waterfront bars and brothels. Here they were easily found and returned to their posts by well-organized shore patrols from the *Richelieu*.

Captain Marzin, blessed with a loyal and disciplined crew, prepared to take the *Richelieu* to sea and make a run for it. He would fight if he must. He told his heads of departments to be ready to get under way at 5 A.M.

If Captain Marzin had been able to carry out his intention, the British would have had their hands full. The *Richelieu* could have made short work of the two British cruisers, and the *Hermes* had too few aircraft for her captain to have any confidence in the outcome.

The British time limit expired, but neither side made a move. Captain Onslow waited several hours on the chance that a French message had been delayed. Shortly after midnight he decided to wait no longer.

A little after 3 A.M. lookouts noticed a small boat making its way through the harbor. It passed close astern of the battleship, dropped something into the water, and withdrew. Highly suspicious, the French investigated carefully but could find nothing amiss.

At 4:30 A.M. alarm bells sounded on the *Richelieu*. The men ran to their posts of battle and their stations for getting under way.

The routine preparations for sea were interrupted by the shout of a lookout. Six British Swordfish planes from the *Hermes* were closing rapidly, weaving and bobbing as they came. The torpedo planes made a concerted attack on both sides of the battleship; only one torpedo hit, but the explosion was so tremendous that the stern of the *Richelieu* was heavily damaged.

It was not until after the war that the French learned what had happened. The boat they had observed earlier had dropped four depth charges near the stern of the battleship. Because the water in the harbor was shallow, they had not exploded then. But when the torpedo went off, its shock wave detonated the depth charges, with disastrous results for the *Richelieu*. The ship settled in the water, down by the stern, in no condition for sea. The French towed her into the inner harbor and moored her to a pier where she served as a floating battery. She gained a measure of revenge two and a half months later when the British returned to Dakar.

* * *

"I have been betrayed by my brothers in arms! They did not believe my word of honor!"

In a fury, Admiral Darlan, consulting no one, ordered the French fleet to attack Force H as it returned to Gibraltar from Mers el Kebir. As far as he was concerned, France was at war with Britain.

> The admiral [wrote one of his friends] woke up in the grip of a terrible passion which he concealed, containing his inner frenzy by an external coldness. He was not the same mentally. He had also changed physically. His speech was brief and very curt, his voice heavy, and his hand trembling. His lips were invisible against his face, and his eyes were unseeing, turned toward the depths of his being as though he were contemplating his devastated soul. A year later when he learned of the loss of the *Hood,* sunk by a lucky salvo from the *Bismarck,* his passion suddenly seized him again and manifested itself by a lively explosion of joy. I remember the man of July 4, the features drawn, the lips compressed, and the uncomprehending look. One must be very superficial or very ignorant of the depths of men's hearts to judge hastily in such a crisis, when it has crushed a soul of such sincerity. The cold rage of Darlan was moving because it was so real. The French Government would have to take into account the feelings of the fleet commander upheld by the entire navy which had been stricken with him.

Hard upon these tragic events came the hour of decision for France. Prostrate before her conquerer, she had been sore wounded by her former ally, while her powerful friend across the sea stood by, not lifting a finger to help her in her agony. Stricken as never before since the Hundred Years' War, she struggled to preserve her integrity as a nation, her unity as a people. Her leaders bore a heavy responsibility.

Under such conditions of trial the wisest men might well err in their decisions. Few wise men gathered that Thursday, July 4, 1940, to decide the fate of France.

Darlan energetically, passionately, led one group. France, he declared, was already at war with Britain. It remained but to recognize the fact, to attack British ships, British bases, British territory with every means at their disposal.

Another group remembered the Germans, who thrice in seventy years had devastated the soil of France. Much as they hated the British for what they had done the previous day, they hated the Germans more.

The war is over, declared others. It can profit nothing for France to take sides. Let us learn to live in the world we have not made.

All day long the bitter debates continued, political leaders struggling for position and influence. Through it all moved Pierre Laval.

Pierre Laval had had a long and stormy career in French politics. Twice Premier of France, Laval, although a socialist, had strong leanings toward totalitarianism. He particularly favored and admired Hitler and the Third Reich. Much to his fury, Laval had been excluded when Pétain took the reins of government. The aging Marshal soon realized that the only thing worse than having Laval in his government was having him out of it, free to make trouble.

Laval became Minister of State. He now had the power and office he needed for his next move: the overthrow of the constitution.

Laval exploited the British actions to their utmost to advance his cause of establishing Marshal Pétain as the dictator of France. With word of Mers el Kebir, Laval demanded war with England. "We decided yesterday," he reminded the Council of Ministers on July 4, "to answer an attack by an attack."

In spite of Darlan and Laval, the Council decided not to dignify the British moves with a declaration of war. Instead they decided "to make official the break in diplomatic relations which have in fact existed between us and England since the departure of Sir Ronald Campbell and all the staff of the British Embassy."

Although they excluded war, the Council of Ministers agreed they must undertake reprisals against Britain. Darlan had several proposals, each more extreme than the last: to attack the British base at Gibraltar, to seize British shipping at sea, to join with the Italian Navy and forcibly release the French ships held at Alexandria, to make a major military expedition against the British base at Freetown on the coast of West Africa. The Ministry of Foreign Affairs vetoed these measures, as inevitably leading to war with Great Britain. To satisfy the honor of France, the Council agreed on symbolic air attacks on Gibraltar. Two such attacks were made. On the nights of June 5 and again on June 6, three aircraft flew over the harbor and carefully dropped several bombs harmlessly in the water.

Meanwhile Laval had toiled insidiously to end the Third Republic. In his role as Vice President of the Council, on July 4, he introduced a resolution to end a type of government he charged with being supine and powerless in emergency.

Article unique: The National Assembly gives all powers to the Government of the Republic, under the signature of Marshal Pétain, President of the Council, to the effect of promulgating by one or several acts the new constitution of the French state.

This constitution shall guarantee the rights of Labor, of Family, and of the Nation. It will be ratified by the Assemblies which it will have created.

After presenting this resolution, Laval stalked out of the meeting. It was not open to discussion. He adroitly rounded up supporters among the weaker members, terrifying them with the consequences unless, in this hour of crisis, France had a strong hand at the helm. Those who might have stopped him were, by a series of chances, not available. Reynaud had been detained by an automobile accident. Mandel and his followers were on the *Massalia,* under practical arrest in the harbor of Casablanca. With no strong man to oppose him, Laval gained steadily in power and influence.

The day of reckoning came on July 10. On that day, the National Assembly voted itself out of existence. Marshal Pétain became dictator of France. Laval would guide the Marshal.

What role did Laval intend France to follow? His will could dominate the bewildered, stubborn old man on whom the hopes of France rested. He confidently propounded his plan.

We have no other path to follow than that of loyal collaboration with Germany and Italy. This policy can be carried out with honor and with dignity. I experience no pain in speaking this way, because I have desired this collaboration during peace time.... It is necessary for us, in all of our territories, to integrate ourselves with courage and sincerity into a European and Continental polity. That is possible, that is indispensable to the condition of preserving always the things which have given us our pride in being French....I declare to you that we have no intention of declaring war on England, but, each time that we can, we shall return blow for blow.

Neither Laval nor the British leaders realized that the men of Vichy had reckoned without the people of France. Collaborators there were, but patriots there were, too. Not Laval, not collaborators, not German brutalities could make the people of France untrue to themselves.

CHAPTER TEN

The Lion at Bay

It is not to be thought of that the Flood
Of British freedom, which, to the open sea
Of the world's praise, from dark antiquity
Hath flowed, "with pomp of waters, unwithstood"...
Should Perish.
Wordsworth, "National Independence and Liberty"

WITH A curious illogic, the average Briton felt more secure after the fall of France than he had before. "We'll do better alone." "There's no one left to let us down." One old lady, who was quoted approvingly, stated, "Oh, well, if the Germans win, at any rate I have my pension, and they can't touch that." Even King George confided in a letter to his mother, "Personally, I feel happier now that we have no allies to be polite to and to pamper."

Such expressions were not bravado. They might be characterized as obtuseness, lack of imagination, blind stupidity, or an inability to face the facts. On the other hand, they might be called courage, determination, faith in themselves, and a refusal to accept the ideas that Hitler stood for. Churchill always claimed that his own great speeches were but an expression of the nation's will. "It was the nation and the race living all around the globe," he said on his eightieth birthday, "that had the lion's heart. I had the luck to be called on to give the roar."

Commented *The Daily Express* on the Mers el Kebir tragedy:

> Churchill has once more shown himself a rough, tough leader of our brave fighting men. He has shown that England, which was thought so old and staid and respectable, still has the smash-and-grab fighting spirit of Drake and Raleigh and Marlborough.
>
> We rejoice in the realism which is not afraid to offend a potential

241

enemy, which makes no pretence that the Bordeaux Government is our friend.

In this war we had been too kind and considerate. We tried to appease Italy. We turned the other cheek and looked the other way when we were insulted.

Now we face all our enemies boldly.

The German attack in the west proved the psychological turning point for the British. Before that date, there had been too much business and play as usual. By a realistic assessment of the situation, Britain stood no chance whatever. Her Army was disorganized, having left huge quantities of equipment in the sands near Dunkirk; her Air Force desperately needed time to regroup and recover from the wounds of the battle just ended. Only her Navy had not been severely mauled. But the Navy had grown circumspect, for it had learned what it meant to operate where it did not have air cover.

Little had been done to organize either the economy or the people for war. A timid tax law was passed in April, but it was immediately derided as ridiculously inadequate by the press. It hit mainly on luxuries, a penny a pint on beer, threepence an ounce on tobacco. Postage rates went up a penny, and telephone charges were taxed at 15 percent.

As time went on, various measures, both sensible and erratic, made their appearance. To guard against paratroops, the Government ordered all road signs taken down throughout the country. Also in villages, names of streets, railroad station signs, and identifying signs in the village were to be obliterated. This caused no little inconvenience to the honest traveler but none at all to the Germans, since they never had a chance to be confused by this measure. About the same time, the Government ordered the roofs of the red London double-decker buses to be painted battleship gray, to make them more difficult to spot from the air. This measure credits the German bomber pilots with uncanny skill as well as odd notions of what is a worthwhile target. They do not seem to have considered the question of how much camouflage value battleship gray has on black asphalt pavements.

A more serious edict, perhaps the most serious of the war, was passed by Parliament on May 22, 1940. The measure gave the Government complete control over every person and all property in the country. *The Daily Telegraph* called it "the most sweeping constitutional measure ever placed before the House of Commons."

No such measure was passed by the Congress when America

entered the war. But the British took it almost without comment. Viewed in retrospect, it is a magnificent act of trust on the part of the people that they welcomed the new legislation. On a less sweeping law, Hitler had gained his dictatorial powers in Germany, powers that had made the word "liberty" a mockery. But in Britain, the people trusted the Government. It never seems to have crossed their minds that these new controls were anything more than wartime measures. Nor did it cross their minds that they would last longer than the war.

The most remarkable thing is that within these manpower and property controls, human liberties and property rights continued to be respected. To save manpower, except in capital cases, juries were reduced from twelve to seven, but trial by jury continued. Commandeered property was paid for, and the right to dissent remained.

Naturally, with tales of spies and fifth columnists in Norway, Belgium, Holland, and France, people began to be suspicious of the odd-looking stranger, and queer conversations began to be reported to the police. General Ironside, who took command of the Home Defences after being relieved as Chief of the Imperial General Staff, added to this kind of suspicion by saying, "My experience is that the gentlemen who are the best behaved and most sleek are those who are doing the mischief. We cannot be too sure of anybody."

It was not long before General Ironside was relieved of this post and passed from the picture. There is no evidence, but it seems not unlikely that someone highly placed in the Government and with a greater understanding of the meaning of human rights than General Ironside possessed may have heard him speak.

Encouraged by such attitudes as Ironside proclaimed, and the Treachery Bill, passed by Parliament also on May 22, the Englishman with time on his hands employed it by spying on his neighbor. "Spying" is perhaps too strong a term, because "Mind Your Own Business" is practically an Eleventh Commandment to Englishmen. Perhaps it would be better to say, "casting sidelong glances at his neighbor."

If most of these self-appointed sleuths were Watsons rather than Sherlocks, it was not for want of trying. The new Treachery Bill was no joke. For six centuries the Treason Acts had protected the accused and had insisted on proof of guilt before conviction. Now anyone committing acts "designed or likely to give assistance to the naval, military, or air operations of the enemy, to impede such operations of His Majesty's forces, or to endanger life" would be subject to the death penalty.

Panicky people persisted in seeing flashing lights, smoke signals, trails of wool, signals in the trees, and such-like flights of imagination. Innocent citizens were detained because someone misunderstood a word in a pub or because someone else thought "he looked German." Gradually sanity was restored, and as the summer months passed without invasion, such behavior became pretty much a thing of the past.

More important than these random activities, measures taken by the Government itself reveal the temper of the time. First, a curfew from midnight to eight in the morning was imposed on aliens in the British Isles. Later, aliens of certain nationalities were interned for a considerable period of time. Since many of those were refugees who hated Hitler and all his works even more keenly than did the British, it was an ill-judged measure.

Actually, like so many activities in bureaucracy, the execution was more severe than the intention. The measure was taken as a screening attempt; in carrying it out, the people responsible found internment the easiest method of screening. Let human dignity and rights go hang! Every man is guilty until he is proved innocent.

A much more popular measure was the arrest under the Treachery Bill of Sir Oswald Mosley and 33 members of his British Union of Fascists. One of those arrested was Captain Archibald Ramsay, a Member of Parliament. Captain Ramsay had been implicated with a Miss Anna Wolkoff, daughter of a former admiral of the Imperial Russian Navy. Miss Wolkoff was involved with extreme right-wing groups and succeeded in getting one clandestine letter through to Germany before she was picked up by the police. She believed, at any rate, that she had succeeded, but the letter was intercepted, examined, and passed on; the police believed that its addressee, William Joyce, would be more deceived than aided by its contents.

William Joyce, the notorious "Lord Haw-Haw," was also a member of the British Union of Fascists. He made his way to Germany before the war and took up broadcasting in English. His broadcasts were much listened to by the British, not because they believed in his brand of poppycock, but because he had become something of a legend. It was said that he would report what time a town clock had stopped as a result of an air raid. No one was ever able to identify the clock or the town, but the habit of listening to Lord Haw-Haw was ingrained. Part of his popularity was his complete lack of understanding of the British character. As an Irishman, Joyce never understood the issues that bothered an Englishman, nor did he understand how an Englishman would react in a given situation. The result was that most people merely thought him funny.

It was in an attempt to straighten him out that Miss Wolkoff wrote her letter. Some of her advice was good: "Stick to plutocracy. Avoid King." (That is, hit at rank and privilege and do not make slurring remarks at the King and Royal Family.) But in the rest of the letter, Miss Wolkoff showed herself as blind to the British feeling as Joyce himself. "There *Kriegshetze* [war fever] only among the Blimps. Workers fed up. Wives more so. Troops not keen. Antisemitism spreading like flame everywhere—all classes. . . . Churchill not popular. . . . Cost of living steeply mounting."

In the last analysis, the Germans had few contacts in England, and their intelligence was faulty in the extreme. Such intelligence weaknesses hampered the Germans throughout the war.

Even though the average Briton shrugged off the perils ahead and listened to German propaganda broadcasts only for amusement, he was not stupidly blind. He knew he was in for a fight. He had no idea how the war might be won, but he had no idea of losing it. He wanted to be given his marching orders.

A recurrent theme in the newspapers during the summer was lack of direction of the war. The strictures were directed not at Churchill but at the bureaucrats who had no idea of how to speed things up. "This is a time for initiative," grumbled *The Times*.

Regulations were issued, some silly and some well considered. John Bull Countryman and Tommy Atkins Bowbells were alike affected, if in different ways. First, everyone had to carry his National Registration Identity Card, which had his name, his 6- or 7-digit number, and spaces for new addresses, the whole adorned with sternest warnings against mutilation, loss, or failure to carry the card at all times. Any of these, or any alteration (how was the holder supposed to enter a new address if he could not alter the card in any way?) was punishable by fine or imprisonment.

Then everyone had his ration card and his coupons for gasoline. If he was lucky enough to have a car, he had to paint the bumper and fenders white so that they could be seen in the blackout more easily. If his car was equipped with a radio, it had to be removed, even though there was no limitation on radios in his home or anywhere else. If he stopped to park his car, he was liable to savage penalties if he did not immobilize it.* It was not enough to lock it. He had to remove the rotor arm from the distributor. Soon everyone, car thieves included, was carrying a spare rotor arm.

In his home or his flat, Mr. Countryman or Mr. Bowbells minimized the possibility of shattered glass from bomb blast by crisscrossing his windows with gummed paper. Some of the decorations achieved by this means were quite artistic. In most rooms buckets of water and sand stood ready for fighting fires, and he had emergency food supplies, even though he was careful not to hoard. He had given up his fireworks into the keeping of the police, sighing as he did so that Guy Fawkes Day would be gloomy this year. Also he turned over his shotguns, sporting rifles, and binoculars for use in national defense. He had an air-raid shelter, if he had room for it; otherwise, he used public shelters. Mr. Countryman, and occasionally Mr. Bowbells, had a bit of land for a vegetable garden, for the posters exhorted him to "Dig for Victory."

Other directives charged him never, *never* to shoot carrier pigeons, and forbade "any person, other than a servant of His Majesty" to fly a kite or a balloon. The directives did not explain how a person was to distinguish a carrier pigeon from any other pigeon, nor how he would shoot when he had turned his weapons in to the police as ordered.

Women were asked to wear low heels, for the wood from which high heels were made, it was said, required 50,000 tons of shipping per year, or 10 average shiploads. Not only high heels became war casualties, but almost all items of clothing and luxury goods were regulated or eliminated altogether. The items which would be subject to rationing (voluntary at first) were "corsets, braces, suspenders, gloves and hosiery, knitted clothes and lace, mattresses, pillows and cushions, carpets, linoleum, rugs and mats, pottery and glassware, metal furniture and fittings, cane and wicker furniture, cutlery, kettles, pots and pans, dishes and bins.

"Handbags, suitcases, trunks, toilet preparations, except such items as soap and toothpaste, vacuum cleaners, electric appliances, refrigerators and lawn mowers, cameras, photographic appliances and films.

"Musical instruments, sport gear and games, toys, lighters and umbrellas, jewellery and ornaments."

* The fine on charge of "failing to secure a motor car" was £50, about $200 at then current rates of exchange.

If there was something of convenience or necessity omitted from this list, it was because the authorities had not thought of it.

Food was rationed, and during the war amounts of various foods became so small as to be near the vanishing point.

On July 9 the British citizen was struck the cruelest blow of all. Tea was rationed. It was easier for him to face the fact that all luxury would go out of meals and that only wedding cakes could be iced. But—tea! The ration was a skimpy two ounces a week, from which an optimistic spokesman estimated that 25 cups might be brewed. Perhaps this spokesman liked his tea weaker than most Britons.

Commented an erudite reader in a letter to *The Times,* quoting an epigram of Martial:

Nec tecum possum vivere, nec sine te.

Suggested translation: "I can't live on my tea ration, and I can't live without it."

Even before the German victory on the continent became apparent, the British expected the attack to fall on them before long. On May 15, Churchill wrote Roosevelt, "We expect to be attacked here ourselves, both from the air [by bombing] and by parachute and airborne troops, in the near future, and are getting ready for them." Part of these preparations was the establishment of a series of volunteer units across the nation, known as Local Defense Volunteers, usually abbreviated L.D.V. In July, at the suggestion of Churchill, the name was changed to the Home Guard. This is another example of how Churchill sensed the feeling of the British people. The term L.D.V. had inspired little unit loyalty or pride of organization. The name Home Guard somehow made the men march a little more erect.

The Home Guard was an immediate success, in spite of mockery and aching muscles. Within six days over a quarter of a million men joined—those too old for the services, or too young, or those engaged in war work. By August, the enrollment was over a million.

Predictable confusion marked the beginnings of the organization. Police stations were swamped with applicants and soon ran out of the necessary forms. Then, they had no idea of what to do with completed applications, for they were ordered to deliver them only to "a properly appointed commander," but until someone analyzed the forms, there was no way of determining who was proper to appoint as commander.

Gradually, however, matters were straightened out, and bands of men, some looking like Falstaff's army, were reviewing basic infantry drill and learning to use weapons, if they had them.

Lack of proper weapons remained the most serious problem throughout the summer. The best rifles, naturally, had to go to the fast-expanding Army forces, so the Home Guard perforce had to make do with what was left over. Some 70,000 more or less modern military rifles were discovered, and the sporting guns patriotic citizens had handed in earlier were reissued. (Perhaps it was at this point that the authorities began to worry about carrier pigeons.) An odd (in every sense of the word) weapon was found here or there, in museums, in the property room of the Drury Lane Theatre, in railway lost-property offices. Some Home Guardsmen marched with assegais, ceremonial sabers, axes, pitchforks, or even a well-weighted golf club.

All sorts and conditions of men made up these Home Guard units. The newspapers called them "Parashots," but the term seems to have gone no further than the pages it appeared on. Retired generals, resplendent in their generals' uniforms, appeared in the ranks as privates, commanded by more recently retired junior officers. One company in Sussex had six generals. The Bishop of Truro belonged to a unit, and was cheered in the House of Lords when he disclosed the fact that he was a regular member of a night patrol. Months earlier the Bishop of Chelmsford had organized a band himself in anticipation of the whole Home Guard idea. Residents of London's West End drilled in Green Park and Hyde Park, denizens of Bermondsey in Southwark Park; suburbanites of Golders Green practiced in Hampstead Heath. Outside the capital, the story was the same. In Leeds and Coventry, in Bristol and Nottingham, in Hadley and Botesdale, they drilled, they guarded bridges, they reported aircraft, they kept an eye out for suspicious strangers. They trained 17-year-olds, who the next year would be called to the colors.

To judge from the German radio, the Home Guard was a real threat to Nazi plans. Nothing could have been more stimulating to these men, armed with inadequate weapons and wearing armbands as the only mark of uniform, to hear hysterical German broadcasters refer to them as "murder bands" and "unscrupulous *franc-tireurs*," who would be shot on sight.

After Dunkirk, the most vital concern to Britons was the danger of invasion. In the week between the conclusion of the Dunkirk evacuation and the German drive into France, everyone from Churchill on down waited to see which way Hitler would move.

Would he turn on France, or would he send clouds of paratroops over Britain, to be followed by infantry across the Channel?

On June 13 an order went out forbidding the ringing of church bells in England. This particularly lovely sound of the English countryside was to be limited to an alert of invasion. Campanologists objected, but the order remained. About the same time the Ministry of Information put out a pamphlet containing seven rules for use by civilians in case of invasion. It is a curious mixture of common sense and naiveté.

(1) If the Germans come by parachute, aeroplane or ship you must remain where you are: the order is "stay put."

If the commander-in-chief decides that the place where you live must be evacuated, he will tell you when and how to leave. Until you receive such orders, you must remain where you are. If you ran away you would be exposed to far greater danger because you would be machine-gunned from the air as were civilians in Holland and Belgium and you would also block the roads by which our armies would advance to turn the Germans out.

(2) Do not believe rumors and do not spread them.

(3) Keep watch. If you see anything suspicious, note it carefully and go at once to the nearest police officer or station, or to the nearest military officer. Do not rush about spreading vague rumors. Go quickly to the nearest authority and give him the facts.

(4) Do not give any German anything. Do not tell him anything.

Hide your food and your bicycles. Hide your maps. See that the enemy gets no petrol. If you have a car or motor-bicycle, put it out of action when not in use. It is not enough to remove the ignition key: You must make it useless to everyone except yourself.

If you are a garage proprietor, you must work out a plan to protect your stock of petrol and your customers' cars. Remember that transport and petrol will be the invader's main difficulties. Make sure that no invader will be able to get hold of your cars, petrol, maps or bicycles.

(5) Be ready to help the military in any way. But do not block roads until ordered to do so by the military or L.D.V. authorities.

(6) In factories and shops, all managers and workmen should organize some system now by which sudden attack can be resisted.

(7) Think before you act. But think always of your country, before you think of yourself.

* * *

Was Hitler coming? Did he have any plans to invade the British Isles?

The answer cannot be an unqualified yes or no. On July 16, 1940,

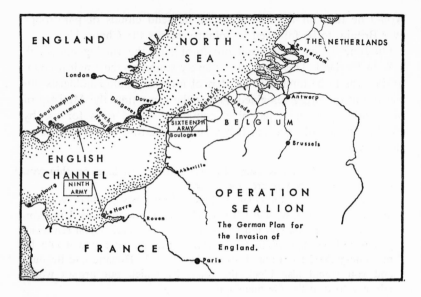

The German Plan for the Invasion of England.

he issued Führer Directive No. 16, which contained the curious, amorphous statement, *"I have decided to begin to prepare for, and, if necessary, to carry out, an invasion of England."*

In the tone of this directive, we sense a feeling of exasperation, even frustration. England had not reacted to the victory over France as Hitler had expected, and he could not understand why.

With the signing of the French armistice, Hitler had a huge army on his hands and nothing to do with it. Already he had ordered a partial demobilization from 160 to 120 divisions, partly because he felt that the Luftwaffe and the Navy could "be given the mission of carrying on alone the war against England."

As early as May 21, the day the Panzers reached Abbeville and the Channel coast, Admiral Raeder brought up the question of possible invasion of England. Hitler, his mind on the land battle, paid little attention, but Raeder had his staff make a study of the problem, because he did not want to be caught short if the Führer should suddenly order him to undertake the onslaught.

But Hitler, at that time, had other ideas. On June 18, he told Goering, "The war's finished. I'll come to an understanding with England."

Hitler had won all he wanted—at the moment—but now he had a bear or, rather, a lion, by the tail. And he did not know how to let go. In his mind, there was no reason the war should go on, and he was prepared to offer Britain a generous settlement, demanding only the colonies that had been taken away in the Versailles settlement. Peace feelers, some of them self-inspired, began to make their way to London from such would-be mediators as the Pope, the King of Sweden, and others. The German chargé d'affaires in Washington, Hans Thomsen, seems to have tried to aid in the peace movement. His encouragement of the isolationists was calculated to produce discouragement in Britain and so make her more susceptible to a peace offer.

Churchill, in his memoirs, says that no consideration was given to seeking peace with Germany after the fall of France; the subject simply did not come up. Although Hitler thought that Churchill's "We shall fight on the beaches" speech was merely gifted oratory, Churchill meant every word of it. His reply to a peace feeler from the King of Sweden was blunt for the language of diplomacy.

> Before any such requests or proposals could even be considered, it would be necessary that effective guarantees by deeds, not words, should be forthcoming from Germany which would ensure the restoration of the free and independent life of Czechoslovakia, Poland, Norway, Denmark, Holland, Belgium and above all, France.

In Hitler's mind Churchill and "his clique" were the principal barriers to peace. To a lesser extent this idea applied as well to King George. If they could only be got out of the way, the German magnanimity would be well received by the British people, who would rally under the leadership of Lord Halifax. For some curious reason, Ribbentrop and Hitler had the idea that Halifax was head of a vast "peace movement in Britain." Nothing could have been farther from the truth. Halifax had opposed war, as Chamberlain had, but when it came, he was prepared to fight it to the end.

A by-product of Hitler's idea of toppling the British leaders was the comic-opera notion of kidnapping the Duke and Duchess of Windsor. The former King Edward VIII had been attached in a liaison capacity in Paris, and when France fell he made his way to Portugal through Spain. The conspirators convinced themselves that once they had him in their hands, they could restore him to the throne he had abdicated, he would then dismiss Churchill, and peace would be signed. Unfortunately for their ideas, the Duke sailed from Lisbon in the American Export liner *Excalibur* to take up his post as Governor of the Bahamas. Even then the Germans convinced themselves that the Duke would work for Germany and made approaches. The

Duke had other ideas and faithfully discharged his duties as Governor. "At no time," he said later, "did I ever entertain any thought of complying with such a suggestion, which I treated with the contempt it deserved."

On July 19, three days after he had issued the order for preparations for the invasion of England, Hitler entered the Reichstag for a major speech and a major ceremony. It was a splendid piece of pageantry. Resplendent generals, bedecked with medals and Iron Crosses, their braid catching the light and glinting it back in golden flashes, filled the first row of the balcony. Hitler on the podium, always a gifted orator, was at his best. William L. Shirer noted in his *Diary*, "Tonight he used his hands beautifully, seemed to express himself almost as much with his hands—and the sway of his body—as he did with his words and the use of his voice. I noticed too his gift for using his face and eyes (cocking his eyes) and the turn of his head for irony, of which there was considerable in tonight's speech, especially when he referred to Mr. Churchill."

The speech was a long one, beginning with a recounting of Germany's woes, Nazi version. At one point, he broke off and with a Nazi salute created twelve new Field Marshals, nine from the Army and three from the Luftwaffe. Goering, already a Field Marshal, was given a new rank invented for the occasion, Reichsmarschall. The twelve accepted their batons with soldierly dignity, but Goering was like a small boy in his delight.

The pleasures of the evening done, Hitler came to the real point of his speech. He was going to give England one last chance. Since he could not move Churchill, he appealed over his head to the British people.

> From Britain I now hear only a single cry—not of the people but of the politicians—that the war must go on! I do not know whether these politicians already have a correct idea of what the continuation of this struggle will be like. They do, it is true, declare that they will carry on with the war and that, even if Great Britain should perish, they would carry on from Canada. I can hardly believe that they mean by this that the people of Britain are to go to Canada. Presumably only those gentlemen interested in the continuation of the war will go there. The people, I am afraid, will have to remain in Britain and . . . will certainly regard the war with other eyes that their so-called leaders in Canada.
>
> Believe me, gentlemen, I feel a deep disgust for this type of unscrupulous politician who wrecks whole nations. It almost causes me

pain to think that I should have been selected by fate to deal the final blow to the structure which these men have already set tottering. . . . Mr. Churchill . . . no doubt will already be in Canada, where the money and children of those principally interested in the war have already been sent. For millions of other people, however, great suffering will begin. Mr. Churchill ought perhaps, for once, to believe me when I prophesy that a great Empire will be destroyed—an Empire which it was never my intention to destroy or even to harm. . . .

In this hour I feel it to be my duty before my own conscience to appeal once more to reason and common sense in Great Britain as much as elsewhere. I consider myself in a position to make this appeal since I am not the vanquished begging favors, but the victor speaking in the name of reason.

I can see no reason why this war must go on.

Shirer recorded that by the time he got to the *Rundfunkhaus* to make his broadcast, the British answer was already in. It was a resounding NO, broadcast by the B.B.C. on its own initiative, with no consultation from the Government. "Can you understand those British fools?" shouted a German official to Shirer. "To turn down peace now! They're crazy!"

There was no mistake. No one answered Hitler officially until July 22, when Halifax stated in a routine broadcast, "We shall not stop fighting until freedom is secure."

That was that. Even Hitler accepted the fact of Britain's stubborn pride. The invasion of England would go forward—if . . .

Operation Sea Lion, the planned invasion of England, had hard going from the first. Although Raeder had been the first to mention it, he never favored it because he knew he did not have the naval strength to bring it off. On July 21, in a conference with Hitler, the matter was discussed at length. Raeder's minutes contain the following:

The invasion of Britain is an exceptionally daring undertaking, because even if the way is short, this is not just a river crossing, but the crossing of a sea which is dominated by the enemy. This is not a case of a single crossing operation as in Norway; operational surprise cannot be expected; a defensively prepared and utterly determined enemy faces us and dominates the sea area which we must use. For the Army operation 40 divisions will be required; the most difficult part will be the continued reinforcement of material and stores. We cannot count on supplies of any kind being available to us in England. The prerequisites are complete mastery of the air, the operational use of powerful artillery in the Dover Straits, and protection by minefields. The time of year is an important factor, since the weather in the North Sea and in the Channel during the second half of September is very bad and the fogs begin in the middle of October. The main operation would therefore have to be completed by September 15; after this date co-operation between the *Luftwaffe* and the heavy weapons becomes too unreliable. But as air co-operation is decisive, it must be regarded as the principal factor in fixing the date. . . .

If it is not certain that preparations can be completed by the beginning of September, other plans must be considered.

The Army, overestimating British strength by some 8 divisions, demanded a force of 39 divisions for the assault, to be landed over a broad front from Ramsgate in the Straits of Dover to Lyme Bay, 75 miles west of the Isle of Wight. This was a front of 237 nautical miles, and was absolutely out of the question in Raeder's view. He urged a front from the Dover Straits to Eastbourne, scarcely more than 75 miles wide. Even then, he was not hopeful. "All things considered," he concluded, "the best time for the operation would be May 1941."

Perhaps he hoped that by that time, Hitler's mind would be on other things.

The Army utterly rejected the proposal for a narrow front. "I might just as well," said Army General Staff Chief General Franz Halder, "put the troops that have landed straight through a sausage machine!"

The two positions were irreconcilable. If the Army persisted in demanding a broad front, then the Navy was perfectly sure the troops would never reach England in face of British sea superiority. If the Navy had its way with a narrow front and a correspondingly decreased number of troops, then they faced defeat on the beaches.

It was almost with relief that they agreed to disagree and tossed the baby to the Luftwaffe. For the Army and Navy *could* agree that no operation was possible unless British air power was knocked out. On August 1, Hitler issued a directive (signed by Keitel as head of OKW) which put the onus on the Luftwaffe.

Preparations for Sea Lion are to be continued and completed by the Army and Luftwaffe by September 15.

Eight to fourteen days after the launching of the air offensive against Britain, scheduled to begin about August 5, the Führer will decide whether the invasion will take place this year or not; his decision will depend largely on the outcome of the air offensive.

And so the Battle of Britain began.

It began in a strange way. On the night of August 1, the bombers came over southeast England, but they carried no bombs. Instead they dropped thousands of copies of a pamphlet printed in English and entitled "A Last Appeal to Reason," a translation of Hitler's speech to the Reichstag on July 19. It was picked up, passed from hand to hand, and read. But not for the reason Hitler had ordered it dropped. Everywhere people were laughing as they read it. A well-known photograph shows four British housewives reading a copy. The broad grins on their faces would not have been to Hitler's or Goebbels's liking, had they but known.

On August 2, Goering ordered the Battle of Britain to begin. It had the single aim of destroying the Royal Air Force so that the Sea Lion troops could cross the Channel. To this end, OKL * assigned priorities to the units principally charged with attacking Britain.

   (a) Enemy aircraft, specifically fighters, in the air and on the ground.
   (b) Main harbors and wharf storage facilities.
   (c) The ground organization of the RAF in the area of London.

For some time, British fighters had engaged the Germans over the Channel in defense of shipping, but now the die was to be cast for quite a different stake. On his Luftwaffe's ability to clear the skies of the Royal Air Force, Goering hazarded his reputation and the outcome of the war. Churchill saw this clearly. "Hitler," he wrote, "knows that he must defeat us here, in this island, or he will lose the war." At the time, those words seemed to be mere whistling in the dark. But, they were in deadly earnest. And they were true.

Having ordered the Battle of Britain to begin on August 2, Goering found himself in the position of a man who has telephoned for a taxi, but the taxi does not come. Day after day, German pilots looked at the weather reports and gazed up at gray skies and rain squalls. Local raids were possible, but nothing on a large scale. Wheat fields were set afire in Essex, and an observer station was knocked out. But there was nothing special.

In England it was quiet, and some places were having sunny weather. People flocked to the parks, to the river, but not to the beaches in the east and south, since they were being prepared, not for tourists, but for invaders.

Goering, nursing his frustration over the weather, set August 10

* *Oberkommando der Luftwaffe,* High Command of the Luftwaffe.

as the date the great attack was to begin. It was to be overwhelming. Drawn up between Cherbourg and Norway, the fat Reichsmarschall had 3,358 aircraft ready for the attack, approximately 75 percent of the Luftwaffe strength. On the realistic basis that two-thirds of them would be ready for service at any one time, approximately 2,240 would be available for "Eagle Day," the mass strike on Britain. These aircraft were organized into three great air fleets (*Luftflotten*). *Luftflotte* Number 2, based in the Low Countries and northern France, was under command of Field Marshal Kesselring; Number 3, also based in northern France, was commanded by Field Marshal Sperrle; and Number 5, based in Norway, was under General Strupf.

On August 12, the weather cleared, and Goering ordered a preliminary attack on Britain, the Luftwaffe flew 440 sorties and the RAF 758, most of them by Fighter Command, planes sent up on call to stop the Germans. The British lost 22 aircraft, and the Germans 32, although both sides claimed heavier casualties inflicted on the enemy. The Luftwaffe claimed 134 for that day. It wasn't long before they began believing their own propaganda and could not understand why the RAF had not been swept from the skies.

August 13 was officially "Eagle Day," and the attack began in earnest.* And it was on this day that Goering made the first of his two great errors that were to cost him the Battle of Britain. Among the targets of the Luftwaffe for August 12 were the radar stations which gave early warning of the enemy approach and enabled the British fighters to be used most efficiently. Five of these radar stations were actually hit that day, and one on the Isle of Wight was knocked out. It remained out of action for eleven days, leaving an embarrassing hole in the radar screen.

But Goering did not know of this success, and he ordered that no more time and effort be wasted on the radar installations. Instead, the attack was shifted to the airfields and their supporting installations. The Germans were not particularly good at selecting their targets, for on one day, out of eight airfields attacked, only three were actually in use by Fighter Command. And it was Fighter Command, more than any other organization, that had to be destroyed if the Luftwaffe was to win.

The British papers paid little heed to events these first few days. More important was the opening of the annual grouse season on

---

* Some accounts place "Eagle Day" on August 15, for this was the date of the heaviest attack on Britain. But, according to Goering's orders, "Eagle Day" was actually August 13.

August 12. Correspondents wrote *The Times* that the cuckoos had never sounded so fine as they had that year.

"You won't have any difficulty finding trouble," the commander of Number 603 Squadron of Fighter Command told his pilots. "The only problem is how to get out of it."

That day, August 15, all three *Luftflotten* from Norway, Denmark, the Low Countries, and France hurled their attacks, sending 801 bomber sorties and 1,149 fighter attacks. They could not all be turned back. The skies were filled with twisting, dodging shapes, British Hurricanes and Spitfires taking on all comers—Dorniers, Stukas, Heinkels, Messerschmitt 109s and 110s. British fighter pilots charged huge formations of enemy aircraft, shooting, shooting, shooting. The sky filled with bits of wreckage, wings, tails, rudders shot off. Small forms leaped from burning aircraft, and above them parachutes blossomed. Sometimes, horribly, they did not open, and the forms fell to earth or into the sea. One can only hope that they were dead when they started to fall.

That day the British shot down 75 German aircraft and lost 34. *Luftflotte* 5 was so badly mauled that it never returned to the battle. The British believed at that time that they had destroyed 182 German planes and probably shot down 43 more. When the news was officially told in the communiqué, it boosted morale everywhere, especially among the hard-pressed fighter pilots.

The fighter pilots of Britain were a breed apart. Only a few years before, many had been pacifists, some of them having signed the famous Oxford Pledge, in which they said they would "never fight for King and Country." Then somehow the fighting spirit had come. Perhaps they had only wanted to fly airplanes, and in the RAF they found not only the planes to fly but a spirit of dedication to service. But they were not men naively following a slogan. They were dedicated to their work, and they fought because they must. It had to be done. They were the elite, and they knew it. They gave no quarter and asked none.

They had to be supremely self-confident, knowing that they could do their jobs. There was no time for self-analysis in the air combat of the Battle of Britain. It was like plunging into a game of soccer or hockey. If you held back for fear of getting hurt, you probably would get hurt. Only by dashing in and forcing the issue could a fighter pilot hope to do his job and come out of it alive.

Flight Lieutenant J. B. Nicholson of 249 Squadron took on a

Messerschmitt 110 near Gosport, but he was a moment or even a second too late. The 110 got off a burst setting Nicholson's Hurricane on fire. But Nicholson refused to bale out, even though the flames were licking around him in his cockpit. He had to get a chance at that German. The nimble Hurricane chased the twin-engined fighter-bomber around the skies. Then Nicholson had it in his sights. A quick burst from his machine guns. But, no. The 110 slid out of the sights. Around again, after him. But the burning Hurricane would no longer respond. Horribly burned, Nicholson leaped out of the falling plane.

His parachute opened, and in agony he slipped down. Then he heard the sounds of firing and thought the Messerschmitt was coming to finish him off. But, no. It was coming from the ground. Home Guardsmen had taken him for a German.

A bullet hit Nicholson, and then he was on the ground. Apologetic Home Guardsmen recognized his uniform, picked him up, and rushed him to a hospital. He became the only pilot of Fighter Command to be given the Victoria Cross during the Battle of Britain.

Perhaps he was given the award as a symbol, for, as he would have been the first to grant, so many others deserved it.

The men of Fighter Command were good, but there were never enough of them. The Battle of Britain was a battle of attrition, but not of aircraft. Britain could produce more planes than it had pilots to fly them. As the days wore on, men were getting worn out, men were making little mistakes that made all the difference, and men were dying. As the experienced pilots were killed or wounded, their places had to be taken by men of less experience. And experience made all the difference. Before you got it, you were very likely to be killed.

But still they went up to meet the Germans—two, three, even seven times a day. For the Battle of Britain went on.

Persistent as they were, the pilots of Fighter Command could never have done it if they had not been helped from the ground. The dedication of the men who serviced the aircraft matched that of the men who flew them. And there were the men and women in the sector command posts who plotted the radar information and saw to it that the planes were in the right spot at the right time. These sector command posts were the nerve centers for the battles waged above.

On August 24, the Germans singled out these sector stations as prime targets.

On the same day the weather broke. Cloudy skies had hampered operations for several days, but now beautiful holiday weather gave the Luftwaffe the opportunity it had been waiting for. For the next two weeks the Germans sent an average of a thousand planes a day against England. Night and day they came. By day they smashed at the sector stations and at the airfields in Kent and other parts of southeast England. By night they turned their attention on industrial centers, ports, and aircraft factories.

And Fighter Command pilots went up to meet them. It got to be harder, because coordination became more difficult. Bombing of sector stations caused delays in vectoring defending fighters. The Germans pressed harder, and the losses mounted on both sides.

But August 24 was a key day in another sense. For the first time, German aircraft dropped bombs on London.

It was a mistake that they did so. The bombers which had been sent against Rochester and the Thameshaven oil tanks got turned around in the darkness and loosed their loads at London Wall, at Tottenham, Finsbury, Stepney, East Ham, and Bethnal Green and several other places. The church of St. Giles, Cripplegate, was hit, and another bomb knocked the statue of Milton from its pedestal. This was the first time since the Gotha raids of 1918 that London had been bombed.

It was not to be the last.

London had been expecting for some time that it would be bombed, but the people were still psychologically unready to believe it. On the afternoon of August 24, as bombers came near London in search of other targets, the air-raid warnings keened. At Regent's Park, where a theatrical troupe was putting on Shakespeare's *A Midsummer Night's Dream* in an outdoor theater, few members of the audience left their places, and the play went on.

Another kind of play did not. For the first time in history, the cricket match at Lord's was interrupted by the air-raid warning. As the noise of the sirens rose, the players walked slowly from the field and the spectators reluctantly followed—all except one man who, wrapped in a red overcoat, kept his place, waiting for the play to resume. The Scots Guards were bowling, and he intended to see it all.

Perhaps this little scene is symbolic. The idea of invasion was abstract. It meant little to the average man. But such an interruption of his way of life made an Englishman furious. It couldn't be allowed to happen. Come war, come invasion, come death and destruction, life must go on, and it had to be life as he knew it. Men continued to gather in the pubs to drink their evening pints of mild or bitter, to play a game of darts, to talk. They worked in their gardens. They played their games.

A golf tournament was held at a club northwest of London. The night before it was to begin, the tournament committee held an emergency meeting to rule on the question: What happens if a member's ball goes in a bomb crater? The committee investigated the rule book, but there was no mention of bomb craters. On the whole, they thought that the players should not be penalized by extra hazards which had been added to the course during the night. Their ruling: Any player whose ball went into a crater was allowed to pick it up and play it from behind the crater without penalty.

On the airstrip at Bircham Newton a squadron of Hampton bombers was poised, the twin engines ticking over. The planes were a part of a group of 81 which would repay the bombing of London, for their target for that night was Berlin.

It was just dusk on the evening of August 25 as the bombers began their 600-mile-long trip to the German capital. British planes had visited Berlin before, but they had always dropped leaflets. This time they had a more sinister cargo to be dropped on the Siemens-Halske Electrical Works in the outskirts. Most of the flight was through cloud, with only an occasional glimpse of the land below.

The clouds did not prevent the German antiaircraft defenses from opening up, and some of the bursts came uncomfortably close. "Twice I had to take evasive action to escape the shells," wrote one of the pilots. "When we arrived over Berlin, there was a formidable concentration of guns and searchlights. We cruised around for half an hour before we located the target and all the time the guns were popping off at us, and accurately."

Squadron Leader R. J. Oxley led the way down, hoping for a break in the cloud. When he was below 5000 feet, he gave it up, but he had not come all that way for nothing. He could go no lower, but his bombs could. "I was keen," he recorded, "but not that keen. I could have brought my bombs back, of course, but I didn't. I left them in Berlin."

On the way back, Oxley ran into trouble. As he was crossing the Channel, one of his two engines quit. Then, over Leaconfield, the other engine gave up the struggle. Fortunately there was an airport below, and there Oxley made a good dead-stick landing.

As he emerged from the plane, the controller, a Pole, gave him a good dressing down for not taxiing the plane to the hangar. Oxley was frustrated at the end of his grueling experience, and made even more frustrated by the Polish officer's inability to understand. Turning away, Oxley snapped at him, "Taxi it yourself, because I can't."

"If a single British bomber attacks Berlin, you can call me Meier." * Goering had made that boast early in the war. Now bombs had fallen, but there is no record that anyone ever called the fat Reichsmarschall "Meier."

William L. Shirer, who witnessed that first bombing of Berlin, described its results in his *Diary*. "The Berliners are stunned. They did not think it could happen. When this war began, Goering assured them it couldn't. He boasted that no enemy planes could ever break through the outer and inner rings of the capital's anti-aircraft defense. The Berliners are a naive and simple people. They believed him . . . And then last night the guns all over the city suddenly began pounding and you could hear the British motors humming directly overhead, and from all reports there was a pell-mell, frightened rush to the cellars by the five million people who live in this town."

The bombing of Berlin went on for night after night, and the propagandists were hard put to explain the facts away. "BRITISH AIR PIRATES OVER BERLIN," reported the *Börsen Zeitung*. Goebbels claimed that "on the personal orders of Churchill," the bombers attacked only non-military targets. And he denied that Berlin itself was hit; because of the splendid work of the defenses, all bombs fell in the outskirts. Berliners seemed to accept this, even though the Tiergarten was roped off, and concentration-camp inmates were working to remove delayed-action bombs. These miserable wretches were promised their freedom if they disarmed a certain number of bombs. In spite of the fact that these men were often cheated in the count, they had nothing to lose but their lives, and these usually were not worth keeping in a concentration camp.

On September 4, stung into reply by the repeated bombings of Berlin, Hitler made a speech. He castigated the "cowardly British," who dared fly over only at night. "When they declare that they will increase their attacks on our cities, then we will raze *their* cities to the ground." His audience screamed in approval. "The hour will come," Hitler shouted, "when one of us will break, and it will not be National Socialist Germany."

Dropping his frenetic role, Hitler turned coy. Referring to the long-expected invasion of England, he mocked: "In England they're filled

* Meier is one of the common Jewish names in Germany.

261

with curiosity and keep asking: 'Why doesn't he come?' Be calm. He's coming! He's coming!"

Coyness aside, Hitler's speech did reveal his plans, for as he spoke plans were well advanced for Sea Lion. Gone was the idea of the broad front demanded by the Army, and the 40 divisions had shrunk to 13, all that the Navy could hope to transport by means of the motley collection of barges, coasters, and small boats which would carry most of the troops. Admiral Raeder pointed out that September 15 was the latest reasonable date for the crossing—the weather dictated that. And he demanded a minimum of ten days for minesweeping and for naval preparations. Thus, if the invasion was to be mounted that year, September 5 was the day of decision.

Yet September 5 came and went, for the Navy was not ready to meet the deadline. Hitler himself set the new date—September 21. It was full speed ahead with the plans. On D-minus-10, that is, on September 10, Hitler would make the final decision. He could not make it yet, for the air war had not yet been won.

British Fighter Command was nearly at the end of its tether. During the crucial fortnight between August 24 and September 6, the British lost 466 fighters, but the problem, as always, was not in aircraft but in pilots. During that same period 103 fighter pilots were killed and 128 seriously wounded. This represented about 25 percent of the fighter pilots available.

"Never," said Churchill in the House of Commons, "in the field of human conflict was so much owed by so many to so few."

But the few were getting fewer.

Then came the great change. Hitler ordered the Luftwaffe to begin the bombing of London. No more were the fighters of the RAF the prime target. No more would the airfields, whence they clawed their way into the air, be bombed into uselessness. No more were the sector stations in the bull's-eye. Now it was the center of the nation, the world's largest city.

The raids began on September 7. That afternoon a special train named *Asia* pulled up on a siding at Cap Blanc-Nez. It was a beautiful train, protected at each end by antiaircraft batteries. The main coach, which was ballasted with lead for a smoother ride, had two sybaritically decorated bedrooms, a small office, and a bathroom. The next car was a lounge outfitted with a movie projector and screen. Behind it came a mobile command post. It is said that it took 171 persons to serve this train and its owner, the gross Siegfried of the

Luftwaffe, Reichsmarschall Goering. He had come to be with his pilots for the great attack on London.

"I have personally taken command of the Battle for Britain," he announced pompously.

As the planes left their bases, Goering nearly broke his neck watching them, wishing he could be with them. But the fat Reichsmarschall could no longer squeeze into the cockpit of a Messerschmitt, and he would not fly a bomber. He gazed after his planes, his heart exulting that he would deliver the blow that would drive Britain from the war. Had not Warsaw and Rotterdam shown what massive bombing could do? Now it was London's turn.

Massive blobs for targets nearly blanked out British radar screens. This was the biggest thing yet! Twenty-three squadrons of fighters were scrambled by 4 o'clock that afternoon.

But the Germans were too many. Over 300 bombers, escorted by some 600 fighters, were headed toward the Thames Estuary and London. Soon the German flyers could look down at the famous U of the Thames between Blackwall Tunnel and Rotherhithe Tunnel. Between them lay the vital docks of London.

Bomb-bay doors opened and bombs began to fall. One blaze after another sprang up, and the rising clouds of smoke acted as beacons for succeeding waves. Docks, houses, Woolwich Arsenal, Bishopsgate Goods Yard began to blaze. Tons of molten sugar caught fire and spread to the area which had escaped the flames. Thousands of gallons of rum spilled from the containers, forming a devil's punch, flames licking along the surface.

In the smashed and blazing buildings, screams of the injured and dying could be heard. A.R.P.* wardens did their best, but it was their first experience, and they could do little. The fires spread, while the London Fire Brigade rushed more and more equipment into the East End.

That night, the bombers came back. They had an easy target, for flames were still dancing from the afternoon raid. But this time, somehow, it wasn't so bad. People were still being killed and property was being destroyed, but the men working in the ruins had the measure of the task. "Most of us had the wind up to start with," remarked one of them later, "but we were all unwilling to show fear. You looked around and saw the rest doing their job."

* A.R.P., *i.e.,* Air Raid Precautions.

Even as the East End was undergoing its second ordeal, someone—some idiot, it was charged later—sounded the code word "Cromwell," which meant that invasion was imminent. Church bells, silent for weeks, began to peal, and men sprang to their stations to watch and wait.

They waited.

Stories began to spread that the Germans had landed, but it was always somewhere else. The Channel was said to have been set on fire. Burned corpses were reported, but none of these things had any truth. No invasion was going on. Hitler had not yet made up his mind. He was still waiting for the Luftwaffe to win over British Fighter Command.

Night after night the bombers came over, an average of 170 per night for 57 consecutive nights. Day raids, meanwhile, slackened off, a godsend for the exhausted fighter pilots. The nearly non-existent antiaircraft defenses of London were greatly strengthened, and though the guns seldom hit anything, the people were heartened to hear them going off. It gave Londoners the feeling of fighting back.

If the Germans had continued to pound at the docks and the crowded East End, they might have achieved both a military and psychological breakthrough. In those days, London was the busiest port in the United Kingdom, and it was being bombed to a standstill. Although the area contained many slums, large parts of it were filled with neat row houses, each with its neatly scrubbed steps, its lace curtains, its windowboxes of flowers. Still and all, it was not a high-income area, and leftist agitators and Russian sympathizers were noising rumors about that there was a gentlemen's agreement between the ruling classes and the Germans to avoid the wealthy and stylish West End.

On September 12, the Luftwaffe attacked the center of London, the City and the West End. Bombs fell on the Embankment, in Trafalgar Square, on Somerset House, along Piccadilly. A delayed-action bomb fell near the great cathedral of St. Paul's. It fell within a few yards of the north wall and penetrated to a depth of 27 feet. There it lay, its infernal mechanism running, a constant threat to Christopher Wren's masterpiece.

Therein lie at rest many of Britain's greatest soldiers and sailors, Wellington and Nelson among them. The entire country, it seemed, watched and waited as experts worked on the bomb to render it harmless. For seventy-two unending hours, each of which was made up of sixty interminable minutes—any one might be their last—Lieutenant

264

R. Davies and his assistant Sapper Wylie worked on the monstrous bomb. At last they won. The bomb was disarmed. The exhausted men became the first to receive the George Cross.

Even as the bomb fell on St. Paul's, another, possibly the most important to fall on England, dropped on Buckingham Palace. The King and Queen escaped injury, but the windows of their apartment were shattered, and they might have been cut to ribbons. The King made light of the matter, but he was exhilarated by the thought of sharing the dangers with his subjects.

The bombs on the West End, and particularly the bombs on Buckingham Palace, soon put a stop to the ugly rumors that only the poor were to be bombed. The people of London developed a feeling that they were all in it together. In piles of rubble tiny paper Union Jacks had been planted in defiance of the raiders above.

It was not easy. It is never easy to see your home destroyed, your friends and family killed, to have no water in the pipes, no electricity or gas, and to know that the next bomb may have your name on it. But the amazing thing is that the people did stand up to it. War theorists had predicted that after a few raids, the people would panic and demand that their Government sue for peace—anything to end the bombing.

But the Londoners of 1940 did not. They kept going, men and women alike. "The womenfolk in particular were amazing," recorded Lord Ismay. "The courage of the charwoman who used to clean my office was typical of her sex. She generally arrived before the last German bombers had left, and for the first fortnight or so she was full of cheerful gossip when she awakened me. But one morning she was in floods of tears. She said that nearly all the houses in her street had been destroyed, that her sister had been killed, that she never got any sleep, and that she could not stand it any longer. I told her that I was just as frightened as she was, and that the only solution that I could think of was to tell Hitler that we could not take it, and that he had better come over and occupy England. Whereupon the old lady gave vent to a flood of the most sulphurous language that I have ever heard. Her description of Hitler's ancestry to the third and fourth generation was a masterpiece. The outburst evidently gave her relief; anyhow, there were no more tears or grumblings."

If Lord Ismay's charwoman was unwilling to have Hitler come, the German dictator was getting less willing to come. On September 11, Hitler postponed the day of decision to September 14, and on that day, he postponed it again to the 17th. Goering had to have a few more days to complete softening up England.

He did not succeed. Raid followed raid, but on September 15, although neither side realized it at the time, the real decision was made. This day, celebrated in the United Kingdom as Battle of Britain Day, was misty at first, but it soon cleared. About eleven o'clock in the morning, large formations of planes began to appear on the British radar screens. Nearly everything Fighter Command had that could fly took to the air.

All day long the fighting and bombing went on. At one point, the last reserve aircraft defending southeast Britain was committed. No new raids appeared; if they had, there would have been nothing to oppose them.

This was Germany's maximum effort against Britain. At the end of the day, the British claimed 185 German aircraft had been shot down. The Germans claimed they had destroyed 78 British Hurricanes and Spitfires. Both sides wildly exaggerated, but it hardly mattered.* The figure "185" became fixed in the British minds, and at the moment, it seemed as big a victory as Trafalgar. They had not won, they knew, but they had not been beaten by the worst the Germans could throw at them.

Infuriated by the lack of a decisive breakthrough, Goering castigated his commanders and ordered the German fighters to stick even closer to the bomber groups. It was an idiotic order, for the fighters, tied down, could do little to parry the attacks of the British fighters. It was another tactical blunder for the fat Reichsmarschall.

Still he begged for just "four or five more days" to finish off the RAF and bomb London into submission.

The weather turned bad the next day, and few German planes flew. But that night 170 planes attacked London. They hit the big department stores this time; John Lewis's in Oxford Street, Bourne and Hollingsworth, and D. H. Evans were hit.

People were beginning to recover their spirits and a certain grim humor, even though more than 30,000 Londoners had been rendered homeless. They sang the popular songs, "A Nightingale Sang in Berkeley Square," and the recent import, "Begin the Beguine." A

---

* The actual losses for September 15 were 52 German and 27 British aircraft. After the war the British admitted that they had exaggerated enemy air losses for the sake of morale, but wryly pointed out that over the period of the Battle of Britain their exaggeration had only been 55 percent, while that of the Germans had been 224 percent.

new version of the former was heard in the clubs and even being sung by those digging in the rubble:

There were six miscarriages,
Under Claridges,
When a screaming bomb fell in Berkeley Square.

On the other side of the Channel there was another miscarriage. Sea Lion died aborning. On September 17, Hitler ordered the invasion of England postponed until further notice, and two days later he ordered the invasion fleet to be dispersed. At the same time, he gave instructions that planning continue, that outward signs of invasion be kept up as long as possible. He hoped these activities would come to the attention of the British. Next spring, he argued, we may try again.

But next spring, he would be far too busy with the plans for the invasion of Russia. Next spring Hitler would repeat the mistake of Napoleon and leave an undefeated Britain at his back. And it would be for the same reason: his plan to invade Britain had failed.

Meanwhile, the blitz went on.

The people were developing a routine. No longer did they run for cover at the first warning, for there would be another, a Red Alert, when they must take cover. Then they would move to the nearest shelters. The Undergrounds were especially popular, being, for the most part, deep beneath the surface. The deepest in the system, the one at Hampstead, was approached only by elevator, but others, at Oxford Circus, Trafalgar Square, Piccadilly Circus, Elephant and Castle were well down yet accessible. Here, on the station platforms, beneath the advertisements for Players and Senior Service cigarettes, Bovril, and Whitbread Ale, men, women, and children bundled in their blankets, brewed tea over spirit lamps, and waited out the raids.

When the All Clear went, the people would go to the streets, do what had to be done, and carry on the work they had to do.

On the night of October 15, the Germans began a new kind of attack. That night they dropped 386 tons of conventional, high-explosive bombs, but they added as a new sort of remembrance a confetti in the form of 70,000 incendiary bombs.

Now Londoners had to take to the roofs in an air raid rather than to the shelters. Fire-watchers, with no protection other than a tin hat, stood ready with sand buckets and other devices for quelling the fires. If these men and women had not been there, the blazes would have been far beyond the capacity of the London Fire Brigade. In peacetime the Brigade considered a 30-alarm night as an all-out emergency. During the blitz, a 900-alarm night was not uncommon.

One day, while Churchill was visiting Ramsgate, for the outlying cities were not spared while London was taking it, he chanced upon a tea shop which had just been hit. Outside the wreckage, sobbing her heart out, was the aged owner. Her livelihood was gone.

"Arrangements must be made for poor people like that to be given immediate compensation in order that they may be able to start up their businesses again," ordered Churchill. And soon a National Insurance arrangement was worked out. During the war £830,000,000 was paid out.

During these trying months, the former Prime Minister, Neville Chamberlain, had faithfully carried out his duties as Lord President of the Council. His fate was not to lead, but to preside. He was not a doer but a conciliator. No word of complaint passed his lips over his loss of power as Prime Minister. He and Churchill had their differences, but Chamberlain kept on working for his new chief.

Then, in August, he could not go on. Learning that he had cancer, he consented to an operation, but on September 17 was back in the House of Commons. He kept grimly to his duties until the end of the month. He met every engagement, faultlessly dressed, somewhat thinner, and no sign of the pain within was allowed to show.

But Churchill was not deceived, and he knew his old friend and former leader was a dying man. "He ought not to be here in this condition," he told Mrs. Chamberlain. "You must take him away till he is well again. I will send all the telegrams to him each day."

From his country home in Hampshire, Chamberlain carried on his work for six weeks. On November 9 the end came. He had died still in the service of his country.

Whatever else history may or may not say about these terrible, tremendous years [said Churchill in his eulogy in the House of Commons], we can be sure that Neville Chamberlain acted with perfect sincerity according to his lights and strove to the utmost of his capacity and authority, which were powerful, to save the world from the awful, devastating struggle in which we are now engaged. . . . Herr Hitler protests with frantic words and gestures that he has only desired peace. What do these ravings and outpourings count before the silence of Neville Chamberlain's tomb?. . . . [We] here assembled this morning, members of all parties, without a single exception, feel that we do ourselves and our country honour in saluting the memory of one whom Disraeli would have called "an English worthy."

It was on the night of November 3 that, for the first time in eight weeks, no bomb fell on London. It was uncanny. People wondered what was wrong. It was a lull, but the blitz was not over. It had merely shifted to the industrial cities. It was a relief to Londoners for a time, but their relief could not last long.

The bombers would be back.

But, while London and Britain were taking it, their armed forces were not idle. They were hitting back around the edges, and some of their blows hurt.

And, across the sea, the American people watched and wondered if Britain could hold out. There were many who doubted it, but there were more who had faith in Britain's courage and determination. Among these were the Republican and Democratic candidates for the office of President of the United States, Wendell L. Willkie and Franklin D. Roosevelt.

CHAPTER ELEVEN

An American Summer

*That they may both perceive and know
what things they ought to do,
and also may have grace and
power faithfully to fulfill the same.*
Book of Common Prayer

BY BUS and train they came. By car, and even by air, landing in the three-day-old Philadelphia airport, came the delegates— there was Good Ole Joe Stubble from Persepolis, and his wife Susie. There were Mike and Evelyn Stabble from Providence, and Art and Alice Stebble from Petersburg. Under the lowering gloomy skies of that Sunday afternoon, young Bill and Maudie Stibble of Pottsville yelled *"Hi,* there" to Bob and Masie Stobble from Pokane.

From far and near they came, a thousand delegates, a thousand alternates, hundreds of workers, well-wishers, wheels, wheels-within-wheels, wheels-within-wheels-within-wheels. There came the party faithfuls, the would-be's, those with an axe to grind, little men and lesser men, great men and greater men. And came the candidates themselves.

Philadelphia was bracing itself for the Republican National Nominating Convention, which was to open the next day, June 24, and there were axes to grind and fences to mend. There were delegates to be wooed and deals to be made.

They crowded hotels and restaurants, lunch counters and bars. In a crowded elevator Les Gubble from Portsville stepped on the toes of Pete Gobble from Pleasantville and was answered with a curse. Les was for Dewey, and Pete was a Taft man.

And so it went. The delegates whooped it up, sweated, nursed sore feet, drank too much Scotch, bourbon, rye, corn, rum, gin, vodka, and other firewaters. They ate too much steak, French fries, fish filets, fried chicken, croquettes, lamb, pork chops, and pie à la mode. Some got sick and repented. Some got sick and went right back to it. They put their heads together and plotted and schemed.

In the Credentials Committee there were the usual fights and compromises. In the Platform Committee there were the usual efforts to produce a platform that would say nothing to offend anyone except the Democrats.

Delegates and supporters wore buttons bearing such names as DEWEY, TAFT, VANDENBERG, MARTIN, GANNETT, MAC-NIDER, HOOVER, MCNARY. And there was another button on which the party pros cast baleful glances. It said WIN WITH WILLKIE.

The presence in town of Wendell L. Willkie, a burly, shambling man of 48, was an unwelcome intrusion on the high spirits of the delegates. From his suite on the 16th floor of the Benjamin Franklin Hotel, he cast a pall over the proceedings. Not that any of the professionals gave him any chance. His campaign headquarters was a crazy quilt of disorganization, run by amateurs, well-wishers, debutantes, stockbrokers, business leaders, tourists, and clubwomen. These so-called campaign workers were so ignorant that they did not know the party faithful and the importance they had.

There was really nothing to worry about from a contender who had none of the party machinery at his beck and call. Still, it was disturbing. There were so many of these enthusiastic amateurs. If a delegate sent his suit to the cleaners, it was likely to come back with a Willkie button on it. In the jostling crowd you might have one pinned on you and never know it until a fellow delegate coldly demanded an explanation. The phone would ring and you would hear only the single word "Willkie," followed by the click of the caller hanging up.

The politicos had never seen anything like it. It was, as one of them put it, "the damnedest convention that ever was." And this was before it had even started. Still, things would be better when they got the delegates into the convention hall. Under the chairmanship of old reliable House Minority Leader Joe Martin, the amateurs would be out of their depth. Let Willkie and his gang have their fun. They won't know what hit them when the convention gets going.

The convention opened quietly enough, in rather drab surroundings, for there was no bunting, no parading bands—only jostling, milling crowds of delegates, unaffected as usual by the chairman's cries of "The delegates will please be seated!" Keynoter Harold E. Stassen, Governor of Minnesota, spoke as though he were seeing his speech for the first time. "We are tragically unprepared," he stated. "We are too woefully weak to give the Allies that material assistance this nation wants to give them. We are sadly wanting in the state of our defenses of this hemisphere."

This was all part of the game. No matter that over the years most Republicans had voted down any increase in appropriations for national defense. It was the Administration of That Man in the White House that was responsible. Besides, That Man had just played the Republicans a dirty trick.

Four days before the convention opened, Roosevelt shocked his own party and the Republicans by appointing Henry L. Stimson as Secretary of War and Frank Knox as Secretary of the Navy. It was unforgivable, for both men were lifelong Republicans. G.O.P. faithfuls charged Roosevelt with trying to saddle the blame for America's lack of preparation on them. They prepared to read Stimson and Knox out of the party. Democrats were equally furious. It was a calculated insult to the party to give two of the most responsible Cabinet jobs to Republicans. There was talk of delaying Senate confirmation of the two for "intensive investigation." It was just talk, but there was a lot of it.

Meanwhile, the business of the convention went on. The platform appeared, and its vague generalities caused some to observe that the weasel ought to replace the elephant as the party symbol.

From the beginning, cries of "We Want Willkie" had resounded from the galleries, disturbing the equanimity of the bosses, but they really felt little alarm, for the votes were on the floor, not in the galleries. There were two men to watch, Senator Robert A. Taft of Ohio and Governor Thomas E. Dewey of New York. There was a chance for Senator Arthur H. Vandenberg of Michigan. All the rest were of little account—Favorite Sons, who would hold their delegations until the proper moment, and then would jump on the proper bandwagon in return for the proper favor. It was always so, and there was no reason it should be different this time.

Then came the business of nominations. Dewey was the first to be nominated, and the organ played, and delegates shouted, and standards were waved. Parades formed, and all was customary pandemonium. Then came the nomination of publisher Frank Gannett of New York. A few scattered handclaps marked the climax of his campaign, into which he had poured half a million dollars of his own money.

Representative Charles Halleck of Indiana was next escorted to the podium by none other than the chairman, Joe Martin. In a speech that struck at everyone's sacred cows, he placed in nomination the name of his fellow Hoosier, Wendell L. Willkie. Here it was that the real split in the convention showed, for the galleries cheered, while the delegates mostly sat silent. Then a few began to move, and the demonstration gathered strength. Finally all 20,000 of those in the hall were on their feet. A parade began, but fights broke out, as well. Someone pulled down Virginia's waving standard, and a fight erupted around it. Police broke up the fracas and other similar melees. But the big states, with the big electoral blocs, stood fast. Watching it all, one of the pros remarked, "Well, there goes your Willkie boom."

There were the other nominations. Vandenberg, Taft, James of Pennsylvania, Martin of Massachusetts, Hoover of California. A few Favorite Sons had their moment of glory.

After the dreary round of seconding speeches, the convention adjourned. The nominations had taken the best part of two days. It was now Thursday afternoon, June 27, and at 4:50, Joe Martin's new lucite gavel succeeded in imposing order.

"The Clerk will call the roll of the states for the nomination of the next President of the United States!"

"A-a-a-l-a-b-a-a-m-a!"

"Alabama casts seven votes for Thomas E. Dewey and six for Robert A. Taft!"

And so they were off. Private tally sheets were marked by delegates, bigwigs, spectators, newsmen, by campaign managers and candidates, and by millions of people all over the country, as the radio brought the voices from Philadelphia into their homes. To win the nomination, 501 votes were required. It was clear no one could win on the first ballot. Too many Favorite Son candidates were cluttering the slate. Dewey had to come in strong, or he was through. Taft expected to gain strength slowly and hoped for some 250 votes on the first tally.

The galleries loudly cheered each Willkie vote, while the regulars looked annoyed. But this, too, would pass, they felt.

The results of the first ballot: Dewey had a comfortable lead, with 360 votes. Taft had 189, and Willkie was a poor third with 105. Vandenberg had 76, and the rest were scattered among Favorite

Sons. Grim-faced Taft-men set about buttonholing delegates as the second ballot began.

When it was over, Dewey had dropped to 338, and the Taft camp cheered up considerably. To be sure, their own candidate had gained only 14 votes to 203, but they were sure Dewey was out of it, for never has a candidate been nominated by either party who has lost ground on any ballot. But the Willkie forces were delighted, for their man had gained 66 votes for a total of 171. The question was, could Taft grab the Dewey votes?

There was time for deals to be made for the third ballot, for at 6:50 P.M. Joe Martin adjourned the convention until 8:30. There would be more conferences, discussions, and arguments than there would be eating. And during those few minutes the delegates began to break away from the party discipline.

When the steamy convention reconvened and the third ballot was taken, Joe Martin released his own supporters, and to a man, they went over to Willkie. So did some from Pennsylvania, New Hampshire, and elsewhere. Taft's deals did not pay off much. He gained only 9 votes. Results of the third ballot: Dewey, 315; Willkie, 259; Taft, 212.

Willkie supporters screamed with delight to see their favorite in second place, and Dewey recognized that he was through. He released his delegates, and it was up to Taft to gather them in if he could. Thus, the fourth ballot was crucial. If Willkie faltered, then the nomination would go to Taft almost by acclamation on the next ballot. Up and down the aisles Willkie-men and Taft-men brushed past each other, buttonholding delegates.

On ballot four, more delegates kicked over the traces, and the results were a sore disappointment to Taft and his supporters. Taft had gained 42 votes, but Willkie had gone ahead 47. The fourth ballot: Willkie, 306; Taft, 254; Dewey, 250.

As the results of the fourth ballot sank in, the pros grew desperate. Willkie had not faded; he had gone ahead. The constant chant from the galleries—"We Want Willkie!—We Want Willkie!—We Want Willkie!"—was getting on their nerves. They united in a grand last minute attempt to put Taft over. The Clerk began the roll call again, and the galleries cheered every vote for Willkie and groaned at every vote for Taft or anyone else.

This time the contenders gained 123 votes each. Willkie now had 429, Taft 377, and Dewey had dropped to 57. The next ballot would probably be it.

The weary delegates started once again. Willkie gained a few votes, as shown on the tally sheets. Then Pennsylvania, which had been casting most of its votes for its Governor, Arthur H. James, asked to reserve its vote until the end. "Deal! Deal!" shouted delegates and galleries alike. But no one was sure what the deal was, or whom it favored.

Howard C. Lawrence, a gray, bespectacled man, made his way to the platform. He was campaign manager for Senator Vandenberg. People sat up. He was obviously about to release the Michigan delegation. He did. Then he announced the result of a poll. Michigan cast 35 votes for Willkie, 2 for Taft, and 1 for Herbert Hoover. The crowd roared. This brought Willkie's total to 499. He needed only two more votes to put him over.

Then Pennsylvania shouted for recognition. Former Senator David A. Reed grabbed a microphone and shouted, "Pennsylvania casts 72 votes for Wendell Willkie!"

It was done. The gangling Hoosier and his crowd of amateurs— "Boy Scouts," the politicos had dubbed them—had confounded the party organization.

As a sop to the professionals, Willkie allowed a party faithful, Senator Charles L. McNary of Oregon, to be named as his running mate. Addressing the convention on Friday, Willkie promised a formal acceptance speech later and crowed a little over his triumph. As the band played his theme song, "Heigh Ho, Heigh Ho, It's Off to Work We Go," he gripped the rostrum waiting. Confetti rained down and he grinned. "Forty-eight days, and only forty-eight days ago, I started out to preach to the American people the doctrine of unity, the doctrine of the destiny of America. . . . The cause is great. We must win. We cannot fail if we stand together in one united fight."

"Now," he added, "I'm going home to sleep for a week!"

* * *

The radio brought the doings of the Republican Convention into the homes of America, for at that time, radio was in its heyday. Some 45,000,000 radio sets were in the homes of 33,000,000 Americans. Television was still in an experimental stage, so it was upon radio that the burden of home entertainment fell. Regular newscasters had their following. Most popular of all was Lowell Thomas, whose broadcasts for Sunoco hit the right note of urbanity and folksiness. Walter Winchell's combination of cynicism and gossip about the entertainment world fascinated listeners from Dubuque to Denver, from Portland to Miami. Drew Pearson and Robert S. Allen gave the low-down on doings in Washington, much to the disgruntlement of Washingtonians, particularly those with anything to hide. Fulton S. Lewis, Jr., with his "That's the top of the news as it looks from here," blasted the New Deal in general and hanky-panky in particular. His extreme right-wing views discredited him with the intelligentsia, but his careful documentation impressed a lot of the folks back home.

Foreign correspondents had their day, as well. In Berlin Howard K. Smith and William L. Shirer fought a constant battle with censorship to bring the straight story to America. Shirer's eavesdropping account of the French surrender in the railroad carriage at Compiègne was one of the most remarkable broadcasts of the war. From London Edward R. Murrow's account of the blitz brought the plight of the British close to the hearts of the American people. Sometimes on his broadcasts you could actually hear the sirens wail and the bombs explode. It put the war in the living rooms of everybody.

Entertainment had its place, too. Soap operas claimed most of the daylight hours. Who can forget the indestructible Helen Trent, who spent her daily stint warding off admirers and wolves, all the while extolling the virtues of true love? There were *Our Gal Sunday, Guiding Light, Road of Life, Woman in White,* and countless others. Comics such as Bob Hope, Jack Benny, Fred Allen, and Edgar Bergen and his Charlie McCarthy pulled the most listeners. Very popular was the program *Information, Please,* in which a panel presided over by the sophisticated Clifton Fadiman included such regulars as Franklin P. Adams, John Kieran, and Oscar Levant. The listeners sent in questions to stump the experts, and if successful were awarded a set of the *Encyclopaedia Britannica.* A rival program began in the summer of 1940; it was called *The Quiz Kids,* and children drawn from Chicago schools took on all comers. At first there were no regulars, the two with the lowest scores being dropped after each program, but soon 7-year-olds Gerrard Darrow and Joel Kupperman became regulars because they could not be unseated. Joel was a genius in arithmetic, and after agonized mumblings, scowlings, and fumblings, he almost always came up with the correct answer.

Music was a big factor on the radio. The Saturday afternoon broadcasts of live opera from the stage of the Met were announced and summarized in the somewhat pedantic tones of Milton Cross. The

Sunday afternoon broadcasts of the New York Philharmonic were the musical highlights of the week for classical music lovers.

Leading popular orchestras were those of Gene Krupa, the Dorsey brothers, Eddy Duchin, Wayne King, Paul Whiteman, Glenn Miller, Benny Goodman, Harry James, Duke Ellington, and Fred Waring. Unfortunately, for a time these artists were not heard much on the radio, for James Caesar Petrillo, President of the American Federation of Musicians, banned broadcasting of records unless live musicians were paid for each broadcast. The feud was not settled until 1942. Thus disc jockeys played uncopyrighted material, such as the tunes of Stephen Collins Foster and Civil War relics.

Irving Berlin reached into a trunk and pulled out a song he had written in 1917 for inclusion in a show improbably entitled *Yip, Yip, Yaphank.* At the last moment, Berlin took it out of the show on the grounds that it was too serious and too heavy for an all-male chorus. Now he issued it again, and it caught on to such an extent that it became an unofficial national anthem overnight. Kate Smith introduced it under the title of "God Bless America," and soon everyone was singing it. The tune was simple and called for none of the vocal gymnastics demanded by the "Star-Spangled Banner."

Classical music was raided for popular songs. A strain from the Overture to Tschaikovsky's *Romeo and Juliet* was used in 1939 to form the tune of "Our Love." Later in the same year "Moon Love" was taken from his *Fifth Symphony.* And in 1940, Tschaikovsky again hit Tin Pan Alley when the theme from the First Movement of his Piano Concerto appeared under the title of "Tonight We Love." One of the most popular songs was "Beer Barrel Polka." Later in the year appeared two sentimental songs growing out of the war, "There'll Always Be an England," and Oscar Hammerstein and Jerome Kern's "The Last Time I Saw Paris." For the youth of America, jitterbugging was the most popular form of dancing under the influence of Glenn Miller and his "new sound."

Bestsellers of the year were Ernest Hemingway's *For Whom the Bell Tolls,* Richard Llewellyn's *How Green Was My Valley,* and Christopher Morley's *Kitty Foyle.* Of substantial worth were Graham Greene's *The Power and the Glory,* a semi-allegory of a priest in a Mexican state where religion was forbidden by law, and Dylan Thomas's *Portrait of the Artist as a Young Dog.*

If you liked the movies, you could see Walt Disney's *Fantasia,* an improbable cartoon commentary on popular concert staples. Shapeless abstractions danced across the screen to Bach's "Toccata and

Fugue in D Minor." Volcanoes erupted and boiling mud plopped for Stravinski's "Rite of Spring." Most tasteless were the animated cartoon centaurs and centaurettes that gamboled to the music of Beethoven's *Sixth* (Pastoral) *Symphony*. The whole production was what might have been expected when Walt Disney and Leopold Stokowsky pooled their talents. Both men were magnificent showmen, but neither was above a little corn.

Charles Chaplin's *The Great Dictator,* a satire on Hitler and Mussolini, somehow ceased to be funny during 1940. In any case, it was not the best Chaplin, although the scene of Charlie shaving a customer and keeping time to Brahms's Fifth Hungarian Dance is one of the finest bits recorded on film. Alfred Hitchcock's *Rebecca* captured all the suspense and flavor of the novel, thanks to the fine acting of Laurence Olivier and Joan Fontaine. Bette Davis led the cast of *Dark Victory,* and there was not a dry eye in any house where it played. One of the finest pictures made that year was *Pride and Prejudice,* with Greer Garson as Elizabeth and Laurence Olivier as Darcy, adapted from Jane Austen's masterpiece. The British-made *Pastor Hall,* the story of a courageous priest in Nazi Germany, provided some fine moments and a good deal of suspense.

But the biggest suspense of the summer was not to be found in the movie theaters. It was being provided in Washington, by That Man in the White House.

* * *

A cadaverous-looking man sat in suite 308-309 of Chicago's Blackstone Hotel smoking a cigarette, his rumpled suit flecked with ashes. Around him were other men, some looking worried, some confident. Others came in, had their say, listened, and went out again. The man was Harry L. Hopkins, Secretary of Commerce of the United States and self-appointed manager of the campaign to win nomination for Franklin D. Roosevelt for a third term as President of the United States.

For months Roosevelt had kept his intentions secret, and they still were. The faithful New Deal crowd had urged him to run for a third term, and the Chief had been noncommittal. Reporters who asked him whether he would run again were told sarcastically to go stand in a corner, put on a dunce cap, and quit speculating. He would make his intentions known at the proper time and place.

All of this was good fun, and the press generally went along with the gag. Cartoons showed the Sphinx with the face of F.D.R., cigarette holder at a jaunty angle. *Time* magazine referred to his supporters as "Third Termites," and many a Republican felt the term apt.

So did not a few Democrats, those who hoped to succeed the "Squire of Hyde Park" in the White House. Several believed they had been given the green light—Postmaster General James A. Farley, Secretary of State Cordell Hull, Vice President John Nance Garner—but they were hearing more than Mr. Roosevelt was saying. Then there were a few hopefuls, such as Maryland's Millard Tydings and Montana's Burton K. Wheeler. But no one could make plans until the Great Man spoke. And he wasn't speaking.

He still wasn't speaking when the Democratic National Convention opened on Monday, July 15. There had been strategy meetings in the White House before the convention began, but they accomplished little, since Roosevelt refused to commit himself. Someone asked him, "Suppose at some point we want to know your directions on strategy —whom do we ask?"

"In that event," replied the President, after a moment's reflection, "if I were you, I'd consult Jimmy Byrnes." But when they got to Chicago, these politicos found that Harry Hopkins had grasped the reins and was laying down the law to the convention. He had an invincible weapon, and that was that no man the Democrats could nominate, other than Roosevelt, had any chance of defeating Willkie in November. It was as simple as that. If the delegates didn't knuckle under, then the Boss wouldn't run, and where would the Democratic Party be? Through Hopkins, with Byrnes's assistance, Roosevelt had an absolute iron grip on the convention, if he cared to use it.

This state of affairs made the situation decidedly unpleasant for the Chairman of the Democratic National Committee, who would preside until the Permanent Chairman took over. It was unpleasant and awkward because the National Committee Chairman was a candidate for the office of President of the United States. This man was James Aloysius Farley, the master mind of Roosevelt's two previous campaigns. Farley had the reputation of never forgetting a name or a face, and he knew the game of politics inside out. He really believed that the mantle had fallen on his shoulders, and he was distinctly irritated with the Chief for not saying so. It was in a rebellious mood that Farley came to the convention. Secretary of the Interior Harold L. Ickes believed that Farley intended to pack the galleries with anti-Roosevelt people in an attempt to stampede the convention for him as had been done for Willkie in the Republican convention.

Other candidates had their little boomlets. Vice President John

Nance Garner believed he had a chance, but no one else did. Isolationist Burton K. Wheeler of Montana had come up to the convention as a candidate, but he pulled out in return for an isolationist foreign policy plank in the platform. Senator Millard Tydings of Maryland was blatantly inconspicuous, waiting for the lightning to strike.

Hopkins's headquarters, by coincidence, were in the same smoke-filled rooms where, in 1920, Warren G. Harding had been selected as the Republican dark-horse candidate. The room was as smoke-filled in 1940 as it had been twenty years earlier, but no deals were being made. Hopkins was laying down the law. Over and over, it was the same thing. Do as I say, or the Boss won't run.

On the afternoon of Tuesday, July 16, Mr. Roosevelt held a press conference, at which he announced, among other things, that the correspondents should listen to Alben Barkley that evening. Barkley would read the convention a message from the President.

Could Mr. Roosevelt give any hint what the message would contain? No.

The Sphinx was being sphinxlike right up to the last minute.

But two newsmen wangled a copy of the announcement and the word spread. By the time the convention was called to order at 9 P.M., Chicago time, only a few people wondered what he was going to say.

Mr. Roosevelt's message was simple: "The President never had, and has not today, any desire or purpose to continue in the office of President, to be a candidate for that office, or to be nominated by the Convention for that office."

In other words, this was the go-ahead. In any other language but that of politics, it would mean *no;* nothing short of an unequivocal refusal means *no* when coming from the lips of a candidate. Sometimes even that doesn't.

Hopkins had planned a vast demonstration when the President's words were read, and then he hoped for Roosevelt's nomination by acclamation, as had happened in 1936. To lead the hoopla, he picked Mayor Edward J. Kelly of Chicago.

But things began to go wrong. Barkley's bumbling voice droned its way through a prepared speech, and it was fourteen minutes before he mentioned Roosevelt's name at all. At their first chance to cheer, Roosevelt supporters began a parade through the convention hall, screaming and shouting. At the head of the parade marched the impeccably dressed Under Secretary of State, Sumner Welles. He looked like a French aristocrat on his way to the guillotine, the Jacquerie in full pursuit. His glacial smile painted on his lips, he did his faithful duty to the Boss and to the democratic process. It was fortunate for his equanimity that he had to do it only once every four years.

The demonstration flagged, and the organist got a signal. He burst into "Franklin D. Roosevelt Jones." The demonstration went on.

It never really came to life. When Barkley shouted into the microphone, asking for a doctor and saying, "A lady has been seriously injured," the uproar stopped as though it had been turned off by a switch. Barkley droned his way through the rest of his speech.

At the end he read Roosevelt's message and waited for applause. There was none. Then Kelly's demonstration got going. It was dubbed by the press, the "voice from the sewers." The parading went on for fifty-three minutes. No one shouted for the nomination by acclamation. The parade petered out. Barkley adjourned the meeting, and the delegates went back to their hotels.

The Hopkins strategy had been upset, but not seriously. The nominations would come at the usual time, and there was nothing to worry about. But to make sure that Roosevelt's name came in first, Hopkins arranged with Senator Lister Hill of Alabama to enter the President's name.

The dull business of the platform reading took up the afternoon session on Wednesday. As is the case with all party platforms, it stood foursquare for virtue, peace, and prosperity. The foreign policy plank was as bad as the Republican one, for it was worded to satisfy both interventionists and isolationists. As a result, it said nothing.

The evening session was what everyone had been waiting for—the nomination of candidates and the roll call to decide upon the man who would oppose Wendell L. Willkie.

When Alabama was called to present names in nomination, Senator Hill made his way to the platform. His speech was so filled with Southern cornpone and " 'lasses" that newspapers throughout the South apologized for days in their editorial columns. He seems to have set the standard of oratory for that session. As Ickes put it, "He made a rotten speech. As a matter of fact, there wasn't a decent speech made that night, and some were almost terrible."

Then Senator Carter Glass of Virginia tottered to the platform to place Farley's name in nomination. He was 82 years old, a man of highest principles, and a firm believer in the sacredness of the tradition that no man should serve more than two terms as President of the United States.

Glass was indignant that he had received two anonymous communications protesting Farley on the grounds that he was a Catholic. Righteous indignation gave Glass such vehemence that Farley's demonstration was quite respectable in strength. However, it didn't last long.

Edward J. Colgan, Jr., of Baltimore, placed Tydings's name in nomination. There was a brief cheer. Then Wright Moody, a burly Texan, presented the name of John Nance Garner. Garner's demonstration was a little more spirited, whipped by the tune, "The Eyes of Texas Are Upon You."

The seconding speeches dragged on. Then the voting began.

There was never any doubt. An hour and ten minutes later, the results were announced: Roosevelt, 946½; Farley, 72½; Garner, 61; Tydings, 9½.

Garner took the results very hard. He remained in seclusion for a week, and then he began to move the tokens and trinkets of 37 years of public life to Texas. He knew that there was no chance under the sun that Franklin Roosevelt would again choose him as his running mate.

Big Jim Farley made the sporting gesture. Striding to the platform, he gripped the microphone and moved that the rules be suspended so that Franklin D. Roosevelt could be nominated by acclamation. There was a roar of assent, and Farley grinned and waved, while the band played, "When Irish Eyes Are Smiling." On that note the convention adjourned for the night.

There was one more item of business facing the delegates, that of selecting the Vice Presidential nominee. At least 17 men had been led to believe that they would get the nod. It is, of course, customary for the Presidential nominee to choose the man he desires as his running mate. Yet, when Roosevelt's selection was announced, it caused a furore. He selected his Secretary of Agriculture, Henry A. Wallace. Every man of power in Washington makes enemies, but Wallace seemed to have a particular gift for making them. Roosevelt's selection of him came as a stunning shock.

In fact, the convention nearly revolted. It took all of Hopkins's abilities to keep the delegates in line, and he might have failed had he not let it be known that President Roosevelt would refuse the nomination if Wallace was turned down.

Confusion and resentment caused the afternoon session to be canceled, so it was not until evening that the convention got down to its final business.

Every time Wallace's name was mentioned it was booed, to the accompaniment of catcalls from the galleries. "Just because the Republicans have nominated an apostate Democrat," * shouted one furious delegate, "let us not for God's sake nominate an apostate Republican!" †

As Roosevelt listened to the shouting, jeering convention over the radio, he was actually preparing a speech refusing the nomination. But the revolt was not quite strong enough. Wallace was nominated on the first ballot by a vote of 627. Nearly half the convention had opposed the nomination, in spite of Roosevelt's power and expressed desires.

Twelve minutes after the convention had swallowed the bitter pill, the lights in the hall were lowered, leaving only spotlights illuminating a picture of the President. From loudspeakers throughout the hall came the voice of Franklin D. Roosevelt, broadcast from Washington.

It is with a very full heart that I speak tonight. . . .

When, in 1936, I was chosen by the voters for a second time as President, it was my firm intention to turn over the responsibilities of government to other hands at the end of my term. That conviction remained with me. . . .

When the conflict first broke out last September it was still my intention to announce clearly and simply . . . that under no conditions would I accept reelection. . . .

It soon became evident however, that such a public statement on my part would be unwise from the point of view of sheer public interest. . . .

Thinking solely of the public good and of the international scene, I came to the reluctant conclusion that such a declaration should not be made before the national convention. . . .

During the past few months, with due congressional approval, we have been taking steps to implement the total defense of America. I cannot forget that in carrying out this program I have drafted into the service of the nation many men and women . . . calling them suddenly from their homes and their businesses. . . . Regardless of party, regardless of personal convenience, they came—they answered the call. . . .

Lying awake, as I have on many nights, I have asked myself whether I have the right, as Commander-in-Chief of the Army and Navy, to call on men and women to serve their country or to train themselves to serve and, at the same time, decline to serve my country

* Willkie.
† Wallace.

in my own personal capacity if I am called upon to do so by the people of my country.

So the race was set. It would be Wendell L. Willkie and Charles McNary for the Republicans against Franklin D. Roosevelt and Henry A. Wallace for the Democrats.

Willkie's reaction to Roosevelt's renomination was, "Good! I want to take on the Champ."

Meanwhile, "the Champ" had other things to do. The war against Britain was building to a climax. Roosevelt's acceptance speech came on the very day that Hitler was making his "final peace offer" to Britain. Roosevelt simply pretended that there was no campaign to bother with. He was more interested in America's defenses and all the aid he could give to Britain in her struggle.

The chief barrier to giving aid to the Allies was the series of Neutrality Acts passed between 1935 and 1939 to keep America out of any European war. The acts reflected the dominant isolationist feelings of Congress, and they proposed to protect America by abandoning the very principle for which she had fought in 1917—freedom of the seas. When the President "found" a state of war existing among foreign powers, he was directed to apply the provisions of the law against the belligerents. If he failed to do it, then Congress had the authority to do it for him. Under the law, American ships were forbidden to carry either freight or passengers to belligerent ports. Such ships could not be armed, and American citizens were prohibited from traveling in ships belonging to nations at war. Further, the President was to proclaim combat zones which Americans could not enter. For a time all sales of munitions and armaments to belligerent powers were completely forbidden, but in 1939, the "cash-and-carry" policy replaced the embargo.

The cash-and-carry policy obviously favored Britain and France, for the tight British blockade kept German ships from coming across the Atlantic to American ports. At the time, the British and French had plenty of foreign-exchange credit, and the "cash" part was no particular burden. The United States Government was ready with loans through the Export-Import Bank.

But the "carry" part was more difficult. In view of the U-boat peril and the catch-as-catch-can antisubmarine measures then in force, the British were taking uncomfortable losses. And with the removal of 92 American ships from the North Atlantic run, the Neutrality

Act "aided the German blockade of Britain as effectively as if all our ships had been torpedoed," as D. H. Fleming put it.

Honestly convinced that Great Britain was the last barrier to complete Nazi domination of Europe, and that such domination would be mortal peril to the United States, Mr. Roosevelt fought for a repeal of the provisions of the Neutrality Acts. Britain had to be sustained, and she could not be under the law. "Give us the tools, and we will finish the job," declared Churchill. But what was on his shopping list?

The British needed nearly everything. The British Isles are not self-sufficient in either food or raw materials. They have no oil. They have no rubber. They must even import the tea which is the very source of life to most Britons.

Their factories and shipyards were humming, but they had started late and the need was now. Britain needed rifles, antiaircraft guns, light and heavy artillery, tanks, trucks, ammunition, oil and gasoline, drugs and bandages, all types of aircraft, fresh, frozen, and dried food, and raw materials. Also, she needed help at sea. If American merchant ships could not enter British waters, could not the United States turn over some old destroyers to help out in the unceasing war against the U-boats?

As early as May 15, five days after he had become Prime Minister, Churchill had cabled Roosevelt asking for "the loan of forty or fifty of your older destroyers to bridge the gap between what we have now and the large new construction we put in hand at the beginning of the war. This time next year we shall have plenty, but if in the interval Italy comes in against us with another hundred submarines we may be strained to the breaking-point."

All during the summer, references to destroyers pepper Churchill's messages to Roosevelt. Sometimes it is "thirty or forty," sometimes it is "fifty or sixty" he requests. But the theme is always the same. Without the destroyers Britain might go under.

Although Roosevelt was most sympathetic, there was little he could do at the time. The laws would not permit the Government to dispose of arms or naval vessels unless the Secretary of War or the Secretary of the Navy, as appropriate, declared such arms or vessels not needed for the defense of the United States. At a time when we were building our own defenses as rapidly as possible, how could *any* ships, arms, or munitions of war be declared excess?

The American public was more emotionally aroused than the responsible officials in Washington could afford to be. Sympathy for Britain was widespread in the United States, particularly during the blitz. One widely organized drive was to send "Bundles for Britain" to the aid of those dispossessed by the bombing. Such bundles contained typically eggs, oranges, coffee, tea, vitamins, and canned meats. Sometimes a home-knitted sweater or scarf would be included; sometimes a little nip of bourbon or gin.

The Committee to Defend America by Aiding the Allies worked largely through influencing newspaper editors and radio broadcasters. There was a smaller organization called the Century Dinner Group which favored more active support, even if it increased the danger of war. The Century Group included such men as Admiral William H. Standley, Lewis Douglas, Ward Cheney, Allen W. Dulles, Herbert Agar, Robert Sherwood, Will Clayton, Dean Acheson, Elmer Davis, and Joseph Alsop. They recommended that food be sent to Britain, even if it meant American convoys to get it through. They also called for the U.S. Navy to protect the United Kingdom and in return demanded that the British fleet be moved to American ports in the event of British capitulation.

The fear of British capitulation acted as a considerable brake on British sympathizers in Washington. Not a few in high places doubted that Britain could long hold out. Among these was the American ambassador to the Court of St. James, the Honorable Joseph P. Kennedy. He kept the cable wires working overtime with predictions that Britain would soon collapse and that over-generous aid would only fall into the hands of the Germans when they took over. "Don't let anybody make any mistake," he cabled; "this war, from Great Britain's point of view, is being conducted from now on with their eyes only on one place and that is the United States. Unless there is a miracle, they realize that they haven't a chance in the long run." Such sentiments, which Kennedy apparently expressed freely in London, scarcely endeared him to the British people who were literally in the front line of the only fighting going on in World War II.*

Against such counsels of despair, a few bright reports were heard. Air Corps Captain Benjamin F. Kelsey, who had been with the RAF, impressed top military headquarters that the British had already foiled the German invasion by inflicting such heavy losses on the Luftwaffe. The foremost exponent of air power, Major Alexander de Seversky,

---

* This unpopularity was long-enduring. On the occasion of the nomination of John F. Kennedy in 1960, a British friend remarked to the author, "If you elect Kennedy, you will have as President the son of the most unpopular ambassador ever to serve at the Court of St. James." Ambassador Kennedy changed his mind after he returned to the United States later in the year.

took much the same line, arguing that Hitler could never invade Britain unless he had a large fleet of new aircraft. And he did not have such a fleet.

Roosevelt moved very cautiously during these times. In spite of his love for Britain, he keenly felt his responsibilities as President of the United States. His enemies have charged that he was maneuvering even at that early date to get America into the war on the side of Britain. Yet, in the light of the documents of the time, this view will not stand up. Roosevelt was anxious to do everything he could to aid Britain, but not to the point where it would endanger the vital interests of the United States.

In June and part of July, the President turned a deaf ear to those who urged him to send destroyers to Britain. He was by no means prepared to go all-out in his support. The tiny capacity of American industry to produce war goods depressed him, but he was not yet moving rapidly to increase it. Perhaps it was the election year, but he still hoped for both guns and butter.

It was hard to see where the war machines were coming from. The fledgling Army Air Corps had none to spare. In May it had only 160 pursuit planes for 260 pilots. But they had ordered 4500 more aircraft of all types. Well and good. But the British had placed orders for 11,000, which were soon upped to 14,000. The British orders alone were for over five times the number of aircraft produced in the United States during the entire year of 1939.

There was a certain amount of surplus equipment in Army warehouses. Rifles, machine guns, and light field pieces left over from World War I might be used by the British, even though they would be useful for training purposes in an expanding American Army. General George C. Marshall, Chief of Staff of the Army, ordered a survey of what could be spared, and by giving the benefit of every doubt to the British came up with half a million rifles, 35,000 machine guns, 500 field pieces, 500 mortars, and some ammunition for each of these weapons.

The problem was how to get them to the British. Under the Neutrality Laws they could not be given directly. There was much head-scratching in the Department of Justice. Acting Attorney General Francis Biddle, with an assist from Secretary of the Treasury Henry Morgenthau and Under Secretary of State Sumner Welles, finally came up with a solution. Marshall would declare the weapons "surplus." Then they could be sold to private business firms, who in turn, under provisions of "cash-and-carry," would sell them to the British. They were on their way by the end of June.*

Churchill acknowledged their receipt in a message which was more of a letter to Santa Claus than a thank-you note: "Tonight the latest convoys of rifles, cannon, and ammunition are coming in. Special trains are waiting to take them to the troops and Home Guard, who will take a lot of killing before they give them up. I am sure that, with your comprehension of the sea affair, you will not let this crux of the battle go wrong for want of these destroyers."

Fear that Britain might succumb put a damper on over-large shipments from the United States. It was a particular bar to Churchill's demand for destroyers. There was no question that Britain desperately needed them, for the toll of their own destroyers had been heavy in Norway and during the Dunkirk evacuation; of the hundred they had begun the war with, fully half had been sunk or damaged. With the entry of Italy into the war, more were needed for the Mediterranean. Convoys and naval units contended for the rest.

From the first, Mr. Roosevelt was highly dubious that there was any way Britain could be given even one destroyer. The trouble lay in a rider the Congress slipped into the appropriation bill of June 28, 1940, that only such war materials could be shipped to belligerents or released for sale as had first been certified not essential for the national defense. Old as they were, these creaking relics of World War I were still warships. And, Mr. Roosevelt felt, so long as the fate of the British fleet remained in doubt, they *were* essential to the defense of the United States. That seemed to be that.

Even if the President could bring himself against his better judgment to declare the destroyers surplus, there did not seem to be a chance in the world that Congress would agree. Various schemes were bandied about, such as selling the destroyers to Canada with the proviso that they be used only in the Western Hemisphere. This would release Canadian destroyers to be used in British waters, but Roosevelt did not even bother to pursue this suggestion.

Three principal obstacles lay in the path of any destroyer deal:

* By the end of October, the following had been shipped under this first "Marshall Plan."
970,000 rifles
200,500 revolvers
 87,500 machine guns (including antiaircraft guns)
    895 field guns (75-mm.)
    316 Stokes mortars
Ammunition for the above in limited quantities.

(1) the Congress, with its strong isolationist sentiments; (2) the Neutrality Acts; and (3) fear that such an action might provoke Germany into declaring war on the United States.

The Century Dinner Group, which had been advocating increased American aid, even at the risk of war, came up in July with the idea which eventually led to success. After careful soundings in Washington among influential Americans favoring the idea, and after an informal approach to Lord Lothian, the British ambassador, a group of three of them sought an appointment with the President. On August 1, Clark Eichelberger, Herbert Agar, and Ward Cheney were ushered into Mr. Roosevelt's Oval Study and laid the proposal before him. In return for the destroyers, Britain would agree that her fleet would never be surrendered or scuttled, but, in the event of Britain's defeat, would be sent to the Empire bases overseas or to America. Also, Britain would cede certain bases in the Western Hemisphere for use by American naval and air forces.

Mr. Roosevelt listened politely, but he was noncommittal. His visitors retired convinced that the political difficulties were uppermost in the President's mind. They never expected to hear anything more of their plan. They felt badly let down.

But Roosevelt was more impressed than his visitors believed. At a Cabinet meeting the next day he brought up the idea, and everyone agreed that it would be an excellent idea if it could be worked out. The question was, how?

Everyone present at the Cabinet meeting believed that Congress would have to agree to the proposed deal. Roosevelt, having no illusions, believed that such a request, "if asked for by me without any preliminaries, would meet with defeat or interminable delay in reaching a vote."

The President, therefore, decided to approach Willkie, to enlist his aid in the destroyer deal. If Mr. Willkie could persuade the Republican minority in the House and Senate to vote the right way, they could grumble as much as they liked for the consumption of the voters back home. Willkie, however, declined to intercede with the Republican leaders in Congress. It probably would not have done much good if he had, for many of them were still nursing their grudges over the way Willkie had been foisted on them by the convention. They were dying to have him ask for favors so they could have the fun of saying no.

The best Willkie would offer was not to oppose the destroyer deal personally and not use it as a campaign issue. He could not have done less, for his position was that not enough was being done to aid Britain.

People all over the country hotly debated the destroyer issue. They were not told of a possible deal; rather, they thought it would be a matter of a loan or a gift. The sentiment was stronger for Britain than the Administration suspected, but there was still the isolationist bloc in Congress.

The isolationists could reject the sentiments expressed in telegrams, letters, and letters to the editor as artificially stimulated by propaganda. And much of it was. The Century Group was busy, and a constant barrage of speeches, letters, articles, and editorials got on the nerves of Borah, Taft, Vandenberg, *et al.* Even the venerated General Pershing was persuaded to speak out in favor of sending destroyers to Britain, and his intervention brought a stream of new demands.

An editorial in the *New York Herald Tribune* put the case thus:

> From every aspect of the actual situation, the one greatest requisite to the defense of the United States—the one thing which could make that defense most certain, the one thing which would do more than all the guns and ships and men we can ever amass for ourselves, the one thing, indeed, which might make many of the present defense plans unnecessary—would be the successful defense of Great Britain.

On the other hand, argued *The Chicago Tribune,* "the sale of the Navy's ships to a nation at war would be an act of war. If we want to get into war, the destroyers offer as good a way as any of accomplishing the purpose."

The impasse continued. Mr. Roosevelt could think of no way of getting Congress to agree to the transfer of destroyers on any terms.

On August 11, 1940, a long, closely reasoned letter appeared in *The New York Times.* It was signed by four prominent American lawyers, Charles C. Burlingham, Thomas D. Thacher, George Rublee, and Dean Acheson. And it showed a way out. The Neutrality Laws forbade a gift or sale of such ships of war, but they could be traded for something that would contribute as much or more to the national defense. And the President had authority to make such a deal. It would not have to be referred to Congress.

After that, things went reasonably smoothly. Everyone agreed that bases were needed for American defense, and the value of such bases would be immensely greater than that of 50 destroyers nearly ready for the scrap heap. As a matter of fact, some destroyers of the vintage under consideration had already been sold for scrap for about four or five thousand dollars apiece.

Britain quickly agreed to the trade, allowing the President to accept the reputation that he had been a smart Yankee horse-trader and had put something over on the British. This helped to quiet the critics when the deal finally came off. The British put in writing (but not for publication) the promise that their fleet would never be surrendered. They agreed to lease for 99 years bases and facilities in Newfoundland, Bermuda, the Bahamas, Jamaica, St. Lucia, Trinidad, and British Guiana. In return, the United States agreed to transfer 50 destroyers to the Royal Navy.

At the last moment, Mr. Churchill nearly wrecked the whole works. He decided that the bases should not be tied to the destroyer deal! He was afraid of British reaction to a one-sided arrangement, so much more valuable in terms of actual money worth to the United States. "We should, therefore," he cabled, "like to give you the facilities mentioned without stipulating for any return . . . Meanwhile, we are quite content to trust entirely to your judgment and the sentiments of the people of the United States about any aid in munitions, etc., you feel able to give us. But this would be entirely a separate spontaneous act on the part of the United States, arising out of their view of the world struggle and how their own interests stand in relation to it and the causes it involves."

Churchill's cablegram caused consternation. As the President later remarked, "We couldn't just up and give 'em to 'em." A compromise ensued. The destroyers would be traded for some of the bases; the others, in Bermuda and Newfoundland, would be Mr. Churchill's "free gift." And so the long debate was over. Secretary Hull and Lord Lothian, the British ambassador, signed the papers on the evening of September 2, and soon the destroyers were bucking the gray Atlantic swells under the White Ensign.

There is a footnote to the story. In preparing the final draft of the agreement, a whole section had been omitted. This included the transfer of a considerable amount of war material in addition to the destroyers: a little matter of 20 torpedo boats, 5 B-17 bombers, 5 PBY naval patrol bombers, a quarter of a million rifles, and 30 million rounds of rifle ammunition. This omission is a good candidate for the biggest typographical error in history.

What to do about it? If the Administration confessed that a slip had been made and a new agreement was necessary, there was sure to be a hue and cry of hanky-panky and dirty dealings at the cross-roads. Finally Roosevelt instructed General Marshall to certify that the rifles could be released and everyone else to try to figure out a way to get the rest of the materials across somehow. Eventually 15 B-17s were sent over for a "test under combat conditions." These tests proved so revealing that later the Army did the same thing with tanks. Both the planes and the tanks were immeasurably improved as a result.

When the destroyers-for-bases deal was announced to the press, it met widespread approval. *The Christian Science Monitor* noted that "history may record September 2, 1940, as the beginning of the ebb of the totalitarian tide. This trade gives notice that the democracies have the courage and foresight to help each other effectively." There were screams from the other side. The *St. Louis Post-Dispatch* ran a full-page ad in *The New York Times* to say:

> Mr. Roosevelt today committed an act of war. He also became America's first dictator. . . . The President has passed down an edict that compared with the edicts forced down the throats of Germans, Italians and Russians by Hitler, Mussolini and Stalin. He hands down an edict that may eventually result in the shedding of the blood of millions of Americans; that may result in transforming the United States into a goose-stepping regimented slave-state. . . . Of all sucker real estate deals in history, this is the worst, and the President of the United States is the sucker.

German leaders grumbled and spluttered, but they did not declare war. They were too busy with other things and hoped that the isolationists would keep American involvement in the war from getting any worse. The War Diary of the German High Command noted simply, "The deal to send fifty American destroyers to England has been concluded."

With the destroyers deal, traditional American neutrality in reality went out the window. Hitler kept a more wary eye on American actions, but on the whole, each side pretended nothing had changed. The myth of American neutrality was allowed to continue.

It was just as well. If the United States had had to fight in September, 1940, there would have been precious few to do the fighting. At that time the authorized strength of the Army was 375,000 men, and including the National Guard, there were probably not more than half a million soldiers in the country. Chief of Staff Marshall wanted another half million as soon as possible and double that number in a year. There was no way to raise such numbers by volunteers. It had to be done by conscription, if Congress could be persuaded to act.

The President refused to take the lead.

It was an election year, and this was a proposal that could strike at the home of nearly every voter in the land. Nor would General Marshall lead the way. If he had done so, he said later, "I would have defeated myself before I started, and I was very conscious of that feeling. If I could get civilians of great prominence to take the lead, . . . then I could take up the cudgels and work it out."

The "civilians of great prominence" turned out to be Senator Edward R. Burke of Nebraska, an anti-New Deal Democrat, and Representative James W. Wadsworth, a Republican from New York. The bill was introduced as the French armistice went into effect, on June 21, 1940. Its effect was rather like throwing a cat into a dog pound.

It was not only the isolationists who howled. William Green, President of the American Federation of Labor, urged "the American way" of voluntary enlistment, and if a draft was necessary, then "working men and women . . . should be assured that they will not be called upon individually or collectively to engage in a foreign war or to be sent abroad to become involved in foreign wars." Said the Reverend Harry Emerson Fosdick, "a conscript army is needed only if we are going to send an expeditionary force to conquer, let us say, Europe or Asia. The well-justified suspicion will not down, that behind this hectic haste to force conscription on us is the policy of the belligerent interventionists."

Isolationist spokesmen were even more lurid. Senator Burton K. Wheeler proclaimed a jeremiad: "Enact peacetime conscription and no longer will this be a free land—no longer will a citizen be able to say that he disagrees with a government edict. Hushed whispers will replace free speech—secret meetings in dark places will supplant free assemblage—labor and industry, men and women will be shackled by the chains they have themselves forged."

The prose style leads one to wonder what kind of blood-and-thunder literature occupied the Senator's spare time.

The reasoned support of Secretary Stimson, General Pershing, General Marshall, and others kept the debate on the level of sanity. Isolationist Republicans had the rug pulled out from under them on August 17, when Wendell Willkie came out for selective service, as it was called, as "the only democratic way in which to assure the trained and competent manpower we need."

As was so often the case before Pearl Harbor, the public was ahead of the leaders. Public opinion polls showed that at the time the Burke-Wadsworth Bill was introduced, 59 percent of the American people favored selective service, at least as a necessary evil. A month later the figure had risen to 69 percent, and by the end of August, it stood at 86 percent.

Finally, after fighting off a series of crippling amendments, Congressional leaders managed to get the bill passed. Earlier, the Congress had given the President authority to call up the National Guard for active duty not to exceed twelve months and for use only in the United States or the Western Hemisphere. On September 14, both Houses passed the Selective Service Act, with the same limitations. The President signed it two days later.

On October 16, all men between the ages of twenty-one and thirty-five registered. To schools, gymnasiums, fire houses they went; to courthouses, armories, dancehalls, to theaters, office buildings, meeting halls. Each man gave his name, date of birth, permanent address, and other vital information. In return he was given a card with the information neatly typed or poorly written. It bore one other vital piece of information, a serial number—say, 158.

Weeks later came the drawing ceremony, to determine who would be snatched first and who would be allowed to pursue his normal way of life. A blindfolded Secretary Stimson drew a capsule containing a slip of paper from a huge jar. He handed it to President Roosevelt. "The first number which has been handed to me is serial number one five eight."

And so six thousand men went to war.

Six thousand more responded to the second number, and so on, through the limit the Army could handle at the time. It was Marshall's despair that he could have the men for only a year. He could not hope to make trained soldiers in so short a time, and if he broke up his trained units to teach the "selectees," October, 1941, might find the United States Army far worse off than it was at the moment.

There was nothing to do but make the best of it. To the training camps throughout the land reported the heartsick, homesick men.*

As America began to mobilize, however feebly, for war, a clear warning came from across the seas.

* For a picture of life of the draftees, see the author's *1942: The Year That Doomed the Axis* (New York: David McKay Company, Inc., 1967).

294

It was September 27, 1940, and the scene was Berlin. In the Chancellery three men were gathered about a table to sign a document which would extend the Rome-Berlin Axis to Tokyo. Foreign Minister Ribbentrop for Germany, Foreign Minister Galleazo Ciano for Italy, and Ambassador Suburo Kurusu put their signature to the Tripartite Pact. It was clearly aimed at the United States.

By treaty Japan agreed to let Germany and Italy have a free hand in carving up Europe, and in return, they let Japan have her way toward the "establishment of a new order in Greater East Asia." Except for the case of Russia, which was specifically exempted, they undertook "to assist one another with all political, economic and military means if one of the three Contracting Powers is attacked by a Power at present not involved in the European War or in the Chinese-Japanese conflict."

In other words, said the pact, the United States had better watch its step in aid to Britain. If Germany decided she had been "attacked," then a declaration of war on her part would bring war in two oceans to the United States.

And the United States was still woefully unprepared.

On July 10, 1940, President Roosevelt laid before the Congress a message calling for total defense. It was a complete package as he saw it at that time. It carried the unheard-of price tag of $4,848,-000,000, which seemed like the moon to the Congressmen, even though the American people would be willing to endure more. They wanted defense, and they were not worrying about the price. They were scared by the swift collapse of "the finest army in the world," and at that moment, no one could foresee that Britain would not quickly follow.

> The principal lesson of the war up to the present time [said the President] is that partial defense is inadequate defense.
>
> If the United States is to have any defense, it must have total defense.
>
> We cannot defend ourselves a little here and a little there. We must be able to defend ourselves wholly at any time.

Congress responded promptly. On July 19, it authorized funds for 1,325,000 tons of new naval construction, and so prepared the way for the future "two-ocean Navy," which would be so sorely needed in 1942 and afterwards. Many of the ships which would carry the war to Japan were ordered under this initial authorization. More would follow.

Roosevelt also demanded an increase in the Army to a strength of 1,200,000 men, with equipment for another 800,000. He hoped the additional men would not be needed and made the promise that "we will not send our men to take part in European wars." He asked another 19,000 planes for the Air Corps, although he did not abate a jot his demand for 50,000 planes a year.

Congress completed its work on the defense legislation on September 9, and authorized more than the Administration had asked. Isolationists and interventionists were able to agree that few votes were lost in voting for defense, so long as the boys were not going "to take part in European wars."

In the diplomatic field as well, the United States was busy. German victories over France and the Netherlands gave cause for alarm that Hitler might demand that his victims cede their colonies in the Caribbean and in South America. Such cession would be a violation of the Monroe Doctrine, possibly the most popular item of American foreign policy—popular in the eyes of American citizens, that is. To forestall such a possible change in sovereignty, the United States called a conference of American States at Havana on July 21, 1940. According to a Gallup Poll of that time, a full two thirds of the American people were ready to fight if Germany came across the South Atlantic and landed forces in any Latin or South American country. Or, there might be internal subversion. The Germans had no plans to send their own troops to South America, but on July 7, the Argentine police discovered plans for a Nazi uprising and establishment of a pro-German government. Ten days later, the Nacista Party of Chile attempted to overthrow the popular front government.

In spite of these clear warnings, the various American governments were still suspicious of the motives of the United States. Of course, it was standard practice for Latin Americans to denounce proposals of the Yankee colossus on the basis of "Dollar Diplomacy," but many honestly feared any extension of United States influence south of the Rio Grande. Argentina saw an opportunity of freeing South America from European influence by granting independence to all European colonies in the Western Hemisphere (Canada excepted). Thus there was considerable opposition to the proposition presented by Secretary Hull that "The American Republics would regard any transfer, or attempted transfer, of the sovereignty, jurisdiction, possession, or any interest in or control over any such region to another non-American state as inimical to their peace, safety, and political independence."

Eventually, on direct appeal to President Roberto Ortiz, Argentina gave way, and the United States proposal was accepted. In an emergency, any signatory was empowered to act, but in practice, this meant that Brazil and the United States were made the policemen, since they were the only countries with sufficient strength to take action.

Problems of Greenland and Iceland were disturbing to both the United States and Canada. It was not clear to what extent the Monroe Doctrine applied to those Danish possessions, but President Roosevelt decided to interpret it loosely. It would apply if Germany showed any signs of moving against either island, but the United States looked the other way when the British sent troops to Iceland and landed "weather observers" in Greenland. These actions made Britain, Canada, and the United States much more comfortable, even if no one wanted to talk about them.

* * *

A crowd of 200,000 people swamped the little town of Elwood, Indiana. It was August 17, and it was hot. The thermometer stood at 102 degrees. In Callaway Park, where the sun beat down mercilessly, these thousands of people were waiting to hear Wendell L. Willkie give his formal acceptance speech of the Republican nomination for the Presidency.

They wanted a rip-roaring attack on the New Deal, on President Roosevelt, and all his works. The husky, slurred voice began, and the crowd stirred uneasily. How could the faithful get excited over such a statement as one promising a campaign "not on the basis of hate, jealousy, or personalities"? He spoke out for the draft, for increases in armaments, and for aid to Britain. In fact, there was little in what he said that anyone could see was much different from what the President was already doing. His import seemed to be, I'll do the same things, but I'll do them better.

Toward the end, he dropped some of his formality, and the crowd began to cheer. "I charge," he shouted, as the sweat poured down his face and his rumpled suit got more rumpled, "that the course this administration is following will lead us, like France, to the end of the road, . . . to economic disintegration and dictatorship. This is a serious charge. It is not lightly made. It cannot be lightly avoided. . . . I have, therefore, a proposal to make. The President stated in his acceptance speech that he does not have either 'the time nor the inclination to engage in purely political debate.' I do not want to engage in purely political debate, either. But I believe that the tradition of face-to-face debate is justly honored among our political traditions. I propose that in the next two and a half months the President and I appear on public platforms together in various parts of the country and on those platforms debate the fundamental issues." But Mr. Roosevelt was too busy. There was too much to do in running the country, with the destroyers deal, arms mobilization, industrial mobilization, psychological mobilization, to be bothered with campaigning. It made Willkie furious, but Mr. Roosevelt kept up the act of the man above practical politics.

And he had to keep his eye on the situation in Europe. The danger of the blitz was by no means over. And who could tell what the volatile Churchill might do to strike back?

Part of Mr. Roosevelt's attitude was an act, a coldly calculated campaign strategy. But another part of it was in deadly earnest, for events across the Atlantic could bring mortal danger to the United States. And no one could tell what the next day might bring.

CHAPTER TWELVE

Dakar Debacle

And enterprises of great pith and moment
With this regard their currents turn awry,
And lose the name of action.
Shakespeare, Hamlet

MR. CHURCHILL was growing restive. So was General de Gaulle. It went against the grain of both men to sit and take it under the nightly German air attacks.

In addition, Churchill was getting his stomach full of de Gaulle. The imperious, autocratic, austere French leader rubbed him the wrong way, and instead of tending to his own Free French business, he was demanding a place in the decision-making at the highest levels of the British councils. It would not have mattered so much, of course, if it had not been for the unhappy, idle Free French forces which had rallied to de Gaulle's appeals. As the summer wore on, they were kicking their heels, with nothing to do but complain and get into trouble.

So it was that when de Gaulle suggested to Churchill that the Free French forces should capture Dakar, he found a willing listener.

Seldom has an operation been so ill-planned, ill-conceived, ill-mounted, and ill-executed as Operation Menace, as the Dakar operation was called.

Dakar is a beautiful city at the westernmost part of Africa. In German hands it would be a major threat to British convoys to South Africa and to the Far East. It could be a springboard for a leap across the South Atlantic to Brazil. With the finest harbor on the west coast of Africa, Dakar offered both a menace and an opportunity. It was not in German hands, but it was under the control of Vichy. Neither Mr. Churchill nor General de Gaulle trusted that arrangement. Dakar's strategic importance was so obvious that neither believed for a moment that Germany could keep her hands off.

They believed, further, that Dakar was longing to be free. As they saw it, only a handful of "Vichy traitors" had betrayed France into surrender. Loyal Frenchmen everywhere were but waiting the opportunity to seize arms and throw off the shackles of Vichy's subservience to the Nazis.

Many colonies were, indeed, ready to break with Vichy. But not Dakar. High Commissioner Boisson supported the Vichy Government and had no use for de Gaulle and his Cross of Lorraine. And where he ordered, the colonists would follow. For Mr. Churchill to have misunderstood this feature of French temperament is perhaps understandable, but for de Gaulle to forget it is incredible. He must have believed, in his arrogance, that he had become the symbol of France, that his presence would overturn any misguided loyalty to captive Vichy.

On August 3, 1940, Churchill informed de Gaulle that the plan for a Free French operation against Dakar had been approved in principle. Psychological warfare was to win other French West African colonies so that a vast Free French territory might be established in West Africa. As General de Gaulle put it: "France could, in the vast spaces of Africa, in effect remake an army and a sovereignty, and, while waiting for the entry into the fray of new allies alongside of the old, reverse the balance of force."

General de Gaulle's original plan did not include a landing at Dakar; instead he proposed to go ashore with his troops at Konakry in French Guinea. There he would collect a magnificent army and march overland against Dakar. Churchill demurred, preferring to move directly against Dakar itself. A slow overland march, he felt, would require British naval support longer than the ships could be spared. Dakar could be taken in a few days and the ships quickly returned to other pressing duties.

As Churchill discussed the project with de Gaulle, his enthusiasm mounted. "Dakar will awake one morning," he declared, "sad and uncertain. Now, under the rising sun, notice how the inhabitants will see the sea covered to the horizon with ships. An immense fleet! A hundred warships and cargo vessels! They will approach slowly, sending messages of friendship by radio to the city, the navy, and the garrison. Some of them will be flying the tricolour. Others will be sailing under British, Dutch, Polish, and Belgian colors. From this squadron there will come a small, inoffensive boat flying a white flag of truce. It will enter into the port and disembark the emissaries of General de Gaulle. They will be conducted to the Governor. They will give him to understand that if he allows you to disembark, the allied fleet will retire and there will be nothing to settle between yourselves other than the conditions of your cooperation. On the other hand, if he desires to fight, he will run a grave risk of being crushed."

In the face of this enthusiasm, de Gaulle allowed himself to be convinced and agreed to Churchill's proposal. He had little choice, for he knew full well that if he insisted on his own plan, the British would act without him and the Free French, rather than run the risk of having Dakar fall under the control of the Axis. If the British took Dakar while the Free French sat idly in England, de Gaulle's influence would be at an end.

British fears of a German move against Dakar were well founded. As early as July 11, 1940, Admiral Erich Raeder, Commander in Chief of the German Navy, had suggested to Hitler the possibility of a German take-over of the town. When the French West African colonies declared for de Gaulle, Raeder, meeting with Hitler in Berlin on September 6, proposed it again. The minutes of the conference are enlightening.

The C.-in-C., Navy, stresses once more the extreme importance of Dakar for Germany in this war. The danger of a British or American occupation of the Azores and Canary Islands is particularly great in the event that Spain or Portugal enters the war . . .

Treatment of the French Colonies.—In the French possessions in Equatorial Africa there is an open break with Pétain's government and a swing over to General de Gaulle. There is danger that unrest and revolt might spread to the French West African colonies. The economic situation in the colonies, particularly as regards foodstuffs, is used by Britain as a means of exerting pressure. An agreement between the colonies and Britain, and revolt against France would jeopardize our own chances of controlling the African area; the danger exists that strategically important West African ports might be used for British convoy activities and that we might lose a most valuable source of supplies for Europe. The danger of an attack on the part of the U.S.A. is not entirely out of the question, in view of the possibilities for such action.

Far-sighted German measures are necessary to counteract any development of this kind. Therefore the Naval Staff agrees in principle to send French naval forces to the areas threatened; to the resumption of merchant traffic between the colonies and neutral countries by means of French and neutral vessels, in order to alleviate economic difficulties; and to the attempt to re-establish merchant shipping between France and her colonies.

For the moment, Germany made no move. The Free French and British were preparing theirs.

The Dakar plan took shape quickly—too quickly. The enterprise was to be entirely French, except that Britain would provide the necessary shipping and naval forces to transport and safeguard the troops. In addition, the British would supply Hurricane aircraft for French pilots. The expedition was to be loaded and equipped so that it could disembark in any French West African port, and finally all negotiations on fighting were to be between de Gaulle's Free French and the local French garrisons.*

Haste was the order of the day. The original plan called for the expedition to sail on August 10, and the operation to be completed by August 28.

The original plan lasted only a few days. Intelligence estimates indicated that the Free French could not provide enough men. Only British troops could make up the deficiency. Desperately anxious to preserve the predominantly French character of the operation, Churchill convinced himself that Dakar would welcome de Gaulle and that the British reinforcements would not need to show themselves. They would be there if the situation turned nasty. So, it would not be a bad thing to have British troops on hand. Something might turn up.

This new concept for the operation meant a totally new plan. Churchill now insisted on a British commander. De Gaulle's objections were brushed aside. It would be a British commander or nothing. Still, the operation was to lose nothing of its all-French character.

Vice Admiral John H. D. Cunningham † was appointed to command the naval forces for the operation, while the military commander was Major General M. N. S. Irwin. General de Gaulle had command of the Free French forces, subject to the orders of General Irwin.

It was August 13 by the time these commanders were appointed. By this time, the ships should have been three days on the way. They would not actually sail for another seventeen days.

The two commanders found little they liked in the hastily prepared

* At this time, de Gaulle had about 2500 infantry troops, a tank company, and several artillery and engineer units as well as fighter and bomber pilots.
† No relation to Admiral A. B. Cunningham, Commander in Chief of the Mediterranean Fleet.

plan. Four of the six landing beaches were exposed to the heavy seas from the Atlantic and well defended by shore gun emplacements. Only 16 landing craft were available. There were no mobile guns except those of the ships, and no tanks; the only motor vehicles were three ambulances.

Someone belatedly remembered that two senior British naval officers had been in Dakar as recently as the end of July. Where were these officers now? Hasty examination of the files in the office of the Second Sea Lord revealed that they were in Freetown, Sierra Leone. A special plane was dispatched to bring these men to London so their special knowledge could contribute to the forthcoming operation. No one thought to inform the commander at Freetown that there was need for haste. He had some errands for the plane to do, and it was several days before he got around to letting it leave with its two important passengers. Before the plane reached London, the final plan had been completed.

Delays continued to plague the operation. The target date, September 8, had to be postponed for ten days to permit the ships to pass Dakar, proceed to Freetown, refuel, and then return to the target. Also, no one had checked the speed of the vessels carrying supplies. Everyone had proceeded on the assumption that they could make 12 knots. When it was finally learned that they could make only 8 to 9, it was so late that it would take more time to unload the slowpokes than it would to allow for their leisurely ways.

These delays nearly wrecked the secrecy of the expedition. While some officers who needed to know, such as the commander at Freetown, were rigidly excluded, others, who had no business knowing, had been told full details. De Gaulle had informed his men, and at a public dinner, French officers lifted their glasses with stirring cries of "Dakar!" A loading crane dropped a bundle of leaflets. The bundle burst, and the leaflets were scattered. Many were not recovered. They began: *"Français de Dakar—joignex-vous à nous pour délivrer la France!"*

It seems a miracle, but in spite of these appalling breaches of security, no word of the impending operation found its way to Vichy or to Berlin.

Finally, on August 30, "Menace Force" sailed in three sections. From Scapa Flow came 3 transports, escorted by the cruiser *Fiji* and 3 destroyers. From the Clyde came 3 Free French sloops, a British destroyer, and H.M. cruiser *Devonshire,* flying Admiral Cunningham's flag. Three additional transports, including the *Westernland,* which carried General de Gaulle, sailed from Liverpool, escorted by 3 destroyers. Other minor vessels and stores ships sailed on OB 204, a regular merchant convoy to Freetown. For naval cover, Admiral Cunningham had been provided with 2 battleships, *Barham* and *Resolution,* another cruiser, the *Cumberland,* the aircraft carrier *Ark Royal,* along with 10 destroyers and several lesser vessels. Air support for the operation was limited to what the *Ark Royal* could carry: 20 Skua fighters and 25 Swordfish torpedo-bombers. In all, some 6900 troops were embarked for the attack, of which about 2700 were French.

Thus sailed from Britain the "immense fleet" which Churchill had so glowingly depicted. On board were the principal commanders, all less than satisfied with the plan, but all willing to go ahead in view of the huge gains to be won if the plan succeeded. Not all ships had copies of the overall plan, and detailed operation orders had not been prepared. In a tiny cabin on board the *Devonshire* a seasick soldier, when he could raise his head from the convenient bucket, pounded an old, battered typewriter, cutting stencils of the operation order as the staff officers wrote their drafts. Under these inauspicious circumstances, the armada headed south.

As planning for "Menace" was entering its final stages, events in French Equatorial Africa seemed to augur well for the success of the expedition. Within the space of three days beginning August 26, the Chad Territory, Duala in the French Cameroons, and Brazzaville, capital of French Equatorial Africa, declared for the Free French. By the time the expedition sailed for Dakar, all of French Equatorial Africa except Gabon had rallied to the Cross of Lorraine. Hopes rose that de Gaulle would be welcomed at Dakar.

But French West Africa and its capital Dakar were not like the other African colonies. Here, firmly in command, were energetic leaders, loyal to Vichy rather than to de Gaulle. They were determined to see to it that French West Africa did not go the way of the colonies farther south. Indeed, they planned to recover the lost territory. One of these energetic leaders, Admiral Landriau, had been sent to Dakar after the first British attack. His orders were to organize defense and to hold French Africa together, by force, if necessary. He could make no move by sea, since he had only one small ship capable of reaching Equatorial Africa without refueling. Nor could he move by land, since the rainy season was imminent. For the moment, there was nothing to be done about the dissident colonies.

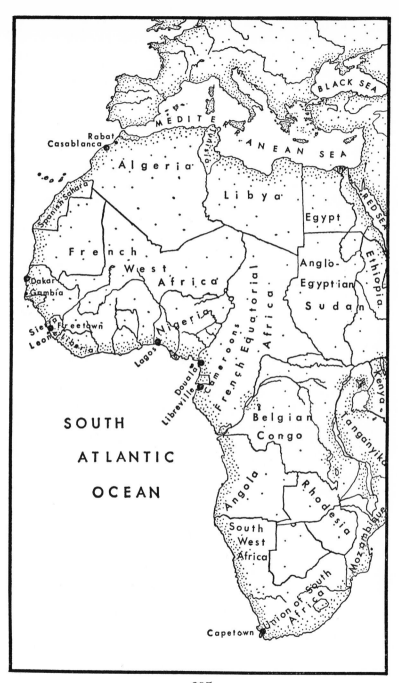

SOUTH

ATLANTIC

OCEAN

He reported the impasse to Vichy.

"I approve your propositions," replied Darlan by radio, "and in particular the immediate goal which is to maintain and safeguard French West Africa more than to deal with French Equatorial Africa. I shall request of the Armistice Commission authorization to send a naval force of three cruisers, but I do not know whether this authorization will be granted."

The permission was granted, as a part of Hitler's aim of driving France into alliance with Germany.

The French Government felt bound to act against the dissidents. If they did nothing, they felt, the Germans would do it for them and claim all French possessions in West Africa as their fee. Pierre Boisson, the Governor General of French West Africa, shared this fear. Although he had originally favored continuing the fight against the Germans, he had become convinced that the only way to keep the French colonies out of the hands of the Nazis lay in loyal adherence to the Pétain Government.

While the Vichy ministers knew nothing of the proposed Dakar expedition, they had ample cause for discontent with the British. They blamed the loss of French Equatorial Africa on the British for supporting the upstart de Gaulle. Then the British took another unforgivable step. On July 31, 1940, they imposed a virtual blockade on France and her colonies. Churchill had warned that this would happen. French leaders had not believed him.

Anglophobia, dormant for nearly a month, flared up again, giving Laval his opportunity. Once again he demanded that France declare war on Britain and throw her lot in completely with Germany. Both Weygand and Foreign Minister Baudouin violently opposed the idea, and since they had the support of Marshal Pétain, nothing came of it. On the other hand, Laval's influence was strong enough to cause Pétain on September 5 to ask Weygand for his resignation as Minister of Defense and to exile him to the newly created job of Delegate General of the Government in French Africa.

The iron hand of the Axis showed when they gave the French permission to move certain naval units to West Africa. All ships were to be disarmed no later than September 30. What the Axis gave with one hand, it more than took back with the other.

The French protested. How they could be expected to maintain the integrity of their colonies if their naval forces were disarmed? General Stülpnagel, German head of the Armistice Commission, coldly replied that the permission to move the ships in no way changed the obligation of the French to disarm them, but that he would consider circumstances at the time, in view of the problem in Equatorial Africa. The interview ended with the ominous statement, "In a case in which the French government has not succeeded in reestablishing order in threatened territories, the German and Italian governments reserve complete freedom of action."

On September 9, 1940, there sailed from Toulon the 3 light cruisers of Cruiser Division Four, the *Georges Leygues, Gloire,* and *Montcalm.* Escorting them were the destroyers *Fantasque, Malin,* and *Audacieux.* The commander of this group, designated Force Y, was Rear Admiral Bourragué, whose instructions were to safeguard the interests of French West Africa, to resist any British attack and, above all, to ensure that none of his vessels should fall into British hands.

According to agreement, the French duly informed the Gibraltar control station of the movements of the French ships. The officer who received the message filed it as a routine movement report! Thus the key force in the entire Dakar operation passed peacefully through the Strait of Gibraltar, answering the challenge from the British signal station with their international call signs.

"Thank you," replied the signal station.

By late afternoon, Force Y had reached Casablanca. There Admiral Bourragué intended to refuel in a leisurely fashion and continue the voyage to Dakar the next day. About 8 P.M. he learned that British ships were off Cape Spartello, a big headland on the African side of the Strait of Gibraltar. This put another face on the matter. Rather than risk being bottled up in port, Bourragué decided to sail that night.

As soon as refueling could be completed, the 6 French warships slipped out of Casablanca harbor, speeding through the dark night for Dakar.

The passage of the French warships out of the Mediterranean caught the British completely by surprise, although at least two warnings reached them. One even came in twice by two different means of transmission. On September 9, the British Consul-General at Tangier received a tip from an undercover agent. He duly reported it to Admiral North at Gibraltar, sending an information copy of the dispatch to the Foreign Office in London. "Following received from 'Jacques.' French squadron may try to pass the Straits proceeding westward for unknown destination. This attempt may be timed to take place within the next seventy-two hours."

Admiral North had been told very little about Operation "Menace." He did know that British forces were en route to Dakar, but he did not know why. He, therefore, felt no alarm at the passage of the French ships. The Admiralty felt that he should have, and after the operation was over, they relieved him of his command for this omission. Yet there is much to be said on his side. What could he have done? He had no naval force at his disposal. Force H, then at Gibraltar under the command of Admiral Somerville, was directly subordinate to the Admiralty. Admiral North felt, with good reason, that if the Admiralty desired Somerville to take any action, they would issue the orders directly to him as they had done on many previous occasions.

The Consul-General information copy to the Foreign Office reached London promptly. Then it lay in some duty officer's basket unnoticed. It was not even deciphered for several days. By that time it had become a historical souvenir.

At 6 P.M. on September 10, hours before the French ships passed the Strait, the French Admiralty officially notified the British naval attaché in Madrid that 3 French light cruisers of the *Georges Leygues* type and 3 destroyers would pass Gibraltar the next morning. The French notification did not specify a destination for these ships. The attaché promptly informed both Admiral North and the British Admiralty by a dispatch with an "Immediate" priority. Admiral North, on seeing the message shortly after midnight, felt it did not concern him, since the Admiralty was the principal addressee. If Their Lordships desired him to act, they would inform him.

The message from the attaché in Madrid reached London at 11:50 P.M. The duty officer at the Admiralty, who was fully informed on the Dakar operation, should have appreciated its importance at once. He did not. Instead of wakening the First Sea Lord, he simply added the message to the pile of routine signals which would go to His Lordship in the morning. For this mistake in judgment, the erring officer later received an expression of Their Lordships' displeasure, a mild enough admonishment, considering the consequences.

Meanwhile H.M. destroyer *Hotspur,* on patrol in the Strait of Gibraltar, had sighted the French squadron, reporting its course and speed and that she was shadowing. At 5:55 A.M., Admiral North ordered the destroyer to break off, since the French had notified him of the passage of these ships. He did, however, notify the Admiralty of the *Hotspur*'s contact, adding a little later that he would "keep in touch with this force by air" in order to "report its probable destination."

Meanwhile Admiral Somerville, who had received a copy of the message from Madrid, was also informed of the *Hotspur's* report. To be on the safe side, he brought Force H to one hour's notice for steam, but took no further action, no doubt assuming, as Admiral North had done, that the Admiralty would issue any necessary orders. His action was merely a measure of prudence. He did not want to be caught short if he did receive urgent orders from London.

It was not until about noon on September 11 that anyone who knew the full picture woke up to the situation. The awakening did not come from the delayed messages from either Madrid or Tangier, but rather from the *Hotspur's* sighting report which had been sent to the Admiralty as a matter of routine. This time a different duty officer recognized the threat to the Dakar expedition at once. He took his career in his hands and immediately routed out Admiral of the Fleet Sir Dudley Pound, the First Sea Lord, breaking into a meeting of the Chiefs of Staff with the Cabinet to so do.

Admiral Pound acted swiftly. He alerted Admiral Somerville and informed him that he might allow the French squadron to proceed to Casablanca. The French vessels were on no account to be permitted to reach any German-occupied ports in metropolitan France. Further, he was to prevent them from going to Dakar. If possible, he was to intercept the ships at sea and learn their destination.

Admiral Somerville took the *Renown* with 6 destroyers to sea at 4:30 P.M. By this time it was too late. The French squadron was already approaching Casablanca. Somerville set up a barrier patrol between Cape Blanco and Agadir. When an inquisitive British plane flew over Casablanca, French antiaircraft guns promptly shot it down as a warning to the others to keep their distance. It was not until dawn on September 13 that the British were able to get a good look at the harbor of Casablanca. No French cruisers were present. They were well on their way to Dakar, 1350 miles to the south.

Only poor visibility averted a clash as the French ships slipped away during the night of September 11/12. Somerville's orders were unequivocal that the French ships must not be allowed to reach Dakar; the French had sailed on the express condition that they resist all British attack. In all probability the battle cruiser *Renown* could have handled the French cruisers without difficulty, but the French destroyers were more powerful than their British counterparts. Such a battle would have ended all possibility that Dakar might be taken without resistance.

Meanwhile the "Menace" forces made their way southward. As

they steamed through waters where the U-boats kept watch, the cruiser *Fiji* was torpedoed on September 1 and had to return to the Clyde for repairs. The *Australia* from the Home Fleet took her place. On September 13, when the force was some 300 miles from Dakar, Admiral Cunningham received word that the French ships had left Casablanca. He was instructed to intercept Force Y. The *Devonshire, Australia, Cumberland,* and *Ark Royal* set up a patrol off Dakar, as soon as they could, on the evening of September 14. But the French were ahead of them. They had entered Dakar harbor that afternoon. Vichy triumphantly announced the safe arrival of their little squadron.

Since the French ships had reached their destinations, Somerville's ships set course south for Freetown, where the other ships of the Dakar expedition were gathering.

In London, the Chiefs of Staff were having second thoughts concerning the prospects of "Menace." Everything seemed to be going wrong.

Everything continued to.

Churchill convinced the War Cabinet that the movement of the French ships sealed the fate of the operation. New orders went out to Admiral Somerville on September 16.

> His Majesty's Government have decided that presence of French cruisers at Dakar renders the execution of Dakar operation impracticable. Alternative plans have been examined here. Landing at Konakri does not appear to offer any chance of success. . . . Moreover, close blockade of Dakar from seaward is not possible with the naval forces available. . . . Best plan appears to be for General de Gaulle's force to land at Duala with the object of consolidating the Cameroons, Equatorial Africa, and Chad, and extending influence of de Gaulle to Libréville. The British portion of the force would remain for the present at Freetown.
>
> Unless General de Gaulle has any strong objections to the latter course, it should be put into operation forthwith.

In spite of everything, Cunningham, Irwin, and de Gaulle all wanted to go ahead with the operation as planned. The arrival of the French ships had, they conceded, undoubtedly stiffened the morale of the French at Dakar, but "Menace Force" was much more powerful than what the French had. The French ships, they added, were peacefully anchored, awnings spread, and would be easy bombing targets if the worst happened.

In the face of these plans, the Cabinet reconsidered, but reached no firm conclusion. At 11:52 P.M. on September 16, Churchill sent a hedging message to Cunningham: "You are fully at liberty," he radioed, "to consider the whole situation yourselves and consult de Gaulle, and we shall carefully consider then any advice you may give."

This reply was less than satisfactory to all three of the commanders. De Gaulle, with characteristic bluntness urged, "At the very least, should the British Government uphold its new and negative decision concerning direct action upon Dakar by sea, I request immediate co-operation of British naval and air forces here present to support and cover an operation which I personally shall conduct with my own troops against Dakar from the interior."

Admiral Cunningham and General Irwin were equally vehement that any action was better than indecision.

Faced with the unanimous recommendations of the commanders on the scene, the Cabinet gave permission to proceed with the operation. At 1:20 P.M. on September 18 the message went off.

> We cannot judge relative advantages of alternative schemes from here. We give you full authority to go ahead and do what you think is best in order to give effect to the original purpose of the expedition. Keep us informed.

Henceforth there was no turning back. The operation against Dakar was to go ahead, come what might.

During the passage from Britain, the two naval officers who had been flown up from Freetown studied the operation plan with mounting dismay. They saw that estimates of gun emplacements, numbers of aircraft, morale of the population, and the overall state of the defenses had all been misjudged, and that all the errors had been on the optimistic side. Both men gave it as their firm opinion that the French at Dakar would *not* welcome de Gaulle. The only way he would set foot ashore would be by fighting.

One of the officers wondered why the intelligence on Dakar that he had sent much earlier had not been incorporated. The query caused consternation. What intelligence? No one had ever heard of it. Fortunately he had another copy of the document with him, a complete plan of the local defense organization. He produced it, and the planning had to be done all over.

Long after the operation had become history, the copy he had sent to London labeled "Most Immediate" was discovered in some staff officer's basket, where it had lain forgotten for weeks.

On the long voyage south, most of the time was spent in preparing and revising, preparing and revising, copies of the plan. As the force approached the Equator, temperatures belowdecks approached a hundred; officers and men found they could work only an hour or so in the oppressive atmosphere before they had to seek the fresher, if not cooler, air topside.

Two days before the force reached Freetown, they sighted and stopped the Portuguese brig *Capatana*. She had just left Dakar a day or so before and provided valuable intelligence to the busy commanders and staff officers. Among other things, the British learned that the French had only just completed laying a new line of hydrophones some 5000 yards from the beach. Such a line would give warning of any vessel approaching the harbor; there was no chance of a ship's approaching closer than two and a half nautical miles without being detected, even in low visibility.*

Barely had the leading elements of the force reached Freetown when word arrived that the troublesome French ships were on the move again. The cruisers and destroyers of Force M, as the naval part of the "Menace" force was designated, gave chase.

Completely unaware of the Dakar expedition, the leaders in French West and Equatorial Africa were devoting their energies to restoring the situation in the Cameroons, Chad, and ports of French Equatorial Africa. In particular, affairs at Pointe Noire in the French Congo caused alarm. A recent recruit to the Free French standard, Pointe Noire now threatened to bring neighboring Gabon into de Gaulle's orbit. The presence of the British cruiser *Delhi* at Pointe Noire gave both influence and authority to the anti-Vichy elements.

High Commissioner Boisson found the situation intolerable. French Africa could not be allowed to go to the upstart de Gaulle. Fully backed by Vichy, Boisson intended to use force if necessary to save Pointe Noire and Duala.

Secretary of State for the Colonies, Admiral Charles Platon, cabled:

> It is important that with the means which have been placed at your disposition you act with energy to reestablish order at Pointe Noire and Duala simultaneously. . . .
>
> The government holds it of the highest importance that these operations should be mounted with the least delay; I repeat, with the least delay, and that all precautions be taken to insure certain success. These operations, once begun, are to be carried through, cost what it may.

* This operation, it must be remembered, was mounted in the infant days of radar, and this electronic device, commonplace three years later, played no part in the events off Dakar.

Besides the fact that they are aimed at attaining objectives of capital importance, you will consider them as tests of our strength and our determination. The world is watching us. I am counting on you and on the military authorities for a rapid and successful execution of these present instructions.

Boisson forthwith issued his orders. An expedition was to set out from Dakar! Admiral Bourragué, Commander of Force Y, was given overall command.

The French, having strengthened Dakar, proceeded to weaken it for the sake of regaining Pointe Noire and Duala. Their ships left Dakar; nothing could have been better for Operation "Menace." But the British chased most of them back again.

The 3 cruisers left Dakar at 6 P.M. on September 18, leaving behind the 3 destroyers which lacked the necessary endurance for the forthcoming operation. Nearer Pointe Noire was another cruiser, the *Primauguet,* with the oiler *Tarn.* Various other vessels, minor warships or auxiliaries, waited for orders in other ports.

The French well knew that the British might interfere in their projected operations. The cruiser *Delhi* was still at Pointe Noire. The carrier *Ark Royal,* accompanied by a heavy cruiser, had been sighted in the waters between Dakar and Freetown. On September 17, the steamer *Poitiers* had been intercepted at sea by the British cruiser *Cumberland.* Recognizing that escape was impossible, her master, in obedience to his orders, attempted to scuttle the ship. As the French crew took to the lifeboats, the *Cumberland* opened up with two warning bursts of machine-gun fire. The effort to escape in the boats came to an abrupt halt. The crew of the *Poitiers* was taken prisoner, and the unfortunate vessel was finished off with gunfire.

Alerted by air searches that the French cruisers were no longer at Dakar, Admiral Cunningham set out from Freetown with his cruisers and destroyers in search. The next morning, September 19, the *Australia* sighted Bourragué's force and, joined by the *Cumberland,* pursued the speedy French ships for the remainder of the day. The French ships were pushing ahead as rapidly as possible, building speed up to 29 knots. His ships racing through the seas, broad, creaming wakes slashing the blue water as far as he could see, Admiral Bourragué noted with satisfaction that the British ships, 12 miles behind, seemed unable to close.

The sun went down. Perhaps in the back of his mind Bourragué had a nagging worry about his one weak sister. It is common that among a group of sister ships, one of them will acquire a reputation for bad luck. She seems constantly beset with mechanical difficulties. Sometimes this is a result of a poor crew or a poor captain. Sometimes it is the fault of the builder. Sometimes early ships in a class will have weaknesses which have been corrected in her younger sisters.

The unfortunate *Gloire* acquired such a reputation soon after her commissioning. In the race on the evening of September 19, however, she seemed to be giving the lie to her bad name. She even tempted the fates by sending a message to Bourragué in the *Georges Leygues* that everything was going well and that she could easily produce a few more turns on her screws if the admiral desired to increase speed.

The fates struck back a quarter of an hour later. On her bridge the watch officer answered the telephone from the engine room. They would have to reduce speed.

The *Gloire* fell far behind as the *Georges Leygues* and *Montcalm* sped on their way through the night. The speed of the *Gloire* dropped to 4 knots. Suddenly, out of the darkness, the *Australia*'s searchlight flooded the French ship in a pitiless glare. Just as though they had not been pursuing her all day, the British politely asked if they could be of any assistance and offered to escort the *Gloire* to Freetown. The French replied, equally politely, that they had had a minor breakdown and were proceeding to Konakry for repairs. Two British destroyers silently came up and took station on either bow of the French cruiser.

Mindful of his orders that under no circumstances was he to permit his vessel to fall into the hands of the British, Captain Broussignac of the *Gloire,* while playing out the game to the full, ordered the lower spaces evacuated so that he could scuttle his ship quickly if he had to.

Still pursued by the *Cumberland,* the other two French cruisers had sped on several miles ahead of their crippled consort while Admiral Bourragué grappled with a dilemma. The *Gloire* would surely be lost if he left her behind. If he turned back to her assistance, he had a choice of presenting his two remaining cruisers to the British as well, or of fighting. In either case his mission at Pointe Noire would be compromised. He had no real choice. His mission must come first. Having confidence in Captain Broussignac, he left the *Gloire* to her fate and turned back north toward Dakar at 30 knots. He had not abandoned his mission, but he saw no chance of success while so many British ships were on the prowl. He would try again another day. As he countermarched, the *Cumberland* turned with him, taking advantage of the maneuver to gain station close alongside the French ships.

As this strange formation rushed northward through the tropical night, each side was careful to avoid violence. The British pleaded with Bourragué not to go to Dakar, obviously the last place they wanted his ships to be. "I am very anxious," Captain Fallowfield of the *Cumberland* signaled, "that a representative of my commander in chief should have an opportunity to talk with you before there is any chance of an incident which we would all regret. Would you consent to a meeting at sea with my admiral? We could send a representative by air to meet you. I urged you to consider this as being very much to our mutual advantage."

Later, as the French admiral gave no sign of agreeing to the British requests, the *Cumberland* signaled plaintively, "Surely we can find a better solution than that of fighting one another."

The battle continued, but by signal searchlight rather than by gunfire. Sometimes it was interrupted by heavy squalls. At length, with daylight approaching, Dakar loomed up ahead. The *Cumberland* gave up and allowed the two French ships to proceed peacefully into port. She turned away and headed back to rendezvous with Admiral Cunningham in the *Devonshire*. She had failed, but she could not have stopped the French without bloodshed. Outnumbered as she was, she might not have been able to stop them at all.

Meanwhile, on September 19, before Bourragué's wild race to the south and north had ended, the cruiser *Primauguet* and the oiler *Tarn,* making their way toward Pointe Noire, encountered the heavy cruiser *Cornwall*. Soon the *Delhi* joined up. She had left Pointe Noire to join in running down the French ships.

The *Cornwall* signaled that she desired to send an officer with a message of the utmost importance. Stopping briefly, Captain Goybet of the *Primauguet* accepted a letter from General de Gaulle addressed to Admiral Bourragué.*

September 1940

Admiral,

As you no doubt know, French Equatorial Africa, a large part of West Africa, and our Pacific colonies have already joined me to carry through the war of honor and liberation. Other French territories are about to follow their example.

---

* Why the *Cumberland* did not have the text is not clear, and it is especially strange since she and the *Australia* actually made contact with the French admiral. At any rate, only Captain Goybet received this message.

315

I have the duty so to arrange things in these territories that everyone may consecrate himself without hindrance to his sacred task.

In no case will I allow Frenchmen who are acting under the influence of the so-called authorities who have fallen under the control of the enemy to attempt to thwart in any way those who have chosen to perform the duty of national defense. I do not know your intentions, but I am obliged to request you to:

Join immediately the Free French Forces under my orders and, as a consequence, carry out my instructions.

Return to Casablanca without delay.

I must further warn you that, with the concurrence of my allies, I have, like them, decided to prevent you, with all means at my disposal, from continuing on your course to any port in French West Africa or Equatorial Africa.

Will you accept, Admiral, the expression of my most distinguished feelings.

De Gaulle

Captain Hamill of the *Cornwall* sent along a letter of almost identical content to show that the British were in the game as well and that the game was deadly serious. But he sent along a more personal letter to Captain Goybet, underlining his friendship for the French, a result of his years as naval attaché in Paris. He hoped Captain Goybet could see his way to joining the Free French, "but yours is a difficult decision, and this letter is not one of propaganda but of friendship."

"I hope with all my heart," his letter continued, "that you will find it possible to do as I ask and return to Casablanca without forcing me to do a thing which I should regret all my life."

Captain Goybet dismissed de Gaulle's letter; de Gaulle, he said, had no official position in the French Government. He could not so easily dismiss the threat of the British cruisers. He could scarcely pit his eight 6.1-inch guns against the eight 8-inch guns of the *Cornwall* and the six 6-inch guns of the *Delhi*. Fighting for time, he requested permission to consult his admiral by radio. Captain Hamill extended his instructions to the extreme limit and granted permission. As a result, Admiral Bourragué was soon reading:

An ultimatum from the *Cornwall* and a *Delhi*-type cruiser requires us either to fight or be underway for Casablanca by 17 o'clock, G.M.T. In view of the international importance of the decision to be made, I request exact instructions.

As he read those words, Bourragué was over a thousand miles from the *Primauguet-Tarn* group and was being trailed by the British himself. He could do nothing to assist. It took him but a few minutes to decide. At 4:07 P.M. he ordered Captain Goybet to accept the British demands. Shepherded by the *Cornwall* and *Delhi,* the French ships made for Casablanca.

The *Gloire,* meanwhile, had accepted her fate. Abandoning his efforts to reach Konakry, Captain Broussignac gave his parole that he would make directly for Casablanca. The British accepted his word, relieved that they were thereby released to take part in the forthcoming operations.

When Captain Broussignac heard of the attack at Dakar on September 23, he considered himself released from his obligations. But by that time he was too far away to be able to do any good, especially with a partially crippled ship. He held on and entered Casablanca on September 24.

Of the 4 French cruisers which might have interfered with Operation Menace, 2 had been peacefully eliminated by British strength and by the use of tact on both sides. However, the other 2 had reached Dakar. Their story had just begun.

September weather off Dakar is normally fair, with bright sunshine and unlimited visibility. Churchill undoubtedly anticipated such a day when he painted his word picture of the huge Allied armada off the French port. Unfortunately for British and Free French hopes, September 23, 1940, dawned with a thick, heavy fog, cutting visibility to less than a mile at times. Early risers in the city that morning heard the sound of aircraft overhead. Glancing up, they could see nothing. Then, fluttering down through the fog, thousands of leaflets fell upon streets and yards. Through these leaflets the citizens first learned of their situation. Dakar was threatened.

> We are coming to defend Dakar with you! [read one of the leaflets]
> We are coming to resupply Dakar. General de Gaulle.

Another, more explicit, said:

> Dakar is menaced by the enemy and by famine.
> Dakar must be saved for France!
> Dakar must be resupplied!
> It is for these things that forces under my orders are arriving at Dakar.
> Powerful allied forces are ready to assist us.
> I urge the civil and military authorities to cooperate with me.

I ask that all elements of the ground forces, the naval forces, and their air forces remain at their posts and establish liaison with the French troops which are coming to reinforce them.

I ask the population to show its patriotism by remaining calm and by welcoming my troops.

Long live French Dakar!
Long live French Africa!
Long live France!

General de Gaulle.

Not all the planes were dropping leaflets. Two of the aircraft had special missions. Like the others, they had flown off the carrier *Ark Royal,* but unlike the others, they were piloted by Frenchmen. They were to land at Wakam Field, Dakar's airport, and rally the garrison to de Gaulle. If the commandant proved intractable, they would seize him and signal to the British that the airfield was ready to receive aircraft from the *Ark Royal.* Then they would commandeer trucks and cars, proceed to the town, and lend assistance.

As their planes touched down at Wakam Field, the Frenchmen were greeted by machine-gun fire, not handclasps. Their grim-faced compatriots surrounded them and led them away to the guard house. No word of their fate reached the "Menace" forces off shore. The fog had swallowed them up.

British leaders had enjoyed high hope that a display of overwhelming force would give the local leaders the excuse they needed to go over to the Free French. The fog destroyed any such hope. The people and their leaders could not be impressed by what they could not see.

Even if the day had dawned fair and bright, so that the full power of the expedition could have been seen, it is doubtful that the French leaders of Dakar would have yielded. The British interception of the French cruisers had alarmed Vichy officials. Darlan was furious. He reaffirmed the order that any British ship within 20 miles of a French coast was to be fired upon. He directed 4 more French cruisers and 5 destroyers to prepare to leave Toulon for Dakar. The Germans and Italians, however, felt this was going a little too far, and the ships stayed where they were.

Of more immediate effect at Dakar, Admiral Darlan precipitately relieved Admiral Bourragué for not resisting to the limit when the British ordered him to go to Casablanca. On September 21, Vice Admiral Lacroix, Commander of the Third Cruiser Squadron, left Toulon by air to take over command of French naval forces in West

Africa. Lacroix had no time for packing and departed with but a single suitcase.

On his arrival, he and Rear Admiral Landriau, the local naval commander, conferred immediately. They agreed that the *Gloire, Primauguet,* and *Tarn* not be ordered to break their paroles; they should continue their voyages to Casablanca. "Any attempt," telegraphed Lacroix to Vichy, "to break this promise would mean an English attack on traffic which is essential to us."

Lacroix and Landriau spent the next day, September 22, investigating the defenses of Dakar. They rapidly reached the conclusion that the presence of so many British ships in the area implied an impending blockade of Dakar or possibly even an attack. Until they got the situation at Dakar under control, French Equatorial Africa would have to wait.

High Commissioner Boisson urged military and air force leaders to be alert and prepared for anything. He also ordered air and sea searches out each night for a distance of 40 to 50 miles to prevent any surprise force from catching the city unaware. These searches, however, were not far enough distant to pick up Force M as it moved through the night toward Dakar.

As the ships of Force M made their slow way north from Freetown, Admiral Cunningham, General Irwin, and General de Gaulle held a last conference. All that remained to be done was to persuade the people at Dakar to join the Free French movement willingly. Force, they agreed, must be avoided. Only if the operation could succeed in no other way could its use be justified.

All of the commanders of "Menace" had by this time shifted their flags to the battleship *Barham*—all, that is, except de Gaulle. The tall, imperious Frenchman, trusting no one wholly, confiding completely in no one, preferred to keep his own counsel. Condemned to death in absentia by his compatriots, regarded by his British allies with mingled admiration, suspicion, respect, and exasperation, this icily aloof general, the symbol of Free France, had been an uncomfortable colleague since the beginning. It was impossible to live with him and impossible to do without him.

On the eve of sailing from Freetown for Dakar, de Gaulle had appeared on board the *Barham* with his British liaison officer, Major General Sir Edward Spears, and demanded equal status with Admiral Cunningham and General Irwin. He could not bear to see the French subordinated in any way to the British.

The British leaders flatly rejected his demand. Churchill would not stand for it. All operations had to be under British control. De Gaulle must consider himself under the instructions of General Irwin. De Gaulle refused. His Free French forces must not come under any control but his own.

General Irwin offered a compromise. If a landing in force should become necessary, de Gaulle and his Free French would make the first try at Rufisque Bay 6 miles east of Dakar. This would be his own show; British troops would be committed only if the operation would fail without them. Mollified by this concession, de Gaulle promised "complete cooperation with the British Commanders in case of need." He refused, however, another invitation to take passage in the *Barham*, preferring to return to his own flagship, the *Westernland*. No doubt Cunningham would have liked to have his difficult associate under his eye, and no doubt de Gaulle was equally anxious not to be there.

The passage from Freetown to Dakar was without incident. Subordinate officers spent their time studying the plans for the operation. The combined forces would appear at dawn. Aircraft from the *Ark Royal* would fly ahead to drop leaflets on the city, while two French aircraft made an attempt to seize Wakam Field. About the same time the Free French sloop *Savorgnan de Brazza* would attempt to enter the harbor and land *parlementaires* under a flag of truce. Their task would be to persuade the authorities to join the Free French.

If these efforts failed, then de Gaulle would make his attempt at Rufisque Bay. This phase of the operation was known as Plan "Charles." Further attempts, to be made by combined British and Free French forces, were successively known as "Rufus," "William," and "Conquerer." Almost self-explanatory voice signals would indicate the situation. "Happy" would be used if the French welcomed de Gaulle. If the opposition was moderate, the word "sticky" would be used, while the word "nasty" would mean that all-out resistance had developed.

At 5:15 A.M. Force M arrived off Dakar. The combatant ships moved close inshore, the transports remaining some 10 miles out to await developments. About ten minutes later the *Savorgnan de Brazza* pulled away from the other ships and headed for the breakwater. Three miles south of the entrance, she stopped and put two boats in the water. In one were nine spokesmen for de Gaulle with eight enlisted helpers under the Free French Commander Thierry d'Argenlieu. The other boat carried an armed security detachment, a strange proceeding, indeed, for men bearing a flag of truce. Both boats flew large tricolors as well as their flags of truce. At 6:06 A.M. both boats set out at 10 knots for the harbor entrance. While the two boats were on their way, General de Gaulle took to the radio to win over the people of Dakar.

General de Gaulle has arrived with his troops to reinforce the defenses of Dakar and to resupply the city. A powerful English squadron and many British troops are here to support him. General de Gaulle has just sent officers of his staff to confer with the authorities of Dakar: the Governor General, the Admiral commanding the naval forces, and the Commanding General. This delegation of General de Gaulle's has the mission of requesting the free debarkment of the French troops and their replenishment. If all goes well, British forces will not be called upon to intervene and will not land. All officers, soldiers, sailors, aviators, and citizens of Dakar are to cooperate in facilitating this operation of preservation.

Commander d'Argenlieu's boats made their way into the harbor without being challenged. Overhead a plane spotted them and notified the reconnaissance control station that two boats flying flags of truce were standing in. As Commander d'Argenlieu's boat pulled up to Pier 2, he was challenged by a security officer. D'Argenlieu stated that he was an unarmed *parlementaire* with important messages from General de Gaulle to the governor general, the commanding general, and the naval commander. The officer requested d'Argenlieu to wait while he sent a message to the admiral.

Admiral Landriau, who had already read one of the leaflets dropped from the air, had no doubts of what his course should be. He ordered that d'Argenlieu should not be received, since there had been no advance notice of the coming of *parlementaires*. The more he thought about it, the angrier he became, and he changed his orders. Any of d'Argenlieu's group who had landed were to be arrested. The rest should be driven off.

Commander d'Argenlieu by this time was standing on the pier arguing with the officer who had brought Admiral Landriau's first answer. The debate was heated in the best Gallic manner. Glancing toward shore, he saw armed men running toward him. Realizing his danger in a flash, he leaped back in his boat, calling his followers to follow his example. As the boats dashed for safety, the shore party sped them on their way with small-arms fire which wounded Commander d'Argenlieu and another officer.

Hearing the firing, Lieutenant Commander Roux took his ship, the *Savorgnan de Brazza,* in close to the harbor to recover the boats more quickly. He depended on the resemblance of his ship to one regularly stationed at Dakar to avert disaster. He had not gone far before the signal station on Gorée Island challenged him. Since he could not possibly reply with the correct recognition code, he calmly went about his work of picking up his boats. He ignored warning shells from the *Richelieu* and the outposts, recovered his boats, and then shaped course for the *Westernland*. Commander d'Argenlieu had much to report to General de Gaulle. "We are faced with an organized and resolute resistance," he radioed. "No reaction whatever of sympathy apparent among the population."

When his representatives were driven off, an irate General de Gaulle made a second broadcast. This time the threat was no longer implicit.

I am waiting for the answer to my questions about debarkation. I am persuaded that I have the concurrence of the garrison and the population. If such is the case, everything can be concluded between Frenchmen. But you have just fired on the *Savorgnan de Brazza*. If such opposition continues, enormous allied forces which are following me will enter the action and this will cause extremely grave consequences. I do not want to think upon it. I am persuaded that good sense and reason will prevail and that everything will work out without any unfortunate incident. I am awaiting your response. Immediately. De Gaulle.

While de Gaulle's message was going out, his patrol minesweepers *Commandant Duboc* and *Commandant Dominé* tried to pretend they were local ships and penetrate the harbor. Even though the commanding officer of the *Commandant Dominé* impudently rendered passing honors to the *Richelieu,* their attempt was no more successful than the previous one; they had to beat a hasty retreat. The *Dominé*'s commander was convinced that shots from the battleship had been more friendly than otherwise. "If they had wished to blow us out of the water," he remarked, "it wouldn't have been difficult."

Aboard the *Barham*, Cunningham and Irwin were facing up to the realization that the operation had turned "sticky." Reconnaissance reports yielded the information that the *Richelieu* and the cruisers *Montcalm* and *Georges Leygues* were raising steam. Two destroyers and two submarines could be seen moving inside the harbor.

To convince the French garrison that they meant business, Admiral Cunningham decided to make a show of force. He ordered the fleet to close the shore and steam parallel to it at 26 knots. A 240-mm.*

* Approximately 9.5 inches.

battery on Cape Manuel opened fire as soon as the British ships broke out of the fog. Almost at once the cruiser *Cumberland* was hit with two shells which damaged her steering cables. The ship swung out of control, cut across the bow of the *Barham,* and headed on a collision course for the *Devonshire.* It was, perhaps, unfeeling of Cunningham to signal: *"Cumberland,* please keep station."

The *Cumberland* barely missed the *Devonshire* and veered erratically through the water. The other ships had to move nimbly to keep out of her way. At length Captain Fallowfield got her under control and headed to Bathurst in British West Africa for repairs. The rest of the British ships kept up the demonstration for three-quarters of an hour and then retired into the fogbank. Admiral Cunningham sent a parting message to the French defenders at Dakar: "Ships are not to leave harbour; if they do so, I will be regretfully compelled to use force to make them return."

A few minutes later, he sent, in some exasperation: "If you continue to fire on His Majesty's ships, I will regretfully be forced to reply with all the guns at my command."

"Unless you remove your ships 20 miles from Dakar," came the discouraging reply, "I will continue to fire to the last."

This message convinced Admiral Cunningham. He had no choice. He ordered his ships to close the beach once again and fire on the French defenses. During this second engagement, which lasted some thirty minutes, the French steamship *Porthos* was damaged in Dakar harbor and the British destroyers *Inglefield* and *Foresight* were both hit and reported casualties.

The French, determined to strike at the aggressors, sent out the patrol vessels *Gazelle* and *Surprise.* They did not get far before they found a British cruiser directly in the way. They scurried back to port. The submarines *Ajax* and *Persée* had better luck and succeeded in getting clear of the harbor, only to be spotted at once by aircraft from the *Ark Royal* at 10:15 A.M. Cunningham cautiously withdrew once more into the fog with his heavy ships, leaving his destroyers to deal with the submarines. "If your submarines sortie," he warned, "they will be attacked."

At 11:23, with no sign of trouble from the submarines, Cunningham cautioned his Swordfish planes against attacking them without further orders. Twenty minutes later, the *Persée* shattered the informal truce by launching two torpedoes at the *Delhi.* The torpedoes missed, and the submarine surfaced between the *Australia* and *Barham.* The battleship enthusiastically greeted her with a rain of 6-inch shells.

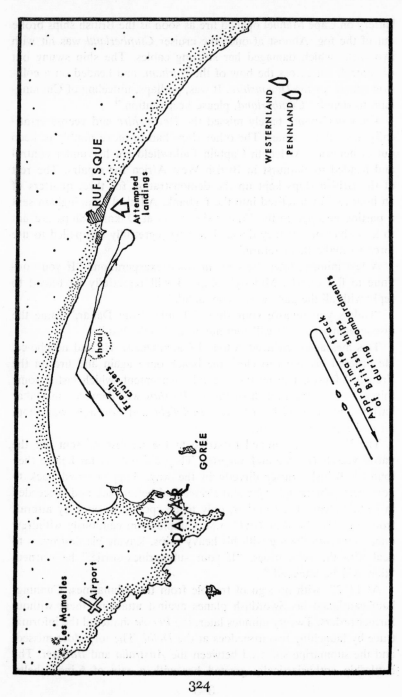

RUFISQUE

Attempted landings

shoal

French
cruisers

GORÉE

DAKAR

Airport

Les Mamelles

WESTERNLAND

PENNLAND

Approximate track
of British ships during
bombardments

Hit three times, the submarine crash-dived, only to be forced back to the surface, fatally wounded by depth charges from the *Fortune*. Before the *Persée* sank, the *Barham*'s chief yeoman of signals leaped on board and rescued the log and code books. The *Ajax* prudently returned to her anchorage.

The captured crew of the *Persée* painted a black picture for the success of "Menace." All the high authorities in the city, they reported, were determined to oppose de Gaulle's Free French forces; the officers were prepared to follow their leaders. Enlisted men and ordinary citizens were confused, but they would obey orders.

There could be little doubt in the mind of any of the Anglo-French commanders that Dakar would be defended, and defended vigorously. Yet, before committing themselves to an all-out assault, they thought they would give Plan "Charles" a trial, hoping that perhaps an all-French attempt would not be opposed as resolutely as the British demonstrations.

At 12:20 P.M., de Gaulle made one final appeal to the Dakar authorities.

> I urge the authorities of Dakar and call upon them to signal that they will not oppose entry into the port of French ships and the debarkation of troops under my orders. In any case, forces under my orders and the allied forces will return the fire of those who oppose them.

Shortly after his message went out, de Gaulle received one from General Irwin: "What about Charles? Now he ought to do well."

What about "Charles," indeed? De Gaulle's flagship was still with the transports, some 13 to 15 miles out. He knew only that his planes to Wakam Field had disappeared as though they had never been and that his representatives led by Commander d'Argenlieu had been fired upon. He could not see the British warships and had not heard the sounds of gunfire.

Poor communications, wishful thinking, and faulty assumptions combined to throw the next events into such confusion that no one on the scene knew exactly what was happening.

The first event was clear enough. Governor Boisson replied:

> We confirm that we will oppose any debarkation by force. You have accepted the responsibility for the shedding of French blood. The responsibility is yours, for that blood has already flowed.

Once de Gaulle had Boisson's reply in hand, he began to set Plan "Charles" in motion. He apparently assumed that the message from the British was an authorization to go ahead, rather than a suggestion for his comment.*

Having nothing to report on the progress of the operation, he made no reply to General Irwin's query. The British asked testily, this time in standard language rather than in slang, what the devil was going on. De Gaulle, realizing he had made an error, replied that he was ending his preparations for the landing. By this he meant he had made up his mind. The British on their part believed that he meant he had *completed* his preparations. Delighted that things were going so well, they fired back a query asking if de Gaulle could land his troops at 3:30 that afternoon. They alerted the fleet to implement "Charles," leaving the time of the landing blank while they awaited de Gaulle's agreement.

The aloof Frenchman kept his own counsel. Nearly two hours went by. Finally, at 2:20 P.M. a message from de Gaulle arrived. Clutching it eagerly, Cunningham and Irwin were confounded. "Am still," it read, "awaiting instructions concerning Charles."

All this time, Cunningham and Irwin had assumed that de Gaulle was maneuvering his ships into position in Rufisque Bay, ready to land at 3:30. Now they wondered: had he moved at all from his previous anchorage? If he had not, there was no hope for landing according to plan. Cunningham immediately answered, "Carry out Charles and report zero hour."

Again there was no answer. Exasperation rising at their irritating subordinate, Cunningham and Irwin decided they had better see for themselves. The admiral ordered his warships to get under way and steam toward Rufisque Bay. On through the fog they groped for two hours, looking for de Gaulle's ships. At 4:20 P.M., having neither heard from de Gaulle nor sighted his ships, they sent messages canceling "Charles."

A few minutes later, one of the British destroyers sighted de Gaulle's errant ships sailing placidly toward Rufisque Bay. They were still some 20 miles from their destination. Cunningham repeated his order to cancel the operation. By this time he had another problem to face. A Swordfish on patrol over Dakar broke in suddenly: "At 1610

* The English text as sent: "What about Charles? Now he ought to do well," was translated by a staff officer in the *Westernland* before it was handed to de Gaulle, as *"Où en est Charles? Cela devrait aller bien maintenant."* The French idiom *"Où en est?"* means "how are things going with?" Thus de Gaulle almost certainly assumed the British thought it was in the works. Since he had done nothing about "Charles," he proceeded at once to repair the omission.

one *Fantasque*-class destroyer, one mile east of Gorée, steering south."

The Swordfish pilot had seen the *Audacieux*. But he had not seen the whole picture, by any means. Following behind were the cruisers *Georges Leygues* and *Montcalm*. The little group was even then speeding toward Rufisque Bay. Was de Gaulle still heading right into a trap?

The *Audacieux*, separated from her companions, fell afoul of the guns of a British cruiser. Hit by an 8-inch shell, the *Audacieux* had to beach herself in order not to sink. She was out of action.

British aircraft had by this time spotted the two cruisers and kept up a steady flow of reports on their movements. Because they were following an unmarked channel, the British did not dare close and could not bring them to action.

The cruisers, arriving at Rufisque Bay after the departure of the British scouting forces and before the arrival of de Gaulle's ships, found it empty. Admiral Lacroix ordered them to return and await developments.

During the brief skirmish, French shore batteries once again engaged the British ships. This time the *Richelieu* joined in. *Ark Royal* planes unsuccessfully attacked the French battleship and the batteries. The French had better luck, hitting the *Resolution* four times.

De Gaulle, meanwhile, was going ahead with "Charles," in spite of the fact that the British had canceled it. He did not bother to inform his British allies. Perhaps he was still offended at being under British orders. Perhaps he wished to avoid British interference. He would show them how a Frenchman would do it. Since he didn't tell the British, he deprived himself of the support that might have led to success.

At 5:30 P.M., de Gaulle's Free French sloops, *Savorgnan de Brazza*, *Commandant Duboc*, and *Commandant Dominé*, stopped and lowered boats. They were close in to the appointed beach in Rufisque Bay, their movements hidden by the fog. Loaded with French marines, these boats comprised the first wave. Where was the second? It was 7½ miles away, embarked in the *Westernland* and *Pennland*. These men of the Marine-Vernerey Brigade could not reinforce their comrades for at least forty minutes.

The first wave headed in. What did it matter that there was no plan for gunfire support? Or for coordination with the second wave? Or for communications between the boat waves and the flagship? *Élan, audace, toujours l'audace*, would carry the day.

327

Then the fog lifted.

Rufisque Bay came to life.

From a battery at the foot of Rufisque beach came the crash of gunfire. The *Savorgnan de Brazza* shuddered from a hit. One man was killed and five wounded. The ships' gunfire quickly knocked out this battery, but their satisfaction did not last long. Word came from the boats: "We are being machine-gunned. It is impossible to continue under the fire."

The fog closed in again. No one could do anything. Sloops and small boats drifted helplessly. At 5:51 P.M., de Gaulle signaled, "Plan Charles terminated."

Such a feeble, ill-planned amphibious assault has seldom been seen in the history of warfare. Had de Gaulle condescended to keep the British informed, he could have had the support of 2 battleships, 6 cruisers, an aircraft carrier, and several destroyers to cover movements to the beach. A single British destroyer had more firepower than all 3 French sloops put together. He might not have had to use this force, but it would have been there if he had needed it. As it was, small-arms fire from the beach repulsed the landing.

The British could not protect de Gaulle's ships if they did not know where they were. It was only by sheer chance that the *Montcalm* and *Georges Leygues* missed the *Pennland* and *Westernland*. If the cruisers had reached Rufisque Bay a few minutes later, they could have wiped out the Free French troops and their brilliantly independent leader with them.

Night fell, and activity ceased. The thoroughly alerted defenders of Dakar stood to their posts, ready for any further threats. The Allied force, retiring to take stock of the situation, dispatched a full and detailed account of the day's proceedings to London, and Churchill replied in a personal message to Admiral Cunningham:

HAVING BEGUN WE MUST GO ON TO THE END. STOP AT NOTHING.

Understanding of the extent of French resistance at Dakar seems to have varied inversely with the distance. The high command in London believed the opposition was only token; it would dissipate, they were sure, in face of a determined, all-out thrust.

Aboard the *Barham* Admiral Cunningham and General Irwin agreed on the all-out thrust but did not believe that the defenders would throw down their arms. The British, this time, would make a major assault. After de Gaulle's debacle, the British commanders wanted him out of the way. His men could form a floating reserve; in that role they could not botch another landing. Nor would they be fighting in a bloody, fratricidal battle between Frenchmen.

As the first step of the new day's plan, at 1 A.M. Cunningham sent an ultimatum to the High Commissioner:

> To the Governor and the people of Dakar.
>
> General de Gaulle informs us, the commanders of the British naval and military forces, that you have prevented him from landing his troops and the revictualling of Dakar. Furthermore your forts and your ships have opened fire on our ships without result. Your attitude gives us every reason to believe that Dakar may at any moment be handed over by you to the common enemy.... Desiring that Frenchmen should not fight against other Frenchmen in a pitched battle, General de Gaulle has withdrawn his forces. Our forces are now at hand; it is for us now to speak. You will not be allowed to hand over the French and Native people who wish to remain free to the slavery to which Germany and Italy would subject them. Yours is the entire responsibility for what may happen. We have the honour to inform you that if at 0600 hours tomorrow morning you have not given your powers to General de Gaulle, the very powerful force at our disposal will take action; when action has begun it will continue until the fortifications at Dakar are entirely destroyed and the place occupied by troops who will be ready to fulfill their duties.... There is no compromise possible. Notify your acceptance before 0600 hours tomorrow and avoid bloodshed.

The French at Dakar were no more willing than their countrymen elsewhere to bow to British pressure. They felt bitter over the assumption that the Axis forces were a threat to Dakar. There were no German nationals in Dakar at the time. Certain German economic commissioners were at Casablanca, but no Nazi military personnel were in any part of French West Africa. Dakar was French, and Frenchmen directed its defense.*

The Dakar authorities met during the night to frame their reply to the British ultimatum. No one had any notion of yielding. It was just a matter of phrasing the reply. Their original impulse had been to render a rude one-word answer. This word, unfortunately, had already been used on another occasion. At length the reply took form:

---

* British conviction that any right-thinking Frenchman would flock to de Gaulle was so strong that the myth of German pressure at Dakar died hard. A few days after these events the B.B.C. proclaimed that the stubborn defense there had been a result of its being directed by German officers.

"France has entrusted Dakar to me. I shall defend Dakar to the end."
Boisson's answer went out at 4:24 A.M., ninety-six minutes before the ultimatum expired. There could be no turning back.

During the night the cruisers *Montcalm* and *Georges Leygues,* screened by the destroyers *Fantasque* and *Hardi,* patrolled in the Bay of Dakar to the east of the city. His 2 remaining submarines, *Ajax* and *Bévéziers,* Landriau ordered on patrol, the latter 10 miles south of Gorée Island, and the *Ajax* a few miles farther east.

When he received Boisson's rejection of the ultimatum, Admiral Cunningham moved his ships to their bombardment stations. When the sun came up, Cunningham saw that the visibility, although somewhat better than that of the day before, would not permit long-range bombardment. There was no other way; they would have to move in.

As the British ships advanced, the French destroyers promptly began to lay smoke screens. The billowing smoke hung like a pall, concealing everything. Cunningham's move had been parried.

Since the British approach course brought them within range of the *Ajax,* the submarine dived and began to maneuver to gain an attack position. Hearing asdic * pings from the British destroyers, the French submarine approached cautiously. There was no sign that his ship had been detected, so Lieutenant Commander Guimont came to periscope depth to take a look around.

He left the periscope up a few seconds too long.

The British destroyers turned toward him, their bows rushing toward the submarine like deadly knives. Frantically scrambling for the depths, the *Ajax* was buffeted by repeated depth charges. Most of the charges went off above her, and she was smashed down, as though by a giant hand, out of control to the bottom, 200 feet below the surface. All electric power knocked out, the crew fought in the darkness to stem the water jetting in through numerous small leaks. Unless Commander Guimont wished to remain down forever, he had to surface at once. Bleeding high-pressure air into the diving tanks, the crew felt their ship begin to rise, slowly at first, and then with a rush. As she broke water, her men hastily abandoned ship and were taken prisoner by the British destroyer *Fortune.* The stricken *Ajax* returned to the depths in her final dive a few moments later.

As the *Ajax* fought her last battle, the Dakar defenders found themselves contending with attacks from the air. The *Ark Royal's* 32 aircraft, and 6 seaplanes from the heavy ships, pressed home a

---

* Asdic: An echo-ranging device for detection of submerged submarines, similar to the American sonar.

bombing and torpedo attack on the ships and shore defenses. French aircraft, meanwhile, left Wakam Field to attack British ships.

As soon as they could see anything to shoot at, British gunners opened fire. French shore batteries and ships replied promptly. At ranges of between 17,000 and 18,500 yards, the British scored no hits; only the destroyer *Malin,* which had joined the French cruisers, was slightly damaged by a near miss.

After thirty-four minutes, at 10:20 A.M., the British withdrew, firing a few final 15-inch salvos at the *Richelieu.* All missed, but a few of the shells fell in the city, causing some casualties. The *Richelieu's* 15-inchers answered, but then her only operational turret jammed. Her 6-inch guns carried on the fight, but without success. Officers of the *Richelieu* cheered when they thought they saw a hit on the funnel of the *Barham,* but British records indicate that they were mistaken.

The air attacks were equally inconclusive. Several dogfights developed, and a number of British planes were shot down by antiaircraft fire.

At 11:53 A.M. the British opened fire again, and this exchange, which lasted until 1:30 P.M., was more intense than the former one. The *Richelieu's* crew had made good use of their time and cleared the jammed turret. Firing no less than 160 rounds of 15-inch shells, they had the satisfaction of seeing four of them smash into the *Resolution.*

By this time the smoke screen had cleared away, so the French destroyers laid another. Firing through clear patches, the British were able to inflict minor damage on the shore batteries. Some ships in the harbor were hit, but not the *Richelieu.* She seemed to bear a charmed life, untouched by the scores of shells of all calibers which fell near her.

Smoke from the guns, from the stacks of the ships, and from smoke screens gradually blotted out everything. The British withdrew out of range once more.

During the afternoon they tried again, this time with the *Ark Royal's* aircraft. Three sections of Swordfish came in low over the water, challenged hotly by the French antiaircraft defenses. Two planes managed to win through to drop torpedoes aimed at the two French cruisers. The *Georges Leygues* put her engines all ahead full and threw her rudder to hard left. The *Montcalm's* watch officer ordered all engines back full and the rudder hard right. The torpedoes passed harmlessly between the ships.

During the afternoon, Admiral Cunningham took the *Barham* out to the vicinity of the waiting Free French ships and invited General de Gaulle to come on board for a conference. At the meeting, the atmosphere was grim. British officials were baffled at the stout French resistance, contrary to all expectations and all logic in the face of a force so manifestly superior. De Gaulle said it showed how the French virtues of courage and discipline had been perverted by the defenders of Dakar to interests contrary to those of France.

"Given the attitude of the city and of the supporting fleet," said Cunningham, "I do not believe that bombardment alone can bring about a solution."

General Irwin stated that he was ready to land troops, but warned that a landing would be fraught with danger to every boat and every soldier.

Both commanders then asked de Gaulle how it would affect the Free French movement if they canceled the operation.

"Up to now," replied de Gaulle, "we have not directed an all-out attack against Dakar. The attempt to enter the city as friends has been checked. Bombardment has decided nothing. Finally, the attempt to land a force of troops and an assault on emplacements will lead to a pitched battle which, for my part, I wish to avoid, and which you, yourselves, have indicated may have a questionable outcome. We must then, for the moment, give over the attempt to seize Dakar. . . . But the blockade ought to be continued in order not to permit freedom of action to the ships currently in Dakar. Then we should get ready for a new attempt to take Dakar by an overland attack, after a debarkation at undefended or lightly defended points, for example, at Saint Louis. In any case, and whatever happens, Free France will endure."

Cunningham and Irwin agreed. On this note the conference ended, and de Gaulle returned to the *Westernland*.

Operation Menace seemed finished. But London intervened to urge yet another attempt. Churchill could not bear to give up. He urged "one more crack" at Dakar. He suggested that the mist which hampered gunnery might mask a landing force. He was, however, willing to leave the decision to the men on the scene. PRAY ACT AS YOU THINK BEST . . . MATTER TO BE PUSHED TO A CONCLUSION WITHOUT DELAY.

Cunningham and Irwin agreed to make one more attempt to bring about victory. Their decision was aided by the disappearance of the mist and fog which had so hampered operations for the last two days. On the morning of September 25, the sun rose clear and bright in a cloudless sky. With it rose British hopes.

Once more the British battleships closed Dakar. Once more their 15-inch guns trained on the port. Once more they shuddered under the recoil as the cordite hurled shells weighing a ton each toward the city. Eyes of all observers peered through the smoke to mark the fall of shot.

At once the French responded to the fire, and all around the British ships colored columns of water arose, marring the smooth surface of the sea. Each battery ashore had its own dye-marking in its shells so that each could apply the proper corrections. Huge black spouts of water marked the 15-inch shells of the *Richelieu.* Closer than all the rest came purple splashes from the 8-inch guns on Gorée Island.

The flagship *Barham* was hit repeatedly, but kept her place in line. A hit amidships by a 240-mm. shell put the destroyer *Inglefield* out of action. From above, French planes dropped bombs on the twisting, turning British vessels.

The real danger was not from above. Early that morning the *Bévéziers,* Dakar's last remaining submarine, had left the harbor and, passing to the eastward of Gorée, set out on a southerly course toward the position where the British battleships had been the two previous days.

With dawn just over the horizon, the *Bévéziers* submerged at 5:45 A.M. to escape aircraft detection. Running along smoothly, she came to periscope depth occasionally to keep an eye out for the British.

At 8:07 A.M. the submarine was again at periscope depth. Lieutenant Commander Lancelot made out a British formation of 2 battleships escorted by destroyers zigzagging toward Dakar. Quickly he read off the range: 26,000 yards; bearing: 140° true. Thirteen miles away in the southeast was the quarry he was waiting for.

To intercept the British ships, which he estimated were speeding toward him at 20 knots, he turned to a course a little north of east. Another glimpse a few minutes later revealed that the British had altered course toward him, so he made a complete circle to avoid passing ahead of the British formation. At exactly 9 A.M., a final observation revealed that he was in perfect position. Four torpedoes leaped out of the tubes and ran toward the British battleships 2700 yards away.

The *Barham* heeled to starboard in response to a rudder full a-port. Holding their breath, the *Barham*'s crew watched the torpedoes streak by, only a few feet away. The *Resolution* was not so lucky. This unfortunate ship, hit on both the previous days, maneuvered radically but could not escape. Three of the torpedoes narrowly missed her, but the fourth caught her amidships. Shuddering to a stop, she lay wallowing in the trough of the sea, smoke and steam pouring from her damaged port side. The destroyers *Fury* and *Foresight* hastened up the torpedo wakes, dropping a rain of depth charges as they gained contact. Although severely shaken, the *Bévéziers* escaped serious injury and made her way back to Dakar, arriving about noon.

The battered *Inglefield* came to stand by her stricken larger sister. The *Barham* and the cruisers *Australia* and *Devonshire* moved in toward shore to draw fire away from the cripples.

At 9:25 A.M., the *Barham* was hit again by a 15-inch shell from the *Richelieu*. This was the final blow. Cunningham gave the recall signal, and all his ships withdrew seaward. The *Resolution* had by this time managed to get some steam to her turbines, and she followed slowly.

Cunningham and Irwin agreed that there was no point in continuing the action. The chances of success seemed no better than they had been from the beginning. Both their capital ships had been damaged, and the *Ark Royal* could no longer furnish air superiority. It was with a sense of relief that they received the following from Mr. Churchill:

> On all the information now before us, including damage to *Resolution,* we have decided that the enterprise against Dakar should be abandoned, the obvious evil consequences being faced. Unless something has happened which we do not know, which makes you wish to attempt landing in force, you should forthwith break off. You should inform us "Most Immediate" whether you concur, but unless the position has entirely changed in our favour, you should not actually begin landing till you receive our reply.
>
> Assuming enterprise abandoned, we shall endeavour to cover Duala by naval force, but we cannot safeguard de Gaulle's forces if they remain at Bathurst. Question of reinforcing Freetown with troops is being considered. Instructions regarding disposal of remainder of forces will be given on receipt of your reply.

Since Admiral Cunningham and General Irwin had already reached the same decision, their reply was simple.

CONCUR IN BREAKING OFF.

That afternoon Force M set course for Freetown, the transports leading the way, while the damaged warship force followed some

10 miles behind to act as rear guard. The defenders at Dakar sent a few planes to speed the unwelcome visitors on their way, and the submarine *Sidi Ferruch* from Konakry attempted to intercept the retreating force. An alert air patrol from the *Ark Royal* spotted the submarine and forced her to submerge before she had come within 10 miles of Force M.

On the morning of September 29 the British and Free French ships entered Freetown. By this time de Gaulle had decided not to undertake an overland campaign against Dakar and asked to be taken to Duala. He busied himself there with consolidating the position of the Free French in Equatorial Africa. Here in Duala he was comfortably removed from the energetic Churchill, who admired him greatly, especially at a distance.

The recriminations over the Dakar episode were widespread. In the House of Commons, in the British, the French, the German, and the American press, sarcastic allusions to the twisting of the British Lion's tail were the clichés of the day. The comparison of David and Goliath was not infrequent.

The effects of the operation were less than might have been expected. Vichy ordered further bombing reprisals against Gibraltar. They took place on September 23 and 24, while the battle for Dakar was still in progress. Four French destroyers from Casablanca made a demonstration off Gibraltar and were attacked. Both the French and the British were half-hearted in these Gibraltar episodes, and little or no damage was done. Three days later the situation had returned to normal in the Strait of Gibraltar, so much so that a small French sloop escorting a small French convoy was allowed to pass with no more challenge than a polite WHAT SHIP PLEASE? from the signal station on the Rock.

Certainly Britain lost credit by the ill-fated Dakar expedition, but less than she had during the retreat from Norway and from France. The news of Dakar was rather swallowed up by the Italian drive into Egypt, which had begun on September 13. Even though the drive stalled a few days later, Italian troops were on Egyptian soil. In the course of a few weeks, the Dakar operation had faded into a backwater of history.

Yet curiously enough, one positive gain to Britain, France, and the United States resulted from Operation Menace. The Germans were so impressed by Dakar's stubborn defense in the face of such odds that they decided the French could be depended upon to resist any British incursion into their African colonies. Accordingly, to conserve troops soon to be needed elsewhere, Hitler decided not to insist on the occupation of French West Africa and Morocco as he had planned. This made all the difference in November, 1942, when the British and Americans landed in French North Africa.

The tragic events of the summer of 1940 poisoned Anglo-French relations for a long time. The Vichy Government became more pro-German, and Laval's strength grew for a time. Within months, however, Laval's influence was on the wane, and the French people learned what it was to live under the Nazi heel. Vichy became a symbol of a divided France, always subject to the threat of German occupation of the whole country.

Instead of encouraging Vichy to declare war on England, the Germans decided she should not be permitted to do so. She was to be no ally; she was to be eliminated from the list of great powers. Besides, Hitler wanted her colonies, and he could have no excuse for taking them if he allowed Vichy to become a partner of the Axis. Cynically and brutally, the Germans imposed ever more severe restrictions on Vichy. If the French demurred, the Armistice Commission threatened that Germany would take over the whole country. Such measures and the calculated brutalities of the SS and Gestapo in Occupied France combined to drive French feeling once more to the Allied side. Gradually the memories of Mers el Kebir and Dakar faded, and the resistance movement grew.

Much would happen before France was free once more. The British were still alone, still stubbornly resisting. They would strike back where and when they could. And they looked across the seas to America. Only from the United States could come the ultimate salvation.

CHAPTER THIRTEEN

Hands Across the Sea

But welcome fortitude, and patient cheer,
And frequent sights of what is to be borne!
Such sights, or worse, as are before me here—
Not without hope we suffer and we mourn.
Wordsworth, "Elegiac Stanzas"

I T was the evening of November 5, 1940. Two men in shirtsleeves waited in a room of a suite on the fourteenth floor of New York's Commodore Hotel. It was easy to see that the men were brothers. There was a new-fangled gadget called a television in the room, and the two men looked at it from time to time. From the next room came the murmur of voices and the chatter of Teletype machines. Although the hour was still early, there was tenseness in the suite.

It was the most important day in the life of one of the two men in the room with the television.

Wendell Lewis Willkie sat with his brother Ed waiting for the news wires and radio and television announcers to tell him whether he would occupy the office of President of the United States.

No man had campaigned harder for the office. In a period of fifty days he had criss-crossed the land and made the incredible total of 560 speeches, all but the first few in a hoarse croak. Who can forget the newsreel clips of him standing on an observation car platform, his freshly pressed suit rumpled in a few minutes, his hair falling over his forehead, and his impatient challenges to the "Presn-Unide-States"?

From the first, his campaign was handicapped, for he had no real issues with Roosevelt. He supported economic mobilization. He supported Selective Service. He approved the destroyers-for-bases deal. In fact, his principal issue was that he would do all these things faster and better.

He lacked enthusiastic support from his own party. Although he had romped home with the nomination, and the party faithful had to support his campaign, they didn't have to like it. And they didn't like it. They viewed him with suspicion as a renegade Democrat who was not to be trusted. Former Senator James E. Watson from Willkie's home state of Indiana put it bluntly. "If a whore repented and wanted to join the church, I'd personally welcome her and lead her up the aisle to a pew, but, by the Eternal, I'd not ask her to lead the choir the first night."

Democratic faithfuls turned on the apostate with glee. Secretary of the Interior Harold L. Ickes led the pack with his witty characterization of the "barefoot Wall Street lawyer." Ickes went on to say:

> I regard him [Willkie] as a very able and resourceful man, but one who is unscrupulous. He has the ability of covering his unscrupulousness with a coating of candor. . . .
>
> Fundamentally, I believe that Willkie is what we know as a "corporation man." By this I mean that he probably holds the theory that the greatest good of the country results from building up and fostering an ever richer class, through which benefits will percolate to those lower down. . . .
>
> And yet, curiously enough, there might be circumstances in which I would openly support Willkie. As I see it, I would support him against any man who conceivably could be nominated on the Democratic ticket except the President himself and Bob Jackson. I would do this on the theory that I would rather have, at the head of the Government, a clever and able opponent of the theories in which I believe than a weak, vacillating, and therefore ineffective—perhaps even a pretended—champion of those theories. One can always reason with a strong, able man, but the other type is like manipulating a bladder that has been filled with air. You push at one point and it bulges at the opposite.

Most infuriating to Willkie was that his opponent refused to campaign. He made no political statements an opponent could challenge. Willkie was shadow-boxing, while "the Champ" wasn't even bothering to put on the gloves. It was maddening.

Willkie did have sincere points of difference with the Administration. He opposed the Roosevelt alliance with Big Labor, believing that Big Business, responsible to its millions of stockholders, was a firmer economic base for the country. He opposed governmental competition with business; this led him into his famous fight against the Tennessee Valley Authority.

He recognized that some regulation of utilities was necessary for

338

the protection of consumers, and he favored most of the New Deal social reforms; but differences in detail, how and when to implement them, made sparse campaign material. As Norman Thomas, the perennial Socialist candidate, put it, "He agreed with Mr. Roosevelt's entire program of social reform—and said it was leading to disaster."

As passionately as anyone, Willkie hated Hitler and all his works. There could be no thought in his mind of opposing any of Roosevelt's defense measures. He believed that Britain was fighting the battle for America, and he supported F.D.R. on attempts to aid the British. In fact, he urged that the Administration ought to do more.

Lacking a real difference, he could only present himself to the American people as the man who could do it better. His real challenge had to be to the man, and the President had most of the cards in that game. The jaunty cock of the head, the boat cloak, the jutting jaw, the gleaming smile, the confident wave of the right arm, the pince-nez eyeglasses, the gaily tilted cigarette holder were all familiar symbols, and millions of people loved them. Other millions hated him. Business tycoons and the patroons of the Hudson Valley considered him a traitor to his class. A Peter Arno cartoon depicts a group of New York society luminaries summoning others of their kind from a club: "Come on! We're all going down to the Trans-Lux * to hiss Roosevelt!"

In contrast, Willkie's bumbling physical appearance, his harsh voice, and his unruly hair cast no spells on the public. His loyal supporters, and he had millions, were drawn by his forthright honesty, his sincerity, his passionate love of his country.

In the early stages of the campaign, Willkie devoted himself to the issues as he saw them. His speeches were well phrased, logical, and cold. His listeners wanted something to cheer about, a "give-'em-hell" approach, and they did not get it from Willkie. In labor areas he stood, a forced smile fixed on his face, as he was booed even before he began to speak. Sometimes he was pelted with eggs, tomatoes, once even with a watermelon. He never lost his temper in the face of such treatment until an egg narrowly missed his wife and splattered her dress and stockings. Reporters noted that his face got red with rage. He started to move toward the graceless lout who had thrown the egg. Then he controlled himself.

As in every campaign, rude signs appeared: "Win *What* with Willkie?" "To Hell with Willkie!" He kept his composure. A little jingle began going the rounds:

* A newsreel theater.

Roosevelt's in the White House,
Waiting to be elected;
Willkie's in the ashcan,
Waiting to be collected.

By the end of September, it became clear that Willkie's campaign was not working. All kinds of polls—Gallup, *Fortune* Magazine, the New York *Daily News*—showed his percentage dropping. Odds against his election went from seven to five to twelve to five. Something had to be done. His advisers urged him to make slashing attacks on the President and on the war program.

He began to yield. He had plenty of provocation from the other side. Although "the Champ" was keeping silent, his henchmen were not. In particular, Willkie was stung by Henry Wallace's feckless statement, "The Nazi support of Wendell Willkie is part of Adolf Hitler's plan to weaken and eventually conquer the United States."

Willkie smashed back. He accused Roosevelt of having promised Churchill that the United States would enter the war right after the election. He pinned the name "warmonger" on the President. He accused him of wanting to be a dictator. Whatever you want to call it, he said, "national socialism, national capitalism or a complete concentration of power in a centralized government of the economic forces of the country. . . . That is the issue."

Worried by the responses to Willkie's new tactics, the President watched and waited. His rating dropped at the polls, and "the Champ" decided to put on the gloves, after all. He announced that he would make five campaign speeches during the period of two weeks just before the election.

On October 23 in Philadelphia, F.D.R. took his case to the American people. He regretted that personal innuendos and falsifications had entered the campaign, but, "I am an old campaigner, and I love a good fight!" Thirty-two times in his speech, he charged Willkie with deliberate distortions of fact. He was sly, sarcastic, witty, ironic, confidential, and tough. The crowd loved it.

They loved it even more a few days later at Madison Square Garden in New York when he took the Republicans over the coals for their hamstringing record of votes on defense appropriations. It was in that speech that he twice symbolized the conservative and isolationist wing of the Republican party by rhythmically joining the names, "Martin, Barton, and Fish."

Roosevelt had repeatedly stated that American soldiers would not be sent overseas to fight, unless America was attacked. Willkie's response had been, "If his [Roosevelt's] promise to keep our boys out of foreign wars is no better than his promise to balance the budget, they're already almost on the transports."

On October 30, Willkie predicted that "on the basis of his past performance with pledges to the people, you may expect war by April, 1941, if he is elected."

Roosevelt snapped back that night in Boston. "And while I am talking to you mothers and fathers, I give you one more assurance. I have said this before, but I shall say it again and again and again: You boys are not going to be sent into any foreign wars."

He had said this before, but he had always added the phrase "except in case of attack." But this was the stuff the people like to hear. And so F.D.R. said it.

As the election neared, the polls showed the candidates running neck and neck. People were crossing party lines so fast you couldn't make solid predictions. The most prominent Democratic defector was John L. Lewis, president of the C.I.O. He urged laboring men and women to vote for Willkie, and added, "President Roosevelt will not be reelected for the third term unless he has the overwhelming support of labor. If he is, therefore, reelected . . . I will accept the result as a vote of no confidence, and will retire as president of the Congress of Industrial Organizations at its convention in November." *

On Tuesday, November 5, 49,579,223 Americans trooped to the polls to cast their votes for Mr. Roosevelt or Mr. Willkie. A few thousand others voted the offbeat tickets—Prohibitionist, Socialist, Communist. Mr. Roosevelt voted at Hyde Park. Willkie cast an absentee ballot in Indiana. Physicist Albert Einstein cast his first vote as an American citizen at Princeton, New Jersey. He did not reveal his choice. In Uvalde, Texas, Vice President John Nance Garner sulked like Achilles in his big brick home and did not go to the polls at all. Roosevelt lost one vote when Mrs. Edward Steele of Peoria, Illinois, changed her mind about going to the polls. She went to the hospital instead, where she gave birth to a boy. He was named Franklin Delano Steele.

That evening, F.D.R. sat in the family dining room at Hyde Park, tally sheets laid out on the table. As the returns came in, he filled up the squares in his sprawling handwriting. Once in a while Harry Hopkins or Judge Samuel Rosenman would put in an appearance. They were looking happier all the time.

* Lewis dutifully kept his promise.

In the Commodore Hotel suite, the atmosphere was getting more and more gloomy. When Ohio was reported lost, Robert B. Hollister, Taft's law partner, and one of Willkie's advisers, recommended an early concession. Willkie refused.

"I can still win," he said grimly.

The hours went on. Finally, just before midnight, a tight-lipped Willkie went down to the ballroom to speak to his workers and supporters. He grinned and waved.

> Fellow workers: I first want to say to you that I never felt better in my life.
>
> I congratulate you in being a part of the greatest crusade of this century.... And that the principles for which we have fought will prevail is as sure as that the truth will always prevail. And I hope that none of you are either afraid or disheartened, because I am not in the slightest.... I hear some people shouting to me, "Don't give up." I guess those people don't know me.... Don't be afraid and never quit. Good night.

And Willkie would not give up. It was not until the following morning that he sent the customary telegram of congratulation to the President.

Even in defeat, Willkie had given Roosevelt a bad scare. Although he carried only ten states * for 82 electoral votes, Willkie had won nearly six million more votes than the Landon total in 1936. It was the narrowest victory Roosevelt had won since his election as Governor of New York in 1928.

In spite of the narrow squeak, a placard outside Hyde Park proclaimed "SAFE ON THIRD."

On November 11, Willkie took to the radio again. He asked those who had voted for him to keep their faith in him and in America. There was no bitterness in his heart, he said, and there should be none in theirs. "We have elected Franklin Roosevelt President. He is your President. He is my President.... Your function during the next four years is that of loyal opposition."

The day after the election, Roosevelt received a telegram of congratulation from one of his strongest supporters—Winston S. Churchill.

* Colorado, Indiana, Iowa, Kansas, Maine, Michigan, Nebraska, North Dakota, South Dakota, and Vermont. Final totals were: *Electoral votes:* Roosevelt, 449; Willkie, 82. *Popular vote:* Roosevelt, 27,245,422; Willkie, 22,333,801.

I did not think it right for me as a foreigner to express my opinion upon American politics while the election was on, but now I feel you will not mind my saying that I prayed for your success and that I am truly thankful for it. . . . Things are afoot which will be remembered as long as the English language is spoken in any quarter of the globe, and in expressing the comfort I feel that the people of the United States have once again cast these great burdens upon you I must avow my sure faith that the lights by which we steer will bring us all safely to anchor.

* * *

The ancient city of Coventry is located about ninety miles northeast of London. Most people know of it from the story of Lady Godiva, who, in the eleventh century, rode naked through the streets at noon to relieve the oppressive burden of taxes imposed by her husband, Leofric, Earl of Mercia. All the townspeople kept indoors with their shutters closed while she rode—all except one, known as "Peeping Tom." According to the legend, he was struck blind for his presumption.

The Germans were not interested in Lady Godiva when they selected Coventry as target for a massive raid. The city lies in the heart of the Midlands, Britain's heavy industrial district. Coventry has been called Britain's "little Essen" by the Germans and Britain's "little Detroit" by Americans.

According to Luftwaffe Field Marshal Kesselring, the targets at Coventry were the armament factories, but "smoke clouds make it impossible to aim accurately." Beginning shortly after dark on November 14, five hundred bombers came over the city. It took them eleven hours. Early in the raid the main water supply was cut, and men stood hopelessly, watching while the center of their city burned to the ground.

One of the proudest accomplishments of Leofric and Godiva was the cathedral begun in 1043. It was pulled down by Henry VIII about 1539. A second cathedral erected nearby was completed in 1433. It stood until November 15, 1940. Its spire stands today.

When incendiary bombs fell on the roof of the magnificent 15th-century St. Michael's Cathedral, there was nothing anyone could do. The flames quickly ate through the wooden roof, destroyed the interior, and left standing only charred bits of masonry and the beautiful spire. It was a loss that sickened everyone.

Before the citizens of Coventry could mourn their cathedral, they

343

had to find some way of keeping themselves going. For at least twenty-four hours, the Administration was at a standstill. No one seemed able to do anything but exchange tales of the horrors of the night. There was little to eat and little to drink. But by the time the King and Queen arrived on November 17, Coventry's newspaper, *The Midland Daily Telegraph,* was able to report that electricity had been restored in many sections of the city. "Marvels of adaptation in wood, cardboard, and roof felting were combined to make premises wind and waterproof—all designed towards minimizing damage."

The cruiser *Coventry* sent a message: COMPLIMENTS OF H.M.S. *COVENTRY.* EXPRESS SYMPATHY WITH CITIZENS IN THEIR ADVERSITY, BUT ASSURE THEM THAT SHIP WILL ENDEAVOUR TO REPAY. Later the crew members sent £105 for relief of the distressed citizens.

The raid killed 554 people and destroyed 32,000 homes. Yet within two months, arms production was back to normal. The Germans threatened to "Coventryize" other cities in Britain, such as Birmingham. But nowhere else was the bombing so vicious, and nowhere else did the destruction cause such revulsion in the minds of free men.

Services continued in the ruins of the cathedral under a vault of sky instead of wood. A rude altar was constructed out of the rubble of masonry blocks, and huge handmade nails were set together to form a cross. Behind the Cross of Nails, now a symbol of Coventry's passion, were words scratched in the stone, "Father Forgive." *

* * *

Mr. Leonard Coatsworth, a reporter for the *News-Tribune* of Tacoma, Washington, was driving his car across the new suspension bridge connecting the Olympic Peninsula with the mainland. Beneath him the bridge bucked, rippled, and swayed, but no worse than usual.

The bridge had been opened in July, 1940, and at once it got a fearsome reputation. Its 2800-foot-long span heaved and swayed like a hammock. Sometimes people got seasick during a crossing.

Yet the engineers swore the bridge was safe. Its twists were more violent in light breezes than in strong ones. Residents decided they would have to learn to live with it.

* The ruined cathedral is still used for services, although it has been embodied in the controversial but magnificent new cathedral designed by Sir Basil Spence. The original Cross of Nails forms a part of the Golden Cross above the main altar.

On November 7, at about 9:45 in the morning, Mr. Coatsworth felt the rippling stop, while shrieks and groans sounded from the supports above. His car hit the curbing. The motion began again, worse than ever. Coatsworth climbed out of his car and was pitched forward on his face. He encountered a student, Winfield Brown, and they tried to make their way off the bridge, both seasick, both frightened to death. All around them the concrete roadbed was popping, snapping, and chunks of it broke away to fall into the water 190 feet below.

Coatsworth and Brown made it off the bridge on the Tacoma end. A man and a woman scrambled out of a logging truck and made their way off. Then with a sound like an explosion, the suspension cables let go and the main span fell into the water below, carrying Mr. Coatsworth's car and pet dog with it.

Although no one was hurt in the bridge collapse, it was a sad blow for Tacoma. Back came the ferries, back came the long waits to get over to the Bremerton Navy Yard, just when the yard was busier than ever.

* * *

At 5 o'clock on the afternoon of June 10, 1940, Italy's *Duce* Mussolini strode out onto the balcony of the Palazzo Venezia in Rome. Strutting like a turkey cock, his jaw thrust arrogantly toward the sky, he snapped his arm out in the Fascist salute. His great moment of destiny had come.

Fighters of land, sea, and air, Blackshirts of the revolution and of the legions, men and women of Italy, of the Empire and of the Kingdom of Albania, listen!

The crowd, whipped up by the *Giovani Fascisti* (Young Fascists) roared *"Duce! Duce!"*

We take the field against the plutocratic and reactionary democracies who always have blocked the march and frequently plotted against the existence of the Italian people. . . .

Our conscience is absolutely clear. . . .

Proletarian, Fascist Italy has arisen for the third time, strong, proud, compact as never before.

There is only one order. It is categorical and obligatory for every one. It already wins over and inflames hearts from the Alps to the Indian Ocean: Conquer!

And we will conquer in order, finally, to give a new world of peace with justice to Italy, to Europe, and to the universe.

Italian people, rush to arms and show your tenacity, your courage, your valor.

He stepped back. The crowd roared, and the great man disappeared. His son-in-law, Count Galeazzo Ciano, recorded in his diary: "I am sad, very sad. The adventure begins. May God help Italy!"

The next day Italian soldiers crossed the French border and immediately ground to a halt.

Mussolini had made his move, and he could claim a seat at the victors' table. But it brought him the contempt of the world, not even excluding that of his Axis partner.

At sea, the British longed to come to grips with the Italian Navy and settle affairs once and for all. But nothing much happened. The Italian ships proved hard to catch, for class by class, they were 3 to 5 knots faster than their British counterparts.

The first blood went to the Italians when a submarine torpedoed and sank the British light cruiser *Calypso* in the early morning hours of June 12. An Italian submarine, however, was not a particularly safe place to be during that time, for by the end of June, 10 of them had been lost. Another 10 went the same way before the end of the year.

Because of the problems with the French fleet, it was not until July 9 that Admiral Sir Andrew Browne Cunningham, Commander in Chief, Mediterranean Fleet, was able to make a move. The Italians had a goodly portion of their fleet at sea, covering the passage of a convoy to their forces in Libya. Similarly, Cunningham in the *Warspite,* with 2 other battleships, *Malaya* and *Royal Sovereign,* the carrier *Eagle,* 5 cruisers, and 17 destroyers, was shepherding a convoy from Alexandria to Malta. The day before, the cruiser *Gloucester* had been bombed by Italian aircraft, so she was unable to take part in the action.

The two opposing admirals were old acquaintances. They had entertained each other during a courtesy call of an Italian squadron to Malta in 1938. Admiral Arturo Riccardi had shown him a book, *The Life of Nelson,* which always lay on a table by his bed. "His subsequent actions," Cunningham noted wryly, ". . . rather showed that he had not greatly profited by his nightly reading."

The Italians had 2 fast battleships, the *Giulio Cesare* and the *Ca-*

vour, 16 cruisers, and a large number of destroyers. The British advantage in capital ships was offset by their lower speed, and the *Malaya* was never able to come into action at all.

The *Eagle* flew off aircraft in an attempt to slow the Italians down, but the attack was ineffective. They did succeed in hitting a cruiser, but the battleships were unscathed. The *Warspite,* meanwhile, was lobbing shells at the *Cavour* and *Cesare.* At 1600, at a range of 26,000 yards, one of the *Warspite's* 15-inch shells hit at the base of the *Cavour's* funnel. A great orange-colored flash could be seen, followed by a surge of smoke. This was too much for Admiral Riccardi, and he turned away under cover of a smoke screen, gleefully pursued by the British destroyers.

By 1800, the Italians had reorganized, but they had no thought of continuing the fight. Cunningham called off the pursuit, since his ships were getting too close to Italy and the planes of the Regia Aeronautica.

The Italian planes duly came out and bombed both sides impartially. It is not recorded that they got any hits, but Cunningham paid tribute to their accuracy. "It was most frightening. At times a ship would completely disappear behind the great splashes, to emerge as though from a dark, thick wood of enormous fir trees."

This little skirmish set the tone of the naval war in the Mediterranean. The British established a moral ascendancy over the Italians that never wore off. Never thereafter did the Italians accept battle with the British fleet if there was a way to avoid it.

Ten days later the Australian cruiser *Sydney* and 5 destroyers encountered 2 Italian cruisers off the north coast of Crete. After a running fight, the Italians got the worst of it, losing the *Bartolomeo Colleloni.*

Admiral Cunningham was not deceived by the success of these two engagements. He knew that there was going to be hard fighting in the Mediterranean, at sea, on land, and in the air.

Smarting from his inability to get a place in the sun by means of war in Europe, Mussolini saw Africa as the opportunity for glory. He had two armies there. In Eritrea and Italian Somaliland were 200,000 men under the Duke of Aosta. They threatened the British position in East Africa, and they could also advance on the Anglo-Egyptian Sudan and menace Egypt from the south.

The second army was in Libya, commanded by Marshal Rodolfo Graziani, with a force of some 250,000 men. The collapse of France had freed him of worries about the Tunisian border, and he could devote his entire attention to Egypt.

347

Mussolini peremptorily ordered both Aosta and Graziani to take the offensive.

The Duke of Aosta obeyed first. He advanced to give desperate battle, for his 200,000 men were opposed strongly by 1500 British and native troops. The outnumbered British conducted a skillful withdrawal and were evacuated from the port of Berbera on August 19. The whole campaign had taken just fifteen days.

Roman propaganda hailed it as a glorious victory. Mussolini's pouter-pigeon chest expanded another inch.

Marshal Graziani, who was ordered to take the offensive at about the same time, managed to stall. There was, after all, a strong British force in Egypt in the area the British called the Western Desert. It would be better, Graziani argued, if the invasion of Egypt should follow Operation Sea Lion, the invasion of England. Unhappily for Graziani's peace of mind, Sea Lion was postponed and postponed. Mussolini began to wonder. The Marshal had always wanted to make the advance from what he called a "firm base." The "firm base" even included a motorized brothel for the delectation of his officers. Was Graziani more interested in his comforts than in the glory Mussolini sought to thrust upon him?

On September 7, Mussolini peremptorily ordered the Marshal to attack in two days at the latest. Graziani obeyed promptly, stepping off on September 13, only four days late. He preceded his advance by a massive barrage on the empty British frontier posts, for the British had withdrawn their main forces to Mersa Matruh, leaving only light forces to keep an eye on the Italians.

Four divisions of the Italian Tenth Army, accompanied by miscellaneous groups of tanks, advanced grandly into Egypt, moving at the rate of 12 miles a day. Small British units harried the flanks, but nothing, *nothing,* was allowed to stand in the way of the magnificent Italian advance.

Finally, at Sidi Barrani, he stopped. He was 60 miles inside Egypt, and still 80 miles from the British Western Desert Force, which Churchill later referred to magniloquently as "The Army of the Nile."

Overcome by his temerity, Graziani erected a monument in Sidi Barrani to commemorate his magnificent feat of advancing virtually unopposed 60 miles into Egypt. And there he stayed. It was perhaps just as well, for at Mersa Matruh the British had prepared a trap for him. Wrote the commander of the Western Desert Force, Major General Richard O'Connor:

348

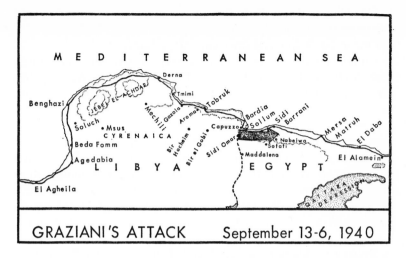

We hoped he would try and advance to the neighbourhood of Matruh, as we had prepared a full-dress counterstroke with all our armour. We worked this out on the ground, and I was greatly disappointed that he never came far enough to put it into execution.

All during October and November, both sides waited. O'Connor was building his forces for an overwhelming thrust westward. Graziani was once again establishing his "firm base." Whether it included the motorized brothel is not recorded.

Admiral Cunningham was not satisfied with a passive role. He needed more strength if he was to accomplish anything worthwhile. After his action with the Italian battleships off Calabria on July 9, where only the *Warspite* had the range of gunfire to equal that of the Italians, he had reported, "I must have one more ship that can shoot at a good range." He also needed a couple of heavy cruisers: "I should dearly like the *York* and *Exeter*."

He did not get *York* and *Exeter,* but he did get ships that delighted him. During August, the Admiralty undertook Operation Hats, under which the battleship *Valiant,* the new carrier *Illustrious,* and the anti-aircraft cruisers *Calcutta* and *Coventry* would cover a convoy through the Mediterranean to Alexandria and then remain as part of the Mediterranean Fleet.

To meet his new comrades-to-be, Cunningham took the fleet to sea, leading a small convoy to Malta. The operation went off as planned, and Cunningham rejoiced in his new strength, the more especially as the *Valiant* and the *Illustrious* had radar. The new-

349

found ability to detect the Italian aircraft at a good range and to send *Illustrious*'s Fulmar fighters after them went a long way toward solving the worst of Cunningham's current problems.

However, the two carriers on the scene could not cope entirely with the Italian Regia Aeronautica. The Italians had several hundred aircraft available, while *Illustrious* carried only 40 to 60, depending on size, and the *Eagle* only 15. More ships were hit, and many more suffered narrow escapes.

Admiral Cunningham knew full well that the little island of Malta was the key to the entire position in North Africa. If Malta fell, there would be no way the British could prevent the free movement of Italian ships across the central Mediterranean to Libya. Malta had to be supplied, especially since years of peacetime neglect had left the defenses in a state that might be described as minimal if one is generous.

By August, Malta possessed three fighter aircraft, Gladiators nicknamed "Faith," "Hope," and "Charity." These venerable biplanes gamely took on the Italian bombers that were coming over Malta daily, and kept casualties from bombing to a smaller number than they might have otherwise been.

However optimistically named, three fighters could not stand off the Italian Air Force, and the British decided to send reinforcements. It was a problem to get them there, for, with France lost, there was no way they could fly direct. No British fighter of the time had the range to fly from England to Gibraltar, nor from Gibraltar to Malta.

The Admiralty made the old aircraft carrier *Argus* available, and 12 Hurricane fighters were flown in on August 12 from a point near Sardinia.

It was a constant battle to keep Malta from starving. One of the most thickly populated areas of the world, the island was utterly dependent on imports for food, oil, and all necessities of life.

And the Axis was going to make it increasingly tough to get things through.

But Malta was going to be held, and was the key factor to winning the war in North Africa in 1942 and 1943.

Following his magnificent victories in Somaliland and in Egypt, Mussolini wanted to extend his empire in Europe. Already he had taken little Albania, in April of 1939, while the Western world watched uneasily. Now, Mussolini wanted more.

Albania has a common border with Greece, and it was across this border that the little Italian dictator proposed to strike. He carefully kept his plans secret from his partner Hitler. The German Führer had given him an inferiority complex by his overwhelming victories in Scandinavia and in western Europe. Just recently he had moved troops into Rumania with the agreement of Ion Antonescu, who had ousted the more liberal King Carol. Antonescu had invited the Germans in, and Hitler lost no time. The move gave him access to Rumanian oil. Also, Rumania borders on Russia, and Hitler would find this position useful the following spring.

Mussolini reacted to Hitler's move into Rumania with petulance, and was the more determined to keep the Greek venture a secret until it was too late.

> Hitler always faces me with a *fait accompli* [grumbled Mussolini to Ciano]. This time I am going to pay him back in his own coin. He will find out from the newspapers that I have occupied Greece. In this way the equilibrium will be re-established.

On October 22, Mussolini ordered the attack on Greece to commence on October 28. He wrote a letter, pre-dating it October 19, to inform Hitler of his action, and routed it so that it would not reach the Führer until too late. He knew perfectly well that Hitler was away on a trip, so he sent the letter to Berlin!

Hitler's trip was an effort to persuade Spain to join in the war against England. He met with the Spanish dictator, General Francisco Franco, at Hendaye on the Spanish-French border on October 23. The wily Spaniard well knew that he owed the existence of his regime to the military aid provided by Germany and Italy during the Spanish Civil War. But, at the Hendaye meeting, he was in no mood to pay the debt. Unimpressed by Hitler's claim that "England is already decisively beaten," he listened impassively to Hitler's offer to assist him in taking Gibraltar and the gift of large chunks of the French African empire "to the extent to which it would be possible to cover France's losses from British colonies."

For nine hours the discussions went on, and at the end, Franco had yielded exactly nothing. "Rather than go through that again," Hitler said later, "I would prefer to have three or four teeth yanked out."

The Führer's special train moved on to Montoire in France, where, the next day, Hitler had a meeting with Pétain. This one went off better; Pétain, his loathing for the British after Mers el Kebir and Dakar exceeding all bounds, agreed to collaborate in bringing Britain to her knees. He and Hitler signed a secret pact, including the statement:

The Axis Powers and France have an identical interest in seeing the defeat of England accomplished as soon as possible. Consequently the French Government will support, within the limits of its ability, the measures which the Axis Powers may take to this end.

France was not to join the war against England. Collaboration was to be the order of the day.

Hitler's special train moved slowly through France. By this time he had got wind that Mussolini was up to something and suggested that they meet to talk things over. Mussolini agreed and set the meeting for October 28 at Florence.

When Hitler's train arrived that morning, a splendid array of glittering uniforms and medals greeted him. And there was *Il Duce,* a smirk on his face, his chin high.

"Führer, we are on the march! Victorious Italian troops crossed the Greco-Albanian frontier at dawn today!"

Hitler was furious, but there was nothing he could do about it. The apple cart had been upset. Putting the best face he could on the matter, he wished his partner well and returned to Germany, fuming about "ungrateful and unreliable friends [Franco], Axis partners [Mussolini], and 'deceiving' Frenchmen [Pétain and Laval]."

The Italian troops in Greece did not remain victorious for long.

At the most undiplomatic hour of 2 o'clock in the morning of October 28, Count Grazzi, the Italian Minister in Athens, roused the Greek Prime Minister, General John Metaxas, and presented him with an ultimatum. Its conditions bore no relationship to reality, and Metaxas promptly rejected it. At dawn Italian Savoia bombers came roaring over the Greek mountains and raided Tatoi Airport near Athens and bombed the bridge over the Corinth Canal. Italian troops followed, and war engulfed Greece.

Metaxas called upon the British for assistance, but it quickly developed he did not desire troops. If British troops landed in Greece, Metaxas feared, it would give Germany the excuse to intervene. Instead, he pleaded for arms, planes, tanks, ammunition, oil, and gasoline—all those things which were in critical shortage in Egypt and in Great Britain itself.

With the consent of the Greek Government, the British established a naval base at Suda Bay on the north coast of Crete, but there was little else they could do. As it turned out, the Greeks did not need much help.

Inside a week, the Italians had been chased out of Greece, and before winter, Greek forces held a quarter of Albania. Mussolini became a laughingstock.

However much he may have resented his impetuous partner's ill-judged and ill-timed expedition into Greece, Hitler realized he could not sit idly by and see Italy defeated. The symbol of Axis power would be shattered, so as early as November, he ordered General Halder to examine the problem of sending troops to support the Italians in Greece and in Africa. But nothing could be done before spring.

And in the spring, Hitler had more important fish to fry—the invasion of Russia.

It is impossible not to speculate that Mussolini's ludicrous attack on Greece may have cost the Axis the war. It sucked German forces into the Mediterranean and delayed the attack on Russia for a month. With an additional month of campaigning in 1941, Germany *might* have brought Russia to her knees. It was a near-run thing as it was, to paraphrase Wellington on the Battle of Waterloo.

Another humiliation lay in store for Mussolini before his cup was full for the year.

The main Italian naval base at Taranto at the heel of the Italian boot was ideally situated to threaten Malta and convoys bound there from Alexandria. Shaped something like a figure 8 on its side, it had an outer and an inner harbor, the Mar Grande and the Mar Piccolo. Here were stationed the main elements of the Italian fleet, except for the rare occasions when they went to sea.

Since he could not get the Italian Navy to come out and fight, Admiral Cunningham decided to hit them where they lay. Now that he had the *Illustrious,* he could strike them by a surprise air attack, the first such carrier raid in the history of naval warfare.*

Originally he hoped to conduct the raid on October 21, in honor of Trafalgar Day,† but a fire on the hangar deck of the *Illustrious* delayed matters. The attack was then set for November 11. It was to consist of strikes from the two carriers *Illustrious* and *Eagle,* but, at the last moment, the *Eagle* broke down as a result of too many near misses in the last months and had to be left behind. It was a

---

* The U.S. Navy had conducted such carrier attacks on Panama and Pearl Harbor as exercises during fleet problems in the Thirties.

† A British fleet under Admiral Nelson defeated the combined French and Spanish fleets off Cape Trafalgar on October 21, 1805.

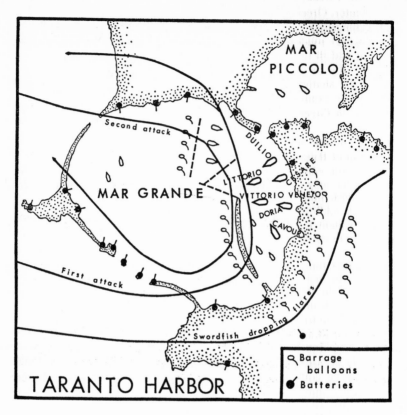

Attack on Taranto, November 11–12, 1940.

bitter disappointment, for the *Eagle* had borne the brunt of the war from the beginning, and her pilots were more experienced than those of the *Illustrious*. But not more skilled, the *Illustrious* pilots maintained.

To enable the *Eagle* to take part, however, 5 of her bombers and 8 air crews were transferred to the *Illustrious*. On November 6, the Mediterranean Fleet left Alexandria. While the *Illustrious* and her escorts were to raid Taranto, the rest would sweep through the Strait of Otranto, where they came upon a small convoy bound for Brindisi. They destroyed 3 of the 4 ships. The two escorting Italian destroyers deserted their charges and fled when one of them was hit.

This little episode was as nothing compared to what was happening at Taranto.

As the *Illustrious* moved to her launch point, there were some scares and alarms. On November 8, seven Italian bombers attacked the fleet. The *Illustrious* promptly scrambled her fighters and succeeded in shooting down two of the intruders, driving the others away.

When the flight leader, Lieutenant Commander C. L. G. Evans, returned to the carrier, he was summoned to the bridge. Wondering what was up, he climbed the endless succession of ladders leading from the flight deck to the pilot house.

"Very good show, Charles," congratulated Captain Denis Boyd, when Evans reached the bridge.

"Oh, I didn't do anything, sir," replied Evans. "My other two chaps shot them down."

Up the long climb came Evans's wingmates.

"I hear you're to be congratulated," said Boyd when the fliers appeared.

"It wasn't us, sir," was the reply. "The C.O. shot them down."

Modesty aside, the pilots managed to keep the Italian bombers at a respectable distance.

Aerial photographs showed that Taranto Harbor would be a tough nut to crack. There were antiaircraft defenses, and the ships were protected with torpedo nets. In addition, the air was filled with barrage balloons, intended to entrap any aircraft which might dive-bomb or make a torpedo attack. But most interesting were the ships. In the outer harbor, Mar Grande, were 5 of Italy's 6 serviceable battleships. In Mar Piccolo were several cruisers and destroyers.

On the afternoon of November 11, an RAF plane from Malta flew over Taranto and took photographs. When these had been interpreted, word was passed to Rear Admiral A. Lumley St. G. Lyster: the sixth battleship had come into the harbor. All the lambs were in the fold.

And the wolf was approaching fast.

The Italians had had a busy day. During the previous night, strong gusts of wind had blown down 60 of the barrage balloons, and they had worked all day to get them back. By the time night fell, 27 of them were in the air. Tomorrow would be time enough for the rest.

Aboard the ships of the Italian fleet, the men had had their hands full. They had had gunnery drills. And then they had sweated and strained at rigging and unrigging the torpedo nets. They left them unrigged. To set them in place again would be the job for tomorrow.

That night there were air-raid alarms. The first one came around 8 o'clock, and the crews went to their battle stations. When nothing had happened by 8:30, the All Clear was sounded.

Back to their battle stations they went at 9 o'clock for another thirty minutes. At 10:25 noises of aircraft were heard again, and the men wearily manned their guns once again. Just as the noise of planes was fading out, another sound could be heard from the south and southeast.

This time it was real. This time it was the first wave of aircraft from the *Illustrious*.

By 8 P.M., the *Illustrious* and her escorts had arrived at the launch point 170 miles southeast of Taranto. The aircraft had been checked and rechecked. The guns were loaded, and flares, bombs, and torpedoes were on board. The visibility was good, with a light breeze and a three-quarter moon high in the sky.

Zero hour arrived. The *Illustrious* swung into the wind. On her flight deck propellers were ticking over as the 12 pilots of the first wave watched for the signal to go.

High in the island of the carrier a green light glowed. Now! Lieutenant Commander Kenneth Williamson, in charge of the first attack, pushed forward the throttle of his Swordfish. The plane lumbered down the flight deck, dipped below the level of the bows, and then clawed for altitude. Eleven other aircraft followed, one by one.

Fifty minutes later, the second wave flew off, 8 Swordfish this time. There were supposed to have been 9, but the last one had an accident to its wing tip and was sent below to the hangar deck.

Two angry, determined men raced to the bridge. Lieutenant Going, the pilot, faced Captain Boyd.

"Sir, we must go to Taranto."

"But, my dear fellow," said Boyd, "you've smashed your bleeding aircraft."

"We can repair the damage in ten minutes if you'll let us go, sir. I know we'll catch up with the others."

Captain Boyd thought a moment. Then he told them to put it up to the Admiral.

Admiral Lyster needed little persuasion. "Well, you're flying the bloody aircraft," he said. "All right, off you go!"

And so, thirty minutes after the second wave had gone, an unofficial third wave consisting of Swordfish L5F set off for the Italian base. And it got there.

By this time, the 12 planes of the first wave were nearing Taranto. Lieutenant Scarlett, in the rear seat of Williamson's leading Swordfish, looked down and said briefly, "There's Taranto."

Two of the planes peeled off and flew to the east of the harbor, dropping flares to silhouette the Italian ships. Others dropped bombs on the oil storage tanks and gun emplacements.

That left 6 Swordfish to attack the Italian battleships. Williamson led the way, passing unscathed between the barrage balloons. In fact, he never saw the cables. Doctrine called for the torpedoes to be dropped from an altitude of 150 feet, but too many things might go wrong at that height. Williamson decided to go lower.

All around him antiaircraft fire was rising to meet the British planes, but it was mostly inaccurate. Williamson decided that he was low enough at 30 feet, and he let the torpedo go. He must have been lower than he thought, for he flew into the splash of water made by the impact of the torpedo. Then his engine quit, victim of an antiaircraft gun. The plane went into the water.

In a few minutes, Williamson and Scarlett were in the wardroom of an Italian destroyer, drinking rum to take off the chill of their swim. They learned they had hit the battleship *Cavour*.

Their squadron mates were doing well, too. When the first wave withdrew, the *Cavour* had been hit by one torpedo and the *Littorio* by two.

Shortly afterwards the second wave came in. Again flares were dropped, and again the harbor was bombed. The torpedo attacks put two more torpedoes into the *Littorio* and one in the *Duilio*.

Then came Going's "third wave." He had no luck with his bombs, but he was able to get a good look at the harbor before heading for the waiting carrier. He reported two of the battleships listing badly and a third down by the bows.

The *Illustrious* recovered her chicks and turned back toward Alexandria. Only two aircraft had been lost in the raid, and when photographs were taken by Malta-based aircraft the next day, the British could hardly believe them. Three of the battleships had sunk at their moorings. In one stroke, 21 obsolescent Swordfish had knocked out half of Italy's battleships.

The *Littorio* and *Duilio* were raised and repaired, returning to service some six months later. The *Cavour* was out of the war.

The best result from Cunningham's viewpoint was that the other 3 battleships were sailed to Naples. This move put them far from the crucial areas where they were needed. They would be hard put to interfere with Malta convoys henceforward.

Cunningham's signal to the *Illustrious* on her return to Alexandria was a masterpiece of British understatement. By flag hoist the flag-ship signaled: *"Illustrious,* maneuver well executed."

* * *

On October 22, General Sir Archibald Wavell reached into a desk drawer and pulled out an order instructing Major General Richard O'Connor to carry out "a five-day raid" on the Italian positions at Sidi Barrani.

O'Connor is the forgotten man of the desert war in North Africa. Even when he was winning spectacular victories, he never got the credit he deserved; all the glory went to Wavell or to Lieutenant General H. M. (Jumbo) Wilson. But neither Wavell nor Wilson commanded the troops in the field. Neither carried out the actual maneuvers. O'Connor did.

Confronted with Wavell's directive for a "five-day raid," O'Connor went to work on plans. He rejected Wavell's suggestion for a sweep with his tanks around the Italian southern flank. "This was the obvious way from the map," noted O'Connor, "but the ground to the south of the enemy positions was quite unsuitable for tanks, so it was not considered."

As O'Connor studied the Italian positions around Sidi Barrani, he noted that they were grouped roughly in two main areas, with a main force from Sidi Barrani on the coast to Nibeiwa some 15 miles inland. Then there was a pocket at Sofafi, 20 to 30 miles southwest. Here O'Connor saw his opportunity. He would drive between Nibeiwa and Sofafi, thus cutting the enemy in two. Then he would head for the sea north to Sidi Barrani and northwest to Buq Buq in hopes of entrapping large numbers of the Italian forces in his enveloping movement. It was a good plan, and it worked.

Rommel was later to imitate it twice.

On December 9, 1940, as soon as it was fully daylight, the British guns began. At the same time, British tanks began to move to envelop Nibeiwa. The Italians were caught by surprise, and some isolated units quickly surrendered. Others put up a stiff resistance. An Italian camp commander was shot down while he was firing a machine gun. He had rushed out so quickly that he was still in his pajamas.

Nothing could stop O'Connor's Western Desert Force. Certainly not the Italians. Everything went according to schedule, and the reports of success came to O'Connor headquarters by the moment. One young officer advised that his column had "reached the second B in Buq Buq."

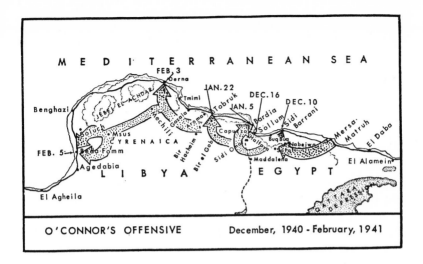

By the evening of December 11, it was all over. The "five-day raid" had turned into a major victory. O'Connor had ended the Italian threat to Egypt, routed the Italian armies, captured 38,000 enemy troops, including 4 generals, and had taken 73 tanks and 237 guns. British losses had been 624, killed, wounded, and missing in action. And O'Connor had started the campaign with only 36,000 men.

The next day, nearly half of his strength was taken from him to mount an attack on Eritrea. O'Connor could pursue the beaten enemy with what he had left.

He lost no time. Pressing on with the Fourth Armoured Brigade on the high escarpment to the south and the Seventh Armoured Brigade on the coastal road, O'Connor pursued the Italians into the fortress town of Bardia. The Fourth Armoured made a wide swing to the west and blocked the two possible escape routes from Bardia, the Trigh Capuzzo and the Via Balbia. Into Bardia hustled 45,000 Italians and their commander, General Bergonzoli, known as "Electric Whiskers." There they were inspired by a message from Mussolini:

I HAVE GIVEN YOU A DIFFICULT TASK, BUT ONE WELL SUITED TO YOUR COURAGE AND EXPERIENCE AS AN OLD AND INTREPID SOLDIER—THE TASK OF DEFENDING BARDIA TO THE LAST.

In rhetoric to match his master's, Bergonzoli replied:

I AM AWARE OF THE HONOR AND I HAVE TODAY RE-
PEATED TO MY TROOPS YOUR MESSAGE—SIMPLE AND
UNEQUIVOCAL. IN BARDIA WE ARE AND HERE WE STAY.

"Electric Whiskers" stayed four weeks. Then his men came out—
as prisoners. He made good his escape to the west. O'Connor had to
wait three weeks to build up his supplies. To replace the Fourth Indian Division he had lost, he was given the understrength Sixth
Australian Division, which was equipped largely with weapons left
over from World War I. He made good use of the Aussies and their
museum-piece ordnance.

On the early morning of January 3, 1941, O'Connor attacked. All
the previous night his tanks had been roaring up and down outside
Bardia, their mufflers removed to add to the noise and deceive the
Italians on the size of the attacking force. O'Connor actually had less
than half the strength of Bergonzoli. The fleet supported the attack,
and after two days of fighting, Bardia fell. O'Connor swept into his
bag another 40,000 prisoners, 400 guns, 100 tanks, and over 700
trucks.

The "five-day raid" was losing none of its magic.

The next target was Tobruk.

But there was a danger to O'Connor's campaign, a danger greater
than anything the Italians could offer. Churchill proposed to take his
army away from him.

From the moment Mussolini had invaded Greece, Churchill, whose
emotions sometimes got the better of his strategic sense, was determined to send British troops to fight alongside the Greeks. There was
only one place where such troops were available, and that was in the
African desert. These were the ones currently engaged in thrashing
the Italians soundly.

Fortunately for the situation in the Western Desert, the Greek
Prime Minister, General Metaxas, would have nothing to do with a
British Expeditionary Force in Greece. In his view, it would only invite the Germans to join the Italians. So, for the moment, Churchill
had to drop the idea, and O'Connor was allowed to proceed. But
early in the new year, it became increasingly obvious that Germany
would have to intervene. He could not afford to let Mussolini be defeated ignominiously. He began to move troops to Bulgaria and
Yugoslavia.

Churchill began to think about Greece again. His minutes to the

Chiefs of Staff and his telegrams to General Wavell begin to sound an insistent note. Two days after the fall of Bardia, he minuted to the Chiefs of Staff: "Although perhaps by luck and daring,"—he seems unconscious of O'Connor's brilliant generalship—"we may collect comparatively easily most delectable prizes on the Libyan shore, the massive importance of . . . keeping the Greek front in being must weigh hourly with us."

Five days later, he was telegraphing Wavell: NOTHING MUST HAMPER CAPTURE OF TOBRUK, BUT THEREAFTER ALL OPERATIONS IN LIBYA ARE SUBORDINATED TO AIDING GREECE. . . . WE EXPECT AND REQUIRE PROMPT AND ACTIVE COMPLIANCE WITH OUR DECISIONS, FOR WHICH WE BEAR FULL RESPONSIBILITY.

O'Connor's offensive was living on borrowed time. It was up to him to make the most of it. And make the most of it he did.

January 20 was O'Connor's selected day for the attack on Tobruk, but at the last moment, his commanders asked for an additional twenty-four hours to work on their tanks. Only a dozen of the big tanks were left, but there were a good number of medium ones and those captured from the Italians. O'Connor readily agreed to the delay, and when the assault on Tobruk began the morning of January 21, some of the Italians were captured before they woke up to the fact that they were under attack. The remainder fought gamely, but they were overwhelmed by the afternoon of January 22. Once again, O'Connor had the problem of dealing with large masses of prisoners. This time there were only 25,000, and with them they had brought some 200 guns, 23 medium tanks, 200 trucks, and enough food to feed the Italian garrison for two months. Best of all for the British offensive was a plant capable of distilling some 40,000 gallons of water daily.

And the British offensive was going on. Even before Tobruk fell, the Seventh Armoured Division was rolling westward toward Mechili. Though Churchill's eyes might be on Greece, O'Connor's were on the next great prize, Benghazi.

The British Chiefs of Staff agreed, and Wavell was authorized to move on Benghazi. O'Connor's offensive was still directing strategy, in spite of Churchill's fuming.

But O'Connor could not move at once. He had the thorny problem of supplies. By improvisation and ingenuity, aided by naval help in opening the port of Tobruk, O'Connor kept the delays to a minimum. In three days he was ready to move, following up the thrust of the

Seventh Armoured Division, now reduced to little more than brigade strength.

He was moving into a very different sort of terrain from that he had traversed. In the squat peninsula outlined by Tobruk, Derna, Benghazi, and Agheila, lie the Jebel Achdar—the Green Mountains. Here there is ample water; the region seems to be a bit of transplanted Greece or Italy. White houses dot the area, most with their own olive groves and gardens. South of the Jebel Achdar are desert wastes for a thousand miles. O'Connor's plan was simple and daring. He proposed to send the Sixth Australian Division along the coastal road, the Via Balbia, through Derna and on to Benghazi. His armor would strike out boldly from its inland base at Mechili, across the base of the peninsula through Msus to reach Beda Fomm and Sidi Saleh, south of Benghazi on the Via Balbia. In this way he hoped to trap the rest of the Italian army in Cyrenaica.

He would have to work fast, for already Marshal Graziani, Governor General of Libya, and Commander in Chief of Italian forces in Africa, gave the orders to evacuate all of Cyrenaica and build up the strength around Sirte for the defense of Tripolitania. He well knew that if the British took the main port of Tripoli, the Italian position in North Africa would be untenable.

British intelligence got wind of the Italian plan, and O'Connor fretted that the Italians might be able to get away from him. He had no desire simply to pursue a retiring enemy as Montgomery was to do after the Battle of El Alamein in late 1942. O'Connor was seeking a battle of annihilation.

Before he could close his trap, O'Connor had to take Derna. This was a natural strongpoint, protected by a wadi—a dry river bed—which in places had a vertical drop of some 800 feet. He hoped to use the attack on Mechili to open a gateway to Derna from the south, but the Italians escaped and entered the fortress. O'Connor had to wait. With all the Italian forces in Derna, he could not make a frontal assault.

As it turned out, he did not have to. The Italians were already pouring out of Derna along the Via Balbia, falling back on Benghazi. Derna fell on January 30, and O'Connor would have to act quickly, or his prey would escape the jaws of the trap he planned to close.

It was time to move. Major General Michael Creagh, commanding the Seventh Armoured Division, got his marching orders. With only 50 medium and 95 light tanks, he was to set out across the desert wastes south of the Jebel Achdar, through completely unreconnoitered country, to reach the sea south of Benghazi. The distance was 150 miles, and the only thing O'Connor and Creagh knew about the terrain was that it was reputed to be bad.

Creagh had a very bad sore throat, but that did not depress his spirits. At dawn on February 4, the move began. The going was rough, even rougher than had been expected. It was slog through soft sand strewn with boulders. Yet they went on, with good spirit.

Off we went across the unknown country in full cry [wrote General Creagh later]. It was definitely exciting and the Division pushing on and on across the desert was a stimulating sight. Some of this desert was very rough and slowed us up; so I sent a wheeled column ahead which was faster than the tracked tanks. This column was to get on to the coast road and hold up any retreating forces until the main body of the Division could go into action.

While Creagh's men were making the terrible march, the Italians were falling back on Benghazi along the coast road. But they did not expect to stop. They were hell-bent for Tripolitania and would get there unless Creagh could cut them off. They were being speeded on their way by Major General Sir Iven Mackey's Sixth Australian Division.

During the evening of February 4, after a conference with Wavell, O'Connor set forth in a staff car, accompanied by Brigadier E. E. Dorman-Smith, a member of his staff. As they drove through the night, they kept coming upon disabled and abandoned British tanks. Creagh had had none too many to start with, and he was losing them mile by mile. A worried O'Connor turned to Dorman-Smith.

"My God, do you think it's going to be all right?" he exclaimed anxiously.

But things were all right. After 50 miles or so, the going got better, and the motorized column under Colonel Combe sped through Msus and on toward Antelat. Air reconnaissance showed the need for haste, for the Italians were close—very close. Would the trap close in time?

At about 10:30 the following morning, Combe reached Antelat and immediately sent forces west and southwest to Beda Fomm and Sidi Saleh. They arrived just at noon and blocked the road. Just half an hour later, men watching the Via Balbia saw the vanguard of the Italian column coming down from the north. O'Connor's trap had closed with just thirty minutes to spare.

It was not yet a very strong trap. With the few men who had arrived, the Italians could have punched their way through easily.

But when the British guns opened up, the Italians took cover, allowing Creagh to reinforce the position at Beda Fomm and also to send a column behind the Italians at Solluch.

The annihilation battle lasted less than forty-eight hours. At 9 o'clock on the morning of February 7, 1941, the Italians surrendered. There was no escape for "Electric Whiskers" Bergonzoli this time. Later in the day, O'Connor paid a visit to the villa where the senior Italian officers were confined and asked to see the senior general. Bergonzoli appeared, resplendent in shining uniform and glittering spurs. He towered over his captor, who was dressed in his usual campaign clothes, corduroy trousers, leather jacket, a scarf with tartan, and only his red-banded cap to show his rank.

"I'm sorry you are so uncomfortable," said O'Connor diffidently in Italian. "We haven't had time to make proper arrangements."

"Thank you very much," replied "Electric Whiskers" politely. "We do realize you came here in a very great hurry."

Once again O'Connor counted his booty. He had captured another 20,000 men, over 100 medium tanks, more than 200 guns and 1500 trucks and other vehicles.

He had driven the Italians out of Egypt. He had driven the Italians out of Cyrenaica. The way to Tripoli lay open.

But it was not to be. While he was waiting for permission to go ahead, O'Connor made his position secure by taking El Agheila on the border of Tripoli. He was poised to go on. Rommel wrote later, "Graziani's army had virtually ceased to exist. All that remained of it was a few lorry columns and hordes of unarmed soldiers in full flight to the west. . . . If Wavell [Like most historians, Rommel fails to credit O'Connor with his accomplishments] had now continued his advance into Tripolitania, no resistance worthy of the name could have been mounted against him—so well had his superbly planned offensive succeeded."

Wavell urged Churchill to permit him to send O'Connor against Tripoli. But Churchill had his eyes on Greece. Metaxas had died, and his successor, Alexander Koryzis, accepted the British offers of help. From that moment, the drive into Tripolitania was dead. In spite of the professional advice of his military advisers, Churchill insisted the matter was a political one.

On February 13, O'Connor learned that his magnificent offensive was at an end. In his 10-week-long campaign, he had advanced 500 miles, taken 130,000 prisoners, destroyed an army of 10 divisions, taken two major fortresses, and seized 400 tanks and 1290 guns.

The British forces had never been larger than 40,000 men, and their losses had been 476 killed, 1225 wounded, and 43 missing.

And now, this glittering success was to be thrown away to send troops uselessly into Greece. The desert war would go on for two years more. There would no longer be a comic opera aspect to it, for it would become professional, and the British would have to learn the ways of desert fighting all over again if they were to recover the positions Churchill's decisions had cast away.

O'Connor's well-trained veterans were dissipated. Some were scattered among other units. Others found themselves boarding transports en route to Greece. Cyrenaica was to be held by a garrison force. This would be adequate against a demoralized Italian army.

But it was no longer a demoralized Italian army that stood in the wastes of Tripolitania.

On February 12, 1941, a relatively obscure German Major General arrived in Tripoli. His name was Erwin Rommel. He was to be followed by crack German soldiers who would make up the Afrika Korps.

Although he did not yet know it, Hitler had sent the first team to Africa.

* * *

Mussolini still had more crow to eat. His magnificent conquests in East Africa were about to be taken from him.

In Kenya, General Sir Alan Cunningham, brother of the Commander in Chief of the British Mediterranean Fleet, had some 70,000 troops, largely Africans with British officers. The defenders in Italian Somaliland were considerably stronger, but Cunningham, like his brother, was not one to be daunted. On February 10, 1941, his men crossed the border, and four days later captured the seaport of Kismayu. Thirty thousand Italian troops were routed, killed, or captured, or they took to their heels.

This success was only the beginning of his campaign. Pushing on without delay, Cunningham took the main seaport of Mogadishu, finding there a vast treasure trove of military supplies, including more than 400,000 gallons of gasoline.

Turning inland into Abyssinia, he made a forced march of 740 miles to Jijiga, which he took on St. Patrick's Day. In a remarkably short space of time, all of British Somaliland was freed of Italians, and he was ready to begin operations to restore Emperor Haile Selassie to his throne.

In these operations, he had support from the north. General Sir W. Platt, commanding British forces in the Sudan, smashed into Eritrea and captured Asmara on April 1 and the principal Italian naval base at Massawa on April 8. He not only took 10,000 prisoners, but he eliminated Italian naval power by seizing their only base. The Royal Navy enthusiastically cooperated, and quickly accounted for the nine Italian destroyers and eight submarines in the Red Sea. Soon President Roosevelt was able to declare the Red Sea and the Gulf of Aden no longer combat zones. American ships were free to enter those waters and bring supplies to Wavell in Egypt.

Another month of fighting followed in Abyssinia, but on May 5 Emperor Haile Selassie was able to reenter his capital of Addis Ababa. The Italian commander, the Duke of Aosta, was captured twelve days later along with the remnants of his army.

Between them, Cunningham and Platt had liquidated forces four or five times their own strength, had captured 185,000 men, had aided in opening the Red Sea to navigation, and had restored an emperor to his throne.

A few small pockets of resistance held out until near the end of the year, but Mussolini's African Empire was no longer of any consequence, either militarily or politically.

As one correspondent put it in a letter to the editor, *"Sic transit gloria Musso!"*

*   *   *

The United States heavy cruiser *Tuscaloosa* made her way slowly through the sparkling waters of the Caribbean. There was no hurry, for her distinguished passenger was aboard mainly to loaf, read, bask in the sun, and shoot the breeze with his cronies. The President of the United States was getting away from it all.

Ever since his reelection, F.D.R. seemed to have lost interest in everything—the war and domestic politics being no exception. Other than make a major policy decision that Britain and the United States would share American war production on a fifty-fifty basis, he had done little to take advantage of the new mandate the country had given him. The *New York Herald Tribune* complained: "One course more disastrous than having no policy at all is to decide upon a policy and then fail to apply it. The United States has decided upon its policy —all aid to Britain short of war. The time has come to implement it."

When Mr. Roosevelt embarked in the *Tuscaloosa* on December

3, 1940, his critics charged him with fiddling or, rather, fishing, while the world burned. Even his loyal supporters were anxious, for he took none of his experts with him. Accompanying the President were only four men, his military aide, Major General Edwin M. Watson, known as "Pa," his naval aide, Captain Daniel Callaghan, his personal physician, Rear Admiral Ross McIntire, and Harry Hopkins. There were three "pool" reporters, but they had little to report. The President seemed to be spending the days enjoying himself.

The ostensible purpose of the trip was to inspect the bases newly acquired from the British, but these inspection trips were perfunctory. The ship called at Guantanamo Bay and the Presidential party laid in a stock in Cuban cigars. At Eleuthera he received the Duke of Windsor, now Governor General of the Bahamas. The *Tuscaloosa* passed by Martinique, and through binoculars F.D.R. examined the French aircraft carrier *Béarn,* now immobilized, but always a worry in case she might try to return to Europe.

In the evenings, Mr. Roosevelt played poker with his friends or watched the movies. Among the films presented were *Northwest Mounted Police,* starring Gary Cooper, Paulette Goddard, and Madeleine Carroll; *They Knew What They Wanted,* with Charles Laughton and Carole Lombard; *I Love You Again,* with William Powell and Myrna Loy; the lengthy *Arizona,* with Jean Arthur and William Holden. Generously the crew gave up their own favorite, *Tin Pan Alley,* which starred Alice Faye, Betty Grable, and Jack Oakie.

The fishing was not very good. Harry Hopkins hooked a 20-pound grouper but had to get Dr. McIntire to haul it in for him. F.D.R. didn't have much luck, even though Ernest Hemingway sent a radio message telling of his own favorite spot and advising the best lure for the fish.

This kind of interlude was often necessary for Roosevelt, a kind of recharging of the batteries, or, as Henry Hopkins put it, a "refueling." Roosevelt had worked hard all summer, worrying over the fate of Britain and France, trying to keep his own domestic programs going in face of the peril across the sea. Then had come the campaign for the Third Term, which had taken more out of him than anyone realized. His fatigue showed in his lack-luster performance in the month since his reelection.

It was just as well that he was able to have this "refueling" period, for just ahead of him lay some of the hardest decisions of his career.

Every so often, a Navy seaplane would land near the *Tuscaloosa* to deliver mail. Even on vacation, the President of the United States can never completely relax. There is legislation to be signed or vetoed. There are state documents which must have his signature. There are intelligence reports his eyes must see. These duties cannot be delegated. Only one man can perform them, the President, whether he is on vacation or not.

The seaplane which arrived on the morning of December 9 looked no different from any of the others. But it carried a letter from the British Prime Minister, a letter which Churchill later described as "one of the most important I ever wrote."

It was a very long document, and it analyzed Britain's position in the war with a frankness that is nearly unparalleled in history. These were state secrets being freely set forth to the President. Yet Churchill knew they would not be misused. He set forth the plans Britain had for carrying on the war and the demands on American production that would be necessary. "Only the United States can supply this need."

Near the end of the letter came the real squeeze. Britain was running out of cash. Under terms of the Cash and Carry Policy, Britain had to pay in dollars for every bullet, every rifle, every plane, every tank, every ship she received from the United States. It would not be long before Britain reached the limit of her ability to pay.

Last of all [wrote Churchill], I come to the question of Finance. The more rapid and abundant the flow of munitions and ships which you are able to send us, the sooner will our dollar credits be exhausted. They are already, as you know, very heavily drawn upon by the payments we have made to date. Indeed, as you know, the orders already placed or under negotiation, including the expenditure settled or pending for creating munitions factories in the United States, many times exceed the total exchange resources remaining at the disposal of Great Britain. The moment approaches when we shall no longer be able to pay cash for shipping and other supplies. While we will do our utmost, and shrink from no proper sacrifice to make payments across the Exchange, I believe you will agree that it would be wrong in principle and mutually disadvantageous in effect if at the height of this struggle Great Britain were to be divested of all saleable assets, so that after victory was won with our blood, civilisation saved, and the time gained for the United States to be fully armed against all eventualities, we should stand stripped to the bone. Such a course would not be in the moral or economic interests of either of our countries. . . .

You may be certain that we shall prove ourselves ready to suffer and sacrifice to the utmost for the Cause, and that we glory in being its champions. The rest we leave with confidence to you and to your people, being sure that ways and means will be found which future generations on both sides of the Atlantic will approve and admire.

If, as I believe, you are convinced, Mr. President, that the defeat of the Nazi and Fascist tyranny is a matter of high consequence to the people of the United States and to the Western Hemisphere, you will regard this letter not as an appeal for aid, but as a statement of the minimum action necessary to achieve our common purpose.

Hopkins later told Churchill that the President took no one into his confidence on the contents of the letter. Instead, he sat alone in his deck chair and re-read the document time after time. He was trying to make up his mind.

It was at this crucial juncture in the war that at the time when Britain was putting all her cards on the table and calling upon America either to put up or shut up, her ambassador, Lord Lothian, died.

Lord Lothian had been a particularly effective ambassador, for he understood the American political system better than most Americans. Most Englishmen, brought up in the British tradition of party discipline, could not see why Mr. Roosevelt could not simply call for any program he desired and have it loyally followed in Congress. Lord Lothian knew better, and he was much missed in the months ahead.

Roosevelt promptly sent a message of condolence to King George, and the next day the *Tuscaloosa* headed for home. Roosevelt was still brooding over Churchill's letter, but he gave no sign to the reporters aboard or even to his friends.

When the ship reached Charleston, South Carolina, the President and his party disembarked and went to Warm Springs, where F.D.R. ate turkey with the young polio victims. He was saying nothing to newsmen. As he boarded his special train for the trip back to Washington, he promised to return next "March, without any question, if the world survives."

On December 17, looking tanned and fit, Roosevelt held a news conference. His ideas had solidified, and he was preparing to put his prestige on the line. And it was a bold course he was proposing.

He began archly with his usual statement, "I don't think there is any particular news." This got its customary laugh. Then he got down to business. "There is," he said, "absolutely no doubt in the mind of a very overwhelming number of Americans that the best immediate defense of the United States is the success of Britain in defending herself." He began to lay his foundation by dismissing two ideas no one had proposed: that the United States lend money to England so

369

that she could buy war goods, or that the United States simply give the materials away. These ideas Roosevelt described as "banal." Neither one would ever have got out of a Congressional committee, and well the President knew it.

"Now, what I am trying to do," he went on, "is eliminate the dollar sign. That is something brand-new in the thoughts of everybody in this room, I think—get rid of the silly, foolish, old dollar sign."

This was a brand-new idea, and everyone wondered how he proposed to go about it. Mr. Roosevelt proceeded to tell them.

> Suppose my neighbor's home catches fire, and I have a length of garden hose four or five hundred feet away. If he can take my garden hose and connect it up with his hydrant, I may help him to put out his fire. Now, what do I do? I don't say to him before that operation, "Neighbor, my garden hose cost me fifteen dollars; you have to pay me fifteen dollars for it." What is the transaction that goes on? I don't want fifteen dollars. I want my garden hose back after the fire is over.

With this simple analogy, Roosevelt stated the idea of Lend-Lease. Many observers have stated that this inspired parable won the victory for it, since it was one that obviously made sense to the American people as a whole. If he had dealt with abstractions, the Lend-Lease Bill might have had rocky times ahead.

Four days after Christmas, Roosevelt took the case for Lend-Lease to the country in a Fireside Chat. Roosevelt wrote a good deal of this speech himself, for it was the first time since midsummer that he had felt he could really let himself go. He was not buying votes this time. He was speaking as a man who had a vital program to sell, a program he believed essential to the survival of the democratic powers of the world.

"This is not a fireside chat on war," began the President. "It is a talk on national security. . . ."

He ran over the crises America had faced in the past. This was the greatest in American history. "Never before since Jamestown and Plymouth Rock has our American civilization been in such danger as now."

Facing the issue directly, after a description of the Nazi aim of world domination, Mr. Roosevelt continued:

> If Great Britain goes down, the Axis powers will control the continents of Europe, Asia, Africa, Australasia, and the high seas—and they will be in a position to bring enormous military and naval resources against this hemisphere. It is no exaggeration to say that all

of us, in all the Americas, would be living at the point of a gun—a gun loaded with explosive bullets, economic as well as military.

We should enter upon a new and terrible era in which the whole world, our hemisphere included, would be run by threats of brute force. To survive in such a world, we would have to convert ourselves permanently into a militaristic power on the basis of war economy. . . .

Some nations of Europe were bound by solemn non-intervention pacts with Germany. Other nations were assured by Germany that they need *never* fear invasion. Non-intervention pact or not, the fact remains that they *were* attacked, overrun and thrown into the modern form of slavery at an hour's notice, or even without any notice at all. . . .

The fate of these nations tells us what it means to live at the point of a Nazi gun. . . .

The President then turned his big artillery on the appeasers, the Woods, the Fords, the Coughlins, the Wheelers, the Lindberghs.

The American appeasers ignore the warning to be found in the fate of Austria, Czechoslovakia, Poland, Norway, Belgium, the Netherlands, Denmark, and France. They tell you that the Axis powers are going to win anyway; that all this bloodshed in the world could be saved; that the United States might just as well throw its influence into the scale of a dictated peace, and get the best out of it that we can.

They call it a "negotiated peace." Nonsense! Is it a negotiated peace if a gang of outlaws surrounds your community and on threat of extermination makes you pay tribute to save your own skins?

Such a dictated peace would be no peace at all. It would be only another armistice, leading to the most gigantic armament race and the most devastating trade wars in all history. And in these contests the Americas would offer the only real resistance to the Axis powers. . . .

After castigating the "unholy alliance" of the Axis powers, he went on to say that the British "are today the spearhead of resistance to world conquest." They were making no demands for an expeditionary force, and the American Government had no plans for one. "You can, therefore, nail any talk about sending armies to Europe as deliberate untruth."

America's role, and its best chance for peace, lay in its productive power, and this production had to be put at the disposal of the British just as much as it had to be put at the disposal of the American Army and Navy. How much will remain at home and how much will go overseas still depend on the military necessities of the moment.

He came to his peroration.

We must be the great arsenal of democracy. For us this is an emergency as serious as war itself. We must apply ourselves to our task with the same resolution, the same sense of urgency, the same spirit of patriotism and sacrifice as we would show were we at war. . . .

I believe that the Axis powers are not going to win this war. I base that belief on the latest and best information.

What "the latest and best information" was, Mr. Roosevelt did not say, and it is as well that he did not, for he had no very cheering information at all. The public knew all the good news. F.D.R. was still keeping Churchill's grim letter to himself and a few selected advisers.

Be that as it may, Roosevelt's Fireside Chat had a remarkable effect on public opinion. The phrase "arsenal of democracy" caught on and was widely quoted, not always approvingly, to be sure.

Hitler tried to drown out the impact of Roosevelt's speech by sending over London one of the heaviest bombing raids of the war. A large part of the City of London, the mile-square financial district which lies in the center of Greater London, was nearly laid to the ground. St. Paul's Cathedral escaped by a miracle. In a cable thanking Roosevelt for the Fireside Chat, Churchill said, "The scenes of widespread destruction here and in our provincial centres are shocking; but when I visited the still-burning ruins today, the spirit of the Londoners was as high as in the first days of the indiscriminate bombing in September, four months ago."

Even the Republican *New York Herald Tribune* called the speech one of the greatest the President had ever made and predicted that if the action was as good as the speech, he would find the Americans unanimous in support of the measures he felt necessary. *The Christian Science Monitor* said that "President Roosevelt's fireside chat . . . clarified and crystallized America's choice, a choice really made long ago."

The Fireside Chat was the second blow in a series of three that F.D.R. threw at the isolationists. The third came in his State of the Union Address delivered to the new Congress on January 6, 1941.

His problem, after the "garden hose" and the "arsenal of democracy," was, what could he do for an encore? The State of the Union message must not be an anticlimax.

As he gripped the lectern and looked out over the faces of the members of the Seventy-Seventh Congress, he must have wondered whether his words would carry the impact he knew they must have. He began quietly enough; it was almost a repetition of the Fireside

Chat. Then he let the isolationists have it once again, right between the eyes.

As a Nation we may take pride in the fact that we are soft-hearted; but we cannot afford to be soft-headed.

We must always be wary of those who with sounding brass and a tinkling cymbal preach the "ism" of appeasement.

We must especially beware of that small group of selfish men who would clip the wings of the American eagle in order to feather their own nests. . . .

After calling for increased production and for national unity, the President looked ahead to the promise of the future, a promise which could be fulfilled if dictatorships could be defeated.

In the future days, which we seek to make secure, we look forward to a world founded upon four essential human freedoms.

The first is freedom of speech and expression—everywhere in the world.

The second is freedom of every person to worship God in his own way—everywhere in the world.

The third is freedom from want—which, translated into world terms, means economic understandings which will secure to every nation a healthy peacetime life for its inhabitants—everywhere in the world.

The fourth is freedom from fear—which, translated into world terms, means a world-wide reduction of armaments to such a point in such a thorough fashion that no nation will be in a position to commit an act of physical aggression against any neighbor—anywhere in the world.

The Champ had done it again. His "Four Freedoms" speech was as highly praised as the Fireside Chat. Its terms have lasted longer, and, although the dream has not yet come true, it expressed an eternal hope of mankind.

The effect of these three major policy statements, all made in a period of less than three weeks, can be measured precisely. Just before the election in November, public opinion polls had shown the country evenly divided on whether to aid Britain even at the risk of war. A week after the State of the Union Address, some 70 percent were willing to risk war in order to aid Britain.

But the question was, would the change in attitude pay off in the Congress, where the Lend-Lease Bill was even then beginning a long and stormy period of gestation?

The Lend-Lease Bill was introduced simultaneously into both

Houses on January 10, 1941. Congressman John W. McCormack of Massachusetts presented it in the House of Representatives, and Senator Alben W. Barkley of Kentucky in the Senate. By a happy but unexplained set of circumstances, it was designated H.R. 1776, for it was what Robert Sherwood later called a "declaration of interdependence."

The bill proposed to place in the hands of the President enormous power to supply American-made arms, ammunition, ships, aircraft, anything and everything, to nations fighting against the Axis. No formal accounting would be kept. The idea was that the Allied nations would give back what they had left at the end of the war. Certainly it got rid of the dollar sign. Many Congressmen were afraid it would get rid of American wealth and substance as well.

As expected, the isolationists cried to the high heavens. Senator Burton K. Wheeler of Montana called H.R. 1776 a "triple-A foreign policy; it will plow under every fourth American boy." This charge made Roosevelt furious. It was, he said, "the most untruthful, the most dastardly, unpatriotic thing that has been said in public life in my generation." He scowled at the attentive reporters.

"Quote me on that!" he snapped.

One of the vocal opponents of the Lend-Lease Bill was the former Ambassador to the Court of St. James, the Honorable Joseph P. Kennedy. In spite of his service in London, Kennedy was still by no means sure that Britain would hold out, and he opposed the blank check embodied in H.R. 1776. He took this attitude even though his second son, John Fitzgerald Kennedy, had recently published a book entitled *Why England Slept*.

In both Houses opposition to the bill rested on two main themes—isolationism and the fear that its passage would commit the United States to war. After all sides had had their say, the bill passed the House of Representatives by a vote of 260 to 165, on February 8, 1941. Exactly a month later it passed the Senate, 60 to 31.

The opposition was more vocal in the Senate than it had been in the House, and it was given academic respectability by the adverse testimony presented by historian Charles A. Beard, who insisted that the title of the bill was "imprecise." It should read, he said:

> All provisions of law and the Constitution to the contrary notwithstanding, an Act to place all the wealth and all the men and women of the United States at the free disposal of the President, to permit him to transfer or carry goods to any foreign government he may be pleased

to designate, anywhere in the world, to authorize him to wage un-declared wars for anybody, anywhere in the world, until the affairs of the world are ordered to suit his policies, and for any other purpose he may have in mind now or at any time in the future, which may be remotely related to the contingencies contemplated in the title of the Act.

The return of Wendell Willkie from a visit to London proved to be a turning point. Willkie had gone over to "see for himself," but he had borne a message from the President to Churchill. Following his testimony, the Senate Foreign Relations Committee cleared the bill. Debate in the Senate dragged on for over two weeks, and Senator Wheeler threatened a filibuster. Mr. Roosevelt wisely kept hands off, and at length the bill came to a vote. Three days later, the House concurred in the Senate amendment by a vote of 317 to 71. The same afternoon the President signed the bill, at the same time sending the British a list of all available weapons and asking them to take their pick.

The Lend-Lease Act is important in many ways. It committed the people of the United States to the Allied cause in an unmistakable way, and it served to draw the two English-speaking nations closer together. But more than Britain's ability to pay was involved. If the United States was committed to the proposition of aiding Britain, then something had to be done to make the aid effective. The under-cover expedients of supplying "test" equipment, of declaring needed equipment "excess," had gone about as far as they could. After the Lend-Lease Act, the issue was faced squarely. Whether it was the right or the wrong decision, the American people, the British people, and, to their shock and dismay, the German and Italian people, knew the policy of the United States Government.

The Lend-Lease Act came just in time. In Europe and in Africa the Germans were about to set the British back on their heels.

CHAPTER FOURTEEN

Mediterranean Meetings

The mountains look on Marathon—
And Marathon looks on the sea;
And musing there an hour alone,
I dream'd that Greece might still be free.
Lord Byron, Don Juan

A DMIRAL SIR ANDREW BROWNE CUNNINGHAM was playing golf. He enjoyed the game, but on this particular afternoon of Thursday, March 27, 1941, it was more than a game. It was a part of a cover plan to keep secret the fact that the Mediterranean Fleet would sail that night. It seems that there was a Japanese consul there in Alexandria who reported every move of the British ships to the Germans and the Italians. Sir Andrew had even carried an overnight bag with him to lull the suspicions of the gentleman from Japan. This time the fleet would be going out unreported.

As he played his game, Cunningham observed the little Japanese on the golf course. He was of an unmistakable shape, short and squat, and with a huge southern exposure when he bent over to putt, so that he had acquired the nickname of "the blunt end of the Axis."

His game over, Cunningham retrieved his suitcase out of sight of the Japanese consul and returned on board the *Warspite*. The fleet sailed at 1900 that evening.

"What the Japanese consul," wrote Cunningham later, "thought and did when he saw the empty harbour next morning was no affair of mine."

There had been an unusual increase in Italian air reconnaissance over Greece and Crete in the previous days. It had even extended to Alexandria. Since it was obvious that the Germans would soon move into Greece, Cunningham was easily able to deduce that the Italian fleet might well be out to cover shipping or troop movements bound for Greece. This could be his opportunity to have another crack at the Italian Navy, which had got off so lightly in the action off Calabria the previous July.

The obvious place for the Mediterranean Fleet was in the waters west of Crete where it could lie in wait to catch the unwary Italians. Bu the increased air reconnaissance would give the game away unless the fleet could slip out undetected and its absence remain unreported for several hours.

Hence, the Admiral played golf.

Hitler was nearly ready to take a hand in the Mediterranean. In January, Italian naval leaders had met with their German opposite numbers at Merano in northern Italy, near the Brenner Pass. The Italian Navy was running short of oil, and it needed German assistance. Since the Germans were about to take over the Mediterranean war, they were prepared to insist that the Italian Navy do something to support the forthcoming drive into Greece. The German method of giving aid was to move in fully equipped units, so that they could eventually subordinate Italian aims to German goals. In February, as the Afrika Korps moved into Tripolitania, the Luftwaffe moved Fliegerkorps X into Sicily.

The Germans did not propose to move naval forces into the Mediterranean at this time. But they did demand that the Italian Navy make a sortie to try to knock out British troop convoys moving O'Connor's veterans to Greece.

Admiral Arturo Riccardi, Commander in Chief of the Italian fleet, was not entirely happy over the proposed operation. Its success lay in the fulfillment of too many things beyond his power to ensure. First, since the operation would take place in waters dominated by the British, he had to have surprise. Then he needed air reconnaissance and air cover. The Italian Navy could provide neither. Mussolini had always vetoed the idea of a carrier, claiming that Italy itself was a gigantic, unsinkable aircraft carrier. The result was that the Italian Air Force had all the planes. It was supposed to cooperate with the navy on request. In practice, it cooperated if it had nothing better to do and when it got around to it.

In view of the political importance assigned to the operation, Admiral Riccardi let his misgivings go by the board. Superaero [the Italian Air High Command] and Fliegerkorps X promised full support. There would be air reconnaissance and air support a-plenty.

When the time came, the Italian ships got absolutely none.

On the evening of March 26, the Italian ships sailed. From Naples came the new battleship *Vittorio Veneto,* a sleek ship mounting nine 15-inch guns. She was fast, having exceeded 30 knots on her trials. She also had a dozen 6-inch guns for close work. With her came 4 destroyers. From Taranto came the First Cruiser Division, consisting of the heavy cruisers *Zara, Pola,* and *Fiume,* escorted by 4 more destroyers. From Brindisi sailed the Eighth Cruiser Division, made up of the light cruisers *Abruzzi* and *Garibaldi.* They had 2 more destroyers with them.

As the *Vittorio Veneto* passed the Strait of Messina, she was joined by the Third Cruiser Division, the heavy cruisers *Trieste, Trento, Bolzano,* and 3 more destroyers. The entire force joined up about 1100 on March 27. The force commander, Admiral Angelo Iachino, did not order a single tight formation. Since the First and Eighth Divisions were to sweep to the north of Crete beginning that night, he let them trail behind, while the Third Division was some miles ahead of the flagship.

About 1220 a British Sunderland patrol plane sighted the 3 cruisers of the Third Division and reported their course and speed. Thus it was not entirely deduction that led Admiral Cunningham to take his fleet to sea that evening. The Italians also heard the report and deciphered the simple aircraft code the British were then using. Supermarina [the Italian Naval High Command] did not call off the operation, but did recall the sweep into the Aegean north of Crete. Thus, the next morning, Iachino had his entire force fairly close together.

On through the night they sped. They hoped the British would have something in their way. They did not reckon that there would be so much.

As the *Warspite* left Alexandria on the evening of March 27, she came too near a mudbank and fouled her condensers. This had the unfortunate effect of reducing her speed from 24 to 20 knots. With the flagship came the battleships *Valiant* and *Barham,* the carrier *Formidable,* which had recently replaced the *Illustrious* in the Mediterranean, and 9 destroyers.

Already a part of Cunningham's force was at sea. Operating in the Aegean was a force of 4 cruisers and 4 destroyers under Vice Admiral H. D. Pridham-Wippell in the *Orion.* Cunningham ordered this force to join him south of Crete. Pridham-Wippell headed on down to the rendezvous and the next morning found himself in a very ticklish

378

situation. Aircraft reported the Italian Third Division, which Pridham-Wippell enthusiastically closed and began to engage at 0812, March 28. Soon, however, further reports from aircraft reported 2 battleships some distance to the northwest. Although the British light forces could deal with the 3 Italian cruisers, there was no sense in taking on even the single battleship that was in the offing.

After nearly an hour of desultory engagement between the British and Italian light forces, the Italians reversed course to fall back on the *Vittorio Veneto*. Pridham-Wippell followed cautiously. Suddenly up ahead there loomed the unmistakable silhouette of the Italian battleship. She opened fire immediately, and the British turned away under a smoke screen.

It was time to get help.

At that time Admiral Cunningham's 3 battleships and 1 carrier were some 45 miles to the east and coming on as hard as they could. But the situation was grim. The *Vittorio Veneto* was capable of 31 knots, and an engineering casualty on the cruiser *Gloucester* of Pridham-Wippell's group had reduced her speed to 24 at best. On one quarter Pridham-Wippell had a battleship firing at him and on the other 3 cruisers. Twisting and turning to avoid shells, the three skippers of the cruisers which could make full speed kept casting glances at their laggard sister. On the *Gloucester,* Captain H. A. Rowley sent for his chief engineer and pointed out the *Vittorio Veneto*. There was no need for words. The engineering force had another try at the engines, and soon the *Gloucester* was making 30 knots through the water.

Cunningham ordered the *Valiant,* his fastest battleship, to rush on alone to support Pridham-Wippell, and soon she began to inch her way toward the head of the formation. It was not to Cunningham's liking to be left behind because of the mud in his condensers. He sent for his Fleet Engineer Officer, Captain (E) B. J. H. Wilkinson, and told him to do something about it. As on the *Gloucester,* necessity accomplished repairs that had seemed impossible. The *Warspite* and *Valiant* sped on together.

The real hope lay in the aircraft of the *Formidable*. Unfortunately for the British, she had to turn back east into the wind to launch her aircraft, so Cunningham sent her off to operate alone. He could not afford to be slowed down.

Flight operations were not the easiest thing in the world for the *Formidable*. Captain A. W. La T. Bisset maneuvered her skillfully,

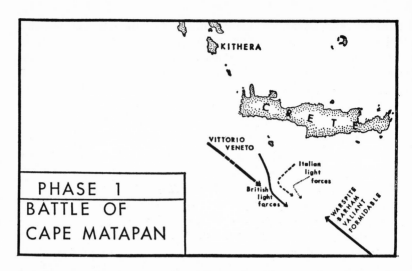

KITHERA

VITTORIO
VENETO

Italian
light
forces

British
light
forces

WARSPITE
BARHAM
VALIANT
FORMIDABLE

PHASE 1
BATTLE OF
CAPE MATAPAN

dodging torpedo-plane attacks while getting his own aircraft into the air. His skill paid off, and the torpedo bombers failed to get a hit.

About 1115, six British Swordfish found the *Vittorio Veneto*. The battleship had to break off from the job of disposing of the British cruisers to defend herself. The pilots of the Swordfish pressed their attacks to a range of 2000 yards and reported one hit on the *Vittorio Veneto*. Athough the report was mistaken, it encouraged Admiral Cunningham, and at 1230 he ordered a second attack.

The Italians were by this time retiring from the fight. The unsuccessful attack of the Swordfish saved the day for Pridham-Wippell and his light forces. He turned around once more toward the west to keep in touch with the retreating Italians.

The second Swordfish attack had no better luck than the first, and it was evident that unless the Italians could be slowed down, they would get clean away. By 1500 the Italian battleship was some 65 miles away and gaining slowly.

Another strike went off from the *Formidable*. This time there were both bombers and torpedo planes, and they made a perfect coordinated attack. First the bombers came over and attracted the attention of the Italian gunners. As the antiaircraft shells soared up into the air, 3 Swordfish came in on the *Vittorio Veneto*. They were so low that they were skimming the water. From three directions at once they launched their torpedoes. Hurriedly corrected antiaircraft fire knocked one Swordfish down, but not before it had released its torpedo from very close range. As the horrified Italians watched, the torpedo came closer and closer to the port quarter. The big ship swung, but not soon enough and not far enough. The torpedo slammed into the port screws. The vessel shuddered to a stop. Over 4000 tons of water came spouting through the hole in the ship's stern, and she began to settle.

Superb damage control stopped the flooding, and after a few minutes the ship was again under control and moving through the water at 10 knots, using the starboard screws only. By late afternoon she had built up her speed to nearly 20 knots and was well on the way to making good her escape.

Aboard the *Warspite,* Cunningham was elated. He hoped to be able to finish off the *Vittorio Veneto* before dark. But as reports kept coming in of her increases in speed, he realized there was no hope of catching her that day. He planned to work around to the northwest to try to get between her and her base at Taranto. Perhaps he could get another crack at her the next morning.

On the flag bridge of the *Vittorio Veneto,* Admiral Iachino was watching the skies anxiously. He had been promised full cooperation from the Italian Air Force and from Luftflotte X. Now, when he needed them, where were the planes? There was nothing to be seen in the skies except the clouds.

Suddenly a lookout reported aircraft. Putting his binoculars on them, Iachino feared the worst. They were coming from the east, not the west. They were British.

Six Swordfish from the *Formidable* and two from Maleme airfield on Crete caught up with the Italian formation and began circling. The British pilots on looking down saw it was going to be tough. Iachino had placed the crippled *Vittorio Veneto* in the center of a formation, guarded on both sides by cruisers and destroyers and by more destroyers ahead and astern. As they flew along, the pilots saw the menacing guns following them implacably.

For an hour the planes stayed out of range, wearing down the nerves of the Italian gunners. The tension mounted on both sides. The sun went down. Still the British planes circled.

Thirty minutes later, they made their move. They broke from their circles and began to weave and sideslip through the air, coming closer and closer. The Italians turned on searchlights to blind the pilots and fired everything that would bear. Torpedoes splashed in the water, and spouts rose from falling bombs. The Italian ships twisted and turned to dodge. Flashes of the guns made it difficult to see what was going on.

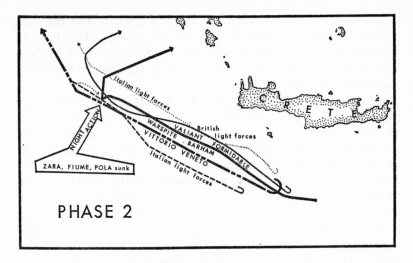

ZARA, FIUME, POLA sunk

NIGHT ACTION

Italian light forces

WARSPITE VALIANT British light forces

VITTORIO VENETO BARHAM FORMIDABLE

Italian light forces

PHASE 2

Admiral Iachino breathed easier when the last of the planes had completed its attack and turned for home. No casualties had been reported. Was it possible that the Italians had escaped unscathed?

Then a report came in. The 10,000-ton heavy cruiser *Pola* had been torpedoed just at the end of the attack and was dead in the water.

About the same time, Supermarina informed Iachino that a British force was about 75 miles from the Italians. For some reason, Iachino believed the British units were destroyers. Instead, it was Pridham-Wippell's group of cruisers and destroyers, and not far behind, Cunningham's 3 battleships were racing to catch up.

Iachino had no certain knowledge that the British battleship force was at sea. He assumed that if it had been, it had turned back to Alexandria. There was no reason for this assumption, but he made it and based his decisions on it. These decisions were to cost him three cruisers.

The *Pola* belonged to Admiral Cattaneo's First Division, and he requested permission to send 2 destroyers to look after the cripple. On his assumption that there was nothing more than a destroyer or two to worry about, Admiral Iachino ordered Cattaneo to go and see for himself, taking his other 2 cruisers, the *Zara* and *Fiume,* and the destroyers *Alfiere, Carducci, Oriani,* and *Gioberti* with him. There was justification for having a flag officer on the scene, for he would be the one to make the decision on whether the *Pola* could be saved or should be scuttled.

Back sped the 6 Italian ships to look after their stricken sister. Admiral Cattaneo must have been convinced, just as Admiral Iachino was, that the British ships were far away, for he proceeded in column formation, the cruisers leading. He thus had no screen to protect him from submarine attack or to give him warning of the presence of surface ships.

He got away with it, however, and reached the *Pola* at 2225.

But he was not alone.

Admiral Cunningham had no reliable information on the results of the last air strike against the Italians. He believed that the *Vittorio Veneto* was more seriously damaged than she was. His hunting instinct was up, and everything urged him to catch her and finish her off. But he also knew that it would be dangerous to forge on ahead with his 3 battleships in the dark with little protection from his light forces. If he had been in Iachino's position, he would have sent every destroyer and cruiser he had against an enemy battle fleet. He proceeded to have dinner while he thought it over.

He decided to take a chance. He ordered destroyers to pursue the retiring enemy at high speed, keeping only 4 to protect the battleships and the *Formidable*.

On they sped through the night. He believed the Italian fleet was about 33 miles away, making good some 15 knots. Actually Iachino was considerably farther away and was making close to 20. Although Cunningham did not know it, there was no hope of catching the *Vittorio Veneto* before she got under the umbrella of short-range bombers and fighters from southern Italy.

At 2103 the *Ajax,* veteran of the *Graf Spee* battle, and now a part of Pridham-Wippell's cruiser group, made radar contact on a stopped Italian ship, which was duly reported to Cunningham in the *Warspite*. The stopped ship was, of course, the *Pola,* but excitement was high in the British flagship that it might be the stricken *Vittorio Veneto*. Cunningham directed Pridham-Wippell to pursue the fleeing Italians at high speed; the *Warspite, Valiant,* and *Barham* would see to the cripple, whatever it might be.

Altering course slightly to port, Admiral Cunningham peered ahead, trying to catch sight of something in the dark. The moments passed. Then, at 2210, the *Valiant* picked up a target on her radar. It was a large ship, over 600 feet in length, according to the radar operators. Could it be the *Vittorio Veneto?* wondered the British. She was only 6 miles away.

The British altered course 40 degrees to port to close. All 3 battleships were at action stations, their guns trained on the correct bearing.

The minute hands of the ships' clocks crept around to 2225. Suddenly the Chief of Staff, Commodore John Edelsten, spoke quietly. He had seen 3 cruisers ahead.

The British ships turned into battle line, their twenty-four 15-inch guns keeping steadily on the Italian ships. It was point-blank range—3800 yards. From the director tower of the *Warspite* Cunningham heard the calm voice of an officer: "Director layer sees the target."

There came the *ting-ting-ting* of the firing gongs. The ship shuddered as the guns roared, spewing a great orange flash and their deadly armor-piercing shells. Searchlights pinned the hapless Italian cruisers in their merciless glare.

The Italians were caught absolutely unaware. The first they knew that there was an enemy within a hundred miles was when the shells smashed into their ships. Half the Italian seamen were busy preparing to assist the *Pola;* aboard the *Fiume* they were faking down the towing cables.

The first salvo from the *Warspite* registered five hits. "The plight of the Italian cruisers was indescribable," wrote Admiral Cunningham. "One saw whole turrets and masses of other heavy debris whirling through the air and splashing into the sea, and in a short time the ships themselves were nothing but glowing torches and on fire from stem to stern. The whole action lasted no more than a few minutes."

Both cruisers were total wrecks. The *Fiume* sank about 2315 and the abandoned *Zara* was sent to the bottom by torpedoes from the *Jervis* about 0200.

The Italian destroyers counterattacked with guns and torpedoes, but were driven off by the British. In the action the destroyers *Alfieri* and *Carducci* were sunk and the *Oriani* heavily damaged.

So far the British had not sighted the cause of it all, the crippled *Pola.* Her men could see the gun flashes and knew their side was getting the worst of it. At any moment they expected the British heavy ships would turn to finish them off, too. They were helpless to intervene in the fight because they had lost all power. Their guns could not be trained, and the ammunition hoists would not operate. Some of the crew panicked and raced about the decks. Others broke into the liquor and wine stores and proceeded to drink themselves into a stupor. The Captain ordered the sea cocks opened, but then shut them again.

About 0300 on the morning of March 29, several of the British destroyers found the *Pola.* The *Jervis* came alongside and rescued 258 survivors before finishing the derelict off with two torpedoes.

So ended the Battle of Cape Matapan. By this time there was no chance of catching the *Vittorio Veneto,* so Cunningham and his heavy ships returned to the scene of the sinking of the three cruisers. They spent the morning in rescue operations, saving altogether over 900 men.

While they were engaged in this work of mercy, the German aircraft, which had been so needed the previous day, put in an appearance. Several JU-88s began bombing the British ships, and Admiral Cunningham felt it would be unwise to tarry longer. As he gathered his units about him to begin the voyage to Alexandria, he radioed in plain language to Supermarina, telling where the men he had been forced to abandon might be found. Supermarina sent out the hospital ship *Gradisca,* which rescued 160 men. A Greek destroyer picked up another 110. But over 3000 lost their lives.

Not a British ship was hit. It is no wonder that Admiral Cunningham ordered a special Thanksgiving Service held on board all ships after their arrival at Alexandria.

The victories in the Libyan desert, in East Africa, and at Cape Matapan marked the high point of British success for a long time to come.

All at once the Germans were striking everywhere. The Mediterranean's eastern shores became the scene of one disaster after another. General Wavell, on whom the responsibility rested, could no longer count victories. There were only defeats. Yet he had to hold on as the Germans threatened him on all sides.

The superb fighting team of General O'Connor was dispersed. O'Connor himself was captured on a patrol behind enemy lines, where he had no business being, but where he characteristically was. The fascinating battle between the two desert masters, O'Connor and Rommel, would never take place.

The Western Desert was held by light garrison forces. Many of O'Connor's veterans were in Greece. They had gone there on another forlorn hope, just as their brothers in arms had gone to Norway. They were there because Mr. Churchill believed that British honor and good faith demanded it.

He also believed, against all logical analysis, that they might succeed in keeping the Germans out of Greece. It was a belief that only a man of great moral courage could hold—or a fool. And Churchill was no fool.

The Greek Premier, General Metaxas, was dead. With him died the idea of keeping Greece free of British troops. On February 8, 1941, his successor, Alexander Koryzis, asked the British Government what help they could give in case the Germans moved on his country.

To the British, the problem was not simply Greece. The entire Balkan position was balanced as delicately as a man on a tightrope. Bulgaria, Yugoslavia, Turkey, and Greece formed an uneasy association of neutrals so far as the Anglo-German war was concerned. If they could be held together, then Hitler would be barred from the eastern Mediterranean. At the very least, Churchill hoped that the Yugoslavs and Turks could be persuaded to form a common front with the Greeks, supported by a handful of British forces wrenched from General Wavell's "Army of the Nile," which O'Connor was even then leading on its rampage through Cyrenaica.

Mr. Churchill seems to have had an exaggerated idea of the strength available to Wavell in his vast Middle Eastern command. Noting that 50,000 troops had been sent to Wavell during January, 1941, the Prime Minister charged that they were sitting in idleness—useless to his grand designs. "Does nothing emerge," he inquired petulantly, "in the shape of fighting units from this reinforcement?"

Admiral Cunningham commented that the men controlling the war from Whitehall were living in a land of dreams. The victories in East Africa by Alan Cunningham and by the brilliant O'Connor in the Western Desert had been heady wine for Churchill. Now he urged more; his telegrams to Wavell and Cunningham bristle with importunities—Operation Mandibles, the occupation of Rhodes; Operation Workshop, the occupation of Pantelleria; Operation Influx, the invasion of Sicily.

To Admiral Cunningham, such operations seemed little short of madness. He was having his hands full trying to maintain the garrison at Malta. Churchill took a great deal of convincing that the seizure of more islands in the Mediterranean would create problems far beyond the resources of the Mediterranean Fleet. In the face of Axis air superiority, Cunningham could not hope to keep the captured islands garrisoned or supplied. They might be taken, but they could not be held.

Mr. Churchill had not yet learned the truth that mere masses of men are useless in war unless they are well supplied and have adequate support—naval, air, or artillery. Confronted with the united opposition of the Middle Eastern commanders, he allowed Mandibles, Workshop, and Influx to be interred. But he was grumpy about it. Meanwhile the Balkan problem remained.

On receipt of Prime Minister Koryzis's feeler for British assistance to Greece, Churchill dispatched Foreign Minister Anthony Eden and the Chief of the Imperial General Staff, Sir John Dill, to the Middle East with full powers to represent the Government in all matters, diplomatic and military, affecting that part of the world and to "initiate any action he [Eden] may think necessary with the Commander in Chief of the Middle East [Wavell], with the Egyptian Government, and with the Governments of Greece, Yugoslavia, and Turkey."

The absence of Bulgaria from this list is significant, for by this time the Government in Sofia was already acting like a member of the Tripartite Pact. Hitler had won already, so far as Bulgaria was concerned.*

Eden and Dill left England on February 12. The Three Fates must have chuckled to themselves, for it was on that very day that General Edwin Rommel arrived in North Africa.

Wavell greeted the emissaries from London full of confidence and enthusiasm. He had been given the time to permit O'Connor to finish the conquest of Cyrenaica. As yet he had no knowledge that the Germans were landing troops in Tripoli, the vanguard of the Afrika Korps. It is even possible that he had never heard of Rommel.

Present at the councils of Wavell, Dill, and Eden was a particular friend and confidant of Churchill, Field Marshal Jan C. Smuts, Prime Minister of South Africa. Smuts was a canny old Boer, never one to go out on a limb unless there was good reason for it. There seemed to be a good reason at the present moment, for success in halting a German advance into Greece would have enormous political, diplomatic, and psychological impact on the entire world.

"We agreed [Eden cabled to Churchill] we should do everything in our power to bring the fullest measure of help to Greeks at earliest possible moment."

As this message was on its way to London, Eden received a reminder and warning from Churchill: "Do not consider yourselves obligated to a Greek enterprise if in your hearts you feel it will only

* On February 8, 1941, Bulgaria reached a military understanding with Germany and joined the Tripartite Pact on March 1. Construction of a bridge across the Danube started February 28, and the bridge was used by German troops March 2.

be another Norwegian fiasco. If no good plan can be made, please say so. But of course you know how valuable success would be."

In spite of every caution, the commanders in chief agreed to go ahead if the Greeks would consent to the presence of British troops in their country. Accordingly Eden and Dill flew to Athens, accompanied by Wavell, Air Chief Marshal Sir Arthur Longmore, RAF commander in the Middle East, and Captain R. M. Dick, representing Admiral Cunningham.

No sooner had their plane landed at the Greek capital than Eden was summoned to the royal palace at Tatoi for an immediate audience with King George. Wasting no time in small talk, His Majesty asked Eden to agree to a private meeting with Prime Minister Koryzis. This proposal was not to Eden's liking, for he preferred to keep the negotiations purely on the military plane. The royal will prevailed, however, and Eden found himself closeted with Koryzis.

Producing a piece of paper with something of a flourish, the Greek Prime Minister proceeded to read a formal statement:

> At the outset of our meeting I wish to repeat in the most categorical manner the declaration I made to the British Government when I succeeded the late General Metaxas as President of the Council. It represents the firm basis of Greek Policy.
>
> Having been given a spontaneous guarantee by Great Britain and having received valuable help from her on the occasion of Italy's unprovoked aggression, Greece is now her faithful ally, and is firmly resolved to continue the war to a victorious conclusion with all her strength at the side of her great ally in whom she has complete confidence.
>
> This determination on the part of the King and Government is shared by the entire Greek nation, and in this complete unity lies the explanation of the brilliant victories gained by the Greek army against an incomparably stronger and better equipped enemy.
>
> We are aware that this resolve on the part of Greece to defend her liberty and integrity is not limited to Italy but applies equally to aggression by Germany. Indeed, Greece is fighting both for liberty and honour.
>
> As for Italy, Greece has been able not only to resist the invader successfully but also to gain a succession of victories over a period of four months, and to penetrate deeply into the enemy's territory in spite of the rigours of winter and the great difficulty of the country.
>
> But in this struggle she has been compelled to use almost all her forces and has only three divisions in Macedonia facing Bulgaria. Therefore the problem—and it is a purely military one—is to decide

the size and composition of the force with which the Greek army must be reinforced to make it capable of offering effective resistance to a German invasion. The Greek Government possesses more or less accurate information about the German armies in Rumania, which are being continually reinforced (there are twenty-five divisions according to the most recent reports), and about the Bulgarian forces, but they do not know the help the British might be able to give within the space of two months.

They do not even know the intentions of Turkey and Yugoslavia, nor what military aid these countries could give, nor when and how it would be sent. This question is not only exceptionally important but also extremely urgent.

In these circumstances Your Excellency's arrival in the Middle East is most opportune, for it will serve not only to clarify the situation but also to turn it to the common advantage of Great Britain and Greece. But let me repeat once again that whatever the future holds in store, and whether there is any hope of repelling the enemy in Macedonia or not, Greece will defend her national soil, even if she has to do so alone.

Eden was struck by the naiveté of this appeal, but he could not help being impressed by the courage and patriotism expressed. It was as well to establish at the outset that the Greeks meant business.

As the military commanders met, wide differences in their thinking quickly became apparent. The Greek Commander in Chief, General John Papagos, was most reluctant to abandon any of the territory his troops had wrested from the Italians. To hold such positions depended on Turkey and Yugoslavia joining the Allies, or at least being benevolently neutral.

The British insisted that there was little chance of winning Turkey and Yugoslavia, and that it was only realistic to make plans based on their own resources. Instead of establishing a defense line well to the north which would depend on Yugoslavian troops, Wavell argued that the so-called Aliakmon Line, based on the position Kajmakcalan-Edessa-Verria-Mount Olympus, would be far safer. If, by any lucky chance, Yugoslavia joined them, then the Allies could give further thought to the Metaxas Line which Papagos had proposed.

Papagos agreed with these conclusions and promised to abandon certain positions in Albania and the Metaxas Line within twenty days. But when the time came, he could not bring himself to leave large areas of Greek territory undefended. Thus he did nothing.

The result was that when the Germans struck, neither the Metaxas nor the Aliakmon Line could be held.

When the conferences with Papagos were over, it was reported in the press that Eden appeared "buoyant." If so, it was a piece of acting worthy of an Academy Award, for there was nothing in prospect to be buoyant about. Neither Eden nor Wavell trusted overmuch the vainglorious Papagos, and neither was under any illusions that the German attack, when it came, would be half-hearted.

There remained the problem of Turkey and Yugoslavia. Even as Eden and Dill had been making their way to the Middle East, Turkey had signed a non-aggression treaty with Bulgaria. The clear interpretation of this pact was that Turkey would have no objection to German troops passing through Bulgaria on their way to attack Greece. It began to appear that not only was Turkey going to remain neutral; she was going to interpret her neutrality on the side of the Axis.

This diplomatic coup was a triumph for the wily Bavarian, Fritz von Papen. As German ambassador to Turkey, he controlled a spy network which penetrated even the British Embassy. Microfilm copies of all correspondence between Whitehall and Ambassador Knatchbull-Hugessen reached von Papen's desk almost as soon as they arrived at that of Knatchbull-Hugessen.

Von Papen's persuasive voice was heard in the highest councils of the Turkish Government. Now that the British were rushing to aid the Greeks—he knew this as well as Churchill did, thanks to his spies—von Papen argued that they had nothing left with which to aid Turkey. Churchill's impulsive promises to send hundreds of planes and thousands of men meant nothing. There were no planes and no men left over from North Africa, East Africa, and Greece.

When Eden arrived in Ankara, he found a courteous reception and not much else. President Ismet Inönü and General Chakmak blandly told him that they would defend their land if they were attacked, that they were prepared to act in concert with Yugoslavia in event of invasion of that country, so why didn't Mr. Eden talk with the leaders in Belgrade? The Turks had received no response from their tentative fair offers. Thank you for coming, Mr. Eden. Good afternoon.

Returning to Athens, Eden sent for Mr. Ronald Campbell, now ambassador to Yugoslavia, in order to learn the latest details of the situation in Belgrade. But, before Mr. Campbell could arrive, word came in that the Germans had entered Bulgaria. This was no great surprise in itself. What was a surprise was that General Papagos had done nothing to keep his promise to evacuate eastern Macedonia in order to garrison the Aliakmon Line.

To compound confusion, Papagos now bluntly refused to do any such thing. His excuse was that the men of Belgrade had not confided their plans to him. Therefore he could make no move until they saw fit to do so. To abandon Salonika, the only port Yugoslavia had on the outside world, would be to drive Belgrade straight into the German camp.

This argument was all well and good, but impossible from a military standpoint. There were simply not enough troops available in the Near East to hold the lengthy Metaxas Line on which General Papagos pinned his hopes.

Summoned to the council, Wavell flew in from Cairo and found Papagos as stubborn as he was unrealistic. Tempers rose, and Eden demanded that the matter be put up to King George of Greece. His Majesty listened calmly to the impassioned pleadings of Papagos and to the cold logic of Eden, Dill, and Wavell.

The British presented three courses of action:

(1) Accept three untrained, newly mustered divisions which Papagos grudgingly offered for the Aliakmon Line instead of the five reinforced veteran divisions he had originally promised. With these green organizations try to build the Line up with British troops as fast as possible.

(2) Accept Papagos's plan of trying to reinforce the Metaxas Line over roads so bad that the men and supplies could arrive only in driblets.

(3) Withdraw the British offer of military support.

The British representatives and the King agreed that both (2) and (3) could lead only to disaster. Only proposal (1) offered any chance of success. It was a pretty slim chance by now, for Papagos's delay meant that the defensive positions had not been prepared. At this late date it was doubtful that they could be.

On one thing the British insisted. The command of the entire Aliakmon Line, both British and Greek forces, must be vested in British Lieutenant General Sir Henry Maitland Wilson, known throughout the British Army as "Jumbo."

No one really liked this plan, but it was the only one they could come up with. At least the country was suitable for rearguard action if the defenders could not hold the position. They could fall back to the sea, and it would be up to the Navy once more.

In London the War Cabinet and the Chiefs of Staff Committee were by this time having second thoughts. But Mr. Eden's sentiments expressed in a telegram to Mr. Churchill could not be denied. "No doubt our prestige will suffer," he wrote, "if we are ignominiously ejected, but in any event to have fought and suffered in Greece would be less damaging to us than to have left Greece to her fate."

Mr. Churchill agreed. "We must share their ordeal."

Now that matters in Greece had reached a decision—no matter that it was less than satisfactory—it was time to turn to the problem of Yugoslavia. If she could be persuaded to join the Anglo-Greek alliance, so much the better, but in any case her neutrality would be a great handicap to Germany. Eden sent Sir Ronald Campbell back to Belgrade to impress upon Prince Regent Paul the horrors that would fall on his country if the Germans entered, either by invitation or as invaders. Also, he should persuade the Prince Regent to send a staff officer to discuss common defense measures with the Greeks.

Before Campbell could reach Belgrade, the Prince Regent, whose "susceptible nature," as American Ambassador Arthur B. Lane put it, made him unlikely to stand up to pressure, had left on a secret visit to Hitler at his "Eagle's Nest" at Berchtesgaden.

A few days later a certain Colonel Perescitch of the Yugoslav General Staff arrived in Athens. His visit was something of a mystery, as he came in mufti, under the name of Mr. L. R. [Last Ray?] Hope. He was empowered to make no specific proposals, nor agree to any. He seemed most anxious to learn specific details of the Greek and British plans for defense. It need hardly be said that he received little satisfaction.

At his meeting with the Führer, Prince Paul received the customary combination of bribes and threats. Salonika would be his if he went along with the German plans; Yugoslavia would be Hitler's if he did not. On a second visit on March 17, 1941, Prince Paul was given a veritable ultimatum. There could be no talk of non-aggression pacts. Either Yugoslavia joined the Tripartite Pact, or she could answer for the consequences. The Prince Regent and the Crown Council decided to yield. On March 25, the Pact was signed in Vienna at a ceremony which even Hitler condescended to grace with his presence.

The agreement with Germany was anathema to most Yugoslavs, particularly the Serbian population. While Churchill urged his ambassador to exploit this feeling, admonishing him to "continue to pester, nag and bite," events for once were ahead of the British Prime Minister. On March 27, General Richard Simovich, Chief of the

Yugoslav Air Force, led a coup which swept the Prince Regent and his opportunist ministers from power. The young Serb officers who adhered to General Simovich installed the young King Peter on the throne and defied Germany to do her worst.

The British, of course, were delighted with the turn of events. Eden and Dill, who had reached Malta on their way home, were directed to return at once to Athens and enter into discussions with Simovich on matters of common defense. When Eden reached Belgrade, however, after a brief stop in Athens, the results proved disappointing. The jubilant Churchill had telegraphed, "Is it not possible that if a united front were formed in the Balkan peninsula Germany might think it better business to take it out on Russia, observing that we have had many reports of heavy concentrations in Poland and intrigues in Sweden and Finland?" Churchill's idea was worthy, but Eden and Dill found that it could not be put into practice. General Simovich and his officers had only the vaguest ideas of plans to defend their country, and they were a little apprehensive over what they had done. They went so far as to assure Germany that they had only peaceful intentions; they were ready to offer to sign a non-aggression pact.

Hitler, however, was beyond reason, beyond agreeing to any form of diplomatic action. Nothing would do but revenge for this daring affront. He vowed, "without waiting for possible declarations of loyalty of the new government, to destroy Yugoslavia militarily and as a nation. No diplomatic inquiries will be made; no ultimatum presented."

He ordered work to be begun at once on planning for the invasion of Yugoslavia to be concurrent with that of Greece. Führer Directive Number 25 was written more in a fit of temper than in the cold logic of the military planning process.

> The military putsch in Yugoslavia [it read] has altered the political situation in the Balkans. Yugoslavia, in spite of her protestations of loyalty, must be considered for the time being as an enemy and therefore crushed as speedily as possible.
>
> It is my intention to force my way into Yugoslavia . . . and to annihilate the Yugoslav Army.

So furious was Hitler that he lost sight of the main objective. The secret records of the OKW record Hitler's perhaps most fateful statement: "The beginning of the Barbarossa operation [the invasion of Russia] will have to be postponed up to four weeks."

And so, on both sides, the fateful decisions were made. Operation

Lustre, the movement of British troops from Egypt to Greece, began, not without serious misgivings on the part of Admiral Cunningham. In fact, he gave orders to begin planning the evacuation even as the first troops were going up the gangways onto their transports. In all, some 50,000 British troops were to be landed in Greece. The First British Armoured Brigade Group (Brigadier H. V. S. Charrington), the New Zealand Division (Major General B. C. Freyberg), and the Sixth Australian Division (Major General Sir Iven Mackey) comprised the expeditionary force. Incredibly its commander, General "Jumbo" Wilson, was required by the Greeks to masquerade in civilian clothes under the alias of Mr. Watt. This absurd disguise, bad enough during the preliminary discussions, was idiocy when the British troops were actually landing and taking up positions in the Aliakmon Line. No effective command can be exercised by a general forced to pretend he isn't there. Additionally, no German spy observing a huge figure dressed in clothes of an obviously English cut moving about the military installations could have come to any conclusion other than that he was gazing on Lieutenant General Sir Henry Maitland Wilson.

On April 6, 1941, a Sunday, at 0545, two German armies slammed into Yugoslavia and Greece. In accordance with Hitler's determination to crush Yugoslavia with unmerciful harshness, the Luftwaffe attacked Belgrade continuously for three days and three nights. At rooftop level the bombers came over, for there was no defense worthy of the name. The Yugoslav Air Force was destroyed in a matter of hours; the antiaircraft defenses of Belgrade lasted little longer. Then it was only bombing practice for the Germans. Flying from airfields in Rumania, they could carry maximum bomb loads. Over 17,000 persons died in the rubble of Belgrade. Even worse, the command structure was paralyzed, and the high command had no way of communicating with its forces actually opposing the German Second Army under Field Marshal Maximilian von Weichs and elements of the Twelfth Army under Field Marshal Sigmund List. Although many of the troops, especially the Serbians, fought heroically, large numbers of Croatians surrendered or deserted to the Germans. After eight days, the Yugoslavian Government had had enough. Surrender took place at Belgrade on April 17, following the escape of King Peter and the Prime Minister to Greece.

The collapse of Yugoslavia made General Papagos's precarious position on the Metaxas Line even more untenable than the British had foreseen in March. It was a natural strongpoint, strengthened by pillboxes, mine fields, and barbed wire. But in two days the line had been breached. The Germans moved quickly to prevent the Greeks from reaching the Aliakmon Line. On April 9, the Germans captured Salonika, and all resistance in northern Greece collapsed. It was now up to Wilson in the Aliakmon Line to try to save Greece from total occupation.

He skillfully met the first German attempt to turn his western flank by sending the First Armoured Brigade to plug the hole at Monastir, exposed by the rapid Yugoslavian collapse. The Greeks moved a cavalry division from Albania to hold the left side of the gap.

It became painfully apparent, however, that the extended front of the Aliakmon Line was too much to be held with the slender resources Wilson commanded. He decided to abandon the position and fall back to a line near Mount Olympus. The Greeks, because of their knowledge of the mountainous terrain, were to move to the west while the British withdrew southward, pinning their eastern flank on the sea. Unfortunately for the Allies, the untrained Greeks were totally inadequate for the complicated movements of passing their west-bound formations through those of the south-bound British. Many Greek units simply evaporated, large numbers of men being captured by the advancing Germans.

The Mount Olympus position remained strong, and early German attacks were beaten off. A nagging cause for worry in Wilson's mind was the western end, which could be more easily turned and was manned by those Greek elements which had survived the retreat relatively intact.

The news of the collapse of the Greek Army in Albania and of the Yugoslavian peace overtures caused Wilson to decide to retreat once more, back to the famous position at Thermopylae where, twenty-four centuries earlier, Leonidas and his band of Spartans had died to a man opposing Xerxes.

General Papagos, now a beaten man, approved the British withdrawal to Thermopylae. He went even further, proposing that the British get out of Greece altogether.

Such a decision was not Wilson's to make. The British had come to Greece as a result of decisions on the highest level of the governments in Athens and London. Those same high officials would have to decide whether the British would leave or stay.

Recognizing that British evacuation would probably be necessary in a few days, Churchill, with the concurrence of the War Cabinet, authorized Wavell to make the decision, provided, and only provided,

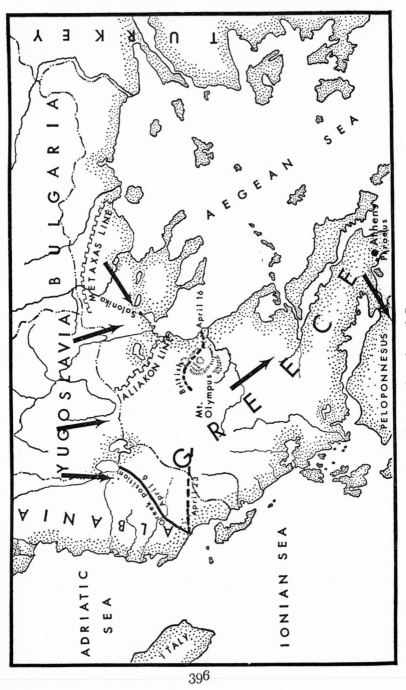

German invasion of Greece.

that the Greek King asked them to leave. Accordingly Wavell flew to Athens, accompanied by Rear Admiral H. T. Baillie-Grohman, who would command the evacuation, if it came to that.

On April 21, Wavell, members of his staff, Ambassador Michael Palairet, Air Marshal D'Albiac, commanding the RAF units in Greece, "Jumbo" Wilson, and Baillie-Grohman met with General Papagos and King George. Absent was the Greek Prime Minister Koryzis, who, only twenty-four hours earlier, had left a cabinet meeting to go to his home and blow out his brains.

Wavell lost no time in getting to the heart of the conference.

"We must know," he stated flatly, "whether the Greek Army can give effective support to General Wilson's left flank in the Thermopylae Line."

Everyone looked at Papagos, who squirmed uneasily in his chair. A tale of woe began to unfold. Some of his generals had been acting like Fifth Columnists. In eastern Macedonia, General Bakopoulos had surrendered to the enemy while his men were still holding out in the frontier forts. Minister of War Papademas had issued an order stating that resistance was no longer possible and ordering the generals to surrender as they saw fit. Someone in the army high command had issued an order granting two months' leave to all those recently called up to face the Germans. Minister of Communications Oeconomou had ordered all Greek aircraft grounded and fuel depots at several airfields destroyed. This edict, amounting to sabotage, had been countermanded by the King when he had learned of it through British sources, but the damage had been done. Misled and misguided, the Greeks were now helpless to resist much longer. Papagos told the pitiful tale of refugees jamming roads, interfering with troops. The British had heard all of this before, but it did not make the fact any less poignant.

"The longer our armies continue to fight," said Papagos despairingly, "the more the defenseless civilians will suffer."

Thinking of how things might have been different if the Greeks had been able to make up their minds at the first British offer of assistance, Wavell stated simply that as long as the Greeks continued to resist, the British soldiers would be at their sides.

"But, Your Majesty," added Wavell simply, "if you and your Government wish us to leave, we will do so. The decision rests with you, sir."

A long silence ensued. Then the King conferred briefly with Deputy Prime Minister Tsuderos. He looked slowly around the table.

"Gentlemen," he said carefully, "we do not think there is time to reorganize our army in Epirus to give support to your left flank before the enemy attacks. Therefore, it is our opinion that the British force should be withdrawn."

He paused to control his emotions before going on. "I want you to know how deeply we regret that it is through us that you and your troops have been placed in this position. But I give you my word that I will do all that I can to preserve order in my country and that I and my Government will delay our departure for Crete until the last possible moment."

Another evacuation was now inevitable. In many ways it would be worse than Dunkirk. There it had been a short run across to the British Isles, and the RAF had been able to dispute German control of the air, so that the Luftwaffe could not devote its entire attention to disrupting the embarkations. At Dunkirk there had been available transports, Channel packets, and the willing aid of private boat owners. Here none of these advantages would exist.

Nor could the major port of Piraeus be used. The evacuation would have to take place from the beaches of many small harbors, mostly fishing ports.

On April 6, as the Germans struck, Piraeus was jammed with shipping. There was not a vacant space at any of the wharves, and ships were anchored out in Phalerum Bay awaiting their turns to unload.

These ships had come in two days earlier as Convoy ANF-24 from Port Said. En route they had been bombed mercilessly, and several ships had sustained damage. The *Northern Prince* had vanished in a shattering roar as her cargo of ammunition went off. High winds and pounding seas had caused cargoes to shift and deck loads to be wrenched from their lashings. Some ships had a crazy list as they rode at their anchorages, boding ill for their stability in the event of another blow.

The simultaneous arrival of all these vessels completely jammed the already creaky organization of the port. The Greeks could not yet comprehend what was happening to them as the Germans descended on their land. Stevedores and port officials worked with their minds partly on their usual way of doing things, partly on the safety of loved ones facing the enemy to the north, and partly on the safety of their own skins. Every time the air-raid alarms sounded, they dropped what they were doing and ran to take cover, even if it meant leaving a sling full of ammunition suspended between ship and shore, a mine or moored bomb that could be set off by a machine-gun tracer bullet.

Confusion became worse as orders were given, countermanded, and counter-countermanded. The frantic Captain of the Port, Scarpetis, did his best, but his authority was limited, and he did not know the things he needed to know if he was to do his job at all. In a war situation, there was no possibility of doing it well.

Captain Herbert Giles, master of the freighter *Clan Fraser,* nosed his ship carefully up to the dock. He had on board a mixed cargo of army vehicles, chemicals for a Greek arms factory, and 350 tons of high explosive. He was anxious to unload and get rid of his dangerous cargo. He had seen what had happened to the *Northern Prince.*

The military authorities intervened and ordered the *Clan Fraser* to shift to Berth No. 6, where railway cars had been sent to take off the explosives. With a sigh, Captain Giles got his ship under way again and found his new berth. But now the First Officer reported that the explosives could not be unloaded until the other cargo had been cleared. There were no facilities at Berth No. 6 for handling anything but the explosives.

Back went the *Clan Fraser* to her original berth. There were no railroad lines here, and no one had thought of sending trucks. Once again the unloading was stymied.

Into the breach stepped the British Assistant Sea Transport Officer, Lieutenant Commander Hook. He prevailed on Greek Army officials to take delivery of the *Clan Fraser*'s cargo and remove it in their own trucks. Soon this unloading was proceeding as well as could be expected.

Hook realized that a commercial dock facility was not an ideal place to handle large quantities of explosives. The obvious place was the naval station at Scaramanga, but the Greek Navy firmly refused to allow any ammunition ships in that area.

In desperation, Hook secured 2 lighters from somewhere, and the *Clan Fraser* soon began to discharge the explosives into them. At least, they could be towed away from the dock and city area. By 6 o'clock that evening, the lighters were almost full, although some 250 tons of TNT remained in the *Clan Fraser.* In vain Captain Giles looked for the promised tugs to come and take the lighters away. Nothing happened. By 7 o'clock there was no chance that the tugs would appear; their skippers had all gone home for the night.

At 8:35 P.M., the air-raid warning sounded for the fifth time that day. The stevedores dropped their burdens and ran for shelter. All unloading stopped, not only on the *Clan Fraser,* but on all other ships in the harbor. Nearby could be seen the *Cingalese Prince* unloading coal, the *Clan Cumming* with general cargo, and 2 ammunition ships, the *City of Roubaix* and the *Goalpara.*

For nearly half an hour, an uncanny silence hung over the harbor. All the ships were blacked out, and no lights showed in the port or the city. The waxing gibbous moon cast a soft glow all around.

About 9 o'clock the first German planes came over. They paid no heed to the port installations or the ships. Ranging out over the harbor, they dropped mines, and the parachutes could be clearly seen in the moonlight.

A little later came the bombers. They made a straight line for the *City of Roubaix* and the *Goalpara*—and the *Clan Fraser,* which still had the death-laden lighters alongside. The selectiveness of the bombers was a clear demonstration of the effectiveness of the German spy system in Piraeus and its excellent communications with the Luftwaffe.

When the attack was over, the *Clan Fraser,* the *Goalpara,* and the *City of Roubaix* were all on fire. At any moment any one of them might go up in a blast that would wreck the port. The *Clan Fraser* lay some yards out in the stream, held to the dock by a single strand of mooring line. The lighters alongside had been miraculously untouched.

There was no possibility of saving the ships, nor, since the Greeks refused to allow any movement in the port because of the newly laid German mines, could they be towed out of the harbor. Commander Buckler, formerly Sea Transport Officer, was determined to remove the lighters if at all possible, rather than sink them where they were. Commandeering a tug, and with a volunteer crew, he made his way cautiously near the *Clan Fraser.* The ship herself was beyond help; by this time her decks were red-hot.

Before Commander Buckler could even get a line aboard the first lighter, the *Clan Fraser* blew up in a huge explosion. The shock wave was felt 15 miles away. The port area was completely wrecked, and pieces of flaming wreckage set fires on other ships and on the innumerable small boats to be found in any harbor. Of Commander Buckler and his volunteer crew there was no trace. They had been blown out of existence as though they had never been.

The entire area of Piraeus seemed to be a single mass of flames.

Fires were completely out of control; they would have to burn themselves out.

Nor was the Calvary of the city yet over. At 2:45 the next morning, the *Goalpara* blew up. This blast flattened the few remaining buildings which had survived the first. Fifteen minutes later, the *City of Roubaix* disappeared in another tremendous explosion which set fire to the *Clan Cumming*.

In all, 11 ships were lost in these three explosions, and the port of Piraeus was rendered utterly useless. There could be no question of using it in Operation Demon, the rescue of the British Expeditionary Force in Greece.

Rear Admiral Baillie-Grohman, in charge of the shore arrangements for the operation, had to decide, and decide quickly, which ports were to be used. Already troops were heading for the beaches. He had to get word to Vice Admiral Pridham-Wippell to send the ships to take the men off.

Originally the evacuation had been scheduled to begin on April 28, but the rapid German advances forced the British to begin it on the night of April 24. Pridham-Wippell had to get the ships there.

Luckily for the British, Operation Demon was made the sole responsibility of Admiral Cunningham's command in Alexandria. No longer would General Headquarters, Middle East Command, have a finger in the pie. The delays involved in getting word back and forth between Alexandria and Cairo had caused too much muddle. From the time Admiral Cunningham assumed command, Operation Demon ran smoothly—as smoothly as the Germans would permit.

The exiguous strength of the RAF in Greece had proved no match for the Luftwaffe. The British pilots, aided by the Greek airmen to the limit of their ability, had fought gallantly, but there were never enough planes. On April 23, the unequal struggle reached its end. Air Marshal D'Albiac and his few remaining pilots took what planes they had left to Crete. They would be of little use in covering the evacuation, and there were no aircraft available in the Middle East to assist them. All the planes Air Chief Marshal Longmore could get his hands on were needed to oppose Rommel, who was by now rampaging through Libya.

Since the Luftwaffe ruled the skies over Greece, there could be no daylight evacuations of troops. Admiral Baillie-Grohman ordered the troop lift to be held each night beginning at one hour after darkness had come and ending promptly at 0300. In this way the ships could make their final run-in to the beaches protected by darkness and could have a good head start on the way to Crete before the sun rose. It would not be an easy task for either the Army or the Navy, but with courage, skill, and determination it might just be done.

For the embarkation there were 4 cruisers, *Orion* (flagship of Pridham-Wippell), *Ajax, Phoebe,* and the Australian *Perth;* 3 antiaircraft cruisers, *Calcutta, Coventry,* and *Carlisle;* about 20 destroyers, 3 sloops, 2 special 14,000-ton Infantry Assault Ships, the *Glenearn* and *Glengyle,* 19 troop transports, and a number of "A" lighters, forerunners of the LCI. Commander Kenneth Michel chartered and otherwise acquired a large number of motorboats, caiques, and other small craft to assist in ferrying the troops out to the ships. There would be no laying the ships alongside the docks at these ports. There was not enough water.

Admiral Cunningham's instructions were succinct: "The object is to embark men, if possible, with arms; but no material must be allowed to take precedence to men. Troop-ships with men embarked to sail direct to Alexandria, except 'Glen' ships which must unload at Suda Bay and do a second embarkation. Destroyers to take their troops to Crete, where they will be transferred later."

None of the embarkation beaches had ever been used for large ships before. Picking one's way through the darkness, with inadequate charts, inadequate buoyage, unknown currents, shallows, bars, and wrecks, is no job for an amateur. The protection from enemy threats the darkness afforded was counterbalanced by the navigational perils it posed.

Some ships grounded on the way in; others after loading found themselves aground as a result of tide changes and the additional weight of the troops aboard. Yet they got off somehow, and so began the hazardous voyage to Crete or Egypt.

Early embarkations were from Raphtina, Raphtis, Megara, and Nauplia. Each port witnessed tales of heroism, despair, and agony. A volume might be written on each.

Let us rather tell of the Dutch ship *Slamat* as representative of dozens of untold tales.

One of several groups of ships was bound for Nauplia and the beach at Tolon, a little farther south. The Infantry Assault Ship *Glenearn,* with its invaluable landing craft, was in company with the large transports *Khedive Ismail* and *Slamat.* Escorting were the cruiser *Calcutta* and the destroyers *Diamond, Griffin, Hotspur, Isis,* and *Havock.*

It had been a long day for most of them, and it was not yet sunset. The destroyers and the *Calcutta* had arrived at Suda Bay on Crete only at 4 o'clock that morning. The cruiser discharged 700 troops and then refueled. The destroyers were busy with various tasks, and the crews had had only an hour's sleep that night.

Just about 1800 that evening, the little convoy entered the Gulf of Nauplia, leaving the open sea behind them. All day long the men had been robbed of any chance of rest by threat of air attacks, even though no planes approached the formation. They had been seen circling in the distance. Now the threat became real.

A group of Stukas and ME-109s came skimming over the hills and dropped bombs all around the ships, but intense antiaircraft fire kept them from making any hits. Then, just at the end of the attack, one Stuka came screaming down in an almost vertical dive. As the pilot pulled out, he dropped a large bomb which headed directly for the *Glenearn*.

It missed—but just barely.

It might as well have hit. The *Glenearn* heeled violently to port and then glided to a stop—all power and lights had been knocked out. There was no possibility of repair on the scene, for the bomb explosion had ruptured several plates below the waterline; both the engine room and the generator room were flooded.

The ship was in no danger of sinking, but she could not go on. She was out of Operation Demon, and with her the precious landing craft for ferrying troops. Captain D. M. Lees of the *Calcutta,* as senior officer present, had to make up his mind what to do about the cripple. He swore to himself. Two hours of daylight remained.

"We can't hang about here waiting for her," he muttered. "Yeoman, make to *Glenearn:* 'Prepare to be taken in tow.' And make to *Griffin:* 'Take *Glen* in tow and return to Suda.' " He turned away, and then an afterthought struck him.

"Add the word 'sorry' to the signal to *Griffin.*"

The *Griffin* needed some word of comfort. Not only would she be losing the opportunity to do her part in the evacuation. She would also be tied to a cripple during hours when the Luftwaffe knew her position and would undoubtedly be back. Then there was the comparatively minor problem of passing the heavy towing hawser to a ship which had no power in her capstan or winches. The problems were at length solved, and the *Griffin* and her tow made it safely to Suda.

Captain Lees did not allow his thoughts to dwell on the *Griffin's* difficulties. He had his own job to do, and that was to pick up as many refugees as he could by 3 o'clock the next morning.

The depleted convoy steamed on.

The darkness did little good when Lees's ships arrived at their destination. The transport *Ulster Prince* had run firmly aground the first night of the operation. Now, two days later, she was still there, burning fiercely from several bomb hits. The crews on the other ships could only hope that she would serve to draw the attention of the Luftwaffe from themselves.

The loading of troops went on amid greatest difficulties. The *Glenearn*'s two types of landing craft could carry 45 and 140 troops respectively. But they were on the mother vessel making inching progress to Suda. The conventional boats of the transports and the warships were continually swamping, the men being thrown into the water. It was up to Commander Michel's little navy of chartered caiques and motorboats to do most of the work, along with one of the "A" lighters.

Man by man the troops arrived aboard the ships. Four hundred went aboard the *Isis*. *Slamat* had only 500, the *Calcutta* 1000, *Hotspur* 500. Pridham-Wippell sent three of his ships to help out, and they picked up another 2000.

The *Khedive Ismail* was still empty, for none of the ferrying vessels had found her in the darkness.

Three o'clock came and went. All ships prepared to sail, but not the *Slamat*. Her Captain, a stubborn Dutchman named Lundinga, ignored all signals to sail.

Perhaps it was a misunderstanding of signals. Perhaps it was a misunderstanding of language. But the *Slamat* was only a quarter full. Captain Lundinga stayed where he was.

At length, Captain Lees sent the *Diamond* alongside with orders that could not be ignored. At 0415 the convoy sailed.

Already it was getting light in the east.

At first all went well. The little convoy was so late that the Stukas were looking for it a good deal south of its actual position. It was too good to last.

About 0700 a lookout on the *Calcutta*'s bridge sighted aircraft, and the whole formation went to action stations. The *Calcutta* moved in between the two transports so she could give them the maximum protection with her antiaircraft guns. The 3 remaining destroyers took positions ahead, shooting with everything they had as they dashed full speed for their stations.

The sky seemed full of diving aircraft as dirty fluffs of smoke dotted the air all around them. Some planes fell, but there were too many. It was inevitable that something would happen.

About ten minutes after the attack began, the *Slamat* took two bombs in quick succession. A sheet of flame shot skyward, followed by bits of metal, wood, and flesh. Everyone on the bridge and in the pilot house was killed, and the blazing wreck of the *Slamat* sheered wildly out of control. She missed the *Calcutta* by no more than four feet and turned bows into the wind. Aided by the fresh breeze, the flames, which had been confined to the foredeck, now raced aft, driving the soldiers into the water. A few of the crew managed to get boats off; others launched Carley floats, but most simply jumped—anything to get away from the inferno sweeping the Dutchman's decks.

The destroyer *Diamond,* having spent most of the previous night patrolling to seaward of Nauplia, had very few troops on board, so Captain Lees sent her to rescue survivors from the *Slamat*. It was to be no easy task.

A little later, 3 destroyers came boiling up from the south, the *Wryneck, Vendetta,* and *Waterhen.* These veterans of the "V and W" class were manned by Australians and had been sent by Pridham-Wippell to relieve the burdened *Hotspur* and *Isis,* who were to proceed at top speed to Suda to unload troops.

The *Diamond* was in trouble. As she set about her errand of mercy, playful Luftwaffe pilots were making great sport of strafing and bombing the men in the water, making an occasional pass at the lifesaving destroyer. Captain Lees sent the *Wryneck* to help out. As he brought his venerable ship on the scene, Commander R. D. H. Lane learned that the *Diamond* had already picked up some 500 men, but that there were still a few for the *Wryneck* to deal with. In a few minutes she had pulled over 50 more of the wretched men aboard. This work completed, the *Diamond* finished off the blazing *Slamat* with torpedoes, and the 2 destroyers set off at 25 knots to rejoin the convoy.

The crews of the 2 ships were busy tending the wounded, helping the shocked and dazed men get into dry clothes, and giving them cups of tea and corned beef sandwiches. About noon a flight of aircraft appeared overhead. They bore markings that everyone on both destroyers interpreted as friendly. At last, they thought, the RAF was able to help out. A few men waved.

Suddenly some of the planes turned toward the ships. They were Messerschmitts. Off guard, both destroyers were easy prey. In a few moments, they were blazing wrecks, sinking rapidly. Men were thrown into the sea, some on fire from the oil soaking their clothes, others

405

wounded. When they were found later the next day, only one officer, 51 sailors, and 8 of the rescued soldiers were still alive.

The rest had paid the price of the *Slamat*'s dilatory sailing and the stubborn courage of Captain Lundinga.

Soon the more northerly ports could not be used. The Germans occupied Athens on the heels of the Greek surrender on April 24. In short order, Port Raphtis, Raphtina, and Megara became useless as embarkation points. Henceforth, all evacuations would have to be from the beaches in Peleponnesus—Nauplia, Kalamata, and Monemvasia.

During these grim days, 25 ships were lost, including 5 hospital ships, but Operation Demon continued through the night of April 30/May 1. In all, about 80 percent of the British Expeditionary Force was finally evacuated from Greece, a total of 50,672. More might have made it if the Germans had not been able to bridge the Corinth Canal so swiftly. Even more might have made it if the authorities in Whitehall had provided adequate air strength in the Middle East. But it was not entirely the fault of the present ministers. In Greece, as in Norway and in France, the common soldiers and sailors paid the price for years of peacetime neglect of Britain's defenses.

Little opportunity was given the British to rest from the rigors of the Greek campaign. Next on the German schedule was Crete, and this island the British expected to hold. And Rommel was by now threatening, or so it appeared, the entire British position in Egypt.

And out in the dark-gray waters of the Atlantic, Britain's lifeline was being endangered as never before.

CHAPTER FIFTEEN

Guarding the Lifeline

> *... outside, beyond the broad seas,*
> *there are the markets of the world*
> *that can be entered and controlled*
> *only by a vigorous contest.*
>
> Alfred Thayer Mahan
> The Interest of America in Sea Power

A TELEPHONE line ran from the office of the Admiralty Operations Room across the city of London, through the county of Middlesex, and on to the north. Past York and Edinburgh, and on to the northern tip of Scotland at John o'Groat's it went. From there it dipped down underneath the sea to reach its end at a buoy in Scapa Flow. Moored to that same buoy was the flagship of the British Home Fleet, the new battleship *King George V*. Another telephone line was connected to the long one extending from London, and it led to the Admiral's cabin on the flagship. A sensitive-looking man wearing the uniform of a full admiral in the Royal Navy was talking into the telephone as his Chief of Staff, Commodore E. J. P. Brind, entered the cabin. The admiral, Sir John Tovey, listened to the voice from London briefly and then hung up.

"There's a German ship on the prowl," he told the Commodore. "Admiralty's afraid it may be *Bismarck*."

At the moment, the Germans could have picked no worse time to send their newest battleship on a foray into the Atlantic—from the British point of view, at least. Their troops had been ousted from Greece and were now embattled in the fight for Crete. Every ship that the Admiralty could lay its hands on was needed in the Mediterranean. Yet each was equally needed in the Atlantic to guard against a breakout of the big German warships: *Scharnhorst, Gneisenau,*

Scheer, Lützow, Hipper, Prinz Eugen, and, greatest threat of all, the immensely powerful *Bismarck.* The Admiralty could not station its ships everywhere at once. It was a matter of the nicest judgment.

Now, at the end of May, 1941, Britain's capital ship force was scattered over the ocean. With him at Scapa Flow, Sir John Tovey had the *King George V* and the battle cruiser *Hood,* considered by naval experts to be the most powerful ship afloat. The battle cruiser *Repulse* was in the Clyde, ready to sail to protect the troop convoy WS-8B, due to sail for the Middle East around the Cape of Good Hope. The battleship *Revenge* was in Halifax, the venerable *Ramillies* was at sea with Convoy HX-127, the *Rodney* was westbound across the Atlantic for an overhaul in the Boston Navy Yard. The *Prince of Wales* was at Scapa, but she was so new that builder's workmen were still aboard checking out her turrets and main engines.

All the rest of the British capital ships were assigned to the Mediterranean, were in refits, or were too far away to be of any use in the forthcoming operations against the *Bismarck.*

It had been so from the beginning of the war. Since Britain had to use her ships to move vital cargoes across the seas, they could not be hoarded at home for the day when Hitler should decide to send one or more of his few warships against the merchant ships that formed Britain's lifeline to the world.

The most serious threat to these merchant ships, of course, came from the U-boat arm. Fortunate, indeed, it was for the British that for the first year of the war, Hitler did not recognize the key role these sea wolves, as the Germans liked to call them, would play in the war at sea. As Reichsmarschall Hermann Goering was in charge of allocations of steel, it is not surprising that his Luftwaffe got its share and more, to the detriment of the navy. After a year of war, Dönitz, the U-boat high commander, had exactly the same number—56—of boats that he had at the outbreak. Replacements had just matched losses.

This unhoped-for period of grace had been a godsend to the British antisubmarine forces, for they had been ill-equipped from the first to deal with a serious U-boat campaign such as had developed in 1917. Between the wars, the Admiralty planners had seemed to take the view that if we don't look at the U-boat problem, perhaps it will go away. When war came and the U-boats struck, it was half-hearted at first, for Hitler gave orders that the U-boat war was to be conducted in accordance with international law, which required the U-boat to surface, stop the ship it was going to sink, inspect the ship's papers, and see to it that the crew had an opportunity to reach a position of safety. Only then was the U-boat at liberty to sink the enemy merchant ship.

Obviously, such measures deprived the U-boat of its greatest advantages, those of secrecy and stealth. Also, if the stopped ship used her radio, it was likely to bring aircraft or destroyers rushing to the scene, a proceeding likely to be very uncomfortable to the U-boat.

Nevertheless, the U-boat skippers, most of them, tried to conform to Hitler's orders. For example, Leutnant Otto Kretschmer, destined to become Germany's leading U-boat ace, on patrol in the North Sea encountered the *Glen Farg,* a small coaster. The vessel refused to stop when challenged, and Kretschmer ordered *U-23's* gunners to put a machine-gun burst across her bows. The coaster speeded up, and the German radio operator called to the U-boat commander. "Target calling for assistance, sir. She is saying *Glen Farg* attacked by U-boat using gunfire."

Both of these acts—refusal to stop and use of wireless—gave Kretschmer the right to sink the vessel without further ado. Kretschmer ordered the machine-gunner to sweep the bridge with a burst. There was a scrambling of men for the boats. Kretschmer gave them time to get clear and then fired a torpedo. A burst of flame followed, and when it died away the *Glen Farg* could be seen sinking rapidly.

Kretschmer nosed *U-23* over to one of the lifeboats. "What ship and what were you carrying?" he yelled.

"Glen Farg, in ballast."

"Right." Then he advised them on their best course for land. "Head southeast and you will get the advantage of the current. Are any of you hurt?"

"No."

"Sorry you are landed in this position. I am leaving now."

After a brief silence, a voice replied from the boat. "Thanks for coming over."

Kretschmer waved and *U-23* slid off into the night.

The war at sea could not long continue on the basis of such gallantry. As defenses against the U-boats improved, the U-boats became more wary and more vindictive. On August 17, 1940, all restrictions were lifted for U-boats operating in waters around the British Isles. As these waters were defined loosely, unrestricted submarine warfare quickly reached out into mid-Atlantic.

While the U-boats were still operating in limited numbers and under restrictions, the British seamen who manned the antisubmarine vessels were learning to be seamen. It was almost a light-hearted improvisation at first, for few regular officers could be spared from the demands of the fleet. Older destroyers, partially manned by regulars, took charge of the convoy escorts, but on the smaller ships, the corvettes, the trawlers, the drifters, it was the reserves who took over and bore the brunt of the war. These ships, converted from peacetime uses, were given a gun or so, a couple of depth-charge racks, a green crew who were given a cram course in working their ship and in looking for U-boats, and then they were sent off to add another tiny measure of protection to the merchant ships on whom Britain's life depended.

Commanding officers of these small escorts were largely drawn from the Royal Naval Reserve, men who pursued the sea in peacetime as officers on freighters and passenger liners. They, at any rate, had a knowledge of the sea, however imperfect their knowledge of the ways of the Royal Navy. Their officers were usually members of the Royal Naval Volunteer Reserve, landsmen hastily trained in essential naval matters. They wore their insignia of rank in a zigzag pattern on the sleeves instead of the straight stripes of the officers in the Royal Navy. The Volunteers were known as the "Wavy Navy."

Taking these small ships to sea in the North Atlantic was no picnic even in peacetime. Their living accommodations were limited, their amenities few, and their motion lively. There was no excuse for taking them out into the deep Atlantic, yet out they went, for it was war, and something had to go to protect the cargoes. Learning as they worked, the former bank clerks, insurance salesmen, college men, barristers, solicitors, clubmen, tradesmen, and factory workers did their best, and gradually they learned to become fairly competent seamen. They learned to use the puny weapons they had, and they began to kill U-boats.

The U-boats were killing ships, too. The first winter of the war, the losses were supportable, and then the Norwegian campaign caused Dönitz to call his U-boats out of the Atlantic to support the German operations in the far north. It was there that the German U-boat skippers learned that they had a faulty torpedo; its magnetic head was subject to premature detonation. It was frustrating to see your torpedo explode before it reached the target. It was frustrating during the Norwegian campaign; later, when the Battle of the Atlantic was at its height, it would have been fatal.

With the fall of France, the U-boats gained a great advantage. Now, instead of making the perilous journey out through the minefields of the North Sea in order to reach their hunting grounds, they could operate at bases much closer to them. Over the next months at Brest and Lorient in France and at Trondheim and Bergen in Norway elaborate U-boat pens were constructed. These were vast concrete structures into which the U-boats could glide. They were so strongly built as to be impervious to bombing. Once a U-boat was inside, the pen provided all the comforts of home. There were barracks for the crews, stores of every description, food, fuel, torpedoes, ammunition, cordage, spare parts. There were recreation areas, including a brothel for the lusty young men of the Reich. It is said that in one case one of these establishments was set aside for the crew and in another "street" one was set aside for the officers. No one was supposed to notice that the two buildings were back to back and that the girls shuttled from one to the other in accordance with the demand.

Because of the U-boat bases in France, the British had to stop using the English Channel for oceanic convoys entirely, routing them instead north of Ireland to ports on the Clyde, particularly Glasgow, and to Liverpool. The task of the escort forces was made the more difficult by the stubborn insistence of the Republic of Eire on maintaining her neutrality, in spite of the fact that her very existence depended on the cargoes carried in British ships. The prejudice of De Valera and his men against Britain was stronger than their fear of German victory. So, throughout the war, Britain was deprived of bases in southern Ireland such as Cobh (Queenstown) and others which had proved to be of such inestimable value in World War I.

Since the oceangoing merchant ships could not use the English Channel, those which could not be accommodated in the Clyde ports and in Liverpool were routed around the north of Scotland to join coastal convoys, which ran every two days to the Thames.

This practice led them to a new danger, that of magnetic mines. Both U-boats and planes of the Luftwaffe laid large numbers of these insidious assassins of ships. They were set off by the change in magnetic field caused by the passage of a steel ship. Nothing happened if a wooden-hulled ship passed over them. They might lurk for days or weeks, unseen, unsuspected, until a luckless ship came close enough to set them off.

The toll from mines might have been worse than it was had not a careless Luftwaffe pilot dropped one in the mudflats at Shoeburyness in the Thames Estuary. The British were able to recover it intact and get it to a shed where it could be examined. There it lay, inscrutable, seemingly impervious, and deadly. With complete disregard for his own safety, Lieutenant Commander J. G. D. Ouvry volunteered to have a go at it. He and the mine were placed in splendid isolation behind a barrier of sandbags. At some distance a man with a pencil and a notebook kept a record of everything that Commander Ouvry reported.

"Now I am going to loosen the screw in the upper left corner of the access plate."

With infinite care, Commander Ouvry then proceeded to apply his screwdriver and to turn gently, oh, so gently.

By this method, if he failed, the next man to make the attempt would know where Ouvry had been right and where he had been fatally wrong.

Nothing went wrong, and the mine was disarmed. Then its secrets could be discovered. The eager scientists went to work and soon discovered how to defeat it. The process involved "degaussing" a ship by passing a cable around the hull and inducing an electric current in the cable. This had the effect of reversing or neutralizing the natural magnetism of the vessel and so thwarted the mine. The discovery led also to a method of sweeping these magnetic mines. It was no small task, and the fleet of minesweepers operating in British waters grew to over 700, but they did succeed in keeping the major ports open.

Even so, mines continued to be a menace, and by the end of 1941, 280 ships totaling 772,586 tons had been sunk by mines. These ships tended to be small, averaging just over 2700 tons, opposed to the ones sunk by U-boats, mostly out in the ocean. U-boat victims averaged slightly over 4300 tons.

Operating from their new-won bases in Norway and later in France, the U-boats entered on what their skippers referred to as "the happy time." In May, 1940, U-boats sank only 13 ships (55,580 tons); the next month, as they began to use the Norwegian bases, their kills shot up to 58 ships (284,113 tons). And so it continued to the end of the year and on into 1941. The 50 overage American destroyers came in the nick of time, for the regular escort forces were being swamped.

As soon as he had enough boats, Dönitz began a kind of attack he had planned ever since he had been taken prisoner in World War I. This was the "Wolf Pack Attack"—*Die Rudeltaktik,* the Germans called it.

A wolf pack consisted of a line of U-boats spread out across the likely path of a convoy's advance. As soon as one boat made contact, it would send off a sighting report to U-boat headquarters at Lorient. Dönitz or his chief of staff would take personal charge of operations and maneuver the other U-boats of the pack into attacking positions. Once everything was in readiness, they would turn the command over to the senior officer on the scene, and the slaughter would begin.

And it was often a slaughter in the early, unprotected convoys. This was the day of the German U-boat aces: Kretschmer, Prien—sinker of the *Royal Oak*—Schepke, Endras, and Frauenheim.

Part of the success of these men resulted from the fact that large numbers of ships were still sailing unescorted. Doubts about the convoy system still remained in high places, and the aggressive Mr. Churchill considered antisubmarine vessels better employed in "offensive patrol" than in "defensive escort work." Fortunately for Britain, Mr. Churchill learned better fairly quickly. Others were slower or did not learn at all.

Yet the convoy system was working. Throughout the war independently sailed ships were lost at about four times the rate of those sailing in convoys. It was largely against independent shipping that the U-boats directed their efforts, for the kills were easier and the danger less. If the U-boats were to strangle Britain, however, they could not avoid taking on the convoys.*

On any given day in the North Atlantic there might be ten or more of these convoys making their painful, plodding way through the ocean, winter and summer, in fair weather and among the foulest that Nature has been able to hurl against man in his puny ships. Outward bound, largely in ballast, the ships often were in danger of

---

* In addition to coastal convoys, there were several different kinds of ocean ones. Outbound from Britain to North America were the fast OB (later ON) convoys terminating in Halifax, Nova Scotia. "Fast" is a relative term, and in this case it meant 9 to 10 knots. Slow convoys over the same run were designated ONS and made 7½ to 8 knots. Most of them called at Sydney, Cape Breton Island, instead of Halifax. Fast and slow convoys eastbound were labeled HX and SC. A number would be added to indicate which convoy it was, and the numbers would run consecutively, except that occasionally when a convoy designation was changed, the Convoy and Routing section of the Admiralty might begin with 51 instead of 1 to confuse the Germans.

Southbound runs were OG to Gibraltar and OS to Sierra Leone on the west coast of Africa. Corresponding runs to the north were HG and SL.

In and of themselves, these designations are not important except that they serve as a convenient shorthand in dealing with individual convoys. Most of the designations given here remained unchanged throughout the war, but many others were added.

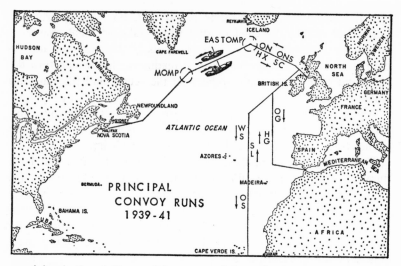

PRINCIPAL
CONVOY RUNS
1939-41

capsizing in the violence of the storms; inbound, often so heavily laden they seemed sure to swamp if they took one more heavy sea aboard, the ships came and went. Around them snuffled the escorts, perhaps five to a 35-ship convoy—their asdic (sonar) apparatus probing, probing, probing for U-boats, their lookouts straining their eyes out, their officers of the watch keeping station in the dark nights by feel rather than any instruments that might aid them, for these little ships rarely carried radar. The escorts chivvied their charges to their stations in the formation, rounded up stragglers, attacked any contact their asdic operators or lookouts reported. These escorts were all things to all men. They occasionally killed U-boats, they protected the merchant ships, and those they could not protect they watched go down, feeling all the time that there must have been *something* they could have done a little differently, *something* that would have saved their sinking charges. The escorts rescued the men in the water when there was time, and sometimes they had to kill them if a U-boat was nearby. Occasionally they were able to pull a German from the water, and often he told them much about the U-boats and their capabilities.

The commonest type of U-boat in the Atlantic war was the Type VIIc, with a surface displacement of 517 tons (750 submerged). These vessels were 213 feet in length and carried usually two deck guns. They had four bow torpedo tubes and one in the stern. In addition to the five torpedoes in the tubes, they carried three complete reloads, for a total of twenty. Surfaced, they could attain a speed of 17 knots, faster than some of the slower escorts. Under water they could make up to 8 knots for short distances, but were more likely to travel at 5 knots or less.

Their slow speed submerged and their speed superiority to the escorts on the surface caused the Germans to adopt the night surfaced attack as their usual method. And, if a well-trained wolf pack was in evidence, the method could be deadly indeed.

Convoy SC-7 was plodding toward Britain west of Rockall Bank on the night of October 16, 1940. The ships were darkened, and the formation was good. To the men aboard these ships, it was just another peaceful night.

But unknown to them, Convoy SC-7 was not alone. As midnight passed, *U-48* picked up the throb of many propellers and began to stalk her prey. Signals flew to Dönitz's headquarters, and soon 5 other U-boats were on their way toward the unsuspecting convoy.

Then a questing escort picked up a contact. Forced to flee for her life, *U-48* lost the convoy. The merchant ships made a drastic alteration of course. For the rest of that night and all the next morning, there was no further sign of U-boats. But the convoy commodore was not deceived. He knew that they might be massing ahead of him.

They were. Although *U-48* had lost the scent, *U-46, U-99, U-100, U-101,* and *U-123* were closing in for the kill. They had placed themselves in a line across the convoy's presumed track, and this plan paid off.

Racing up and down the columns of the convoy after dark, fully surfaced, their guns blazing, and torpedoes leaping from their tubes, the U-boats could not miss. Columns of smoke and flame shot up. A tanker laden with thousands of tons of high octane gasoline illuminated the scene like a giant torch from Hell. An ammunition ship was hit and simply disintegrated. There were no survivors from that ship, but for them the end was quick. They were more fortunate than some others who were burned to death by the flaming gasoline spreading over the surface of the water. Men saw their fate advancing on them, driven by the wind faster than they could swim. They screamed once or twice and were gone.

Seventeen ships were sunk from that convoy before the U-boats were finished. The shattered remnant of Convoy SC-7 staggered on while the U-boats paused to take stock of the situation and look for new victims.

U-99, U-101, and *U-123* had expended all their torpedoes and were ordered to return to base, but *U-46, U-48,* and *U-47,* the last skippered by the redoubtable Prien, joined *U-100,* which was still following after the convoy.

Prien's *U-47* turned up bigger game, however, that same morning, and the boats prepared to attack that night. This time the victim was fast convoy HX-79. The story was the same. There were the same wild charges through the convoy columns, the same sinking ships, the same drowning men. Before HX-79 could make its escape, 14 more ships had gone to the bottom.

But this was not the end of the story. As the U-boats withdrew to catch their breath, a second section, Convoy HX-79A, stumbled on the scene. With their torpedoes nearly depleted, the U-boats could account for only 7 more ships before breaking off the action.

In this series of actions, known to the Germans as the "Night of the Long Knives," 8 U-boats sank 38 ships without getting a scratch themselves. For the British it was the worst convoy disaster of the war. In the space of two nights, they had lost more ships to submarines than they had in each of six of the previous thirteen months of the war.

October was even worse, but then some relief began to be felt. The 50 American four-pipers began to come on the scene, and shortly thereafter new British destroyers and other antisubmarine vessels began to take their places in the escorts. Air coverage was extended, which forced the U-boats to operate farther out in the Atlantic. But most important was the shortsightedness of Adolf Hitler. Even after a year of war, he still did not understand the use of sea power, and submarines were allocated a very low priority. By the end of 1940, Dönitz had only 22 U-boats fit for operations. This meant that at most 8 could be on station at any one time; these did their best, but they were not enough.

U-boats were aided by surface raiders, both disguised merchant ships, such as the *Atlantis,* and warships making brief forays out against British shipping.

The *Atlantis* was skippered by Captain Bernhard Rogge, who proved himself to be as much a master of disguise as Sherlock Holmes at his best. Known in the German naval records as "Ship 16," the *Atlantis* was converted from a German freighter of the Bremen Hansa Line. She displaced 7860 tons, was 500 feet in length, and could make a top speed of 17½ knots. Hidden beneath such camouflage as artificial deck houses, dummy booms, and fake winches were six 6-inch guns, a 3-inch warning gun, two 37-mm.

antiaircraft guns, four 20-mm. general-purpose guns, and a torpedo tube. She could carry 92 magnetic mines, and Number 2 hold had been converted into a hangar for a seaplane. Rogge managed to get two planes assigned to the ship, one assembled and ready for use, and the other disassembled, in crates. That way the two would just fit.

The *Atlantis* sailed from Bremen on March 31, 1940, disguised as a Norwegian ship, and escorted by a U-boat. After darkness fell, the crew set to work, removing a dummy funnel and making other, more subtle, changes in her appearance. The next morning she appeared to be the Russian auxiliary ship *Kim*. For the next few days she held her course as though bound for Murmansk. After crossing the Arctic Circle, she bade farewell to her U-boat escort and passed through the Denmark Strait between Iceland and Greenland.

The bitterly freezing weather turned to blazing tropical sun as the *Atlantis* made her way through the Atlantic narrows en route to the Cape Town area, where she would begin her attacks on shipping. Once south of the Equator, she changed her disguise once more, as the presence of a Russian ship in the South Atlantic was highly suspicious. After poring through Lloyd's Register of Shipping for a suitable model, Captain Rogge decided his ship should become the Japanese freighter *Kasil Maru*. Stages were slung over the side, and the crew went to work with paintbrushes. The hull became black, the masts yellow, the ventilators yellow outside and red inside, while the black funnel bore a large white "K."

Even the crew was disguised as Japanese. One of the smaller members put on women's clothes and pushed a baby carriage up and down the deck, while six "passengers" dozed in deck chairs.

The play-acting went on for some time, and it was not until May 3 that the *Atlantis* claimed her first victim. She was the British freighter *Scientist,* and she was caught completely by surprise. After a few rounds, the crew took to the boats, except for the master and first officer, who remained in icy calm to await the boarding party.

The *Atlantis* rescued all the crew of the *Scientist* before sinking her. Two men who were wounded received expert medical care. Captain Rogge was determined to conduct his raiding activities as humanely as possible.*

---

* This humanity was characteristic of the captains of all the German disguised merchant raiders with the conspicuous exception of Captain von Ruckteschell, commanding the *Widder* and later the *Michel.* His ruthlessness led to his conviction at Nuremberg as a war criminal.

The *Atlantis*'s career lasted over twenty months. She existed by taking on fuel, food, and stores from supply ships sent out to meet her, from prizes, and wherever else she could find what she needed. She ranged throughout the Indian Ocean for nearly a year. Once she doubled back into the Atlantic. The Indian Ocean seemed a better hunting ground, so Rogge took her back. Once she believed she had sighted the liner *Queen Mary,* but on that date the big ship was in Sydney. What it was that was seen by Rogge has never been determined. Once she came near to being spotted by the battleship *Nelson,* and it was only by luck that she made her escape.

Rogge decided to return to Germany by way of the Pacific. The *Atlantis* sank one more ship during the crossing. On the way she passed near Pitcairn Island, home of the descendants of the *Bounty* mutineers. Then the foul-weather clothes came out again, for the *Atlantis* was approaching Cape Horn.

As he entered the Atlantic, Rogge learned that the supply ship serving U-boats in the Cape Town area had been sunk and offered the services of his ship for this purpose. In a matter of hours, he was ordered to rendezvous with the first of several U-boats. It was this errand that led to his downfall, for while he was refueling *U-126,* H.M.S. *Devonshire* came on the scene. It was quickly over. All but seven of Rogge's crew were saved by the U-boats, and Rogge reached home to tell of his adventures. During the long cruise he had sunk 22 ships. But the disruption of naval plans he and his fellows caused was far more important than the tonnage they sank.

By no means was the *Atlantis* the only successful disguised merchant raider—she was merely the most famous. The *Orion* had a cruise of 510 days in the Atlantic, Pacific, and Indian Oceans, the *Pinguin,* finally sunk by H.M.S. *Cornwall* after a marauding cruise which extended as far south as the Antarctic Ocean, sank 17 ships and 11 whaling vessels. Other raiders were the *Widder, Thor, Komet,* and *Kormoran.*

Other than the *Atlantis* and *Pinguin,* none of these disguised merchant raiders did as much damage as the big warships when Hitler let them go out. After losing the *Graf Spee* in Montevideo and the *Blücher, Karlsruhe, Königsberg,* and 10 destroyers in Norway, the Führer was reluctant to risk the big fellows. Combined with Hitler's reluctance was the necessity for extensive repairs to most of the surface navy after the Norwegian campaign, so it was not until late in 1940 that the *Admiral Scheer,* first of the new wave of raiders, was able to sail. She was sister ship to the sunken *Graf Spee* and was destined to be far more successful. She got home.

Leaving Germany on October 23, 1940, under command of Captain Theodore Krancke, the *Scheer* slipped through the Denmark Strait between Iceland and Greenland, to reach the freedom of the broad Atlantic. Two weeks after she had sailed, she came upon her first victim, the independently routed *Mopan,* which failed to get off the "RRR" warning signal of a surface raider. Had she done so, she might have averted a great catastrophe. But the world would have been robbed of a great tale of heroism.

It was unbelievable weather for the Atlantic in November. The sun was shining brightly, casting bright reflections on the smooth sea, scarcely ruffled by a gentle south-easterly breeze. It was the kind of weather passengers hope for when they set out on an ocean voyage, and the kind of weather men in wartime convoys learned to hate. In such weather there was no concealment from a ruthless enemy.

Convoy HX-84 was steaming peacefully through these peaceful waters in 52°45′ North latitude, 32°13′ West longitude, almost the middle of the Atlantic. Steadily, hour by hour, the 38 ships in nine columns were approaching Britain. In their holds and tanks, they were bringing, not the wealth of India, but the wealth of the New World, the food, the oil, the gasoline, the machines, the guns, the ammunition, that Britain needed to keep going a little longer. Eleven of these ships were tankers; they were especially vulnerable and had been placed in the center of the formation. The ships were of all sizes, from the 17,000-ton *Rangitiki,* belonging to the New Zealand Shipping Line, to the *Puck,* a tiny cargo tramp of a thousand tons, seeming scarcely large enough to venture so far from land. There was the convoy commodore's 7300-ton flagship, *Cornish City,* the *Stureholm,* belonging to neutral Sweden, but joining in the fight for freedom. Then there was the *Jervis Bay.*

The only warship in the convoy, the *Jervis Bay* was carried on the Royal Navy List as an "armed merchant cruiser." In peacetime, this 14,000-ton vessel had carried passengers and freight between Britain and Australia. Belonging to the Aberdeen and Commonwealth Line, she was a veteran of eighteen years' service. When the war broke out, the Royal Navy had taken her over, installed a few elderly 6-inch guns in Singapore, and commissioned her for service as a warship. Now, on November 5, 1940, she was the only protection for Convoy HX-84; not for hundreds of miles would the convoy pick up its antisubmarine escort to take it the final miles to the United Kingdom.

On her bridge was a tough, craggy-browed Irishman, Captain Edward Fogarty Fegen. At forty-seven years of age, Captain Fegen was still a bachelor. The Navy was in his blood. He was the son of an admiral, the grandson of a captain, and the sea had been his life.

On this lovely afternoon, he was in his usual position on the bridge of his ship. There had been no trouble, and there was no reason to expect any.

Suddenly a lookout spoke. There was a ship 15 miles away to the north, broad on the port beam. At that moment, Captain Fegen probably realized what was in store for him and his ship. Even at that distance, he could see that the stranger was a warship. He knew no British ship should be in that position. It might be American, but the chances were that it was German.

Fegen turned to his chief yeoman of signals.

"Make the challenge."

The chief yeoman clacked the shutters of the Aldis lamp. Everyone on the bridge peered intently toward the stranger. There was no reply.

"Make it on the ten-inch searchlight," ordered Fegen.

The chief yeoman moved over to the big signal-searchlight. Once again the challenge flashed northward.

Again there was no reply.

"Make it on the searchlight!" commanded Fegen.

There was no possibility that the stranger could fail to see the flashes of the brilliant searchlight. By this time, Fegen scarcely needed to look.

He knew there would be no reply.

Fifteen miles to the north, Captain Krancke peered through his binoculars at the convoy. He could see no signs of any warships that might stand in his way. He could take the *Admiral Scheer* down on it like a wolf descending on a flock of sheep. There would be just time to finish off most of the convoy before darkness fell in a couple of hours. He ordered 25 knots to close the enemy ships and get the job over as soon as possible, before the darkness of night would close in to hide his victims.

"Action stations!" ordered Captain Fegen. "Hoist the signal to the convoy: 'Prepare to scatter.' " Alarm bells sounded, and men rushed to man the obsolete guns which were all that stood between the convoy and the *Scheer's* six 11-inch modern rifles—all that stood between the convoy and destruction.

The convoy commodore ordered a turn directly away to the south at the same time as Captain Fegen ordered his ship to turn directly to the north. In those few moments he had made up his mind to die.

There was no chance whatever that the *Jervis Bay* could stand up to the *Scheer*. In some cases, even the bravest David is no match for the Goliath. Fegen could only hope to slow the German down enough to give the convoy a precious few minutes more to scatter and escape. Every minute gained was a minute nearer darkness, a minute nearer safety for the ships of HX-84.

Already shells were falling among the convoy. The *Rangitiki* was straddled, but escaped damage by some miracle. The tanker *San Demetrio* took an 11-inch shell. Her crew hastily abandoned her, but the next day she was still afloat. Another crew boarded her and sailed her home in triumph.

Captain Krancke swore softly. Here was a fool of a merchant cruiser heading toward him, determined to spoil the game. Very well. The fool should have his lesson.

Captain Fegen was no fool, and there was no lesson to be learned. He knew full well that there was no hope of survival for him or for his ship. The 100-pound shells his pop-guns could throw would not even dent the armor of the *Scheer*. A few of the 650-pound shells of the German pocket battleship would make a sieve of the frail hull of the *Jervis Bay*.

As the guns of the *Scheer* swung round toward the *Jervis Bay*, the range had closed to 11 miles. Then it happened. The third German salvo crashed home. At one instant, the foremast was shot away, the gun-control station demolished, the range-finder wrecked, and the bridge all but destroyed. Amid the dead and dying stood Captain Fegen, his left arm shot off just below the shoulder, arterial blood pumping his life away from the shattered stump.

Refusing all aid, Captain Fegen struggled to regain control of his stricken ship. The *Scheer*, satisfied that the *Jervis Bay* was out of the fight, turned back to the convoy. But Captain Krancke reckoned without his adversary. In terrible agony, Captain Fegen calmly and courteously issued the orders that would once again interpose his

421

ship between the German and the convoy. The range closed, and the ancient guns could now reach the target. In local control, trained and elevated painfully by hand, the guns roared their defiance. Even at best, those relics were too inaccurate to be of much use. Under the circumstances, Captain Krancke never saw the fall of shot from the stubborn British ship commanded by an even more stubborn Irishman.

But she was in the way again, this *Jervis Bay*. This time there would be no respite for her. She would be destroyed.

The *Scheer's* guns swung back on the tormentor. A shell severed the cables between the bridge and the rudder. Ordering steering shifted aft, Captain Fegen painfully—supporting himself with his remaining arm—made his way from the bridge to the after control station, every inch of his progress marked by a trail of blood from his stump. The red contrasted brightly with the blackened and charred decks.

His face now dead-white, Captain Fegen found himself too weak to climb up to the secondary bridge at the after station. But his commands could be heard, and he got his ship back on course. He dropped smoke pots to help hide the convoy and then turned to make his way back to the bridge. Above the roar of the flames, he could hear the groans and screams of the dying, but he had done his job, and his men had done theirs. The ship still had way on, and nearly an hour had passed since the *Scheer* had been sighted. Incredibly, both captain and ship still survived.

He glanced aft and saw that his battle ensign had been shot away. He sent a seaman to hoist another. Appropriately enough, this was the ensign reserved for burial of the dead.

The convoy was scattering, and darkness was coming on. The *Scheer* was still occupied with the *Jervis Bay*.

As he neared the bridge, Captain Fegen finally lost his personal fight. Another shell landed near him. He never knew what happened. His pain-wracked body was instantly disintegrated.

But the *Jervis Bay* was still afloat and still headed to cut off the *Scheer*.

It could not last. The German shells reached her engines, and the former liner drifted to a stop, listing, burning, down by the stern.

She and her captain were both finished, but their job was done. For exactly 22 minutes and 22 seconds, the *Jervis Bay* had held off the *Scheer*. The convoy was scattering rapidly; there was no longer any chance that the German warship could annihilate it. Captain Krancke would have to settle for less, much less.

In the remaining moments of daylight, the *Scheer* moved upon her victims, sinking five before darkness and shortage of ammunition caused Krancke to break off the action. He had already used one third of his supply of shells, and he was sure that his position was known to the British. Utterly alone in a sea where every man's hand would be against him, Krancke decided to put as much distance as possible between himself and the grave of the *Jervis Bay*.

Later that night, another ship approached the spot where the *Jervis Bay* had gone down. With infinite caution, Captain Sven Olander, master of the *Stureholm,* brought his ship through the darkness. It was a fantastically dangerous thing that he was doing, for no one could know the *Scheer* was gone for good, and there was every reason to believe that she had summoned U-boats to finish off the convoy. But Captain Olander was a determined man. He knew how much he and all the others owed to Captain Fegen and the *Jervis Bay,* and he was determined to discharge that debt, so far as he was able. He was looking for survivors from the *Jervis Bay*.

By the time dawn revealed nothing but broken and burned bodies and bits of wreckage, the *Stureholm's* crew had pulled 65 men out of the water. It was from them that we were able to learn the story of the last hours and minutes of the *Jervis Bay* and of Captain Fegen.

"I wonder if the captain survived," murmued Captain Krancke as he watched the gallant armed merchant cruiser go down. "God knows, those men have put their country forever in their debt."

When the details became known, all a grateful country could do for Captain Fegen was award him the Victoria Cross posthumously. But the crews of 32 merchant ships would know to the end of their lives just what it was that he had done. Their knowledge would have been more precious to Captain Fegen than any medal, even one whose inscription reads "For Valour."

After her encounter with HX-84, the *Scheer* sped south, looking for shipping in the Freetown area before rounding the Cape of Good Hope and prowling the Indian Ocean. By means of aid and resupply from ships sent out to meet her, she managed to remain at sea for five months, sinking 10 more ships during the period. During the last week of March, 1941, she once again eluded the British patrol lines and reached Bergen, Norway, on March 30. Two days later she arrived at Kiel, where she delighted Admiral Raeder, not only by her success, but by the dinner of steak topped with eggs she provided for him. These had come from the captured British refrigerator ship *Duquesa*—as Krancke put it, a kind of involuntary gift from Winston Churchill.

The heavy cruiser *Hipper* made two sorties into the Atlantic during this period. Her first cruise, lasting for three weeks in December, 1940, was completely unproductive, and she retired to Brest, where she remained for two months. On February 1, she set out again, operating in the waters between the Azores and Portugal. Here it was that she encountered, on February 12, the unescorted convoy SLS-64. There was no *Jervis Bay* to help out this time, and she was able to sink 7 ships for a total of 32,806 tons before fuel and ammunition shortages forced her captain to break off the action and return to Brest.

Once she had returned, the German Naval Staff became nervous about her because of the risk of British bombs, so they ordered her to return to Germany by making a wide sweep out through the Atlantic, passing through the Denmark Strait. She preceded the *Scheer* on this journey by a few days and reached Kiel on March 28. She was not spotted by the British, who had their hands full with the cruise of the two battle cruisers, *Scharnhorst* and *Gneisenau*.

These two vessels had left Kiel on January 23, 1941, under the command of Vice Admiral Günther Lütjens. Attempting to break through into the Atlantic east of Iceland, Lütjens was spotted by a British patrol, but turned back to the north before definite contact could be made. It was lucky for him that he did so, for beyond the cruiser *Naiad,* which caught a fleeting glimpse of the German force, lay the two 16-inch-gun battleships *Rodney* and *Nelson* and the battle cruiser *Repulse*. There would have been no possible escape for the German squadron. But they survived to fight again later, and Admiral Lütjens had a rendezvous with the *Rodney* four months later.

Refueling north of Iceland from a supply ship, the German battle cruisers passed through the Denmark Strait and at dawn on February 8 encountered the eastbound fast convoy HX-106. Lütjens immediately split his force in order to attack simultaneously from the north and the south. As the two ships were making their approach, the water creaming around their bows, their wakes extending toward the horizon, a lookout in the *Scharnhorst* sighted the fighting top of a battleship. This put another complexion on the affair, so far as Lütjens was concerned, for he had orders not to engage enemy warships if it could be avoided. He turned away, and convoy HX-106 was allowed to proceed unmolested. The *Ramillies,* escorting the convoy, had sighted only one ship and reported it as a *Hipper*-class cruiser, which seriously misled Admiral Tovey and the Admiralty. They took positions to intercept a returning ship, not an outbound squadron. For this reason, Lütjens's squadron moved on undetected.*

After replenishing from a waiting supply ship, Lütjens lurked in the waters used by the Halifax convoys for several days, but luck was against him. He moved westward, and on February 22, encountered the smoke of several ships, recently dispersed from a westbound convoy. Here was game to his liking, and the two German battle cruisers quickly disposed of 5 ships, for a total of 25,784 tons. This success was marred by the fact that several ships got off raider contact reports. Wireless operators in the German ships did their best to jam the transmissions, but they clearly heard the station at Cape Race acknowledge one of the signals. Lütjens realized that the Admiralty would quickly be aware that a powerful force of German ships was at sea in the North Atlantic.

It was time for him to move on.

Not only would pickings be slim, because the Admiralty would quickly reroute all shipping, but he could expect a swarm of British warships around him if he stayed where he was.

He headed south to operate in the neighborhood of Sierra Leone, picking up two of the waiting supply ships as he went.

Off the Cape Verde Islands, he encountered the convoy SL-67, but was deterred by the presence of the battleship *Malaya.* Knowing he had been sighted and reported, Lütjens headed north once more, back to the Halifax route. Here, on March 15 and 16, he met his greatest success, sinking 16 ships, totaling 82,000 tons. While the Germans were enjoying their target practice against the defenseless merchant ships, Lütjens had a bad fright, for his squadron was sighted by the battleship *Rodney.* Turning his stern on the enemy, Lütjens headed for the horizon. The *Rodney* lost touch with the Germans and broke off the chase to pick up survivors from the sunken ships.

The Admiralty made an all-out effort to hunt down and bring the Germans to action, but they eluded all searches. Because the German Naval Staff had plans for a more ambitious operation with these two

---

* All the big German ships had similar silhouettes, and their resemblance caused mistakes on several occasions. The most serious took place during the battle between the *Hood* and *Prince of Wales* and the *Bismarck* and *Prinz Eugen,* as will be told shortly.

ships a little later, Lütjens was ordered to head for Brest in Occupied France. He made the passage without difficulty, although his ships were sighted by planes from the *Ark Royal* and by a Hudson bomber of Coastal Command. In each case, the British forces were too far away to intercept. The *Scharnhorst* and *Gneisenau* entered the port of Brest on the morning of March 22.

British Coastal Command aircraft did not discover them for six days. Bad weather had hampered searches, and it was by no means certain that Brest would be the port selected by the Germans. Once they were discovered, however, the two ships were subjected to heavy raids by the RAF. The *Gneisenau* took several bomb hits and required extensive repair. The *Scharnhorst*'s time had not yet come, and she escaped all damage. She did require considerable work before she would be ready to go to sea again, and so neither ship could be used in May for the grandiose operation Raeder and Lütjens planned.

Lütjens journeyed to Berlin. He would soon return to the North Atlantic, and there he had a rendezvous with the *Rodney* and the *Ark Royal*. He had escaped them once, but the next time, Fortune would be on the other side. These two ships would be instrumental in destroying him and the new flagship he was so proud to have under his orders.

Lütjens's future was mercifully concealed from him as he and his staff stepped onto the quarterdeck of the *Bismarck*. On hand to greet him, his stiff salute a model of military correctness, was Captain Ernst Lindemann with other officers of the brand-new battleship. Since the beginning of the year, she had been conducting trials and working-up exercises in the Baltic; now she was fully ready, poised for her first foray out into the Atlantic. She would be accompanied by Germany's newest heavy cruiser, the *Prinz Eugen*.

At this time, naval experts considered the *Bismarck* to be the most powerful ship in the world. Although she was officially listed as 35,000 tons, her actual standard displacement was 42,345 tons, and at full load she displaced nearly 53,000 tons. Over 10,000 tons of this weight was devoted to armor plate of specially hardened steel. Below the main deck, her hull was honeycombed into hundreds of watertight compartments, making the ship as near to unsinkable as man can devise. She had eight 15-inch guns in four twin turrets, each capable of hurling a shell weighing a ton a distance of 20 miles or so.

She could make over 30 knots, and she mounted the finest equipment that German skill could give her.

For this, her first cruise, she was taking several officers assigned to her sister, the *Tirpitz,* as yet unready for operations, and a number of naval cadets. These boys of sixteen and seventeen were expecting to get sea experience. They got far more than they bargained for.

The only ship in the Royal Navy that was near the *Bismarck* in speed and firepower was the battle cruiser *Hood.* She mounted the same number of 15-inch guns, but her speed was at least 2 knots slower. Also the *Hood,* now twenty-one years old, was, in the British expression, "a bit long in the tooth." She was a product of the design experience of the pre-Jutland period, whereas the *Bismarck* embodied the latest in naval architecture. Also, the *Hood* had a fatal weakness. Her magazines were not well protected against shells coming down nearly vertically—plunging fire, as it is called.

The Royal Navy had 2 battleships which could destroy the *Bismarck* by gunfire, the *Rodney* and the *Nelson.* Each mounted nine 16-inch guns, making their projectiles half again as heavy as those of the *Bismarck.* But they were limited to 22 knots. If they were to come into action against the German battleship, someone else would have to slow her down first.

Secret agent reports reached the Admiralty that two heavy German units had passed the Skaw heading north. Although there was no solid evidence, the First Sea Lord, Sir Dudley Pound, decided to assume the worst, that it was the *Bismarck* and some consort setting out on a raid into the Atlantic.

In this assumption, Pound was perfectly correct. Before sailing, Lütjens had summoned Captain Lindemann and certain other officers into his cabin.

"Gentlemen," he stated flatly, "we put to sea in two hours. To disguise our departure, our sister ship, the *Tirpitz,* will berth here tonight. We enter Norwegian waters tomorrow morning, refuel quickly at Bergen, and then join forces with the *Prinz Eugen,* which will operate along with us. Our job is to attack merchant shipping in the Atlantic. Orders from the Supreme Naval Command are to avoid clashes with enemy warships as far as possible.

"I have no doubt that the enemy is fully informed as to the *Bismarck's* firepower and range of action. They will throw everything they have at us. We shall either return victorious or not at all."

It was to be both victorious and not at all.

The German admiral's statement was not quite accurate, for the

Prinz Eugen joined before the *Bismarck* reached Bergen, Norway. And it was there that the British discovered her and learned for certain that it was the *Bismarck* they had to contend with.

In view of the intelligence reports of movements of German warships to the north, the Admiralty ordered a search of Norwegian ports by specially equipped long-range Spitfires belonging to the Coastal Command Photographic Reconnaissance Unit. Off went the aircraft about 1100 on May 21. A little over two hours later, Pilot Officer Suckling passed over Grimstad Fjord, just south of Bergen. There he saw two warships in a secluded cove. Circling around for a better look, he photographed the vessels and then set off for home.

When he landed about 1445, he reported that he had seen two cruisers, but his photographs proved better witnesses than he. Careful examination by experts revealed that the two ships were the *Bismarck* and a *Hipper*-class cruiser.

Pilot Officer Suckling was not the first man to be confused by the similar appearances of German warships, nor would he be the last. Such confusion would have more serious consequences when Vice Admiral L. E. Holland made the same mistake three days later from the flag bridge of the *Hood*.

The easiest way to attend to the *Bismarck* would be by air attack, but the British were not to be permitted so simple a way out. Shortly after Pilot Officer Suckling returned from his mission, the weather deteriorated. Driving rain swept over the North Sea, and no break was forecast by the meteorologists. Pilots sat in their briefing rooms watching the water run down the windows and flood down their runways. It was frustrating, but there was nothing they could do.

The same foul weather that frustrated the bombing attacks robbed Admiral Sir John Tovey of priceless information. In his cabin aboard the Home Fleet flagship, *King George V,* he contemplated the problem. The Admiralty might give advice, but the *Bismarck* was entirely his problem. He had to find her and, if possible, bring her to action and sink her. And at that moment, he had no idea where she was.

She might still be swinging around her anchor at Bergen, or she might have sailed the moment the Spitfire had left. She might be headed back to Germany, or she might be breaking out into the Atlantic.

If he moved too soon, Admiral Tovey's ships would be wasting fuel and would be in no state to engage the *Bismarck* even if they found her. If he moved too late, she might get clean away. Lacking information, he had to be very careful.

One thing he could do at once. He could send a force to cover the two most likely escape routes, to the east and west of Iceland. If necessary, the ships could refuel at Hvalfjord. The question was, which ships should he send?

He resolved to keep the flagship where she was until the last possible moment. The telephone line that connected him to the Admiralty was too valuable a source of information to be lightly cut off. That left the *Hood* and *Prince of Wales* at his disposal as the only ships capable of engaging the *Bismarck*. He hesitated before sending the *Prince of Wales* out, for she was too new. She had not yet had time to conduct the exercises so necessary to make a ship a fighting unit. Her machinery was untested, and builder's workmen were still aboard. Yet, he decided, she would have to go.

Midnight approached. Accompanied by six destroyers, the *Hood* and *Prince of Wales* left their anchorages at Scapa Flow and stood out to sea. The same lashing rain that kept the RAF grounded was beating onto the windscreens of the ships as their bows lifted to the Atlantic swell. It was a dirty night.

The next morning brought no improvement in the weather. It was now eighteen hours since Admiral Tovey had received any reports of the *Bismarck* and *Prinz Eugen*. They could still be at Bergen; they could be well on the way back to Germany, or they could be five hundred miles on their way toward the North Atlantic.

By this time, the Admiralty had assigned the new carrier *Victorious* and the battle cruiser *Repulse* to Admiral Tovey's force. Like the *Prince of Wales,* the *Victorious* was too new; her air squadron had never operated as a squadron before, and many of the pilots were completely inexperienced. Nevertheless, Admiral Tovey felt he had to use her if he could. As the *Victorious* entered Scapa Flow, Admiral Tovey signaled her commanding officer, Captain H. C. Bovell, to come on board the flagship. Could the *Victorious* attack the Germans in Bergen, or at any rate discover whether they were still there?

Captain Bovell regretfully concluded that his 80-knot Swordfish were unlikely to be able to do much good in a place so strongly defended as Bergen.

Admiral Tovey's face clouded. Is the *Victorious,* he wanted to know, fit to proceed to sea at all in the operations against the *Bismarck?*

Captain Bovell hesitated. In his own mind, he knew that his ship

PRESTON PUBLIC LIBRARY

was *not* ready for war operations. But he could not bring himself to say so. He hedged. Could he send for his flying commander and the squadron leader? They could give sounder advice than he on the conditions of the airmen assigned to the *Victorious*.

Commander H. C. Ranald and Lieutenant Commander Eugene Esmonde, when they arrived, were strongly in favor of being allowed to sail with the fleet. Admiral Tovey still hesitated, but he needed every ship he could lay his hands on, and the only other carrier that could conceivably be used was the *Ark Royal,* over a thousand miles away at Gibraltar. It had to be the *Victorious* or nothing.

The Admiral made up his mind. The *Victorious* should go.

Knowing how desperate Admiral Tovey was for information, Captain H. L. St. J. Fancourt, commanding the Naval Air Station at Hatston in the Orkney Islands, decided to see whether there was something he could do. He had some experienced pilots, and he felt that if any airmen could make it to Bergen in the thick weather that hung over the sea, his men could do it.

Commander G. A. Rotherham was just such a man. He had been a Fleet Air Arm observer for years and years, and most of those years had been before the days of complicated navigation devices. Rotherham was the kind of flier who could find his way by the smell, by the touch of wind on his cheeks, by the direction of the waves.

When he was asked, Rotherham was eager to make the attempt, and he suggested Lieutenant N. N. Goddard, RNVR, as the pilot. Fancourt supplied them with a Maryland bomber, and with the blessing of Coastal Command, sent them on their way.

Rotherham's idea was to fly as close to the water as possible, so he could observe the direction of the wind and know which way the aircraft was being set. Rotherham planned to use the old navigational device of the deliberate error, heading for a point some miles south of Bergen. Then, when he hit the coast, he would be in no doubt which way to turn.

About 1630 on the afternoon of May 22, the Maryland took off and headed out across the gray seas. At first the going was not bad, but the plane ran into mist, and Goddard found the strain of keeping the aircraft at 200 feet far too much to endure for the entire crossing. Up he went to 3000, but soon Rotherham wanted to go back down to get another glimpse of the water. So went the trip, up and down, up and down. After several such roller-coaster effects, the confident Rotherham announced that they were within ten minutes of their destination. Now the only problem was to keep from flying into a mountain.

Just at the right moment, the clouds cleared away, and dead ahead Rotherham saw the very landmark he had been heading for. The plane made a turn to port and headed north. They quickly found the fjord where the *Bismarck* and *Prinz Eugen* had been reported.

It was empty.

As they dropped down for a better look, every antiaircraft gun in Norway opened up on them—at least, so it seemed. Out they roared across the city, skimming the rooftops, astonished that they were still alive.

Immediately the radio operator tapped out the message: BATTLESHIP AND CRUISER HAVE LEFT.

Then Rotherham and Goddard settled down to a comparatively relaxed trip back to Hatston.

When he received the report, Admiral Tovey decided to wait until he could interrogate the pilot. It would result in little delay, and he could be certain that there was no error.

As the admiral and his staff were sitting down to dinner in his cabin on the *King George V,* the telephone call to Rotherham went through. There was no doubt about it. The Germans had sailed.

For some time, the fleet at Scapa Flow had been at two hours' notice for steam, and it being near 2000, Admiral Tovey ordered the sortie for 2200. By 2300 all ships had left their moorings and were standing down Pentland Firth toward the Atlantic.

That he might be heading in the wrong direction, he knew full well, but Admiral Tovey had to act to counter the action of the enemy that would pose the greatest danger to Britain. Clearly this greatest danger was the chance of the two German ships escaping out into the ocean to prey on the ships in the Atlantic lifeline. If the Germans had returned to Germany, no harm would have been done except for the waste of fuel oil.

There were four possible routes into the North Atlantic from the Arctic Ocean, but two of them lay so close to Scapa that they could be watched by smaller ships. The two most likely were the Iceland-Faroes passage, some 200 miles wide to the east of Iceland, and the Denmark Strait, between Iceland and Greenland. The latter was 120 miles wide, but in May was limited to about half that width by pack ice extending eastward from the coast of Greenland. The British had narrowed it even farther by a minefield extending northwest from Iceland. This was, however, the route all German surface raiders had

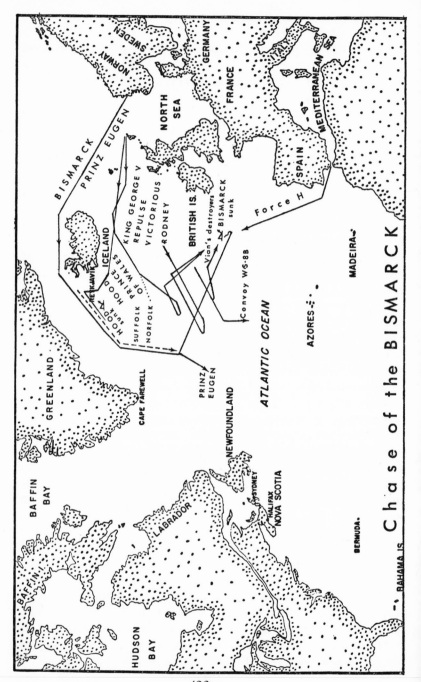

Chase of the BISMARCK

used before, and it seemed likely that the German admiral would use it again.

In any case, Admiral Tovey had his big ships well disposed to cover either eventuality. The *Hood* and *Prince of Wales* could reach the Denmark Strait by the time the Germans could, thanks to his foresight in sailing them early. He, with the *King George V*, the *Victorious*, and the *Repulse*, which had joined his force on the morning of May 23, could cover the Iceland-Faroes passage and could reinforce the *Hood* and *Prince of Wales* in a pinch.

At any rate, he had done all he could.

Able Seaman Newell was on duty as after lookout on the cruiser *Suffolk*. It was bitterly cold as the ship plunged and rolled in the disturbed waters of the Denmark Strait. Every so often, he would lower his binoculars and slap his arms across his chest to restore the circulation. At that moment, Admiral Tovey was eating his dinner westbound from Scapa Flow. Newell had had his own dinner some time earlier, and was now looking ahead to the end of the second dog watch, when he would be relieved to go below and get warm. The time was 1922 on May 23.

He raised his binoculars to his eyes again and swept the northern horizon once more. At that time of year, in those latitudes, it never gets entirely dark. A twilight hung in the air, and would remain with little change until morning. He could see nothing to port; a heavy mist reduced visibility to nothing. On the starboard quarter, he had more scope. There the visibility was nearly unlimited.

Suddenly his steady sweep of the horizon stopped. Did he see something? One could never be sure in these waters, for the mirage played funny tricks. There was something out there, but it might even be a reflection of their sister ship, the *Norfolk*, which was some little distance to the southwest of them. Newell looked again and made up his mind.

"Ship bearing green one four oh!" he shouted.

A moment later he corrected his report. "Two ships bearing green one four oh!"

On the bridge of the *Suffolk*, Captain R. M. Ellis rushed to the starboard side and peered through his own binoculars. There was no doubt about it. There they were. No British ships could be in that vicinity. The *Bismarck* and *Prinz Eugen* were found.

His first thought was to get his ship under the protective cover of the fogbank. The *Bismarck* was only about 14,000 yards away, and her guns could shoot 20 miles. At any moment, 15-inch shells might come crashing down upon him. He put his rudder over instantly and breathed a sigh of relief when the comforting mists closed about his ship.

His next job was to get off a sighting report. His immediate superior, Rear Admiral W. F. Wake-Walker in the *Norfolk,* was not far away, and he had to be alerted. The Admiralty and the Commander in Chief, Admiral Tovey, all needed to know what was happening. Even as the fog and mist were beginning to conceal the *Suffolk,* a radio message was going out: ONE BATTLESHIP, ONE CRUISER IN SIGHT BEARING OH TWO OH DEGREES DISTANT SEVEN MILES. COURSE TWO FOUR OH DEGREES.

For some reason, only the *Norfolk* received this message, perhaps because the transmitting antennas were wet. As more and more messages went out, the *Suffolk* could be heard by the *Hood* and the *King George V* and by the Admiralty in London.

It was no part of the duty of the two cruisers to fight the German force. Their role lay in shadowing and keeping in touch so the big ships could bring them to action.

Captain Ellis slowed down and allowed the two German ships to pass him. So far they had given no sign that they knew of his presence. They held their course steadily toward the southwest.

Because of a recent refit, the *Suffolk* had the latest in detection radar, and it was on her that the main burden of the shadowing rested. The *Norfolk*'s radar was much more limited, functioning only in a narrow arc dead ahead. Her captain, A. J. L. Phillips, contented himself with taking station on the opposite quarter of the Germans from the *Suffolk.* Before she got into the fog, she was narrowly missed by four 15-inch salvos from the *Bismarck.* The German shooting was entirely too good for comfort.

Admiral Wake-Walker sent a more complete report of the German warships, and this was the first inkling that Admiral Tovey and the Admiralty had that they had been found.

The forces began to close in on the *Bismarck* and her consort.

Aboard the *Hood,* Vice Admiral L. E. Holland considered the situation. His force of the *Hood,* the *Prince of Wales,* and 6 destroyers was some 300 miles almost due south of the enemy. His staff did a little plotting, and the Admiral ordered a course change to 295° and and a speed of 27 knots. That change should bring battle early the next morning.

As Holland's force increased speed, the destroyers were finding it heavy going. Spray and occasionally green water were breaking over their bridges, and their hulls shuddered to the crashing seas. Holland was conscious of their difficulties, but he was not going to slow down for them.

IF YOU ARE UNABLE TO MAINTAIN THIS SPEED [he signaled] I WILL HAVE TO GO ON WITHOUT YOU. YOU SHOULD FOLLOW AT YOUR BEST SPEED.

The destroyers were not going to give up. They hung on, accepting damage to boats, lifelines, and deck gear, rather than miss out on the opportunity of seeing action against the most powerful battleship in the world.

The chase went on. The *Bismarck* and *Prinz Eugen* held their southwesterly course, the two British cruisers tagging after them like wolves. Across their bows, still far off, lay the *Hood* and *Prince of Wales*.

Just before midnight, in a blinding snowstorm, the *Suffolk* lost contact. Before she could regain it, Admiral Holland had come to the conclusion that the Germans might have doubled back on their tracks. If so, they would escape him altogether if he held his westerly course. He decided to try to cover both possibilities. He slowed to 25 knots and headed due north.

It was over two hours before the *Suffolk* regained contact with the *Bismarck* and found that she had held her course steadily all the time. Admiral Holland turned back to the southwest, but his change of course had put him somewhat behind the Germans, so that the next morning he would come upon them from abaft the beam. His destroyers, for some reason yet unexplained, held on to the north, so as he prepared for battle, he had only the *Hood* and *Prince of Wales* in company. He thereby limited his range of vision, since he no longer had any scouting vessels ahead of him.

Aboard the two British capital ships, all hands were sent to their battle stations shortly after midnight, but the men were allowed to sleep in relays at their posts. As the men on deck made their bodies comfortable on the steel plates, cushioned only by their heavy clothing, they could see above them the huge battle ensigns flapping in the dim light.

All during the remaining hours of the night, the various forces held on as they had been steaming. Frequent reports from the *Suffolk* and *Norfolk* kept Admiral Holland constantly informed of the position of the enemy.

Shortly after 0400 the visibility began to improve. The German squadron was then estimated to be about 20 miles away. Action could come at any time. Half an hour later, it was possible to see about 12 miles from the bridge of the *Hood,* and lookouts redoubled their efforts.

At 0510, Admiral Holland ordered instant readiness for action. Men sprang to their feet, rubbing the sleep from their eyes. The big guns on both ships swung around to starboard, pointing in the suspected direction of the enemy. Eyes peered keenly into the lightening horizon.

On the *Bismarck* and *Prinz Eugen,* German eyes were also seeking the enemy. Neither Admiral Lütjens nor Captain Lindemann could know that a powerful British squadron was so close, but they knew one might be. They had heard the *Suffolk*'s radio messages and knew that she was leading battleships to the scene of action. The question in the minds of both captain and admiral was: can we get through before British forces reach us, or will we have to fight our way out?

At 0535 the questions were answered on both sides. Almost simultaneously, the British and Germans caught sight of each other. Admiral Holland ordered an immediate turn toward the enemy to close the distance. The *Bismarck* and *Prinz Eugen* held their courses, but their guns were aimed and ready.

This was the moment when Holland's turn to the north during the night became so important. He could no longer close the German ships at a sharp angle, for if he did, they would get away from him. He had to make an oblique approach which robbed him of the use of his after guns. He held the *Prince of Wales* in close formation with him, so that her after guns were masked, as well.

Thus he had the worst of both worlds. He could not close rapidly enough to minimize the danger until he was at his chosen battle range, nor could he use all his guns. If he had closed more slowly, he could have used all of his weapons, but he would have presented a broader target to the *Bismarck*'s excellent gunnery. If he had freed the *Prince of Wales* to conform to his movements generally, one ship could be closing the range rapidly while the other kept the *Bismarck* busy.

As Admiral Lütjens prepared his squadron for action, the *Prinz Eugen* was leading. This put the *Bismarck* in the post of danger, for it enabled her to cover threats from the two likely directions, northeast and southeast. He could see his adversaries quite clearly by now and correctly identified the *Hood.* He thought her consort was the

436

King George V, and it is under this name that the *Prince of Wales* appears in the German records of the battle.

His time to meet the *King George V* would come.

His error in identification was not important. However, Admiral Holland was about to make an error which may have cost him the battle and his life.

As the British squadron approached the Germans, the *Bismarck* was slightly more distant than the *Prinz Eugen,* and, as had happened before, the similar silhouettes confused the British. From the yardarm of the *Hood* came a signal to engage the left-hand ship (*Prinz Eugen*). Captain Leach of the *Prince of Wales,* certain that the admiral had made a mistake, disregarded the signal and took the *Bismarck* as his target. Three minutes later, Holland apparently recognized his error and signaled a shift of one target to the right. Simultaneously, at 0552, the *Hood* opened fire, and her shell splashes fell around the *Prinz Eugen.* At the same instant, the *Bismarck's* main battery belched smoke and fire; almost instantly the *Prince of Wales* followed suit.

Within the space of a minute, all three capital ships had opened fire. The *Prinz Eugen* contributed her bit with her 8-inch guns, and, according to German reports, was the first ship to obtain a hit. About the time of the third *Bismarck* salvo, a glow of fire sprang up at the base of the *Hood's* mainmast. It was a pulsating, orange flame, possibly cordite burning but not exploding.

Three minutes after fire was opened, the *Bismarck* fired her fifth salvo. While the shells were in the air, Admiral Holland ordered his ships to turn together 20 degrees to port.

The *Hood* never completed her turn.

Horrified watchers on the *Prince of Wales,* the *Suffolk,* and the *Norfolk* saw a flame leap hundreds of feet into the air from the *Hood.* It was gone in an instant, and a pillar of smoke hung over the ocean. Huge pieces of wreckage dropped back into the sea. A turret was blown completely free of the ship and sent up an enormous splash as it entered the water.

Of the *Hood* all that could be seen were the bow and stern sticking out of the water like a broken toy. Then they were gone. In the flash of an eye, the pride of the Royal Navy had been destroyed. A shell from the *Bismarck* had penetrated to her magazine, and the *Hood* had simply disintegrated. Violently churning water, broken bodies, bits of wreckage, and the lingering column of smoke were all that were left.

The *Hood's* grave is in 63°21′ North latitude, 31°50′ West longitude, 500 miles south of Cape Farewell on the southern tip of Greenland. With her lie the bodies of 94 officers and 1321 enlisted men. By some miracle, three of her crew survived, Midshipman W. J. Dundas, Able Seaman R. E. Tilburn, and Ordinary Signalman A. E. Briggs.

On the bridge of the *Prince of Wales,* Captain Leach watched with disbelieving eyes. It simply couldn't be happening.

But there was no time to mourn the *Hood.* He had to come hard right to avoid the wreckage. In a moment, German shells would be crashing down on his own ship.

The roar of the *Prince of Wales*'s guns never ceased, and her shells kept dropping all around the *Bismarck.* The German was lucky, and no hits were scored at first. It took but a short time for the *Bismarck*'s gunnery officer to shift his fire to the *Prince of Wales,* and about 0602, a 15-inch struck her compass platform. In an instant, Captain Leach found himself standing alone in the wreckage. Every other man there was killed or wounded.

Ordering smoke, Captain Leach turned away. The newness of the *Prince of Wales* had demanded its price. Less than half his battery was operating; at the moment, his ship was no match for the *Bismarck.*

The *Bismarck,* with some assistance from the *Prinz Eugen,* had defeated two British capital ships.

Rear Admiral Wake-Walker in the *Norfolk* had done his full duty in bringing the *Bismarck* under the guns of the *Hood* and *Prince of Wales.* Once the action had been joined, his role had become that of spectator. Now he was once again senior officer on the scene, and once again the full responsibility for the *Bismarck* fell on his shoulders.

He decided against ordering Captain Leach to re-engage the *Bismarck* with the *Prince of Wales.* From first to last, the German fire had been rapid and accurate; furthermore, it showed no signs of slackening. Clearly, in her present state of training and efficiency, the British battleship was of little use.

He decided to resume shadowing. He kept the *Prince of Wales* with him—just in case.

Although Captain Leach and Admiral Wake-Walker had no way of knowing it, one of the last salvos from the *Prince of Wales* had resulted in three hits on the German battleship. Two of these were unimportant, but the third penetrated an oil bunker on the port side, forward. This hit not only caused the loss of all the fuel in that tank, but it contaminated adjoining tanks, reducing the range of the ship severely. Although Captain Lindemann wished to carry on with the operation, Admiral Lütjens decided to take the ship to a French port where repairs could be made. He reasoned that even if they were successful in rendezvousing with a waiting tanker, his fuel capacity was permanently limited until repairs were carried out. Besides, he might be able to come out again with the *Scharnhorst,* and possibly the *Gneisenau,* if she could be put in shape. Then he would have a force the British would be hard put to withstand.

The British were having enough trouble with the *Bismarck* alone.

When the signal HOOD HAS BLOWN UP arrived at the Admiralty, it was like a death in the family. In the Operations Room, everyone had had good cause for satisfaction, having brought two capital ships to the scene where they could engage the enemy. Now it was defeat, total and utter disaster.

Almost everyone in that room had served in the *Hood.* All had friends on board, or brothers, or sons. Even though the fighting in Crete was at its height, even though the Mediterranean Fleet of Admiral Cunningham was in its hour of greatest trial, nothing was allowed to stand in the way of bringing the *Bismarck* to action and sinking her.

Even Churchill added his voice and resolution to the chase. Some critics say that he added too much, busying himself in matters he did not understand. But everyone was agreed. The *Bismarck* must be destroyed.

The sinking of the *Hood* caused major reshufflings of the British naval strength in the Atlantic. It became painfully obvious that the *King George V* and *Repulse* might prove incapable of stopping the *Bismarck* by themselves. On paper, these two ships constituted a weaker force than the one the *Bismarck* had already defeated. The *Prince of Wales* and *King George V* were sister ships, mounting ten 14-inch guns, as we have noted. The *Repulse* was a smaller version of the *Hood,* mounting only six 15-inch rifles as her main battery. The officers in the Operations Room set little store by the carrier *Victorious,* new as she was. Clearly Admiral Tovey, now some 330 miles southeast of the enemy, needed reinforcement.

Even before the loss of the *Hood,* a message had gone to Admiral Somerville at Gibraltar. He had been rather expecting a summons to move to the eastern Mediterranean to help out in Cretan waters, so it was no surprise to him to receive orders from London. But it was something of a surprise to find himself ordered out into the Atlantic.

439

While all ships of Force H at Gibraltar were brought to short notice for steam, search parties roamed the length of Gibraltar's Main Street, through the shops, honky-tonks, and bars, sending the men back to their ships. By 0200, May 24, Somerville in the *Renown,* sister ship of the *Repulse,* was leaving Europa Point astern and heading out with Cape Spartello on the port beam. With him were the carrier *Ark Royal,* the cruiser *Sheffield,* and 6 destroyers.

With the loss of the *Hood,* the Admiralty resorted to sterner and more dangerous measures. They ordered the battleship *Revenge* to leave Halifax and head for the central North Atlantic, where she might be useful, especially if the *Bismarck* made for the American side of the ocean. The cruisers *London* and *Edinburgh* were pulled off convoy and patrol duties to join the search. They could extend the eyes of the fleet that much farther.

Were there any big ships that could be brought up?

Far to the south, escorting an 8-knot convoy, was the ancient *Ramillies.* The only reason this battleship had not fought at Jutland was that she had been damaged in her launching and was delayed in completion. At best she could do about 22 knots. Still, her eight 15-inch guns would be useful if they could be brought within range of the *Bismarck.* She was ordered to leave her convoy and head for an intercepting position. As she pulled away, her 27-year-old boilers emitted great clouds of black smoke. Captain A. D. Read was a little embarrassed, since he had spent several hours on previous days rebuking the merchant ships for doing the same thing.

When the *Ramillies* was detached, the Admiralty changed the orders of the *Revenge* to take over the escort of the convoy left by her sister.

One other big ship was available. This was the *Rodney,* at that moment about 500 miles west of Ireland, bound for an overhaul in the U.S. Navy's Boston Shipyard. She had 4 destroyers with her, and they were escorting the liner *Britannic.* The *Rodney* and her sister ship *Nelson* were two of the strangest-looking battleships ever built. Because of the limitations imposed by the Washington Treaty, these ships had all their guns forward, as near to the center of buoyancy as possible. In this way they could carry the massive weight of three triple 16-inch turrets without exceeding the limitation of 35,000 tons imposed by the politicians. Although their best speed of 22 knots could not catch the *Bismarck,* their gun power could prove decisive if they could get in range.

Only the *Rodney* was available at this time, and on receipt of the

Admiralty signal, Captain F. H. G. Dalrymple-Hamilton left the *Britannic* the single destroyer *Eskimo* as a guardian.

The cruiser *Dorsetshire* was escorting a convoy northward from Sierra Leone. At the moment, she was too far away to do any good, but she might come in handy later.

All the big ships that had any chance of making contact were now closing in on the *Bismarck*. There was little doubt that she could be brought to bay if she did not elude the stalking forces of the *Suffolk, Norfolk,* and *Prince of Wales.*

All day long, after the disastrous encounter between the *Bismarck* and *Hood,* the *Suffolk* held the German ships pinned with the invisible radar beams. In the late morning she nearly lost her quarry when the ships ran into a fogbank and the *Bismarck* slowed and altered her course from southwest to south.

Occasionally the *Bismarck* made other radical changes of course, sometimes to try to catch the British shadowers napping and blow the two cruisers out of the water. Sometimes the turn was made in an attempt to elude pursuit. During one of these radical turns, when the *Bismarck* fired a few salvos at the British cruisers, the *Prinz Eugen* slipped away to carry on the raiding by herself.*

During the afternoon, Admiral Tovey decided to make a try with the *Victorious* against the *Bismarck.* He ordered the carrier to proceed to a position approximately 100 miles from the German battleship and send off strikes while daylight lasted. By 2200 that night, Captain Bovell estimated that he was nearly 120 miles from the enemy and ordered a strike flown off. Nine aircraft were sent, led by Lieutenant Commander Eugene Esmonde, and about 2330 they spotted what they thought was their target. Down they went through the clouds, and when they broke out into the clear, they were astonished to find not the *Bismarck* but a strange vessel steaming peacefully on her way in the middle of one of the greatest sea hunts in history.

The strange vessel was the U.S. Coast Guard cutter *Modoc,* peacefully keeping her Atlantic ice patrol. It is hard to say which was more surprised, but no harm was done.

The British aircraft went on their way, and their next contact was the right one. They pressed home their attack in face of heavy anti-aircraft fire and had the satisfaction of seeing one torpedo hit. Highly elated, they set out on the homeward run.

The homing beacon on the *Victorious* chose that moment to fail

---

* The *Prinz Eugen*'s cruise was a failure. She refueled and then returned to Brest, arriving ten days after she had parted from the *Bismarck.*

completely, but the inexperienced pilots, by superb navigation, reached the carrier. Despite all predictions, they all managed to land safely aboard, even though not one of them had ever made a night landing before.

Although the pilots had no way of knowing it, their gallant attack had done no damage to the *Bismarck*. The torpedo struck on the armor belt on the starboard side and did no more to the ship than shake a few barnacles loose.

But the Germans did not escape entirely unscathed from this attack, for the concussion of the torpedo explosion killed one man, Boatswain Heiners. He was the first to die on the *Bismarck*. He would not be the last.

Some four hours after this attack, the *Suffolk* lost contact with the German. She had done a magnificent job of shadowing for over twenty-four hours, and perhaps had grown careless.

At any rate, the *Bismarck* was gone. The hunt would have to begin all over.

Admiral Tovey was again faced with a terrible anxiety. If he guessed wrong, the *Bismarck* would escape him with all the consequences that would mean. As he saw it, the German admiral had three choices: he might disappear into the broad Atlantic to continue commerce raiding; he might head back for Germany; or he might head for a French port.

In addition, Admiral Tovey's ships were running low on fuel oil. The *Repulse* shortly had to be detached to go to Iceland, and there was a question of how long the flagship herself could hold out. If Admiral Tovey failed to anticipate the *Bismarck*'s future movements, he would not have enough fuel for a high speed chase, perhaps not enough to get him home.

Then it was that Fate took a hand in the game.

Because the *Suffolk* had done such a superb job of shadowing for so many hours, Admiral Lütjens did not know that she had lost contact. He kept right on using his radio freely, allowing radio direction stations to get a series of bearings on him. Properly plotted, these would have established his position within a few miles.

Not content with this first joke, Fate played another one. The British plotted the *Bismarck*'s position wrong.

This error led Admiral Tovey to believe that the German ship was heading back to Germany. He abandoned the thought of covering a breakout into the Atlantic or a run for French ports and headed to intercept the battleship on her return to the Fatherland.

But the *Bismarck* was heading for Brest.

For several hours the principal strength of the British Home Fleet steamed in the wrong direction. Then someone in the Admiralty replotted the radio bearings and the truth came to light.

With little hope, Admiral Tovey swung his ships around. He was a long way behind by now, and there was no chance of catching up unless the *Bismarck* could be located and slowed down.

Before Admiral Tovey was really committed to his new course of action, he did some reshuffling of his fleet. The *Repulse* was sent to Iceland, while the *Prince of Wales,* too low on fuel to continue, was told to return to Scapa Flow. The cruisers *Suffolk* and *Norfolk* were out of the chase, as well.

Of all the ships near enough to be effective, only Admiral Somerville's Force H and the *Rodney* continued as they had been going.

If the *Bismarck* could be found, Force H was the one unit that had any prospect of slowing her up. Only the *Rodney* could add enough strength to the *King George V* to destroy her.

First, she had to be found.

"Z for Zebra" Catalina of the 209 Squadron, Coastal Command, was flying out over the Atlantic on the morning of May 26. It had been a long flight, for they had taken off at 0300 that morning from Lough Erne in Northern Ireland. It had been a dull flight, as well.

About 1030, reported Pilot Officer D. A. Briggs, "George [the automatic pilot] was flying the aircraft at 500 feet when we saw a warship. I was in the second pilot's seat when the occupant of the seat beside me, an American, said, 'What the devil's that?'

"I stared and saw a dull black shape through the mist which curled above a very rough sea.

" 'Looks like a battleship,' he said. I said, 'Better get closer. Go round its stern.' I thought it might be the *Bismarck,* because I could see no destroyers round the ship and I should have seen them had she been a British warship.* I left my seat, went to the wireless operator's table, grabbed a piece of paper, and began to write out a signal."

Briggs's signal was not undisturbed, for the *Bismarck* promptly opened up with all her flak. No one was hit in the Catalina, but her hull had several holes punched in it, as they discovered when the aircraft got back to Lough Erne.

* It is ironic that the pilot identified the *Bismarck* by the fact that she had no destroyers with her. At that time, the *King George V,* approximately 100 miles away, had no destroyers with her, either.

Now Admiral Tovey knew where the *Bismarck* was, and there was little to be cheerful about. There was no chance whatever that the *King George V* and *Rodney* could catch up before the German reached waters commanded by the Luftwaffe. The British had the rest of the day and all the coming night to stop the *Bismarck*. After that, she would be safe.

Everything depended now on Force H. Admiral Somerville did not have a surface ship which could stand up to the enemy battleship, but he did have the *Ark Royal*. She was no infant like the *Victorious*. Her crew and her pilots were all experienced, and if anyone could stop the *Bismarck,* they could do it.

Two *Ark Royal* Swordfish headed for the position reported by the Catalina and held on until they were relieved. Since holding contact by aircraft was a chancy business, Admiral Somerville sent the cruiser *Sheffield* on ahead to make radar contact and shadow. If necessary, the *Sheffield* could dog the enemy until the big ships could catch up.

Recovering the aircraft on the *Ark Royal* was no easy task that morning, for the weather had turned vile. The ship was rolling and pitching wildly, and it was an act of monumental airmanship to make a landing on her decks. Just as a pilot was making his approach nicely, the deck would fall away and there was nothing for him to do but pour on the coal and try again. Once, the opposite happened. The deck rose sharply under a landing aircraft. The pilot got out all right, but the plane was matchwood and steel scrap. The deck crew had to sweep it over the side before landings could continue.

While the pilots were having a bite to eat, their Swordfish were being refueled and rearmed. Each plane was loaded with one of the new torpedoes triggered by magnetic pistols. With them, the pilots would not have to get a hit. If the torpedo came close enough, the magnetic effect of the *Bismarck*'s hull would set it off.

By 1440 all pilots were in their planes and had started engines. Ten minutes later take-offs began, with the ship still plunging wildly in the angry sea. All got away successfully and headed for the enemy. The pilots had been told that the *Bismarck* was all alone. They could attack anything they saw.

A few minutes after the aircraft had taken off, the *Ark Royal* received a message that the *Sheffield* had been sent off to shadow the *Bismarck*. Since Admiral Somerville was in the *Renown* and had sent instructions to the *Sheffield* by flashing light, this was the first word Captain Maund had received that the cruiser was no longer with them on the other side of the formation.

Immediately he thought of the instructions given his pilots to attack anything they saw on that bearing. Now there was real reason to believe that they might attack their own "chummy ship" which had accompanied them on so many voyages in the Mediterranean.

He hastily sent out a signal to all aircraft: LOOK OUT FOR SHEFFIELD. His anxiety was so great that he let discretion go and broadcast in plain language.

It was too late. The Swordfish spotted the *Sheffield* and began an attack. Horrified, Captain C. A. A. Larcom ordered his ship not to fire back and maneuvered wildly to avoid the torpedoes.

Here Fate took a hand once again. The magnetic pistols, which had been so confidently loaded and confidently dropped, proved to be defective. Some exploded as they struck the water. Captain Larcom was able to dodge the others. The pilots of the last three aircraft recognized the *Sheffield* in time to avoid dropping their own torpedoes.

As they turned away, one pilot signaled apologetically to the *Sheffield:* SORRY FOR THE KIPPER.

It was a chagrined bunch of pilots that returned to the *Ark Royal,* but Captain Maund wasted no time in recriminations. He encouraged them and promised them another chance a little later. The thing for them to do now, he said, was to get something to eat and a little rest.

Nonetheless, it was in a grim mood that he reported to Admiral Somerville laconically: NO HITS.

In the *King George V,* which had just been joined by the *Rodney,* Admiral Somerville's report made sober reading. There was only one chance left to get the *Bismarck,* and there was no reason to believe that the *Ark Royal's* second attack would prove any more successful than the first. In addition, the fuel situation was now getting critical. Unless the *Bismarck* could be stopped in the next few hours, the two British battleships would have to give up the chase and return to port. Sir John Tovey reported to Admiral Somerville that he would have to leave at midnight unless the *Ark Royal* managed to do the impossible and bring the *Bismarck* to bay.

About 1830, the pilots were being briefed again and were getting ready for the last chance. Their planes were once again being loaded with torpedoes, but not with the magnetic pistols this time. The old, reliable mechanical exploders were installed, to the relief of everyone.

A little after 1900 the 15 Swordfish took off. They headed for the *Sheffield,* which had made contact with the *Bismarck.* This time they did not tarry over the British cruiser but went on in the direction she indicated: THE ENEMY IS TWELVE MILES DEAD AHEAD.

The weather had not improved, and rainstorms swept across the heaving sea. It was hard to see a ship at any distance, and it was hard to see an airplane from the decks of the *Bismarck*.

Because of the bad weather, the Swordfish could make no coordinated attack. For the most part, the planes acted individually, darting in whenever they saw an opening through the cloud and flak. The *Bismarck* twisted and turned, avoiding torpedoes in the water and keeping the Swordfish at a distance by the very mass of the antiaircraft fire. At one point she lashed out with her 15-inch guns at the *Sheffield* 12 miles away. The first salvo was a long way off, and officers on the bridge of the cruiser made some mocking comments on the quality of German gunnery. Their sneers stopped abruptly a moment later, when the *Bismarck*'s second salvo was a straddle. Splinters wounded a dozen men, of whom three died later. Captain Larcom promptly headed for cover behind a smoke screen. Beset as she was by air attack, the *Bismarck* was still no laughing matter.

After half an hour of attacking when they could, the Swordfish had expended all their torpedoes. The flight leader led the way back to the *Ark Royal* and wirelessed despondently: ESTIMATE NO HITS.

When this signal reached Sir John Tovey, he gave up all hope of bringing the enemy to action. He began to lay his plans to get his fuel-thirsty ships back to base.

Yet there was a puzzle. The *Sheffield* had reported the *Bismarck* was steering 340°. This was a course directly away from safety and one toward her enemy. He concluded that the *Sheffield*'s officers had made the common error of mistaking a ship's course by 180°.

Then a report came in from a shadowing aircraft. The *Bismarck* really was steering northwest.

Could the Swordfish have made a hit after all? Could the *Bismarck* be so damaged that she had to turn into the seas? Had something happened to her rudder?

Whatever the answer, Sir John Tovey concluded that there was a chance, after all. He began to lay plans for action the next morning.

Aboard the *Bismarck,* everyone from Admiral Lütjens down to the lowest rating was painfully aware of the trouble. One of the torpedoes had struck in the steering engine room and jammed the rudder 20 degrees to port. For hours divers struggled to free the rudder, working in the icy water that chilled them to the bone in a minute or two. But the damage was beyond repair. Disheartened, the men returned to their quarters, being strictly enjoined not to tell the men of the *Bismarck.*

Admiral Lütjens ordered the word passed over the ship's loudspeakers: "Steering gear damaged. Repairs in progress. Prospect that the damage can be made good."

But he knew better. Just before midnight, he sent three radio messages to the *Seekriegsleitung.*

1140: SHIP UNMANEUVERABLE. WE SHALL FIGHT TO THE LAST SHELL.

1158: TO THE FUEHRER OF THE GERMAN REICH, ADOLF HITLER. BELIEVING IN YOU, MY FUEHRER, WE SHALL FIGHT TO THE LAST AND IN UNSHAKABLE CONFIDENCE IN GERMANY'S VICTORY. FLEET COMMANDER.

1159: ARMAMENTS AND ENGINES STILL INTACT. BUT SHIP CANNOT BE STEERED WITH THE ENGINES. FLEET COMMANDER.

No one needed to be reminded what these messages really meant. They were a sentence of death to nearly every man aboard the *Bismarck.*

Such news could not long be withheld from the crew. Inevitably it leaked out, so when the official announcement was made, it came as no surprise. Then the ship's stores and canteens were opened, with everyone allowed to take what he wanted for no payment. There were few takers. Some took a bottle or two of brandy or some canned pineapples. Even though Death was paying the bill for the canned hams, the cologne, the cigarettes, these men now had little appetite for such things. They wrote letters which would never be mailed; they prayed; they sat in silence. Some got drunk. There was little sleeping.

During the small hours of that endless night that would end too soon, the loudspeakers hummed once more and an invisible voice began to read:

> I thank you in the name of the whole German people. All Germany is with you. What can be done will be done. The exemplary manner in which you have carried out your duty will fortify our nation in its fight for life. Adolf Hitler.

That there was little sleeping aboard the *Bismarck* that night was not merely in anticipation of battle. The Germans were not to be left in peace for their last night of this life.

Captain Philip Vian, still in the *Cossack,* which had cornered the

Altmark in Norway, was commanding the escort of a troop convoy. Suddenly he received orders to leave the transports and join the *King George V* and *Rodney,* which had no protection of any kind from U-boat attack. En route, Vian learned that the *Bismarck* had been slowed and was steaming northwest. He decided, on his own responsibility, that he had better take his 5 destroyers to keep tabs on the *Bismarck* rather than join the 2 British battleships. He hoped to use his torpedoes to damage the German further and so assure the result of the morning battle.

He informed no one of his decision, observing strict radio silence, and dashed at high speed toward the *Bismarck.* The same vile weather that was hampering everyone vented its full fury on his little ships. "The heavy following sea," he wrote, "made conditions horrible; the ships yawed up to 140° from their course, and in some cases, although spread a mile apart, found themselves exchanging places in the line. Reports reached me of men being hurt, and in one case of being washed overboard, but there was nothing to be done."

On the way in, Vian sighted the *Ark Royal,* and a little later the *Sheffield.* At 2200, the Polish destroyer *Piorun,* one of Vian's force, opened fire on the *Bismarck.*

In view of the terrible weather, Vian abandoned the idea of a concerted torpedo attack. He stationed his ships around the battleship and ordered them to attack individually as opportunity offered. Each time one of the destroyers tried it, she was driven off with highly accurate, radar-controlled gunfire.

But they kept on trying.

By morning, each ship had made at least two attacks, but the German records deny that any hits were made. In the weather prevailing, it is not surprising that the torpedo attacks failed, but the important thing to remember is that the ships of Vian's force hung on all night. There would be no need to search for the *Bismarck* when the morning of May 27 dawned.

Now the scene is set for the main event. From all points of the compass, ships were converging on the damaged German battleship. Although she could not steer, she could still fight, and Admiral Lütjens and Captain Lindemann meant to carry on the battle so long as there was a gun working and a man to load it.

Admiral Tovey did not repeat the mistake of Admiral Holland and tie the *Rodney* closely to him. Each of the two British battleships was free to maneuver independently, taking care not to foul the other's range. Sir John brought his ships into action from the west in order to silhouette the *Bismarck* against the rising sun. At 0847 the *Rodney* opened fire at a range of about 21,000 yards. The *King George V* and the *Bismarck* followed suit almost immediately.

The first German salvos straddled the *Rodney,* but as the British shells began hitting, the German gunnery fell off rapidly. Soon there was nothing to the battle but target practice. Admiral Lütjens was among the first to die, but soon others, many others, joined him in death. Almost until the end, Captain Lindemann stood amid the wreckage of his shattered bridge, controlling the battle of his stricken ship.

At 1015, the *Bismarck* a burning, shattered wreck, with all her guns silent, Admiral Tovey signaled the *Rodney* to fall in astern of him and leave the scene of action. He could stay no longer, if his ships were to reach port. He had already overstayed the time of prudence by a wide margin.

The cruiser *Dorsetshire* was the only ship with any torpedoes left, and Captain B. C. S. Martin did not need the admiral's signal to finish the *Bismarck* off. He was already taking the *Dorsetshire* into firing position.

He loosed two torpedoes into the starboard side of the wrecked battleship, but still the *Bismarck* refused to sink. She had absorbed more punishment than any ship in the history of naval warfare, and she was still afloat.

Only one torpedo remained. Captain Martin took the *Dorsetshire* around to the port side of the *Bismarck* and let it go. It ran hot, straight, and normal and hit the leviathan's hulk squarely. There was an explosion deep below the waterline, and slowly the *Bismarck* slipped under the turbulent waves, her colors still flying.

Just then, at 1040, Captain Martin received Admiral Tovey's signal telling him to do what he had already done. It gave him great pleasure to be able to reply that the *Bismarck* had been sunk.

The cruisers and destroyers on the scene turned to rescue work, pulling some 130 men out of the water until a U-boat alarm caused them to break it off.

The U-boat picked up two other men. She had been forced to stand by helplessly all through the battle. It was Fate's final joke.

She was out of torpedoes.

The *Hood* had finally been avenged, and the German surface navy had been driven from the Atlantic. But the cost had been high in lives, in ship damage, in human endurance. President Roosevelt took

449

a serious view of the *Bismarck*'s operations so close to the waters of the Western Hemisphere, and his reaction brought the United States and Germany one little step closer to war.

The British had no time to relax and enjoy their triumph. The war was going on with no let-up. German planes were again over Britain, and in the Mediterranean the struggle was reaching new heights of ferocity.

On May 27, 1941, as the *Bismarck* carried over 2000 men to the bottom of the sea with her, the British faced stark defeat in the Near East. Rommel stood on the Egyptian border. The British Expeditionary Force had been driven out of Greece and, on that very day, was preparing to evacuate Crete.

The British triumphs of the winter had all been undone.

CHAPTER SIXTEEN

The Summer of Discontent

> *We have a very daring and skilful*
> *opponent against us and may I say,*
> *across the havoc of war, a great general.*
> Winston S. Churchill,
> Speech in House of Commons
> *January, 1942*

EVERYONE WAS jittery in Italian headquarters in Tripoli. O'Connor's relentless drives had forced the Italians back and back. Who knew where he would stop? The line was stabilized—for the moment—at El Agheila, five hundred miles to the east, but—you never could tell. Most officers had their bags packed, ready for a quick return to Italy.

On February 12, 1941, a single German aircraft swept in and landed on the airstrip at Castel Benito, south of Tripoli. Leutnant Heggenreiner, the local German liaison officer, ran up and helped open the door. Out of the plane stepped the man whose name would be ever more associated with the war in North Africa, Lieutenant General Erwin Rommel.

A few days earlier, Rommel had been enjoying a brief leave at home at Wiener Neustadt with his wife. He was allowed only two days before the telephone rang. Rommel was to report to Chief of Staff von Brauchitsch and to the Führer immediately.

Because of the Italian rout by O'Connor, Hitler had decided to stiffen the Axis position in North Africa. Two divisions would be sent, one light motorized, and one Panzer. Command of this, the Afrika Korps, would be entrusted to Rommel, who was to proceed to Tripoli in Libya to get acquainted with the ground and prepare for the arrival of his troops. The first detachment would come in mid-February; the Fifth Light Division should arrive by mid-April, and the Fifteenth Panzer Division by the end of May.

After a stop in Rome for consultation with the *Comando Supremo,* Rommel went on to his new task. He found on arrival that Marshal Graziani had given over command of Italian forces in Africa and had left affairs in the hands of his chief of staff, General Gariboldi.

Rommel's arrival was a rude shock to Gariboldi. Instead of setting the defense line against further British advance at Tripoli, Rommel planned to move it 250 miles eastward to Sirte, where the Italians had a weak rearguard force. "The defense works around Tripoli were totally inadequate," noted Rommel caustically. "They could possibly have been defended with some hope of success against insurgent Senussi or Arab tribesmen, never against the British."

Gariboldi suggested that Rommel could not possibly have any notion of the difficulty of fighting in the desert. Perhaps Rommel should have a look at it before he came up with any more grandiose ideas.

"It won't take me long to get to know the country," rejoined Rommel. "I'll have a look at it from the air this afternoon and report back to the High Command this evening."

Rommel was firmly determined to have nothing to do with the kind of half-hearted campaign the Italians had been conducting in North Africa. Yet his position was certainly questionable. A comparatively unknown German general, he had landed with only a tiny staff at a time when there was not a single German soldier in Africa. Gariboldi looked upon him as an interloper and was determined to give him as little authority as he could. The troops Rommel proposed to use in the early days were Italian. Only the Luftwaffe represented German strength in Africa, and it was not under Rommel's command.

The orders Rommel had received from von Brauchitsch and Hitler had been tentative and cautious. Both men conceived of the German commitment to North Africa as merely a sop to the Italians. Neither one realized the opportunities or the dangers to the Axis which existed in the Mediterranean. If Hitler had been willing to assign to the North African Theater one-tenth * of the strength he committed to the Russian front, he could have driven the British from Alexandria and Egypt. Then the southern way to the oil of the Middle East would be his for the taking. The doorway to southern Russia would lie open. With the oil of Persia and the wheat of the Caucasus, Hitler would

* Actually about one-fiftieth of the strength engaged in the Russian campaign was committed to North Africa.

be near his dream of the Reich that would endure a thousand years. An Allied victory in North Africa would expose what Churchill would later call "the soft underbelly of Europe." Italy could be driven from the war; France would think again about being a silent partner in German-dominated Europe. Fortunate it was, indeed, for Britain and the United States that the German High Command never grasped the strategic possibilities of the Mediterranean.

Rommel understood his opportunities in the North African Theater well enough. While his instructions from Berlin were to take no risks, to confine himself to reconnaissance in force, Rommel decided to make the most of his chances. His superiors had cautiously suggested he might be able to seize Benghazi. Rommel realized that Benghazi could not be held by itself. Because of the peculiar nature of war in the desert, he would have to occupy all of Cyrenaica.

Although the newspapers of both sides rejoiced for every gain through the sands of the Sahara, their jubilation was from ignorance. Positions in the desert mean little more than positions at sea. The featureless landscape stretching for mile after mile offers neither concealment for the attacker nor strongpoints for the defender. In only a few places, where the escarpment comes close to the sea—such as Halfaya Pass—can a force successfully hold a defensive line to bar eastward or westward progress. This simple truth Rommel grasped at once; his superiors in Berlin seem never to have learned it.

For his first month in North Africa, Rommel could do little except stiffen the Italian defenses of Sirte. He would have too few troops for anything else. He shrewdly grasped that the British were far weaker in the Western Desert than anyone supposed. He did not know that Wavell, under pressure from the Prime Minister, had stripped the defenses of Cyrenaica to the absolute bone. The disastrous Greek campaign had first priority. Every man, every gun, every tank which could be spared, and then double that number, had been withdrawn. Lieutenant General Sir Philip Neame, who had taken over from O'Connor, laid low with stomach trouble, commanded only raw troops in observation posts rather than the sharp veterans who had beaten the Italians so dramatically.

Wavell felt comparatively safe in stretching thin his forces in the Western Desert. His intelligence sources in Tripoli kept him well informed on Axis strength, and it seemed incapable of drastic action in the near future. Also, British Intelligence in Berlin was well aware of the restrictive orders given Rommel. No grave risk, therefore, could be anticipated in North Africa.

In making this estimate, both Whitehall and Alexandria reckoned without a Rommel. No hint could come from Berlin of plans for an offensive through Libya, because Berlin didn't know of any such plans. Rommel had carefully not confided his intentions to the Führer or to OKW. They would be as surprised as Wavell and Neame when the time came.

On March 24, after initial probing attacks, Rommel struck. In a few hours El Agheila, with its fort, airfield, and water supply, fell to the Third Reconnaissance Battalion of the German Fifth Light Division. Rather than hold in such an exposed position, the British garrison made a skillful withdrawal to the commanding heights at Mersa el Brega and the salt marsh at Bir es Suera.

If he waited until the end of May for his Panzer division to arrive, Rommel would be allowing the British time to establish minefields, wire defenses, pillboxes, and tank traps to supplement the natural defense features of the area.

The course of boldness suggested pushing on against Mersa el Brega with the small forces Rommel had at his disposal. Rommel, being Rommel, chose to move, quickly and hard, before the British could dig in. On March 31, Rommel threw his strength against Mersa el Brega. After a day of fierce fighting, the Germans had made little progress, until a flanking attack through the rolling sand hills took possession of the key defile.

Wavell had foreseen what might happen the moment the Germans seized El Agheila. He ordered Neame to fall back to Benghazi if hard pressed and even to evacuate that port town if necessary. After a day's stand at Mersa el Brega, Neame decided to pull out.

It was more important to preserve the Western Desert Force than it was to hold useless territory. A stand could be made later, when lines of supply were shorter and reinforcements from Egypt could be brought up. This stand might well be made at Sollum on the Egyptian border, or possibly at Tobruk.

A retreat is the most difficult of maneuvers for inexperienced troops. Everyone has a tendency to look over his shoulder on the chance that the pursuing enemy may be just behind. In the desert, water is more precious than booty, and the trail of a retreating force becomes littered with discarded souvenirs whose weight has become insupportable. Rumors fly of one's own reverses and of enemy exploits. Someone begins to run and is sharply rebuked by a sergeant. Shamefaced, he resumes his place and sullenly marches on with his unit.

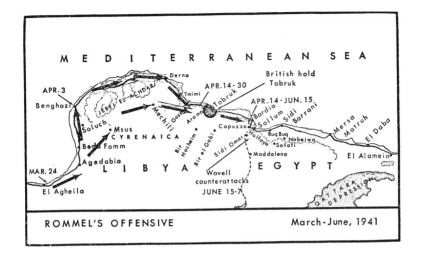

ROMMEL'S OFFENSIVE   March-June, 1941

Men begin to drop out. Units break up, and a spirit of *sauve qui peut* permeates the ranks.

To some extent this was the picture of the British retreat across Cyrenaica. Some units maintained their traditions proudly, but others disintegrated.

Rommel could not know this. He simply knew that British resistance was vanishing before him and that the opportunity was not to be missed. Hurriedly he sent a column north along the coast road to seize Benghazi while he prepared to set off across the neck of the peninsula through Msus to Mechili and on to Derna. He was paying an unconscious compliment to O'Connor by repeating his maneuver in reverse.

General Gariboldi was furious. This johnny-come-lately German general was daring to put the Italians to scorn by succeeding brilliantly where they had not dared to venture. When Rommel returned to headquarters, Gariboldi shouted invective at him. He ordered Rommel to stop where he was, particularly since Rome had forbidden any risky action. At the very least, Gariboldi insisted that Rommel wait for approval from Rome before his troops advanced a step farther.

Rommel refused. Delay would give the British a chance to consolidate, to strengthen defenses. He intended to do exactly what he felt the situation demanded, and Gariboldi was not going to tell him otherwise.

At that very moment, so aptly that a novelist would not dare use it, a signal came in from the German High Command giving Rommel complete freedom of action. Even worse, according to Gariboldi, was an order from Rome putting several Italian units, including their finest, the Ariete Division, under Rommel's command.

After that, there was no stopping Rommel until he had regained almost all the territory O'Connor had wrested from the Italians.

Wavell realized that the inexperienced Neame was fast losing control of the situation. There was only one British soldier in North Africa with the knowledge of desert warfare and with the imagination and daring to cope with Rommel. *Marlbrough se va t'en guerre!* Back to the fray went O'Connor.

A diffident and sensitive man, O'Connor suggested to Neame that he not take over in the height of a battle, and Neame gratefully agreed. On April 6, he and O'Connor were riding in the command car, a Humber of uncertain vintage. Suddenly they came upon a group of German motorized infantry. The driver grabbed his rifle but was cut down at once. The two generals looked at each other in horror and slowly raised their hands.

All obstacles to his advance removed, Rommel pushed on with breathtaking speed. His dash surprised everyone, friend and foe alike. He was everywhere at once, it seemed, now driving along in a command car, now viewing the scene from his "Mammoth," a captured British armored command car, now in his "caravan," a truck fitted out with living accommodations. Sometimes he flew above the battle or from one of his detachments to another. He used a German Storch, a light passenger-carrying aircraft somewhat resembling the old Jenny so beloved of barnstorming pilots. On other occasions he flew in an Italian Ghibli, a somewhat larger plane. Sometimes Rommel's visits were rather tempestuous, as he prodded, urged, commanded, exhorted, and drove his men to further efforts. Since the word "ghibli" means tempest or sandstorm in Arabic, many of his men felt the name of the aircraft was appropriate for its dynamic rider.

On one occasion Rommel learned that the Fifth Light Division had stopped its advance. The commander proposed to take four days to replenish. This was too much for Rommel, who ordered the division commander to unload all his vehicles and send them to a supply dump. There they were to load with all the gasoline, rations, and ammunition they could carry and rush back to the division bivouac. In twenty-four hours the division was to be ready to go.

The division moved off in less than the allotted twenty-four hours.

The success of Rommel's drive across North Africa is legend. On April 3, Benghazi fell. Three days later, it was the turn of Msus. The key to the whole position south of the Jebel Achdar, Mechili, became part of the German booty on April 8 and, on the same day, his greatly over-extended forces were at Derna. Allowing no time for rest, Rommel pushed on toward his next major objective—Tobruk.

As the Panzer Gruppe Afrika approached Tobruk, Rommel was highly confident of success. He expected it to fall in two or three days at the most. He had no way of knowing that it would withstand his attacks for 242 days before being relieved by General Neil Ritchie. It would be 467 days before German troops would enter the fortress in triumph.

On April 9, Wavell made the decision to hold Tobruk. He was spurred on by a telegram from Churchill: "Tobruk . . . seems to be a place to be held to the death without thought of retirement." On that afternoon, Wavell sent his temporary Director of Military Operations, Brigadier E. E. Dorman-Smith, to fly up to Tobruk with an order that the port was to be held at all costs. Landing in a blinding sandstorm, Dorman-Smith handed over the order and then set off on the return journey. On the way back he observed from the air something that made the order academic. German troops were well east of the city. There was no possibility of retreat. Tobruk had to be held.

His inability to capture Tobruk was frustrating to Rommel. He could not advance beyond the Egyptian border so long as it remained in British hands. The only roads which could support a massive attack on Egypt led through the beleaguered town. Rommel ordered repeated attacks on the city, culminating in an all-out assault lasting from April 30 to May 4. Tobruk held, and Rommel was forced to stop. Just beyond his advance positions lay the road to Alexandria and Cairo, but he could not travel it.

Except for an abortive British attack, appropriately code-named Brevity, war in the desert settled down into a stalemate. Sporadic patrolling represented all the activity there was until mid-June, when the ill-fated Operation Battleaxe began.

It was just as well for the British that the lull came when it did, for troubles were besetting them all at once. Crete, Syria, Iraq all became trouble spots. In April the Luftwaffe resumed heavy attacks on Britain, hitting at Coventry again, but concentrating on the ports such as Plymouth, Portsmouth, Liverpool.

457

On May 10, the Luftwaffe returned to London, attacking with incendiary bombs. They seemed to be everywhere, and over 2000 fires were set. Nearly 150 fire mains were destroyed, and their loss, combined with low tide in the Thames, seriously hampered fire-fighting.

Back came the old routine: the A.R.P. wardens urging people to take cover, the *crump-crump-crump* of antiaircraft guns in the distance, the roar of exploding bombs, the crash of falling buildings, the long lines of men, women, and children taking shelter in the tube stations, the screams of the wounded, the grieving of those whose loved ones had perished.

Five docks were hit, and all but one of the main railway stations were put out of service for weeks. Travel was seriously hampered, and many a soldier and sailor on a brief leave was seriously delayed in reaching his destination.

The historic meeting chamber of the House of Commons was destroyed in that same raid. No lives were lost, but the room that had heard the debates of Pitt and Newcastle, the Younger Pitt and Fox, of Disraeli and Gladstone, of Lloyd George and Baldwin, lay in ruins. For the rest of the war, Parliament would have to conduct its business elsewhere.

Although no one in Britain could know it, the attacks of mid-May ended the blitz on Britain until 1944. Hitler was moving east, and the German air fleets were getting ready to follow. Soon they would be ranging over Russian rather than British skies.

On that same night of May 10, Churchill was spending the weekend at Ditchley. According to his custom, he dined late, and then the entire party sat down to watch a Marx Brothers movie. Twice Churchill left the showing to inquire about the air raid on London. After a few moments, a secretary appeared at his elbow with the message that the Duke of Hamilton was telephoning from Scotland and had an urgent message. Churchill, unwilling to disturb himself a third time, sent Brendan Bracken to speak to the Duke.

Bracken soon returned with astonishing news: "Hess has arrived in Scotland."

Rudolf Hess, for years Hitler's closest personal friend, Deputy Führer of the Reich, Member of the Secret Cabinet Council for Germany, Reich Minister without Portfolio, Member of the Ministerial Council for the Defense of the Reich, and Leader of the Nazi Party, had taken off in a plane from Augsburg and had dropped by parachute near the estate of the Duke of Hamilton.

He was first discovered by David McLean, a Scottish plowman. "I was amazed and a bit frightened," reported McLean, "when I saw a parachute dropping slowly downwards through the gathering darkness." McLean took Hess to his house, where he lived with his mother and sister, and offered him tea, which Hess refused. "He was most gentlemanly in his attitude to my old mother and my sister and stiffly bowed to them when he came in and before he left. He thanked us profusely for what we had done for him."

Hess did not reveal his identity to David McLean, and when he was taken away by Home Guardsmen Jack Peterson and Robert Gibson, he demanded to see the Duke of Hamilton. His Grace refused to see him and instituted the call to Churchill.

The problem was to avoid official recognition, which might confer on Hess the status of a herald or give him some form of diplomatic immunity. By various stages he was removed to the Tower of London and then to a place of confinement near London. There he remained until the end of the war, when he was brought to trial at Nuremberg along with other Nazi leaders.

Hess's motives for his flight remain obscure to this day. He seems to have believed that in the Duke of Hamilton he would find a sympathetic hearer for the idea of peace between Britain and Germany. He insisted that peace could be secured if only the British would turn Churchill and his Government out of office. Perhaps he hoped to enlist the British on the German side in the forthcoming invasion of Russia. If so, he was overly indirect, for he gave no hint of it to his questioners. It is possible that he knew nothing of Hitler's plans for Russia, because he had been dropping from the Führer's confidence ever since the war had begun.

The official German attitude was that Hess was insane. The announcement was terse and cold. "It is officially announced by the National Socialist Party that Party Member Hess [a quick demotion for Hess, who was officially Leader of the Nazi Party], who, as he was suffering from an illness of some years' standing, had been strictly forbidden to embark on any further flying activity, was able, contrary to this command, again to come into possession of an aeroplane . . .

"A letter which he left behind unfortunately shows, by its distractedness, traces of mental disorder, and it is feared that he was a victim of hallucinations."

Another German reaction to Hess's flight was to ban all vaudeville acts by astrologers, soothsayers, crystal-gazers, and fortune tellers.

Hess had been fond of such acts, and Hitler believed they had given him his hallucinations.

Hess was certainly a victim of hallucinations if he believed that the Duke of Hamilton or the British people were ready to throw Churchill out and make a peace with Germany on any other terms than complete victory.

The British kept their sense of humor as the war neared the end of its second year. Shortages grew worse as the U-boats took their toll of shipping, and bureaucracy seemed to add its quota of blunder in aggravating conditions. A letter writer complained in *The Daily Telegraph* that the distribution of eggs was so badly handled that even those stamped "new laid" were fit only for cake baking. What ordinary eggs must have been is best left to the imagination.

Official stupidity showed itself again in a Ministry of Food order that all persons who raised more than twelve chickens would have to turn over *all* their eggs to a food control center. This edict produced a rash of letters to editors from suburbanites who pointed out that the sole result would be the slaughter of chickens in excess of twelve so that they might keep a few eggs for themselves. Later, in June, the limit was raised to fifty chickens, in order to separate the amateur and the professional farmer.

Most meats were simply unavailable, except on rare occasions. Officially each person was allowed between a shilling and one and six pence worth a week for meat. Fish formed a substitute, even though an official reported that herring were likely to be rare in 1941. He concluded on the optimistic note that eels were plentiful. By the end of the year, canned meats were rationed on a point system which allowed each person a pound a week of desirable pork, beef, lamb, mutton, salmon, lobster, tuna, or sardines, down to four pounds a week of canned beans in sauce or gravy.

The milk ration was set at seven pints a week for children and expectant and nursing mothers. The rest were allowed half that amount. Toward the end of the year, the ration was reduced to two pints a week for adults and six pints for children and mothers.

In view of these shortages, the newspapers and the Ministry of Food published recipes for dishes based on root vegetables and a suggestion of meat. The newspaper recipes were generally matter-of-fact and helpful. The writers for the Ministry of Food tried to add a bit of cheer in their suggestions.

If anyone should care to try the standard of living of wartime

Britain, here are a few recipes. The first two are from *The Daily Telegraph*.

CARROT CASSEROLE

3 carrots	1 flat teaspoonful ground ginger
1 heaped teaspoonful of salt	3 potatoes
½ flat tablespoonful of pepper	1 onion, if available
1 tablespoonful brown sugar	

Scrub the carrots and grate them on a coarse vegetable grater. Put them into an earthenware casserole with the potatoes scrubbed and sliced, and the onion, chopped. Cover the bottom of the casserole with vegetables. Then put in half the salt, pepper, sugar and ginger. Add the rest of the vegetables with the rest of the seasonings. Add *no* water. Put the casserole in the bottom of the oven and bake about 1½ hours in a low heat. The time varies according to the age and freshness of the carrots. 1½ to 2 hours is the average time. Serve straight from the casserole.

POTATO AND LEEK SOUP

6 large potatoes	½ pint of milk
3 leeks	salt and pepper
1 quart of water	1 oz. Special Margarine

Wash the leeks well and cut them in thin slices. Scrub the potatoes, scrape them and cut them in small pieces. Put the vegetables into a saucepan, cover them with cold water, and add salt and a little pepper. Cook gently for an hour. Put through a wire sieve, add boiling milk, re-heat, put the Special Margarine in the soup tureen and pour boiling soup over. Serves 4–5.

The Ministry of Food produced a recipe for a comestible which it had the temerity to call "Patriotic Pudding."

You need 8 oz. flour, 2 oz. grated raw potato, 2 oz. suet, a pinch of salt and just enough cold water to mix to a soft dough. Roll out into a neat oval. Spread with 1 lb. chopped root vegetables (whatever you have), salt and pepper and either 1 rasher of bacon finely diced or a sprinkling of gravy powder. Roll up either in margarine paper or a floured cloth and steam for about two hours (potatoes and greens can be steamed at the same time). Or you can boil the pudding in a jam jar with a margarine paper cover. Serve with brown gravy or a pastry sauce. Quantities given make enough for four people—a patriotic pudding that will give them energy and vitamins in a way they will like.

Since fire-watching had been made compulsory for all persons from 16 to 60 years of age who were not in the armed forces, there was a steady demand for equipment such as shovels, sand buckets, and portable pumps. The "Bestobell Fire-Fighting Outfit" at fifty-seven shillings and sixpence was widely employed. It came with its own carrying case and included a face protector with neck guard and mica eye shield. Also included were an apron with asbestos cords and asbestos gloves. If you were bombed out, you could sleep on the "Sacco Air Bed" made by the Self-Controlled Air Cushion Company.

Even the family dog was protected. The firm of O. S. Warn of Bradford offered dog gas masks at five shillings for toys, six shillings for medium-sized dogs, and seven shillings for large ones.

Double Summer Time began on Sunday, April 4, and extended until August 10. The usual grumbles were heard, but in general the British people had too many other things to worry about to become upset over the clock. Clothing was severely rationed, but if one lost his wardrobe to enemy action, he would be given enough coupons to buy one overcoat, one suit, one pair of slacks, three shirts, two pairs of shoes, five undershirts, five underpants, six pairs of socks, six handkerchiefs, and two neckties. If he wanted galoshes or slippers, he could sacrifice a pair of underpants.

His wife, similarly bereft, could be supplied with two wool dresses, two skirts, two blouses, two pairs of shoes, three slips, three bras, six panties, six pairs of stockings, one overcoat, and six handkerchiefs. Second-hand clothes were not rationed, but were not generally available. Some persons were desperate enough or ghoulish enough to follow casualty lists and try to purchase the civilian wardrobes of the men killed in action.

One needed the wool suits or dresses to keep warm, for coal was strictly limited to one ton a month during the winter months. A footnote to the order stated that this was a maximum amount and could not be guaranteed.

Owners of small homes or semi-detached houses did not suffer excessively under the coal ration, but the stately homes of England became dreary places indeed. The householder had the choice of keeping the mansion at a temperature of about 40 degrees or of heating only one or two rooms. In either case, a night visit to the bathroom had a certain resemblance to Scott's Antarctic explorations.

If you could afford them, auctions for charity might give you a few luxuries. In one held at the Comedy Theatre in London, 100 cigarettes sold for £42. Eight bottles of Scotch brought the same price, while a basket of fruits, eggs, and ham was knocked down for only £11.

It was during the summer of 1941 that the famous "V-for-Victory" campaign caught on in Europe. No one knows how it started, but the British were quick to take advantage of it in broadcasts to occupied lands. Churchill adopted it with his famous two-fingered gesture. Since the Morse code for the letter V (three dots and a dash) corresponds in rhythm to the opening notes of Beethoven's *Fifth Symphony,* the B.B.C. used a few bars of it for an opening theme in broadcasts to occupied Europe.

The Germans found the symbol of "V-for-Victory" nearly intolerable. The letter cropped up everywhere, under their very noses. It was chalked or painted on doors, walls, official German pronouncements, the sides of troop trains, freight cars, buses, sidewalks—anywhere you cared to look. A town clock in Belgium was stopped with its hands pointing at 11:05. When the German officials investigated, they found that the clock works had been sabotaged and the hands could not be moved.

In another town, the local German commander announced that any householder would be held personally responsible if the hated letter was found painted or chalked on his house. The next morning, the commander's own house was literally covered with V's. They had to be blacked out with tar.

No prosecutions were made.

The V-Campaign worked so well on its own that the British decided to give it official recognition. They proclaimed that July 20, 1941, would be V-Day.

All day long, throughout Europe, the Germans were hectored by the V. Small boys chalked the letter on the uniforms of German soldiers and then darted away before they could be caught. In restaurants and movie theaters, patrons tapped out the Morse code for V. In Belgium, stickers with a large V and the words *Victoire* and *Vrijheid* were attached to German uniforms, cars, and letters.

A writer with a better flair for propaganda than for poetry wrote some words which were sung to the opening of Beethoven's Fifth:

> Do not give way,
> Never despair;
> We'll get them yet.
> Hitler, beware!

There being no possibility of stamping out the V-Campaign, Joseph Goebbels, Nazi Minister of Propaganda, decided to claim it for the Germans. He proclaimed that the V was for the German word

Viktoria, and all the V's pointed to a German triumph, that the British had stolen the symbol.

The B.B.C. nailed this absurd claim by reminding its listeners all over Europe that the German word for victory is *Sieg.*

Broadcasts by the B.B.C. were sometimes getting on the Germans' nerves. Goebbels's henchmen tried frequent jamming, not always successfully. On October 13, the regular 9 o'clock program of B.B.C. news was constantly interrupted by a mysterious voice, presumably German. It spoke such comments as:

"Do you know how much money Churchill is being paid by the Jews?"

"We are being led up the garden path and sold to America."

"Churchill will never be a Duke of Marlborough."

The voice was not finally silenced until the B.B.C. shifted to a program of bagpipe music. At that the man gave up.

No one was ready to give up in Britain during that summer, and the ever-growing American support kept hopes for final victory very much alive. The American correspondent Quentin Reynolds made a broadcast as part of the program at the premier performance of the film *Britain Can Take It.* Along with Edward R. Murrow, Reynolds was much respected by the British people, not only for the quality of his reporting, but also because he had "taken it" during the blitz. Reynolds left his listeners in no doubt where he stood, although his language must have bewildered many a listener on the continent:

Listen to this, Dr. Goebbels!

When Slap-happy Hermann's little men come over now, the people of Britain no longer take their medicine with complacency. Today the people of Britain are giving it, not taking it.

My country believes with England, and has not been backward lately about showing belief, that they cannot live in peace and in Christian unity so long as your kind of pagan philosophy dominates half the world.

Keep listening, doctor, and one night—I hope soon—you'll hear a new song. Behind it you'll hear the voices of 130,000,000 united people singing the song of freedom.

I mean the anthem, doctor, that takes its name from the flag of my country—a country which this time will be proud to fight. . . .

Hess is a rat who left a sinking ship. . . .

Take very good care of yourself, doctor. We'll be seeing you soon. Perhaps not this summer—perhaps not next autumn, or next winter, but sooner or later. And when we do see you, we want you to be in very good health.

Some B.B.C. staff members considered Reynolds's broadcast "too warlike."

If the B.B.C. staff members still believed that war in 1941 was still played by gentlemen's rules, they should have been assigned to cover the fighting in Crete. When the British were driven out of Greece, Mr. Churchill was determined to save Crete at all costs and believed that it could be done. Wavell was not so hopeful, even though the redoubtable General Bernard Freyberg was assigned to command in the island. A New Zealander, General Freyberg had enjoyed a long and arduous career in the Army, earning the Distinguished Service Order with two bars and the Victoria Cross. Churchill regarded him highly. "Freyberg, like his only equal, Carton de Wiart, deserved the title with which I acclaimed them of 'Salamander.' Both thrived in fire, and were literally shot to pieces without being affected physically or in spirit."

What did Freyberg think of the prospects of holding Crete?

> Forces at my disposal [he cabled to Wavell] are totally inadequate to meet attack envisaged. . . . I cannot hope to hold out with land forces alone, which as a result of campaign in Greece are now devoid of any artillery, have insufficient tools for digging, very little transport, and inadequate war reserves of equipment and ammunition.

The British made every effort to remedy these weaknesses, but there was too much to do and too much opposition by German air. About 27,000 tons of ammunition and equipment were sent to Crete during the first three weeks of May. Only 3000 tons of these reached the island. Another 3000 tons went to the bottom, and the rest were sent back to Alexandria. To defend an island 18 miles long and 65 miles wide, Freyberg had about 27,500 British troops and 14,000 Greeks. His artillery was meager, to say the least. He had forty-six field guns, sixteen 3.7-inch antiaircraft guns, thirty-six 44-mm. guns, and twenty-four antiaircraft searchlights.

The greatest weakness was in the air. There were only 36 aircraft in all available for the defense of the island, and only half of them were serviceable. The Germans were preparing to employ over 1200 aircraft, including over 600 transports and gliders. The situation was so clearly hopeless in the air that on May 19, all the British aircraft which could fly were sent to Egypt.

Crete, the land of the mythological King Minos, had been the site

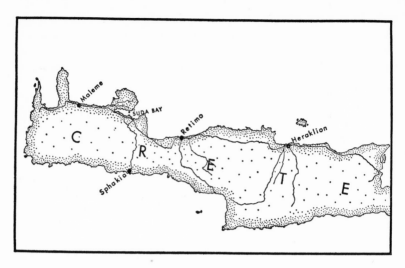

of one of the world's oldest civilizations. It had known many wars in the three and a half millennia since the Minoan civilization had been at its height. But it had never known any attack as ferocious as that which fell upon it on May 20, 1941.

The island offered almost insoluble problems for a defender. At that time there was only one road capable of carrying military traffic. It ran along the north coast of the island, past the airfield at Maleme, passing Suda Bay, Retimo [Rethimnon], and Heraklion, and on to the eastern end. There were only foot trails leading north and south. One went to Sphakia and Plaka Bay, the only deep-water ports on the southern coast.

Because of the terrain and the poor roads, Freyberg could not maintain a reserve force centrally located. Instead, he had to establish three strong resistance points at Maleme, Retimo, and Heraklion, where vital airfields were located. The Maleme and Retimo complexes protected Suda Bay, and the Heraklion defenses guarded the eastern harbor.

The three airfields at Maleme, Retimo, and Heraklion were essential to the defense of Crete. The Germans knew well that they could not hope to pass a significant number of troops across the sea. Instead, they planned a massive air assault by paratroops, transport aircraft, and gliders. If they could win control of any of the three airports, then they could pour in troops, expand from the airhead, and pin the other garrisons against the sea.

Because Hitler did not want to waste a single day in the Balkan and Mediterranean area, he ordered Goering to throw in men regardless of losses. He entrusted overall command to the fat Reichsmarschall, since the assault was a new concept in military operations, to cross over a sea barrier and seize control of strongpoints from the air.

In the early morning of May 20, operations against Crete began. An intensive bombing and strafing attack against Maleme airfield drove the defenders to cover and quickly destroyed the few antiaircraft guns defending the area. Even as these attacks were going on, gliders loaded with troops began to land to the west of the airfield. Freyberg's defending forces opened up with machine-gun and rifle fire. Most of the Germans simply died as they left the machines. Many of the gliders crashed, and the screams of the injured and dying went unheeded as the British defenders fought off succeeding waves of airborne troops.

About 0800, parachute troops began dropping in the area east of Maleme. To expose them to enemy fire for as brief a time as possible, the Germans were dropped from heights below 600 feet. Sometimes this was not enough. Men could be seen tugging frantically at ripcords until a hideous thud put an end to their efforts. The defenders managed to kill or wound most of the parachute troops, but more kept on coming, regardless of losses.

One of the paratroopers was heavyweight Max Schmeling, the only boxer ever to defeat Joe Louis.

Slowly the number of Germans safely on the ground increased, although most of the day they were outnumbered by the dead. By 1500, there were enough Germans alive on the ground to make a coordinated attack on the Maleme airstrip. By nightfall the Germans had established a position on the northwestern and northern edges of the field.

The next day was worse. The Germans began to use Maleme field to land transport aircraft, even though the British field guns and mortars swept the runways, inflicting severe casualties on the Germans. But there was no stopping the onrush. By May 22 the Fifth New Zealand Brigade, which had been defending Maleme, had been driven back 10 miles.

Now German reinforcements could come in freely—by air.

At sea it was a different story. In spite of the danger of operating in the waters north of Crete, Cunningham sent two light forces to sweep through those areas after dark each night. Since it was entirely possible that the Italian Navy might intervene in the Cretan operation, he stationed a heavy force to the west in a position to stand guard.

At 2300 on May 21, light forces under Rear Admiral J. G. Glennie intercepted a large German convoy consisting of many caiques and a number of steamers. About 15 of these vessels were destroyed, while the rest fled. Over 4000 German troops were drowned.

Some four hours later, another light force under Rear Admiral E. L. S. King mauled another German convoy and forced the survivors to turn back. So it went throughout the Cretan campaign. Not a single German soldier reached Crete by sea until after the British had left.

The Royal Navy paid a terrible cost. With no air support of any kind, they lay open to savage attacks by the Luftwaffe. For hour after hour crews manned their air defense stations. Thousands upon thousands of antiaircraft shells were hurled up into the sky, and still the German airmen came on. Glennie's flagship, the cruiser *Dido,* expended nearly three-quarters of her antiaircraft ammunition that first day. Other ships had comparable experiences.

The Germans were not always killed or driven off, despite such heavy fighting. In a three-day period, the cruisers *Gloucester* and *Fiji* were sunk, as were the destroyers *Greyhound, Kashmir, Juno,* and *Kelly.* Commanding the last of these was Captain Lord Louis Mountbatten, later to become famous as head of Special Forces, better known as Commandos. The battleship *Warspite,* the cruisers *Naiad* and *Carlisle,* and 4 destroyers were seriously damaged. The Battleship *Valiant* was also hit, but was able to continue her duties.

"I came to dread every ring on the telephone," wrote Cunningham, "every knock on the door, and the arrival of each fresh signal."

He tersely informed the Chiefs of Staff: "Sea control in the Eastern Mediterranean could not be retained after another such experience."

The fighting ashore was growing more vicious. Once the Germans had obtained their bridgehead at Maleme, they expanded it rapidly. On May 26, Wavell telegraphed the Chiefs of Staff:

Telegram just received from Freyberg states only chance of survival of force in Suda area is to withdraw to beaches in south of island, hiding by day and moving by night. Force at Retimo reported cut off and short of supplies. Force at Heraklion also apparently almost surrounded.

Fear we must recognise that Crete is no longer tenable and that troops must be withdrawn as far as possible. It has been impossible to

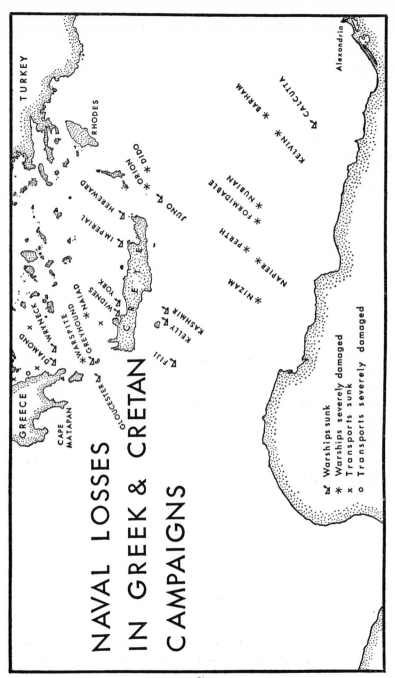

NAVAL LOSSES
IN GREEK & CRETAN
CAMPAIGNS

GREECE

TURKEY

CAPE
MATAPAN

RHODES

GLOUCESTER

DIAMOND

WRYNECK

WARSPITE

GREYHOUND

NAIAD

WIDNES

YORK

IMPERIAL

HEREWARD

ORION

DIDO

JUNO

C R E T E

KELLY

KASHMIR

FIJI

NIZAM

NAPIER

PERTH

FORMIDABLE

NUBIAN

KELVIN

BARHAM

CALCUTTA

Alexandria

↙ Warships sunk
* Warships severely damaged
× Transports sunk
○ Transports severely damaged

withstand weight of enemy air attack, which has been on an unprecedented scale and has been through force of circumstances practically unopposed.

Reluctantly the War Cabinet took the decision to evacuate Crete. No one believed it would be easy. For the troops lay ahead the incredible hardships of crossing the island by foot trails to Sphakia where the majority would be taken off by the Navy.

The retreat over the mountains toward Sphakia was protected by a strong rear guard consisting of two Commando units and remnants of the Fifth New Zealand Brigade and the Seventh and Eighth Battalions of the Sixth Australian Division. It was a grueling grind, but the majority of the forces from the Maleme-Canea-Suda Bay area made it through to Sphakia.

Inevitably there were stragglers, and these the Germans hunted down mercilessly. Any of the local residents who aided the British received short shrift. In Kystomadon, three men were buried alive. Their families were forced to give dinner to the German murderers, who laughed uproariously and mocked the new-made widows.

Food was short during the retreat. An Australian sergeant reported:

> I'll say we were hungry. I know men who had had no food for three days before they were evacuated. I came off from Sphakia, and the night before I left I saw men eating donkey's flesh. They had slaughtered the donkey in a *Wadi* and were hacking lumps off the beast and roasting them over a fire. I saw other men eating the raw flesh from fowls they had killed.

Another Australian described the suffering inflicted by the pitiless bombing of the retreating soldiers.

> I saw scenes in Crete which make me thank God for my luck. I saw men who had had their arms blown off staggering along toward the coast in the hope of being evacuated. I saw a Maori, whose foot had been shot through by a bullet, limping along with the rest of the troops. He was in agony, but not a word of complaint passed his lips.

As the troops neared Sphakia, the RAF did its best from bases in Africa to give all the support it could. The support was painfully little, but it helped some.

It was on the Navy, however, that the chief burden fell. Once more the scene of exhausted, disheartened troops and over-pressed and battered ships had to be repeated. Again only the night hours could be used, and again the losses were heavy in both ships and men.

Despite the fearful cost he had paid in the last few days, it never occurred to Admiral Cunningham to abandon the Army. "It takes the Navy three years to build a new ship," he declared. "It will take three hundred years to build a new tradition. The evacuation will continue."

On the night of May 28/29, the cruisers *Orion, Ajax,* and *Dido,* escorted by 6 destroyers, ventured to the north side of the island to pick up four or five thousand men at Heraklion. It was then or never for the Army forces there, for Heraklion was to be strictly a one-night stand. Under heavy attack on the way in, the force suffered the loss of the *Ajax,* which was damaged and had to return to Alexandria. The embarkation went smoothly, and by 0300, May 29, the force set out for Egypt. Then the damaged destroyer *Imperial* had to be sunk after she went out of control. The unfortunate delay caused the little group of ships to be caught at daylight the next morning. Fierce air attacks lasted from 0600 to 1500, when the force had come within 100 miles of Alexandria.

The delay caused the ships to miss contact with the fighters sent out to cover them. As a result, the ships had to endure the German onslaught absolutely alone. The destroyer *Decoy* was hit, and the *Dido* took a bomb on her forward turret. There was little damage. The *Orion* was hit twice. The first attack mortally wounded her captain, G. R. B. Bach. In the second, the bomb penetrated to the mess deck, which was jammed with rescued soldiers. In a single explosion, 260 men died and much oil fuel was contaminated.

"I shall never forget the sight of those ships coming up the harbour," Cunningham wrote, "the guns of their fore-turrets awry, one or two broken off and pointing forlornly skyward, their upper decks crowded with troops, and the marks of their ordeal only too plainly visible."

In contrast, the evacuations from Sphakia went comparatively smoothly. Several ships were damaged by air attack during the three nights of the operation, but only one, the antiaircraft cruiser *Calcutta,* was sunk.

In all, some 16,500 men were evacuated from Crete. Nearly 1000 more escaped later through their own ingenuity or the aid of submarines and Commando raids. On the other hand, some 13,000 British and Greek soldiers were killed, wounded, or captured. Estimates of German losses run as high as 15,000.

Germany paid highly for a Pyrrhic victory in Crete. Although the British Mediterranean Fleet was so weakened that the Italians might have been able to win control had they tried, the British were able to hang on. In the process of taking the island, the Germans lost their only airborne division. It was so thoroughly cut to pieces that it never was restored to effectiveness; Hitler reached the conclusion that the value of paratroops was negligible, and no more were formed. The following year he refused to consider the use of German airborne troops in the planned capture of Malta.

The occupation of Crete did not ease the German supply problem in North Africa. Only the capture of Malta could do that, and that operation was not undertaken. Axis ships sailing near Crete were too vulnerable to British air and sea attacks from Egypt.

Hitler never understood the problems of war in the Mediterranean. The opportunities there were golden, but he was not interested. His eyes were on the east.

* * *

"The situation in Iraq has turned sour." Churchill was writing to Mr. L. S. Amery, Secretary of State for India, asking him to send troops to Basra, the main port of Iraq on the Persian Gulf.

Ever since 1930, Britain had enjoyed treaty rights to maintain air bases near Basra, and Habbaniya, together with the necessary right of transit of military forces and supplies. In time of war, these rights were extended to shipping and rail facilities.

In the decade following this treaty, Iraqi attitudes grew to be more and more pro-German, and in March, 1941, the Anglophobic Rashid Ali became Prime Minister. With three prominent officers who shared his sentiments, he formed a cabal known as the Golden Square and forced the pro-British regent, Emir Abdul Illa, to flee for his life. Ali promptly appealed to Germany for aid.

It was slow in coming.

Although Wavell had his hands full enough, he had to undertake yet another campaign. Rashid Ali moved against the British establishment at Habbaniya on May 2. The defenders held their own, and a relief force from Basra arrived on May 18, quickly putting the Iraqi dissidents to flight, in spite of the presence of a few German aircraft, moved belatedly to the rebel support. German enthusiasm was somewhat dampened when the Luftwaffe commander assigned to Iraq did not emerge from his plane after it had come to a stop at the end of the runway. Upon investigation, he was found dead with a bullet in his brain. A zealous rebel whose marksmanship was better than his judgment had placed it there.

Rashid Ali tried to carry on the rebellion from Baghdad, but the British followed him there. Deciding that a whole skin was better than political power, Ali and his cohorts took refuge in Persia. The regent came back, and order was quickly restored, with the British better off than they had been before. At least one thing went right for Britain in that dark May.

* * *

Admiral Darlan was ever a sailor with a watchful eye to windward. Whatever happened, he was determined that France would be on the winning side in the war. If this meant alliance with a former enemy and turning on a former ally, then so be it.

In May, 1941, it became clear to Darlan that Germany was going to win. In his role as second to old Marshal Pétain, he turned his efforts toward bringing France into the Axis.

In November, 1942, he changed his mind. Then he thought the British, Russians, and Americans would win.

Darlan's attitude was not typical of Frenchmen everywhere. Most prayed for an Allied victory, and the men and women of France were prepared to risk their lives to aid downed airmen and to hinder the Germans in any way they could. In particular, the people in Occupied France, daily subject to Nazi repression and discipline, hated the Boche with all their hearts. A few, of course, proved venal and collaborated, but the prayer was, "Let the British win!"

In Vichy France, where anti-British propaganda was distributed by their own Government, the French modified the prayer slightly: "Let the British swine win!"

Admiral Darlan set about allying France with Germany to the extent that he felt he could. In May, Darlan met with Hitler and other Nazi officials. Hitler was willing to make certain concessions in return for the use of French ships in the Mediterranean, for landing rights at airfields in Syria and in French North Africa, and for French trucks to be delivered to Rommel.

By the time Hitler got his hands on the French items that he demanded, most of the concessions were forgotten.

Having been balked in their hopes of getting a force to the east of the British in the Mediterranean by the failure of the revolt in Iraq, the Germans saw another opportunity in French Syria.

When Rashid Ali sought aid from Hitler, the Führer took the

473

opportunity of moving a few Luftwaffe elements into the Levant. With the concurrence of Admiral Darlan, the Axis sent about 100 German and 20 Italian aircraft into Syria. The French High Commissioner and Commander in Chief, General Dentz, reacted in typical Vichy fashion by assisting the Axis where he could and preparing to oppose any British or Free French reaction.

The presence of Axis air power in Syria and the prospect that Syria would become a German-Vichy French base were totally unacceptable to the British and Free French. The British position in Palestine would be in grave danger. Aircraft from Syrian fields could bomb the Suez Canal, the oil refineries at Abadan, and the naval base at Alexandria. The fact that the Germans could move into the Levant would have had the gravest political effect on the neutral governments of Egypt and Turkey.*

At first Churchill hoped that the Free French could handle the situation by themselves, and de Gaulle, back from his African exile, was enthusiastic. Then Churchill began to have second thoughts. Above all, Britain must avoid another Dakar. Reluctantly the Prime Minister asked Wavell to shoulder yet one more burden.

The drive into Syria began on June 8, after the conclusion of the Cretan campaign. Units of the RAF and 2 cruisers and 10 destroyers of the Mediterranean Fleet supported the ground forces.

For the first week, all went well, but then General Dentz consolidated his defenses, and Wavell had to hustle in reinforcements. Fortunately for the British, the units which had settled Rashid Ali were available. Marching across the desert, they closed in on Palmyra from the southeast and then swung west toward Tripoli and Damascus. They saw no visions on the road to Damascus, but the troops from the south and east seized the ancient city on June 21. The end of French resistance was clearly in sight, although General Dentz managed to hold out until July 12.

And what of the German aircraft that had begun it all? They left the Vichy French to fight for themselves. The Germans had a date to keep in Russia.

* * *

In Churchill's mind a Tiger was burning bright. "Tiger" was the code name of a special convoy sent through the Mediterranean to

* Although the British were using Egyptian facilities and fighting was going on in Egyptian territory, Egypt was technically neutral. The British were in Egypt by treaty rights.

relieve a serious shortage of tanks in Egypt. No convoy had gone straight through the Mediterranean since the spring of 1940, and the defense leaders in London were highly dubious of success. But Wavell's needs were so great and Churchill so persuasive that the convoy was sent.

Five fast merchant ships carrying 307 tanks passed through the Strait of Gibraltar on May 6, escorted by Admiral Somerville's Force H. Also in company were the battleship *Queen Elizabeth* and the cruisers *Naiad* and *Fiji,* intended as reinforcements for Cunningham's Mediterranean Fleet. In a matter of days, the *Fiji* would find her grave in the waters off Crete.

On May 8, the convoy ran into a minefield and one merchant ship was sunk and another damaged. The cripple, however, was able to continue with the convoy. Near Malta, Force H turned back, leaving the convoy to rendezvous with Cunningham, who had brought a powerful force to meet the "Tiger." On the way he had sent detachments to bombard Benghazi. At the same time he had shepherded a convoy with supplies for the relief of Malta.

The Tiger convoy reached Alexandria on May 12 without further loss, in spite of heavy air attacks. "We did not altogether congratulate ourselves," recorded Cunningham, "being fully aware that the success of the operation must be ascribed to the thick and cloudy weather, which, for that time of year in the Mediterranean, was unprecedented."

Having got his tanks to Egypt, Churchill immediately thought of putting them to use. Wavell had asked for them in order to be able to defend Egypt from the new German armored division then being landed. Churchill thought otherwise. "No German should remain in Cyrenaica by the end of the month of June," he telegraphed to Wavell.

Even Churchill was sufficiently occupied by the events of the disastrous month of May to keep him from sending more than occasional telegrams to Wavell about the need to drive Rommel back to Tripoli. But he never forgot it. He never let Wavell forget it.

A limited British offensive in mid-May gained control of Sollum and Halfaya Passes, the only places in the region where it was possible to go from the coastal plain up onto the escarpment that stretched limitlessly southward. The British could not enjoy their triumph for long, however; Rommel promptly threw them out.

The Desert Fox had problems of his own. He could not advance as long as Tobruk held out. And he could find no way to take Tobruk.

He could only stay where he was and await the inevitable British counterattack.

Churchill demanded action. The Tiger convoy had arrived and the Tiger Cubs—Churchill's whimsical designation of the tanks it had brought—had been unloaded. Why were they not in use? Wavell drily reminded him that even Tiger Cubs have teething troubles.

Against his better judgment, Wavell agreed to begin operations against Rommel on June 7. "I think it right to inform you," he warned, "that the measure of success which will attend this operation is in my opinion doubtful."

When the offensive had to be postponed until June 15, Churchill was furious. He expected great things from the offensive, which he had personally named Battleaxe.

Selected to command the operation was General N. M. de la P. Beresford-Peirse. He had about 25,000 men and 180 tanks. Included in his command was the famous Seventh Armoured Division, the spearhead of O'Connor's triumphal drive. But, alas for the British, Beresford-Peirse was no O'Connor, and the Seventh Armoured was not what it had been. After its withdrawal from O'Connor's command, the division had been stripped of its equipment. Its personnel had been scattered into other units. Only recently had it been reorganized, re-equipped, and some of its men returned. It was still diluted with green recruits, and it had had no opportunity for its men to train together.

Beresford-Peirse was a conventional general of the old school. His narrow-slitted eyes peered intently across the desert, while the stub of a cigar protruded from his firm mouth. He was completely orthodox, completely unimaginative, and he had never before commanded armor.

His battle plan was completely orthodox. Halfaya (Hellfire) Pass was the key to the attack, and he planned two frontal drives on it, one from the coastal plain and one along the escarpment. The coastal plain attack bogged down completely, and an effortless riposte by Rommel caught the 22nd Guards and the Fourth Armoured brigades in the flank as they turned the corner at Capuzzo. In three days it was all over. Rommel had a nasty surprise for Beresford-Peirse, and he had used it in opposing Battleaxe. It was the 88-mm. gun. British tanks simply could not stand up to it, and Rommel used the guns so successfully that the British could not get close enough to knock them out. In this sense, it was the Germans, not the British, who had the Battleaxe.

The failure of Battleaxe depressed Churchill severely. He would not realize that his own decisions had imperiled the whole British position in the eastern Mediterranean. It was he who had stripped the Western Desert in order to send troops to Greece; it was he who had made the decision to try to hold Crete; it was he who had ordered a premature offensive in Cyrenaica.

Instead of recognizing his own errors, Churchill found them in other men. Especially, he reached the conclusion that Wavell was tired. Wavell had every right to be tired, having run seven separate campaigns in the space of a few months. In four of them he had won, but he had lost his last—Battleaxe. For that he was to be relieved.

General Sir Claude Auchinleck came from India to take over as Commander in Chief. When he arrived in Cairo, he noted, "Wavell showed no signs of tiredness at all. He was always the same. I think he was first class; in spite of his silences, he made a tremendous impact on the troops. I have a very great admiration for him . . . but he was given impossible tasks."

No sooner was Auchinleck installed than Churchill began pressing him for a resumption of the offensive. The "Auk," as he was known, proved unreceptive to Churchill's enthusiasms, so he was summoned to London to fall under the spell of Churchill's personal eloquence. The journey was a failure from Churchill's point of view. Auchinleck, rather than being converted, converted his critics, all but the Prime Minister. "He certainly shook my military advisors," recorded Churchill, "with all the detailed argument he produced. I was myself unconvinced."

In these months Churchill showed himself at his worst as a wartime leader. Unable to accept any notion of defeat, he could not accept lesser goals than his vision produced. Being no ordinary man, Churchill could not understand the limitations of ordinary men or the limitations imposed by circumstances. His imagination soared, and he had scant patience with the realities which stood in the way. For him, to imagine was to dare, to dare was to do, and to do was to accomplish. Britain could not have survived without him in those years, but his harried advisers sometimes wondered if Britain could survive him.

Fortunately all around, he soon had a larger scope for his driving energies. On June 22, 1941, Hitler cynically tore up the Non-Aggression Pact he had signed with Russia less than two years earlier. On that date some 130 German divisions, supported by more than 2700 aircraft, hurled themselves at Russia.

Britain was no longer fighting alone, but her ally was not the one she hoped or expected to have.

The United States still stood on the sidelines.

CHAPTER SEVENTEEN

Clear and Present Danger

And not by eastern windows only,
When daylight comes, comes in the light;
In front the sun climbs slow, how slowly,
But westward, look, the land is bright.
Arthur Hugh Clough,
"Say Not the Struggle Nought Availeth"

FRANKLIN DELANO ROOSEVELT was up to his old tricks. He was being enigmatic. After the passage of the Lend-Lease Act, he had done little positive in either preparing the country for war or in giving aid to Britain. His leadership faltered. He read the daily situation reports. He corresponded with "Former Naval Person" Winston Churchill. He found time to toss out the first ball in the American League opener, which the Washington Nats lost 3–0 to the Yankees. He presided over the annual White House egg-rolling Easter lawn party.

But what was going on in the country? Where would Roosevelt lead America?

Lend-Lease supplies were beginning to move to Britain, but they moved in British-controlled ships, because the Neutrality Acts barred American vessels from the war zones. Some pro-British officials urged American convoys to protect Lend-Lease goods, but Roosevelt parried all such suggestions. "But convoys mean shooting," he told a visitor, "and shooting means war."

It was as though Mr. Roosevelt had seen the specter of war in front of him if he continued his course of "all aid short of war" to Britain. He was not prepared to lead the country into war, and he knew the country did not want war. Isolationist sentiment might be lessening in numbers, but it was louder than ever. While an increasing

479

number of people believed that war would come, only a tiny minority was ready to fight in the spring of 1941.

In his news conferences, Mr. Roosevelt dodged all questions artfully. Reporters came away mystified and irritated. The President went fishing. He talked to his cronies. He made no major speech after his January State of the Union Address.

As disasters overwhelmed Britain, one after another that spring, Mr. Roosevelt made no comment. He was not ready to move further toward the thin edge that would separate "all aid short of war" from actual shooting.

Events could not remain as they were. The Atlantic Fleet was strengthened and patrols moved regularly, keeping an eye out for U-boats and for German surface vessels. Inevitably there would be brushes. American merchant ships were kept busy on runs around Africa to Egypt, on runs to South America. They sailed boldly, lighted at night, floodlights playing on large American flags painted on their hulls.

Mr. Roosevelt's inertia was finally given a jolt by the report that the American destroyer *Niblack* had depth-charged a German U-boat near Iceland.* On April 15, two days after the incident, Mr. Roosevelt summoned his advisers to decide whether to go to convoy operations or to increased patrol operations.

After listening to the arguments of the aggressive Chief of Naval Operations, Admiral Harold R. Stark, and to those of the cautious Mr. Cordell Hull, the President ruled against escort of convoys. American naval vessels were to increase their patrols west of the twenty-sixth meridian.† If an American ship contacted a German vessel, it was to follow and broadcast its position to the British. The general idea was to make operations in the western Atlantic as dangerout as possible for the Germans without Americans actually engaging in gunfire.

With the Russian campaign coming soon, Hitler was anxious to avoid incidents with the United States. He ordered Grand Admiral Raeder to ensure that no American ships were molested. In spite of these instructions, American ships were attacked and American lives were lost.

Later in April, the Egyptian steamer *Zamzam* was sunk by a Ger-

---

* Apparently the *Niblack* depth-charged a whale. The German records reveal no attack on a German submarine in that area on that date, nor was any U-boat lost at that time.
† Roughly, west of Iceland.

man raider. Among her passengers were 135 Americans. This incident caused little stir, but the following month brought a real confrontation.

The American freighter *Robin Moor* was steaming peacefully through the South Atlantic in the early morning hours of May 21. The watch had changed, and dawn was just breaking over the gray sea. The American flags painted on her sides were clearly visible.

A light began to flash in the distance. Carefully the men on the bridge spelled out the letters: STOP. SEND OVER A BOAT. The *Robin Moor*'s master came to the bridge, still clothed in his pajamas. The *Robin Moor* drifted to a halt and lowered a boat. The chief officer and four men rowed over to the long, low shape of *U-69*, a mile or so away, while the people on the *Robin Moor* waited tensely.

At last the boat returned, and the chief officer reported grimly, "They're going to let us have it."

The master ordered the other three boats put in readiness and lowered. The eight passengers, including three women and a child, were awakened and told to get into the lifeboats. After everyone was clear, the U-boat fired a torpedo and then began shelling the helpless derelict. Twenty-three minutes later she went down, stern first, in a position 750 miles west of Freetown.

The U-boat moved closer, and a sailor passed over some canned food. The commander of *U-69* shouted, "I'm sorry, but you were carrying supplies to my country's enemy."

For eighteen days the boats drifted under a blazing tropical sun. One boat wandered away from the others and was picked up by a passing freighter somewhere near the coast of South America. Survivors in the other three boats were rescued by a British freighter bound for Cape Town.

The American people knew nothing of the sinking until mid-June. Then they responded with a combination of shock and outrage. But not the isolationists. Commented Senator Nye, "It would not be wholly impossible for the British themselves to engineer little programs of that kind. . . . We have rather been issuing engraved invitations for an incident of this kind."

Even before word of the *Robin Moor* sinking had reached him, Mr. Roosevelt had stirred from his seeming lethargy and had taken a major step toward putting the country on a war footing.

German naval activities in the western Atlantic had infuriated the President, and he felt that there was little point in shipping Lend-Lease cargoes if the German U-boats were going to be permitted to sink the ships carrying them before protecting escorts took charge.

The sinking of the *Hood* in the waters west of Iceland, well within the proclaimed American Defense Zone, gave the President the pretext he needed.

A few hours after the *Bismarck* went down, Mr. Roosevelt was scheduled to address the ambassadors and ministers of Latin America and Canada in a Pan-American Day address. That evening these gentlemen gathered in the East Room of the White House. Outside on Pennsylvania Avenue, Communist anti-war pickets plodded up and down under the watchful eyes of the police and the White House guards.

Mr. Roosevelt was wheeled into the room to face the battery of microphones that would carry his voice to the nation and the world. It was later estimated that he commanded an audience of 85 million persons.

Since the President had made no major address for five months, he devoted a good portion of his broadcast to a review of the events of the intervening time and the measures the Government had taken to protect the interests of the United States. He tended to be conciliatory toward the isolationists and reasoned and logical with his critics. As a result, he tended to be somewhat dull. Some of the distinguished gentlemen in the East Room politely concealed yawns. Even the President himself seemed a little bored with what he was saying.

At length he came to his thesis—the heart of the matter. "Control or occupation by Nazi forces," he said, "of any of the islands of the Atlantic would jeopardize the immediate safety of portions of the continental United States itself."

After dealing with the problems of Britain's need to keep control of the seas, he grew more forceful, if no more specific.

> Our patrols are helping now to ensure the delivery of the needed supplies to Britain. All additional measures necessary to deliver the goods will be taken. Any and all further methods or combinations of methods which can and should be utilized are being devised by our military and naval technicians who, with me, will work out and put into effect such new and additional safeguards as may be needed.
>
> I will say that the delivery of needed supplies to Britain is imperative. I say this can be done; it must be done; it will be done.

Having reached a premature climax, the President lapsed into dullness again. He raised the blood pressure of both business and labor leaders by castigating them for putting self-interest ahead of the duty of rearming the nation. He warned both that "this Government is determined to use all its powers to express the will of the people, and to prevent interference with the production of materials essential to our nation's security."

Whatever heads might have been nodding in this, one of Mr. Roosevelt's least-inspired speeches, were snapped back to full attention by his concluding words.

> Therefore, with profound consciousness of my responsibilities to my countrymen and my country's cause, I have tonight issued a proclamation that an unlimited national emergency exists and requires the strengthening of our defense to the extreme limit of our national power and authority.

Before the President retired for the night, the first telegrams in response to the speech were pouring into the White House. Mr. Roosevelt confided jubilantly to Robert E. Sherwood that 95 percent were favorable. He had, he confessed, counted on no more than an "even break." If this percentage of response could be believed, the people were more ready than the President suspected to respond to firm direction in the preparation for war.

But by the time he had read the morning papers, Mr. Roosevelt apparently began to get cold feet. Although quite a few members of Congress agreed with the proclamation, the isolationist voice was shrill. Representative Hamilton Fish of New York, one of the arch Roosevelt-haters, stated, "It was a typical Rooseveltian speech to promote further war hysteria and fear to break down the will of over eighty percent of the American people who are against involvement in European and Asiatic wars." Senator Robert A. Taft charged that Roosevelt "in dictator style" was taking "warlike action without submitting to the people the question of whether or not we shall go to war."

At his press conference later that morning, the President was in a bad humor. He said he had no plans to ask Congress for repeal of the Neutrality Acts. The Navy was not planning to escort merchant ships. One reporter asked what he would do if labor and management did not respond to his appeal of the previous night. Mr. Roosevelt dismissed the question as "iffy." He had no plans to issue the executive orders that would make effective the proclamation of unlimited national emergency.

The entire press conference was frustrating to most of Mr. Roosevelt's official family. It was clear evidence that the President was not prepared to challenge the isolationists in open battle. He would go on as he had before, working behind the scenes.

The Sphinx of 1600 Pennsylvania Avenue had become enigmatic again.

Two of the islands Mr. Roosevelt had been worried about were Iceland and Greenland. Both lay near the convoy runs, and both would be invaluable to the German U-boat campaign if they were in Nazi hands. In May, 1940, the British, at the invitation of the local government, had sent Army units to defend Iceland from possible German occupation on the orders of the captive Danish Government.

British troops kept Iceland free of Nazi occupation, but the Germans made several attempts to land weather observers on Greenland. The United States Coast Guard was assigned the duty of turning these parties out as part of what the newspapers called an "unofficial protectorate over Greenland." Because of this activity, the Germans were denied the weather information that would have been useful in planning the operations of their U-boats. This activity on the part of the Coast Guard intensified after the sinking of the *Bismarck* and continued throughout the war under the leadership of Commander (later Captain) Edward H. Smith, known throughout the Coast Guard as "Iceberg" Smith.

One of the "additional measures" to be taken by the United States was the replacement of the British garrison in Iceland with U.S. Marines. The Marines came from a camp in California and were sent to Charleston, South Carolina, where, much to their astonishment, they were issued long, woolen underwear. They had been expecting Caribbean duty.

On June 22, 1941, the Sixth Regiment of the Second Marine Division, with a total strength of 194 officers and 3714 enlisted men sailed for Reykjavik, Iceland.

This, the first U.S. expeditionary force to be sent out in World War II, was embarked in 6 transports with a heavy naval escort, including 2 battleships and 2 cruisers. On the way, the destroyer *Hughes* rescued fourteen survivors from a torpedoed Norwegian freighter. Four of those rescued were American nurses who had been bound for England with the Harvard Red Cross Unit.

Iceland became increasingly important in the Battle of the Atlantic. In addition to the naval base at Hvalfjordur, there were air bases, British, Norwegian, and later American. From these, the ships and planes went out to come to the assistance of the hard-pressed convoys.

At first the Icelanders and the Marines had difficulty in adjusting to each other. The tendency of most Americans to look upon different customs and ways of life as inferior caused many hard feelings. But over the months, the generosity of both sides eased tensions. Dances, exchange dinners, an impromptu Marine jazz orchestra all made their contributions, and it was not long before Americans were welcome guests in Icelandic homes. A few of the Marines even married local girls.

One Navy man, on learning that his girl's family had never heard of a watermelon, decided to do something about it. He had a buddy on a supply ship, and on the next trip, the buddy brought in a large, succulent watermelon.

The sailor gave the fruit to the girl to take home one morning and that night showed up for dinner. He found the family deep in gloom. His hostess led him to the kitchen, where the melon was in the largest cauldron the woman owned.

"It's been boiling since noon," she explained apologetically, "and it's still tough."

Watermelons apart, the value of Iceland became increasingly apparent as the U-boat operations entered their second summer. After the success of the operations against the convoys SC-7, HX-79, and HX-79A,* U-boat operations received a series of setbacks. During the winter of 1940/41, the undersea hunters were largely foiled by a combination of bad weather, skillful defense by convoy escorts, and evasive routing of convoys. By the end of the year Dönitz found that new construction had barely replaced the losses of 31 U-boats.

The U-boat building program was moving ahead, however, and Dönitz determined to make a frontal assault on British convoys. He dispatched his three aces to conduct the blitz in the Northwest Approaches Area. These aces were Lieutenant Commander Joachim Schepke in *U-100*, Lieutenant Commander Günther Prien in *U-47*, and Lieutenant Commander Otto Kretschmer in *U-99*. These three men had the largest scores of any U-boat commanders, and Prien still enjoyed special esteem for his feat in penetrating Scapa Flow and sinking the *Royal Oak*.

On the night of March 6, *U-47* and three other boats made contact with westbound convoy OB-293. Attacks lasted for twenty-four hours, and at dusk the next evening, Prien had the misfortune to encounter

* See pp. 415–416.

H.M.S. *Wolverine*. A barrage of depth charges put an end to *U-47* and her illustrious commander.

A week later, Schepke and Kretschmer happened upon convoy HX-112 and pressed home a skillful attack. Schepke accounted for the *Erodona,* a 10,000-ton tanker, but then activity ceased until the night of March 16. Making a concerted assault, Schepke and Kretschmer crept in. In his customary night-surfaced attack, Kretschmer bent on the knots and raced down the columns of the convoy, blazing away with his deck guns and firing torpedoes as he went. He hit four tankers and two merchant ships in this daring attack, but it was his last. A year earlier, such an attack would have thrown the convoy into complete confusion. This time, discipline prevailed. The surviving ships kept on their way, closing the gaps as they went, while the escorts set out to punish the intruders.

The likely place to look after such an attack was astern of the convoy, and this time the defenders struck it rich. Commander Donald Macintyre in H.M.S. *Walker* spotted Schepke's *U-100* creeping along on the surface and promptly rushed after her. *U-100* crash-dived and escaped for the moment, but other destroyers joined the hunt and turned the water to a maelstrom with repeated depth charge patterns. Schepke's boat was forced to the surface, and the destroyer *Vanoc* promptly rammed her. The hull of *U-100* was split wide open, and she quickly went down in her last dive.

Macintyre was not idle during these moments, and a short time later depth charges from the *Walker* blasted *U-99* to the surface. A lively battle ensued, both the *Walker* and *U-99* firing their guns as fast as possible, until a message from *U-99,* "WE ARE SUNKING [*sic*]," brought an end. Kretschmer and his men hastily abandoned ship, and *U-99* went to the bottom. Macintyre maneuvered his ship to pick up survivors. Among them was Kretschmer. Because of the crowding in small ships, Macintyre was forced to house his unexpected guest in his own day cabin, which he never used at sea. Sharing the cabin with the U-boat ace were the master and chief officer of the freighter *E. B. White,* which Kretschmer had sunk that same night. All three being gentlemen, and the fortunes of war being what they were, they made the best of it and settled in to enjoy their favorite recreation— bridge. The chief engineer of the *Walker* made the fourth. "It was the only decent game of bridge I had during the entire war," he remarked later.

Three aces trumped in a little over a week gave an enormous lift to the spirits of the weary British escort crews. News of the loss of their three greatest skippers was a major setback to the U-boat Command.* The attrition of U-boats suddenly rose to 20 percent, and Dönitz had to shift his hunting to softer spots farther west. This move naturally increased the danger of encounters with American ships.

* * *

No such sense of outrage gripped the American people over the *Robin Moor* affair as had occurred over the sinking of the *Lusitania* in World War I. Most people wanted to be left alone. Let Europe stew in her own juice. To be sure, most Americans sympathized with Britain in her agony, but involvement was something else. According to the polls, a substantial majority of the people expected the United States would be drawn into the war, but only a handful were willing to declare war, even to save Britain from total defeat. Business went on as usual, even though the Federal Government was beginning to get into the act, like the camel getting its nose in the tent. Defense orders were beginning to squeeze on civilian production, but not seriously. The word "shortages" was beginning to be heard in governmental offices and in the conversation of businessmen. Aluminum, zinc, and nickel were high on the list of scarce items, and steel was running short for Mr. and Mrs. John Q. Citizen. By August, the Government had put steel under mandatory priorities. No one could buy steel without a Federal permit, and permits were hard to come by. Automobile manufacturers were still getting an adequate quantity for cars, and they looked ahead to the 1942 model year as one of the brightest in history. The Chevy, the Ford, and the Plymouth made up the low-priced three, ranging in cost from $659 to $800 F.O.B. Detroit. Top-of-the-line Cadillacs and Lincoln Zephyrs (with the "revolutionary V-12 engine") ran around $2000.

Production of automobiles was no longer the sole concern of Ford, General Motors, Chrysler, and Studebaker. Those were the only plants in the country with the capacity to begin to meet the demands of President Roosevelt for 50,000 planes a year. General Motors contracted to build the twin-engined B-25, designed and hitherto produced solely by North American Aviation. Ford began production of the B-24 Liberator four-engined bomber, and Chrysler set to work on Glenn Martin's B-26. Studebaker concentrated on turning out aircraft engines.

---

* Kretschmer's record of 266,629 tons sunk is the highest for any submarine commander of any nationality in any war. After the war, Kretschmer became head of the submarine arm of the Federal German Navy.

With the arrival of Government contracts, Henry Ford faced the fight of his life. The Ford Motor Company had never been unionized for the simple reason that Mr. Ford would never deal with a union. He prided himself on his fair labor dealings and on his wages, which were publicized as the highest in the industry. Organized labor had often tried to get a foot in the door, but this time it had an ally. The Supreme Court had given the National Labor Relations Board authority to order union elections in defense plants. Mr. Ford did not mean to budge. "We do not intend," he growled, "to submit to any union, and those who belong to one are being fooled. . . . Occasionally outside agitators try to keep our employees stirred up, but the men know they will be treated fairly by the company, without outside intervention."

In the spring of 1941, however, the forces of change were to prove too much for Mr. Ford. In April the United Auto Workers called a strike against Ford's main plant in Dearborn, Michigan. A brief outbreak of violence flared between strikers and non-strikers. The weapons were iron pipes, knives, straight razors, large bolts, and wooden clubs. After about a week, Mr. Ford agreed to allow elections. He privately expected that his workers would reject a union, but he was to be sadly disappointed.

When the election was held a few weeks later, only 2 percent of the 80,000 workers voted for no union at all. Nearly 70 percent opted for the C.I.O. over its arch-rival, the A.F. of L. Walter Reuther proclaimed a great victory. Harry Bennett, Ford's strong-arm man in charge of plant security and labor relations, had another idea. "A great victory for the Communist Party," he grumbled.

Other labor disputes in defense industries plagued the nation, especially in the spring. It is remarkable how they fell off after the German invasion of Russia. The most serious were wildcat strikes in the logging industry, in San Francisco shipyards, and in the North American Aviation plant in Inglewood, California. In each case, responsible labor leaders repudiated the strikers, but in each case the strikers defied their leaders and the Federal Government. Philip Murray was booed right off the platform as he tried to plead with the men at North American to go back to work. President Roosevelt threatened to seize the plants. A rebellious spokesman for the strikers defied him: "Armed forces will not break our strike," he pontificated. "Bombers can't be made with bayonets."

Nothing daunted, the President acted. Two battalions of troops moved in on North American. A few hours later, workmen were streaming into the plant, and production resumed.

Strikes among the loggers and the shipbuilders lasted longer, but the men eventually went back to work after far too much production had been lost.

The greatest labor pontificator of all was ponderous John L. Lewis. In rolling jeremiads, he denounced the New Deal and Franklin D. Roosevelt, whom he regarded as a traitor to Labor. After rumbling and snorting most of the summer, he called a strike of 53,000 workers in the captive coal mines * for late November. The issue was the closed shop. Said F.D.R. to a glowering Lewis, "I tell you frankly that the Government of the United States will not order, nor will Congress pass legislation ordering a so-called closed shop."

The miners struck, and the strike spread to other mines, even those under contract.

Nonsense, proclaimed Mr. Lewis. It would not hurt defense production. Six days later, Lewis suddenly called the whole thing off, after thousands of tons of coal had been lost to industry. He agreed to submit the whole dispute to arbitration, in the obvious expectation that the arbitration board would decide in his favor.

It did.

It handed down its decision on the evening of December 7, 1941.

Mr. Lewis was not the only one to put limited and selfish interests above national defense. In his case it might be characterized as short-sightedness, a blindness to anything but the attainment of his goals for his miners. The same cannot be said for profiteers and operators in budding black markets in scarce commodities. Prices began an inexorable rise.

Because he knew that prices would soon be a problem, Roosevelt decided to create an agency to do something about them. Being Roosevelt, he declined to give the new agency any real power. It was designated the Office of Price Administration and Civilian Supply, quickly changed to OPACS by the headline writers. Its leader was Leon Henderson, who soon succeeded in getting everyone irritated with him. He argued with business leaders, who went right on raising prices. He submitted a price-control law which Congress promptly tore to shreds. He spoke against excess profits, and *The Wall Street Journal* rebuked him, saying "Profits . . . are not the business of Mr. Henderson."

---

* These were the mines owned by the steel companies to produce coal for their own use.

489

Sighed Henderson, "The honeymoon is over." If there ever had been one, it had not been apparent to anyone but the leader of OPACS.

*   *   *

As German troops moved ever deeper into Russia,* leaders in Washington grappled with the implication of Germany's turn eastward. Military experts argued over whether it would take Germany three weeks or three months to defeat the huge but disorganized Soviet armies. Although England had promptly offered Russia all the aid in her power, American leaders were not so sure. There was little point in making enormous sacrifices to aid the Russians, only to see the equipment fall into the hands of the victorious Nazis. In addition, the ideological distrust of international Communism was so great among the American people that many of them almost preferred a Hitler victory to one by Stalin.

Most of F.D.R.'s advisers urged that the United States take advantage of the great opportunity to strike on the western front, to hit the Führer while his back was turned. Secretary of the Navy Knox expressed it in an address to the Conference of Governors on June 30.

> For the first time since Hitler loosed the dogs of war on this world, we are provided with a God-given chance to determine the outcome of this world-wide struggle.... While his back is turned, we must answer his obvious contempt with a smashing blow that can and will change the entire world perspective. If, while Hitler is assaulting Stalin, we can clear the path across the Atlantic and deliver, in safety, the weapons our factories are now producing, ultimate defeat for Hitler is certain.

Mr. Roosevelt had other ideas and decided to send his Lend-Lease coordinator and closest political friend, Harry Hopkins, across the Atlantic to confer with Churchill in order to coordinate efforts of the two great democracies.

Hopkins, a frail man at best, whose very existence was something of a medical miracle, crossed the Atlantic as a passenger in a B-24 Liberator bomber being ferried to Great Britain under the Lend-Lease Program. Never designed for comfort, the Liberator was a great strain on Mr. Hopkins, and he was seriously ill when he reached Scotland. As always, his spirit was far stronger than his gaunt body, and Hopkins insisted on proceeding without delay to his meeting

* The military operations of the German invasion of Russia appear in the author's *1942: The Year That Doomed the Axis.*

490

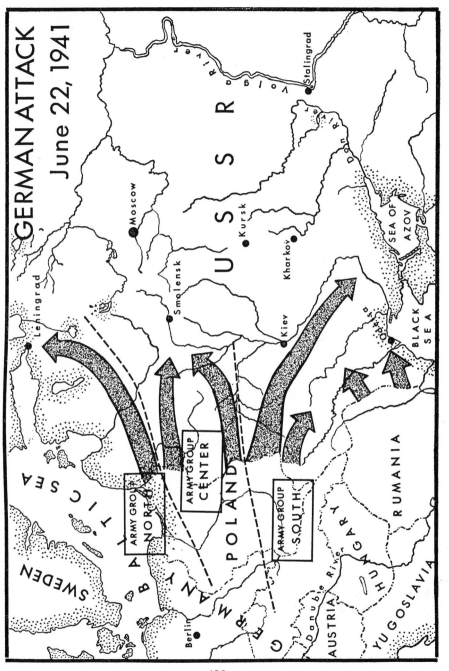

GERMAN ATTACK
June 22, 1941

Volga River

Stalingrad

Don River

Moscow

Kursk

Sea of Azov

Smolensk

Kharkov

Leningrad

Kiev

Black Sea

Odessa

Baltic Sea

Sweden

Army Group North

Army Group Center

Poland

Army Group South

Germany

Berlin

U S S R

Danube River

Hungary

Austria

Rumania

Yugoslavia

with Churchill at Chequers, the Prime Minister's official country residence, where Churchill spent his weekends.

As unalike as any two humans could be, Hopkins and Churchill had certain things in common. Both were men of enormous courage, and neither would admit the possibility of defeat. Both were ready to give everything to the cause of liberty. Both were convinced that Britain could hold out until the final victory came.

They argued, but the arguments were over methods, not over principles. The meeting accomplished an enormous amount of detailed work over Lend-Lease shipments and requirements. It eased misunderstandings and it brought the Governments of the United Kingdom and the United States together more closely than ever before. Without such a preliminary understanding, the Combined Chiefs of Staff system which later enabled the two nations to work as one in strategy would have been impossible.

It nearly was impossible as it was, because the British Chiefs of Staff and their mercurial leader had one set of ideas and the United States leaders another. But they did work together, as will be seen, and their cooperation led to victory.

Mr. Hopkins knew that Churchill and Roosevelt were planning to meet at Argentia, Newfoundland, the following month, and it was at his suggestion that Roosevelt brought his military and naval leaders with him. In a sense, this was the first meeting of what would become officially known as the Combined Chiefs of Staff, representing the highest commands of Britain and America.

On the conclusion of his conversations with Churchill, Hopkins decided that he would go to Russia to interview Stalin and find out for himself the spirit and determination of the Russian people. There was only one way for him to get there, and that was by a Coastal Command patrol plane, an American-built PBY Catalina, from Invergordon, Scotland, around North Cape, and on to Archangel. It was a ghastly trip for Hopkins, lasting twenty-four hours. The plane lacked all amenities for a comfortable flight, and Hopkins spent long hours in the tail blister, looking out through the uncomfortably good visibility for signs of the enemy. He had been briefed on the operations of the machine gun, but fortunately his marksmanship was not put to the test.

At Archangel, Hopkins had his first encounter with Soviet hospitality to visiting dignitaries. He recorded his own description of it later.

It was monumental.

It lasted almost four hours. There was an Iowa flavor to it, what with the fresh vegetables, the butter, cream, greens. For some reason the cucumbers and radishes surprised me. They were grown on the farms that hem in the city. Anyway the dinner was enormous, course after course. There was the inescapable cold fish, caviar and vodka. Vodka has authority. It is nothing for the amateur to trifle with. Drink it as an American or an Englishman takes whiskey neat and it will tear you apart. The thing to do is spread a chunk of bread (and good bread it was) with caviar, and, while you are swallowing that, bolt your vodka. Don't play with the stuff. Eat while you're drinking it—something that will act as a shock absorber for it.

The feast broke up at one o'clock in the morning, and three hours later, Hopkins had to leave by plane for Moscow. He made no protest at being allowed only two hours' sleep that night after the hard journey from Invergordon, but when he arrived in Moscow, American Ambassador Laurence A. Steinhardt put him to bed for the rest of the day.

In two days, Hopkins had two long discussions with Stalin. He was impressed by Stalin's grasp of the details of the fighting, by his precise knowledge of his country's needs in armaments and supplies. But most of all, he was impressed by the determination of the Russians to keep on fighting, come what might. Hopkins realized and he made the American leaders realize that there was no possibility of an early Russian collapse.

The flight home to Britain was even more harrowing than the one to Russia because someone had forgotten to bring the little bag of medicines that Hopkins needed to remain alive. The flight was rough, and Hopkins suffered severely, but he was able to sleep for seven hours of the time. The PBY landed in the water at Scapa Flow and Hopkins was immediately taken aboard the *Prince of Wales*. Admiral Sir John Tovey took one look at his distinguished guest, ordered him taken to his own day cabin, and summoned all the doctors he could find. It seemed highly likely that Tovey would have a corpse on his hands when Mr. Churchill arrived on board the next day.

After being drugged into a good night's sleep, Hopkins was up and about the next day in time to see a distinguished party from London arrive on board. Leading the way was the Prime Minister.

Churchill spotted Hopkins at once.

"Hello, Harry!" he exclaimed. "How is our friend Joe?"

"Joe is looking very well, Winston, and is sorry he didn't take your advice." *

"Joe has a lot of work to do now."

"I guess he knows it now," said Hopkins.

"He should have taken my advice. *Everybody* should take my advice. At all times."

It was not diplomatic courtesy that brought Britain's Prime Minister to the *Prince of Wales* to greet Hopkins on his return from Moscow. Much bigger things were in prospect.

Churchill was about to cross the Atlantic to meet President Roosevelt, to confer with him on the progress of a war in which the United States had officially no part.

Mr. Roosevelt announced he was going on a fishing trip. The Presidential yacht *Potomac* was waiting for him at New London, Connecticut, and the President embarked on August 3. The *Potomac* stood out to sea, but off Martha's Vineyard, Mr. Roosevelt transferred to the cruiser *Augusta,* flagship of the Atlantic Fleet. In company with the cruiser *Tuscaloosa* and a division of destroyers, the *Augusta* set off for Argentia, Newfoundland.

The *Potomac* continued to cruise leisurely along the coast. As she passed through the Cape Cod Canal, an individual vaguely resembling Mr. Roosevelt sat on the quarterdeck, smoking cigarettes and waving genially to the crowds which had assembled to watch the yacht go through. The deception fooled everyone, even the White House press secretary, Steve Early, who had been left out of the planning.

On the morning of August 7, the *Augusta* and *Tuscaloosa* came to anchor off Argentia. The American Chiefs of Staff, Admiral Stark, General Marshall, and General Arnold, came over from the *Tuscaloosa,* and many conferences were held. Admiral Ernest J. King, Commander in Chief, Atlantic Fleet, had his hands full with all his high-ranking guests, but Mr. Roosevelt had time to go fishing in a small boat, accompanied by his personal physician, Admiral Mc-Intire, and White House aide "Pa" Watson. They had little to show in the way of fish, but at least the President had not lied to the public. He had been on a fishing trip.

On the morning of August 9 the *Prince of Wales* entered the harbor, looming up out of a fog, being shepherded into the anchorage by American destroyers which had been sent out to escort her on the

* A reference to the warnings Churchill had sent Stalin of the coming invasion of Russia.

494

last leg of the voyage. It was a dramatic and stirring moment. Ceremonial honors were exchanged. The band on the *Prince of Wales* rendered the "Star-Spangled Banner," which was answered by "God Save the King" from the *Augusta*.

At 1100, Mr. Churchill came aboard the *Augusta,* dressed in the uniform of an Elder Brother of Trinity House. He was accompanied by Sir Alexander Cadogan, Permanent Under-Secretary for Foreign Affairs; Lord Cherwell, head of scientific war activities; Admiral of the Fleet Sir Dudley Pound, First Sea Lord; General Sir John Dill, Chief of the Imperial General Staff; Air Chief Marshal Sir Wilfred Freeman, Vice Chief of the Air Staff, and other members of Churchill's party. The President was there to greet them, standing on the quarterdeck, supported by his son Elliott. There followed meetings, lunches, conferences. The President and the Prime Minister lunched alone, but no record remains of their conversation.

That evening Roosevelt entertained Churchill and the British dignitaries with a state dinner which lasted until almost midnight. Churchill was effusive in his thanks for a gracious gesture Mr. Roosevelt had made earlier in the day.

While Churchill and Roosevelt had been having their lunch, a boat had crossed from the *Augusta* to the *Prince of Wales*. It carried hundreds of boxes which were distributed to the British crewmen. In each box was a carton of cigarettes, two apples, an orange, and half a pound of cheese. There was a printed paper reading, "The Commander in Chief, United States Navy, sends his compliments and best wishes. Franklin D. Roosevelt, President of the United States, August 9, 1941."

Most of the British seamen had not seen an orange for nearly two years, and to have one in their possession meant immeasurable riches.

The next morning, the President embarked in the destroyer *McDougal,* which took him and his party to the *Prince of Wales* for church service on the after deck. The senior British and American chaplains shared the service from the Book of Common Prayer, and men of both nations were intermingled in the congregation. Mr. Churchill had chosen the hymns himself, including "Eternal Father, Strong to Save," "Onward, Christian Soldiers," and ending with "O God, Our Help in Ages Past." Everyone who participated in the service would remember it for the rest of his life.

Half of them were soon to die.

The remaining days of the conference were business affairs, the military staffs considering the situation in Europe and Africa, the

Battle of the Atlantic, and the rising menace of Japan in the Far East. If Churchill hoped for a promise of American involvement in the war, he was sadly disappointed. Roosevelt got Churchill to agree to the so-called Atlantic Charter, a statement of war aims. In its eight points it proclaimed the right of people to choose their own forms of governments, freedom from trade barriers, freedom from fear and want, freedom of the seas, and the abandonment of the use of force in international affairs. It proclaimed that neither nation had any territorial desires, and it pledged the destruction of Nazi tyranny.

On August 12, 1941, the conference was completed. The *Prince of Wales* and the *Augusta* got under way and stood out of Argentia. Once clear of the sea buoy, the *Augusta* set course for Maine, where the *Potomac* was waiting for the President. The *Prince of Wales* swung around to port, bound for Iceland and Scapa Flow.

Soon after her safe arrival home, she was detached from the Home Fleet and sent with the *Repulse* to the Far East as a deterrent to Japan. On December 10, she and the *Repulse* were caught alone by Japanese aircraft and sunk. She had a short career in the Royal Navy, and it was starred with ill luck. She had been beaten by the *Bismarck* and forced to retire, and she was lost ineffectually to the Japanese. The high point of her brief existence was that Sunday service at Argentia.

The United States Navy was being drawn ever closer to the war. It was well enough for the politicians to pretend that the United States was not involved against the Germans, but the sailors knew better. Already American ships were escorting American convoys which took supplies to Iceland, "including shipping of any nationality which may join such United States or Iceland flag convoys." On September 4, American ships began escorting British convoys for a part of the trip across the Atlantic.

As a convoy sailed from Halifax or Sydney, it would be escorted by Canadians to a point south of Argentia, where the American destroyers would take over. They would shepherd the merchant ships for several days until they reached an eastern-ocean meeting point, unfelicitously abbreviated EASTOMP.* There the British would hand over a westbound convoy to the Americans and take the eastbound one on to the United Kingdom. Under these circumstances, it could

---

* The point for the first rendezvous had an even worse abbreviation—MOMP—mid-ocean meeting point.

be only a matter of time until a United States warship had an encounter with a U-boat.

Oddly enough, the first brush came, not as part of convoy operations, but when the U.S.S. *Greer* was steaming independently toward Iceland. On the morning of September 4, 1941, she spotted a British patrol plane, which drew near to send a message. A U-boat was athwart her course some 10 miles ahead. Lieutenant Commander L. H. Frost began zigzagging and increased speed to 20 knots. As he drew near the position, Commander Frost sent his ship to General Quarters and slowed to 10 knots to allow his sonar gear to work efficiently. Almost at once, the sonar operator picked up contact, and the *Greer* held on, pinging off the hull of *U-652* for three hours. She kept the U-boat on her bow, but made no effort to attack.

Before the British plane departed for base, it dropped depth charges more or less at random. This may have disturbed the U-boat captain, but he made no move to reply. He kept on trying to evade the nerve-shattering *"ping-g-g-g-g!"* of the *Greer*'s sonar.

Finally he had enough. He turned on his tormentor and let fly a torpedo. The *Greer* dodged it easily enough and counterattacked with depth charges. A few minutes later the U-boat fired another torpedo. The *Greer* sidestepped this one also, but in the process she lost sonar contact. After searching for three hours more, Frost called it off and headed for Iceland.

A week later, President Roosevelt took to the air in a "Freedom of the Seas" address. He called the attack on the *Greer* "piracy" and added, "When you see a rattlesnake poised to strike, you do not wait until he has struck before you crush him." He warned Hitler and Mussolini in the strongest terms: "From now on, if German or Italian vessels of war enter the waters the protection of which is necessary for American defense, they do so at their own risk."

Other American ships were being attacked, but the next serious incident took place on the night of October 16/17, 1941. Slow Convoy SC-48, consisting of some 50 ships, had run into trouble, and a division of 5 American destroyers was assigned to help out. The light from a burning ship silhouetted the U.S.S. *Kearny*. As she stopped to avoid a collision, a torpedo struck home on the starboard side. The detonation tore open the side of the ship and wrecked the starboard wing of the bridge. The forward stack was bent back. It seemed that the ship was screaming in pain; the steam siren was jammed open.

Lieutenant Commander Anthony L. Danis took quick stock of the situation. Eleven men were dead or missing, and many more were wounded. But the ship would still float. Escorted by the *Greer,* she limped into Iceland.

The next day, the House of Representatives voted to repeal the Neutrality Act barring American ships from entering war zones. The vote was 259 to 138. President Roosevelt used the occasion of the annual Navy Day Address to state:

> I say that we do not propose to take this lying down.
> Our determination not to take it lying down has been expressed in the orders to the American Navy to shoot on sight. These orders stand.

Senator C. Wayland Brooks was scornful, declaring, "You cannot shoot your way a little bit into war any more than you can go a little bit over Niagara Falls."

On October 31, as though in defiance of Mr. Roosevelt's "shoot on sight" policy, the Germans struck again. This time the victim was the old destroyer *Reuben James,* the first United States naval vessel to be lost in World War II. She was a part of the escort of Convoy HX-156. Just as dawn was breaking, *U-562* sent a torpedo her way which hit on the port side and probably ignited a magazine. The entire forward part of the ship was blown away; the stern section floated for about five minutes and then went down, depth charges going off as it sank, killing several of the survivors in the water. Of the complement of 160 men, only 45 were saved, and no officers.

The loss of the *Reuben James* gave impetus for Senate action on repeal of the Neutrality Act. It came on November 7, but the vote, 50 to 37, was closer than Mr. Roosevelt hoped for. At that, it was better than the vote on the extension of the draft the previous August, where a single vote in the House of Representatives had preserved America's Army only months before Pearl Harbor.

As 1941 drew to its end, American attention was becoming diverted more and more to the Far East, where Japan was beginning to sound more and more ominous. Here American interests were more directly threatened than in Europe, and here the American flag flew over lands which lay in the path of the Japanese.

The British could not concentrate exclusively on either part of the world. The Japanese threatened their possessions in Malaya, Hong Kong, and, above all, Singapore. But in Europe, the Western Front was inactive, while all eyes turned to the furious drive toward Moscow and the siege of Leningrad.

In North Africa, Rommel still stood at the door to Egypt, and it was an intolerable situation for Churchill. He had relieved Wavell from command in the Middle East after the failure of the Battleaxe offensive. Now he was importuning Auchinleck to take the offensive, to relieve Tobruk and drive the Afrika Korps back out of Cyrenaica.

But Auchinleck refused to be hurried. It infuriated Churchill, but there was nothing he could do about it short of relieving his new commander.

Although Churchill wished to assume the offensive in Libya in August or September, it was not until November that Auchinleck would consent to move. For his ground commander, he selected General Sir Alan Cunningham, the victor of East Africa, whose reputation was enormous following that dramatic campaign.

Unfortunately, General Cunningham had never commanded armor.

It was the team of Cunningham, Cunningham, and Coningham * that was to spearhead Operation Crusader, as the drive was called. Admiral Cunningham had the job of protecting his brother's seaward flank and providing him with fire support as needed. Air Vice Marshal Coningham had the 16 fighter squadrons, 12 medium bomber squadrons, and 5 heavy bomber squadrons that made up the Western Desert Air Force.

Three days before the battle was to begin, Churchill telegraphed jubilantly to Auchinleck: "For the first time British and Empire troops will meet the Germans with an ample equipment in modern weapons of all kinds."

Rommel was not expecting the British attack, being involved in preparations for another effort against Tobruk. All summer long, Tobruk had stood in his way, imperiling his flank and barring any further advance eastward. An inshore squadron under Admiral Cunningham had kept it supplied and garrisoned, in spite of the worst the Luftwaffe could throw at it. Losses had been severe on the Tobruk run, but the position had held.

At the moment of the British jump-off on November 18, Rommel was actually in Rome. It was during this absence that one of the most daring commando raids of the war took place. Major Geoffrey Keyes, son of Admiral of the Fleet Sir Roger Keyes, and Colonel Laycock led a raid on the house that Rommel was supposed to be living in. They were landed by submarine and made their way into the German headquarters. After much rough fighting, Keyes was cut down by

---

* Air Vice Marshal Sir Arthur Coningham, RAF commander, Middle East.

gunfire. Only Colonel Laycock and a sergeant eventually made their way back to the British lines.

The sacrifice was in vain. Rommel was in Rome, and the house was not particularly important. No intelligence information of any value was collected.

Impressed by the daring of the raid, even though it had been directed at his own life, Rommel ordered that Keyes be buried with full military honors. The British government awarded him a posthumous Victoria Cross.

Cunningham proposed to make a sweeping drive toward Sidi Rezegh with the Twenty-Second Armoured Brigade, drawing Rommel south to meet him at Gabr Saleh. There he would fall upon him with his reserves and annihilate his armor. But Rommel refused to be drawn. Returning from Rome soon after the battle had started, he would not be diverted at first from his project of taking Tobruk.

Cunningham became increasingly anxious. He made the fatal mistake of splitting his armor into three parts, one to capture Sidi Rezegh, one to wait at Gabr Saleh, and one in reserve. The result was that when Rommel turned to the attack, he was able to fall upon the exposed Twenty-Second Brigade and drive it back in confusion. As the British fled, units became separated. The Germans made a good haul of British vehicles which they repaired and put to their own use. A few German trucks were in turn captured, so that no one knew what was what or who was who. On one occasion a British truck driven by a German and filled with British prisoners of war met an Italian truck. Out of the latter jumped a platoon of New Zealanders, who promptly rescued their allies.

Rommel followed up his success with a wide sweep to the southeast, recalling Jeb Stewart's raid around McClellan in the Civil War. He drove down the El Abd track, passing the Egyptian border near Bir Sheferzen, hoping to take Sollum from the south. But he outran his supplies and had to turn back. By November 27, he was back in Sidi Rezegh. His stroke had failed; but it had come perilously close to succeeding.

While Rommel was striking with his customary daring, Auchinleck made one of the great decisions of the war. He flew to Cunningham's headquarters on November 23 to discuss prospects. He found Cunningham discouraged, about to order a retreat back to the lines the British had held all summer. But where Cunningham saw dangers, Auchinleck saw an opportunity. Realizing that Rommel was overextended and out of position, he ordered the advance to continue.

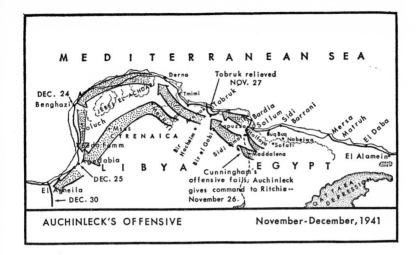

Cunningham was to retake Sidi Rezegh and relieve the Tobruk garrison.

It was a bold decision, one which might have lost the entire British position in Egypt if it had gone wrong. Auchinleck knew the new phase of the battle, the second chance, had to be commanded by someone who believed in victory, someone whose thoughts were on the offensive. And Cunningham was not that man. As Auchinleck cabled Churchill, Cunningham had begun to think defensively. "I have decided to replace General Cunningham temporarily by General Ritchie, my present Deputy Chief of Staff. This is not on account of any misgiving as to the present situation in my mind, but because I have reluctantly concluded that Cunningham, admirable as he has been up to date, has now begun to think defensively, mainly because of our large tank losses."

General Neil Ritchie regrouped his army and proceeded at once to the relief of Tobruk. On the night of November 26, contact was made briefly between Ritchie's troops and the Tobruk garrison, but it was not until the morning of the 29th that the Commander of the Thirteenth Corps, General Godwin-Austen, was able to send a message: CORRIDOR TO TOBRUK CLEAR AND SECURE. TOBRUK IS AS RELIEVED AS I AM.

After the relief of Tobruk, Rommel knew there was nothing for it but retreat. Back across the gains of the spring went the Afrika Korps, to come to a halt on the Tripolitan border, back where it had all started.

But with Rommel, you never knew how long he would stay put. Already he was at work planning his next advance.

Although the year ended with the British triumphant in North Africa, there was an equal amount of mourning to offset the desert victory. On November 12, *U-81* torpedoed and sank the famous carrier *Ark Royal,* which German propaganda had sunk at least half a dozen times before it actually became true. It was the *Ark Royal's* planes which delivered the blow that crippled the *Bismarck* and brought her to bay.

Two weeks later, *U-331* sent the battleship *Barham* to the bottom with a loss of over 500 men. Then, on the night of December 18, an Italian submarine penetrated the anchorage at Alexandria. She launched three "human torpedoes," each controlled by two men. These daring raiders attached limpet bombs to the hulls of the *Queen Elizabeth* and the *Valiant.* The next morning, the bombs exploded, and both battleships were damaged so severely they were out of action for months. The Mediterranean Fleet was reduced to a few destroyers and 3 cruisers. It was finished as a fighting force unless it could be reinforced and reinforced quickly.

* * *

To Americans these events were rather remote. Now that Germany was occupied with Russia, the pressure on Britain seemed less to the man in the streets; there was less need to rush to her aid. Losses to American ships were outrageous, but the men lost were professional sailors, and they were paid to take risks. At this time, there was little sense of identification of the people with the armed forces. Inside a year, when every family had a relative or a friend in the services, it would be different. Now it was "they" who were fighting; a year later, "we" would be.

As ever, the average American turned to sports for his relaxation. Heavyweight boxer Joe Louis was at the height of his career. He was fighting an average of once a month during 1941, mostly pushovers. His opponents were described as "The Bum of the Month Club." Buddy Baer gave Louis a respectable fight in late May before losing on a TKO in the sixth round. The following month, Billy Conn almost toppled the champ. For twelve rounds, he outboxed Louis, jabbing stinging blows at the face and body. Then, in the thirteenth, he threw it all away. As he emerged from his corner for the thirteenth round, he sneered, "I got you, Joe." Joe said nothing, waiting for his chance. It came quickly enough as Conn abandoned his jabbing and began swapping punches. Near the end of the round, the experienced Louis saw his opening and sailed in with a bewildering tattoo of rights and lefts. Just before the bell, Conn was on the canvas for a count of ten.

Louis fought once more that year, knocking Lou Nova out in the sixth round. It was not much of a fight, but it drew 60,000 people who were looking for the chance that the champ might be upset. They would have to come back later.

The baseball season ended with the Yankees, as usual, winning the American League race comfortably. The National League contest went right down to the wire, with the Brooklyn Dodgers coming out on top at the last moment.

It was their first pennant in twenty-one years, and Brooklynites were certain that their beloved "Bums" would win the series as well. Bookmakers, less sentimental and more practical, quoted odds of two to one on the Yankees to win.

The fourth game of the series was being played at Brooklyn's Ebbetts Field. The Yankees had already won two games and Brooklyn one. Now the Bums were about to even the series. Brooklyn was ahead four to three.

It was the ninth inning. Two Yankees were already out, and no one was on base. There were two strikes on Tommy Henrich. Brooklyn pitcher Hugh Casey went into his wind-up and threw. Henrich swung and missed, but catcher Mickey Owen dropped the ball. Before he recovered from his confusion, Henrich was on first, and the umpire was calling for the game to go on.

That was all the Yanks needed. The rattled Casey allowed four runs before he got the last batter, and the Yankees won seven to four.

The next day, the Yankees went on to win, three to one, and became the World Champions for the fifth time in six years. To the heartbroken Brooklyn fans, it seemed that even the Fates were against their beloved Bums.

Perhaps the Brooklynites could take comfort from the song popular that summer, "Tell Your Troubles to the Breeze." "Hearts Don't Lie" was another favorite, but the two most popular discs turned out were Glenn Miller's recording of "Perfidia" and "The One I Love," and Tommy Dorsey's rendering of "Marcheta" and "Deep Night." The greatest craze in the crazy-song department was the unintelligible "Hut-Sut Song." No one knew what it meant, but everyone was singing and humming it.

On Broadway, the year's most popular shows were *Pal Joey,* the story of a Broadway hero-and-heel, who sponged on women and made them like it; *My Sister Eileen; Lady in the Dark,* with Gertrude Law-rence; and Lillian Hellman's stark *Watch on the Rhine.* But the greatest success of all was *Arsenic and Old Lace.* One of the leading characters was an international killer, disguised by his plastic-surgeon friend to look just like Boris Karloff of the movies. The part, natu-rally enough, was played by Boris Karloff. One of the cast described the play as what could be expected "if Strindberg had written *Hellzapoppin."*

Another popular play was William Saroyan's *The Beautiful People,* which nearly won the New York Drama Critics' award as the season's best American play. It may have seemed profound then; re-read today, it seems a collection of improbable schmaltz.

Hollywood turned out its usual fare, still untouched for the most part by the war. The most discussed movie of the year was *Citizen Kane,* starring Orson Welles. Its story of a corrupt newspaper editor was so close to the life of William Randolph Hearst that many theaters refused to book the film at all. Hearst papers refused to men-tion any R.K.O. films, even in advertising, but the picture went on to success and was named Best Picture of the Year. *Philadelphia Story* and *Meet John Doe* were popular, the first for Katharine Hepburn and Cary Grant, and the second for Gary Cooper. Cooper also starred in another film that year, *Sergeant York,* based on the story of Alvin Cullum York, a sniper who picked off 20 German machine-gunners at the Battle of the Meuse-Argonne and persuaded an entire salient to surrender. The real-life York specified that Cooper portray him in the film biography.

Those who stayed home from the movies had the radio or books and magazines to entertain them. One era ended in June, 1941, when the program *Pot o' Gold* went off the air, allowing millions of persons to do something on Tuesday evenings other than wait for the phone to ring. The serials kept on pouring out their mixture of sentiment, old-fashioned virtue, Perils-of-Pauline-style drama, homely humor, and God-and-motherhood morality in the name of Lux, Palmolive, Ivory, and assorted other soaps. Among the most popular, continued front runner *The Goldbergs* kept on going. Others were the *Aldrich Family* and *One Man's Family.* Every night, it seemed, was family night. Helen Trent continued to wring tears from housewives during the day.

Popular band leaders Kay Kyser, Tommy and Jimmy Dorsey, Benny Goodman, Glenn Miller, Artie Shaw, Harry James, and Guy

Lombardo were heard on the radio when they could tear themselves away from playing for college dances all over the country.

Comics Charlie McCarthy (with his straight man Edgar Bergen) and Jack Benny continued to lighten evenings at home. Listeners were saddened by the death of comic Joe Penner. His "Wanna buy a duck?" and "Oh, you nasty man!" had become trademarks much imitated by small boys to the irritation of their parents.

Another death mourned throughout the land was that of "Iron Man" Lou Gehrig, who had played first base for the Yankees a total of 2130 straight games.* His string had come to an end in 1939 when he was stricken with amyotrophic lateral sclerosis after fourteen years of playing in every Yankee game. Gehrig's innate modesty and his courage under his affliction endeared him even to millions who had not followed his career on the diamond.

Franklin D. Roosevelt suffered bereavement in the death of his mother, Sara Delano Roosevelt. F.D.R. had always been particularly close to his mother. Her death early in September saddened him more than even his closest associates realized, for he permitted no sign to appear on the surface. He went to Hyde Park for the funeral and then got back to work.

The literary world was hard hit during the year with the deaths of F. Scott Fitzgerald, James Joyce, Sherwood Anderson, and Virginia Woolf. Arthur Koestler brought out a penetrating analysis of the Communist mind in the novel *Darkness at Noon*. The depravity of man under the press of ideologies was vividly revealed in a book, *Out of the Night*, by a man who called himself Jean Valtin. His real name was Richard Krebs, and he claimed to have been at one time or another an ex-German Communist, a former agent of the Communist International, an ex–co-worker of the OGPU, an escaped prisoner of the OGPU, and an escaped prisoner of the Gestapo. His descriptions of torture under the ministrations of the Gestapo are not for the squeamish.

The inside story of Germany under Hitler came out in William L. Shirer's *Berlin Diary*. As a correspondent and radio commentator, Shirer had been in Germany since 1934. The book is a graphic picture of the state of mind of the German leaders and German people as far as Shirer could determine at the time. Even his wide experience with the Germans left him unprepared for the bestialities of Auschwitz and Belsen when they came to light after the war.

* He played a few of those games in the outfield.

The popular A. J. Cronin hit the jackpot again with the simple, sincere story of a Catholic priest seeking the roots of his faith, *The Keys of the Kingdom.* Another phase of human behavior was explored by James M. Cain in *Mildred Pierce,* a sensational story of a California housewife, her two lovers, her business, and her bedroom life. Tame by today's standards, the book was a major sensation then.

Gypsy Rose Lee also wrote of sex, but it was a singularly passionless book. Her *G-String Murders* was a witty, lurid, surprisingly competent detective story set backstage in a New York burlesque theater. Two strippers are strangled in their own G-strings, while another is peeling down to the buff onstage. Gypsy's own life was not without incident that year, for she divorced her husband on the grounds that he had knocked her down twice.

There were those who had been knocked down harder and more permanently than Gypsy Rose Lee. These were the victims of polio. F.D.R.'s affliction had publicized the heart-rending disease, and the March of Dimes program had enabled doctors to conduct massive research into the disease. Mr. Roosevelt was accustomed to spend some of his vacations in Warm Springs, Georgia, where the famous sanitarium tried to nurse crippled children back to some semblance of use of their limbs.

Sister Elizabeth Kenny, an Australian nurse, devised a new treatment for polio victims. Instead of immobilizing the crippled limbs in splints, she stressed exercise, hot water, and massage. Several times a day, she would flex the patients' muscles, and strangely enough the treatment brought some relief. Because Sister Kenny was not a doctor, the treatment caused much controversy in the medical profession, but her treatment was eventually endorsed by the National Foundation for Infantile Paralysis. Promise of her treatment brought new hope to thousands of parents all over the world.

Far less enlightened than Sister Kenny, Governor Gene Talmadge of Georgia snapped his red galluses once too often and brought his state to the scorn of educators everywhere. Pressuring the Board of Regents at a meeting in Atlanta, Talmadge brought about the ouster of Professor Walter D. Cocking as Dean of the School of Education at the University of Georgia. Then, for good measure, he turned out President Marvin S. Pittman of Georgia State Teachers College and Vice Chancellor J. Curtis Dixon of the State University system.

The charge? They had proposed defiling higher education in Georgia by admitting Negroes.

The Southern Association of Colleges and Secondary Schools protested political interference. Governor Talmadge was unrepentant, setting off merrily on a campaign against "furrin" textbooks—meaning textbooks written by non-Southern authors. In December, the Association voted to black-list the University of Georgia, Georgia Tech, and eight other State institutions. The suspension was not lifted until the following year when Governor-elect Ellis Arnall promised legislation to protect academic freedom.

In all these doings, there was a sense of unease. People would have liked to forget the war, but the headlines in the daily papers and the voices of the radio commentators would not allow them to forget. Even going to the movies brought no relief, for the newsreels projected pictures of a suffering world before the eyes of those who wanted to get away from it all.

And now the eyes of the cameramen and of the reporters were turning westward, toward the Philippines, China, Indochina, and Japan. Japan was about to embark on its plan, *Hakko Ichiu*—"bringing the eight corners of the world under one roof."

CHAPTER EIGHTEEN

"Things Are Automatically Going To Happen"

"I didn't even know they were mad at us."
Remark of an American sailor
at Pearl Harbor after the attack

S. S. *Tatsuta Maru,* crack liner of the Japanese Lines, steamed aimlessly off the coast of California. She had been due to dock at San Francisco on July 25, but suddenly, only a dozen miles from the Golden Gate, she had turned out of the channel and disappeared into the fog.

The reason for her strange behavior was to be found in Tokyo, Vichy, and Washington.

In March, 1941, Japan had served as mediator in the undeclared war between Thailand and French Indochina. Her price for this service to pliant Vichy was a monopoly over the rice crop of northern Indochina and the right to establish an airfield at Saigon. Provided with this leverage, Japan found it simple enough to move troops in around the Hanoi area in preparation for the next move.

Mr. Roosevelt and his advisers knew that Japan had its eyes on the rest of Indochina and that the Vichy Government was unlikely to offer any but token opposition, now that Japan and Germany were allies of a sort, as a result of the Tripartite Pact. At the request of the Cabinet, Under Secretary of State Sumner Welles had an order prepared which would freeze all Japanese assets in the United States.

When, on July 25, Vichy agreed to the occupation of Indochina by the Japanese, the order went out forthwith. At once, all Japanese ships disappeared from the seas. Like the *Tatsuta Maru,* they simply turned off course and waited to see what would happen.

A large liner like the *Tatsuta Maru* could not steam around indefinitely. She had to do something. Therefore, when U.S. Government spokesmen announced that she would not be seized and would be allowed to depart without hindrance, she entered San Francisco harbor on July 30 and tied up at Pier 25. She had spent the intervening six days in a voyage to nowhere. Her 252 passengers had been well treated, although they fretted considerably. They could receive radio messages but send none; part of the time news broadcasts were blacked out. But they were well fed at the expense of the line, and they landed none the worse for their experience.

When time came for the ship to sail, the Treasury and Justice Departments got their signals mixed. Collector of Customs Paul R. Leake cleared the ship, but even as Captain Toichi Takahata was getting ready to cast off the lines, Deputy U.S. Marshal Joseph Kennedy and U.S. Marshal George Vice mounted to the bridge and posted a writ of attachment. Several importers had laid claim to her cargo. Under admiralty law, the ship owners would be required to post bond for double the value of the claim. Since the writ totaled $2,500,000, it was a question where the money was coming from, with Japanese assets frozen.

As the legal maneuvers progressed, the ship was picketed by anti-Japanese organizations. On a tip that she had a million dollars' worth of contraband U.S. currency aboard, customs men subjected her to a surprise and unusually stringent search. Nothing was found.

The comedy of harassment came to an end on August 3 when, on orders from Tokyo, the Japanese ships in American harbors surrendered all the silk they carried, about $4,000,000 worth, in exchange for clearance of all the ships. The *Tatsuta Maru* finally sailed about 4 o'clock the next morning.*

It was all good fun while it lasted, but it did nothing to ease Japanese-American relations.

Probably nothing could have eased Japanese-American relations that summer and fall. Japan saw her great chance in Southeast Asia. To exploit that chance would bring her into direct conflict with American interests. So be it. American interests would have to be sacrificed.

The combination of the inferiority imposed upon Japan by the various naval treaties and the American Immigration Act of 1924 gave militarists their opportunity. The centuries-old tradition of the

* She was sunk by the U.S. submarine *Tarpon* on February 1, 1943, near Tokyo Bay.

feudal caste of the Samurai warrior had given the Army a special place in Japanese life. The Navy was distinctly the junior service and was popularly regarded as inferior.

Little did the Japanese people realize that the Samurai tradition had been diluted in the modern Army. Huge numbers of men drawn from inferior social ranks had made the Army a career. Their code was *Bushido,* the traditional "way of the warrior." In practice, this meant that these career officers and men employed the ruthless brutality of the Samurai code with none of the leaven of responsibility toward a station in life the code imposed. As early as 1927, persons of middle-class, rural background made up 30 percent of the officer corps, and that percentage was growing. Insular, ill-educated, arrogant, they dreamed of turning the clock back to the feudalism which had been given its death blow by the opening of Japan.

These men were all fanatically loyal to the Emperor. Their highest ambition was to die a warrior's death in battle and so become one of the guardian spirits that watched over Japan. Yet it was not the Emperor in actuality who commanded their loyalty; it was the Emperor as they thought he ought to be. The moderate leaders, those who believed that Japan should take her place in the affairs of civilized nations, were anathema. They led the divine Emperor astray; they weakened Japan; they turned people from deeds of glory to money-grubbing in pursuits unworthy of the Sons of Heaven.

The Army had an incredible influence over Japanese life—incredible, that is, to persons brought up in Western ideas. Every male served a minimum of twenty years (two years of active service and eighteen in the reserves) in one of the armed forces. Service life was brutal, but it ingrained attitudes which enabled the Army especially to influence the decisions of the Government, even to dictate them on occasions.

After World War I, Japan had a series of liberal governments which did much to westernize the country. Military budgets were severely cut back, and the money saved was put to social and economic developments.

The excuse of the 5-5-3 ratio, which fixed Japanese naval tonnage at 60 percent of that of the United States or Great Britain, and the exclusion of Japanese immigrants from the United States gave the militarists their opportunity. Proclaiming the "Showa Restoration," the lower-middle-class officers set out deliberately to destroy the liberal tendencies which they believed were ruining Japan. The Showa Restoration was sometimes called *Kodo-Ha,* "the Way of the Emperor," and its aims were destruction of the rich industrialists, hatred of all foreigners, military supremacy at home, and conquests abroad, all to achieve *Hakko Ichiu,* domination of the world.

Admittedly, this was a difficult program, but the fanatical militarists were determined men. Opponents who could not be coerced could be assassinated, and secret societies, such as the famous Black Dragon, were fostered and flourished. Several high officials were cut down, and the Army obtained a veto power over the appointment of the Cabinet. Only an active-service general could serve as Minister of War, and no general would serve unless the Army approved of the make-up of the cabinet.

Incident after incident followed: "The Manchuria Incident" in 1931, the "China Incident" in 1937, the *"Panay* Incident" in 1937. In connection with each of these, the Japanese Government reaffirmed its dedication to peace.

In this affirmation, they were not acting as hypocrites. It depended on what you meant by peace. To the Japanese militarists, the *Kodo* men, the term meant feudal rule by a Japanese overlord class set over all the inferior peoples of the world. If the inferior peoples objected and opposed peaceful Japanese domination, then it was they who were breaking the peace, not the Japanese. Even as the Japanese were fighting in China, moving into Indochina, and threatening Thailand, in the imperial edict of December 8, 1941,* announcing the opening of the war with the United States, they claimed that America had placed barriers "in the way of peaceful commercial endeavors of the Empire" and added that their war aim was "everlasting peace in East Asia."

At the beginning of 1941, Japanese diplomats were still working to avert war with the United States, while the Army and Navy were preparing plans for the war that would come. No sinister motives should be attributed to such planning. All countries prepare contingency war plans against all likely enemies. The United States had been preparing plans for use against Japan since 1921. The American ones, however, were kept in a file cabinet for use if necessary. The Japanese officers were actively studying theirs.

War between the United States and Japan became inevitable with the action of President Roosevelt in freezing Japanese assets and the concurrent embargo on oil. The order was actually signed on July 26, 1941, although it was announced the previous day.

* December 7 in the United States because of the International Date Line.

Admiral Isoroku Yamamoto had been planning the attack on Pearl Harbor since January.

The story of the diplomatic and political moves that led to the war is too well known to need recounting. Less well known is the history of the Japanese plans for the war and what they hoped to gain through military action.

While high-ranking naval officers, who had in the course of their duties seen something of the world outside Japan, were skeptical of Japan's chances of success in a war with the United States, the more provincial Army officers discounted American power. Americans, they argued, lacked the spirit which makes a warrior. American industrial power could never make up for the weakness in moral fiber that characterized American life.

Admiral Yamamoto had served in Washington as naval attaché, and he knew better. He had studied the American people and American industry, and he knew that his countrymen in the Army and some in the Navy underrated both. He had no illusions about what might happen. Shortly after the signing of the Tripartite Pact, he had told Prince Konoye, then Premier:

> If I am told to fight regardless of consequence, I shall run wild considerably for the first six months or a year, but I have utterly no confidence for the second and third years. The Tripartite Pact has been concluded and we cannot help it. Now that the situation has come to this pass I hope you will endeavor for avoidance of an American-Japanese war.*

In spite of this warning, Yamamoto saw that war was coming and proceeded to do something about planning to run wild for the first six months or a year. Japan desired above all else to acquire the riches of Southeast Asia, a move which would bring her into inevitable collision with Britain and the United States. Britain had her hands full in Europe and could be pretty much ignored. The United States was another matter. In spite of her preoccupation with the Atlantic and aid to Britain, America possessed a powerful naval force in the Pacific Fleet (until recently named the United States Fleet). The Japanese knew or could guess that in the event of war, the American plan would be to advance through the mandated islands, the Marshalls and Carolines, to bring relief to the Philippines. Somewhere east of Luzon,

* This somewhat fractured English translation is taken from the Japanese edition of the memoirs of Prince Konoye. No other English-language edition has appeared.

in the Philippine Sea, would occur a great naval battle which would go a long way toward settling the war.

Yamamoto welcomed the idea of a naval battle, but he reasoned that Japan could win without it if the Pacific Fleet were eliminated first. Then Japan could take the Resources Area in Southeast Asia at leisure, build a strong defensive perimeter of "unsinkable aircraft carriers" in the islands to the east, and let the Americans batter themselves to pieces against such strongpoints. Surely the Americans would tire of the war and settle for Japanese hegemony in what they were pleased to call their "Greater Resources Area."

Hence Pearl Harbor was to be attacked at the outbreak of the war. No warning would be given, for this was not the Japanese way. Deceit, regardless of promise or oath, was part of the Code Bushido. It had served them well in the Russo-Japanese War, and it would serve again.

Early in his period of high command, Admiral Yamamoto had been struck with the offensive power of aircraft carriers. While official Japanese doctrine, like that of Britain and the United States, was to employ carriers as platforms to provide air umbrellas over the battleships, Admiral Yamamoto saw a better use for them. Some American carrier men had seen other possibilities, also, and they had demonstrated their theories in completely successful simulated attacks on the Panama Canal and on Pearl Harbor during Fleet War Games. In 1937, the carriers *Lexington* and *Saratoga,* under the command of Ernest J. King, completely knocked out the Pearl Harbor defenses (in theory) by a carrier attack from the north, just as the Japanese were to do nearly four years later. Umpires ruled that the two carriers had not lost a plane.

Thus, the Americans showed Yamamoto just how it was done. When, in January, 1941, he set Rear Admiral Takijiro Onishi to work to begin planning the Pearl Harbor attack, one of the first things Onishi did was take out the intelligence reports on the American Fleet Problem of 1937.

Onishi asked for the aid of Commander Minoru Genda, an officer with wide experience in carrier operations and in carrier staff work. Genda had spent two years in London recently as assistant naval attaché and had become thoroughly familiar with the details of the British carrier raid on Taranto. Thus he was in the position of a man who had seen a daring carrier raid work and knew of the possibilities of surprise. With one carrier the British had sunk or crippled three Italian battleships. What might the Japanese achieve with six?

Genda and Onishi insisted that for any chance of success, all six of Japan's big carriers must be used. This would leave four smaller ones to support the five simultaneous operations in Southeast Asia which would be the main show. These were invasions of Thailand, Malaya, the Philippines, the Netherlands East Indies, and Guam and Wake Islands. The Army and the Naval Staff would naturally oppose any dilution of the strength of the southern drive, but Yamamoto was determined to have his way.

The six carriers Onishi proposed to use against Pearl Harbor were the *Kaga* and *Akagi* (Carrier Division 1), the *Hiryu* and *Soryu* (Carrier Division 2), *Shokaku* and *Zuikaku* (Carrier Division 5). For ships bound on such a warlike mission, they had strangely peaceful names: *Kaga* (Increased Joy), *Akagi* (Red Castle), *Hiryu* (Flying Dragon), *Soryu* (Green Dragon), *Shokaku* (Soaring Crane), and *Zuikaku* (Happy Crane).

Genda also insisted that only the most skilled commanders and pilots should be assigned to the operation and that complete secrecy must be maintained at all times. If word of the operation leaked, the carrier force could find itself under heavy land and carrier-based attack far from any support. It might even be annihilated.

Despite Genda's warning, something did leak. On January 27, 1941, Ambassador Joseph C. Grew sent this message to Washington:

The Peruvian minister has informed a member of my staff that he has heard from many sources, including a Japanese source, that in the event of trouble breaking out between the U.S. and Japan, the Japanese intend to make a surprise attack against Pearl Harbor with all their strength and employing all their equipment. The Peruvian minister considered the rumors fantastic, but he considered them of sufficient importance to convey all this.

How was Grew's report received in Washington?

The Division of Naval Intelligence places no credence in these rumors. Furthermore, based on known data regarding the present disposition and deployment of Japanese naval and army forces, no move against Pearl Harbor appears imminent or planned for the foreseeable future.

One of the chief problems that Genda faced was one the British had already solved in the Taranto raid. Aerial torpedoes may plunge 100 feet or more underwater if launched in the ordinary way. To keep them from hitting the bottom in the 42-foot depth of Taranto Harbor, the British had installed special wooden fins. They had worked. The

Japanese believed they could do as well at Pearl, where the water was 45 feet deep.

Because of the American practice of mooring the battleships in pairs, one alongside the other, Genda realized that the inboard ship would be protected from torpedoes. Therefore he devised a kind of bomb made from a 16-inch armor-piercing shell. Dropped from any height, this would have nearly the velocity of one which had been fired from a gun and would penetrate deep into the ship's vitals before exploding. These two improvised weapons gave the Japanese their main chance of inflicting overwhelming damage on the Pacific Fleet.

Accurate intelligence of locations of ships in Pearl Harbor was essential to the attack, so Yamamoto sent a spy in the person of Ensign Takeo Yoshikawa. Yoshikawa had been forced to retire from the Navy because of ill health but had worked for the Department of Naval Intelligence. He had studied English intensively for four years and was reasonably fluent. Arriving in Honolulu under the name of Vice Consul Morimura, Yoshikawa worked for the consulate during regular office hours, but evenings and weekends, he spent long hours gathering data that would prove useful to the planners in Tokyo. Each week he sent a report on the movement of naval ships in and out of Pearl Harbor. He frequented a Japanese restaurant, the Shuncho-ro, where he could get a good view of the harbor. He went to dances and other social affairs of the Nisei people, but he was disappointed that the Japanese-Americans he tried to pump there were uniformly loyal to America. He talked to sailors in bars.

Shortly before the attack, Lieutenant Commander Suguru Suzuki, who had come to Honolulu disguised as a steward on a merchant ship, sought out the Consul General, Nagao Kita, and slipped a tiny piece of paper into his hand. In minuscule writing were 97 questions planners in Tokyo wanted answered. The key one was: "What day would most ships be in Pearl Harbor?"

Kita passed the inquiry on to Yoshikawa, who replied at once, "Sunday—Kimmel brings his fleet into Pearl Harbor every weekend."

As the plan took shape, Onishi began to have cold feet about it, but Yamamoto would not hear of abandoning it. During war games in the big plotting rooms in Tokyo, the Pearl Harbor attack was tried, with only a few senior officers informed of what was going on. The attacking fleet theoretically lost two carriers. This dampened the spirits of some of the supporters, but Yamamoto was not disheartened. He ordered the planning to go on.

Yamamoto might have been discouraged had he known that the Americans were reading the Japanese code. The cryptographic section of the Army had made a major breakthrough in cracking the Japanese "Purple" code, used principally for high-level diplomatic messages. Since no word of naval operations was allowed to enter the messages to Washington, and since Ambassador Nomura and later Special Ambassador Kurusu were deliberately excluded from knowledge of the Pearl Harbor attack, information from the "Purple" intercepts was not as useful as it might have been to American leaders. Intelligence officers considered that knowledge of American success in code-breaking must be kept secret at all costs, so those permitted to read the "Purple" messages were few in number. In addition to the intelligence personnel who processed the messages, only the President, the Secretary of the Navy, the Secretary of War, the Chief of Naval Operations, and the Chief of Staff of the Army were permitted to read them. A messenger would deliver a locked pouch, would stand waiting while the official read the message, returned it to the pouch, and handed it back. Then the messenger would take it to the next person on the list. When routing was complete, only one copy was kept in a top secret file.

The result was that no one ever had an overview of all the "Purple" messages at once. Bits and pieces of information came in the midst of the unceasing flow of papers to all these busy men, and it would have taken superhumans to remember each scrap in relationship to what had gone before.

The decryption of the Japanese code was called "Magic," and it would have been magic, indeed, under the distribution system if effective use had been made of the information it contained.

Yamamoto was determined to carry through with his plan in spite of all obstacles, all objections. He knew that intensive training of pilots would be necessary, in recognition and in attacking in close quarters. He had a mock-up constructed of Pearl Harbor on a 1-in-100 scale, complete with ships, navy yard, buildings, piers, and water to scale depth. Men waded around, moving the ships according to the latest intelligence reports. Pilots studied this mock-up and photographs until they knew the area better than the people of Oahu.

Near Kagoshima Bay on the southern tip of Kyushu, selected pilots underwent special training. The bay closely resembled the tight confines of Pearl Harbor. Each pilot made at least 50 flights, skimming low to release torpedoes, making sharp turns, diving on targets placed in the water to simulate ships. They made repeated carrier landings and take-offs, in all sorts of weather. They had no idea of what they were training for; all they knew was that something big was going to come off.

In Tokyo, it was by no means certain that something big was going to come off. When Yamamoto submitted his plan to the Naval General Staff, it met almost unanimous rejection. It depended entirely on surprise, and surprise could not be assured. They felt that the American Pacific Fleet could be so damaged in its passage through the Mandated Islands that it would pose little threat to the Japanese in Southeast Asia if it did make for the Philippines. They believed that there would be little chance to do the necessary refueling of the Pearl Harbor Attack Force, since the northern waters chosen for the approach averaged only seven suitable days a month for such an operation. The rest of the time, it would be too rough. They knew that the Americans had recently extended patrols out 600 miles from Hawaii, and that the Attack Force would have to get within 200 miles before it could launch planes. Also, any hint that such an operation was brewing could wreck negotiations in progress toward a peaceful settlement between the United States and Japan.

Yamamoto brushed all such considerations aside, in spite of the fact that his chosen carrier commander, Vice Admiral Chuichi Nagumo, was among those steadfastly opposed to the Hawaiian operation. When he received the Naval General Staff's objections to his proposal, he exploded. He sent his operations officer, Rear Admiral Kamahito Kuroshima, with a letter displaying more fury than tact.

The presence of the U.S. Fleet in Hawaii is a dagger pointed at our throats. Should war be declared, the length and breadth of our southern operations would immediately be exposed to a serious threat on its flank.

The Hawaii operation is absolutely indispensable. Unless it is carried out, Admiral Yamamoto has no confidence that he can fulfill his assigned responsibility. The numerous difficulties of this operation do not make it impossible. Weather conditions worry us most, but as there are seven days a month when refueling at sea is possible, the chance of success is by no means small. If good fortune is bestowed upon us we will be assured of success.

Should the Hawaii operation by chance end in failure, that would merely imply that fortune is not on our side. That should also be the time for definitely halting all operations.

If this plan fails, it will mean defeat in war.

Although deeply impressed by this letter, the Naval Staff still objected to the proposal. Kuroshima phoned Yamamoto aboard his flagship. "Tell them," replied the Commander in Chief, "I will step down as Commander in Chief and take over the carriers to direct the attack personally."

Kuroshima returned with this message, and, although the members of the Naval Staff were shaken, they would not budge from their position. The carriers were needed for the attack to the south. After an hour-long argument, Kuroshima called Yamamoto once more.

When he returned this time, he was white-faced. "I have the authority of the Commander in Chief to tell you if you do not agree to his plan, he must resign from his position and retire into civilian life."

This threat was too much for the Naval Staff. Declaring that Admiral Nagano, Chief of Naval Staff, must decide, they adjourned the meeting.

Nagano reluctantly approved. The Hawaiian operation would go forward. There would be the day which would "live in infamy."

In Washington, of course, no one could know of these plans. General Marshall and Admiral Stark pleaded with Cordell Hull to delay a showdown with Japan as much as possible. American armed forces were not ready. Even the delay of a few months would make all the difference. Doggedly Hull and his associates kept the conversations going. There was little prospect of success. The Americans demanded that Japan withdraw from all her conquests of the last four years, while Japan required the United States to recognize those conquests and to lift the oil embargo, to boot. There was no middle ground.

In desperation, to gain the time the Army and Navy demanded, Hull tried to work out a *modus vivendi*. Even though it gave China what Churchill called "a very thin diet," Hull realized that the Japanese would never accept it. With the approval of President Roosevelt, he did not even submit it to the two Japanese ambassadors.

Through the "Magic" intercepts, Roosevelt, Hull, Marshall, and Stark knew that time was running out. Originally the Japanese Government had told Nomura and Kurusu to conclude the diplomatic surrender of the United States by November 25.

Suspecting that the Americans were working on a new plan (the ill-fated *modus vivendi*) Tokyo extended the deadline four days, to November 29. Premier Tojo warned that this was the last possible extension. "After that, things are automatically going to happen," he cabled.

American leaders were sure that if no settlement was reached in the next few days, war would ensue. Japan would strike. All signs pointed to the Far East. Ship movements in that direction were reported. The resources Japan needed were there. The Pacific Fleet based at Pearl Harbor was a long way away.

Even as the talks were progressing—or rather, failing to progress— Admiral Yamamoto's Hawaiian Attack Force was assembling in Tankan Bay in the Kurile Islands, a thousand miles from Japan. Here, in these bleak surroundings, the ships took aboard barrels of extra fuel oil to be used in case the weather prevented refueling at sea. Pilots studied intelligence reports; officers prepared, distributed, and studied operation orders; navigators checked courses, speeds, and distances. Orders went out for 27 submarines to move to Hawaiian waters to be ready to pick off ships the carrier planes missed. Five of these submarines carried piggy-back miniature 2-man submarines which were scheduled to penetrate the harbor itself.

At 1800 on November 26, 1941 (East longitude date), the Task Force sortied from Tankan Bay bound for a launching point 200 miles north of Oahu. If, by any miracle, negotiations succeeded, the ships could be recalled. Final word to go ahead with the attack would come in a coded message: "Climb Mount Niitaka."

Mr. Roosevelt and his advisers believed war was inevitable. When and where it would come was the big question. No one thought it would be at Pearl Harbor.

It was a normal, peaceful Sunday morning on Oahu. Preparations had been taken against sabotage, and planes had been drawn up in neat, orderly rows on airstrips; they were easier to guard that way. Some people slept late. Others prepared to play golf. Admiral Husband E. Kimmel, Commander in Chief of the Pacific Fleet, was one of these. His companion would be General Walter Short, Army commander in the islands.

In Washington Ambassador Nomura received a message to present the latest Japanese note, one breaking off negotiations, at 1 P.M., Washington time. That would be 7:30 A.M. in Honolulu.

To the north of the islands, laboring through foul weather, the 6 Japanese carriers were getting ready to launch aircraft. The flight leader, Commander Mitsuo Fuchida, sat in the cockpit of his plane on the flight deck of the *Akagi*. Someone handed him a white headband called a *hashimaki*, a symbol he must be prepared to die. From the masthead of the flagship flew the same Japanese ensign which had been flown from the battleship *Mikasa,* flagship of Admiral Heihichiro Togo in the Battle of Tsushima on May 27, 1905. A green light flashed on the *Akagi*'s deck, and the first plane roared down the deck and took to the air.

The time was 0615, on December 7, 1941.

In another hour and forty minutes, the United States would be at war.

No one could foresee the end. Everyone knew that there would be hard fighting, there would be privations, there would be sorrows. Allied forces would be driven back everywhere for a time, but they would return to the fight stronger than ever, with new determination to ensure, in Admiral Halsey's words, that after the war was over, "the Japanese language will be spoken only in Hell."

Nor could anyone foresee that in a little over a year, the Axis would be on the defensive all over the world. Ahead lay the agonies of Bataan and Corregidor, of Singapore, of Java, of the Coral Sea and Midway, of Guadalcanal, of El Alamein, of Stalingrad, of the North African landings, of bloody North Atlantic convoys. But in a little over a year, the way to victory would be clear.

But first the price of wishful thinking and complacency would have to be paid at Pearl Harbor.

Bibliography

The bibliography that follows is a highly selective list based on two criteria: authority and general interest. Some books written during the war cannot pretend to authority, but they have sufficient topical interest to be read today. Some by participants have a natural bias, but their statements of feelings, ideas, reasons for decisions are valuable.

Extensive use has been made of magazine and newspaper files. *The London Times, The London Daily Mail, The Daily Telegraph, The Daily Express, The Midland Chronicle, The New York Times, The Washington Post, The San Francisco Chronicle, Time, Life, Newsweek, U.S. News, The Saturday Evening Post,* and *The New Yorker* have been especially valuable.

Ansel, Walter, *Hitler Confronts England.* Durham, N.C.: Duke University Press, 1960.

Arnoult, P., *et al., La France sous l'occupation.* Paris: 1959.

Auphan, Amiral, *The French Navy in World War II,* trans. by Captain A. C. J. Sabalot. Annapolis: U.S. Naval Institute, 1959.

————, et Jacques Mordal, *La Marine Française pendant la Seconde Guerre Mondiale.* Paris: Hachette, 1958.

Barnett, Corelli, *The Desert Generals.* New York: The Viking Press, 1961.

Baruch, Bernard, *The Public Years.* New York: Holt, Rinehart and Winston, 1960.

Baudouin, Paul, *Neuf mois au gouvernement.* Paris: 1948.

Baumbach, Werner, *The Life and Death of the Luftwaffe,* trans. by Frederick Holt. New York: Coward-McCann, 1960.

Benoist-Méchin, Jacques, *Soixante jours qui ebranlèrent l'occident.* Paris: 1956.

————, *Sixty Days that Shook the West: The Fall of France: 1940.* New York: G. P. Putnam's Sons, 1963.

Bernotti, Romeo, *La Guerra sui mari.* 3 vols. Livorno: Società Editrice Tirrena, 1953.

Bernotti, Romeo, *Storia della guerra nel Mediterraneo* (*1940–1943*). Rome: 1960.

Berthold, Will, *The Sinking of the* Bismarck. London: Longmans, Green & Co., 1958.

Bouthillier, Yves, *Le drame de Vichy*. Paris: 1950.

Bradford, Ernle, *The Mighty* Hood. Cleveland and New York: World Publishing Co., 1959.

Bragadin, Commander Marc Antonio, *The Italian Navy in World War II*. Annapolis: U.S. Naval Institute, 1957.

Brennecke, Jochen, *The Hunters and the Hunted*. London: Burke, 1958.

Bryant, Arthur, *The Allanbrooke Diaries*. Vol. 1, *The Turn of the Tide*. New York: Doubleday & Co., 1957.

Buchanan, A. Russell, *The United States and World War II*. 2 vols. New York: Harper & Row, 1964.

Bullock, Alan, *Hitler: A Study in Tyranny*. Revised ed. New York: Harper & Row, 1962.

Carell, Paul, *The Foxes of the Desert*. New York: E. P. Dutton, 1961.
————, *Hitler Moves East*. Boston: Little, Brown & Co., 1965.

Charles-Roux, François, *Cinq mois tragiques aux affaires étrangères*. Paris: 1949.

Churchill, Winston S., *History of the Second World War*. 6 vols. Boston: Houghton Mifflin Co., 1948–1953.

Ciano's Diary, 1939–1943, Malcolm Muggeridge, ed. London: Heinemann, 1947.

Crisp, Major Robert, *The Gods Were Neutral*. New York: W. W. Norton & Co., 1960.

Cunningham, Admiral of the Fleet Viscount Cunningham of Hyndhope, *A Sailor's Odyssey*. London: 1951.

Davis, Kenneth Sydney, *Experience of War: The United States in World War II*. New York: Doubleday & Co., 1965.

Deakin, F. W., *The Brutal Friendship: Mussolini, Hitler, and the Fall of Italian Fascism*. New York: Harper & Row, 1962.

De Gaulle, Charles, *Memoires de guerre*. 3 vols. Vol. 1, *L'Appel d'honneur*. Paris: 1954.

La Delegation française auprez de la Commission allemande d'armistice de Wiesbaden. 5 vols. Paris: 1949.

Derry, T. K., *The Campaign in Norway*. London: Her Majesty's Stationery Office, 1952.

Devins, Joseph H., Jr., *The Vaagso Raid*. London: Robert Hale, 1967.

Divine, David, *The Nine Days of Dunkirk*. New York: Ballantine Books, 1959.

Eisenhower, Dwight D., *Crusade in Europe*. Garden City, New York: Doubleday & Co., 1948.

Fleming, Peter, *Operation Sea Lion*. New York: Simon and Schuster, 1957.

France during the German Occupation, 1940–1944. A Collection of 292 statements of Petain and Laval, trans. by Philip W. Whitcomb, Stanford, California for the Hoover Institution on War, Revolution, and Peace. Stanford: Stanford University Press, 1958–1959.

Frank, Wolfgang, *The Sea Wolves.* New York: Rinehart & Co., 1955.

————— and Captain Bernhard Rogge, *German Raider* Atlantis. New York: Ballantine Books, 1956.

Frischauer, Willi, and Robert Jackson, *The Navy's Here.* London: Victor Gollancz, 1955.

Führer Conferences on Matters Pertaining to Naval Affairs. In Brassey's *Naval Annual, 1948.* London: 1948.

Fuller, Major General J. F. C., *The Second World War, 1939–1945.* New York: Duell, Sloan & Pearce, 1949.

Gainard, Joseph A., *Yankee Skipper: The Life Story of Joseph A. Gainard, Captain of the* City of Flint. New York: Frederick A. Stokes Co., 1940.

Goutard, Colonel A., *The Battle of France, 1940,* trans. by Captain A. R. P. Burgess. Foreword by Captain B. H. Liddell Hart. New York: Ives Washburn, 1959.

—————, *1940: La guerre des occasions perdues.* Paris: Hachette, 1956.

Greenfield, Kent R., ed., *Command Decisions.* Washington, D.C.: Office of the Chief of Military History, Department of the Army, 1960.

Grenfell, Captain Russell, *The* Bismarck *Episode.* New York: The Macmillan Co., 1949.

Guderian, Heinz, *Panzer Leader,* trans. by Constantine Fitzgibbon. Foreword by Captain B. H. Liddell Hart. New York: Dutton & Co., 1957.

Heckstall-Smith, Anthony, *Greek Tragedy 1941.* New York: W. W. Norton & Co., 1961.

—————, *Tobruk.* New York: W. W. Norton & Co., 1959.

Hollis, Sir Leslie, *War at the Top.* London: Michael Joseph, 1959.

Hull, Cordell, *Memoirs.* 2 vols. New York: The Macmillan Co., 1948.

Ingersoll, Ralph, *Report on England, November, 1940.* New York: Simon and Schuster, 1941.

Ismay, Hastings, *The Memoirs of General Lord Hastings Ismay.* New York: The Viking Press, 1960.

Johnson, Group Captain J. E., *Wing Leader.* London: Chatto & Windus, 1956.

Jullian, Marcel, *The Battle of Britain.* New York: Grossman Bros., 1967.

Kammerer, Albert, *La Passion de la flotte française.* Paris: Librairie Arthème Fayard, 1951.

—————, *La tragedie de Mers el Kebir.* Paris: 1945.

—————, *La verité sur l'armistice.* 2nd ed. Paris: 1945.

Keitel, Wilhelm, *The Memoirs of Field-Marshal Keitel,* Walter Dörlitz, ed. New York: Stein and Day, 1966.

Kemp, Peter, *Victory at Sea*. London: Frederick Muller, 1957.

Kennedy, Major General Sir John, *The Business of War*. London: Hutchinson, 1957.

Kenney, William, *The Crucial Years, 1940–1945*. New York: Macfadden Books, 1962.

King, Ernest J., and Walter Muir Whitehill, *Fleet Admiral King: A Naval Record*. New York: W. W. Norton & Co., 1952.

Kirkpatrick, Ivone, *Mussolini, A Study in Power*. New York: Hawthorn Books, 1964.

Langer, William L., and S. Everett Gleason, *The Challenge to Isolation, 1937–1940*. New York: Harper & Bros., 1952.

————, *The Undeclared War, 1940–1941*. New York: Harper & Bros., 1953.

Lawson, Don, *The United States in World War II*. New York: Grosset & Dunlap, 1964.

Leason, James, *War at the Top: Based on the Experiences of General Sir Leslie Hollis*. London: Michael Joseph, 1959.

Liddell Hart, B. H., ed., *The Other Side of the Hill*. London: Cassell & Co., 1948.

Lohman, W., and H. H. Hildebrandt, *Die deutsche Kriegsmarine*. 3 Vols. Bad Nauheim: 1955–1964.

Macintyre, Donald, *Narvik*. New York: W. W. Norton & Co., 1959.

McKee, Alexander, *Strike from the Sky*. Boston: Little, Brown & Co., 1960.

McSherry, James E., *Stalin, Hitler, and Europe, 1933–1939*. Cleveland and New York: World Publishing Co., 1968.

Manstein, Field Marshal Erich von, *Lost Victories*. Chicago: Henry Regnery Co., 1958.

Martienssen, Anthony, *Hitler and His Admirals*. London: Secker and Warburg, 1948.

Montgomery, Field Marshal the Viscount, *Memoirs*. Cleveland and New York: World Publishing Co., 1958.

Montmorency, Alec de, *The Enigma of Admiral Darlan*. New York: 1943.

Moran, Lord, *Churchill: Taken from the Diaries of Lord Moran*. Boston: Houghton Mifflin Co., 1966.

Mordal, Jacques, *La Bataille de Dakar*. Paris: 1956.

Morison, Samuel E., *The Battle of the Atlantic*. Boston: Little, Brown & Co., 1954.

Murrow, Edward R., *This is London*, Elmer Davis, ed. New York: Simon and Schuster, 1941.

Nicolson, Harold, *The War Years, 1939–1945*, Nigel Nicolson, ed. New York: Atheneum, 1967.

Omang, Reidar, *Altmark-Saken, 1940*. Oslo: Gyldnendal Norsk Forlag, 1953. (Note: Although this book is written in Norwegian, there is a useful summary in English at the end. Documentation is in the original languages.)

Pack, S. W. C., *The Battle of Matapan*. New York: The Macmillan Co., 1961.

Pogue, Forrest C., *George C. Marshall: Education of a General, 1880–1939*. New York: The Viking Press, 1963.

———, *George C. Marshall: Ordeal and Hope, 1939–1942*. New York: The Viking Press, 1966.

Pope, Dudley, *The Battle of the River Plate*. London: William Kimber, 1956.

Potter, E. B., and Fleet Admiral Chester W. Nimitz, eds., *The Great Sea War*. Englewood Cliffs: Prentice-Hall, 1960.

———, *Sea Power*. Englewood Cliffs: Prentice-Hall, 1960.

Raeder, Erich, *Mein Leben*. 2 vols., Tübingen-Neckar: 1956.

———, *My Life*. Annapolis: U.S. Naval Institute, 1960.

Reynaud, Paul, *Au coeur de la mélée*. Paris: 1951; New York: Simon & Schuster, 1953.

———, *In the Thick of the Fight*, trans. by James D. Lambert. London: 1955.

Robertson, Terence, *Night Raider of the Atlantic*. New York: E. P. Dutton, 1955.

Rollins, Alfred B., Jr., ed., *Franklin D. Roosevelt and the Age of Action*. New York: Dell Publishing Co., 1960.

Rommel, Erwin, *The Rommel Papers*, B. H. Liddell Hart, ed. New York: Harcourt, Brace & Co., 1953.

Roosevelt, Franklin D., *Nothing to Fear*, Benjamin D. Zevin, ed. New York: World Publishing Co., 1946.

Roskill, S. W., *The War at Sea*. 3 vols. in 4. London: H. M. S. O., 1954–1961.

Ruge, Vice Admiral Friedrich, *Sea Warfare*. London: Cassell & Co., 1957.

Schramm, Percy E., ed., *Kriegstagebuch des Oberkommandos der Wehrmacht, 1940–1945*. Vol. 1, 1940–1941. Frankfurt am Main: 1965.

Sherwood, Robert E., *Roosevelt and Hopkins*. 2 vols. New York: Harper & Bros., 1948.

Shirer, William L., *Berlin Diary*. New York: Alfred A. Knopf, 1941.

———, *The Rise and Fall of the Third Reich*. New York: Simon and Schuster, 1960.

Slessor, Marshal of the Royal Air Force Sir John, *The Central Blue*. London: Cassell & Co., 1956.

Somerville, Admiral of the Fleet Sir James, *Fighting Admiral*. London: 1961.

Spears, Major General Sir Edward, *Assignment to Catastrophe*. Vol. 1, *Prelude to Dunkirk*. Vol. 2, *The Fall of France*. London: Heinemann, 1954.

Stamps, T. Dodson, and Vincent J. Esposito, *A Military History of World War II*. 4 vols. West Point: 1956.

Taylor, Telford, *The Breaking Wave: The Second World War in the Summer of 1940*. New York: Simon and Schuster, 1967.

————, *The March of Conquest: The German Victories in Western Europe, 1940*. New York: Simon and Schuster, 1958.

Thompson, Laurence, *1940*. New York: William Morrow & Co., 1966.

Thompson, Walter H., *Assignment: Churchill*. New York: Farrar, Straus, & Cudahy, 1955.

Trevor-Roper, H. R., ed., *Blitzkrieg to Defeat*. New York: Holt, Rinehart and Winston, 1964.

Turner, E. S., *The Phoney War on the Home Front*. London: Michael Joseph, 1961.

Vian, Admiral of the Fleet Sir Philip, *Action this Day*. London: Frederick Muller, 1960.

Vulliez, Albert, *Brest au combat, 1939–1944*. Paris: 1950.

Warlimont, Walter, *Inside Hitler's Headquarters, 1939–1945*. New York: Praeger, 1964.

Werth, Alexander, *De Gaulle: A Political Biography*. New York: Simon and Schuster, 1965.

Weygand, Maxime, *Rappelé au service*. Paris: 1950.

Wheatley, Ronald, *Operation Sea Lion*. Oxford: Oxford University Press, 1958.

Wilmot, Chester, *The Struggle for Europe: World War II in Western Europe*. New York: Harper & Bros., 1952.

Wood, Derek, and Derek Demster, *The Narrow Margin*. New York: McGraw-Hill, 1961.

Ziemke, Earl F., *The German Northern Theater of Operations, 1940–1945*. Department of the Army Pamphlet No. 20-271. Washington, D.C.: 1959.

Index

Index

British Coastal Command, 38, 427
British Coastal Command Photographic Reconnaissance Unit, 428, 430
British Expeditionary Force,
  in Belgian operations, 101, 104, 114, 115, 116, 117, 118, 120, 121, 124, 125
  in Greece, 360, 401–406, 450
British Guiana, 291
British Home Defence Force, 114
British Home Fleet, 10, 66, 71, 81, 114, 189, 407, 443
British Home Guard, 247–248, 258, 288
British Navy. *See* Royal Navy.
British Somaliland, 365
British Union of Fascists, 244
Brittany, 161, 164, 167, 169
Brooke, Gen. Alan, 32, 116, 122, 125, 159, 169
Brooklyn Dodgers, 503
Brooks, C. Wayland, 498
Broussignac, Captain, 314, 317
Browder, Earl, 137, 145
Brown, Winfield, 345
Brussels, 102
Bryant, Chief Engineer W., 15, 17
Buckingham Palace, bombing of, 265
Buckler, Commander, 400
Budd, Ralph, 151
Buenos Aires, 18, 25, 28, 29–30
Bulgaria, 360, 386, 387, 390
"Bundles for Britain," 286
Buq Buq, 358
Burke, Edward R., 293, 294
Burke-Wadsworth Bill, 294
Burlingham, Charles C., 290
Byrnes, James, 279

Cadart, Rear Admiral, 234
Cadogan, Sir Alexander, 495
Cain, James M., 506
Calabria, 277, 349
Calais, 117, 121, 123–124, 128
Calcutta, H.M.S., 349, 402–405
Callaghan, Capt. Daniel, 367

Calypso, H.M.S., 213, 346
Cambrai, 114, 115, 118, 121
Campbell, Sir Ronald, 173–174, 176, 189–190, 238, 390, 392
Campinchi, César, 190–191
Camus, Albert, 197
Canary Islands, 301
Cap Blanc-Nez, 262
Capatana, 312
Cape Blanco, 309
Cape Breton Island, 413n
Cape Manuel, 323
Cape Matapan, battle of, 378–385
Cape Race, 425
Cape Spartello, 307
Cape Town, 18, 417, 418, 481
Cape Verde Islands, 425
Capuzzo, 476
  Trigh, 359
Carducci, 382, 384
Carlisle, H.M.S., 402, 468
Carol II, King of Rumania, 351
Caroline Islands, 512
Carroll, Madeleine, 367
Carter, Leading Seaman C., 86–87
Carton de Wiart, Maj. Gen. Adrian, 77–78, 465
Carvin, 118
Casablanca, 233–234, 309, 317, 318, 319
  Force Y at, 307
  French leaders meet in, 191
  German economic commissioners in, 329
  Jean Bart in, 193, 231, 232
Casey, Hugh, 503
Casino de Paris, 31
Castel Benito, 451
Catapult, Operation, 192, 198–212, 215–224, 231–232, 235
Cattaneo, Admiral, 382–383
Cavour, 346–347, 357
Cayla, M., 233, 234
Century Dinner Group, 286, 289, 290
Cesare. See Giulio Cesare.
Ceylon, 18
Chad Territory, 304, 310, 312
Chakmak, Gen., 390

Codoner, Cadet Officer Manuel, 12
Colgan, Edward J., Jr., 282
College of the City of New York, 145
Collinet, Captain, 211
Cologne, 35
Combe, Colonel, 363
Comedy Theater, London, 462
Commandant Dominé, 322, 327–328
Commandant Duboc, 322, 327–328
Commandant Teste, 197, 211, 212
Commandos (Br.), 468, 470, 471
Committee to Defend America by Aiding the Allies, 139–140, 286
Communist Party of the United States, 137, 145–146, 341
Compiègne, 183
Conant, James B., 140
Congo, French, 312
Congress of Industrial Organizations, 488
Coningham, Air Vice Marshal Arthur, 499
Conn, Billy, 502–503
Conservative Party (Gt. Brit.), 91–94, 96, 98
Convoys, 8–10, 413–416, 496–497
ANF-24, 398
HX-79, 416, 485
HX-84, 419–423
HX-106, 424–425
HX-112, 486
HX-156, 498
OB-204, 304
OB-293, 485–486
SC-7, 415, 485
SC-48, 497
SL-67, 425
SLS-64, 424
Cooper, Alfred Duff, 191
Cooper, Gary, 367, 504
Copenhagen, 54
Coral Sea, 520
Corap, Gen. André-Georges, 104, 110
Corinth Canal, 352, 406
Cork and Orrery, Lord, 72, 73–76, 83, 87
Cornish City, 419
Cornwall, H.M.S., 315, 316–317, 418

Cornwall-Jones, Capt. A. T., 113
Cornwallis, Lord, 123
Corregidor, 520
Cossack, H.M.S., 41–43, 447–448
Coughlin, Father Charles E., 137–138, 140
Council Bluffs Nonpareil, The, 147
Courageous, H.M.S., 10
Courbet, 224
Coventry, 343–344, 457
Coventry, H.M.S., 344, 349, 402
Cracow, 7
Crawshay, Capt. J., 118
Creagh, Maj. Gen. Michael, 362–363, 364
Crete, 457, 465–466, 347
battle of, 407, 439, 466–472
British naval base on, 352
Italian air reconnaissance over, 376
Crimean War, 5, 59
Cripplegate, 259
Cromwell, Oliver, 93
Cronin, A. J., 506
Crosby, Bing, 142
Cross, Milton, 276
Cross of Lorraine. *See* Free French.
Crusader, Operation, 499–502
Cumberland, H.M.S., 25, 304, 310, 313–315, 323
Cunningham, Gen. Alan, 365, 386, 499, 500–501
Cunningham, Adm. Andrew Browne, 191–192, 193, 302n, 386, 499
escorts Tiger convoy to Alexandria, 475
in action against French fleet at Alexandria, 214–224
in action against Italian forces, 213–214, 346–347, 349–350, 353, 376–385
in battle of Crete, 467, 471
Cunningham, Vice Adm. John H. D., 302–303, 304, 310–311, 312
Cyprus, 214
Cyrenaica, 362, 364, 365, 386, 387, 453, 455, 475, 499. *See also* names of specific cities.

538

541

Hale, Lt. Commander, 70–71
Halfaya Pass, 453, 475, 476
Halifax, Lord, 42, 94, 97–98, 251, 253
Halifax, Nova Scotia, 413, 496
Halleck, Charles, 273
Halsey, Adm. William F., 520
Hamar, Norwegian government at, 60–61
Hambrò, Carl, 45
Hamburg, 53
Hamill, Captain, 316
Hamilton, Capt. F. H. G. Dalrymple-, 441
Hamilton, Duke of, 458–459, 460
Hamlet, The (Faulkner), 34
Hamlet (Shakespeare), 141
Hammer, Operation, 80–82
Hammerstein, Oscar, 277
Hangö, 48
Hanoi, 508
Hardi, 231, 330
Harding, Warren G., 280
Hardy, H.M.S., 66–68, 87
Harriman, Mrs. J. Borden, 14
Harris, Captain F. C. P., 15, 17
Harstad, 73, 74, 76, 84, 85
Harwood, Commo. Henry, 18–26, 28
Hats, Operation, 349–350
Hatston, 430, 431
Havana, conference of American states in, 296
Havock, H.M.S., 67, 69, 402
Hawaii, 519. *See also* Pearl Harbor.
Hawaiian Attack Force, 519
Hearst, William Randolph, 137, 504
"Hearts Don't Lie" (song), 503
Heatter, Gabriel, 34, 35
Hebrides, 2
Heidkamp. See Wilhelm Heidkamp.
"Heigh Ho, Heigh Ho, It's Off to Work We Go" (song), 275
Heggenreiner, Leutnant, 451
Heiners, Boatswain, 442
Helen Trent, The Romance of, 276, 504
Hellfire (Halfaya) Pass, 453, 475, 476
Hellman, Lillian, 504
Hellzapoppin, 504

Helsinki, 49
Hemingway, Ernest, 277, 367
Hendaye, Hitler and Franco meet in, 351
Henderson, Leon, 151, 489–490
Henrich, Tommy, 503
Henry VIII, King of England, 343
Hepburn, Katharine, 504
Heraklion, 466, 468, 471
Hereward, H.M.S., 107
Herjangsfjord, 65, 68, 83
Hermes, H.M.S., 233, 235, 236
Herriot, Édouard, 171
Hess, Rudolf, 183, 458–460
Heye, Capt. Hellmuth, 56
Hill, Lister, 281
Hillman, Sidney, 151
Himmler, Heinrich, 8, 107n
Hinnøy, 73
Hipper, 55–56, 84, 408, 424
Hiryu, 514
Hitchcock, Alfred, 278
Hitler, Adolf, 8, 62, 89, 103, 121, 187, 227, 351, 372, 377, 416, 452, 472, 473. *See also* Germany.
abrogates naval treaty with Britain, 91
admired by Father Coughlin, 137
and *Admiral Graf Spee,* 27–28
and Operation Sea Lion. *See* Sea Lion, Operation.
and U.S., 480
approves Operation Juno, 84
at signing of armistice with France, 183
attitude toward British, 36–37, 180–181
decides to invade Norway, 43, 45–46
decides to invade Yugoslavia, 393
declares Doorn out of bounds for German personnel, 106
Franco and, 195–196, 351
Goering and, 47
meets with Welles, 143
presents Iron Cross to Prien, 11
satirized, 278
Stalin and, 48

Preston Public Library

F R A N C E

Toulon

Genoa

CORSICA

Rome

I T

SPAIN

BALEARIC IS.

SARDINIA

M E D I T E R R A

Bizerte
Tunis

SIC

Gibraltar

Bone

SPANISH
MOROCCO Oran

Algiers

ALGERIA

T
U
N
I
S
I
A

Gabes

GUL

FRENCH

MOROCCO

T
R
I
P

L

PRESTON PUBLIC LIBRARY